Literature, Religion,
and the Evolution of Culture
1660–1780

Literature, Religion, and the Evolution of Culture 1660–1780

HOWARD D. WEINBROT

The Johns Hopkins University Press
Baltimore

This book was brought to publication with the generous contribution of the
William Freeman Vilas Trust of the University of Wisconsin.

© 2013 The Johns Hopkins University Press
All rights reserved. Published 2013
Printed in the United States of America on acid-free paper
2 4 6 8 9 7 5 3 1

The Johns Hopkins University Press
2715 North Charles Street
Baltimore, Maryland 21218-4363
www.press.jhu.edu

Library of Congress Cataloging-in-Publication Data

Weinbrot, Howard D.
Literature, religion, and the evolution of culture, 1660–1780 / Howard D. Weinbrot.
p. cm.
Includes bibliographical references and index.
ISBN 978-1-4214-0516-2 (hardcover : acid-free paper) — ISBN 978-1-4214-0860-6 (electronic) — ISBN 1-4214-0516-4 (hardcover : acid-free paper) — ISBN 1-4214-0860-0 (electronic)
1. English literature—Early modern, 1500–1700—History and criticism. 2. English literature—18th century—History and criticism. 3. Religion and literature—Great Britain. 4. Literature and society—Great Britain. 5. Great Britain—Intellectual life—17th century. 6. Great Britain—Intellectual life—18th century. I. Title.
PR428.R46W45 2013
820.9'382—dc23   2012035553

A catalog record for this book is available from the British Library.

Special discounts are available for bulk purchases of this book. For more information, please contact Special Sales at 410-516-6936 or specialsales@press.jhu.edu.

The Johns Hopkins University Press uses environmentally friendly book materials, including recycled text paper that is composed of at least 30 percent post-consumer waste, whenever possible.

For Dawn

CONTENTS

Acknowledgments   xi

Introduction. The Groundwork of Change   1
   Eighteenth-Century Evolutionary Theory   2
   Practical Awareness   3
   The Chapters and a Definition   11
   A Note on Notes   16

PART I. THREATS TO THE SPECIES: Madness, Discontent, and the Danger of Dissolution

Chapter 1. Causation and Contexts of Hatred: Savage Beasts Mortal and Deadly   23
   Conjuring Up Reasons: Original Sin, Fragile Connections, Church and State   27
   Aristocratic Historiography: Advocacy and Resistance   32
   Metaphorical Enhancements: Floods, Propagation, Legions, and Dutch Treats   36

Chapter 2. Madness, Extirpation, and Defoe's *Shortest Way with the Dissenters*   55
   Madness   55
   Root and Branch   57
   Defoe's *Shortest Way*, Sacheverell's *Political Union*, and Religious Conflict   66
   The Shortest Way: The Bible and Other Clues beyond the Obvious   73
   Response and Judgment   80
   Defoe as a Character of His Own Creation   84

PART II. TAKING THE CURE AND IMPROVING THE SPECIES: Sermons, Compulsion, and Methodists

Chapter 3. The Thirtieth of January Sermon: From Extermination to Inclusion   105
   The Thirtieth of January Sermon and Royalist Law   105
   The High Church Response and the Beginning of Change   109
   Higher Church and Moderate Responses to the High Church Response   116
   Raising the Decibels in a Lowered Church   119
   State, Not Church   123
   God's Hand, William's Hand, and the Divine Right of Government   127
   Retrospective   132

Chapter 4. "Compel Them to Come In," Luke 14:23: From Persecution to Persuasion; Against Augustinian Compulsion   144
   Revocation of the Edict of Nantes: Response and Rage   146
   Contexts Changed and Augustine Charged   156
   Happy Had His Works Not Been Preserved   159
   Persuade Them to Come In   165
   Adopt Men From All the Nations of the Earth: Equiano's Conversion   168

Chapter 5. Methodism: From Antagonist to Relation   181
   The Spreading *Fog*   182
   Reforming the Reformation? Reforming Reform?   188
   Grudging Acceptance   200
   Humphry Clinker: Joining the Family   207

PART III. EVOLUTIONARY REVERSION: The Gordon Riots, Return to Rage, and Reinventing a Cure

Chapter 6. Déjà Vu All Over Again? The Gordon Riots; Bedlam Revisited, Restoration of Order, and a Trial on Trial   237
   Repeal, No Popery, and the Gordon Riots: Destruction and the Puritan Redivivus   238
   Renovating the Language of Cultural Regress   243
   Church, State, and Political Causation   249
   Strategies of Defense and Alternative Responses   257
   "What Is to Depose the Sword?": The Return to Order; Debate, Arrest, Trial, and Consequences   261
   The Trial of Lord George Gordon for Treason, 1781   268

Chapter 7. A Very Near Thing: State Terrorism, the Fury of the Aggrieved, and
	Incompatibility with the Safety of Millions 289
  A River Too Far   291
  The Trials of Lord George Gordon, 1786–1787, and Excommunication   294
  The Trials of Lord George Gordon, 1786–1787: Libeling France and Britain   298
  Aftermath: Flight, Conversion, and Sentence   310
  True Colors: Robert Watson's *Life of Lord George Gordon*   315

Chapter 8. Coping, Repairing, and Dickens' *Barnaby Rudge*   330
  How to Cope? The World after the Gordon Riots   330
  Dickens' *Barnaby Rudge*: To Point a Moral but Not Adorn a Tale;
    The Victorian Retrospective and Punishment by Neglect   332

Conclusion, Summary, Implications   343
  A Brief Summary of a Long Book   343
  Illustrating Evolution   346

Index   357

ACKNOWLEDGMENTS

Acknowledgments are among the most congenial parts of an author's job. The Department of English at the University of Wisconsin–Madison was my home for some forty-two years. From 1984 I had the privilege of memorializing Wisconsin's great tradition of eighteenth-century studies as Ricardo Quintana Professor of English. From 1987 I had the comparable privilege of being one of the university's William Freeman Vilas Research Professors in the College of Letters and Science. These chairs allowed me both the time and the research budget to work in some of the great libraries in the English-speaking world, as well as in France and Germany. It is a pleasure to acknowledge my debt to the Department of English, to the Vilas Trust, and to Paul de Luca, the most recent of the university provosts who have shepherded the Vilas Professors. I also thank the many colleagues who have provided intellectual and social friendship and constant challenges that helped me to earn my keep before I was transmogrified into an emeritus professor.

My research has been performed primarily at the University of Wisconsin Memorial Library, the Houghton Library at Harvard, the Huntington Library in San Marino, California, where I now am a reader in residence, and, of course, the British Library with its richly productive collections. Occasional trips to the Newberry Library in Chicago, the Beinecke Library at Yale, and the Library of Congress also have been deeply rewarding. I began work on this book in 2005–6 as a Visiting Scholar in the Department of English at Harvard University, where I enjoyed the hospitality both of colleagues in that department and at Leverett House. The book was enormously aided by fellowships at the Huntington Library and at the William Andrews Clark Library of UCLA. I am grateful to all of these splendid institutions and to the foresight and generosity of public- and private-sector stewards of the vast body of Anglophone letters and culture—a tiny part of which I consider in this book.

Over the years many friends, colleagues, and students have done their best to preserve me from various conceptual and factual errors, the inevitable residue of which I alone am the perpetrator. In Madison, Richard Begam, Phillip Harth, Eric Rothstein, and Elliott Sober have been exemplary, as have James Engell, Rob Hume, Misty Anderson, Cedric D. Reverand II, the Reverend Canon Dr. Jane Steen, Debbie Welham, and James Woolley from distant venues. I have presented various versions of work at several meetings of the American Society for Eighteenth-Century Studies, at the admirable Johnson Society of the Central Region, at Harvard, at the Huntington, and at several European universities, including Oxford, Bonn, Düsseldorf, and Münster. I thank all of them for the chance to audition my work and, I hope, to improve it through vigorous exchange.

Portions of the discussion of Defoe's *Shortest Way with the Dissenters* appeared as "'Root out this Cursed Race': Defoe's *Shortest Way with the Dissenters* and His Longer Way with Himself," in *Anglistentag 2006 Halle: Proceedings*, ed. Sabine Volk-Birke and Julia Lippert (Trier: Wissenschaftlicher Verlag, 2008), pp. 7–23. I also draw on portions of "The Thirtieth of January Sermon: Swift, Johnson, Sterne, and the Evolution of Culture," *Eighteenth-Century Life* 34 (2010): 29–55. I thank the editors for permission to recycle, and now to somewhat change, those pages. I am equally grateful to my exemplary graduate students at Wisconsin. For many years they were both partners in sometimes Socratic, sometimes pedagogical, and always instructive exchange, in which I learned as much as I hope they did. I want especially to thank Heather King, Stephen Karian, David Nunnery, Katie Price, Michael Gadaletto, and Morgan Strawn for research, editorial, and friendly support over the years. Several of these students now are friends and distant colleagues. Brava and Bravo.

Above all, I thank my wife, Dawn, for her precious contribution to all aspects of my life. This book is dedicated to her with more than love. *Semper collaetemur.*

ns, and the Evolution of Culture
1660–1780

Introduction

The Groundwork of Change

How did seventeenth- and eighteenth-century England survive, heal, and prosper in spite of civil war, regicide, and multiple dynastic changes? One of many answers to this question suggests analogy with evolutionary processes. At its best, such evolution fosters improvement and reduces danger to the species. In this case, that species called England, and then Great Britain as a United Kingdom, was a complex, turbulent, nation competing with other complex turbulent nations, many of whom did not wish it well. Indeed, many within the nation did not wish it well in certain of its modes of proceeding. How, again then, did England survive, heal, and prosper in spite of dramatic internal and external conflict from, say, 1660 to 1780? In the simplest terms, during those years England chose collectively, painfully and partially, to evolve rather than to self-destruct.

To begin, I offer a radically simplified version of some defining elements of Darwin's *On the Origin of Species* (1859) as modified by subsequent research. Evolutionary theory assumes that inherited traits within a large population's organisms change over successive generations. These new traits emerge in a variety of ways. There may be normal variations within the organism as it interacts with its environment; there also may be cognate beneficial accident from which over time the organism improves. Birds that sip honey develop long thin beaks; birds that crack nuts develop short sharp beaks. A fish that fears predators crawls onto land, learns to eat insects or grass, and develops legs that allow it greater mobility. So long as the environment remains stable, natural selection improves the organism and produces more organisms that fit the environment; these in turn are chosen by other improved organisms, thus diminishing the gene pool's less useful traits for survival and reproduction. Along the way, the organism continues to adapt to and alter its environment. Genetic drift nonetheless may occur and enhance or impede the process of benign natural selection. There thus is no Eureka Moment, in which genetic light conquers genetic darkness. Indeed, according to some evolutionary biologists, such gradual progress is a function of groups' and individuals' cooperating on the basis of benevolent, shared ways to achieve benevolent ends. According to others, those groups and individuals are guided by perceptive human beings whose actions for thousands of years hope to guide us toward the better rather than the worse.[1] Failure to cooperate toward those ends can have malevolent evolutionary consequences. That was a lesson it took the British clerical and political classes a century to learn.

Eighteenth-Century Evolutionary Theory

Such biologically and cooperatively based concepts of evolution are adaptable to aesthetic, literary, and broadly cultural concerns. Few this side of Pollyanna could think that human progress is a handsomely forward movement on a straight road. Few this side of Darth Vader could think that human progress has not taken place on that road, however much its windings are spewed with potholes, expensive tollbooths demanding blood, and dangerous reverse directions that require attention, regret, and correction. "Progress," after all, can mean progressively more efficient ways to destroy ourselves. Part of the battle between the Ancients and the Moderns turned on whether such advances were possible and whether one side or the other had indeed helpfully advanced. Our eighteenth-century ancestors also were aware that *evolution* stemmed from the Latin *evolutio*, "to unroll," as in a scroll, or more properly for later readers, "the opening of a book." The term came to take on three basic meanings, each of which in its way suggested movement, awareness, acquisition of knowledge, and even matters of life and death.

One basic meaning of *evolution* was "a rolling or reading over," "an unfolding, unrolling," or the related "to turn over or unfold." Dyche and Pardon's *New General Dictionary* (1735) enlarges that frequent definition with real-world action: "in common Affairs, the unfolding, unrolling, &c. of Wares, Cloths, &c." Samuel Johnson also saw both the verb and the noun unfolding, opening, or disclosing. His illustrative quotation for the second meaning of *evolution*, however, makes overt what was covert in the term's inherent action. That illustration both sharply differentiates human from divine perception and makes plain that human life is defined by movement through time. "The whole *evolution* of ages, from everlasting to everlasting," Johnson says from More, is "collectively ... represented to God at once, as if all things which ever were, are, or shall be, were at this very instant, and so always, really present and existent before him."[2] Our world develops slowly; God's perception of it is "at once."

A second definition was not so theologically laden. In algebra, evolution is "the Extraction of Roots," and more commonly in geometry as recorded by Ephraim

Chambers it is "the unfolding, or opening of a Curve, and making it describe an *Evolute*." Johnson's 1755 illustrative quotation for his third definition of the noun later was borrowed by at least one familiar successor. John Harris shows how a circle or other curve unbends in evolution, "so that the same line becomes successively" less arched and finally turns "into a strait line."[3]

The most energetic of the definitions concerned military tactics, especially for the infantry but also for cavalry and even naval maneuvers. Edward Phillips' *New World of Words* is typical: "Evolutions are doubling of Ranks or Files, Wheeling or other motion made by a Body of soldiers, that change their posture or Form of drawing up; either to attack the enemy, or receive their Onset more Advantageously." Johnson adapts this, but its greatest extension is in Diderot and d'Alembert's *Encyclopèdie* and its seventy-five folio double columns (6:1756). *Evolution* there denotes the deployment of troops for battle to direct them to their different sides, and their division or reuniting into their varied units. These actions finally give soldiers the most advantageous disposition to fight, following whatever circumstances in which they might find themselves.[4]

The several unfoldings, extractings, turnings into, and wheelings show both movement through time and space and problem solving—as in the presentation of one's ware, the extraction of roots, or the preparation to attack or defend. Johnson's quotation from More on the evolution of ages from everlasting to everlasting is of course on a grander, if less physically dangerous, scale than the movement of troops. As the *Encyclopèdie* notes, these nonetheless must evolve properly or they will be a confused mass whose parts mutually entangle themselves. Proper evolution significantly reduces danger, remedies inconvenience, and provides coordinated movement that protects one army and threatens the other.[5]

Practical Awareness

Eighteenth-century commentators on evolution thus lacked the modern term's meaning but not the broader concept of cultural, chronological, and temporal "evolutions" that suggest problem resolution. Evolution then was linked to the concepts of progress, of improvement, and ultimately of God's design. Virgil's third *Georgic* dealt with breeding of cattle and of horses; Linnaeus understood plant hybridization; in England Robert Bakewell had begun selective breeding of animals by 1760 and developed the New Leicester breed of sheep. Erasmus Darwin's *Loves of the Plants* (1789) was written in part to propagate Linnaeus' system of classification and plant reproduction, whose evolutionary improvements seemed a microcosm of civilization's improvements: "Perhaps all the products of nature are in their progress to greater perfection? an idea countenanced by the modern discoveries and deductions concerning the progressive formation of the solid parts of the terraqueous globe." Buffon's *Histoire naturelle, générale et particulière* began to appear in 1749. Relevant portions appeared in English and also discussed breeding and crossbreeding.[6] Many nonetheless were aware that nature could be incomprehensible. John Ray's widely read *Wisdom of God Manifested in the Works of the Creation* (1691) was a popular physio-theological text. Ray knew that "there is nothing but what is artificially and wisely contrived and formed." Of course man cannot fully understand that wisdom. Johnson defines *hybridous* as "begotten between animals of different species." He cites portions of Ray's awareness of the coupling between a mule and a horse: why they should so mingle, "but also generate an Animal, and yet that that hybridous Production should not again generate, and so a new Race be carried on; but Nature should stop here and proceed no further, is to me a Mystery and unaccountable." The *Encyclopaedia Britannica* (1776) includes a long article on horses' different breeds, functions, and national origins. The several kinds of British horses were drawn from many countries, but no country can equal British racers, "they having been bred from what are called barbs," horses from Barbary.[7]

Britons preferred to deal with the more complex human species, able to make conscious moral choices. The older Tory sense of a modern decaying civilization inferior to ancient grandeur gradually became less persuasive or even attractive as confidence in native achievement grew. Johnson enhanced and exemplified this change in his preface to *Shakespeare* (1765) and its estimate of how to evaluate literary greatness. We revere old writing "not from any credulous confidence in the superior wisdom of past ages, or gloomy persuasion of the degeneracy of mankind." We do so as "the consequence of acknowledged and indubitable positions that what has been longest known has been most considered, and what is most considered is best understood." Johnson later objects both to Pope's and to Swift's posturing, which makes them and their friends the only virtuous men in England: "They show the age involved in darkness, and shade the picture with sullen emulation."[8] For Johnson, the post-Swift/Pope generation's exclusionary ideological rigorism has evolved into something better; it has been replaced by sensible people making sensible judgments based on empirical standards.

Hence the approximately mid- and later eighteenth-century terms commonly used regarding human cultures included *improvement* and *progress*.[9] Each of these suggests evolution as moving toward a superior adaptation, though with some backward turns. That evolution often denoted a joining of the best of the past in order to enhance the present, as in two literary examples from John Dryden. In 1687 he praised Henry Higden's paraphrastic version of Juvenal's tenth satire, which blended Horace's smiles with Juvenal's rage: he was able

"To joyn the Vertues of Two Stiles in One." Shortly thereafter, Dryden raised the level of evolved literary greatness with perceptive "Lines on Milton":

> Three *Poets*, in three distant *Ages* born,
> *Greece*, *Italy*, and *England did adorn*.
> The *First* in loftiness of thoughts Surpass'd;
> The *Next* in Majesty; in both the *Last*.
> The force of *Nature* cou'd no farther goe:
> To make a *Third* she joyn'd the former two.[10]

Milton also provided other eighteenth-century critics with an example of progressive joining. Johnson defines *improvement* as "Melioration; advancement of any thing from good to better." It is also the "Act of improving; something added or changed for the better; sometimes with *on*." His compelling illustrative quotation is from Addison's *Spectator*, No. 273 (1712), one of the influential numbers concerning *Paradise Lost*. Homer's variety of characters is more impressive than Virgil's limited group and types—with one exception: "The parts of Sinon, Camilla, and some few others, are *improvements on* the Greek poet." In Addison's text, *fine* modifies *improvements*, but this small change is not as important as the nature of the *Spectator* from which Johnson quotes. Addison examines the genealogy of characterization in the classical and Miltonic epic. Homer is extraordinary for his variety, novelty, and dignity. Virgil "falls infinitely short of *Homer*" in those areas. Milton has both models in mind as he contemplates how a Christian epic should function in relation to its pagan ancestors. Though he has only two main "human" characters, dramatically they are four and are extended emotionally. He portrays each in an unfallen and a fallen state and of course makes plain that they are our ultimate parents. These "are not only more magnificent, but more new than any Characters either in *Virgil* or *Homer*, or indeed in the whole Circle of Nature." Johnson focuses on a passage in which Milton inherits a literary genealogy that he modifies in order to improve. The consequence is something "more magnificent" than its predecessors or, as Johnson had defined his term, "something added or changed for the better." The line clearly is not smooth and straight, since Virgil had lapsed away from Homeric novelty and variety, but it is in a generally forward direction.[11]

The same is true for *progress*, in definitions of the noun as "Advancement; motion forward" and as "Intellectual improvement; advancement in knowledge; proscience." Two illustrations are especially powerful. Johnson's quotation from Thomas Burnet's *Sacred Theory of the Earth* (1681, 1684) again largely is accurate but, as often for the sake of space, omits the lines I italicize. These make clear that evolution is part of the divine scheme:

> And whosoever understands the progress and revolutions of Nature, will see that neither the present form of the Earth, nor its first forms, were permanent and immutable *forms, but transient and temporary by their own frame and constitution; which the Author of Nature, after certain periods of time, had design'd for change and for destruction.*[12]

An illustration from Locke adds that "it is impossible the mind should ever be stopped in its *progress* in this space."

Whether or not Locke thought evolution part of God's design, he did think that God's gift of reason functioned in a roughly comparable way: postlapsarian human beings try different adaptations, see which is best, and if possible advance accordingly after such a determination. His posthumously published "Examination of P. Malebranche's Opinion of Seeing All Things in God" rebukes le Père for thinking that we partake of God's "infinite and universal Reason." That is false. Locke shares Ray's familiar and sensible view that human reason cannot comprehend God's reason. An omniscient and omnipotent God indeed does not reason; human beings engage in that "laborious and gradual Progress in the Knowledge of things." We compare ideas, find the relations among them, and in such searching "may" find "the Relation we desire to know, which sometimes we find, and sometimes not."[13] Gradual progress, regress, trial, error, and uncertainty define the human situation, which nonetheless has a crudely positive ark of melioration and advancement. We see a good example of this in Edmund Burke's late-1750s fragment "An Essay Towards an History of the Laws of England."

For Burke there is scarcely anything "more rational than the origin, the progress, the various revolutions of human Laws."[14] He does not mean progress in the largely neutral sense of Dryden's essay "The Original and Progress of Satire," prefaced to his translation of Juvenal (1693). There, a genre naturally changes as it moves through changing times rather than toward the fulness of a perfected form. Dryden prefers Juvenal to Horace, but politics contributes to this aesthetic judgment. In contrast, Burke sees the body of English law "enriched" by foreign conquest, softened by peace, "improved and exalted by commerce," by social relations, and by science (p. 322). He indeed uses the word *revolution* (pp. 323, 324) as a virtual synonym for what I call evolution. English jurisprudence is not overthrown but accreted. It gradually melds Saxon law in general with the slightly different specifics of West Saxon, Mercian, and Danish law (pp. 328–29). Burke adapts a metaphor that is the opposite of the one we will see used by the frightened High Church confronting torrents of rage and disorder bursting over England. His composite, fertilizing, English jurisprudence "waters and enriches whole nations with so abundant and copious a flood" (p. 322). Moreover, that northern torrential law ran impetuously, uprooted customs, suited itself to the different nations, and "formed, as it were, the great body and main stream of the Saxon laws" (p. 331). All this blends, improves, and joins into a "heterogeneous mass" appropriate for the heterogeneous English language and people.

The native legal system nevertheless was subject to further improvement by means of an unforeseen historical event characterized in another water image: "The Norman Conquest is the great era of our Laws. At this time the English jurisprudence, which hitherto had continued a poor stream, fed from some few and those scanty sources, was all at once, as from a mighty flood, replenished with a vast body of foreign learning" (p. 331). Such massive changes were for the better. New courts, new names for officers and their functions, new land rights and tenants, and even a new language improved the heterogeneity into a coherent system. Like many of Burke's predecessors, he regards these historical accidents, such as the Norman invasion that improves British/Saxon law, as part of a nobler plan. In so tracing the improvement of law he traces "the advances of men, in an attempt to imitate the Supreme Ruler in one of the most glorious of his attributes" (p. 322). Frail humans often blunder, but they also often strive to improve law, on which improved government depends. Burke later objects to the schismatic French Revolution (1790) because it dissolved, tore, exploded, and ridiculed generations of advances. Destructive fantasy replaced ancient, earned, political power hitherto made gentle, obedient, liberal, and harmonious. Now, "every thing seems out of nature in this strange chaos" in which prosperity and tranquillity revert to a "monstrous" scene.[15]

For Burke, synthetic progress is a virtually ordained historical evolution subject to benign accident that helps to advance culture in spite of grievous, reversionary setbacks. This view was so powerful that it sustained itself even during the French Revolution's Terror and mass serial murder. "Progress" then evoked what the marquis de Condorcet's editor called virtues whose influence required "religious veneration."[16] In 1794 Condorcet was awaiting an appointment with Dr. Guillotin's efficient blade, initially designed as an egalitarian and merciful mode of death.

Condorcet wrote his enthusiastic *Esquisse d'un tableau historique des progrès de l'esprit humaine* (1794) in prison. Perhaps his lingering shade could have read its English version one year later as *Outline of an Historical View of the Progress of the Human Mind* (1795). Condorcet knew that the major improvements among individuals were reflected in group and national improvement among generations. Each advance in the present, though, "depends upon . . . the preceding" advance and influences those that follow (p. 3). There is no limit to human improvement, which could culminate in a world of long-lived reasonable men governed by perfect or at least perfectible shared law and language. Progress can "never be retrograde"

(p. 4). The leaders of such government will be a class of men "considered as the friends of human kind," who exert themselves to advance and improve our happiness (p. 15). Condorcet agrees that progress is not only a group and social movement. At any given time the world is improved by "the accident which has produced in the midst of it [as a nation in space and time] any of those extraordinary men" who so affected their own and future ages (p. 218). Indeed, as Locke said, new ideas at first incoherent, disorderly, and "suggested by accident" soon are accepted "without reflecting on their nature" (p. 241). Healthy accident thus improves the natural growth of culture and becomes a building block for greater elevation of the species.

The man awaiting his own death by state terrorism of course also knew about the several thousand others so murdered in France's grim dystopia and the vast number of deaths in consequent revolutionary wars. With words applicable to the Gordon Riots of 1780, Condorcet insists upon the philosopher's consolation, his knowledge that the human race will be free from chains, chance, and "the enemies of progress," who cannot finally arrest steps "in the paths of truth." He nonetheless laments "the errors, the flagrant acts of injustice, the crimes with which the earth is still polluted." Error clearly remains but, he believes, cannot "restore the reign of prejudice and slavery" (p. 371).

Condorcet's sweetly hopeful views of such progress are touching under deathbed circumstances. Not everyone will be as keen as he was for what seems, at best, like benevolent despotism by an unelected collective body of "extraordinary men" who tell the less ordinary how to behave. He nonetheless has outlined a cultural evolution consistent with this book's argument: gradual improvements from generation to generation are passed on to successive generations. Improvements thereby are solidified and in turn improved by mingled art and accident soon incorporated into national and international social, political, literary, and other cultural gene pools. These developments denote a slow but broad advance that of course has its enemies, errors, injustices, and crimes so humiliating for human pretensions to improvement—as with the French Revolution for example. Granted, indeed insisted upon; but even so, for Condorcet there is a positive "eternal chain of the destiny of mankind" that leads to consolation and "the true delight of virtue" (p. 371). We note as well that much of this moral advancement depends upon groups of individuals acting on behalf of other, larger groups. The cooperative element enhances the biological imperative of survival.

Whether one responds to this with *splendide mendax* or *lux et veritas* is for wiser heads than mine to determine, or not, as the case may be. Clearly, however, whatever progress there is in general human or specific national circumstances is built on blood, destruction, and the desire to avoid further blood and destruction if possible—as in Dryden's angry and frustrated attack upon the Whigs and the Earl of Shaftesbury in *The Medall. A Satyre Against Sedition. By the Author of Absalom and Achitophel* (1682). Dryden wants his readers to know that he wrote that earlier poem, in which David/Charles learned about the superiority of proper statecraft to improper fathering both of his nation and of his darling son Absalom/Monmouth. The poem ends with David's divinely inspired speech that sets all right, restoring him to himself, the nation to its best governed self, and Charles to the benign days of 1660, when he was beloved and master of politics. Achitophel, alas, has been only temporarily quashed. His arrest is nullified by a Whig jury that frees him; the Whigs celebrate with a commemorative medal that rejoices in Shaftesbury and their own triumph; and Dryden fears that England again verges on anarchy and perhaps civil war. *Absalom and Achitophel*'s temperate tone surrenders to *The Medall*'s anger. It does so in part because the Whigs' individualism, collapse of restraint, and freedom from a coherent religion encourage them "To the next headlong Steep of Anarchy" (line 122). They have learned nothing from the horrors of the interregnum, which they indeed are likely to repeat. In contrast, the wiser moderate royalists built upon such lessons and sought to avoid them by means of the evolved, limited, constitutional monarchy. The Whigs think that everyone can be a God almighty in his turn:

> A Tempting Doctrine, plausible and new:
> What Fools our Father were, if this be true!
> Who, to destroy the seeds of Civil War,
> Inherent right in Monarchs did declare:
> And, that a lawfull Pow'r might never cease,
> Secur'd Succession, to secure our Peace.
> Thus, Property and Sovereign Sway, at last
> In equal Balances were justly cast. (Lines 111–18)

By the end of the poem, those "seeds of Civil War" have bloomed into a "Harvest of Rebellious Rage" (line 292), in which religious and political sects suffer disruption on a biblical scale. The only respite seems to be in physical and moral exhaustion and, finally, rest "on a rightfull Monarch's Breast" (line 322).[17] So far as Dryden could tell, moderate royalists sought to evolve away from anarchy to "equal Balances." Shaftesbury's Whigs preferred genetic drift back in to the bad old ways. The terminology changes, but that battle between progress and regress is built into the human situation.

If we backtrack, we can see why *evolution* is one appropriate term for how some versions of literature and religion develop between about 1660 and 1780. These start from an unstable base that attempts to become stable and fails. The culture, perhaps unwittingly, perhaps by design as its grandees replace James II with William III, or perhaps both, sees an unacceptable amalgam that can only lead to more anguish. It gradually tries to move away from the emotional, political, and religious brutality that was harming the organism. What Johnson called "the contentious turbulence of King James's reign" extended at the least through Queen Anne's tenure and could not be sustained in a civilized country.[18] As *The Medall*'s example makes plain, that contention was a regular threat. A series of historical accidents both complicate and finally, it would ultimately seem to most, improve or at the least stabilize the situation: William and Mary die without issue; Queen Anne dies without issue; distant German Protestant relatives are available, so that a Catholic putative James III can be excluded; the German Hanoverians have large enough families to provide issue for generations; the bishops appointed by William, Anne, and the Georges are lower church than the bishops they replaced. In short, the organism called the United Kingdom or Great Britain changes as a series of failures and successes teach it varied paths to take, to avoid, and to rectify if it cannot avoid a failure. Of course none of this is as genial as the evolution of wolf to dog, from predator to loyal pooch with unqualified love for the two-legged leader who, in dog theology, a benevolent God created to feed and care for *fidissimus*. To say that the messy human history is a far more imperfect and partial "progress" is to state what is necessary, obvious, and in a sense irrelevant. The arithmetic of two steps forward and one step back still takes us one step forward, after all.

By affirming the existence of that one step, however, I also reject what I think are two historical errors, whether as assumption or as mode of proceeding. One is what Quentin Skinner long ago called "the mythology of coherence," whether in a specific author like Hobbes or Johnson or in definitive historical movements.[19] Johnson, for example, regularly changed his mind, as in the differences between his *Plan* (1747) of the *Dictionary* and its preface, which denied the possibility of fixing the English language. History also regularly changes direction, as in Europe's revulsion from its world war beginning in 1936 (the Spanish Civil War) to 1945 and its Eurozone, born in 1998. "Europe" sought to ensure a peaceful future by breaking with its violent past.

The other error is the putative "Whig interpretation of history," the triumph of Protestantism and British liberty so allied to the exclusion of Catholicism and "slavery" after 1688. That powerful concept dominated much British historiography well into the twentieth century and, long after Butterfield, continues to need correction. It nonetheless serves as an interesting complication to a theory of cultural evolution: its inherent bigotry existed alongside its antidote. Specifically, Henry Hallam's *Constitutional History of England* (1827) is confident that duplicitous, alien

Catholicism had to be defenestrated in order to establish English national identity. The years in which Hallam was writing that *History* also were the years in which the Catholic Relief Act of 1829 was solidified.[20] We can regard history as an aggregate of connected disconnected events. To evoke the *concordia discors*, history may be a series of contingent events that culminate in the noncontingent, like the end of slavery in nineteenth-century Britain and America.

This book posits and traces some of these changes through religion and politics. Nonetheless, we may not need always to attach such progress to a religious or a political agenda. Samuel Johnson observed the natural tendency of cultures to improve themselves, perhaps without awareness of what they were doing but also by means of conscious moral exhortation. In the *Adventurer*, No. 137 (1754), he argues that the world remains "full of fraud and corruption, malevolence and rapine," but such corruption also is a matter not only of degree but of changing degree over time, as intelligent affirmation intelligently affirms civility over savagery:

> The progress of reformation is gradual and silent, as the extension of evening shadows; we know that they were short at noon, and are long at sunset, but our senses were not able to discern their increase; we know of every civil institution that it was once savage, and how was it reclaimed but by precepts and admonition? . . . How has knowledge or virtue been increased and preserved in one place beyond another, but by diligent inculcation and rational inforcement.[21]

Some may be surprised to see Johnson enlisted on the side of moral Whiggery, but he clearly is on the side of moral progress. As I hope to make clear, so demonstrably "optimistic" a view was not the hypothesis with which this book began or upon which I thought it had much basis until well into its progress. I offers some genealogy and explanation of an academic conversion experience.

The Chapters and a Definition

Readers of this book will notice that I define the term *literature* broadly. Texts like Defoe's *Shortest Way with the Dissenters* (1702), Clarendon's *History of the Rebellion and Civil Wars in England* (1702–4) together with its prefaces by Laurence Hyde, Earl of Rochester, Smollett's *Humphry Clinker* (1771), and Dickens' *Barnaby Rudge* (1841) fall into variously familiar literary canons. I include *Barnaby* within the framework of 1780 because of course it is about 1780, if from a Victorian point of view.

This book also includes an understudied and often brilliant, if on our standards sometimes morally suspect, area of discourse, the Restoration and eighteenth-century sermon. Understandably, few regard the arts of men like Henry

Sacheverell, Charles Leslie, and Luke Milbourne as stylistically important. Fiercely metaphorical writers like these and so many others nevertheless moved their audiences to action and to anger both for and against real or desired events. Biblical commentaries are not likely to make the secular heart beat faster, but as intellectual texts and markers they demonstrate important cultural movements. Reading Lord George Gordon's attacks upon the British legal system again turns us toward polemic as literature and texts that emerge from strident and often fatal contexts. I can only hope that readers will find the connections connected. I can only hope as well that the "evolution" of this book will interest those concerned with scholarly method and the trial and error by which one conceptualizes, gathers materials, writes, and reconsiders the road's final destination. I regard this process of formulating, testing, and, where necessary, modifying a hypothesis as a matter of intellectual urgency.

This book had its vaguely formulated genesis as I was finishing *Menippean Satire Reconsidered: From Antiquity to the Eighteenth Century* (2005). Like many students of the eighteenth century, I then more or less accepted the notion of an increasingly secular and "enlightened" age. The social, psychological, political, and religious brutality cognate with the battle between the Ancients and the Moderns disabused me of that happy view. Its counternotion of an eighteenth century still wed to the divine right of kings, passive obedience, an imposingly dominant High Church of England, and Jacobites crowding the pubs, government, and Church also seemed to me a learned but parochial and often xenophobic outgrowth of 1980s boutique historiography. At one point in such scholarship we even find George I likened to Hitler. Bishop Francis Atterbury's co-conspirators lied to government ministers, the Commons, and the Lords, all of whom represented "a German king." These brave victims, we read, "were much in the same position as members of the Resistance in Europe in the years 1940–44 who were questioned by the Germans."[22] As in Atterbury's case, then, there was indeed a clear sign that some High Churchmen sought again to dominate British culture and to restore a Stuart monarch and his presumably divine right. As with the '45 and other instances, Atterbury's plot lacked popular or fuller ecclesiastical support. Another civil war might benefit the Stuarts and France; it could not benefit Britain.

The late seventeenth and earlier eighteenth-century political and religious fear and often loathing reflected a world peering into an abyss. Despair and rage seemed palpable among all groups, whether beleaguered churchmen, latitudinarians, Dissenters, and sects springing from any of these. For many, either Chaos or even the devil himself was ready to reclaim the world collapsing at both its center and its margins. Even the confidently avuncular narrators of *Joseph Andrews* (1742) and *Tom Jones* (1749) responded sternly to the inherent dangers of a renewed political and religious civil war upon the Jacobite invasion of 1745. Fielding then writes *A Dialogue Between the Devil, the Pope, and the Pretender.* "We are indeed Joint-Workers" in destruction, the pope says of that unholy trinity. Fielding's *True Patriot*, No. 25 (1746), is politically different from Swift some thirty years earlier, but it shares Swift's dark, angry, and frightened tones. Fielding excoriates the incomprehensible and unnatural selfishness of the '45 itself, as well as those who either supported it or were tepid in opposing it. These and other "detestable Vices" reverse the divine inclusion of sympathy and sociability in the human spirit and spread corruption "thro' all Ranks and Degrees of Men."[23]

The repeated vision of human darkness within and without led me to an almost inevitable source for such matters: Conrad's *Heart of Darkness* (1902). We remember that according to Marlow, Kurtz has gone over the edge and has looked into places from which normal human beings retreat. His judgment of his own heart, the colonialist's heart, and the human heart is "The horror! The horror!" Upon Marlow's return to Brussels he visits the still mourning home of Kurtz's Intended, whose name we never learn. After some minor chat, she asks about Kurtz's last words, which, in an emotive triplet, she must have: "'His last word—to live with,' she insisted. 'Don't you understand I loved him—I loved him—I loved him!'" Marlow is faced with a nearly shattering choice of love or death and needs to pull himself together. As the consequent dash in Conrad's prose suggests, Marlow hesitates even into the answer itself: "The last word he pronounced was—your name." The Intended bursts out with "an exulting and terrible cry." It is "of inconceivable triumph and of unspeakable pain. 'I knew it—I was sure!'. She knew. She was sure. I heard her weeping; she had hidden her face in her hands." Marlow is troubled by his lie but cannot tell the truth. "It would have been too dark—too dark altogether." Marlow has chosen a version of light over darkness and distance from the edge over which Kurtz stepped. He also has chosen to preserve a myth of love and, loosely, of civilization, in which one's certainty of being remembered and loved, of loving and being loved beyond the grave, remains exultingly vibrant. Whatever the horrors of colonial Africa, of the English Thames valley, once so colonized by imperial Romans, or in the human heart, the scene in Brussels ensures that one person preserves love and memory: "Don't you understand?"[24]

Much crystalized around that one exchange, which unwittingly returned me to certain great eighteenth-century figures and their ability to look into the heart of darkness, which seemed so powerful in their own times. The working title of the book that developed was "Hearts of Darkness: Swift, Johnson, Burke, and Confrontations with Evil in the Eighteenth Century." Swift was the Kurtz character, for whom the human race was so grimly unconscionable that he could find reason only in horses unpolluted by Europe's civilization. Johnson was the Marlow character, as able as Swift to see human darkness but willing to step back, to tell us that yes, we may fail, but that the real failure is in not trying to succeed. The French Revolution, the grim Indian situation, and the Warren Hastings trial returned Burke and his generation to the earlier world of collapse of values and decency in Europe and in a colonial enterprise. Things changed but stayed the same.

It soon became apparent to me that Burke needed to be saved for another time or to be considered by hands and heads more comfortable with the massive problems of postcolonial literature and analysis. What I thought of as the "Tory" bias of the book still remained in the contrast between Swift and Johnson—dark visions with different responses, a Kurtz and a Marlow, one stepping over the edge and one perhaps awkwardly stepping away. As the book progressed, however, it became increasingly clear that eighteenth-century culture also had "progressed," that Ned Ward's earlier eighteenth-century concept of *All Men Mad*, characterized in the first two chapters, would be reconsidered. Chapter 3 taught me that the thirtieth of January sermons excoriating Dissenters and urging the divine right of kings changed; many preached a version of limited tolerance, the divine right of government, not kings, and in some cases even a legitimate regicide if the monarch was a tyrant. By chapter 4, biblical interpretation of Luke 14:23, "Compel them to come in," had changed from Augustinian compulsion by force to Christian moral suasion. Methodists, in chapter 5, at first thought yet another crackpot sect, were accepted, if often grudgingly, as part of the mainstream Protestant religious order. Even Smollett's Methodist Humphry Clinker ends that novel with almost physical placement within the gentry/Matt Bramble's Anglican church. The darkly Tory beginning of my study had become a mid-project quasi-Whig enterprise, after which it no longer was possible to write the book that I had begun years earlier. Eighteenth-century British culture indeed had changed, perhaps for the better, but where would it go after, say, *Humphry Clinker* in 1771?

Not to a good place, it seemed in chapters 6 and 7. The violent "No Popery" Gordon Riots in 1780 threatened at the least to disrupt moral progress, as well as to destroy much of London and the commercial power on which national dominance rested. Within a decade, though, Britain restored itself from its distant American collapse, its immediate urban rubble, and its moral disintegration, in which martial law was an undesirable but necessary final embarrassment. It would fight a successful, almost world war against its Great Satan across the Channel. How it endured the Gordon Riots, restored itself, but nonetheless engaged in state terrorism against Lord George became objects of inquiry regarding his pamphlets and of literary analysis for Dickens' *Barnaby Rudge*. My sense of that restoration was reinforced by Britain's vigorous debates regarding Catholic emancipation in 1829 and the abolition of slavery in 1833, neither of which could have happened a hundred years earlier. British culture during that time remained deeply connected to religious roots, but those roots were more varied and produced fruit very different from that hitherto on ancestral soil. Chapter 1 begins with a quotation from Ned Ward's *All Men Mad: Or, England a Great Bedlam* (1704). One subtitle of chapter 6 is "Bedlam Revisited," and one repeated image in *Barnaby Rudge* in chapter 7 is London's madness in its riots. In spite of that painful incursion, Britons made a collective decision that sanity was preferable to insanity. Bedlam was not a good place to be. Cerebration and the ability to learn from errors, good sense, and basic decency provided a curative cocktail for mental illness.

I have discussed, above, the concept of evolution, which soon intruded itself within this book's evolving conceptions. I use the term in what I hope is a largely anodyne way. An organism changes, indeed progresses, through time as it often haltingly adapts to its environment; it preserves its better results by choice, by benign accident, or both. Those who adapt best are more likely to survive, so that over time the later organism differs significantly from its earlier form. The Gordon Riots represented a reversion that British culture chose not to accept. Its choice of Hercules was stark: to simplify, the choice between difficult Virtue or easy Vice. Of course, life lacks the static parable in a painting or a poem, and nineteenth-century Britain scarcely was a moral nirvana. As a watershed, though, the hundreds dead after the Gordon Riots, the hanging of children, the broad presence of redcoats, and the fires, rubble, and mindlessness of lunatic drunken crowds made the choice relatively easy, if nonetheless larded with depravities. The cooperative aspect of evolution urged British culture to correct flaws the Gordon Riots painfully illumined: a police force is better than martial law; debate regarding how best to deal with a religious minority is better than mob unrule, for example. The book that once had been called "Hearts of Darkness" itself became what it now is: *Literature, Religion, and the Evolution of Culture, 1660–1780*.

Given such a conversion experience and the learned readers about to begin this book, it is perhaps appropriate to end the Introduction with words from two great men. John Dryden speaks to those with *Absalom and Achitophel* before them. Some may violently oppose Dryden's temperate estimate of Absalom, "but they are not the Violent, whom I desire to please. The fault, on the right hand, is to Extenuate, Palliate and Indulge; and, to confess freely, I have endeavour'd to commit it." In 1765 Johnson lamented critics' need to waste paper "in confutation . . . to demolish the fabricks which are standing" in others' efforts. This further slows the already "slow advances of truth." I thus, generally, have let other "fabricks" remain fabricated in place, let my text speak for itself, and relegated sources of disagreement either to notes or to the aether. At the end of the *Dictionary*'s preface Johnson modestly listed himself among the "candidates of inferiour fame. I must now stand the judgment of the publick; and wish that I could confidently produce my commentary as equal to the encouragement which I had the honour of receiving. Every work of this kind is by its nature deficient."[25] I am grateful that this book has forced me into vast new fields of inquiry, in which I nonetheless assume that I remain deficient and insufficiently informed. Perhaps my readers also will make Dryden's benevolent right hand's fault of extenuating, palliating, and indulging.

A Note on Notes

This is a heavily annotated text. It is so in part because I hope to make consequent research in primary and secondary sources easier for others. I have tried to emulate Johnson on Shakespearean criticism: "I can say with great sincerity of all my predecessors, what I hope will hereafter be said of me, that not one has left Shakespeare without improvement, nor is there one to whom I have not been indebted for assistance and information." Rather than further annoy readers with yet more such notes, where appropriate I have bunched several citations into one longer note. Parenthetical tag words identify the works quoted. This method occasionally may seem ambiguous, but it will save considerable bobbing of heads, flipping of pages, and yet more troublesome little numbers that might otherwise go into triple digits. Johnson on Shakespeare again offers typical wisdom: "Notes are often necessary, but they are necessary evils." He adds that "the mind is refrigerated by interruption; the thoughts are diverted from the principal subject." Given this truth, Johnson recommends that we read the entire play and then return to the notes for necessary elucidation.[26] I suggest a similar procedure for those with this book in hand. Either read the entire section or chapter and then proceed to the notes, or read the notes and then proceed to the section or chapter. Either way will warm the refrigerator and, perhaps, be less diverting from the principal subject.

NOTES

1. For a small proportion of the useful books on the history of evolution, see Carl Zimmer, *Evolution: The Triumph of an Idea* (London: HarperCollins, 2001); Stephen Jay Gould, *The Structure of Evolutionary Theory* (Cambridge, MA: Belknap Press of Harvard Univer-

sity Press, 2002); and Edward J. Larson, *Evolution: The Remarkable History of a Scientific Theory* (New York: Modern Library, 2004). Buffon and Lamarck in France, of course, had significant impacts, some reconsidered, on evolutionary theory. For two helpful guides, see Pietro Corsi, *The Age of Lamarck: Evolutionary Theories in France, 1790–1830*, trans. Jonathan Mandelbaum (Berkeley: University of California Press, 1988); and Jacques Roger, *Buffon: A Life in Natural History*, trans. Sarah Lucille Bonnefoi, ed. L. Pearce Williams (Ithaca, NY: Cornell University Press, 1997). For discussion of the cooperative or group elements in evolution studies, see Martin A. Nowak with Roger Highfield, *Supercooperators: Altruism, Evolution, and Why We Need Each Other to Succeed* (New York: Free Press, 2011). For the conscious acts of individuals over long periods, see Raymond Tallis, *Aping Mankind: Neuromania, Darwinitis, and the Misrepresentation of Humanity* (Durham, UK: Acumen, 2011); Tallis accepts Darwinism but not Darwinian evolutionary psychology, which denies free will. I am scarcely new in adapting the concept of evolution to literary and broader matters. See Carey McIntosh, *The Evolution of English Prose, 1700–1800: Style, Politeness, and Print Culture* (Cambridge: Cambridge University Press, 1998).

2. Elisha Coles, *An English Dictionary* (London, 1708) (rolling); Nathan Bailey, *An Universal Etymological Dictionary* (London, 1721) (unfolding); Thomas Dyche and William Pardon, *A New General Dictionary* (1735), 2nd ed. (London, 1737) (common); Samuel Johnson, *A Dictionary of the English Language* (London, 1755) (whole). These definitions are regularly repeated throughout various editions and throughout the century. That is true as well regarding the two other variant meanings.

3. *Extraction* is in numerous lexicons, including Edward Phillips, *The New World of Words* (London, 1706); John Kersey, *Dictionarium Anglo-Britannicum* (1708), 2nd ed. (London, 1715); Dyche and Pardon, *New General Dictionary*; and Ephraim Chambers, *Cyclopaedia: Or, An Universal Dictionary of Arts and Sciences* (London, 1728, with several reprints). For the borrowing from Johnson, see Egbert Buys, *New and Complete Dictionary of Terms of Art. . . . Dat is: Nieuw en Volkomen, Konstwoordenboek* (Amsterdam, 1768), s.v. "evolution." Johnson's 1755 illustrative quotation os from John Harris, *Lexicon Technicum: Or, An Universal English Dictionary of Arts and Sciences*, 2nd ed. (London, 1710), s.v. "evolution."

4. Denis Diderot and Jean le Rond d'Alembert, *Encyclopèdie, ou dictionnaire raisonné des sciences, des arts et des métiers* (Paris, 1756), 6:169–206: evolution is "les différens mouvemens qu'on fait exécuter aux troupes pour les former ou mettre en bataille, pour les faire marcher de différens côtés, les rempre ou partager en plusieurs parties, les réunir ensuite, & enfin pour leur donner la disposition la plus avantageuse pour combattre, suivant les circonstances dans lesquelles elles peuvent se trouver" (6:169). Military evolution appears often in Thomas More Molyneux, *Conjunct Expeditions: Or Expeditions That have been carried out jointly by the Fleet and Army* (London, 1759).

5. Diderot and d'Alembert, *Encyclopèdie*: on avoiding confusion, "Sans la connoissance & la pratique de ces regles, une troupe de gens de guerre seroit qu'une masse confuse, dont toutes les parties s'embarrasseroient réciproquement" (6:169); on the advantage of coordination, "c'est principalement dans ces sortes de cas [dans evolution], c'est-à-dire lorsqu'on peut approcher de l'ennemi & le charger, que l'on peut tirer de grands avantages de la colonne" (6:195).

6. For Robert Bakewell, see Roger Wood and Vitezslav Orel, *Genetic Prehistory in Selective Breeding: A Prelude to Mendel* (Oxford: Oxford University Press, 2001). Darwin's *Loves*

of the Plants also appeared as part 2 of *The Botanic Garden . . . Containing The Loves of the Plants, A Poem. With Philosophical Notes* (Lichfield, UK, 1789), 2:[ix] and [xiv] for two of the overt evocations of Linnaeus; see the note to line 65 for the quotation. Erasmus Darwin soon became part of the chain of evolutionary progress: see Samuel Butler, *Evolution, Old and New: Or, The Theories of Buffon, Dr. Erasmus Darwin, and Lamarck, as Compared with that of Mr. Charles Darwin* (London, 1879). Maureen McNeil considered Erasmus Darwin's scientific contexts in *Under the Banner of Science: Erasmus Darwin and His Age* (Manchester: Manchester University Press, 1987). Jennifer S. Uglow has characterized the intellectual energy of the Lunar Society, in which Darwin played a key part: *The Lunar Men: The Friends Who Made the Future, 1730–1810* (London: Faber, 2002). For Buffon, see George Louis Leclerc, comte de Buffon, *The Natural History of the Horse. To which is added, that of the . . . Sheep . . . with Accurate Descriptions of their several Parts. . . . Translated from the French of the Celebrated M. De Buffon* (London, 1762), p. 95 on horses and "the judicious choice of the stallions and mares" for breeding and p. 257 on sheep and a consequent "intermediate breed" when stronger, foreign sheep mated with smaller, local French sheep.

7. John Ray, *The Wisdom of God Manifested in the Works of the Creation, In Two Parts*, 3rd ed. (London, 1701), sig. A8^v (nothing), 306 (generate). This book went into a thirteenth edition in Glasgow in 1756. The *Encyclopaedia Britannica* entry is in volume 2, s.v. "Equus." The barbs were brought to Spain by the Moors and are relatives of the modern Arabian racehorse. Iago calls Othello a "Barbary horse" (1.1.110).

8. The Yale Edition of the Works of Samuel Johnson, vol. 7, *Johnson on Shakespeare*, ed. Arthur Sherbo (New Haven, CT: Yale University Press, 1968), pp. 60–61 (hereafter cited as YE by volume, title, and editor); Johnson, *The Lives of the Most Eminent English Poets*, ed. Roger Lonsdale (Oxford: Clarendon Press, 2006), 3:60 (Pope), 4:212–13 (Swift). Johnson is using *emulation* in the sense of ugly and jealous competition. For discussion of both emulation and rising British confidence, see Howard D. Weinbrot, *Britannia's Issue: The Rise of British Literature from Dryden to Ossian* (Cambridge: Cambridge University Press, 1993), pp. 91–113 (emulation) and passim.

9. For some useful guidelines to "progress," see Jules Delvaille, *Essai sur l'histoire de l'idée de progrès jusqu'à la fin du XVIIIe siècle* (Paris: F. Alcan, 1910); J. B. Bury, *The Idea of Progress: An Inquiry into Its Origin and Growth* (London: Macmillan, 1920); Charles Frankel, *The Faith of Reason: The Idea of Progress in the French Enlightenment* (New York: King's Crown Press, 1948); R. V. Sampson, *Progress in the Age of Reason: The Seventeenth Century to the Present Day* (Cambridge, MA: Harvard University Press, 1956); W. Warren Wagar, "Modern Views of the Origins of the Idea of Progress," *Journal of the History of Ideas* 28 (1967): 55–70; and Ronald S. Crane, "Anglican Apologetics and the Idea of Progress, 1699–1745" (1934), reprinted in Crane, *The Idea of the Humanities and Other Essays Critical and Historical* (Chicago: University of Chicago Press, 1967), 1:214–87. David Spadafora's impressive book *The Idea of Progress in Eighteenth-Century Britain* (New Haven, CT: Yale University Press, 1990) moves the debate from France to Britain. It includes a useful bibliographic essay on the subject. Among other studies, see Pierre-André Taguieff, *Le Sens du progrès: une approche historique et philosophique* (Paris: Flammarion, 2004).

10. The California Edition of the Works of John Dryden, vol. 3, *Poems, 1685–1692*, ed. Earl Miner and Vinton A. Dearing (Berkeley: University of California Press, 1969), p. 116, from "To my Ingenious Friend, Mr. Henry Higden, Esq; On his Translation of the Tenth

Satyr of Juvenal," and p. 208, "Lines on Milton" (1688) (hereafter cited as CD by volume, title, and editor). Dryden uses a similar concept in his 1693 "To my Dear Friend Mr. Congreve." He both combines and overmatches Fletcher's excellent dialogue with Jonson's judgment, as well as all the beauties of the present age's Etherege, Southern, and Wycherley (lines 20–29).

11. Joseph Addison, *The Spectator*, ed. Donald F. Bond (Oxford: Clarendon Press, 1965), 2:563.

12. Thomas Burnet's Latin *Telluris theoria sacra* appeared in 1681. For this quotation, see his *Theory of the Earth: Containing an Account of the Original of the Earth, and of All the General Changes Which it hath already Undergone* (London, 1684), p. 39. It was broadly reissued, as in Glasgow in 1753.

13. John Locke, "An Examination of P. Malebranche's Opinion of Seeing All Things in God," in *Posthumous Works of Mr. John Locke* (London, 1706), pp. 206–7 (hereafter cited parenthetically in the text). I have not identified the source of Johnson's quotation from Locke.

14. Edmund Burke, "Fragment, An Essay Towards an History of the Laws of England," in *The Writing and Speeches of Edmund Burke*, vol. 1, *The Early Writings*, ed. T. O. McLoughlin and James T. Boulton, textual editor William B. Todd (Oxford: Clarendon Press, 1997), p. 322 (hereafter cited parenthetically in the text).

15. Edmund Burke, *Reflections on the Revolution in France, and on the Proceedings of Certain Societies in London Relative to that Event* (London, 1790), pp. 117 (dissolved), 11 (every thing, monstrous), 10 (prosperity).

16. Jean Antoine Nicolas de Caritat, marquis de Condorcet, *Outlines of an Historical View of the Progress of the Human Mind: Being a Posthumous Work of the Late M. De Condorcet. Translated from the French* (London, 1795), preface p. ii (hereafter cited parenthetically in the text).

17. John Dryden, CD 2, *Poems, 1681–1684*, ed. H. T. Swedenberg Jr. and Vinton A. Dearing (1972), pp. 46 (Anarchy, Tempting), 52 (seeds, rightfull). The best discussion of this set of poems remains Phillip Harth's *Pen for a Party: Dryden's Tory Propaganda in Its Contexts* (Princeton, NJ: Princeton University Press, 1993).

18. Samuel Johnson, "Life of Roscommon," in *Lives of the Most Eminent English Poets*, 2:19.

19. Quentin Skinner, "Measure and Understanding in the History of Ideas," *History and Theory* 8 (1969): 16. "The writing of the history of ethical and political philosophy is pervaded by this mythology." That was true as well during the height of the New Criticism in literary studies. It has been replaced by the mythology of contradiction and incoherence. Neither monism is adequate before the complexity of human literary practice.

20. For the relevant texts, see Herbert Butterfield, *The Whig Interpretation of History* (London: G. Bell, 1931); and Henry Hallam, *The Constitutional History of England from the Accession of Henry VII to the Death of George II* (London). Hallam's (1777–1859) achievement suggests the difficulty of pigeonhole categories: the Old Etonian and Christ Church (1799) Whig grandee also was a fervent enemy of the slave trade. Michael Bentley has well discussed the longevity of the Whig interpretation in his *Modernizing England's Past* (Cambridge: Cambridge University Press, 2010).

21. Samuel Johnson, YE 2, *The Idler and the Adventurer*, ed. W. J. Bate, John M. Bullitt, and L. F. Powell (1963), p. 489.

22. Eveline Cruickshanks and Howard Erskine-Hill, *The Atterbury Plot* (Houndmills, Basingstoke, Hants: Palgrave Macmillan, 2004), p. 198.

23. The Wesleyan Edition of the Works of Henry Fielding, *The True Patriot and Related Writings*, ed. W. B. Coley (Middletown, CT: Wesleyan University Press, 1987), pp. 85 (Joint, from *A Dialogue*), 266 (detestable), 267 (Ranks, both from *True Patriot*).

24. For these exchanges, see Joseph Conrad, *Heart of Darkness: A Case Study in Contemporary Criticism*, ed. Ross C. Murfin (New York: St. Martin's Press, 1989), pp. 90–93. I have dealt with this issue in "Hearts of Darkness: Swift, Johnson, and the Narrative Confrontation with Evil," in *But Vindicate the Ways of God to Man: Literature and Theodicy*, ed. Rudolf Freiburg and Susanne Gruss (Tübingen: Stauffenburg Verlag, 2004), pp. 205–23.

25. John Dryden, CD 2, *Absalom and Achitophel*, in *Poems, 1681–1684*, p. 4 (they are not), in italics; Samuel Johnson, "Preface to *Shakespeare*," in YE 7, *Johnson on Shakespeare*, pp. 99 (confutation, slow advances), 112 (candidates).

26. Johnson, YE 7, *Johnson on Shakespeare*, pp. 101 (I can say), 111 (Notes, the mind).

PART ONE

THREATS TO THE SPECIES

Madness, Discontent, and the Danger of Dissolution

CHAPTER ONE

Causation and Contexts of Hatred

Savage Beasts Mortal and Deadly

I begin with two contradictory remarks. In 1702 the fire-breathing High Church Tory Henry Sacheverell explained both why humanity needed a check upon its darker instincts and how that check could take place:

> Nature, by itself, is a meer State of Anarchy and Confusion, of Ruine, Rapine and War; and tho' it be Regulated, Restrain'd, and Tyed up by *Political Laws*, yet These Reach not to the *Intellectual* Part, the most Dangerous, Active, Busy, and Destructive part of Man. These take Cognizance only of *Evil in Act*, when it is Brought forth and Produc'd: it must be Religion alone that can Stifle it in the Birth, and Destroy the Seeds and Original Causes of Impiety and Injustice.

Two years later, Ned Ward considered whether religion had indeed stifled such destructive impulses.

> Religion, which we us'd to prize
> Above all things beneath the Skies,
> With the grave Saints as well as Ranter,
> Is now become a common Banter:
> Some use it to improve our Fears,
> And set the Nation by the Ears.
> Others, to cloak their ill Designs,
> And hide their Antichristian Mines,
> Prepar'd to blow up Church and State,
> The only Objects of their hate.[1]

Ward's lament suggests major contexts for young Jonathan Swift and his contemporaries. The religion of peace, which once was a cause of literal war, now was a cause of figurative war and broad cultural confusion. Each side thought the "Other" at the least Beelzebub's vicious lapdog, and the two sides often used similar weapons. In 1709, for example, a Whig/Low Church cartoon showed the Pretender in a coach driven by the devil in petticoats, with Sacheverell on the lead horse. They drive over the figures of Moderation, Toleration, Liberty, and Property. The High Church responded with a similar cartoon, in which perhaps Cromwell's coach behind the same devil and Hoadly on the lead horse rolls over Monarchy, Liberty, Loyalty, and Episcopacy.[2] One year later Hoadly and Joseph Trapp wrote mirror-image attacks on their opposing parties. Trapp's *True, Genuine Modern Whigg-Address* (1710) tells Queen Anne, "It is with Grief that we have observ'd of late a mighty Zeal to appear for the Monarchy which we have labour'd so long to Extinguish" (p. 1). Hoadly's *True, Genuine, Tory-Address* (1710) in turn tells her, "It is with Grief that We have observed of late, a mighty Zeal to appear for the REVOLUTION, which We were in good hopes had been by this time forgotten" (p. 1). A few years later, the thirtieth of January sermon *Whigs No Christians* (1713) was answered by *Whigs Truly Christian* (1713). Such point and counterpoint were regular occurrences in regularly unpleasant confrontations.

Dissension thus was rife even within Protestant ranks. Establishment fought Dissent. Dissent fought Establishment. Dissent fought Dissent. High Church fought Low Church. Low Church fought High Church. Schism, deism, heresy, and atheism seemed everywhere, and for Bishop Atterbury among others, "the bad were never worse." Even one's own group often seemed to have a fifth column sapping from within and undermining virtue's fortress. As William Penn said of his "*Treacherous*" Quaker apostates, "Let them go for Enemies to *Christianity*, and Murderers of Natural Affection." Atterbury, however, regarded that sect as an unChristian font of "damnable errors" within "a complicated system of Deism and Enthusiasm," a view of those uniquely idiosyncratic people Jonathan Swift shared.[3]

Rather than the center not holding, many could not know where the center was in so hostile and disorienting a climate. By 1687 Gilbert Burnet lamented that Christianity now had created "the most implacable *Society* that has ever yet appeared in the World." Edmund Hickeringill put it this way in 1707: "A great deal of Bustle and Noise, a great deal of Murther, Rapine, and Ruine is made in the World about Religion, more than any other matter or Thing in the World." All schismatics disagree, and all use scripture badly interpreted to justify themselves. Protestant sects are numerous, varied, and curse and damn "each other to the Pit of Hell. And before they can thrust them into the *Bottomless Pit*, they fairly *deliver* one another *to the Devil*, in this Earth by *Excommunication*; and then cut one anothers Throats for Religion."[4] No wonder Ned Ward titles his poem *All Men Mad: Or, England A Great Bedlam*. No wonder it includes "Church and State" as in danger and cries, "The Church is in her self divided, / And by her grumbling Sons derided." No wonder it observes that the church's best advocates "In the most dang'rous Times desert her" and "Side with a factious Brood that hate her" (pp. 16–17). *All Men Mad* sadly concludes with "We know not who to Love, or who to Trust" (p. 27).

How did the world, apparently so optimistic upon the restoration of Charles II in 1660, become so pessimistic for so long thereafter? What happened to turn the putative force of restraint into an actual force of multifaceted and often scabrous language and behavior? There are several possible answers. Ward's cry that "we're all but in Confusion still" (p. 10) was a function of turmoil in that uncomfortably manacled couple church and state.

A simple recitation of key dates and events within about seventy-five years of English history offers the bare bones of at least a partial explanation. A civil conflict at once religious, political, and social begins in earnest in 1641; it culminates with the beheading of Charles I in 1649 during a Puritan theocracy; it unravels in 1658 with the death of Oliver Cromwell and the inability of his son to maintain paternal discipline. With the restoration of monarchy in 1660 Charles II returns to the throne, but bitter arguments regarding religion continue and culminate in the Exclusion Crisis, which sought to bar the legitimate heir, his Catholic brother James, Duke of York, from assuming the throne. Events worsen in 1685, when Charles II dies as a Catholic. The worse apparently becomes the worst upon the accession of James II, who allows toleration of Dissenters further to separate them from the Church of England, to encourage the power of fellow Catholics and, many feared, the forced conversion of his subjects. Events become yet more dangerous in 1688, when Parliament invites the Dutch Calvinist stadholder Willem Hendrik Prinz von Orange and his wife, Mary, a Protestant daughter of James II, to invade England and assume the throne, which James II then "abdicates" and flees to France. Willem becomes William and introduces an Act of Toleration, which like its predecessor gives new power to Dissenters and evokes the resignation of Archbishop Sancroft and eight other bishops, who refuse to read the Act of Toleration from their pulpits. William engages England in a long and costly Continental war with Louis XIV that enlarges Whig strength and England's military reputation but angers and solidifies the growing Tory opposition. James' younger Protestant daughter, Anne, becomes queen in 1702, assures the Anglican Church that she is its friend, and by 1713 brings the War of the Spanish Succession to a close. She dies one year later, and George I, the Lutheran Elector of Hanover, is crowned as George I. Some of the nation's most exalted aristocrats at home and abroad either overtly or covertly support the Old Pretender, the nominal James III, whose family had been domiciled in France and Rome for some twenty-seven years. In 1715 Jacobites launch a failed invasion on his behalf. In 1722 Francis Atterbury, bishop of Rochester and former dean of Christ Church, the most royalist and conservative Oxford college, is arrested for high crimes against the state. After a sometimes juridically irregular trial, he is properly found guilty and exiled to France as the leader of another Jacobite invasion scheme. Well might a new Shakespearean Henry V have said of such exalted traitors: "I will weep for thee, / For this revolt of thine methinks is like / Another fall of man" (*Henry V*, 2.2.238–39).

Within a relatively short period of time, then, Anglican England loses one monarch to the victorious usurper's ax, loses that victor to age, and restores an Anglican king who is a closet Catholic. Thereafter, an aggressively Catholic monarch is forced out for a Dutch Calvinist who seems to threaten episcopal dominance but whose death later restores an English Anglican queen. Her own death brings a German Lutheran to the British Anglican throne. Constitutional and religious fevers remain dangerously high, and portions of the Church of England itself seem to be or are enemies of the pending Hanoverian dynasty. Ned Ward's *All Men Mad* again has it right regarding the terrible consequences of such often religious conflict. It breeds discontent, disruption, and rebellion. It alienates subject and Crown, which it also endangers. It creates family strife "and makes Mankind hate one another" (p. 20).

Of course there were many examples of attempted mediation between sides, many temperate exercises in reason and good sense, and searches for a middle way of compromise by reasonable people who agreed to disagree. There also was much recognition that Britons overwhelmingly embraced a shared Christian religion. Dryden's *Religio Laici* (1682) and *Hind and the Panther* (1687) and Archbishop Tillotson's sermons are among the handsomely sane displays of the spiritual and theologically irenic. In 1695 the editor D. Cumyng tells readers of *Two Sermons* that those in both the established and dissenting churches worship the same God, honor the same king, and support the same government. Why, then, "may they not live in mutual Peace and Love?" Why may they not "regard each other as belonging to the same *Commonwealth of Israel?*" In some cases the argument extended as well to High Church and lower church. In Addison's *Spectator*, No. 106 (1711), Sir Roger de Coverly gives his country clergyman an eclectic book of sermons that includes latitudinarian Tillotson and altitudinarian Calamy. This *Spectator*'s clergyman himself reads a sermon from Low Church William Fleetwood on Sunday morning and from High Church Robert South on Sunday afternoon.[5]

In spite of the peaceful gestures, however, polemicists emphasized the differences and the importance of those differences for church-state relations. Apparent moderation thus often was denigrated as lies by soldiers hiding their arms before a merciless assault designed to ruin church and state in 1701 as they had in 1641. The High Church spitfire Charles Leslie insists that "there can be no *Neuters* in this War." Men may cry *"Peace, Peace!* When there is no *Peace;* and our *Enemies Preparing War* against us." Philip Stubs' sermon in 1702 clarifies the stakes: *For God or for Baal: Or, No Neutrality in Religion.* Philo Basileus complains about "canting hypocritical Exhortations to Moderation." The Philo Britannus behind *Popery and Schism Equally Dangerous* (1715) also uses a martial metaphor. Presumed moderates who urge occasional conformity are like "Postern Gates" that open to a "secret Enemy, in the Disguise of a Friend within . . . the Walls of a besieg'd City." Daniel Defoe's *Moderation Maintain'd* (1704) understandably laments that moderation was met by "the most bitter Invectives, and the most biting Sarcasms."[6] For Defoe the plea was fruitless. For Leslie it was hypocritical.

Hatred seeks excuses rather than reasons, but there were several such reasons other than political disruption for this garrison spirit and pandemic hostility from at least the mid-seventeenth century to about the third decade of the eighteenth century. One reason surely was perceived and inherent human depravity, what Swift called "the corrupt Sentiments of the Heart of Man." Ammianus Marcellinus long ago had seen that corruption at work among bloody warring Christians: "No savage beasts are so noisom and hurtful to men, as Christians are to themselves, and for the most part of them mortall and deadly."[7] Those remarks of the late third century were all too appropriate for the European seventeenth and earlier eighteenth centuries.

Conjuring Up Reasons: Original Sin, Fragile Connections, Church and State

Religious groups often saw little but decay, disillusion, danger, and a return to the terrible moral, political, and theological disorder that civil war represents. Controversialists looked into the gulf and saw what they thought was the heart of darkness. They indeed expected such darkness from a race infected with the original sin that still omnipresent Augustinian theology taught all political sides to find in human corruption. Edward Stillingfleet was sadly confident that the "best of Mankind have guilt enough upon them." In 1708 High Church Luke Milbourne preached a stern thirtieth of January sermon and offered a clear theory of causation for regicide and moral anarchy: "I am involved in *the Sin of Adam*, at the distance of a thousand Generations. The Sin of *Adam* corrupted the *Fountain* of human Life, and the Streams will therefore always run muddy" and always will add to the main stream's "Breadth and Strength, and to its Filthiness." The Whiggish and at the least Low Church physician Peter Paxton viewed his world of civil war, repression, schism, constant threat to freedom, and attempted extirpation of congregants in alternative religions as in France. He moans: "Oh

Horror!" Like the High Church Milbourne, Paxton knows that "such is, and hath been the Depravity of Humane Nature that even the dreadful Threats our Blessed Religion denounces, are not always sufficient to deter Men from persuing their worldly Desires." No sect can keep its members "from falling into the Vices common to the corrupt state of Mankind." Joseph Trapp also laments that "the Nation is so shatter'd and divided" by the ferocity of religious conflict that "Destruction approaches."[8] In such an inevitably corrupt world, religion indeed plagued and disunited the state it was supposed to unify.

Another shared reason for fear was the assumption that all things were interconnected: deviation from one norm inevitably meant deviation from all norms. The theory included a pedagogical genealogy that appears again in the Anglo-French battle between the Ancients and the Moderns in general and in Swift's *Tale of a Tub* (1704) in particular. Roger Ascham's *Scholemaster* (1570) warned against rejecting "the best mens iudgementes, in liking onelie their owne opinions." Dissent from Aristotle in logic and Cicero in rhetoric "will, from these steppes, likelie enough presume, by like pride, to mount hier, to the misliking of greater matters" in religion or politics. Ascham knew "a student in Cambridge, who, for a singularitie, began first to dissent, in the scholes, from *Aristotle*, and sone after became a peruerse *Arrian*, against Christ and all true Religion ... whereby the Church of Christ, was so poysened withall." Swift later would warn against "new doctrines and disciplines" in the church or state that must lead to a destructive Babel.[9]

One recognizes the fragility of culture in so enmeshed a world and its fear of singularity. Deviation from Aristotle leads to heresy; deviation from episcopacy and the established church leads to religious and political anarchy. The true Catholic Episcopal Protestant Christian Church based its governance on ancient Hebraic rites, the Apostles' practice, and the church fathers' writings. God placed his authority in the bishops' hands; only they in turn could ordain other priests and authorize modes of worship, church discipline, and the proper relation of church to state. Henry Dodwell became a non-juror after 1689, but he spoke for the orthodox view of the high and low Restoration Church of England: "the very name of the *Episcopat* implies a Supreme Power, immediately next to that of God and Christ." He knew that one "sins against Christ the Invisible Bishop, who refuses to pay due Obedience to the Visible Bishop, who still represents the Person of Christ." Latitudinarian Anglicans added that for their church to be properly comprehensive, certain liturgical acts, like genuflection before the altar, crossing, and infant baptism, were matters indifferent. These should be left to the individual conscience and the parish's shared practice. Both sides agreed, however, that only bishops could ordain priests, establish church government and discipline, and provide a via media between the twin dangers of Rome and enthusiasm. To do otherwise would invite blasphemy, sin, and attempted deicide—what Ascham called a poisoned church of Christ, often through bad learning. The author behind *A Step to Oxford* (1704) likens the university to a fountain. Once it is tainted, its "Springs and Rivolets" spread "Universal and Epidemick" corruption.[10]

High Churchmen and other Tory writers were especially aware that the first step in yielding to latitude was the first step on the road to perdition, indeed to uncreation. Roger L'Estrange's *Short Answer To A Whole Litter of Libellers* (London, 1680) insists that the government must not permit Presbyterianism. It is "like a *Sea-breach* to your *Grounds*: / Suffer but *One Flaw*, the *whole Country Drowns*" (p. 3). The author of *Toleration and Liberty of Conscience considered and . . . Impossible* (London, 1689) uses a scientific allusion to make a similar point. He says of Dissenters and their dangerous plea for toleration: "Give them but this Spot to fix their Engine upon, and, like *Archimedes*, they . . . shall be able to remove the Earth from off its Hinges"—that is, to threaten the church and monarchy with destruction unless they get their way (p. 7). George Smalridge indeed built much of his thirtieth of January sermon for 1702 around the concept of degree. Good men must not collaborate with bad men, who will inevitably corrupt them. That was what happened when honorable parliamentarians were seduced by the regicides. They were "carried on step by step to those Extremes, which at their first setting out they could not have thought it possible for them ever to have arrived at."[11]

Shortly thereafter, Samuel Grascome (or Grascombe) writes *The Mask of Moderation Pull'd off the Foul Face of Occasional Conformity* (London, 1704). Let those "moderates" define accidental matters of worship, and they soon will define away "the *Essentials*" of religion: "take away the *Fences*, and the Vineyard it self would quickly be trodden down" (p. 54). Without those fences, Thomas Rennell knows in *The Nature, Causes, and Consequences of Divisions* (London, 1705), the body of the Church "will be no more; for it will be all rent into loose and scatter'd Limbs." The Church then well may reflect a world "of *Hobbes*'s making" (p. 29). Henry Sacheverell understood what such eradication of fences meant. He and other High Churchmen alluded to Matthew 5:17–18, in which Jesus says that he comes not to destroy but to fulfill the prophets: "For verily I say unto you, Till heaven and earth pass, one jot or one tittle shall in no wise pass from the law, till all be fulfilled. Who so ever therefore shall break one of these least commandments, and shall teach men so, he shall be called the least in the kingdom of heaven." For Sacheverell, "whosoever presumes to *Recede* the least *Tittle* from the *express Word of God*, or to explain the Great *Credenda* of Our *Faith* in *New-fangl'd Terms* of *Modern Philosophy*, must publish a *New Gospel*, *Un-God* his Saviour, and *Destroy* his

Revelation." Even a relative moderate like William Baker insists that "when a Breach is made, no one Knows where the Inundation will stop." Hence once decent men "were led Step by Step to much Greater Lengths than they Intended, till they found Themselves Insensibly Seduc'd into Actions they at First, and at a Distance Abhorr'd."[12]

This rage at broken links was extensive and neither gender- nor sect-specific. L'Estrange urges that Quakers and other schismatics begin by rejecting popish lords, which soon generates into no bishops, no lords, no House of Commons, "And in the *Conclusion, No King.*"[13] Mary Astell's *Impartial Enquiry into the Causes of Rebellion and Civil War in this Kingdom* offered a familiar tale of Dissenters' gradual increase in demands until they destroyed the church and king: "the Encroachments are small at first, and industriously concealed" until the unwary people are trapped and destroyed, for "the Sword being drawn, the Scabbard must be thrown away." Francis Bugg's *Quakerism Drooping, And its Cause Sinking* (London, 1703) in turn lambastes that dangerous splinter group, whose members refuse to remove their hats as a mark of respect for the social order. They also deny the divinity of Jesus, the validity of baptism, the scriptures, and episcopal or other authority external to their own. Such diabolical characters threaten to destroy "the very Foundation of the Christian Faith" (p. 27). The foundation metaphor is equally appropriate for encroaching papists, who want to destroy the Protestant "Bastion or Bulwark," which they seek "to undermine" by splintering the Church of England: "no Doubt they will pursue it *in infinitum,*" Philo Britannus warns.[14]

Lower churchmen and Dissenters gave as good as they got. William Penn's *Judas and the Jews Combined against Christ and his Followers* (1673) enlarges a catalog of insults that includes *bastard, murder, rapist,* and *slander* and makes plain that only true Quakers are true Christians. The others surely shall go to hell, where God's "Rod of his Fury" (p. 64) punishes apostates and non-Quakers and binds them "in chains of Darkness" (p. 85). Their evil returns "from whence it came, even the Bottomless Pit" (p. 91). Only those who seek "to bring People into *Atheism*" vilify the Quakers (p. 81). John Dennis' *Danger of Priestcraft to Religion and Government: With Some Politick Reasons for Toleration* (London, 1702) responds to Sacheverell's church-state screed *The Political Union* (1702) and laments the designs of his "restless Party" and its dangerous attempts to conflate its own power with religion (p. 4). Priestcraft, Dennis knows, "has done more harm to the Christian Religion even than open Immorality" and encourages rampant deism and atheism (p. 7). He lists High Church desire for secular power, clerical greed, "Rage and Malice, and the Fury of Persecution" and asks whether these embody "the True, the Christian Catholick Priesthood. No, these are so many Antichrists" (pp. 9–10). Such creatures long had made gradual incursions on native liberties. In *The Life of the Right Reverend Dr. White Kennett, Late Lord Bishop of Peterborough* (London, 1730), William Newton describes his subject's shrewd recognition of Charles I's errors. These stemmed from his popish queen and corrupt ministers, "who had been taking many Steps towards a more Arbitrary Government, that by Degrees, might have gone into absolute Tyranny" (p. 39).

As several such remarks connote or denote regarding connections, the Church of England and the Crown of England required mutual loyalty. Perceived threats to such joined cousins was another reason for fear. Thomas Bennet's *Discourse of Schism* (1702) makes plain that "*Schism* in the Church or Spiritual Body Politic, is the same with Sedition, Faction or Tumult, in the State or Civil Body Politic." S. E. adds: "He that is untrue to his God, and unsettled in his Religion, can never be Just to his Prince, or firm to the Interest of his Country," about which he will prevaricate and betray. Shortly thereafter, John Savage adds that latitudinarians seek to level the power of church and state. Attacks upon these holy institutions are a product of "ill designs against the Crown; it being a very natural Conclusion, that they who invade the Rights of God, should have but little regard to those of Princes." Mary Astell more bluntly says that "Schism in the Church begets a Schism in the State." Luke Milbourne's *Moderate Cabal* (1710) rhymes the commonplace: "He who forsakes his God, will quickly bring / His Disposition to desert his King."[15]

Most Low Churchmen, Erastians, and Dissenters in general agreed that loyalty was urgent, but they also modified the relationship between church and state. Daniel Defoe's(?) *Occasional Letter Number 1* (1704) grants that a few Dissenters may have collaborated on 30 January 1649; but Whigs and Dissenters as a party "*Abhor and Disown* it as much as" the Tory Party does. Indeed, Defoe also says in *Moderation Maintain'd*, the state's true enemies are the high flyers, but since 1688 the Dissenters have been quiet and loyal, "not so much as lifting up a Finger against the Government, either in Church or State, and continue so to do." In 1705 Edmund Hickeringill argued that the "*Church is in, but* not *above* the *State.*" Moderate churchmen are loyal, but grasping High Church priests will rebel if they are not given power "to the utter disobliging" of Queen Anne's "other Subjects." As the broadside *High-Church and the Doctor out of Breath* put it in 1711, "No truer Loyalty ever was seen, / Than by the Low Church will be shewn to the Queen." That loyalty strengthened itself through exercise on behalf of the queen and also the Hanoverians, both of whom Bishop William Beveridge was glad to celebrate in 1706.[16]

The presumed connection between schism and disloyalty nonetheless was long remembered and long proclaimed. The angry Tory behind *The Moderation and Loyalty of the Dissenters* (1710) knew that once the earlier schismatics had their first requests granted, their "Ostentation of *Loyalty* concluded in the subversion of the *Monarchy*, as, under the colour of a *Reforming Zeal*, they overturn'd the Church." There was "a direct Line from the Pen to the Scaffold." Jonathan Swift put it this way in 1726: under Elizabeth the "wicked Puritans" began "to quarrel only with surplices and other habits, with the ring in matrimony, the cross in baptism, and the like; thence they went on to further matters of higher importance, and, at last, they must needs have the whole government of the church dissolved."[17]

Aristocratic Historiography: Advocacy and Resistance

These arguments on connection, dissolution, and growing demands were reinforced by the aristocratic eminence of Clarendon's *History of the Rebellion and Civil Wars in England, Begun in the Year 1641* (1702–4). Each of its three Oxford volumes was dedicated to Queen Anne and prefaced, unsigned, by Clarendon's son and editor, Laurence Hyde, Earl of Rochester, Lord Lieutenant of Ireland, and in 1702 and 1703 a member of Queen Anne's Privy Council. His Tory resentment was enhanced upon his dismissal from that council, and he used his prefatory matter for political statements. He hoped to stiffen her Majesty's spine, rally the faithful, justify himself and his distinguished father, and supply both ammunition and authority for royalist and High Church beliefs. He would oppose and perhaps even check the growing Whig power in court, church, and state.

Readers were initiated as soon as they saw the *History*'s title page in 1702. It offers the first of each volume's identical images of Britannia armed for battle, her shield embossed with an ominous Medusa's head as an emblem of the horrors of war. A fallen caduceus, a globe, an open book, and scientific implements are to her left. A fallen laurel crown and another open book are to her right, with Oxford's Sheldonian Theater behind her. The sciences and arts collapse, and learning in general is but a backdrop during a civil war. Both the place of publication and its appearance "at the THEATER" also remind us that Clarendon was chancellor of loyalist Oxford during part of the time after, as the subtitle puts it, *"the KING's blessed RESTORATION, and RETURN."*[18] Clarendon's *History*, illustrative icons, and editor made plain that such loyalty was abandoned at a high price.

The *History* indeed was recognized as what it never sought to hide—a defense of the High Church and of a strong, if parliamentary, monarch. In 1704 Mary Astell thus knew that "my Lord *Clarendon* has so unluckily [for the regicides] display'd the whole Contrivance" of their schemes. Like Astell, Samuel Grascome borrows Clarendon to attack White Kennett's apparently "wicked Palliation" of Charles I's execution. A few years later Jean le Clerc's Englished *Account of the*

Earl of Clarendon's History of the Civil Wars (1710) acknowledged its "too odious a Turn" to the parliamentarians' conduct and "a too favorable one to the Actions of the King; without perceiving it." He "bestows infinite Praises" on the Caroline clergy and is confident that Archbishop Laud best "shews that the Religion of the Protestants, is the assured way to arrive at Salvation." This partiality even could be turned to the Dissenters' use. The Presbyterian James Anderson tells readers of his thirtieth of January sermon, *No King-Killers* (1715), that he has been helped by historians who "are supposed to favour the *other side* most, especially the *Earl of Clarendon*." John Withers comparably clears the Presbyterians of king-killing, with Clarendon's authority.[19]

Clarendon's text was of course the main event, but it was introduced by Rochester's more compact and politically comparable editorial action, which evoked reaction. Reluctant absorption by Dissenters to the contrary, the *History* remained a powerful and popular royalist document. In 1727 John Oldmixon says that though he long thought Clarendon's book a misrepresentation, he delayed writing against it because "for several Years . . . no Body would have given a Hearing to any one, who should have said a Word against it." Now that Echard's comparable distortion has appeared, it is time to speak out.[20] Oldmixon probably overstates, but like le Clerc he makes plain that Clarendon's bias was inconsistent with modern Whig ideology. The historian supposes that the church and Crown had the rights to spiritual and secular tyranny, so that persecution could be justified "if they were again put in Practice," as Charles II wanted (p. vii, in italics). That is why in the *History* all the "Wise, Virtuous, and Valiant Men listed in the Cause of Persecution and Oppression, and so many Blockheads and Poltrons [sic] in that of Religion and Liberty" (p. ix). Oldmixon not only thinks that the apparently unrecognized Rochester altered Clarendon's text with "Razures and Interpolations" (p. vi). He also argues that the several dedications and prefaces embody Clarendon's own odious politics. Those documents talk "either Nonsense or Treason" (p. xxiv) and include "an open Attack of the Revolution, and Queen Anne's Title to the Crown" (p. xxv). They are "sacrifices to Arbitrary Power" (p. xxvi), lack "Judgment, Modesty, and Conscience" (p. xxviii), and are absurdly argued (p. xxxi). Yet worse, they are "afraid of Liberty" (p. xxxiv) and replace true "*Revolution Principles*" with false High Church principles of "*Passive Obedience, and Non Resistance, Hereditary Right*, and every Principle which would have kept a Popish King in the Throne, and a Protestant Prince out of it" (p. xxx). For Oldmixon, Rochester's too-long-admired prefatory matter before Clarendon's too-long-admired *History* is resolutely un-British: "He intimates, that the Constitution of the *State* was weaken'd by destroying *Absolute Power*; and that of the *Church*, by destroying Persecution: which is what these worthy Gentleman always mean by Church and State, and nothing else. I do not know whether what follows is Treasonable or Nonsense" (p. xxxv).

Whichever it was or was not, Clarendon's books were demonstrably controversial. On 31 January 1704 White Kennett delivered his sermon *A Compassionate Enquiry into the Causes of the Civil War*. Its apparent apology for the parliamentarians caused an uproar and publication of at least five impressions or editions. One of its lines found itself confronted by Clarendon: "If the Body of a good natur'd *English* People had but *thought* themselves secure in their Legal Rights and Tenures, they could never have been seduced into that Unnatural Rebellion." Rubbish, Samuel Grascome soon replies as he quotes and mocks Kennett's lines, because "I believe the E. of *Clarendon*'s Authority in that, or any other Case, may be as great, at least, as Dr. *Kennet*'s." Lord Rochester enters the fray with the preface to volume 3, whose Oxford imprimatur is dated 16 October 1704. Rochester praises Queen Anne, who can restore the "good Nature (for which the *English* Nation was formerly so celebrated)."[21] Rochester as editor and polemicist thus is very much part of the response to Clarendon's *History*.

Volume 1's preface includes familiar Tory topics. The dates 1641 and 1660 almost bracket the first sentence's first clause (1:1). Here and elsewhere (e.g., 3: sig. c2^v) church and Crown are one concept and one part of the "old Principles" Clarendon and his associates maintained (1:ii). The *History* was begun at Charles I's request but is truthful, impartial, and fair even to the scions of the great men who "were engaged in the Quarrel on either side." The work thus should be "received rather as an Instruction to the Present Age, than a Reproach to the last" (1:iii; all prefatory matter is in italics). The preface also is predictably anti-Catholic, antienthusiast, and warmly Anglican. It is the best church in the world, against whom, adapting Jesus to Peter in Matthew 16:18, the "Gates of Hell were not to prevail" (1:xiv). Like other men, Charles I was not perfect, but he was a good monarch who loved his people and Parliament and was destroyed by an evil faction.

The preface is personal and political in other ways. Its noble defense of Clarendon as a man and as a statesman alludes to Rochester's own difficulties in Queen Anne's moderate government. For example, he regularly excoriates courtiers and courts as unreliable, ungrateful, vicious places with "secret Engines that Actually consummate the Mischiefs, that others, in a more publicke way, have been long in bringing to pass" (1:xx). That court could not have been pleased to see its former independent self now represented as the home of "obsequious" courtiers (1:viii), as bad as the perpetrators of "continued Calumny, and Back-biting" (1:xvii). They finally "hunted down, and unavoidably destroyed" the father (1:xii), as in a less ominous way they did the dismissed son, who also sought to "redress, and correct any mistakes" in royal judgment (1:xi).

These mistakes clearly related to modern Whig as to earlier republican errors. Clarendon hopes to "Awaken Men to that Honesty, Justice, Loyalty, and Piety, which formerly English Men have been valuable for" and now lack (1:iv). Indeed, the loyalty to church and Crown is so deeply eroded that within fifty years of the murder of pious Charles I some are uncertain "on whose side was the Right, and on which the Rebellion is to be charged" (1:iii). His lordship is not shy about suggesting the source of such moral laxity: his is a dangerous time "when a Revolution hath been thought necessary to make a Reformation" (1:x)—surely a sneer at William of Orange, whose invited Crown rejected the passive obedience that Rochester knew was right and proper (1:vi). That monarch initiated the War of the Spanish Succession, wrongly, he implies, continued by Queen Anne and wrongly, he more than implies, prosecuted by Marlborough on land rather than on the natural triumphant English element, the sea (1:viii–x). Her Majesty's counsels include "unaccountable improvidence" on that score (1:ix). To engage France on land is folly, for Louis "must be, for many Years, at least, invulnerable" (1:ix), says the editor, unable to predict Marlborough's great and consistent, if bloody, victories.

Rochester enhances this attack on Whig policies by also attacking Whig political theory, which Tory writers regularly found obnoxious. He excoriates the "wild Notions of appealing to the People out of Parliament (a Parliament sitting) as it were to a fourth Estate of the Realm; and calling upon them to come and take their share in the direction of the publick, and most important Consultations." That attack upon the "ancient and true Constitution" returns one to past violence (1:viii). By 1703 and the second volume of the *History*, Rochester would be asked to leave her Majesty's Privy Council, but he saw a world in which Whig authority and English royal and ecclesiastical collapse were cognate. Indeed, both in 1703, when Rochester was free of the court, and again in the 1704 third volume, he offered a virtual précis of Tory complaint consistent with the complaints by High Church and sympathetic political commentators that I have outlined earlier.

Much of the 1703 preface is a sub-rosa attack upon the never mentioned William of Orange. Rochester reiterates the urgent unity of church and state (2: sig. a2^v), as if to remind Queen Anne of the danger of Toleration. It encourages unrepentant antimonarchic and illegal dissenting academies, which teach "an industrious Propagation of the Rebellious Principles of the last Age," desecration and mockery of the thirtieth of January sermons on behalf of the blessed royal martyr, and of course the "very Expensive War" (2: sig. b1^v) that Queen Anne inherited and continues. Rochester again just suggests the cause of that war by praising Queen Mary, whose "power indeed was more limited and dependent" but whose death allowed Anne's "*English* Heart . . . so *Entirely English*" to assume "more unrestrain'ed and Soveraign Authority... resign'd to Your self alone" (2: sig. b2ʳ). Anne's husband, the Prince of Denmark, is subservient, as Mary's Dutch husband, William, was not. In spite of that backhanded compliment, the dedication understandably angered Queen Anne, who thought it negatively "extraordinary" and inappropriate: "it is very wonderfull that people that dont want sense in some things, should be soe rediculous as to shew theire vanity."[22]

Rochester's ridiculous vanity was enameled by rhetoric and imagery that we will see in numerous other Tory documents. Both *A Tale of a Tub* and the third volume of Clarendon's *History* appeared in 1704. That volume laments all the "noble and innocent Blood" shed in the rebellion and dislikes Whiggish substitution of religious principle by "a levelling principle" (3: sig. c1ᵛ). It sees "the madness of Men" returning "once again to overthrow the Monarchy, and then to perpetuate the destruction of it" (3: sig. c2ᵛ). It knows that the numerous dissenting academies are places "where the fiercest Doctrines against Monarchical, and Episcopal Government, are taught and propagated" and that this "Torrent" must be resisted "by the whole Legislative Authority" (3: sig. d1ʳ). Within the disloyal masses one finds "Atheism, and Profaneness," which are "diligently cultivated" and produce a crop of prostituted "Manners in contempt of all Government" (3: sig. d1ᵛ). Though "these Mischiefs have been still growing," they also are starving the Church of England, ineffectually "put to Nurse" (3: sig. d2ʳ).

Many like-thinkers shared Rochester's sense of danger, betrayal, and return to past depravity. An army of madmen were about to push the decent and loyal subjects into a deadly sea of political and religious vice. Comparable language, however, was a weapon in the other side's rhetorical arsenal as well. It was not a jolly world-view, whichever world one viewed.

Metaphorical Enhancements: Floods, Propagation, Legions, and Dutch Treats

Clarendon and Rochester at the least seeded already fertile ground. Swift's, and others', image of dissolution was joined by equally dramatic clusters of dark images that reflected and enhanced fear and loathing. Two of these images paradoxically conflate the destruction and death of the good with the propagation and increase of the bad. Enemies are everywhere and will commit any sort of evil. One basic metaphor in the cluster is that of what Rochester called a torrent. It also could be a flood, deluge, or inundation that contrasts tellingly with God's severe but ultimately cleansing cataclysm. Thereafter, his rainbow and olive branch–bearing dove signal a bond between the human and the divine, land and water. Reconciliation, repopulation, and a second chance for a race sinking in a sea of its own sin then follow. Works like *For God or for Baal; Or, No Neutrality in Religion* in 1702 and *All Men Mad* in 1704 use only the punitive part of that story. They transfer the power of inundation from the benevolent God to the malevolent devil or his agents.

These uniformly hostile floods threaten to drown the benign church, letters, true believers, and, for High Church Tories, the divinely ordained monarchs, who had long labored on their subjects' behalf. For lower church Whigs and Dissenters the floods came from altitudinarian absolutists, who seemed scarcely different from the French and the papists they secretly supported. We recall Roger L'Estrange's image of the single flaw in a sea wall that leads to flooding of the entire nation. So far as many advocates of the higher or lower church could see, the breach already had taken place, caused in part by indifference to the law of unintended consequences. William Fleetwood put the issue in touchingly domestic and agrarian terms: "He who breaks down the Bank of a great Water, occasions the Overflow, it may be, of a great deal of Ground, the Fall of a House, the Death of a Child, and the Drowning of many Cattle. *Who would have thought it?* is a Fool's Excuse, when things follow naturally, closely, or easily."[23]

As in so many other cases, the image came from the Old Testament as well as from observation of nature. In 1735, for example, the conservative but staunch Whig William Crowe preached a thirtieth of January sermon based on Proverbs 17:14: "*The beginning of Strife is as when one letteth out Water; therefore leave off Contention before it be meddled with.*" Like his higher church colleagues, he warns that a river "having once broke its banks, it grows an impetuous torrent, and runs thenceforth without measure, and without controul." It will rush "furiously, and . . . with a violence and impetuosity not to be withstood"—as happened once the strife between Charles I and his Parliament finally led to regicide.[24] Crowe is a demonstrable trimmer, almost equally troubled by each side in the 1640s and by the contention among his fellow subjects in 1735. He urges respect for government and avoidance of the strife and contention that modern politics regrettably includes. Many of his recent clerical predecessors were more darkly colorful regarding the unleashed floods of vice.

The metaphor of the flood as deluge of vice was sadly familiar. Charles Leslie asks God to forbid a second attempt to remove religion as a bulwark against another "*Deluge* of *Immorality, Heresy,* and *Atheism.*" In 1703 Francis Bugg knows that such persecutors "would have a Sea of Blood." Shortly thereafter, Thomas Sherwill laments what a "Deluge of Absurdities in Religion overspread the Land" during the rebellion. Samuel Grascome comparably sees that "an Inundation of Faction, Libertinism, and Wickedness" has broken in and is resisted by few. One of Luke Milbourne's many harsh sermons excoriates earlier rebels who shed "*vast*

Seas of Blood" and created "prodigious Floods of *Generous and Noble Gore.*" The pseudonymous J. Silvius well evoked such sanguinary scenes. Bishop Sancroft's ghost laments the "Seas of Blood" necessary for atonement to God's anointed monarch: their "Neighbouring Plains, once more will glutted be, / With Human Blood, Sickness and Poverty." Ned Ward's verse, Clarendon influenced, *History of the Grand Rebellion* (1713), drew rebels who "waded through a crimson Flood / Of Loyal, Innocent, and Royal Blood."[25]

Low Church and dissenting writers were equally troubled by attacks upon the bulwark of Protestantism in England but naturally used the relevant image for their own purposes. Thomas Cotton preached *A Sermon . . . to the Societies for Reformation of Manners* (1702) and noted that until God sent William III to save England, "Popery and Slavery [were] bearing hard in like a Deluge." The author of *High-Church Politicks* (1710) saw that James II, divine right, and popery threatened "the Church and State with an entire Inundation." James Anderson later concurred. In 1715 he saw that the parliamentarians had removed the "great Danger of being . . . swallowed up by a Deluge of Popery." Some Whig writers shared their Tory adversaries' vision of an incarnadined sea. Edmund Hickeringill insisted that "by Priest-craft, floods of Blood and Ruine have deluged Christendom," which now "is deluged in Blood at this day, above and beyond any part of the Earth." As John Withers reiterated, under the odious Charles I "Lawless Tyranny" forced "the Sword out of its Scabbard, and made it drunk with the *Blood of Thousands.*" None of this impressed High Church opponents. Luke Milbourne exemplified comparable language by like-minded polemicists keen to blame their enemies for national collapse. He berated rebels who made Britain and Ireland "*one great Field of Blood*" and "made way for that fatal Inundation of *Tyranny, Heresy, Superstition, Blasphemy*, and worse than *Paganism* in these Nations."[26]

Of course the ugly image gets uglier still when reinvoked during the Jacobite threat of 1715. The Congregational minister Thomas Bradbury stipulates that bad churchmen want to see "the Liberties, that have been seal'd with the Blood of our Fathers . . . quite drown'd in our own."[27] At one point the image becomes almost comically ghoulish. The author of *A Tale and No Tale: That is to say, A Tale, and No Tale of a Tub* (London, 1715) may or may not be commenting on Swift. He certainly is commenting on the invading putative James III and his plans, which Saxon— that is, free and anti-Roman—George I must stifle. The Pretender proclaims:

> My *Right Hereditary* to maintain,
> I'll wade thro' Blood of new-born *Infants* slain;
> And when the Stream's advanc'd above the Chin,
> I'll Heav'n applaud, and thirsty gulp it in. (P. 21)

Some of these images of inundation included implicit theories of causation, one of which related to William of Orange. Attitudes toward Dutch William were indeed another basic source of brutal conflict that would not be resolved until well into the Hanoverian era. For the High Church, William was the alien invader whose alien religion and alien Toleration were dangers to the English nation, church, and values. These churchmen were so troubled, in part, because William's empowerment of Dissenters was like the empowerment for which James II was forced from his legitimate throne. In 1702 Charles Leslie remarked that "the *Toleration* granted by K. *James*, (and for which, the most of any one thing, he was *Abdicated*) has *Enlarg'd*, and much more *Encourag'd*" dissent. The consequence was "the great encrease of the *Faction*" in number, power, insolence, and threat to the Church of England. He later added that William favored and elevated Dissenters and may have done so either to encourage popery or because he himself was a Dissenter and occasional conformist. Such conduct is all too typical of the Dutch "Faulty *Policy* . . . to intermeddle with the *Government* of their *Neighbours*." As Leslie fears in *The Principles of the Dissenters concerning Toleration* (1705), William's unfortunate Act will "destroy all Religion" and is "that by which the Devil would . . . lay a foundation for his Kingdom to all Generations." The consequence already was clear in empty pews, stifled reform, unsettled church discipline, and increased schism, division, and religious incoherence. In what Leslie must have thought a dreadful insult, he insists that "the famous City of *London* is become an *Amsterdam* . . . *Toleration* is cryed up, Authority asleep."[28]

One expects such jeremiads from Leslie and those many other altitudinarian divines. They almost certainly agreed with Leslie that, as James Owen paraphrased him, William, Mary, Archbishop Tillotson, "and a great Number of the *Bishops* and *Clergy conspired with the Dissenters to destroy the Church*." Mary Astell's *Impartial Enquiry into the Causes of Rebellion* makes clear why such an English aberration happened. Presbyterians and Whigs join "and tend to the same End, who place the Supreme Power originally in the People." When they are powerful enough they will "put their *Thoughts* and Fancies in Execution." In fact, "the People have no Authority over their own Lives, consequently they can't invest such Authority in their Governours." However that may be, Francis Atterbury later adds, "the People," a false *vox dei*, were responsible for the rebellion and the murder of Charles I.[29]

Other like-minded High Churchmen agreed. Henry Sacheverell knew that such *"Religious Liberty"* as a *"Civil Right"* was the *"Encroaching Monster"* designed for that purpose. All this, Luke Milbourne added as he urged the "utter Extirpation of Tyrants and their Families," was consistent with theories that removed political and religious power from the throne to that amorphous and ugly fantasy called the people. They somehow had an unrecorded contract with someone somewhere at some time that allowed them to depose a divinely anointed monarch who had displeased them for some reason. Milbourne saw such dangerous folly in writings by men like Knox, Buchanan, Milton, Baxter, Sidney, Locke, and similar "Agents of Darkness." Their principles are "fit for Nothing, but to *Ruin Kingdoms* and *Common-wealths*, to *overturn Churches*, to *extirpate Christianity*, and if God would permit the Infection to spread so far, to *depopulate the Universe*."[30] Such views were familiar.

Sackville Tufton thinks that William and his adviser Sunderland were traitors to church and state. Tufton is pleased by William's death because it advanced a queen "to the Throne, whose *Heart was entirely English*" and who was therefore devoted to the Church of England, as a foreigner could not be. Hostility to "foreign" indeed becomes a scarcely veiled code for hostility to William and the Dutch. Charles Leslie wrote his *Now or Never* circa 1696. He feared for "the total Subjection or *Conquest* . . . of the Nation, by the Importation of Greater Numbers of *Foreigners*; and these under a *Foreign* General, who commands in *England*." Such aliens should not be naturalized. The angry author of *A Letter Out of the Country* (1710) is even more overt. He rages at the Whig "Managers Pro and Con" for its use of "FOREIGNERS AS WELL AS BRITAINS. . . . By Foreigners as well as Britains!" to oppose the theory of nonresistance. They won't stop "*'till We have a* Dutch Government, *as well as a* Dutch Alliance" well supported "*in the* Amsterdam Gazette." No wonder Benjamin Hoadly's *Voice of the Addressers* (1710) complains that these men are "fighting against the *States of Holland*, and not the Monarch of *France*." No wonder as well that in January of 1706 the Whig third Earl of Shaftesbury unfairly but understandably told Monsieur van Twedde that "if you would discover a concealed Tory, Jacobite or Papist speak but of the Dutch and you will find him out by his passionate railing."[31]

These are not happy men. Dissenters and lower churchmen, though, indeed urged that the "People are the original and end of Government." In William they found the bright sun of a new day that allowed life and spirit to flourish. As one author put it, "His Highness the Prince of *Orange* came" to rescue the "People" so alienated from James II. We recall that Thomas Cotton, among others, regarded William III as God's Dutch emissary to protect the Church of England and Protestant liberty. That familiar view helps to initiate the Whig interpretation of history. Edmund Hickeringill, for example, knows that heaven sent William's Act of Toleration to stop priestcraft, muzzle the malicious High Church dogs, and enhance lower church authority. He thus proudly and aggressively affirms that unlike the antichrist, mendacious, and diabolical papists and high flyers, "*Christ*'s true *Church* and *Churchmen* are the *Low-Church*, made up of Meekness, Moderation, Lowliness, Brotherly-Kindness, even to *Gainsayer and Enemies*." That demonstrably Erastian church is ordered by Williamite bishops, who neither domineer nor persecute and are subservient to the state.[32]

Given such contrasting attitudes, response to William and such Whig views were easy markers to identify apparent High Church aberrations. The author of *The High-Church Bully, or The Praise of Mr. [Francis] Higgins* (London, 1707) observes that this Irish Sacheverell damns "our Dutch *Redeemer* and his *Cause*" (sig. A1ᵛ). The ironic ventriloquist, perhaps Daniel Defoe, behind *A Letter from A Gentleman At the Court of St. Germains, To One of his Friends in England* (1710) encourages his local propagandist to instill fears of the Dutch and of William of Orange, "the great Cause of all our Misfortunes." One thus should lessen British esteem for him and "blacken his Memory as much as possible." That nasty monarch acted only for power and ambition: "This Article is so much the more essential, because if we can once make the Revolution odious and black, all that is built upon it will fall of course; and we cannot begin better than by giving the People bad Impressions of him who was the Author of it."[33]

Moreover, it is scarcely a new insight to say that both Swift and Alexander Pope had little good to say about William of Orange or about the Dutch in general. *An Essay on Criticism* (1711) includes lines lamenting England's imported, presumably casual Williamite religion (lines 544–59). The third book of *Gulliver's Travels* (1726) ends with a Dutchman trampling on a crucifix. Pope's later *Dunciad Variorum* (1729) includes the Dutch and flooding images that, as it were, floated throughout many of the anti-Toleration tracts. "Proceed, great days! 'till Learning fly the shore," he says. Pope's note warns us not to be securely contemptuous of the apparently "weak agents" he describes: "but remember what the *Dutch* stories somewhere relate, that a great part of their Provinces was once overflow'd, by a small opening made in one of their dykes by a single *Water-Rat*." The stark term probably alludes to the Hanover rat thought to have crossed the water with George I, but the reference also evokes William of Orange and the flooding of Britain with presumably lax new ecclesiastical doctrines and discipline and new forms of national government. I suspect that such an attitude also was behind two other remarks. In one, Mary Astell observed that many "think it highly necessary to secure the Dykes against the Inundation of Error and Schism . . . And consequently of Faction and Sedition." We find another remark in *The Proceedings Of Both Houses of Parliament . . . 1704, Upon the Bill to Prevent Occasional Conformity* (1710). This author joins colleagues who are convinced that the slightest deviation from ecclesiastical or political orthodoxy will be fatal, as in the broken dyke that leads to inundation: "If one picks at a great Dyke that keeps out the Sea, it will be thought how small a Breach soever he makes at first, that he designs a total Inundation."[34]

However dreadful all such regal, episcopal, latitudinarian, dissenting, enthusiast, agnostic, atheistic, deist, skeptic, or other evildoers are, they seem immune to death by water or by seas of blood. Instead, they regularly propagate, are nursed, grow, propagate again, and repeat the terrible cycle with yet greater numbers that parody God's benign decree to go forth and multiply. In one scenario the villains threaten to overwhelm the few decent defenders of faith, fragile order, and the divinity, if not of kingship, certainly of government itself. Francis Atterbury is among those who see cause and effect, insemination and its consequences. Quakers' "damnable errors . . . have been embraced and propagated" by many more evil Quakers. Charles Leslie (1702, 1704), Henry Sacheverell (1704), Thomas Bennet, Mary Astell, and Jonathan Swift are among the other Tories who lament such malign fertility. For Leslie, the dissenting faction "now more than ever, come out Thick and Threefold upon us every Day, to *Propagate* their Abhorr'd *Principles* of *Schism* and *Rebellion*." They indeed have "a *Fiery Zeal* to propagate" schism and false inspiration in order to overturn the world. Bennet knows that schism threatens Protestantism, has "occasion'd the birth and growth of numberless wild and curs'd Opinions" hostile to Christianity, and has caused "infinite other disorders." Astell sees that "the *Forefathers*" of 1649 transmitted "the same Causes, by which their *Offspring* were influenc'd." Both Swift's *Tale of a Tub* and the several versions of Pope's *Dunciad* comparably employ the image of powerful sexual energy, propagation, and the vast power that threatens stable culture. For many, we know, such procreative threat included the dangers of "moderation" so dangerous to the established church and state. In 1711 Henry Welstead placed that evil term in its mock-biblical but evil genealogy: "*Calvin* begat Presbytery, and Presbytery begat Separation, and Separation begat Independency, and Independency begat Quakerism, and Quakerism begat Scepticism, and Scepticism begat Atheism, and Atheism begat Moderation."[35]

Whigs and Dissenters again used comparable images for their own purposes. Gilbert Burnet asks us to be "the Sons and lovers of Peace" in order to live decently. Peter Paxton's thoughtful *Civil Polity* in 1703 tries to establish the relationship between religious and political freedom. He regards good political propagation as a normal part of normal government and spiritual concerns: "A Multitude of . . . Calamities" follow when a government establishes one religion and forces its subjects to obey or to be regarded as enemies of the state. Such bad and autocratic governments will refuse to allow "Religious Opinions" to be "so far propagated as thereby to form a Sect." Consequently, such governments "can never Regularly perform their Natural functions" and will become disorderly. This repression also violates the usual workings of the human mind. We are naturally fond of our own opinions, think them true, and therefore also think it "desirous to Propagate them." A few years later, *High-Church Politicks* returns to propagation as an emblem of the wickedness of religious contention, for which higher churchmen are responsible. The mischief of the last age's "Divisions," its bitter rhetoric of High Church versus Low Church and Dissent, "is entail'd, it is propagated with their Beings, as if Contention was the common Inheritance of a degenerate Clergy." In contrast, White Kennett scolds Sacheverell's brutal sermons and praises Queen Anne's ability "to propagate Christian Knowledge and Morality at home and abroad." That is quite different from the High Church ranters, who, Thomas Gordon says in 1718, have "no other intent, than to propagate . . . Confusion, and Affront the Government."[36]

As the image of entail suggests, propagation requires continuity. Leslie saw that evil *"Nurseries"* spread about the lies regarding bishops and clergy. For Joseph Trapp, Whig Dissenters propagated "Lewdness and Irreligion" and "are presently at work to improve [ridiculous religious notions] against Christianity in general." In time these deviants like Quakers "are Grown to be a *Rich* and *Numerous*, and therefore a *Dangerous* People." As the author of the broadside *Character of a Quaker* (1704) put it, the now fifty-year-old *"Animal* is . . . grown to a formidable as well as monstrous Bulk, being nourish'd by Contradiction, Lying, Worldly Interest, and Self-Conceit." Atterbury again darkens and embellishes the image: "Infidelity hath taken deep root, and, being cultivated with care, hath spread its branches wide, and shot up to an amazing height, and brought forth fruits in great abundance." On the other hand, for the Whig Paxton bad governments, inadequately nursed with freedom and diffusion of power, are "like Monstrous and disproportionate Births." Shortly thereafter, stern Defoe quotes Charles Leslie on the Dissenters but expects sympathetic readers to apply the image to Leslie and his allies: they "have had leisure to Grow, and soon produce a new Crop of Devils."[37]

The monster also could be a plague of locusts, or a vast crew capable of "numberless mischiefs" and "numberless wild, and cursed Opinions" against true Protestants, or like "the Devils in *Milton's Pandaemonium*," or a spreading infection.[38] Perhaps the most grimly evocative allusion was to the biblical term drawn from the destructive Roman legions, and more immediately from Mark 5:9. Jesus asks the possessed man: "What is thy name? And he answered, saying my name is Legion; for we are many"—that is, devils who ravage the human spirit.

As is consistent with the image of propagation, each side also regularly accuses the other of being so numerous and possessed. Hickeringill knows that *"the Devil's* Name [is] *Legion."* He also sees his powerful High Church adversaries, whose "Names are *Legion,* for they are many" but nonetheless cannot defeat him. Defoe premises his *High-Church Legion* (1705) on the same biblical concept made political for the "meer *Church Legion*" and "the Party's *Legion.*" Luke Milbourne and Charles Leslie surely were among Defoe's enemy party, but they too saw that their own dissenting fanatic opponents had strength in numbers, "in their *Legion,* for *they are many.*" Milbourne saw legions of brutes allied with Beelzebub and who flattered and factionalized. For Leslie the legion has "long *Possess'd* the Deluded *People,*" with its antimonarchic mob principles, and also has "set up . . . against the *Commons.*" He further expands the metaphor to conclude the second part of the *New Association.* Upon the Restoration, "the *Legion* which had so long *Possess'd* the Deluded *People*" was briefly "*Driven* but not *Rooted* out." The devils were neglected, indulged, and "have had Leisure to Grow, and soon Produc'd a New *Crop* of *Devils*; who are *Enter'd* into the *Herd* of *Swines*" who recently grunted in the Kentish Petition.[39]

One of Charles Leslie's other allusions makes clear the High Church grievance, embattlement, and anger that suggest despair. In *The Wolf Stript of His Shepherd's Cloathing* he complains about the unprecedented harsh language with which "Moderate" Whigs and Dissenters abuse the Church party. They are represented as unprincipled men, unworthy of life and practitioners "of the *Grossest Immoralities.*" Why such treatment? "Because these are the Men that stand in the Gap, and hinder the Builders of *Babel* from Performing *All that they have Imagin'd to do,* both as to *Church* and *State.*"[40] Leslie has conflated two horrendous Old Testament observations. In Genesis 11:1–9 God punishes and disperses the once linguistically, politically, and morally pure people who build Babel. In Ezekiel 22:30–31 the angry God again sees nothing but vice within Israel and "sought for a man among them, that should make up a hedge, and stand in the gap before the land, that I should not destroy it; but I found none." The people then are consumed with the fire of God's wrath. Leslie seeks to answer God's call, and is destroyed not by God but by the malicious Whigs and Dissenters characteristically perverting divine purity.

Earlier remarks by Astell, Swift, and others make plain that these many diabolical, heretical, violent men had performed deeds that long were remembered and regularly were trundled out as part of what was called the "entail" of High Church hostility. High Church polemicists well knew that Dissenters began their assault upon episcopacy under Elizabeth and began their final drive in 1641. That date rings like an angry knell in many tracts and sermons and their consequent savaging of latitudinarian and lower church false brethren. These groups want to overthrow and eliminate the Church of England. They seek "to destroy the *Outward,* or whole *Body* of *Religion*; and Reduce it all to a *Skeleton* or a *Ghost,* upon Pretence of giving Preference to the *Spirit* or *Inward* Part of *Religion.*" Inversion, abolition of ancient ritual, and retreat from verifiable reason typified events of 1641, in which then as now, the argument went, moderation was a mask for violent excess. Henry Dodwell knows that true religion requires external "Bonds and Securities" to avert such threatened dissolution. Alas, every zealous "Pragmatical Medler" with an illicit "Chimerical pretense" of internal light again seeks "to invade the rights of the supreme Power."[41]

This fear of such repeated malicious history echoes through religious and political discourse and often is class based. In 1694 Peter Birch lamented that during the civil war "we beheld Servants on Horses, and Princes walking as Servants on the Earth" and "distress and perplexity still remains upon the Nation." Robert South worried that the "upstart aspiring Mushrooms" of sedition were sprouting again late in the seventeenth century: "we have seen such new Rebellions springing out of the Ashes of the Old; a sufficient Demonstration doubtless that the Fire is not yet put out." Mary Astell too well knew the answer to her own harsh question, "Would the Dissenters have us forget the Great Rebellion and all the dismal Consequences of it, many of which affect us to this very day?" Milbourne looked behind the question and said that seditious Dissenters were ready "to act the *same Tragedies* over again" and that "what has been may be." Francis Atterbury saw deluded enthusiastic levelers who "thrust themselves into the Estates they have no Title to."[42]

What "may be" included demands for complete control of church and state. The new association of Whigs and Dissenters seeks "to Pull down the *Church*" through illicit Toleration, encouragement of papists, and destruction of monarchy. In so doing, the modern Whigs indeed "have far *Out-stripp'd* their *Fathers of Forty One*" and must be stopped or the nation will be destroyed: "We can never be in *Peace*, till the *Door* be *Bar'd* against them." The Whigs and Dissenters' *"guilty Politicks"* requires *"that the whole Government shall be put into their Hands, and that they shall have the Rule over all."*[43]

"What has been" included dreadful violence and moral ravage. William Cave recalls that when the Church of England was destroyed, "Hell seemed to have broke loose, and to have invaded all Quarters." Hell's hoplites used the weapons they brought with them. Robert South's sermon on Romans 1:32 lambastes "the Devil's Prophets and Apostles," who preach against the Anglican church and state and encourage a return to civil war. Such creatures will cut throats, seize estates, and let "the Rabble . . . loose upon the Government once again." Charles Leslie's colorful language was familiar to his readers. There was "hardly a Family in the Kingdom" that had not lost a relative, been destroyed or plundered or imprisoned or undone "in that Cursed *Rebellion*; Whose *Scars* Sixty Years have not worn out." In another work Leslie embellishes his embellishment and laments the "*Millions* of *Souls* that have been sent to the other World" during the horrid rebellion in which three nations were covered in *"Blood* and *Desolation."* Henry

Sacheverell agreed that these indeed were "*Insatiable, Mercenary Blood-Hounds*" who continue to hunt the Crown's loyal Anglican subjects. Johnathan Edwards spoke for many when he cried, "Good God! what an Age do we live in." For Atterbury that was an age in which "the Voice of the People is the Cry of Hell, leading to Idolatry, Rebellion, Murder, and all the Wickedness the Devil can suggest."[44]

Dissenters and Whigs often shared the lament but denied the theory of causation for that terrible event and its consequences. They gained voice as they gained power, would not be silent when called monsters by monsters, and answered the monstrous charges with their own strident tones. They held up a mirror that showed a world very different from the one so glorified by high flyers. The mirror also showed currents of blood that they attributed to groups other than their own.

The Whigs and their allies used three related responses to their High Church tormentors. One was to paint them with their own brush in a portrait of violent absolutists, enemies to the British constitution, and friends to France, the papacy, and slavery. Edmund Hickeringill's survey of the earth finds darkness, corruption, and priests who regularly subvert government. He asks: "Have we not suffer'd enough already by *Highflyers*?" They are plagues, murderers, and upstarts who raise themselves above "the *Queen, Parliament*, and *all her good Subjects*." They derive their priestcraft "from their Father, the *Father of Lyes . . . the Devil*."[45] The High Church devil suffered the malign fruits of his labors in 1641, but he should have thanked Archbishop Laud and his evil accomplices, who corrupted the church. Hickeringill has had quite enough of altitudinarian excess and repetition: "Let me hear no more hereafter of *Forty One, Forty One*, except you also mention the *Highflown Politicks* of *Laud* and his *Chaplains*." They poisoned King Charles' with lies, absolutism, and illegal taxation, "'till the People *Roar'd* again . . . and then they were *Whipt* for *Roaring*." Finally,

> Oppression made them *Mad*—in *Forty One, Forty One*. And the *Irish Papists* Massacred 200000 Men, Women and Children, and in *England* more Blood and Treasure were lost then ever since it was a Nation; by strugling for Life and Liberty, as *English* Men and Christians; and never 'till the Reign of King *William* III. secured to us. (P. 47)

This inflammatory response to inflammatory response suggests the two other Whig modes of proceeding and their mirror image of High Church complaint. What the Laudian tyrants did, their heirs will try to do again. Henry Sacheverell's violent sermons and consequent indictment for high crimes and misdemeanors provided a fine opening for such an effort. In 1710 an unnamed author thus reprinted the 1683 *University Loyalty* as a comment on the Sacheverell trial. The High Church uses verbal "Drawn Swords" designed to ruin church, state, and the legitimate monarch, whom they will replace with the Pretender and his "despotick *Power*," which his corrupt religion and education have inculcated. That education indeed is consistent with what is taught at Protestant and liberty-hating Oxford and its *"unnatural Spiritual Vipers."* Sacheverell and his associates are repeating the errors of 1641 and are the real cause of rebellion "or something like it by their Sermons and Writings."⁴⁶ The author of *Loyalty* saw a simile, but *An Appeal from the City to the Country* (1710) saw presumed fact. It knew that Sacheverell had "laid a Train [of gun powder] over all *England,* and is now going to blow it up" and will throw "Fire balls among us." In the process, he and his fellow Jacobites would blow up the Revolution settlement, retrospectively murder King William, deny the Hanoverian succession, and threaten Queen Anne's throne: "is it not bidding Defiance to her Majesty's Authority and the very Sketch of Rebellion?" Most certainly, and for Whig writers, we recall, most certainly encouraged by Clarendon's editor Lord Rochester and his apparently "open Attack of the Revolution, and Queen *Anne's* Title to the Crown."⁴⁷

Most certainly as well, an English world without William of Orange would be bereft of the true English values that High Church hates and Low Church loves. Thomas Cotton's nightmare Pisgah site reveals demolished Protestant churches, papal tyranny, banished, imprisoned, or executed Protestant clergymen, confiscated estates, dragooned subjects, and "our *Children* torn from us; our *Wives* and our *Daughters* abus'd and murder'd." If James II had remained on the throne, another author says, he surely would have followed the example of Mary Queen of Scots. She hoped for the "Ruin and final Extirpation" of Protestants and sentenced "a large Number of pious *Protestants* to Death by burning of them." All that of course was to be expected from the Laudian and Sacheverellian spirits whom John Mortimer saw amidst the "Cruelties, Persecutions, Conspiracies, Massacres, Inquisitions, and designs to persecute and destroy" anyone different from themselves.⁴⁸

An Appeal from the City to the Country in 1710, then, had over a decade's worth of feverish language behind it when its title page cited *"Dr Sacheverell,* and his High-Church Faction" as enemies of the state and church. The author uses the familiar concepts of connection and fragility to warn against that faction's incursions: "when once the Fence is broke we shall all suffer alike" (p. 24). The blessed Canaan-like green and pleasant land will be seized by strangers. Cotton tells his readers in language worthy of genocidal Henry V to the governor of Harfleur (3.3): your homes will be burned or captured by papists, your cattle stolen, "and your stately Structures, built for the Grandeur of your Families, turn'd into Monastries, Nunneries, and Convents, for well-fed *Popish* Monks and Priests to satiate their Lusts in, upon the Chastity of your tender Virgins." They also will see "your innocent Childrens Brains dashing out; your own Throats a Cutting, by those who look upon us with no other Regard than Heretical Dogs." Like the High

Church polemicists, this author sees that such conduct is "what the Devil himself would do, were he here upon Earth," but now is acted by his "Agents the *Papists, Non-jurors,* and *Absolute Non-resistance*-Men" who attempt "to Subvert our present Establishment" (pp. 25–26). "Good God! What an Age do we live in" indeed. Such people on each side thought those on the other side irrational lunatics capable of the worst of horrors. Many even contemplated a final solution.

NOTES

1. Henry Sacheverell, *The Political Union. A Discourse Shewing the Dependence of Government on Religion in General: And of the English Monarchy on the Church of England In Particular* (Oxford, 1702), p. 23; [Edward Ward], *All Men Mad: Or, England A Great Bedlam. A Poem* (London, 1704), p. 19 (hereafter cited parenthetically in the text). Sacheverell's view of the need for cultural and psychological restraint by means of religion was familiar. See also Samuel Parker's antitoleration *Discourse of Ecclesiastical Politie: Wherein the Authority of the Civil Magistrate Over the Consciences of Subjects in Matters of External Religion is Asserted* (London, 1670). For example, he warns against *"Liberty of Conscience"* (p. xlvi) because of man's erratic nature: it is "absolutely necessary . . . that there be set up a more severe Government over mens Consciences and Religious perswasions, than over their Vices and immoralities" (pp. lii–liii, in italics). There "is not the least possibility of setling a Nation, but by Uniformity in Religious Worship" (p. 325). Students of the later seventeenth century will want to see Steve Pincus, *1688: The First Modern Revolution* (New Haven, CT: Yale University Press, 2009). Pincus, controversially, argues that James was warmly received upon his arrival to the throne, that his "modernization" rather than his Catholicism forced him from the throne, and that religion in general was not the major cause of such action.

2. John Miller, *Religion in the Popular Prints, 1600–1832* (Cambridge: Chadwyck-Healey, 1986), pp. 140–44.

3. William Penn, *Judas and the Jews Combined against Christ and his Followers* (London, 1673), p. 43; Francis Atterbury, "Representations of the State of Religion . . . in March, 1710–11," in *The Miscellaneous Works of Bishop Atterbury with Historical Notes by J. Nichols* (London, 1789), 4:314 (never worse, damnable). See also Atterbury, "The Petition Allowing the Quakers to Affirm rather than Swear an Oath," 2:166, and "Protests on the Quaker Bill," 5:7, 8, 17, for the Quakers as "no Christians." For Swift, see *The Prose Works of Jonathan Swift*, vol. 7, *The History of the Four Last Years of the Queen*, ed. Herbert Davis, intro. Harold Williams (Princeton, NJ: Princeton University Press, 1951), pp. 106–7 (hereafter cited as *PW* by volume, title, and editor): Quakers believe "the most absurd Heresy that ever appeared in the World" and are a "deluding or deluded People . . . singular from all the rest of Mankind, who live under Civil Government."

4. Gilbert Burnet, *A Relation Of the Death Of the Primitive Persecutors. Written Originally in Latin by L. C. F. Lactantius. . . . To which he hath made a large Preface concerning Persecution* (Amsterdam, 1687), p. 15; Edmund Hickeringill, *Miscellaneous Tracts, Essays, Satyrs, &c. In Prose and Verse* (London, 1707), in which are collected Hickeringill's separately

published works, including *Priest-Craft, Its Character and Consequences*, p. 14 (Bustle) and *The Survey of the Earth, in its General Vileness and Debauchery*, 2nd ed., p. 7, new pagination (damn each other). Given the separate pagination, the booksellers probably had numerous sets of earlier issues that they could newly bind.

5. D. Cumyng, ed., *Two Sermons Preach't . . . On the Sad Occasion of the Death of Our Late Gracious Queen. The Former, by Mr. J. Boyse, The Latter, by Mr. Nath. Weld* (Dublin, 1695), sig. A3^r, with the title page as A1^r, italics and roman type reversed. For Addison, see *The Spectator*, No. 106 (1711), in *The Spectator*, ed. Donald F. Bond (Oxford: Clarendon Press, 1965), 1:441–42. For further discussion of the breadth of unity in the eighteenth-century Anglican Church, see William Gibson, *The Church of England, 1688–1832: Unity and Accord* (London: Routledge, 2001), passim, and Gibson's introduction and several articles in *The Church of England, c. 1689–c. 1833: From Toleration to Tractarianism*, ed. John Walsh, Colin Haydon, and Stephen Taylor (Cambridge: Cambridge University Press, 1993). Gibson makes plain that Sir Roger's clergyman was characteristic of country parishes that discouraged division and dispute (p. 56).

6. Charles Leslie, *The Snake in the Grass: Or, Satan Transform'd into an Angel of Light* (London, 1696), p. lxiv; Leslie, *The New Association Of those Called Moderate-Church-Man, With The Modern-Whigs and Fanaticks, To Under-Mine and Blow-Up The Present Church and Government. . . . By a True-Church-Man* (London, 1702), p. 2; Philo Basileus, *Remarks on Dr. West's Sermon Before the Honourable House of Commons, On the 30th of January 1709–10. In A Letter to the Doctor* (London, 1710), p. 21; [Philo Britannus], *Popery and Schism Equally Dangerous to the Church of England, As by Law Establish'd* (London, 1715), p. xxii, in italics; D. F. [Daniel Defoe?], *Moderation Maintain'd, In Defence of a Compassionate Enquiry Into the Causes of the Civil War, &c. In a Sermon Preached by White Kennett, D. D.* (London, 1704), p. 2.

7. Jonathan Swift, *PW* 8, "A Modest Enquiry . . . Appendix A," in *Jonathan Swift. Political Tracts 1713–1719*, ed. Herbert Davis and Irvin Ehrenpreis (Oxford: Basil Blackwell, 1964), p. 195. For Ammianus' *Res gestae divi augusti*, see *The Roman Historie, Containing such Acts and occurrents as passed under Constantius, Iulianus, Iovianus, Valentinianus, and Valens, Emperours*, trans. Philemon Holland (London, 1609), p. 193, at the end of 22.3; in the modern Loeb edition it is at 22.5. See *Ammianus Marcellinus . . . II: History*, trans. John C. Rolfe (London: William Heinemann; Cambridge, Mass.: Harvard University Press, 1937), pp. 202–3, where Ammianus characterizes Julian the Apostate's attitude toward Christians: "nullas infestas hominibus bestias, ut sunt sibi ferales plerique Christianorum expertus" (no wild beasts are such enemies to mankind as are most of the Christians in their deadly hatred of one another).

8. Edward Stillingfleet, *A Sermon Preached before the King, February the 15 1683/4* (London, 1684), p. 8; Luke Milbourne, *The utter Extirpation of Tyrants and their Families. A Sermon Preached at St. Ethelburga's, Jan. 30. 1707–8* (London, [1708]), p. 13; Peter Paxton, *Civil Polity. A Treatise Concerning the Nature of Government. . . . And Remarks made upon the Changes in our English Constitution* (London, 1703), p. 95 (Horror), sig. bi^r (Depravity, from falling); Joseph Trapp, *The Mischief of Changes in Government; and The Influence of Religious Princes to Prevent Them* (London, 1705), p. 25.

9. Roger Ascham, *The Scholemaster*, in *English Works*, ed. William Aldis Wright (1904; reprint, Cambridge: Cambridge University Press, 1970), pp. 243–44; Jonathan Swift, *PW*

9, *A Sermon on the Martyrdom of K. Charles I.* . . . *Jan. 30, 1725–26*, in *Irish Tracts, 1720–1723* . . . *And Sermons*, ed. Herbert Davis and Louis Landa (Oxford: Basil Blackwell, 1963), pp. 225–26.

10. Henry Dodwell, *An Admonitory Discourse Concerning the Late English Schism* (London, 1704), pp. 215 (very name), 231 (sins; see also pp. 249–50); *A Step to Oxford: In which is Comprehended An Impartial Account of the University* (London, 1704), p. 9. For further discussion of the broad agreement between higher and lower Anglican churches, see John Spurr, *The Restoration Church of England, 1646–1689* (New Haven, CT: Yale University Press, 1991).

11. George Smalridge, *A Sermon Preach'd before the Honourable House of Commons . . . Jan. 30, 1701/2. Being the Anniversary Fast of the Martyrdom of King Charles I.* (London, 1702), p. 14.

12. Henry Sacheverell, *The Perils of False Brethren, both in Church and State* (London, 1709), p. 9. See also Smalridge, *A Sermon Preach'd. . . . Jan. 30, 1701/2*, p. 6; and William Baker, *A Sermon Preach'd before the Honourable House of Commons . . . On Monday, January 30. 1720*, 2nd ed. (London, [1721]), pp. 26, 28. The sermon's familiar image of destructive surging water was drawn from Proverbs 17:14, on the violent letting out of water. See below, under "Metaphorical Enhancement," for further discussion of torrential vice sinking all before it.

13. L'Estrange, *Short Answer*, p. 5; see also Atterbury, "Protests on the Quakers Bill," in *Miscellaneous Works*, 5:9, where the Quakers' refusal to pay tithes leads to violation of other laws.

14. Mary Astell, *An Impartial Enquiry Into the Causes of Rebellion and Civil War in this Kingdom: In an Examination of Dr. Kennett's Sermon, Jan. 31. 1703/4. And Vindication of the Royal Martyr* (London, 1701), pp. 41 (Encroachments), 63 (Sword); [Philo Britannus], *Popery and Schism*, pp. 2 (Bastion), 3 (undermine), 5 (Doubt).

15. Thomas Bennet, *A Discourse of Schism*, 2nd ed. (Cambridge, 1702), p. 6; S. E., *The Clamours of the Dissenters Against the Bill To Prevent Occasional Conformity Examined* (London, 1703), p. 7; John Savage, *Security of the Establish'd Religion, the Wisdom of the Nation. A Sermon* (Cambridge, 1704), p. 17; Mary Astell, *Moderation truly Stated: Or, A Review of a Late Pamphlet Entitul'd, Moderation a Vertue. With a Prefatory Discourse to D^r. D'Avenant* (London, 1704), p. 60; Luke Milbourne, *The Moderate Cabal. A Satyr* (London, 1710), p. 27.

16. Possibly but improbably by Daniel Defoe, *The Occasional Letter. Number I. Concerning several Particulars in the New Association* (London, 1704), p. 29; D. F. [Defoe?], *Moderation Maintain'd*, p. 23; Edmund Hickeringill, "Of Blasphemy," in *Essays. Part II* (London, [1706?]), p. 67. Hickeringill often repeats this or similar terms, especially when the High Church seems to place itself above the state. William Beveridge, *A Sermon Preach'd before the Lords Spiritual and Temporal, In Parliament Assembled . . . On the 30th Day of January, 1705/6* (London, 1706), pp. 27–28. Beveridge suggests the importance of Queen Anne to High Church interests. He adapts Jesus to Peter in Matthew 16:18 on the inability of hell to defeat the new Christian Church: "By *God*'s Grace and Blessing upon Her *Majesty*'s Care and Conduct, she will Preserve, Defend and Uphold it, in Spight of all the Powers of Hell, through the whole Course of Her Reign" (p. 27).

17. *The Moderation and Loyalty of the Dissenters, Exemplify'd From the Historians, and other Writers of their Party, as well as from their late Proceedings* (London, 1710), p. 6; Swift, *A Sermon on the Martyrdom of K. Charles I.*, in *PW* 9, *Irish Tracts . . . And Sermons*, pp. 225–26.

For further discussion of Swift's sermon, see Howard D. Weinbrot, "Swift's Thirtieth of January Sermon: Politics, the Pulpit, and the Choice of Strife," in *Papers from the Fifth Münster Symposium on Jonathan Swift*, ed. Hermann J. Real (Munich: Wilhelm Fink Verlag, 2008), pp. 223–42.

18. All quotations are from Henry Hyde, Earl of Clarendon, *The History of the Rebellion and Civil Wars in England, Begun in the Year 1641. . . . Written by the Right Honourable Edward Earl of Clarendon*, 3 vols. (Oxford, 1702–4) (cited parenthetically in the text).

19. Astell, *Impartial Enquiry*, p. 16; N. N. [Samuel Grascome (Grascombe)?], *Remarks on a Sermon, Preach'd January the 31st 1703/4 by White Kennett* ([London, 1704]), p. 5; Jean le Clerc, *Mr. Le Clerc's Account of the Earl of Clarendon's History of the Civil Wars. . . . Part I*, trans. J[ohn] O[zell] (London, 1710), pp. 3–4 (odious, favourable), 22 (bestows, shews); James Anderson, *No King-Killers. A Sermon Preach'd in Swallow-street, St. James's on January 30. 1714/15* (London, 1715), sig. A2^v, with the title page as A1^r, italics and roman type reversed in this "Dedication to the Reverend Daniel Williams D. D."; John Withers, *A Vindication of the Dissenters From the Charge of Rebellion, And being the Authors of Our Civil Wars*, 2nd ed. (London, 1719), p. 18. Withers' *Vindication* was written and delivered some nine years earlier in Exon and adapted to the new monarch and dynasty.

20. [John Oldmixon], *Clarendon and Whitlock Compar'd. To which is occasionally added, A Comparison Between the History of the Rebellion and Other Histories of the Civil War* (London, 1727), p. xix (hereafter cited parenthetically in the text).

21. White Kennett, *A Compassionate Enquiry into the Causes of the Civil War* (London, 1704), p. 18; N. N. [Grascome (Grascombe)?], *Remarks on a Sermon*, p. 5; Rochester in Clarendon's *History*, 3: sig. d2^v.

22. The italic and roman type are reversed in the quotations from volume 2 (1703) of Clarendon's *History*. For Queen Anne's indifferently spelled remark, see Edward Gregg, *Queen Anne*, 2nd ed. (New Haven, CT: Yale University Press, 2001), p. 168.

23. William Fleetwood, *A Sermon Preach'd before the Right Honourable the Lords Spiritual and Temporal, January the 30th 1709/10* (London, 1710), p. 4. The dyke as an uncertain barrier against cultural drowning was a familiar image.

24. William Crowe, *The Mischievous Effects and Consequences of Strife and Contention. A Sermon Preached before the Honourable House of Commons. . . . January 30, 1734–5* (London, 1735), pp. 1 (beginning), 8 (having).

25. [Charles Leslie], *The Regal Supremacy in Ecclesiastical Affairs Asserted* (London, 1701), p. 81; Bugg, *Quakerism Drooping*, p. 163; Thomas Sherwill, *Church-Conformity Asserted and Vindicated. A Sermon . . . Upon the Feast of St. Simon and St. Jude* (Cambridge, 1704), p. 21; Grascome, *Mask of Moderation Pull'd off*, p. 59; Milbourne, *Utter Extirpation of Tyrants*, pp. 10 (vast), 12 (prodigious); J. Silvius [pseud.], *Bishop Sancroft's Ghost. With His Prophesie of the Times And the Approach of Antichrist* (London, 1712), p. 9; Edward Ward, *History of the Grand Rebellion* (1713), 1:602.

26. Thomas Cotton, *A Sermon Preached to the Societies for Reformation of Manners . . . October 5. 1702* (London, 1702), p. 49; *High-Church Politicks: Or The Abuse of the 30th of January Considered. With Remarks on Mr. Luke Milbourne's Railing Sermons, and on the Observation of That Day*, sometimes attributed to Daniel Defoe (London, 1710), p. 16; Anderson, *No King-Killers*, p. 11; Hickeringill, *Priest-Craft*, in *Miscellaneous Tracts*, p. 26 (Priest-Craft), and *The Survey of the Earth*, p. 13. Blood, wounds, deluges, and hatred of

High Church and other presumed oppressors fairly punctuate these tracts. Withers, *Vindication of the Dissenters*, p. 19. Luke Milbourne, *The Danger of Changes in Church or State; Or, The Fatal Doom of such as love them and their Associates. In a Sermon Preach'd January 31, 1714/15* (London, [1715]), pp. 1, 2.

27. Thomas Bradbury, *Hardness of Heart, the certain mark of a Ruin'd Party. Open'd in Two Sermons*, 2nd ed. (London, 1716), p. iv, in italics.

28. Charles Leslie, *New Association Of those Called Moderate-Church-Man*, p. 25; Leslie, *The New Association. Part II. With farther Improvements* (including attacks upon Defoe's *Shortest Way With the Dissenters: Or Proposals for the Establishment of the Church* [London, 1702]), 2nd ed. (London, 1705), pp. 12 (William), 60 (Faulty); Leslie, *The Principles Of the Dissenters concerning Toleration and Occasional-Conformity. . . . With Seasonable Advice to the Dissenters. In a Preface* (London, 1705), pp. 9 (destroy), 35 (Devil), 16 (famous). The attack upon the Dutch also had its own poem-pamphlet war. See John Tutchin, *The Foreigners* (London, 1700) and then *The Apostates* (London, 1701). The first was answered by John Dennis in *The Reverse: Or, The Tables Turned* (London, 1700) and more powerfully by Daniel Defoe in *The True Born English-man* (London, 1701) and answers to it.

29. [James Owen], *Moderation still a Virtue: In Answer To Several Bitter Pamphlets* (London, 1704), p. 91; Astell, *Impartial Enquiry*, pp. 48–49 (tend, Thoughts), 34 (People); F[rancis] A[tterbury], *The Voice of the People, No Voice of God: Or, The Mistaken Arguments of a Fiery Zealot. . . . By F. A. D. D.* ([London], 1710), p. 13. Atterbury responds to the popular unsigned *Vox populi, vox dei* (London, 1709), often reprinted as *The Judgment of Whole Kingdoms and Nations, concerning the Rights Priviledges, and Properties of the People* (London, 1710). This has been attributed to John Lord Somers and to Daniel Defoe, neither of whom seems to me probable. The text understandably became popular in near-rebellion New England, with reprints at the least in Philadelphia (1773) and Rhode Island (1774). For another such reply to *Vox populi*, see [Edward Fisher], *An Appeal to the Conscience, As thou wilt answer it at the great and dreadful Day of Judgment* (London, 1710). The divine right of kings requires submission and forbids rebellion, "the sum of all sins." Fisher lists eleven, "plus all manner of wickedness what so ever" (p. 39). The attribution is based on information from ECCO, presumably in turn drawn from the copy reproduced from the Boston Public Library. The text does not specify an author.

30. Sacheverell, *Perils of False Brethren*, pp. 18–19; Milbourne, *Utter Extirpation of Tyrants*, p. 19. The commonplace of lack of proper causation would be negatively applied to the concept of the divine right of kings. See, for example, *A Discourse on Government and Religion, Calculated for the Meridian of the Thirtieth of January. By an Independent* (London, [1749?]): "What king did ever come from heaven! that any of them should presume to claim a divine right to any kingdom on earth? Or what commission was ever given from *heaven* to any man, to possess a kingdom on *earth*. The *divine right* of kings to rule over people, without, and against their consent, is a *profane jest*" (p. 12).

31. Sackville Tufton, *The History of Faction, Alias Hypocrisy, Alias Moderation, From its first Rise down to its Present Toleration in these Kingdoms* (London, 1705), pp. 82, with sig. A3^r, 74, and 91 among attacks on foreigners; Charles Leslie, *Now or Never. Or, The Last Cast for England* (London, 1696), p. 4; *A Letter Out of the Country, To the Author of The Managers Pro and Con, In Answer To his Account of what is said At Child's and Tom's In the Case of Dr. Sacheverell* (London, 1710), sig. A1^v–2^r; [Benjamin Hoadly], *The Voice of the Addressers: Or, A*

Short Comment Upon the Chief Things Maintain'd, or Condemn'd, in our Late Modest Addresses (London, 1710), p. 19; Shaftesbury, as quoted in Geoffrey Holmes, *British Politics in the Age of Anne* (London: Macmillan, 1967), p. 67, from PRO 30/24/22/2.

32. *A Short History of the Kings of England* (London, 1692), pp. 3 (People), 48 (His Highness); Cotton, *A Sermon Preached*, p. 49; Hickeringill, *Miscellaneous Tracts: The Survey of the Earth*, p. 44 (Christ's), *Essays. Part II*, pp. 32–33. See also *Essays*, pp. 47–48, and *The Second Part of Priest-Craft*, p. 91, for other aspects of Hickeringill's Erastian preference. He is fiercely anti-Catholic and High Church.

33. *A Letter From A Gentleman At The Court of St. Germains, To One of his Friends in England; Containing A Memorial about Methods for setting the Pretender on the Throne of Great Britain. Found at Doway, after the Taking of that Town. Translated from the French Copy, Printed at Cologne by Peter Marteau* (London, 1710), pp. 14 (great), 5 (blacken), 15 (Article). Both the full title and the lack of a printer's name on the title page suggest the author's and the bookseller's concerns.

34. Alexander Pope, *The Twickenham Edition of the Poems of Alexander Pope*, vol. 5, *The Dunciad*, ed. James Sutherland, 3rd ed. (London: Methuen & Co.; New Haven, CT: Yale University Press, 1963), pp. 191 (3:329), 192 (3:337n); Astell, *Moderation truly Stated*, p. 53; *The Proceedings Of Both Houses of Parliament, In the Years 1702, 1703, 1704, Upon the Bill To Prevent Occasional Conformity* (London, 1710), p. 38, said to be spoken by the "Bishop of S----" (p. 33), presumably Gilbert Burnet, bishop of Salisbury, or Sarum.

35. Atterbury, *Miscellaneous Works* (n. 3 above), 4:314; Charles Leslie, *The Wolf Stript of His Shepherd's Cloathing. In Answer to a Late Celebrated Book Intituled Moderation, a Vertue* (London, 1704), pp. 3 (now), 82 (Fiery); Henry Sacheverell, *The Nature and Mischief of Prejudice and Partiality Stated in a Sermon Preach'd at St. Mary's in Oxford*, 2nd ed. (London, 1704), pp. 24, 54; Bennet, *Discourse of Schism*, p. 44; Astell, *Impartial Enquiry*, p. 43. For some aspects of Swift's and of Pope's fear of being overwhelmed by darkness, see the chapters on *A Tale of A Tub* and *The Dunciad* in Howard D. Weinbrot, *Menippean Satire Reconsidered: From Antiquity to the Eighteenth Century* (Baltimore: Johns Hopkins University Press, 2005). For Henry Welstead, see *The Modern Moderation set in a true Light. In a Sermon Preach'd before The Reverend Dr. Nicholas Clagett. . . . With a Vindication of the Sermon, in a Letter to Obadiah Moderation, Gent.* (London, 1711), p. 8.

36. Gilbert Burnet, *A Sermon Preached before the Aldermen of the City of London . . . Jan 30. 1680/1* (London, 1681), p. 24; Paxton, *Civil Polity*, pp. 87 (Multitude), 89 (Religious), 88 (can never), 93 (desirous); [Defoe?], *High-Church Politicks*, p. 55; [White Kennett], *A Visit to St. Saviour's Southwark, With Advice to Dr. Sacheverell's Preachers There. . . . By a Divine of the Church of England* (London, 1710), p. 7; [Thomas Gordon], *A Political Dissertation Upon Bull-Baiting and Evening Lectures. With Occasional Meditations on the 30th of January* (London, 1718), p. 24.

37. Leslie, *New Association. Part II*, p. 15; Joseph Trapp, *The Character and Principles of the Present Set of Whigs*, 2nd ed. (London, 1711), pp. 41 (Lewdness), 44 (presently); Charles Leslie, *A Reply to a Book Entitul'd Anguis Flagellatus, Or, a Switch for the Snake* (London, 1702), p. 7; Atterbury, *Miscellaneous Works*, 4:310; Paxton, *Civil Polity*, p. 88; [Defoe?], *Occasional Letter. Number I*, p. 27.

38. Grascome, *Mask of Moderation Pull'd off*, p. 16 (plague); Bennet, *Discourse of Schism*, pp. 43–44 (numberless); Trapp, *Character and Principles of the Present Set of Whigs*, p. 42 (Devils); Atterbury, *Miscellaneous Works*, 4:316, 322 (infection).

39. Hickeringill, preface to *Essays*, in *Miscellaneous Tracts*, sig. A3ᵛ (Devil's), and *Essays. Part II*, in *Miscellaneous Tracts*, p. 53 (Names); Daniel Defoe, *The High-Church Legion: Or, The Memorial Examin'd. Being A New Test of Moderation* (London, 1705), pp. 2 (meer), 7 (Party's); Milbourne, *Moderate Cabal* (n. 15 above), p. 3; Leslie, *New Association Of those Called Moderate-Church-Man*, p. 13 (many); Leslie, *New Association. Part II*, pp. 38 (long, Driven out), 36 (Leisure).

40. Leslie, *Wolf Stript*, p. 75.

41. Leslie, *Snake in the Grass*, p. xcv (destroy); Dodwell, *Admonitory Discourse Concerning the Late English Schism*, pp. 210–11.

42. Peter Birch, *A Sermon Preached before the Honourable House of Commons* (London, 1694), p. 19; Robert South, *Twelve Sermons and Discourses on Several Subjects and Occasions* (London, 1724), 6:72 (upstart), 78 (seen): "I am sure it can be of no Mans Duty to obey" such creatures (72); Astell, *Moderation truly Stated* (n. 15 above), p. 110; Milbourne, *Utter Extirpation of Tyrants*, pp. 15 (act), 17 (What); A[tterbury], *Voice of the People*, p. 24.

43. Leslie, *New Association Of those Called Moderate-Church-Man*, pp. 3 (Pull), 17 (have far), 19 (can never); Francis Bugg, *News from New Rome: Occasioned by the Quakers Challenging of Francis Bugg* (London, 1701), sig. B2ʳ (guilty), B2ᵛ (whole).

44. William Cave, *A Serious Exhortation . . . to the present Dissenters* (London, 1683), p. 23. Much of Cave's section 7, pp. 20–27, includes such tones, including the familiar image of inundation: "The Fences of Order and Discipline in the Church of *England* being broken down, what a horrid Inundation of all manner of Vice and Wickedness did immediately over-flow the Land?" (p. 23). Robert South, *Twelve Sermons Preached upon Several Occasions. . . . The Second Volume* (London, 1694), pp. 286 (Devil's), 298 (Rabble). South's familiar harshness in this section was abstracted in the unsigned *Papists of all Sorts Working with the Dissenters of all Sorts, for the Subversion of the Establish'd Church* (London, 1707), p. 76. Leslie, *New Association Of those Called Moderate-Church-Man*, p. 10 (hardly); Leslie, *Wolf Stript*, p. 54 (Millions); Sacheverell, *Nature and Mischief of Prejudice and Partiality*, p. 46; Jonathan Edwards, *The Exposition Given By My Lord Bishop of Sarum, Of the Second Article of Our Religion Examined* (London, 1702), p. 23; A[tterbury], *Voice of the People*, p. 6.

45. Hickeringill, *Survey of the Earth*, in *Miscellaneous Tracts*, pp. 20 (Have), 42 (Queen), 45 (Father) (hereafter cited parenthetically in the text).

46. *University Loyalty: Or, The Genuine Explanation of the Principles and Practices of the English Clergy* (London, 1710), sig. A2ʳ⁻ᵛ (Drawn, despotick), pp. 1 (unnatural), 52 (something).

47. *An Appeal from the City to the Country, For the Preservation of Her Majesty's Person, Liberty, Property, and the Protestant Religion* (London, 1710), pp. 10 (Train), 12 (Fire), 12 (blow up), 11 (bidding) (hereafter cited parenthetically in the text); [John Oldmixon], *Clarendon and Whitlock Compar'd* (n. 20 above), p. xxv (open Attack).

48. Cotton, *A Sermon Preached*, p. 55 (hereafter cited parenthetically in the text); *An Address to the People of England: Shewing the Unworthiness of their Behavior to King George* (London, 1715), pp. 15 (Ruin), 14 (large); John Mortimer, *Some Considerations concerning the Present State of Religion; With Some Essays towards our Love and Union* (London, 1702), p. 6.

CHAPTER TWO

Madness, Extirpation, and Defoe's Shortest Way with the Dissenters

There was, then, stern regular disagreement on principles and stern regular agreement on the evil of the "Other." Even one's own coreligionists could be apostates, antichrists, or false brethren. This world of mistrust encouraged the demonizing and madness that seemed clear to all sides in the squabble when each side thought that only it was sane and knew the Truth. Jonathan Swift claimed that "a very great Majority of the Kingdom" believed that the Church of England's "open Enemies" included "Dissenters of all Denominations" and that the church's "secret "Adversaries" were "Whigs, Low-Church, Republicans, Moderation-Men, and the like."[1] Though that claim was demonstrably false, many High Churchmen hoped to make it true by affirmation.

Philip Stubs, for example, urged absolute belief in his episcopal church because irresolute principles led to "Eternal Misery" and "to *Bedlam*." John Edwards extended the argument to fashionable skepticism, a "mad Notion" of atheist followers of atheist Hobbes and Spinoza. "Let none persuade you that Nonsense and Raving are Sacred, and that *Bethlehem-Hospital* is the best Divinity-School." Many nonetheless seemed to be so persuaded and thus to encourage the world of *The Age of Wonders* in 1710: "Nature's run mad, and Madmen rule, / The World's turn'd upside down."[2] How did lunacy seem to become a staple of religious life?

Madness

One reason was inherent in the dangers of the Reformation's central assumption of personal belief and personal evaluation of the Bible. Such response valued individual rather than institutional judgment, threatened the authority of collective wisdom, and subverted the marmoreal assumption within the later *Discourse on Government and Religion* (London, [1749?]): "Upon the rock of private judgment and liberty of conscience, stands the reformation" (p. iv). For Charles Leslie, an agent of darkness like John Locke urged "toleration" and potential independence both from the Church of England and from the ancestral alliance of subject with monarch. There was no historical precedent for the *"Original Independence* of *Mankind"*; the Dissenters therefore invented that and other irresponsible fictions. Many regarded these fictions as irreligious, for God created monarchy when he created Adam. Leslie also joined those for whom private judgment, liberty, and heresy were dangerous and insane. "Since the *Reformation, England* has suffered more by [the Dissenters] than by the *Papists.*" Samuel Grascome adds that satanic false light leads enthusiasts to believe that one may worship God according to one's own conscience. After wild search and separation, one ends "in Anarchy." Henry Sacheverell knows that such anarchy stems from blasphemous false principles that ignore the basis of the law in God and his constraints upon us. Denial of divine right was a denial of God.[3]

Such dangerous absurdity also begins in pride. Enthusiasts, among others, assume that unaided human reason can indeed fully grasp Christian dogma and the human situation. Yet worse, Charles Leslie insists, they proudly aspire even to be *"Equal* with *God."* Leslie thinks that attempt so depraved and deprived "of all *Sense* and *Reason"* that not "even in *Bedlam"* could such foolishness be conceived. These Quakers' "*Lyes* and *Deliriums"* make clear that they are "Mad and Blasphemous," harbor "Black-mouthed and *hellish* Venom," and are in league with the devil himself. Enthusiasts "cannot hide the *Cloven-Foot.*" Sacheverell unsurprisingly supports Leslie's view. Atheism, fanaticism, and other damnable sins were encouraged by diligent application to *"Apostles* of *Darkness,* and *Emissaries of the Devil"* in their *"Hellish Cause."* The devil hates divine order and light, and so he seeks a return to the inchoate world prior to creation. The Whigs are glad to help his cause. "As to their *Scheme of Government,*" Joseph Trapp says, "it is of the old *Chaos-*make, *without form and void,* and *Darkness is upon the Face of it.*"[4]

Chaos indeed is a synonym for enthusiast-Whig-Dissenter minds. They flit from idea to idea, lack the true church's moral anchor, and, Leslie affirms, have no rules "but their own *Fansie* (which is strongest in *Mad-Men*)." They mistake that fancy "for *Inspiration.* And then their *Madness* is at the height" and is "inconstant as the *Wind.* They know not their own Minds" and cannot be coherent for "an hour together." This theory of causation is as clear as the fragility of the spiritual embodied in the secular: "When once we leave the *Institutions* of God, there is no *Stop,* and our *Imagination* is our only *Rule.*" That distorted imagination lacks "all sound *Reason,* and the *Sobriety* of Religion." The flighty enthusiast seeks to soar yet higher, freezes reason and judgment, and is a prisoner of that *"Fleeting* and Rolling" unfixed fancy: "When *Imagination* is upon the *Wing,* nothing can be so *Irksome* as to *Clogg* it with *Reason,* and Prescribe *Compass* or a *Helm* to it!" In such a case, clouded reason responds only to a man's "present *Impulse.*"

Leslie again says that for enthusiasts a *"roving Imagination (which is strongest in Mad-Men)"* becomes "the *Immediate Command* of *God"* that the lunatic "might come at last to believe himself."[5] Tories and High Church polemicists thus saw madness as a sign of an uncontrolled religious, moral, and political imagination, so dramatically portrayed in Swift's *Tale of a Tub* (1704). By its conclusion malicious invention has mastered method, reason, and the fleeing Anglican Church.

Low Church Whigs and Dissenters were not the only ones thought to be howling under the post-Reformation full moon. Those Whigs countered with a theory of madness induced by and reflected in their opponents' uncontrolled rage. For example, by 1691 there was a backlash against the often ferocious thirtieth of January sermons that lamented the murder of Charles I. Edmund Ludlow then writes about this *"General Madding'Day."* He is "provoked, by the reading the many Idle, Malicious and Lewd Expressions" against Whigs and Dissenters. One year later he again writes to complain about such *"red-hot Zeal"* by the *"high-flown Brethren"* and their choler: "I doubt you will *run mad* before your next *MADDING DAY."* In 1703 Defoe complains that "these furious People ... in Print and in Pulpit, Entitle the whole Church and Government to the Extasies of their Passions." He later adds that mad Sacheverell "raves" and disgraces "the Ministerial Function."[6]

The concept of raving soon became commonplace regarding High Churchmen. Edmund Hickeringill knows that those who write "spitfire *Oxonian* Sermons and," he says misreading Defoe, *"Short-ways ...* must be mad." These priests "are mad, stark mad, raging mad because" the Act of Toleration limits their power and they now are *"Madcaps."* Like Sacheverell, they in turn make "half the People run mad." The author of the radically hostile *Character of a Modern Tory* ([1713]) growls that thanks to hypocritical, treasonous, High Church Tories, the "worst and greatest Part of this unhappy, distracted Nation are under a *Delirium,* which makes them giddy-headed." Thomas Gordon comparably believes that *"High-Church Lunaticks"* induce madness in their parishioners. These crackpots, John Withers says in 1719, are *"fitter* for BEDLAM than a *sober Confutation."* What to do in such a world? When all men are mad, religion creates rebellion and "Makes Mankind hate one another."[7] An apparently reasonable response in the face of such hatred was to exterminate the brutes. All sides were willing executioners.

Root and Branch

Commentators were aware of the harsh history of religious violence. Peter Paxton lamented the blending of religion, politics, civil power, and the almost inevitable actions "as cruel as the Tyger, and as merciless as the Vulture." France thus "rooted out" and "extirpated" its Protestant subjects, and Spain was able "to root out the Relicts of *Judaism* and *Mahometism.*" John Shute Barrington's *Dissuasive from Jacobitism* (1713) put a number on Spanish depredations: some forty million "harmless *Indians.*" The commentators also were aware of what they regarded as the positive side of such severity and its precedent. In 1682 Philip Browne noted that the ancient Hebrew magistrates "settled, maintained, and defended that which was the true Religion, and extirpated and rooted out all false Religions." Constantine and his successors also exercised that power to suppress "dangerous Errours" and "Heresies and Schisms."[8]

Along the way, these and other Augustinian writers distinguished between improper Continental genocide, pre-Reformation attempts to keep the body of Christ's church unblemished, and post-Reformation attempts to annihilate the true reformed Church of England. This last step also was exemplified in the British Isles when foreign-influenced Catholic monarchs were no better than they should be. Mary Queen of Scots burned to death "a large Number of pious *Protestants.*" Later papist Stuarts surely would have done the same or worse. Charles II and James II, for example, sought "the extirpation of Protestancy" and the rise of English "Servitude to the Triple Crown." John Toland agrees that Charles II created political and religious parties to help his bishops "oppress and extirpat" all Dissenters and that James II resolved "to dash" all his Protestant subjects "in pieces against one another." They were forced to become "like so many Gladiators" in combat.[9]

The argument would extend to the alien Jacobite Pretender and his native allies. Oxford education leads one to "*the* extirpation *of the* Protestant Religion" and its rights and liberties. This cry was especially loud before the accession of George I in 1714 and upon fear of a Jacobite invasion. Readers of Shute Barrington's *Dissuasive from Jacobitism* thus knew that the Catholic Pretender would turn Britain "into a Desert, rather than Protestantism shall not be extirpated." The Jacobite monarch will insist that "his Protestant Subjects are still sure to be destroyed." A remark in 1714 epitomizes this widely shared view regarding a popish king and his church: they will think "that *it is their Duty to extirpate Heresy*; that is, to destroy *Protestants* by the most cruel *Persecutions.*"[10] Extirpation and heresy were scarcely limited to the conflict between main-line Protestants and Catholics.

Several responses by and to the Quakers make plain that they were both target and targeter of genocide. We recall the Quakers' early martial and verbal behavior: they were labeled anti-episcopal, antimonarchic, and insulting. William Penn extravagantly abused those who opposed or resisted Quakerism and who should and shall be perpetually chained in the bottomless pit. Henry Pickworth knew that criminal enemies like Francis Bugg represented "Babylonish Trumpery," or malice, villainy, corruption, venom, disease, and poison. "We are very far from returning to Communion with one, whose Fellowship is with the Father of Lies,"

Joseph Wyeth says. We again recall that all this was taken as both personal and national threat. Charles Leslie thus spoke with characteristic crescendo: "When the *Quaker sword* is drawn, it spares none! *Protestants, Papists, Turks,* it is all one." Leslie's High Church indeed thought itself in grave danger from those violent, soon to become pacifists, Dissenters in general and the Low Church Whigs who fathered dissent. Their putative moderation seemed to be the smiling mask that covered the bloody fangs sharpened in 1641. The Dissenters and their associates "Extended their *Spiritual Sword* (like the *Pope*) to all sort of *Temporals*." Leslie and comparable thinkers know that the Dissenters threaten blood unless they are free "to Root *Prelacy* and *Monarchy*" out of the land "and, after that, a Great deal more, in *Cool* Blood—as Before." They will "*Crush* to *Death* all that *Oppose* them, even tho' in *Thoughts*" and will reenact the "Crimes and Calamities of Forty One." They once more seek to overthrow church and state with the sword they laid down only when "it was glutted with the Blood of their Opposers." The title of one of Leslie's books uses a familiar martial metaphor to characterize attacks upon true Anglican orthodoxy: *The New Association Of those Called Moderate-Church-Man, With The Modern-Whigs and Fanaticks, To Under-Mine and Blow-Up The Present Church and Government.* . . . They indeed are allies of the papists and Jacobites, whose invasion must be deaf to "all the dying Groans of Obstinate Hereticks" whose dead bodies, we hear elsewhere, become "the Steps by which" they ascend the throne.[11] Fear of clever and duplicitous erosion and siegelike undermining joined with fear of rebellion as elements of High Church concern.

These commentators were sadly confident that the Whigs and Dissenters planned utterly to destroy the true church. We remember their apparently mendacious plea that they only wanted small reforms of matters indifferent to avoid schism. Luke Milbourne thus knew that Gilbert Burnet preached reformation but would "quickly Blood and Extirpation teach." Leslie saw that the nominal moderates sought "a *Step*" toward the overthrow of church and state. Moderation was merely the "*Scaffolding* to Pull down the *Church.*" Their plea for toleration was "the first step . . . towards Destroying the *Church* of *England*" and authorizing popery. Terms like these abound: the Dissenters will "*pull down* the Pales of *the Church*" or "pull down your *Hierarchy*" or "Undermine the *State*" or "by degrees . . . destroy" the church. Mary Astell epitomizes the sense of the death that Dissent seemed to threaten. Dangerous innovation, novelty, and violation of sacred order must be resisted at once and forever or the civil war that Clarendon chronicled would come again. Dissenters will use "plausible pretenses" to introduce novelty. They then will "improve it to their advantage" and in time "give it new Views and . . . draw from it Inferences that were never intended, too many instances of which you have in that excellent History."[12]

That "excellent History" also helps to explain the anger and power behind the repeated terms of destructive uprooting that we have heard and that are consistent with its cousin *extirpation*. Charles Leslie of course understands that if Dissenters gain power, they will "neither leave Root nor Branch" of the established church and state. They will "make *Root and Branch work with Episcopacy*"; nothing will please them "but the *Destroying of Episcopacy*, Root and Branch." They will "root out our Churches." The Presbyterians sought to destroy the Church of England "*Root* and *Branch*." As Lord Clarendon reported, in 1641 a group of parliamentarians "were believ'd to be for Root and Branch, which grew shortly after a common Expression"—that is, to bury episcopacy beneath the rubble of the undermined Church of England.[13]

This reminder of temporal humiliation was enlarged by the term's dreadful use in several places in the Old Testament's final, darkly prophetic book. Malachi 4:1–3 characterizes an angry God willing to destroy the unrepentant people of unrepentant Jerusalem:

> For, behold, the day cometh, that shall burn as an oven; and all the proud, yea, and all that do wickedly, shall be stubble: and the day that cometh shall burn them up, saith the LORD of hosts, that it shall leave them neither root nor branch.
>
> But unto you that fear my name shall the Sun of righteousness arise with healing in his wings; and ye shall go forth, and grow up as calves of the stall.
>
> And ye shall tread down the wicked; for they shall be ashes under the soles of your feet in the day that I shall do this, saith the LORD of hosts.

From the High Church point of view, the Dissenters had usurped the divine voice. They had proclaimed the established church the wicked Israelites, who would be burned to ash and trodden underfoot by the righteous Dissenters. It was not an insult churchmen could endure. They struck back with both relatively modest proposals and, like the Quakers, with their own language of annihilation. William Tilly raised this rhetorical question in 1705: "Is there any such *Charity* due to a vicious, lewd, profligate, factious Combination of Men?" It would be both sinful and foolish to answer yes.[14]

The lesser schemes in dealing with dangerous dissent derived from the Augustinian concept of *compelle intrare*. Those outside the true church are properly subject to force as a way to correct the mind and soul. Dissenters thus should be reeducated and, if necessary, threatened with "the *Divine Vengeance* for their Disobedience" to man and God. Their books should be prohibited or burned, and they should be subject to unspecified kinds of restraint if they continued to spread their errors.[15]

High Church polemic well displays the anger of a group that thought itself correct, maligned, and defenders of the best values of the best faith of the best nation.

The reward for their stewardship seemed to be death by the sword, by inundation of bloody waters, or by overwhelming numbers of endlessly propagating evildoers. So far as they were able, they would invoke divine sanction or state violence to stop either form of death. As in other cases, they used dramatic metaphors to suggest the appropriate, often terminal, response to danger. Latitudinarian Whigs and especially Dissenters are *"Apostles* of *Darkness"* who deserve "Condign Vengeance." What they have *"Sown in Dissimulation,* they shall *Reap* in ... *Damnation."* They seek to "Propagate a *Generation of Vipers,* that will eat through the very *Bowels* of our *Church";* the Oxford assize judges therefore must *"Execute Wrath upon* them." Dissenters are *"Insatiable, Mercenary Blood-Hounds,* whom the *Hebrew* Law of *Retaliation* can alone Restrain." These extravagant, lewd, vicious, hissing snakes deserve neither divine nor human charity. Such "Incendiaries of *England"* should suffer more than hanging for their wish to "set a whole Kingdom on Fire."[16]

As these remarks at the least imply, metaphor both spurred and reflected policy in which the state's martial arm also was its religious arm. Charles Leslie insists that the spiritual incendiaries must be suppressed by "Civil Authority" and asks the Commons: "Shall it be lawful for Magistrates to punish those that destroy mens Bodies, but not those that destroy mens souls?" Heresy and schism must be extirpated by the restraints of law. As another churchman says, those who absent themselves from ordained religious worship should be "severely lash'd and censur'd, even to Anathema's"—that is, excommunicated and cursed to damnation and destruction. It would be sinful not to "severely punish such Blasphemous Antichristian Actions, such Treasonable Positions." Roger Altham knows that the "Just and Pious Magistrate" will punish such public evil by the "Roughness of Authority." Piety should proceed with "the Thunder of Spiritual Censures," and Justice should be armed "with the Sword of Vengeance," but, he assures us, *" 'tis only to the Evil."*[17]

Two such works serve as paradigms of the extreme high-flying sermon. Luke Milbourne's title is a severe preview of a severe text read on 30 January 1708: *The utter Extirpation of Tyrants and their Families.* It is based on parts of Isaiah 14:20–21: *"Because thou had destroyed thy Land, and slain thy People: the Seed of Evil Doers shall never be Renowned. Prepare Slaughter for his Children for the Iniquity of their Fathers; that they do not Rise nor Posses the Land."* For Milbourne, his countrymen once "enjoy'd our *Religion* in its Apostolical *Purity,* our *Laws* with just *Liberty,* and our *Estates* and *Fortunes* with an Inviolable *Security."* All that was destroyed by murderous, heretical, atheist, sacrilegious, hypocritical rebels who were endlessly wicked and, like the malicious king of Babylon whose fate the prophet chronicles, they are sent to hell, cast out of the grave, thrust through with a sword, and their names and families cut out of the nation. This indeed happened with the rebels of 1641 and ought to happen now. "The Blood of *one single Person* shed unrevenged, tho' the Person be ever so mean, renders a Land *Polluted* in the Eyes of an All-Just God." He knows how brutal those rebels were and requires vengeance to remove the nation's otherwise permanent taint. Israel followed such divine direction against the Canaanites and Amalekites, namely, "to destroy *Infant* and *Suckling* for the Sins of their *Predecessors* as well as for their own."[18] The Jews themselves were punished in perpetuity for their role in the Crucifixion, and comparable justice now is meted out to traitors through death or bills of attainder, "by which whole Families are rendred uncapable of any Office or Honour, for the Crimes of the Heads of them, and their Children are ruined for ever for the Transgression *of their Fathers*" (p. 15). Milbourne implicitly retreats from "*utter Extirpation*" and the destructions of infants and sucklings, for he will not inflict real penalties or remove their "*legal Indulgence*" so long as these traitors cannot rise again (p. 17).

Henry Sacheverell was reluctant to make even that modest concession. His perhaps most famous, or infamous, sermon was *The Perils of False Brethren, both in Church and State* (London, 1709). He will speak necessary truth to a nation in danger of being silenced, affronted, reviled, and threatened by attacks upon the Crown, the constitution, and the national church. Such silencing includes attempts to remove the pulpit from politics "in order the more *effectually to* Undermine *and* Destroy *Us*." Sacheverell will "*Sound a Trumpet in* Sion" to deliver God's message (sig. A2^r, italics and roman type reversed): church and state are as one, the external rituals and discipline of the church "are the *Exterior Fences* to Guard the *Internals* of *Religion*" (p. 8); the least deviation from "those Sacred *Boundaries* of the *Church*" is heresy and treason (pp. 9–10); attacks upon the church are attacks upon the Crown; and passive obedience is God's will (p. 14). Those who believe otherwise are false brethren and false members of the Church of England. How to treat such apostates?

Sacheverell's biblical citation is from the Old Testament, Joel 2:1–3. The prophet tells the trembling Israelites to sound the trumpet, for God is coming to judge them: "A fire devoureth before them; and behind them a flame burneth . . . and nothing shall escape them." Joel 2:15 gives the other option: "Blow the trumpet in Zion, sanctify a fast, call a solemn assembly," and then God will relent and reward their return to virtue. Sacheverell clearly prefers the first citation, for he takes it as his duty, not to preach peace, but to follow God's command "to *Cry aloud, and Spare Not*" (sig. A3^v, italics and roman type reversed). This was taken as an attack upon the government, but its chief target is the presumably rebellious Dissenters, whom Sacheverell knows are at it again. They thus need the wrath of God as transmitted through the civil magistrate to get them sorted out—or worse.[19] Sacheverell also cites Queen Elizabeth's dealings with the Puritan *"Headstrong* and *Encroaching Monster,"* whom she "utterly *Suppress'd*: Which, like a *Prudent Princess,* She did by *Wholesome Severities"* that ensured her reign's prosperity. If King James had followed "Her *Wise Politicks,* his Son had never fall'n a *Martyr"* to Puritan fury from *"Miscreants, Begot* in *Rebellion, Born* in *Sedition,* and *Nurs'd* up in *Faction"* (pp. 19–20).

Since pulpit rhetoric could be accompanied by official or mob action, Dissenters properly feared, or claimed to fear, far worse than enforced catechisms, scolding sermons, or bonfires. They objected to being jailed, having their homes and farms plundered, and being subject to "the great Terrour" inflicted on fellow Protestants. As William Bisset saw it, Sacheverell would induce *"Robberies*; *Burnings*; and *intended Murthers"* of those he thought *"Church-devouring malignant Traytors"* and *"Incarnate Devils."* He would "dispatch us like Dogs, by hanging, or knocking us o' th' Head." Another author complained that Sacheverell's cronies "attack'd" individuals and menaced, reproached, and violently sermonized "to appear Formidable" and threatening. Sacheverell, we read in *The Politicks of High-Church* (1705), *"has already past Sentence upon the Occasional Conformists, viz.* A Gallows here, and Damnation hereafter." John Mortimer characterizes Dissenters' response to such perceived and ongoing threats: The vengeful High Church zealots seek "the destruction of Humane Society, . . . the ruine of the Nation, and of Religion it self." They foster "Cruelties, Persecutions, Conspiracies, Massacres, Inquisitions, and designs to persecute and destroy all that differ" from them. A comparably threatened Dissenter labeled "Wholesome Severities" as hanging, burning, confiscation, and prison. Moreover, such absolutism and extreme royalism "would shake and undermine the very Basis of our present glorious Establishment, as it is founded upon Revolution Principles, and totally blow off all our Prospects and future Hopes, in the Protestant Succession of the *Hanoverian* Line."[20]

In spite of such impassioned outcries against verbal and real violence, Dissenters and lower churchmen scarcely were powerless. Their High Church enemies thought them unscrupulous vast barbaric hordes sweeping down upon the few brave and lonely defenders of God's word, nation, and religion. As was so common in these ugly exchanges, however, roles were reversed, but language remained the same. For Dissenters, the High Church became the unscrupulous, morally barbaric hordes nonetheless smelling of incense, clothed in gaudy silks, and armed with secular weapons in order to root out true British Protestantism.

The responders were likely to include at least three overlapping complaints together with repeated scare terms. One was that the High Church really was a mask for papists, Rome, France, the Pretender, and horrible consequences from a horrible fate. *University Loyalty* (1683) was reprinted in 1710 to coincide with the trial of Henry Sacheverell for high crimes and misdemeanors. Its author laments the High Church "Drawn Swords" to destroy the constitution, civil rights, and the legitimate monarch in order to bring in the despotic papist Pretender. Oxford education indeed is "entirely tending to the *extirpation* of the *Protestant Religion*" and English rights. James Owen's *Moderation a Virtue* (1703) agrees with his *University* colleague. Jacobites under "the *French King*" will seek to destroy and subvert Protestantism and liberty in England as they did in Europe. Even some English monarchs betrayed their trust. As the unsigned *Mystery of Iniquity* (1689) put it, Catholic Charles II and James II sought both the extirpation of Protestantism and English servitude to Rome. John Toland later described a more Machiavellian royal route to the same goal: Charles II purposely created combative political parties to encourage his Bishops to extirpate *"Protestant Dissenters* of all sorts." James II then enhanced the process in order to dash his Protestant subjects "in pieces against one another." Matthew Tindal extended the argument to Sacheverell's verbal excesses and hatred of dissent and moderate Anglicanism. If his principles "had been follow'd at the time of the Revolution," and as some want now, "the Protestant Religion wou'd have been extirpated, and the whole Nation involv'd in Popery and Slavery." Objections to the theory of Papist *ad exemplum regis*, backed by French-style dragooning, had episcopal authority. In 1715 Gilbert Burnet told his audience that James II desired "the total Extirpation" of the English Protestant religion.[21]

A second concern was indeed that the state would use its secular power on behalf of a religion in danger of becoming papist. We know, in figures well remembered during the Gordon Riots in 1780, that Catholic Spaniards were presumed to have killed some forty million Indians, and Catholic Irish some two hundred thousand Protestants. Such are the monsters to whom the High Church would lead endangered England, where "Protestant Subjects are still sure to be destroy'd." Those outside of the High Church feared for their specific as well as general Protestant cause. Oxonian spitfires and even less lofty allies would engage judicial and punitive strength to coerce conformity, to punish nonconformity, or to attack political enemies. That was the position even of the relatively moderate High Church Jonathan Swift. In *The Publick Spirit of the Whigs* (1714) he virtually excommunicates the lower church Whig Richard Steele. Swift denies that clerical piety and wisdom are adequate supports in so evil an age "without the Assistance of *Secular Power*" and without miracles. Properly to have such events, he thinks that "they want a little *Enlargement of Assistance from the Secular Power*, against *Atheists, Deists, Socinians*, and other *Hereticks*."[22]

Quakers were among those who used a third argument. They extended fear of such state power and drew what they thought appropriately horrid conclusions.

James Wyeth elevated Charles Leslie to the role of Rome's depraved emperor: like Nero regarding Romans, he wished that Dissenters had "all but one Neck; and then their dispatch would be speedy." For the marginally optimistic Thomas Ellwood, the only way totally to suppress Quakers is "by *Cutting our Throats*, or *Knocking out our Brains*." Does the House of Commons want "this Inhumane Piece of *Butchery*, to *defile* their hands in the *innocent Blood* of so many *Thousands*"?[23]

More conventional dissenting Protestants feared that someone could be coming for them as well. Edmund Hickeringill saw that the High Church defended itself with the full catalog of state artillery: "*Jaylors, Bumbayliffs, Tackers, and Hangmen*, the *Pillory, Fire and Fagot, Cropt Ears, Dragoons*, and a *Halter*." John Dennis in turn was sadly confident that Sacheverell's sermons meant that the High Church intended to murder its opponents if it could. William Bisset was yet louder, familiar with classical history, and regarded Sacheverell as genocidally murderous. He would hang, brain, burn, and put Dissenters "*in one Burning Cauldron together*" or have the magistrate "*draw the Sword*," as Nero would have against Rome's single neck. John Mortimer comparably saw High Church rage that sought "Cruelties, Persecutions, Conspiracies, Massacres, Inquisitions, and designs to persecute and destroy" those with whom High Churchmen disagreed. Since such designs needed the mask of legal warrant, one ironic author has a nonce English friend at the court of Saint-Germain tell his friend at home that they will elect "Members of Parliament as wou'd willingly have voted their [nonconformists] Extermination in the House." In the broadside *The High Church Champion Pleading His Own Cause* (1710) Sacheverell is flanked by the pope and the devil. His allies dethrone princes, start civil wars, unsettle Parliament, "And cry High Church, is ruin'd and undone / If Persecution, don't through BRITAIN run."[24]

Some Dissenters and lower churchmen borrowed the High Church response to religious danger. Both Whigs and Tories were in fact well peopled with thugs. John Oldmixon was scarcely unique when in 1714 he used Sacheverell, indeed *Shortest Way* Defoe-like language to lament the government's lenity and moderation toward the dangerous Tory faction. "We are told in Divine Writ, that *Mercy* is sometimes *Cruelty*," as it certainly would be to the government's enemies. They should be treated with the ancients' "wise *Severity*." They not only beheaded their enemies but demolished their homes, lands, family names, their "whole *Race*," and buried "even their very Memories in their *Rubbish*," presumably as Greece did to Troy and Rome did Carthage. Seditious authors, their publishers, and street hawkers for that elevated faction should be arrested and punished. In the same year the Congregational minister Thomas Bradbury urged that George I behave like David in the Psalms: destroy his enemies and "*beat them as small as Dust before the Wind . . . cast them out as Dirt in the Streets.*"[25]

The context of Defoe's *Shortest Way with the Dissenters* thus clearly included unironic and violently immodest proposals. His contemporaries lacked the word but not the concept of genocide. Defoe's great errors in *The Shortest Way* were to seem to be such a thug himself, to be politically foolish, rhetorically abusive, and too clever by half. The consequences were especially severe during so dangerously corrosive a time in his nation's history and, from the autumn of 1702, when the bill for occasional conformity increased tensions between the zealous House of Commons and the more moderate House of Lords. George Chalmers later lamented those times when "the minds of men were inflamed against one another, and how little the virtues of mutual forbearance and personal kindness existed amid the clamour of contradiction."[26] *The Shortest Way* nonetheless was a courageous and important response to that clamor, if not in the way Defoe had hoped.

Defoe's *Shortest Way*, Sacheverell's *Political Union*, and Religious Conflict

Let us clear our minds of a central assumption regarding Defoe's incendiary pamphlet. Specifically, we should forgive those few of his early readers who failed at once to recognize *The Shortest Way*'s irony, though we can blame them for not seeing it shortly after they started. Irony can be difficult to identify when its position is at once outrageous and plausible. The unsigned *Billa Vera* (1703) falls into that class. The author seriously laments the political and religious contention pandemic in British culture, and the consequent atheism, deism, and ridicule that threaten "an end of all Religion" (p. 6). Since, following Locke, all impressions on the mind are based on use and custom, education of the young in Church of England principles is the long-run answer. So far so good. Then comes the counterpoint: the monster Dissent is multiheaded, too strong for us to kill by the sword, and will breed more and worse monsters if blooded. For proper annihilation, "chain, fetter, and imprison him, and then suffer him to Starve, Perish, and Expire for Nourishment" (p. 9). There is good reason to think this "straight," a metaphor for avoiding martyrdom and schism and, on modern standards, merely politically grotesque. Given the overheated religious and political world of 1703, there also is good reason to think it ironic, a version of Defoe's *Shortest Way* in which the implications of High Church rhetoric are made explicit: *Billa Vera* would draw our attention to the monstrosity of thinking a different religion monstrous and worth destroying by long starvation. Without benefit of an author's name and biography, the textual meaning here remains uncertain.

Defoe himself often engaged the technique of using plausible premises for excessive purposes. His *Bold Advice: Or, a Proposal For the entire Rooting out of*

Jacobitism in Great Britain (London, 1715) is murderously stern. Treasonous Jacobites should be banished (p. 26), disarmed, verbally constrained by law, and if necessary "stopp'd, Trampled under Foot, and bury'd in Dirt" (pp. 26–27). They are "a poisonous weed in the Ground, which must be pull'd up by the Roots" (p. 33). Unless the lower clergy is restrained by law, there may be an "*Extrajudicial* method" against them (p. 41). He also urged an extreme form of censorship: tearing down or closing down the wicked theaters.[27]

Whether or not such remarks are ironic, as I think they are not, they are consistent, though not congruent, with the familiar rage on either side. We recall Roger Altham's 1702 sermon and its desire to see disobedient evil Dissenters "Corrected by the Roughness of Authority," by the spiritual aided by the magistrate's "Sword of Vengeance."[28] In turn, a Whig behind the 1715 unsigned *Justice and Necessity of Restraining the Clergy in their Preaching* regards those High Churchmen as heretical traitors, as in sermons by "*Sacheverell, Welton, Higgins, Brett, Smith, Milburn, Lamb, Swift* and the like" (p. 1). England never can prosper until the clergy and the universities "are restrain'd from spreading *Sedition*" (p. 8). His key allies suggest his intention: "If there is one of the *High-flying* disaffected Priests, who is not only deficient in *Morals* as well as Principles, I will give up this Cause" (p. 58). That is the language of *Genesis* 18:22–33, in which God would spare Sodom for the sake of one good man. The *Justice* author is Lot, guided to safety by angels. Both Altham and the Whig are serious. Without knowing Defoe as author of the *Bold Advice*, it is reasonable to think of his work as an aggressive, overstated, but not wholly serious proposal. Once we know that it is by Defoe, we must at the least suspect that in fact it was a lamentably serious program, one consistent with Crusoe's later call for a crusade against non-Christians serving the devil. In such a holy war the "Priests and dedicated Persons of every kind, by whatever Names or Titles know[n]; or distinguished, should be at least removed, if not destroyed."[29]

As we have seen, and will see again, the High Church party genuinely felt that Dissenters sought the "utter Extirpation of the *Establish'd Government*" and its established church.[30] Regicide and forced abdication concentrate the mind almost as wonderfully as hanging, and the High Church mind was wonderfully concentrated. It felt justified in calling for that sword of vengeance as an act of self-defense, which in turn evoked Defoe's aggressive defense.

For Defoe, the final of final straws was Henry Sacheverell's 1702 *Political Union*. Sacheverell proclaimed both a high-flying political creed of divine right and the relationship and mutual dependance of church and state. His text in the sermon-discourse was based on Proverbs 8:15, "*By Me Kings Reign, and Princes Decree Justice*" (p. 1). Monarchy and episcopacy are necessary for secular and spiritual order, or the nation will degenerate into lawless atheism and all its malign consequences. Hypocritical enemies of the established church hide behind the mask of moderation and would remove the church's "Fence, and . . . Its *Land-Mark*." Evildoers blur all distinctions, debunk divinity and discipline, allow anyone to believe anything, and even tolerate "Its Worst Enemies" (p. 49).

The Political Union well adapts High Church apocalyptic language. Dissenters and latitudinarians are "Treacherous *False Friends*, who endeavour to Degrade and Sink" the church and to divide it from the supportive state—"the One [is] undermin'd through the Foundations of the Other." This is not a mere squabble, but potentially "*Fatal*" and "*the Greatest Danger*" (sig. A2^v, with the title page as A1^r). Among other scare words, the opposition are Machiavels (p. 2), encroachers (p. 8), murderers (p. 9), vermin, filth, corrupt (p. 17), anarchists (p. 27), Babel-creating Nimrods (p. 36), moths, cankers (p. 41), prostituted, ignorant, unworthy traitors (p. 45), subverters of church fences, dangerous (p. 48), innovators, potential traitors (p. 50), vipers (p. 52), foreigners (p. 53), rebels (p. 54), extirpaters, and Bastard Spawn (p. 55). Most ominously, the true friends of the Church and state "ought to Hang out the *Bloody Flag*, and *Banner* of Defiance" (p. 59). That is the English equivalent of imperial Rome's *debellare superbos*, war to the end against the proud resisters. William Bisset indeed chronicled a partial effort in that direction. He recalls having seen "Officers entring into Houses, and haling Men and Women, committ them to Prison; Shops forcibly broken open, and the working Tools, i. e. Peoples Bread, seiz'd by Distress, for not coming to hear, (for such he was) a very ignorant Sot; and this was not Mob-Justice, as these last Twelve Months, but by Warrant from Magistrates." Bisset is likely also to have been thinking of French dragoons at work prior to the revocation of the Edict of Nantes, for he is especially horrified that such actions "should be done in a Protestant Country."[31]

Sacheverell was demonstrably hostile to Queen Anne's moderate Tory government, whose ministry he harshly castigated as ignorant mercenaries willing to betray the church for selfish secular designs (p. 45). To shield himself from potential prosecution, he uses the future and the conditional tenses. "When" public justice and the morally unified church and state collapse, "We should see" dreadful depravity (p. 44). In another place he uses the present tense to praise the native-born Queen Anne's adherence to his notions: "yet, Blessed be God, there is now a Person on the Throne, who so justly Weighs the Interest of Church and State, as to Remove so false an *Engine*, that Visibly Over-turns Both" (p. 62). William Wake, bishop of Lincoln as he then was, later said that such words "serve as a Back-Door, to slip out at, when he should be call'd to Account." That probably resolves Bisset's puzzlement. He does not understand how the ministers could prosecute Defoe because "he had Insinuated as if the Church of England would use rigorous Methods with Protestant Dissenters" and not prosecute Sacheverell, "who had then actually hang'd out the Bloody Flag; and since openly declar'd his Judgment for having all Dissenters drawn, hang'd, and quarter'd; besides consigning them to the bottomless Pit, and leaving them there with the Devil and his Angels."[32]

The Political Union's targets thus are part of a vast army of enemies at the gate. The repeated image of undermining or removing foundations is drawn from siege terminology (pp. 24, 34, 42, 48, 54, 61). In a partial reversal, Sacheverell knows that God permits his enemies "to proceed in their courses, so as to Destroy and Blow up Themselves, whilst They are Undermining others" (pp. 33–34). Samuel Johnson's main definition of the verb *undermine* in his *Dictionary* (1755) is "To dig cavities under any thing, so that it may fall, or be blown up; to sap." Two of his eleven illustrative quotations for the verb and the noun concern religion, and two concern government. Denham (for the verb) tells us that "Though the foundation on a rock were laid, / The church was *undermin'd* and then betray'd." South (noun) reports that the "most experienced disturbers and *underminers* of government, have always laid their first train [of gunpowder] in contempt, endeavouring to blow it up in the judgment and esteem of the subject." Sacheverell thus imports Queen Anne herself to defeat the enemy's dangerous "False . . . engine." That term denotes "A military machine," or in the plural, *enginery*, "Engines of war; artillery" guided by an engineer, "who directs the artillery of an army." Johnson quotes Fairfax saying that "This is our *engine* towers that overthrows; / Our spear that hurts, our sword that wounds our foes." However merely tactical, Sacheverell's rhetoric shows Anne's Crown "justly" in support of her church.

Dissenters are not Sacheverell's only targets. "Treacherous" Whig "*Latitudinarians*, ought to be Stigmatiz'd, and Treated Equally as Dangerous Enemies to the *Government*, as well as *Church*" (p. 49), for infestation in one body carries over to the other (p. 50). Defoe later will take a cue from the violent image of the stigmata, but Sacheverell's immediate target is Gilbert Burnet, who had been William of Orange's adviser, crossed the English Channel with him, later was appointed his chaplain, and was created bishop of Salisbury on Easter, 1689. Burnet was a regular target of High Church anger, perhaps no place more so than in his *Exposition of the Thirty-nine Articles of the Church of England* (1699). Altitudinarian discomfort would have started with the epistle dedicatory to William III. He is "*Defender of the Faith*"; he has "the Best of Claims" to the Crown, as opposed to those with "Designs of Overturning" it; he is the benign monarch "supporting and securing This Church" against infidelity and impiety; he seeks to heal breaches among Protestants. Such a triumph will establish him as history's "Brightest and Perfectest Character." Burnet hopes to promote that end in his *Exposition*. In contrast, Sacheverell was among the High Churchmen who thought that William appointed "none but Fanaticks Bishops" and was "an Enemy to the Church of England."[33] The High Church was even more troubled by Burnet's explanation of his method and the reason for his book.

Burnet's preface at once acknowledges modern Anglican distance from its Augustinian past. One reason there has been so little printed discussion of the Thirty-Nine Articles is that they "seemed to be so plain a Transcript of St. *Austin's* Doctrine." Yet the vast majority of Anglican divines "is believed to be now of a different Opinion," as Burnet himself is regarding article 17, on predestination (pp. i, vi). From his point of view, however, that is an advantage, since he plans candidly and objectively to lay out the grounds of interpretation on which competing views are based. The *Exposition* is a microcosm of what Burnet hopes for the Church of England and the nation, to reconcile differences regarding matters indifferent. So irenic a practice is consistent with "the Meekness of Christ." He thus fosters "a better understanding of one another and a mutual Forbearance in these matters." Each side, Lutherans and Calvinists, for example, will see that their opponents' arguments are not contemptible or dangerous "but are such as may prevail on wise and good men: Here is a Foundation for Charity." Once we agree upon general principles, we also can agree that men who differ may have their own beliefs, but with the obligation of judging "charitably and favorably of others" and making communion with those who differ from them (pp. vi–vii). As he later says, the church "has not been peremptory," and "a Latitude has been left to different Opinions" (p. 170). Burnet concludes with the words of an unnamed distinguished German Lutheran: "Let the Church of *England* heal her own Breaches, and then all the rest of the Reformed Churches will with great Respect, admit of her Mediation to heal theirs" (p. x).

Rubbish, his enemies insisted. German Lutherans and Whig latitudinarians had no business changing the very nature of holy, fixed interpretation. William Binckes soon spoke for the Lower Convocation, with whose then uncharitable sensibility Sacheverell surely agreed. Burnet's mode of proceeding subverts Anglican authority and offends "the Generality of the Clergy." The church defines what is properly orthodox. "If the Sense deliver'd varies from the known Doctrine and practice of the Church, it is in effect to frame new Articles of Religion" and threatens to put "the Reformation upon a new foot." At the least it changes church boundaries "and alters the Terms of Communion." On Burnet's standard, one could subscribe an article and not believe its stated words. That path to unacceptable comprehension must not be taken. The church insists "that such as subscribe to the Articles, should agree in the things therein contain'd." Binckes uses familiar High Church language to characterize Burnet's pamphlet. It is among the many designed "to undermine the Church, throw down its Walls, and lay all open" to contemplate liberty of opinion regarding religion. As Binckes says elsewhere, the *Exposition* favored non-Anglican persuasions and indeed was written "rather against, than in favour of the establish'd Religion."[34] For Sacheverell, Binckes, and their associates, Burnet was among the many Anglican false brethren who could destroy the church and the state.

There were ample responses to Sacheverell's rejection of fellow Anglicans and Dissenters of all sorts. These later reached a head in the ministry's anger and fear evoked by his fire-breathing 1709 sermon *The Perils of False Brethren: Both in Church and State*. His consequent trial for high crimes and misdemeanors brought a modest punishment and virtual victory lap in March of 1710. Some eight years earlier, however, Defoe tried Sacheverell in *The Shortest Way with the Dissenters*. It is a brilliant piece that too well captures what gradually becomes clear in Sacheverell's *Political Union*, so often based upon martial metaphors, near defamation of Anne and her government, and shrewdly protective grammatical turns. Defoe would not be so clever, but he well mimicked and indeed heightened Sacheverell's tone and technique. Some were confused and took *The Shortest Way* as a proper High Church response with a proper solution to a proper mess. Those numbers surely must have been few if readers paid minimal attention to regular clues that regularly exploited well-known biblical texts and political events. Some recent revisionist readers nonetheless have argued that Defoe really intended that his little book be perceived as genuine High Church agenda and that his later claim of irony was a defensive invention. One critic "has to wonder how even a careful reader could detect Defoe's irony." Another cannot "turn up plausible 'signals' of irony" and believes that *The Shortest Way* was designed as "an intentional fake not mean to be decoded."[35]

Defoe, though, almost certainly meant *irony* in the classical and consequent eighteenth-century lexical and rhetorical sense. The sixth edition of Edward Phillips' *New World of Words* appeared in 1706 and provided the familiar definition of *irony*: "Oratours, when they speak contrary to what they mean, so as to make a shew of praising an Adversary, and at the same time to scoff and despise him." Namely, in *The Shortest Way* Defoe speaks in the highest High Church voice the better to scoff and despise it, to demonstrate that such views were blameworthy, not praiseworthy. He thus pretends to affirm the values of a Sacheverell clone, but as John Tutchin perceived, "Herein those People are drawn to the Life, and those who know their Marks and Character, will the better know how to avoid 'em."[36] As I hope to show, Defoe proceeds by means of outrageous overstatement and misrepresentation, designed to be seen and, he surely thought, impossible to be missed. As George Chalmers put it long after the heat had cooled, *The Shortest*

Way was a "piece of exquisite irony, though there are certainly passages in it that might have shown considerate men how much the author was in jest."

We shall see that one reader who chose not to speak out annotated his copy with all of its errors—which could not be there but by design. John Tutchin comparably noted errors, which he thought characteristic of the foolish High Church "*Inferiour Clergy.*" Defoe soon realized that, as Maximillian Novak has put it, he "had slipped over the edge of the abyss." However much falling, Defoe could not have thought himself invisible and unidentified. Tutchin soon announced what others probably knew. The *Observator* for 30 December 1701–2 January 1702 implicitly proclaimed Defoe's authorship, just one month after *The Shortest Way*'s publication on 1 December. That evil book, the radical Whig Tutchin proclaimed, was by "the Reputed Author of *The Legion Letter*," that is, Defoe's *Legion's Memorial Presented to the Speaker of the House of Commons* (1701).[37] Several fairly dim, or perhaps merely brutal, High Church readers thought the pamphlet a wise statement of what should be done. Some Whigs comparably feared that such in fact was what the high flyers planned to do. Dissenters feared that it would yet further increase High Church hostility toward them. The government feared that it could stir serious civil disruption. Charles Leslie reports that "all over the *Town*, among all sorts of People" every one thought that a churchman and not a Whig had written it. Leslie's circle of acquaintances, however, consisted largely of like-minded Jacobite, nonjuring Tory High Church associates. At first they were pleased by the apparent "*Stile* of a *Church-man, with an Air of* Wit and a great deal of *Truth.*"[38] Simple error or, more probably, wilful blindness says more about the blind than about what the sighted choose not to see.

The hypothesis of invisible irony rests upon such familiar and repeated evidence, which is in turn contradicted or at least significantly challenged by other evidence. A heavily annotated copy of *The Shortest Way* in the British Library makes plain that this reader, surely among many others, promptly or at least reasonably soon saw through the speaker's presumed persona.[39]

We cannot determine when the annotator purchased the copy or whether his annotations were made before or after Defoe's sentence to the pillory. The verso of the title page, though, includes a note detailing the guilty plea and the sentence against Defoe, "a supposed Dissenter," with whom the annotator clearly sympathizes. For example, Defoe writes that under James I "the worst they [Dissenters] suffer'd" was at their own request to go to New England, about which the annotator writes "*Exile*" next to "suffer'd" (p. 5). *The Shortest Way* observes that "Charity and Love is the known Doctrine of the Church of *England*," which the annotator corrects to the Church of "Scotland." *The Shortest Way* claims that its program wrongly may be thought "Cruelty in its Nature, and Barbarous to all the World," to which the annotator replies, "it cannot be otherwise esteemed" (p. 18). He twice modifies *The Shortest Way* with the same pejorative that puts the onus on the High Church. The Church of England cannot "justify our *bearing*" Dissenters' insults, and they surely will not "*suffer* Gallows and Gallies" rather than convert. In each case the annotator's underlined word is answered by a marginal substitution of "Imposed." No wonder, then, that the final manuscript note identifies Defoe as a "Champion for the moderate Church of England . . . in opposition to Jacobite & non Juror + the High Church men of passive obedience." As this evidence suggests, if Defoe was briefly thought by Charles Leslie and others to be their voice and ally, he also was thought by others to propose an odious agenda designed to reveal a "Champion" of moderation. This reader not only recognized Defoe's irony, his representation of an objectionable point of view that he pretends to find attractive; he also makes plain that Defoe's targets clearly were perceived as Defoe's targets.

That targeting proceeded by means of the lexical irony of inversion. Defoe thus amplifies biblical and other allusions that should have alerted readers to the dangers of the screeds he castigates. Much of the power of these allusions apparently has been lost to many secular modern readers. Defoe nonetheless certainly designed them to be found by his own contemporaries, as some did, however much they misread irony for actuality.

The Shortest Way: The Bible and Other Clues beyond the Obvious

Defoe enlarges Sacheverell's key device of excess, as in two grossly distorted Old Testament examples. At this rate, *The Shortest Way* tells us, the church is to be shattered by schism and confused, the government engrossed by foreigners, and the "Monarchy dwindled into a Republic." To spare the next generation such horrors, it would be more rational "to summon our own to a general Massacre." Moses "was a merciful meek Man," yet he practiced this sacrificial method in Exodus 32:27–29. There he descended from Mount Sinai with the Ten Commandments, saw the golden calf the Israelites had made in his absence, and smashed the tablets: "with what Fury did he run thro' the Camp and cut the throats of Three and thirty thousand of his dear *Israelites*, that were fallen into Idolatry." It was "Mercy to the rest, to make these be Examples, to prevent the Destruction of the whole Army" (pp. 20–21).

The impressive illustration is designed to be absurd on the face of it. Assume that it takes a mere six seconds to "run" after, seize, and cut the throat of each of thirty-three thousand individuals. Assume that no one prefers to run away and needs to be caught. Assume that among the thirty-three thousand no one resists or knows that the odds of thirty-three thousand to one are in their favor. After these at the least amusing improbabilities, assume also that Moses spent some 198,000 consecutive seconds, or nearly six hours, running, cutting, stepping over or on corpses, never resting, never needing a potty break, never changing knives that dulled after such perpetual exercise, never washing his hands, never changing his bloody garments soon stiff with gore, never saying a few nice words to assure his grateful army that this was for their benefit—assume all this and one might indeed assume that more than a few wilfully misguided readers did not detect the impossible scenario. Neither Defoe nor even almost all of the even marginally educated would accept Moses as the scarcely exhausted Pheidippides of marathon slaughter, after which he uttered *"Yesh l'anu echad,"* the Hebrew equivalent of the moribund Greek's *Nenikékamen*, "we have won."

Moreover, Defoe obviously improves biblical casualties from "about three thousand" (Exodus 32:28) to thirty-three thousand and distorts the relevant chapter. Young Defoe transcribed all five books of the Pentateuch in shorthand, in fear that James II would destroy written scripture while forcing Catholicism and priests upon the nation. Charles Morton regularly inculcated Bible reading and interpretation while Defoe was a student at Newington Academy. Protestants generally prided themselves on biblical knowledge, and Dissenters in particular were keen on the Old Testament and its God of the chosen people. Defoe's Mosaic passage surely warns against inflated High Church anger that would deal with Dissenters as crudely as it dealt with the Bible. For example, both dissenting and Anglican readers knew that Moses was neither merciful nor meek. The young Moses slays "an Egyptian smiting an Hebrew, one of his brethren." After he flees, he defends the daughters of Midian, who sought to draw water for their father's flock but were attacked by shepherds who refused to share (Exodus 2:11–12, 17). When Moses becomes God's instrument in Egypt, he speaks God's truth to secular power, invokes dreadful plagues, the loss of first-born sons, and the destruction of Pharaoh's army. He later elevates the divinely empowered staff that allows the Israelites to rout the Amalekites (Exodus 17:10–13). Moses asks God to judge Korah, Dathan, and Abiram when they rebel against his—that is, God's—authority. He swallows and buries them and 250 of their sympathizers (Numbers 16:1–35). Meek and mild indeed. Those individual acts, however, scarcely justify his personal slaughter of thirty-three thousand Israelite backsliders.

Like Dissenters, lower church Whig and High Church Tory also knew that the deaths in Exodus were as the sacred text, not *The Shortest Way*, claimed. In 1701 Whig but loyal Church of England man Thomas Bennet wrote that "three thousand were slain for worshipping *Aaron's Calf, Exod.* 32. 20." Thereafter, altitudinarian Francis Atterbury reiterated that God "gave commission to the Sons of *Levi*, who sanctify themselves, by executing 3000 of the offenders . . . [32] v. 35."[40]

Furthermore, though Exodus 32 includes abundant slaughter, it largely concerns Moses' mediation between God and man and the Israelites' fall from and return to favor. The passage invites ultimate mercy, not vengeance, as Moses becomes a type of Christ. Specifically, while Moses is on Mount Sinai the angry God warns him that the Israelites have again corrupted themselves, his anger will consume them, and he will make only Moses the progenitor of "a great nation." Moses beseeches God not to do Pharaoh's work for him: Please remember your promise to Abraham, Isaac, and Israel to multiply their seed "as to the stars of heaven" and give them the promised land for ever. God accepts Moses' plea for mercy. The omniscient God also knows what will happen once Moses sees the golden calf and incessant celebrations on its behalf and on behalf of freedom from obligation to the liberating God. Moses both breaks the tablets on which God inscribed the Ten Commandments and "stood in the gate of the camp, and said Who is on the LORD'S side? *Let him come* unto me. And all the sons of Levi gathered themselves together unto him" (32:27). Moses has offered all of Israel a chance to repent and join God, but only the Levites answer the call. Since Moses was a Levite, their decision exemplifies loyalty to family as well as to God. Bishop Simon Patrick embodies received wisdom and makes plain that their destruction of some three thousand sinners stems from God's authority: because Moses was serving "under God," he was permitted to pass sentence "without the common Process in Courts of Judgment, as Mr. *Selden* observes."[41] The act embodies a chain of connection from God to Moses to Levites "on the LORD'S side." Sacheverell's plan demands forced and no doubt insincere conversion. Moses' plan demands moral choice to accept God. The vast majority of Defoe's readers could not have been ignorant of the demonstrable distortion in the High Church ranter's *Shortest Way*.

Defoe's allusion to Exodus 32 thus clearly rejects any Sacheverell-like assumption of personal or institutional vengeance. Moses implores: "Consecrate yourselves to day to the LORD" (32:29). Both Moses and the Lord then seek to reconcile, not to annihilate. Moses blames his people for their sins but adds that he will go to the Lord and "make an atonement" for them. Forgive them, he asks, but if not, "blot me, I pray thee, out of the book which thou hast written" (32:30–32). God splits the difference. He will punish those who have sinned but grants part of what he had already granted, namely, survival of the nation as it moves toward its new land: "go, lead the people unto *the place* of which I have spoken unto thee: behold mine Angel shall go before thee" (32.34). Readers even marginally familiar with the Old Testament would know far more than that the warrior Moses scarcely was meek. They would add what Atterbury obviously knew: (1) that Moses sought God's mercy both before and after he left Mount Sinai; (2) that Moses was not furious but judiciously offered reform before he asked the repentant to exercise God's punishment; (3) that the Levites, not Moses, did the killing as God required; (4) that the number was one-tenth of thirty thousand; and (5) that God punished the sinners but instructed his guiding angel to lead the Israelites to the promised land. Familiar biblical commentary supports such views.

Several significant interpretations solidified response to the passage in Exodus that Defoe evokes to discredit High Church rage. They would multiply deaths by ten and annihilate mercy as they would annihilate Dissenters. Samuel Wesley's poem *The History of the Old and New Testament* (London, 1704) epitomizes parts of the scene and concludes with the Bible's own conclusion: "Thousands of th' Unjust [were] by Zealous *Levi* slain." Others agree with Wesley and add that, as Matthew Poole put it, Moses asks, "Who will take God's part, and plead his Cause against Idolatry and Idolators"; the Levites do. That tribe indeed was "designed by God for his immediate service." They thus killed only those who rejected God's cause and those who chose to stay in sin. Moses is God's prophetic voice and is neither personally furious nor, in this instance, bloody. By 1710 Matthew Henry comparably added that Moses asked, not who was on his side, but "on the Lord's side." Poole reiterates that the Levites chose only those hardened in sin, in the streets, "and the Ring leaders to others in this mischief" rather than those in their tents and "ashamed and grieving." In judgment as in martial execution of rebellious ringleaders, the Levites consecrated to God had a divine commission. Henry later reiterates that God punished only those of "wilful Disobedience ... not the Innocent for the Guilty."[42]

We recall that Moses goes far beyond prophetic declarations of divine will regarding sinners. After the punishment, he again takes it upon himself to mediate between the angry God and the sinful Israelites. He asks forgiveness and offers himself in exchange for their sin, so that, as Atterbury observed, Moses "obtains Mercy from the Omnipotent, that they may not all perish." Such an offer inevitably evoked the greater sacrifice that it anticipated. Matthew Poole knew that Moses was "the Type of the true Mediator, Jesus Christ, who was in effect to suffer this which *Moses* was content to suffer." A few years later Matthew Henry added that there "are more Types of Christ in this Book, than perhaps in any other Book of the Old Testament." Jesus is an even more successful mediator, but in John 10:11 Moses is "a Type of the good Shepherd," who sacrifices himself for his sheep.[43]

Such broadly available information was both challenged and buttressed in a different way by John Locke's important *Letter concerning Toleration* (1689). The

Letter regularly insists upon the separation of church and state, anger at the magistrate using fire and sword to compel adherence to a state religion, and cognate anger at revocation of the Edict of Nantes. Locke frames his opponents' counter-argument in order to refute it. After all, "by the Law of *Moses* idolaters were to be rooted out. True indeed, by the Law of *Moses*; but that is not obligatory to us Christians." No one believes "that every thing, generally, enjoyed by the Law of *Moses*; ought to be practised by Christians." The Mosaic laws applied to the Israelites, who were governed by God. They thus apply "only to that People. And this Consideration alone is Answer enough unto those that urge the Authority of the Law of *Moses* for the inflicting of capital Punishments upon Idolaters." As a theocracy, the early Jewish nation was "different in that from all others."[44]

Defoe adds yet more abuse of basic positive knowledge that discredits his speaker's moral, religious, and political standing. Two further examples and the book's conclusion suffice. Protestants deplored Louis XIV's revocation of the Edict of Nantes in October of 1685. Anyone supporting that deprivation of Protestant rights would have been demonstrably disloyal. Defoe's *Shortest Way* reverses that assumption, yet further discredits High Church zealotry and associates it with France and presumed papist tyranny. Are the Dissenters too numerous to be suppressed? No. "THEY are not so Numerous as the Protestants in *France*, and yet the *French* King effectually clear'd the Nation of them at once, and we don't find he Misses them at Home" (p. 12). England is being punished "for not utterly extinguishing them long ago" (p. 13). This nonsense was noted and condemned by Anglican and dissenting, Whig and Tory, commentators. John Tutchin, for example, is outraged because Defoe apparently "commends the Discipline of *Lewis* the 14th towards the Hugonots, throughout his whole Book; and Recommends the *Gallies*" to bring men into the Church of England. Mary Astell's 1704 *Fair Way with the Dissenters and their Patrons* was troubled by this insult "towards the Queen and Church of *England*" and "odious Comparison" with Catholic France (pp. 20–21). Both the comment and the concept behind it remained in mind a decade later. The angry John Anderson responds to Thomas Rhind's apologia upon leaving the Presbyterian for the Anglican confession: Presbyterianism is an unacceptable civil and religious institution and should be suppressed as a national enemy. Anderson's long attack upon Rhind promptly turns to Defoe and to French conduct. Several years earlier "THAT Unhappy Fellow *DeFoe* . . . put all *England* in a Ferment" with his *Shortest Way*. It really "was the Immediate Use" of Rhind's doctrine so generally "in all the Controversial Books, and . . . the Sermons of *High-Church*," which has the will but not the power to enact tragic deeds. In fact, the troubled Anderson asks, if the Presbyterians are so wicked, should not the state deny their legal rights and *"crush a Society of so Dangerous a Constitution"*? That is what papist countries do, and "what less should be expected from a Party, which justifies all that carnage the *French* King has made of his *Protestant* subjects?"[45]

Defoe already had considered an appropriately hostile response to that French carnage and denial of rights through revocation of the Edict of Nantes. His *Lex Talionis* (1698) was reprinted in 1703 as part of the unauthorized *Collection of the Writings Of the Author of the True-Born Englishman*, where it was a companion piece to *The Shortest Way*. Defoe understandably did not reprint it in his *True Collection . . . . Corrected by Himself* (1703). Upon reading it one understands how Defoe could so well mimic Sacheverell's version of ethnic cleansing: he was keen on practicing it himself toward Catholics.

Lex Talionis is fiercely anti-Catholic and anti-French. Defoe bases his law of retaliation both on biblical precedent and on equality of response. If Catholic nations expel Protestants, Protestant nations should expel the same number of Catholics.[46] So much the better to be unified in a superior, peaceful religion whose nations will benefit from immigration of skilled foreign coreligionists (pp. 24–25). As for domestic Catholics, good riddance: they "have been always uneasie to the Governments they have lived under." History is filled with their treasons, rebellions, deluges of blood, regicides, and "innumerable Protestants Massacred and Butchered in Cold Blood" (p. 13; see also p. 14). Louis XIV's papist "*French* have Dragooned Three Hundred Thousand of their Protestant Subjects to *Mass*, and hurry'd Three Hundred Thousand more out of their Country, to seek Comfort from the Charity of Neighbour States" (p. 12). France surely will miss Protestants, who "are the Trading People of the World" and thus enrich the nations to which they are so loyal (p. 26).

The Shortest Way clearly distorts Exodus and clearly praises France for revoking Protestant civil rights and for denigrating and depopulating its Huguenot subjects. These are among the several red flags so different from but nearly as mischievous as Sacheverell's. I offer a final example of what also must have appalled readers not wearing ideological blinders.

"Had King *James* sent all the Puritans in *England* away to the *West-Indies*, we had been a national unmix'd Church; the Church of *England* had been kept undivided and entire" (p. 6)—read, certainly rid of modern Dissenters. The West Indies evoked images of punishment, death, and slavery. Swift thought that religion could be advanced if bad clergymen were "dismissed to the *West Indies*; where there is work enough for them, and where some better Provision should be made for them." That provision was in a place redolent of brutality and its consequences. In 1712 Mr. Spectator noted the dreadful "Mortality of the Place." Its "detestable" commanding officer so "oppressed his Subjects that he was heartily hated by every Man under his Command." Such hatred was sadly familiar and sadly harsh. The title of a pamphlet in 1713 includes the *"short, but True, Account of the most horrid, barbarous, and bloody MURTHER and REBELLION committed at Antego in the West-Indies, against Her Majesty and Her Government."*[47] Nathaniel Crouch elaborated upon the social and economic system that produced this disorder. Barbados was divided into three parts: masters lived well; servants were indentured for five years and then were freed to "employ their time to their own advantage"; but the black slaves and their children were "in Bondage for ever ... and used with such Severity" that they were about to start a fatal rebellion until one of their number disclosed the conspiracy: "Many of them were put to death, as a Terror to the rest." This behavior continued well into the eighteenth century. As late as 1777 Samuel Johnson toasted "to the next insurrection of the negroes in the West Indies." For over a century, being sent to the West Indies was, as Johnson said in 1756 of Jamaica in particular, to go to "a place of great wealth and dreadful wickedness, a den of tyrants, and a dungeon of slaves"—and with a painfully high mortality rate.[48] Defoe's speaker did not wish that James I had merely exiled Dissenters to the West Indies; he wished that James had killed or enslaved them.

Readers who arrived at the last page without knowing what Defoe was up to would have to be more than dense. If so, even they should have seen the perversion of Luke 23:32–43 in "Now *let us Crucifie the Thieves*. Let her Foundation be establish'd upon the Destruction of her Enemies" (p. 29). In that portion of Luke, the suffering Christ is crucified between thieves; he forgives his destroyers, for they know not what they do. He also exercises divine mercy upon the repentant thief, who acknowledges his divinity and asks to be remembered: "Truly, I say to you, today you shall be with me in Paradise." The mournful episode exemplifies the possibility of repentance and Christ's power to spare and to reward in the face of excruciating pain and temptation. By naming *"us"* as the crucifiers, Defoe transforms the Church of England into the tormenting Romans, who rule "with the Rod of Iron" (p. 29). Moreover, I suspect that Defoe is alluding to William Binckes' thirtieth of January sermon to the Lower Convocation in 1702. Binckes there wonders "whether either the Prayers of our Saviour on the Cross, or of our Royal Martyr on the Scaffold, and in his Closet" obtained forgiveness for the regicides. Binckes soon resolves his own question: "we shall quickly find that it did not."[49] Binckes has limited Christ's ability to intercede on man's behalf, denied God's omnipotence and infinite mercy, and implicitly, if unintentionally, denigrated Anglican Christianity. No wonder the House of Lords censured him, and no wonder Defoe could suggest that High Church "Destruction of her Enemies" also meant destruction of the Church of England as a moral force. Defoe had excellent reasons to repent much of his *Shortest Way with the Dissenters*. The inability of a few readers to fathom his intention should not have been among them.

Response and Judgment

A few High Church readers, as well as some Whigs and Dissenters, nonetheless thought *The Shortest Way* either a genuine High Church screed or at the least inflammatory. Edmund Hickeringill, we know, placed it within the Oxonian spitfire class.[50] John Dunton's *Shortest Way with Whores and Rogues* (1703) acknowledged that Defoe might be ironic but found the appalling work typical of Defoe as "*a* Mighty Critick in the Works of Darkness." He has libeled "*the best Queen in the World*," slandered the "Honest Men" who serve her government, and made the Dissenters think the government should "*Hang 'em all once.*" Defoe deserves hanging, Dunton says before challenging him to a duel. Like Dunton, the author of *Reflections Upon a Late Scandalous and Malicious Pamphlet* (1703) thinks *The Shortest Way* especially repellant and libelous. Queen Anne insisted on preserving the Act of Toleration. Defoe has slandered the established church, so unlike Laud's; he disturbs moderates and Dissenters by claiming that the queen and ministers "design'd their Destruction," *Reflections* says about a work that encourages discord. One suspects that Dunton was scarcely unhappy when in 1707 he characterized a High Churchman's attitude toward Defoe: "Yes, *Foe*, he takes the *Shortest Way with you.*"[51]

Dunton and the Reflector isolate key responses to Defoe's provocative *Way*: it abuses the moderate queen and government; it ignores her stated preference for peace and Toleration; it rudely tries to instruct her and her ministers; and it seditiously promotes civil unrest. The queen offered a reward for Defoe's arrest, after which he was properly interrogated and punished.[52] Overt High Church response made some of the same points but added presumed motivation consistent with its view of violent dissenting and lower church modes of proceeding.

The Tory and High Church reaction of course expressed fear, loathing, and contempt for Whigs and Dissenters, who regularly sought to ruin church and state. An incendiary behind *The Fox with his Fire-brand* (1703) rejected the laughable notion that Defoe was "free from any *seditious Design.*" The author repeats *sedition* at least eight times within twenty-three pages and complains that Defoe seeks "to bring us back again into the same Circumstances" of violent civil war. The angry author of *The Safest-Way with the Dissenters* (London, 1703) regards *The Shortest Way* as a serious statement but thinks it unsafe and pernicious "for any Government to Hang up so many of its Subjects" (p. 3). Defoe wickedly creates animosity "by proposing such Barbarous Usage to Dissenters" (p. 4). The best way to deal with those odious schismatics is to kill them with kindness rather than with number-enhancing persecution. Toleration will absorb them into the establishment, make them miserable courtiers, and render them harmless because sycophantic placeseekers (pp. 5–8). For sterner critics, Defoe's scheme was a "blowing the Trumpet of Sedition, and crying out, *To your Tents ye men of Israel*" in order to stir up division, dissent, and rebellion against the House of Hanover. Much of this was seconded by the author of *Reflections* upon Defoe's pamphlet: his "invenom'd *Libel*" could "set the Nation in a Flame, and . . . engage us in an intestine War" that would encourage Jacobites, the Pretender, and France.[53]

The usual High Church suspects blended their voices into the chorus. In *The Wolf Stript of His Shepherd's Cloathing* Charles Leslie insists that Defoe viciously labeled the High Church as "not fit to Live upon the Face of the Earth, Men of *Damnable Lusts* of *No Principles*. . . . I know not that ever there was so much *Venom* thrown at any sort of *People*, upon any Occasion!" Leslie and Mary Astell understood the apparent rationale behind the ironic rhetoric. For Leslie, Defoe wanted the Dissenters to believe that the High Church would cut "all their *Throats*," the better to prompt "the *Dissenters* for their own *Preservation* to begin with us." Defoe sought "to prepare the *Mobb*" to attack the church party. For Astell in *Impartial Enquiry* (1704), one of the Dissenters' "Arts is to lay their own Designs of overturning the Government, at the Door of those very Men, who are it's most faithful Supporters." Whatever the disguise, she says in *Moderation Truly Stated*, the Dissenters are "for a *short way with the* Church." *The Shortest Way*'s real message is clear: "it is natural enough to suppose that Other Men will deal with us as we would have dealt with them."[54]

Queen Anne, her government, and their supporters also felt dealt with. When *The Shortest Way* mentions or alludes to the queen, for example, it praises her as a "Constant Member of, and Friend to the Church of *England*." Hence, as for the Dissenters who wrongly flourished under "the Stranger, . . . their Day is over" (p. 2). The Dissenters once had "your *Dutch Monarch*," but this native monarch "will have a care of you" (p. 4). Yes, she promised to maintain the alien Toleration, but not "to the Destruction of the Church," which now can "destroy her Enemies" with a Parliament protected by the queen (pp. 16, 17). We may overturn and suppress "the Destroyers of the Nations Peace" under "such a Parliament, such a Convocation, such a Gentry, and such a Queen as we never had before" (pp. 25, 26). Failure to act will bring posterity's condemnation if we do not "root out this cursed Race from the World, under the Favour and Protection of a true *English* Queen" (p. 19).

The court had good reason to be troubled by a pamphlet that misrepresented and threatened them. Queen Anne succeeded to her brother-in-law William's throne on 8 March 1702. She made her first speech to Parliament on 30 March and there said that she supported both the Church of England and the Act of Toleration. Above all, she sought peace and a reduction in strife among her differing subjects at war with Europe's greatest power. At the insistence of her nephew and Clarendon's son, the annoying High Tory Earl of Rochester, she also said that her heart was "entirely English." The phrase easily, if wrongly, was taken as a comment on her Dutch predecessor and, by extension, as a rejection of his Act of Toleration and appointment of latitudinarian bishops.

Though she herself was relatively High Church, her administration was essentially moderate. She supported the Occasional Conformity Bill of 1702, but her chief ministers, Marlborough and Godolphin, voted for it in the House of Lords without speaking on its behalf. Her husband, Prince George of Denmark, loyally voted for it but told opponents he was on their side. Marlborough and Godolphin were nominal Tories but were moving toward Whig positions, and Harley, in the wings, was an equally moderate Tory who soon employed and protected Defoe as his propagandist. When an aristocratic Tory like Rochester became too demanding, she dismissed him. When a High Church zealot became abusive, her justice punished him. James Drake's unsigned *Memorial of the Church of England* (London, 1705) seemed to question Queen Anne's control of the church. The real and possible authors were sought and interrogated, the queen herself publicly labeled it malicious, and the book was burned by the common hangman. The lower churchman White Kennett put it this way in response to Henry Sacheverell's fierce sermon on 5 November 1709: "The Queen is in Royal Goodness, as well as in the Constitution of her Government, an Enemy to Persecution; and yet this Doctor is whetting a Sword for her, and pointing out her Friends to fall under the Edge of it."[55] By mimicking Sacheverell, Defoe seemed to behave like Sacheverell and to implicate Queen Anne in a scheme to murder those decreed doctrinally impure. The government interrogated, imprisoned, pilloried, and bankrupted Defoe for that insult.

I have suggested two domestic reasons for such anger: Defoe's assertion of royal and ministerial collusion in genocide and its potential to start a civil war, or at least further to disturb a restless wartime population. Thanks to a discovery by J. D. Alsop, there is a third reason for their concern: distribution of the pamphlet in Holland during a sensitive time in Anglo-Dutch military relations. Defoe's bad judgment, or worse, made him part of an international incident. Whether he was an innocent bystander or a conspirator, he had thrown oil on a fire. As the author of *The Safest-Way with the Dissenters* said, "The present State of the Government of England, and . . . the State of our Allies Abroad, require the greatest Union of Her Majesties Subjects at Home" (p. 4). Defoe's indifference to that truth cost him dearly.

Marlborough of course was at once chief minister and leader of a fractious military alliance against the Bourbon dynasty, headed by the Great Satan, Louis XIV. The Protestant Dutch also were principals in that alliance both because of William of Orange and because they feared French domination. The Dutch, though, lacked a large army and feared that their English allies might tire of the ground war and leave them to bargain at a disadvantage. As the Marlborough-Godolphin correspondence makes clear, the English in turn feared that the Dutch would supply too little too late or would seek to negotiate advantageous terms only for themselves.

For example, on 10 August 1702 Marlborough writes that though the Anglo-Dutch alliance "is absolutely necessary for the common cause," Dutch negligence will make the siege of Venlo difficult and threatens the success of the campaign. On 31 August he writes that if Dutch leadership does not improve, "it is impossible the war can be carryed on" as it should. On 17 September he adds that two thousand new Dutch troops should have been available "at the beginning of this campaign." On 18 November he observes that Dutch concern with French war preparations has made them keen to join England in hiring troops: "they are fully persuaded, that if the French have the superiority . . . that the next campagne may prove fatal."[56]

Defoe insisted that he was not part of a conspiracy, but he, his publisher, or another like-minded person sent numerous copies of *The Shortest Way* to Holland, alarming both the local British community and its Dutch hosts. I note first that by 29 April 1699 John Vernon had alerted William's ministry to John Toland's "Incendiary" and "malitious representations" in Holland. He was to be carefully observed in order to determine "his Encouragers either here or abroad" in such undertakings.[57] Association with Toland thus denoted association with treason.

On 18 January 1703 an unnamed correspondent in Utrecht wrote to an English friend with information that reached the secretary of state, the Earl of Nottingham. He read that the anti-Christian, antimonarchic John Toland recently was in the Hague, Amsterdam, Harlem, and Leiden and distributed copies of *The Shortest Way* in high places and "in every Town all over Holland." He rails at "Our Government and Governours to every Body & in every Place where he is." The correspondent thinks that the "unworthy Book was certainly contrived & hatch't by Stronger heads than the pretended author Danl. Fooe." Such men sought to "Frighten & Terrifie them [Dissenters] into . . . Desperate Fooleries." They "contrived that Book" and "Toland calls himself Agent for them, . . . what Judgment can a Man make of this, what can be said in favour of such Proceedings"? The letter from Utrecht ends with, "Pray dear S^r informe me of the Truth as near as you can."[58] That is what Nottingham must have sought, on behalf of both Queen Anne and the ever-tenuous Anglo-Dutch relations and hostility to France. Defoe's work, after all, would have offended the Calvinist ally troubled to read that an English monarch sought mass murder of non-Anglicans. Whether or not Defoe colluded with Toland, *The Shortest Way* was as foolish politically as it was brilliant rhetorically. In later months and years, Defoe often returned to that work and engaged in shifting characterization that foreshadowed the great novelist he would become. The process had four, sometimes overlapping phases.

Defoe as a Character of His Own Creation

The first phase of Defoe's personal novelizing attempts to repair self-inflicted damage and includes amelioration, clarification, explanation, and defense. The title page of that undated but 1703 *Shortest Way* more fully explains the work's nominal sources in hopes of making Defoe's rhetoric more credible. It also distances Defoe from religious terrorism: *The Shortest Way With the Dissenters: [Taken from Dr. Sach . . . l's Sermon, and Others.] Or, Proposals For the Establishment of the Church. By the Author of the True-born English-Man*. The pamphlet proper is followed by "A Brief Explanation," in which aggrieved Defoe joins defense, apology, and criticism. He laments readers' inability to see what he claimed was obvious. Surely it was "impossible to imagine it should pass for any Thing but a Banter upon the high-flying Church-Men" (p. 17). Yet worse, it was hard that "this should not be perceiv'd by all the Town," whether Anglican or Dissenter (p. 20). He only intended to make overt what was scarcely covert regarding High Church intentions "in their printed Books, *tho' not in Words so plain, and at Length*, and by an *Irony, not unusual*." Those authors and works remain unpunished (p. 18). Defoe repeats that claim in a later *Review*: everything "Ironically said in that Book" was accurate and was maliciously, earnestly, and with impunity said "a hundred times before" by High Churchmen.[59]

Defoe also knows that he is in a pickle, that he cannot only blame his audience and that he must confront reception as well as defend his presumed intention. He thus insists that *The Shortest Way* is neither seditious nor an attempt to destroy the Dissenters or to encourage violence against the High Church (p. 17). Indeed, he warns that party not to continue its verbal severities against the Dissenters or, with a remark he amplifies in later works, simply state outright "that they would have them all hang'd, banish'd, and destroy'd" (p. 19). Defoe then contradicts his words in *The Shortest Way*: if the High Church so writes, "it will not go down, the Queen, the Council, the Parliament, are all offended to have it so much as suggested, that such a Thing was possible to come into their Minds"

(p. 19). Defoe implicitly apologizes for his success and again adds that if there was anything in the paper "which may offend either the Government, or private Persons," he begs pardon, stresses his honest design, and asks that the booksellers not be punished for his errors (p. 20).

In other texts Defoe praises those whom he had insulted, urges that he has learned his lesson, and avoids some incriminating evidence. We know that the *True Collection of the Writings of the Author of The True Born English-man* excludes Defoe's earlier *Lex Talionis* and its argument that Protestants should inflict on papists whatever ravages papists inflict on Protestants. The preface to the *True Collection* rejects any notion that he wrote disrespectfully of the queen and insists that he always addressed "her Majesty with all the Deference of a dutiful Subject." If ever he slipped in private, which he denies, "I shall not fail of such humble Acknowledgments as become me" (sig. A5^{r-v}, in italics). "The Shortest Way to Peace and Union" in the *True Collection* observes that Queen Anne has testified her "Abhorrence of destroying, hanging, or banishing all the Dissenters" (p. 456), a view "the Government" shares if the High Church does not (pp. 456, 457). The *Lay-Man's Sermon upon the Late Storm* (London, 1704) also praises Queen Anne's government, angrily seeks moderation in religion, and plainly labels Defoe's chief enemy as innocent of that virtue: "If Mr. *Sacheverell*, with his Bloody Flag, and Banner of Defiance, were Indicted for Moderation, I verily believe no Jury would bring him in Guilty" (p. 12).

The year 1705 yielded a bumper crop of corrections. Defoe then dedicated *The Paralel* (Dublin) to the queen, with a request that she exercise her splendid judgment and desire for peace and union "to protect the Protestant Interest without Distinction." In that year Defoe also dedicated *The High-Church Legion* to Godolphin, whose unprecedented "Integrity . . . and Success" allow Britons to share "the Blessings" of his "exquisite Management of the Nations Treasure." In this phase of the apologia Defoe defends both Queen Anne and Godolphin from attacks by the "Abettors of a Faction." Her moderate Majesty is incapable of destructive thoughts toward her subjects.[60] He turns to her once again in 1705's *The Experiment* with *"an Appeal to your Justice"* to protect the Dissenter Abraham Gill from persecution. In that same year he also tries to remove *The Shortest Way* from religious controversy. The "Challenge of Peace. Address'd To the whole Nation" seeks to shift the argument from the church to the state. Who is more loyal to her majesty? The High Church or the Dissenters? He knows the answer. If the nation can unify, "We should no more be cutting of Throats about religion, and sending one another to the Devil for not going to Heaven our own way." That, he says, "would be the Shortest-Way with the Dissenters and *S----rell*'s bloody Flag would be a Fool to it." Defoe continues this ameliorative or transforming process in 1715. His *Friendly Epistle By Way of Reproof* impersonates an outraged Quaker who scolds Thomas Bradbury for, amusingly, sounding like Daniel Defoe. That dissenting minister's angry screeds bear "false witness against" the moderate and religious queen who so cared for her people. Bradbury indeed does what both Whigs and Tories accused Defoe of doing in 1702: he excites the people to verbal and martial war, as if "thou wast a Preacher of Sedition, an Incendiary, and one that moved to Wrath, and to shedding of Blood."[61]

Defoe clearly was chastened. He knew that he had walked near the edge and almost fallen in. As he says in the *True Collection*, "I shall be very wary how I prescribe more *Short Ways* without the Direction of my Superiors" (p. 459). Nonetheless, by surviving near the edge he grew bolder, almost reckless, and yet angrier at Sacheverell's regular calls to arms against Dissenters. This is the second phase of his post–*Shortest Way* self-portrait.

Yes, he admits, I was imprudent to imply that a moderate queen and her ministers could contemplate the horrors of extermination; but I also was right to say that the High Church zealots wanted what Anne refused. As early as the "Brief Explanation" he insisted that "the Persecution and Destruction of the *Dissenters* [is] *the very Thing they drive at*" (p. 18). He also lambastes the violent clerical lunatics, especially Sacheverell, as "the proper Authors of the *Shortest Way*." *The Paralel* again attacks "Sacheverel's *Oxford Sermon*" and concludes that "there must be some Plot against the Dissenters *as such*." *The Consolidator* (1705) then notes the "few hot-headed Men" who sought the Dissenters' "*Destruction*." Such men also said of the Scots, "*down with them the shortest Way*, declare War immediately, and *down with* them." *The High-Church Legion* will insist that Sacheverell's "Bloody Flags and Destruction of Dissenters" was preached as High Church duty in order to doom them "to the Devil *the Shortest Way*." *The Experiment* brings the case down to the victimized Dissenter, Abraham Gill, who was persecuted, wrongly tried as a forger, found guilty, verbally and physically abused, and shipped off to the army to be killed in combat. This was "a Push made at the Dissenters, a Sally of the Method call'd *The shortest Way*." Defoe's recollection of his trauma was enhanced in 1709, when Sacheverell's *Perils of False Brethren, both in Church and State* burned its way into print in London. William Bisset was among those who tried to label that pamphlet for what it was, but it also gave Defoe another chance to vindicate himself and the accuracy of his *Shortest Way*. He appears to mock Bisset's *Modern Fanatick* (1710) by claiming that he should be grateful to Sacheverell for making High Church intentions so clear: "The real Design was *hanging and drowning the Dissenters*, and sending both Ministers and People to the GALLOWS and the GALLEYS—And they would not believe us—POOR *DEFOE* with his *Shortest Way*, how did they use him, for fathering such a Thing upon" the High Church.[62]

The third phase, in 1712, includes Defoe's warm praise of his own benevolent power. In *The Present State of the Parties in Great Britain* he looks back upon his adventures with *The Shortest Way* and hugs himself for it and for his remarkable success in changing the nature of English monarchic, ministerial, and clerical reactions. Both the earlier recognition of his political blunders and his acceptance of responsibility disappear. Defoe replaces contrition with triumph. The prophet spoke truth to power, fooled the fools, and reoriented national politics.

England, we hear, once was painfully contentious, with High Church predators in hot pursuit of Dissenters. "An Author, till then not much known," wrote *The Shortest Way*, which seemed to preach "the Absolute Necessity of Rooting out the *Dissenters* from the Nation." This pleased and deceived the highest "*Churchmen* in the Nation," but the equally fooled moderate churchmen disapproved and condemned the book and its Sacheverell-like values. Its true ironic and satiric design soon became clear and had a remarkable "Effect upon the whole Nation." The High Church was embarrassed and forced to condemn its principles as "a horrible Slander upon the *Church*," while also answering "the Author's End the more" by implicitly condoning the genocide they wanted. They were forced at least publicly to soften their principles.[63]

The author alas was fined, imprisoned, pilloried, and ruined, but he preserved his "Contempt of them, even under all his Sufferings" (p. 21). Defoe published his derisive *Hymn to the Pillory* (1703) while so punished; he was praised by the common people and by moderate churchmen and Dissenters and softened the national mood. All agreed that "the whole Nation had receiv'd a New Tincture," that High Church zeal had been checked (p. 21), and that the queen and her government "gave a full Turn to the popular Humour" (p. 22). She was persuaded that the High Church sought to destroy the Dissenters. Her next speech to Parliament rejected such views, affirmed the Toleration and her friendship for Dissenters, and sought national peace and union (pp. 22–23). Moderation increased at court, and the zealous Tory High Churchmen were dismissed. Defoe concluded this romance by explaining his method in *The Shortest Way*. He purposely avoided marginal notes to indicate Sacheverell's relevant hostile words. That "would have justify'd" his own remarks but limited his ability to "cut the Throat of a whole Party" by making them unwittingly acknowledge the book as their own, though in Defoe's words. Not to see that was not "to see the Design of the Book at all" (p. 24).

Defoe's narrative inadvertently supports the High Church judgment of one intention in *The Shortest Way*: he wanted to "cut the Throat of a whole Party." We recall that both Mary Astell and Charles Leslie recognized such an intention. For Leslie, Defoe encouraged Dissenters to cut the throats of churchmen. William

King reiterated this belief in 1711. He placed Defoe in a fancied group that "unanimously voted . . . the Death and Destruction" of High Church Tories.[64] Defoe did not often turn to massacre as a fictive device, because he was a pacifist vegan, but if he was, he must have been sorely disappointed.[65]

The High Church not only emerged with its throat intact. It responded with more of Sacheverell's flame-throwing sermons; with Charles Leslie's frequent attacks upon Whigs and Dissenters; with Luke Milbourne's and other angry thirtieth of January sermons that accused Dissenters of the blackest of crimes; with Mary Astell's intellectually rigorous attacks upon Whig dogma; with Francis Atterbury's attempts to control convocation and his savaging of Low Church Erastian Hoadly. There were hundreds of other sermons, pamphlets, and political machinations against Dissenters, together with the usual political horse-trading, in which Whigs and Tories collaborated to get what they wanted. Defoe thought that he knew the consequences of such tergiversation. Within a few years, all the sweetness and light disappeared in the fourth phase of his response to the consequences of *The Shortest Way* response. The key was his disappointment upon passage of the Schism Bill in 1713–14. He says in *The Weakest go to the Wall, or The Dissenters Sacrific'd By all Parties . . . as it respects either High-Church or Low-Church* (London, 1714): never "expect any thing from the Quarrels of Parties, and the Heats and Feuds of the States, except . . . to be destroyed and devoured" (pp. 31–32). Defoe tried to create a world that he could manipulate, about which he could fantasize, and within which he would be exonerated for others' inability to read his texts properly. He failed.

There is further support for the hypothesis of erroneous tactics within brilliant rhetoric and shifting visions of reality. Defoe's *Review* essays for 21, 24, and 26 February 1713 attack the Earl of Nottingham, who Defoe thought was the author of *Observations on the State of the Nation* (1713).[66] He soon was confronted by the formidable William Wotton, the lower church chaplain, eminent scholar, and tutor to Nottingham's family. The unsigned *Vindication of the Earl of Nottingham From . . . Vile Imputations, and Malicious Slanders* (London, 1714) insists that those attacks were a function of Defoe's lingering "Rage" toward the secretary of state. Wotton reiterates persistent anger at *The Shortest Way*, a "Libel" designed "not *to amuse*, but to *inflame a distracted Nation*." Defoe's defense could not save him from deserved arrest and punishment, because he sought "to have thrown us into Confusion at that Time" (p. 41). Parliament was divided about the Occasional Conformity Bill; Dissenters were convinced that it threatened their Toleration; war with France had just begun; and Marlborough's great success was then unimaginable. Defoe's tactics could have encouraged the many dissenting tradesmen to withdraw their money from government coffers: "That would have weakened the Common Cause exceedingly" and helped France and the Pretender. Nottingham was acting as her Majesty's servant and was an honorable man who supported the Act of Toleration (pp. 42–43). Then and now, Wotton says, Defoe sought "to inflame the Dissenters against... their best Friends," who have secured the Toleration that Defoe endangered (p. 44). Wotton was Nottingham's client, but he also saw the dangerous shoals through which Nottingham navigated and saw that Defoe was more hindrance than help to his own cause.

The shape of Defoe's several responses to *The Shortest Way* suggests the ongoing danger in early eighteenth-century England's heated religious and political milieus. We see an exercise in public reaction and both misunderstanding and recognition of the consequences of excessive zeal. We then move to an exercise in state bureaucracy—police, arrest, interrogation, trial, punishment, and bankruptcy. That process changes to mingled authorial remorse, acceptance of responsibility, apology, and defiance. By 1712 Defoe invents a mythic adventure in which the lone and hitherto unacknowledged warrior for truth changes a nation for the better, shames and silences evil, nurtures and empowers virtue, preserves his integrity in the face of assault, and earns fame and money in the process. By 1714, though, he admits the self-delusion, again shades his vision, and again is attacked as an incendiary.

Defoe in part reflects an often unsuccessful human effort to reduce rage by labeling rage. After his stern *Short Way* he at least attempts to narrate amelioration rather than confrontation, however much he fails. We find a similar but more fruitful shape in the long progress of the thirtieth of January sermons that commemorate the murder of the Holy Martyr Charles I on 30 January 1649. Some clergymen were eager to speak of hellish events to ears polite. Others later became eager to redefine hell or even to obliterate the regicide, as they would obliterate original sin and some of the basic assumptions of Augustinian theology. The consequence reflected and enhanced major though gradual evolutionary changes in eighteenth-century Britain's ecclesiastical and political tones. These also were reflected in the contributions of major literary and intellectual men of letters.

NOTES

1. *The Prose Works of Jonathan Swift*, vol. 8, *Some Free Thoughts Upon the Present State of Affairs. Written in the Year 1714*, in *Jonathan Swift. Political Tracts 1713–1719*, ed. Herbert Davis and Irvin Ehrenpreis (Oxford: Basil Blackwell, 1964), p. 88 (hereafter cited as *PW* by volume, title, and editor as appropriate).

2. Philip Stubs, *For God or for Baal; Or, No Neutrality in Religion. A Sermon Against Occasional Conformity* (London, 1702), p. 16; John Edwards, *A Free Discourse concerning Truth and Error, Especially in Matters of Religion* (London, 1701), pp. 3 (mad), 289–90 (none); *The Age of Wonders: To the Tune of Chivy Chase* (London, 1710), p. [1].

3. Charles Leslie, *The New Association. Part II. With farther Improvements*, 2nd ed. (London, 1705), p. 47 (Original); Leslie, *The New Association Of those Called Moderate-Church-Man, with The Modern-Whigs and Fanaticks, To Under-Mine and Blow-Up The Present Church and Government. . . . By a True-Church-Man* (London, 1702), p. 10 (Reformation); Samuel Grascome (or Grascombe) (who makes similar arguments in several of his other works), *Occasional Conformity a Most Unjustifiable Practice. In Answer to a Late Pamphlet, Entituled, Moderation a Virtue* (London, 1704), p. 23; Henry Sacheverell, *False Notions of Liberty in Religion and Government destructive of both. A Sermon Preach'd before the Honourable House of Commons. On Friday May 29, 1713* (London, 1713), p. 10.

4. Charles Leslie, *The Snake in the Grass: Or, Satan Transform'd into An Angel of Light* (London, 1696), pp. cci (Equal, of all Sense, Bedlam); xiv (Deliriums), ccxcix (Mad), xvii (hellish). These terms often are repeated. Leslie knows that enthusiast, blasphemous, heretical, wicked Quakerism stems from the *"Doctrine of Devils"* (pp. 7–8) and reflects *"Luciferian* Pride" (p. 50). Leslie, *New Association Of those Called Moderate-Church-Man*, p. 5 (Cloven-Foot). Henry Sacheverell, *The Nature and Mischief of Prejudice and Partiality Stated in a Sermon Preach'd at S. Mary's in Oxford*, 2nd ed. (London, 1704), p. 12. Joseph Trapp, *The Character and Principles Of the Present Set of Whigs*, 2nd ed. (London, 1711), p. 5.

5. Leslie, *Snake in the Grass*, p. 168 (Fansie, Inspiration, inconstant, hour together); Leslie, *New Association. Part II*, pp. 18 (when once), 30 (Fleeting), 21 (sound, Imagination); Leslie, *The Wolf Stript of His Shepherd's Cloathing. In Answer to a Late Celebrated Book Intituled Moderation, a Vertue* (London, 1704), p. 83 (present); Leslie, *Snake in the Grass*, pp. lxxxvi–lxxxvii (roving).

6. Edmund Ludlow, *A Letter From Major General Ludlow to Sir E. S. Comparing the Tyranny of the first four Years of King Charles the Martyr, with the Tyranny of the . . . four Years Reign of the Late Abdicated King* (London, 1691), p. 2, with *"General Madding'Day"* on the title page in gothic letters; Ludlow, *A Letter From General Ludlow to Dr. Hollingworth, Their Majesties Chaplain At St. Botolph-Aldgate* (Amsterdam, 1692), p. 9; Daniel Defoe, "A Brief Explanation of . . . The Shortest Way with *Dissenters*," in *A True Collection of the Writings of the Author of The True Born English-man. Corrected by Himself* (London, 1703), p. 456; Defoe, "More Short-Ways With the *Dissenters*," in *A Second Volume of the Writings of the Author of the True-Born Englishman. Some whereof never before printed* (London, 1705), pp. 280–81, 288.

7. Edmund Hickeringill, *The "Survey of the Earth," in its General Vileness and Debauchery* (London, [1705?]), pp. 52 (spitfire), 43 (mad), 56 (Madcaps). These and comparable terms also appear in Hickeringill's other works. *Seldom Comes a Better: Or, A Tale of a Lady and Her Servants* (London, 1710), p. 5 (half); the title page epitomizes the work's tone in *The Character of a Modern Tory; In a Letter to a Friend. By which it is evident, that he is the most Unnatural and Destructive Monster (both in Religion and Politicks) that hath yet appear'd in any Community in the World* (London, [1713]), p. 6; [Thomas Gordon], *A Political Dissertation upon Bull'Baiting and Evening Lectures. With Occasional Meditations on the 30th of January* (London, 1718), p. 30; John Withers, *A Vindication of the Dissenters From the Charge of*

Rebellion, And being the Authors of our Civil Wars, 2nd ed. (London, 1719), p. 78; [Edward Ward], *All Men Mad: Or, England A Great Bedlam. A Poem* (London, 1704), p. 20 (Makes).

8. Peter Paxton, *Civil Polity. A Treatise Concerning the Nature of Government. . . . And Remarks made upon the Changes in our English Constitution* (London, 1703), pp. 86 (cruel), 625 (rooted out), 626 (extirpated), 628 (root out). Note also Louis XIV's "Zeal for the extinguishing the Hugonots" (625). [John Shute Barrington], *A Dissuasive from Jacobitism: Shewing in general What the Nation is to expect from a Popish King; and in particular, from the Pretender* (London, 1713), p. 12. Perhaps Robinson Crusoe had the figure of forty million in mind when he rescued a Spanish sea captain. His first word upon being saved from cannibals was Defoe's ironic "Christianus." Philip Browne, *The Sovereign's Authority And the Subjects' Duty, Plainly represented in a Sermon Preached . . . April the 12th. 1681* (London, 1682), pp. 3–4.

9. *An Address to the People of England: Shewing The Unworthiness of their Behaviour to King George* (London, 1715), p. 14 (large); *The Mystery of Iniquity Working in the dividing of Protestants, In order to the subverting of Religion and our Laws For almost the space of 30 Years last past, plainly laid open By a Protestant and true English-man* ([London], 1689), p. 3 (extirpation, servitude); John Toland, *The Art of Governing by Partys: Particularly, In Religion, in Politics, in Parliament, on the Bench, and in the Ministry* (London, 1701), pp. 13 (oppress), 18 (dash), 27 (Gladiators).

10. *University Loyalty: Or, the Genuine Explanation of the Principles and Practices of the English Clergy* (London, 1710), sig. A2^v (extirpation); [Shute Barrington], *Dissuasive from Jacobitism*, pp. 12 (Desart), 4 (Protestant); *Address to the People of England*, p. 14 (Duty).

11. William Penn, *Judas and the Jews Combined against Christ and his Followers* (London, 1673), p. 91. Henry Pickworth, *A Narrative of A Charge Against Francis Bugg, and His Evasions and Shufflings* (London, 1701), p. 21 (Babylonish); "Babylonish" also was among Penn's favorite and often repeated insults, as in *The Christian Quaker and his Divine Testimony Vindicated by Scripture, Reason, and Authorities* (London, 1674). Joseph Wyeth's angry *Anguis Flagellatus, Or A Switch for the Snake* (London, 1699) responds to Leslie's *Snake in the Grass*. It mentions Francis Bugg forty-two times. Wyeth lambastes Leslie as "a *Necessitous and Malicious Priest*." See his *Primitive Christianity Continued in the . . . Quakers* (London, 1698), his answer to Leslie's *Primitive Heresy Revived . . . in the Quakers* (London, 1698). It is a blessing that neither man had "the magistrate" at his disposal. For Leslie, see *Snake in the Grass*, pp. cccviii (Quaker sword [often set against the avenging "Sword of the Lord"]) and ccxcviii with "Inundations of Blood" congenial to Quakers; Leslie, *New Association. Part II*, pp. 33 (Extended), 54 (Root); and Leslie, *Wolf Stript*, p. 53 (Crush). [Thomas Carte], *The Irish Massacre Set in a Clear Light*, 2nd ed. (London, 1715), p. 2 (Crimes). Henry Sacheverell, *The Rights of the Church of England Asserted and Prov'd* (London, 1705), p. 40 (glutted). [Shute Barrington], *Dissuasive from Jacobitism*, p. 3 (dying), and see p. 14. [John Harris], *The British Hero: Or, A Discourse, Plainly shewing, That it is the Interest, as well as Duty, of every Briton, publickly to avow his Courage and Loyalty to his Most Sacred Majesty King George* (London, 1715), p. 53 (Steps). Dissenters of course made clear their resentment of what they regarded as false historical parallels and predictions. William Bisset so indicates in his attack upon Sacheverell's 1710 inflammatory sermon. It was wrong for such a clergyman "to tell the Parliament on the 30th of *January*, that there are many in the Neighbouring City that would act the same Tragedy over again." See William Bisset, *Remarks on Dr. Sach-------s Sermon at the Cathedral of St. Paul, November the Fifth* (London, 1710), p. 4.

12. Luke Milbourne, *The Moderate Cabal. A Satyr* (London, 1710), p. 16 (extirpation); Leslie, *New Association Of those Called Moderate-Church-Man*, pp. 2 (Step), 3 (Scaffolding), 6 (first); Trapp, *Character and Principles of the Present Set of Whigs*, p. 29 (Pales); Leslie, *New Association. Part II*, p. 55 (Hierarchy); Sacheverell, *Nature and Mischief of Prejudice and Partiality*, sig. A3ʳ (Undermine), with the title page as A1, italics and roman type reversed; William Shippen, *Moderation Display'd: A Poem* (London, 1704), p. 10 (degrees); Mary Astell, *Moderation truly Stated: Or, A Review of a Late Pamphlet Entitul'd, Moderation a Vertue. With a Prefatory Discourse to Dʳ. D'Avenant* (London, 1704), p. 90. Leslie and others liked the image of scaffolding. See Leslie, *Snake in the Grass*, where Quaker pleas for liberty of conscience are "but scaffolding to pull down our Church, and to build their own" (p. cxvii, in italics). See also Humphrey Mackworth, *Peace at Home: Or, A Vindication of the Proceedings of the Honourable House of Commons, On the Bill for Preventing Danger from Occasional Conformity*, 4th ed. (London, 1703), p. 11, where Dissenters' pleas for liberty of conscience are "Tools and Scoffods, to raise themselves, destroy our Constitution, and Extirpate the true Christian Religion out of the Kingdom."

13. Various citations by Leslie, *New Association. Part II*, p. 15; Leslie, *Wolf Stript*, p. 48; Leslie, *The Principles of the Dissenters concerning Toleration and Occasional-Conformity. . . . With Seasonable Advice to the Dissenters. In a Preface* (London, 1705), sig. A4ʳ; Henry Gandy, *Some Remarks, Or Short Strictures, upon a Compassionate Enquiry into the Causes of the Civil War. In a Sermon Preach'd . . . By White Kennet* (London, 1704), p. 10 (Presbyterians, Root); Henry Hyde, Earl of Clarendon, *History of the Rebellion and Civil Wars in England, Begun in the Year 1641. . . . Written by the Right Honourable Edward Earl of Clarendon* (London, 1702), 1:184 (believed).

14. William Tilly, *The Nature and Necessity of Religious Resolution in the Defence and Support of a Good Cause in Times of Danger and Trial. A Sermon*, 3rd ed. (London, 1705), p. 22.

15. *Billa Vera: Or, The Natural Way To Prevent Occasional Conformity, And Effect a Union in Religion* (London, 1703), p. 7 (reeducation) (hereafter cited parenthetically in the text); Francis Higgins, *A Sermon Preach'd at The Royal Chappel at White-Hall; On Ash-Wednesday, Febr. 16, 1706/7* (London, 1707), p. 15 (Divine); Robert Marsden, *Zeal for the Duty's of the Christian Religion as Establish'd in the Church of England. . . . A Sermon* (London, 1713), pp. 13–15 (prohibited or burned); Leslie, *Principles of the Dissenters*, p. 28: those who "trouble the publick peace . . . are to be restrained." I deal more fully with Augustinian *compelle intrare* and Luke 14:23 in chapter 4.

16. Sacheverell, *Nature and Mischief of Prejudice and Partiality*, pp. 12 (Apostles, Condign), 15 (Sown), 23 (Propagate), 34 (Execute), 46 (Insatiable); Leslie, *Principles of the Dissenters*, p. 17 (Incendiaries).

17. Leslie, *Principles of the Dissenters*, pp. 18 (Civil authority, lawful) 25 (Heresy and schism), as parts of the pamphlet's general tone and harsh response to vocal dissent. Such propagators and proselytizers of religious and political dissent "are to be restrained" (p. 28). *A Letter Out of the Country, To the Author of The Managers Pro and Con, In Answer To his Account of what is said At Child's and Tom's In the Case of Dr. Sacheverell* (London, 1710), p. 27 (severely lash'd); Higgins, *A Sermon Preach'd*, p. 17 (severely punish); Roger Altham, *The Just and Pious Magistrate. A Sermon Preach'd at St. Lawrence's Church, September the 29ᵗʰ. 1702, Being the Day of Election for the Right Honourable the Lord-Mayor* (London, 1702), p. 11.

18. Luke Milbourne, *The utter Extirpation of Tyrants and their Families. A Sermon Preached at St. Ethelburga's, Jan. 30. 1707–8* (London, [1708]), pp. 1 (enjoy'd), 2–3, 10–11 (Blood), 14 destroy (hereafter cited parenthetically in the text). Readers would have understood such evocation of violence, often indeed associated with the thirtieth of January sermon, regicide, and just retribution. Both the more temperate White Kennett and Richard Eyre in sermons to the House of Commons identified Saul's assassin as an Amalakite. See Kennett, *A Sermon Preach'd before the Honourable House of Commons* (London, 1706), p. 3; and Eyre, *A Sermon Preach'd before the Honourable House of Commons* (London, 1708), p. 15. Each speaker identifies the Amalakite as "a Stranger." Joseph Trapp carried the allusion into his unsigned *Tragedy of King Saul. Written by a Deceas'd Person of Honour* (London, 1703), sig. A3^v. The preface makes plain how disturbing apparent changes in attitudes toward the regicide were becoming, or were thought to be becoming: "The *Amalakite* has the Reward of his Demerits, and is Punish'd with Death for lifting up his Hand against the Lord's Anointed, a Crime that in our time is dismiss'd without Censure, nay is even Approv'd of, and had in Reverence by those that frequent our Calves-Head Assemblies, and keep Feasts for that Royal Blood the Nation never do enough Penance for" (italics and roman type reversed).

19. Richard Chapman cites the allusion to Joel 2:1–3 and scolds Sacheverell for leveling his wrath against "establish'd Government." See *Public Peace Ascertain'd; with some Cursory Reflections upon Dr. Sacheverell's Two late Sermons. In a Sermon Preach'd on Tuesday, Nov. 22. 1709* (London, 1709), sig. A1^v, with the title page as A1^r. Ferdinand Fina used the term *trumpet* to characterize God's punishment of sinners and as a call to root out individual and collective sin: *A Sermon On the Occasion of the Late Storm. Preach'd in Spanish, Before the Worshipful Society of Merchants Trading in Spain* (London, 1704), pp. 10–11. John Moult invoked Joel to warn evildoers in Dublin: *Warnings of the Eternal Spirit, To the City of Dublin* (Dublin, 1710), title page and p. 2. The trumpet's meaning remained known and cited. See George Coade, *A Letter to a Clergyman, Relating to his Sermon on the 30th of January. . . . By a Lover of Truth, who wishes the perpetual Peace and Prosperity of Great-Britain* (London, 1746), p. iv. Coade complains that Bishop Hoadly was wrongly savaged: "The Trumpet was sounded in *Sion*, the Pulpit gave the Alarm. Those who professed themselves Ambassadors of Peace breathed nothing but War."

20. *The Justice and Necessity of Restraining the Clergy in their Preachings* (London, 1715), p. 54 (great Terrour) (hereafter cited parenthetically in the text); William Bisset, *The Modern Fanatick. With A Large and True Account of the Life, Actions, Endowments &c. Of the Famous Dr. Sach--------l* (London, 1710), p. 3. This also appeared under the title *The Immorality of the Priesthood: Being an Historical Account Of the Factious and Insolent Behaviour of the Inferiour Clergy, ever since the Reformation.* See also Bisset, *Remarks on Dr. Sach-------s Sermon*, p. 2; *The High Church Mask Pull'd Off. Or Addresses Anatomized* (London, 1710), p. 3 (attack'd); *The Politicks of High-Church: Or, A System of their Principles About Government* (London, 1705), sig. A2^v, and see also *An Appeal from the City to the Country, For the Preservation of Her Majesty's Person, Liberty, Property, and the Protestant Religion* (London, 1710), pp. 12, 22, 27; John Mortimer, *Some Considerations Concerning the Present State of Religion; With Some Essays towards our Love and Union* (London, 1702), p. 6; *Appeal from the City to the Country*, pp. 26–27 (Wholesome), 12 (shake).

To be sure, some responded to the entire Sacheverell matter with A Plague on Both Your Brainless Houses. See "The History of the Imp——nt; Or, The Nation gone mad. A new

Ballad," in *A Collection of Poems, For and Against Dr. Sacheverell* (London, 1710), pp. 9–11. The nation always had signs of madness, "but now they are out of their Wits" (p. 9). Such title pages nonetheless must be viewed with caution, as in *Fau[l]ts on both sides. Or Whether the Church or Dissenters are in Fau[l]ts* (London, [1710?]). The author clearly seeks "to preserve us from Whiggish intentions, not forgetting the Tyranny we groaned under in Forty Eight" (p. 2). In almost obligatory siege imagery, we read that the Whigs "have purchased all the Tools, they could to batter and undermine the Prosperity of the Church and State" (p. 16).

21. *University Loyalty*, sig. A2^{r-v}, italics and roman type reversed; James Owen, *Moderation a Virtue: Or, The Occasional Conformist Justify'd from the Imputation of Hypocrisy* (London, 1703), p. 35; *Mystery of Iniquity* (n. 9 above), p. 3; this extirpation of course also means "a servitude to the Triple Crown" (p. 3); Toland, *The Art of Governing by Partys*, pp. 13 (Protestant), 18 (pieces); Matthew Tindal, *A New Catechism, with Dr. Hickes's Thirty Nine Articles* (London, 1710), p. vii, in italics; Gilbert Burnet, *The Revolution and the Present Establishment Vindicated. In a Memorial Drawn by King William's Special Direction* (London, 1715), p. 12.

22. [Shute Barrington], *Dissuasive from Jacobitism*, p. 4 (Protestant); Jonathan Swift, *PW* 8, *Publick Spirit of the Whigs*, in *Political Tracts 1713–1719*, p. 42.

23. Wyeth, *Anguis Flagellatus*, p. 22; Thomas Ellwood, *A Sober Reply On Behalf of the People called Quakers* (London, 1699), p. 14.

24. Edmund Hickeringill, *Priest-Craft, Its Character and Consequences. The Second Part*, in *Miscellaneous Tracts, Essays, Satyrs, &c. In Prose and Verse* (London, 1707), p. 80 in a separately paginated text. He uses a similar catalog in part 1 of *Priest-Craft*, pp. 5, 42, 89. John Dennis, *The Danger of Priestcraft to Religion and Government: With Some Politick Reasons for Toleration* (London, 1702), p. 22; Bisset, *Remarks on Dr. Sachev-------'s Sermon*, pp. 3 (hang), 4 (Burning); Mortimer, *Some Considerations Concerning the Present State of Religion*, p. 6; *A Letter from a Gentleman at the Court of St. Germains, To One of his Friends in England; Containing A Memorial about Methods for setting the Pretender on the Throne of Great Britain. Found at Doway, after the Taking of that Town. Translated from the French Copy, Printed at Cologne by Peter Marteau* (London, 1710), p. 16 (Members); *The High Church Champion Pleading His Own Cause. Or The Pope and the Devil Vanquish'd By A Flurt from the Doctors Pen* (London, 1710).

25. John Oldmixon, *The False Steps of the Ministry After the Revolution*, 2nd ed. (London, 1714), pp. 4 (We are told), 29 (wise, whole, even), for censorship of the press, pp. 32–34; Thomas Bradbury, *The True Happiness of Good Government: Explain'd in a Sermon on the Fifth of November, 1714*, 2nd ed. (London, 1714), p. 6.

26. George Chalmers, *The Life of Daniel Defoe* (London, 1790), p. 18.

27. *Defoe's Review: Reproduced from the Original Editions*, ed. Arthur Wellesley Secord (New York: Columbia University Press for The Facsimile Text Society, 1938), 3:76 (1706), 6:65 (1709–10).

28. Altham, *Just and Pious Magistrate*, p. 11. The full context may help us further to understand Defoe's concerns. Obedience to the self rather than to the king leads to chaos and moral corruption: "Every Sinner therefore, of what kind soever, does by this means become a Publick Enemy, a Common Disturber of all Peace and Order, and therefore such as ought to be Corrected by the Roughness of Authority" (p. 11). Altham was a chaplain to the well-connected, royalist Henry Compton, bishop of London, who counted Francis Atterbury and Henry Sacheverell as his protégés (*ODNB*).

29. Daniel Defoe, *Serious Reflections during the Life and Surprising Adventures of Robinson Crusoe* (London, 1720), p. 265, in Crusoe's voice. There is of course uncertainty regarding whether Crusoe and Defoe share these views. Crusoe is far more tolerant in *Robinson Crusoe* itself, and the later Crusoe is more of an enthusiast than Defoe himself probably was. Nonetheless, Crusoe's preface regularly insists that everything in all three *Crusoe* volumes is historically true and not fiction. These stern remarks, however, are part of Crusoe's long discussion of the virtues of a crusade for God and against the devil (pp. 256–66). Given his emphasis upon destruction of idols, the subtext probably suggests a Protestant war against Catholics as well. At the very least, Defoe's presentation of so genocidal a program suggest its plausibility, though scarcely its sense, decency, or humanity.

30. For some of the Walpole administration's attacks upon the press, see Howard D. Weinbrot, "Alexander Pope and Madame Dacier's *Homer*: Conjectures concerning Cardinal Dubois, Sir Luke Schaub, and Samuel Buckley," *Huntington Library Quarterly* 62 (2000): 1–23; Henry Sacheverell, *The Political Union. A Discourse Shewing the Dependance of Religion in General: And of the English Monarchy on the Church of England In Particular* (Oxford, 1702), p. 57 (hereafter cited parenthetically in the text, with italic and roman type reversed where appropriate). See also Sacheverell, *The Nature and Mischief of Prejudice and Partiality*: the enemy seeks the "Extirpation of Our *Law, Nation,* and *Government*" (p. 56).

31. Bisset, *Modern Fanatick*, p. 34.

32. Bisset, *Modern Fanatick*, pp. 34 (Back-Door, quoting Wake), 36 (Insinuated).

33. Gilbert Burnet, *An Exposition of the Thirty-Nine Articles of the Church of England*, 3rd ed. (London, 1705), sig. A3^r–4^r, italics and roman type reversed; Bisset, *Modern Fanatick*, p. 30.

34. [William Binckes], *A Prefatory Discourse To An Examination Of A late Book, Entituled an Exposition Of The Thirty Nine Articles of the Church of England, by Gilbert, Bishop of Sarum.... By a Presbyter of the Church of England* (London, 1702), pp. 1 (Generality), 5 (sense, alters), 11 (subscribe) 2 (undermine), and see p. 63; [Binckes], *An Expedient Propos'd: Or, The Occasions of the late Controversie in Convocation Consider'd.... By a Country-Divine* (London, 1701), pp. 15 (non-Anglican), 21 (against). Binckes' rural persona was unconvincing. He already was a Cambridge DD, was well connected, became the voice of the Lower Convocation, and was installed as dean of Lichfield Cathedral on 9 June 1703. Binckes scolded his archbishop for constraints upon the Lower Convocation in *An Expedient Propos'd*. He was sternly answered by Edmund Gibson's *Reflexions Upon a Late Paper, entitule'd An Expedient Propos'd* (1702). John Hoadly comparably responded on Burnet's behalf in the unsigned *Defense of the Right Reverend the Lord Bishop of Sarum, In Answer To a Book, Entituled, A Prefatory Discourse* (1703): Binckes' cunning book was designed to "Impose upon the *Reader*" and was rude and uncharitable to Bishop Burnet (sig A2^r, italics and roman type reversed).

35. See Kate Loveman, *Reading Fictions, 1660–1740: Deception in English Literary and Political Culture* (Aldershot. Hants, UK: Ashgate, 2008), p. 134 (has to wonder); and Ashley Marshall, "The Generic Context of Defoe's *The Shortest-Way with the Dissenters* and the Problem of Irony," *Review of English Studies*, n.s., 61 (2009): 243 (turn), 235–36 (intentional). Marshall cogently summarizes her conclusion: *The Shortest Way* is "a religiopolitical satire, much of which operates by way of simulation, impersonation, and paraphrase." It is "a counterfeit rigged to project an extreme position that would alarm dissenters and disturb moderates" (p. 257). All this surely is true. There is, however, no contradiction

between, say, impersonation and irony, as Pope's Horatian voice in his *First Epistle of the Second Book of Horace Imitated*, to Augustus (1737), makes clear. It too was briefly thought a compliment rather than complaint.

36. John Tutchin, *The Observator . . . From Wednesday December the 22d, to Saturday January the 26th, 1701 [1702]* (news sheet).

37. Chalmers, *Life of Daniel Defoe*, p. 18; Maximillian Novak, *Daniel Defoe, Master of Fictions: His Life and Ideas* (Oxford: Oxford University Press, 2001), p. 178; on pp. 174–75 Novak cites a British Library copy heavily annotated with *The Shortest Way*'s presumed errors. Tutchin, *The Observator . . . From Wednesday December the 22d, to Saturday January the 26th, 1701 [1702]*; Tutchin, *The Observator . . . From Wednesday December the 30th, to Saturday the 2d, 1701/2*. The heading alerts readers to discussion of *The Shortest Way*. For information regarding Tutchin, see J. A. Downie's good brief biography in the *ODNB*.

38. Leslie, *New Association. Part II*, p. 6. He soon realized that Defoe designed "to *Blacken* the *Church-Party*, as Men of a *Persecuting* Spirit. And indeed it had this Effect all over the *Town*." See also [William King], *A Vindication Of the Reverend Dr. Henry Sacheverell, From the False, Scandalous and Malicious Aspersions Cast upon Him in a late Infamous Pamphlet, Entitled, The Modern Fanatick. . . . In a Dialogue between a Tory and a Whig* (London, 1711): "The Book was writ so artificially that a great many well-meaning People began to believe it" and thus pitied the Dissenters and joined the putative moderate men (p. 12).

39. [Daniel Defoe], *The Shortest Way With the Dissenters: Or Proposals for the Establishment of the Church* (London, 1702), British Library, shelf mark 110, f. 27 (hereafter cited parenthetically in the text). A manuscript note on the title page reads, "by Daniel de Foe." I am indebted to Maximillian Novak for bringing this annotated copy to my attention.

40. Thomas Bennet, *A Confutation of Popery, In III Parts* (Cambridge, 1701), pp. 232–33. Bennet, though, emphasizes the exemplary nature of these deaths, "undoubtedly . . . for a terror to the others" and a blessing to the slain, who if repentant would be rewarded in heaven (pp. 232–33). F[rancis] A[tterbury], *The Voice of the People, No Voice of God: Or, The Mistaken Arguments of a Fiery Zealot. . . . By F. A. D. D.* ([London], 1710), pp. 7–8. The passage from Exodus also was cited in the Book of Common Prayer's catechism (London, 1703) as the second commandment's warning against graven images. That is an implicit warning against Catholicism as well (sig. C3^r). See also William Sheridan, *Several Discourses. . . . All Preach'd on Particular Occasions at St. Patrick's in Dublin and elsewhere* (London, 1705), pp. 107–8, 109. These evocations of Exodus 32 and the three thousand deaths easily are multiplied.

41. Simon Patrick, *A Commentary upon the Second Book of Moses, Called Exodus. By The Right Reverend father in God, SYMON, Lord Bishop of ELY*, 2nd ed. (London, 1704), p. 652.

42. Samuel Wesley, *The History of the Old and New Testament Attempted in Verse* (London, 1704), p. 120; Matthew Poole, *Annotations Upon the Holy Bible. Wherein the Sacred Text is Inserted and Various Readings Annex'd* (Edinburgh, 1700), vol. 1; Matthew Henry, *An Exposition of the Five Books of Moses. . . . With Practical Remarks and Observations* (London, 1707).

43. A[tterbury], *Voice of the People*, p. 8; Poole, *Annotations Upon the Holy Bible*; Henry, *Exposition of the Five Books of Moses*. The quotation regarding the frequency of types of Christ in Exodus is from the *Exposition*'s introductory "Practical Observations," in italics. Poole and Henry agree in all matters relevant for illumination of Defoe's *Shortest Way* and the allusion to Moses.

44. For Locke, see *A Letter concerning Toleration* in *The Works of John Locke, Esq;* (London, 1714), 2:247. Both Paula Backscheider (n. 53 below) and Maximillian Novak (n. 37 above) have discussed aspects of Locke's influence on Defoe. Backscheider discussed this in an earlier article: "The Verse Essay: John Locke and Defoe's *Jure Divino*," *ELH* (1988): 99–124. Katherine Clark offers various overviews of Defoe's positions in political theory in *Daniel Defoe: The Whole Frame of Nature, Trade and Providence* (Houndmills, Basingstoke, Hants: Palgrave Macmillan, 2007). Manuel Schonhorn, however, argues that Defoe is more anti-Lockean: *Defoe's Politics: Parliament, Power, Kingship, and "Robinson Crusoe"* (Cambridge: Cambridge University Press, 2006).

45. Tutchin, *The Observator . . . From Wednesday December the 22d, to Saturday January the 26th, 1701*; John Anderson, *A Defence of the Church-Government, Faith, Worship & Spirit of the Presbyterians. In Answer to . . . Mr. Thomas Rhind* (Glasgow, 1714), pp. iii–iv, italics and roman type reversed. See also pp. 73, 239–41. Anderson responds to Rhind's *Apology for Mr. Thomas Rhind. Or, an Account of the Manner how . . . he separated from the Presbyterian Party* (Edinburgh, 1712). Defoe also regarded *The Shortest Way* as a defense of Presbyterian church government and could do so with amiable mischief and self-promotion. He puts on the mask of William Bisset's enemy in *A Letter to Mr. Bisset . . . In Answer to his Remarks on Dr. Sacheverell's Sermon* (London, 1710): Bisset is wrong to say that Sacheverell has harmed the Dissenters, when in fact he has helped them. "I wish it does not appear that this Sermon is another of *De Foe*'s SHORTEST WAYS, and that the Dr. is in a Plot with the phanaticks, to make the *Church* of *England* appear Odious and Hateful to the World" (p. 7). Dissenters long had complained that the High Church had the will but not the power to destroy or exile them. See William Penn, *Judas and the Jews Combined against Christ and his Followers* (London, 1673), p. 5: "they only want as much Power, as Will, *to send us and our Principles to* New England *for a Venture*."

46. Daniel Defoe, *Lex Talionis: Or, An Enquiry into the most Proper Ways to Prevent the Persecution of the Protestants in France* (London, 1698), pp. 19–20 (hereafter cited parenthetically in the text).

47. Jonathan Swift, *A Project for the Advancement of Religion and the Reformation of Manners* (1709), in *PW* 2, *Bickerstaff Papers and Pamphlets on the Church*, ed. Herbert Davis (1966), p. 55; *The Spectator*, No. 493 (1712), in *The Spectator*, ed. Donald F. Bond (Oxford: Clarendon Press, 1965), 4:248–49; *Truth brought to Light; Or, Murder will out; Being a short, but True Account* (London, 1713), regarding the murder of Daniel Parke in 1710.

48. Nathaniel Crouch, *The English Empire in America. . . . By R. B.* (1685), 5th ed. (London, 1711), pp. 184–85; Crouch discusses local cannibalism as well on pp. 166–67. Samuel Johnson, in *Boswell's Life of Johnson Together with Boswell's Journal of a Tour to the Hebrides*, ed. George Birkbeck Hill, rev. L. F. Powell (Oxford: Clarendon Press, 1934–50), 3:200; Johnson, The Yale Edition of the Works of Samuel Johnson, vol. 10, *Political Writings*, ed. Donald J. Greene (New Haven, CT: Yale University Press, 1977), "An Introduction to the Political State of Great Britain," p. 137. For further discussion of Johnson and slavery and the slave rebellions in the West Indies, see James G. Basker, "Johnson and Slavery," in "Johnson after Three Centuries: New Light on Texts and Contexts," ed. Thomas A. Horrocks and Howard D. Weinbrot, special issue, *Harvard Library Bulletin* 20 (2009): 29–50.

49. Interpretation of the passage was stable. Henry Hammond, for example, said of the repentant thief: "Immediately after thy death, thou shalt go to a place of bliss, and

there abide with me, a member of that my kingdom which thou askest for." See Hammond, *A Paraphrase, and Annotations Upon all the Books of the New Testament, Briefly Explaining all the Difficult Places thereof,* 7th ed. (London, 1702), p. 233. William Burkitt emphasized repentance and grace: "O the powerful Efficacy, and adorable Freeness of the Heart-changing Grace" portrayed on the cross. See Burkitt, *Expository Notes, with Practical Observations, on the New-Testament of Our Lord and Saviour Jesus Christ,* 3rd ed. (London, 1707). The words stay about the same throughout the century and into North America. See the *Expository Notes* (New Haven, CT, 1794), p. 299. The argument that the Church of England was like Jesus crucified between thieves probably was a familiar High Church complaint. See Robert South, "A Sermon Preached before King Charles II . . . on the Thirtieth Day of Jan. 1662/3," an impassioned sermon for the anniversary of Charles I's regicide, in South, *Twelve Sermons and Discourses on Several Subjects and Occasions* (London, 1717), 5:102–3: "the Church of *England,* which at this time is so much struck and railed at, and in danger (like its first Head) to be crucified between *two Thieves"* should be made more secure. It is the only Christian church "whose avowed Principles and Practices disown all Resistance to the Civil Power." I am indebted to Phillip Harth for bringing this text to my attention. For William Binckes, see *A Sermon Preach'd on January the 30th. 1701/2. . . . Before the Reverend Clergy of the Lower House of Convocation* (London, 1702), pp. 15–16. See chapter 3, at n. 12, for the House of Lords' severe response to Binckes' sermon.

50. Hickeringill, *Survey of the Earth,* p. 52, in *Miscellaneous Tracts.* The man behind *Reflections Upon a Late Scandalous and Malicious Pamphlet* (London, 1703) thinks the author of *The Shortest Way* probably is *"a Papist"* or *"a Nonjurant Parson"* whose anti-Dissent and anti-William language he uses (sig. A2^v).

51. [John Dunton], *The Shortest Way with Whores and Rogues: Or a New Project for Reformation. Dedicated to Mr. Daniel de Foe, Author of The Shortest Way with Dissenters* (London, 1703), sig. a1^v (ironic, Mighty), a2^r (Queen, Honest; see also A2^v), a2^v (hanging, duel), a1^v (Hang 'em); *Reflections,* pp. 20 (Toleration), 16 (Laud), 19–20 (design'd); John Dunton, *The Pulpit fool. A Satyr* (London, 1707), p. 11.

52. [Dunton], *Shortest Way with Whores and Rogues,* sig. a2^v.

53. *The Fox with his Fire-brand Unkennell'd and Insnar'd. Or, a Short Answer to Mr. Daniel Foe's Shortest Way with the Dissenters* (London, 1703), pp. 3 (seditious), 21 (bring us back); *The Shortest-Way With the Dissenters: . . . With its Author's Brief Explication Consider'd . . . and His Hellish Designs set in a True Light* (London, 1703), pp. 7 (blowing), 23 (rebellion, Hanover); *Reflections,* p. 22. Readers concerned with *The Shortest Way* can profit from several sources, certainly including two recent biographies: Paula R. Backscheider, *Daniel Defoe: His Life* (Baltimore: Johns Hopkins University Press, 1989), pp. 94–105, 109–14, 126–35, and Novak, *Daniel Defoe, Master of Fiction,* pp. 126–35, 173–87. I have found the following especially and variously helpful: Novak, "Defoe's *Shortest Way with the Dissenters:* Hoax, Parody, Paradox, Fiction, Irony, and Satire," *Modern Language Quarterly* 27 (1966): 402–17; Miriam Leranbaum, "'An *Irony Not Unusual':* Defoe's *Shortest Way with the Dissenters,*" *Huntington Library Quarterly* 37 (1974): 227–50; Paul K. Alkon, "Defoe's Argument in *The Shortest Way with the Dissenters,*" *Modern Philology* 73 (1976): S12–23; J. A. Downie, "Defoe's *Shortest Way with the Dissenters:* Irony, Intention and Reader-Response," *Prose Studies* 9 (1986): 120–39, which also cites the designed error in the num-

ber of Israelites Moses supposedly killed; J. S. Horsley, "Contemporary Reactions to Defoe's *Shortest Way with the Dissenters,*" *Studies in English Literature* 16 (1976): 407–20; and D. N. DeLuna, "Ironic Monologue and 'Scandalous *Ambo-Dexter* Conformity' in Defoe's *The Shortest Way with the Dissenters,*" *Huntington Library Quarterly* 57 (1994): 319–35. See also Loveman, *Reading Fictions*; Marshall, "Generic Context"; and Howard D. Weinbrot, "'Root out this Cursed Race': Defoe's *Shortest Way with the Dissenters* and his Longer Way with Himself," in *Anglistentag 2006 Halle: Proceedings,* ed. Sabine Volk-Birke and Julia Lippert (Trier: Wissenschaftlicher Verlag, 2008), pp. 7–23. Some of this information is included within this chapter.

54. Leslie, *Wolf Stript*, pp. 75 (not fit), 71 (Dissenters); Leslie, *New Association. Part II,* p. 6. See also Leslie's *Cassandra. (But I Hope not) Telling what will come of it. Num. I,* 2nd ed. (London, 1705), p. 13, and its attack on Kennett. Mary Astell joins in with *An Impartial Enquiry Into the Causes of Rebellion and Civil War in this Kingdom: In an Examination of Dr. Kennett's Sermon, Jan. 31. 1703/4. And Vindication of the Royal Martyr* (London, 1701), p. 7 (Defoe[?] defends Kennett's sermon in the unsigned *Moderation Maintain'd, In Defence of a Compassionate Enquiry Into the Causes of the Civil War, &c. In a Sermon Preached by White Kennett, D. D.* ([London, 1704]) and defends Queen Anne's moderation on pp. 1–2 and passim); Astell, *Moderation truly Stated,* pp. 79 (short way), 72 (natural). Astell attacks *"Short-Ways"* as well in *A Fair Way With The Dissenters and Their Patrons* (London, 1704) and refers to Defoe on pp. 3, 7, and 22; on p. 7 she says that he "spares ne'er a Sovereign Prince in *Christendom.*" Astell has recently been well studied. For useful discussion and overviews, see Hilda Smith, *Reason's Disciples* (Urbana: University of Illinois Press, 1982); and Ruth Perry, *The Celebrated Mary Astell: An Early English Feminist* (Chicago: University of Chicago Press, 1986). See also Astell's *Political Writings,* ed. Patricia Springborg (Cambridge: Cambridge University Press, 1996). For other studies, see Joan M. Kinnaird, "Mary Astell and the Conservative Contribution to English Feminism," *Journal of British Studies* 19 (1979): 53–79; Patricia Springborg, "Mary Astell and John Locke," in *The Cambridge Companion to English Literature, 1650–1740,* ed. Steven N. Zwicker (Cambridge: Cambridge University Press, 1998), pp. 276–306; and William Kolbrenner, "'Forced into an Interest': High Church Politics and Feminine Agency in the Works of Mary Astell," *1650–1850: Ideas, Aesthetics, and Inquiries in the Early Modern Era* 10 (2004): 3–31.

55. See Edward Gregg, *Queen Anne* (London: Routledge & Kegan Paul, 1980), pp. 152–54 for the contexts regarding her speeches, pp. 162–63 for occasional conformity, and pp. 159–60, 168, for Rochester. J. A. Downie has discussed *The Memorial of the Church of England* in his *Robert Harley and the Press: Propaganda and Public Opinion in the Age of Swift and Defoe* (Cambridge: Cambridge University Press, 1979), pp. 80–100 on the burning of the book, 99 and 212n89 for Queen Anne's response. [White Kennett], *A True Answer to Dr. Sacheverell's Sermon Before the Lord Mayor, Nov. 5. 1709. In a Letter to one of the Aldermen,* 2nd ed. (London, 1709), pp. 20–21. Jonathan Swift also was aware of the controversy and alluded to the polarization of response among parties and readers and to Defoe in the pillory. See Swift, *Sentiments of a Church-of-England Man,* in *PW* 2, *Bickerstaff Papers,* p. 13, and the *Letter. . . . concerning the Sacramental Test,* p. 113. For one of the many Anglican praises of Queen Anne's moderation, see John Edwards, *The Preacher. A Discourse, Shewing what are the Particular Offices and Employments of those of that Character in the Church* (London, 1705), p. v.

56. John Churchill, Duke of Marlborough, and Sidney Godolphin, Earl of Godolphin, *The Marlborough-Godolphin Correspondence*, ed. Henry L. Snyder (Oxford: Clarendon Press, 1975), 1:100 (absolutely), 110 (impossible), 117 (beginning), 147 (fully).

57. Daniel Defoe, *The Letters of Daniel Defoe*, ed. George Harris Healey (Oxford: Clarendon Press, 1955), p. 8, for Defoe's disclaimer regarding a conspiracy. For the letter by Vernon, see British Library, Add. MSS 40773, [James Vernon] to the Earl of Portland, Whitehall, 29 April 1699. I am indebted to J. A. Downie for this discovery and thank him for permission to make it known in this context. Toland surely was not someone with whom Defoe under interrogation wished to be associated. The paper trail of suspicion was enhanced by the paper trail of other powerful attacks. Swift often places Toland in the antimonarchic, anti-Christian, anti–Church of England camp. In *An Argument Against Abolishing Christianity* (1708; pub. 1711) Swift calls Toland "the great Oracle of the Anti-Christians," and in the *Examiner*, No. 39 (1711), he lists Toland among the enemies of episcopacy and monarchy and a justifier of Charles I's murder. See, respectively, Swift, *PW* 2, *Bickerstaff Papers*, p. 37, and *PW* 3, *The Examiner and Other Pieces Written in 1710–11*, ed. Herbert Davis (1966), pp. 142–43. The author of *The Fox with his Fire-brand* also made the connection between Defoe and Toland; see pp. 13–14.

58. J. D. Alsop, "Defoe, Toland, and *The Shortest Way with the Dissenters*," *Review of English Studies*, n.s., 43 (1992): 247. Alsop transcribes and quotes from PRO, SP84/225/65, dated "from Utrecht 18th January 1702/3."

59. *Defoe's Review* (n. 27 above), 5:376 (1705).

60. Daniel Defoe, *The Paralel: or Persecution of Protestants the Shortest Way to Prevent the Growth of Popery in Ireland* (Dublin, 1705), sig. A2^r; see also p. 16. This was reprinted in *A Second Volume of the Writings of the Author of the True-Born Englishman*, pp. 382–416. Defoe, *The High-Church Legion: Or, The Memorial Examin'd. Being A New Test of Moderation* (London, 1705), pp. [iii] (Integrity, in italics), iv (Abettors, in italics), and 1, 9, 12, on Queen Anne's moderation. For example, "No Age can parallel the Moderation of the present Government" (p. 1). This of course contrasts with the wicked, snarling, threatening, reproaching "Faction."

61. Daniel Defoe, *The Experiment: Or, The Shortest Way with the Dissenters Exemplified. Being the Case of Mr. Abraham Gill, A Dissenting Minister in the Isle of Ely. . . . Humbly Dedicated to the Queen* (London, 1705), sig. A1^r; [Defoe], "A Challenge of Peace. Address'd To the whole Nation," in *A Second Volume of the Writings of the Author of the True-Born Englishman*, p. 242; Defoe, *A Friendly Epistle by Way of Reproof From one of the People called Quakers, To Thomas Bradbury, A Dealer in many Words*, 3rd ed. (London, 1715), pp. 23 (false witness), 7 (Preacher).

62. Defoe, *True Collection*, p. 456 (proper); Defoe, *Paralel*, p. 4; Defoe, *The Consolidator: or Memoirs of Sundry Transactions From the World in the Moon* (London, 1705), pp. 245 (hot-headed), 341 (down); Defoe, *High-Church Legion*, pp. 11 (Bloody), 18 (Devil); Defoe, *The Experiment*, p. 58. Defoe's *Experiment* was answered by at least two pamphlets. The unsigned *An Impartial Survey of Mr. De Foe's Singular Modesty and Veracity* (London, 1710) calls Defoe characteristically impertinent, deceitful, and "full of Malice and Falshood" (p. 3). He seeks "openly and barefacedly to traduce the Church and Clergy" (p. 5). *The Shortest Way* itself is among Defoe's many "scandalous" and "pernicious" writings (pp. 17, 21). [James Hugh], *An Answer to a late Pamphlet, Entitled, The Experiment* (London, 1707), labels Defoe's

many "*Misrepresentations, Falsifications, Forgeries and Perjuries, Counterfeit and Imposture... in that Pamphlet*" (title page). He really designed "the shortest way with the Church" (p. 2) in his "*villainous Piece*" (p. 18). For Defoe on Bisset, see *Letter to Mr. Bisset*, p. 11; see also pp. 5, 7, for specific references to *The Shortest Way*, though all of the pamphlet concerns it. The first lines of Bisset's preface to his *Modern Fanatick* immediately concern themselves with contemporary violence and threats to Dissenters. I am indebted to George Starr for bringing Defoe's *Letter to Mr. Bisset* to my attention. See also [Daniel Defoe?], *The Occasional Letter. Number I. Concerning several Particulars in the New Association* (London, 1704), p. 28, where the author observes that the High Church paints the Dissenters in such dark colors in order to make one think that they are "too dangerous and too wicked" to live. They deserve "*Hanging* or Banishment" for the public safety.

63. Daniel Defoe, *The Present State of the Parties in Great Britain: Particularly An Enquiry into the State of the Dissenters in England, and the Presbyterians in Scotland* (London, 1712), pp. 18 (Absolute, Church-men), 19–20 (fooled, horrible, Author's), 21 (soften) (hereafter cited parenthetically in the text).

64. [William King], *Mr. B----t's Recantation: In a Letter To the Reverend Dr. Henry Sacheverell* (London, 1711), pp. 2–3. See also King's fuller discussion of *The Shortest Way* in *Vindication Of the Reverend Dr. Henry Sacheverell*, pp. 11–12. Defoe, he says, was deservedly punished for encouraging Dissenters to tear down their own meeting houses under the guise of the High Church.

65. See, for example, *Lex Talionis, The Shortest Way*, its numerous adaptations, Defoe's general anger, and *Bold Advice*, as on pp. 24–28: require oaths of abjuration and banish or trample under foot and bury (p. 28) those who refuse or who violate their oaths. Apparent irony well can be a mask for a genuine "modest proposal." Charles Owen was among those who seriously recommended a *lex talionis*. If exercised too harshly, it would be inhumane. "But the Law of Retaliation, subject to certain Restrictions, may perhaps, and with equal Success, be executed without offering Violence to the Maxims of Religion and Reason." See Owen, *An Alarm to Protestant Princes and People, Who are all struck at in the Popish Cruelties at Thorn, and other Barbarous Executions abroad* (London, 1725), p. 22, and see all of the pamphlet's "Section III," pp. 21–26. There was a second edition in the same year. Charles Gildon recognized that Defoe's violence in *The Shortest Way* was consistent with Swift's in *A Tale of a Tub* (1704): the *Tale* has "certainly discover'd the Shortest way with Controversy." Charles Gildon, "The Epistle Nuncupatory to the Author of *A Tale of a Tub*," in *The Golden Spy: Or, A Political Journal of the British Nights Entertainments of War and Peace, and Love and Politics* (London, 1709), sig. A7^v.

66. Nottingham denied the attribution, which nonetheless remains probable. The Harvard/Houghton copy less probably attributes it to Wotton. His *Vindication* also attacks the *Examiner* for 30 March 1712.

PART TWO

TAKING THE CURE
AND IMPROVING THE SPECIES

Sermons, Compulsion, and Methodists

CHAPTER THREE

The Thirtieth of January Sermon

From Extermination to Inclusion

The creation and evolution of the thirtieth of January sermon was a central response to the regicide of Charles I on 30 January 1649 (n.s.). For most, that horrendous act violated every canon of decent English religious, moral, political, and civil life. Crucifixion excepted, for most English subjects it seemed the darkest look into the darkest human action. The regicides, they knew, murdered a monarch whose defenders thought him at the least a saintly paragon of a saintly faith. Divine punishment was appropriate and necessary for the regicides, their supporters, their offspring, and the nation in which the horror was enacted. Surely, it seemed to the restored Charles II, his church, and Parliament within the now properly fixed order, the nation needed a perpetual reminder of its failed duty. The thirtieth of January sermon was established for that purpose. Its gradually changing nature reflected the gradually changing nature of English and British political and religious cultures. Those changes in turn affected the ways in which clergymen and other men of letters viewed the job of writing their own different sermons on a nominally shared topic of terrible implications.

The Thirtieth of January Sermon and Royalist Law

These sermons were mandated by Charles II, Parliament, and Convocation in 1662 as one of the thanksgiving days. Every Anglican cathedral, parish church, and collegiate chapel was required to read prayers and present a sermon. The requisite wording was included at the end of the Book of Common Prayer and was amended toward severity under James II in 1685.[1] Arguments concerning the continuity of the law and the nature of the sermons began within a decade of its creation. It nonetheless lingered until 1859, when the marketplace settled the issue. By then the entire service long had fallen from public or ecclesiastical grace. The sermons generally were neither commissioned nor presented, and when they were, parishioners chose neither to attend nor to hear that they shared the blame for ancestral depravity, from which they thought themselves innocent and about which they scarcely cared. While the law was enforced, the sermons were to be read on 30 January unless that was a Sunday, in which case the following Monday was so designated. In 1685 Francis Turner, bishop of Ely, said that three thousand such sermons were preached every year. If the law was fully enforced, that number was more than conservative given the approximately ten thousand Anglican parishes in the British Isles. There thus could have been about one million thirtieth of January sermons merely in the century from 1662 to 1762.[2] As we shall see, we may allow for casual enforcement. There also were parishes without a resident priest, vicar, or even a functioning church; harsh winter travel in rural areas inhibited both the congregants and the ministers; these certainly recycled old sermons, borrowed others from printed sources, or made accommodations if the pews were empty.[3] Whatever the diminished numbers, the thirtieth of January sermons offer a staggeringly large and largely ignored area of intellectual and literary inquiry.

The task is made more complex by the quantitatively impressive but proportionally small number of printed sermons available to us. The major proportion of that small proportion were variously official: they were addressed to the monarch, the Lords, the Commons, one of the houses of Convocation, the Lord Mayor and Aldermen of the City of London, and at a major urban venue. Even if attendance was increasingly sparse, sermons for such places were prestigious, normally were printed, and thus had enhanced authority. Moreover, after William Stephens' rousing Lockean, or worse, sermon to the Commons in 1700, that body invited speakers only with the dignity of dean or with a doctorate of divinity.[4] The Lords invited one of their own spiritual peers, a bishop, to address them. The Establishment chose to hear only what it hoped were Establishment voices.[5]

Given the vast number of sermons, it was inevitable that various formulae evolved. Thomas Bradbury's pamphlet in 1714 opposed Luke Milbourne's angry sermons. Bradbury had read many such similar efforts in which, from his point of view, there was "very little new in 'em but a Transposition of Terms." He sees "Schismaticks, Atheists, Rebels, Traitors, Miscreants, Monsters, Enthusiasts, Hypocrites" on one side and "Lord's Anointed, Sacred Majesty, God's Vicegerent, impious, blaspheme, Damnation" on the other. Stir them together within a hot head, rearrange them, ignore reality, "and your Work is half done."[6]

The sermons nevertheless fell into more classes than Bradbury acknowledged, and the genre even was available for an early version of the academic term paper. In 1730 John "Orator" Henley's *Light in a Candlestick . . . Or, The Impartial Churchman* studied that year's sermons by William Bradshaw, bishop of Bristol, before the Lords, Samuel Croxall before the Commons, and Joseph Trapp before the Lord

Mayor and Alderman. Henley evaluates neither the writers' different politics and theology nor the genre's value. Instead, he offers a lesson in rhetorical evaluation and order, a receipt for making a thirtieth of January sermon, and a "Method of Judging" the sermons. He concludes by "doing Justice to the Virtues of the three Preachers."[7]

Whatever the receipt, by 1757 most, but certainly not all, sermons were too familiar to be evocative. Edward Cobden reports the tale of "A little Nymph" who had just read Tom Thumb before going to church on 30 January, when the preacher elaborated on Charles I's manifold misfortunes: "Miss, upon her Return Home with a deep Sigh, utter'd this melancholy Reflection. Sure nobody ever suffer'd so much as" Tom Thumb and the "Royal Martyr."[8] Whether Charles was elevated or denigrated by the association with his diminutive colleague was left to wiser heads to determine.

There were disturbances in the process of selecting the speakers and responding to them, often in more confrontational ways than by Henley or the little Nymph. The speakers sometimes were scolded either by their hosts or by their troubled readers when the sermons were discussed or printed. In 1710, for example, Richard West's sermon to the Commons seemed to Philo Basileus an attack upon monarchy, Charles I, and the thirtieth of January sermon itself. The House authorized its printing only by a "very small Majority," and so it was fair game for "the impartial Judgment of all Readers." A reader of the Huntington Library's copy annotated it as "A Scandalous Sermon rather vindicating this villany."[9] Luke Milbourne in print, Francis Hare to the Lords (1731), William Berriman to the City's Lord Mayor (1733), Thomas Pickering at Saint Paul's (1750), and as late as 1793 Bishop Samuel Horsley to the Lords were among the many sermons that were scrutinized, criticized, and often vilified.[10]

Indeed, whether by High Church, lower church, or dissenting opponents, the terms of discourse often were harsh. Henry Gandy was enraged by White Kennett's *Compassionate Enquiry into the Causes of the Civil War*, a thirtieth of January sermon delivered to his congregation at Saint Botolph Aldgate in 1704 that Gandy claimed angered the "wisest and best Men." The sermon "savours more of a conventicle, than a Church" and was truly "an Invective against Charles I. or, A Justification of his Murderers." Kennett "must give Scandal and just Offence" to all who abhor the regicide. Some clergymen both anticipated and gloried in attacks as a badge of honor. Ralph Skerret delivered a moderate Whig sermon before the Lord Mayor and Aldermen in 1715. Upon publishing the sermon he expected "the very Worst Treatment" but was not troubled by the "Frowns of the Disaffected."[11]

The houses of Parliament themselves could weigh in and make clear when a sermon before them or before another body was unacceptable. High Church William

Binckes delivered his memorial sermon on 30 January 1702 to the comparably High Church lower house of Convocation. We recall that Binckes likened Charles I's regicide to Jesus' crucifixion, but he so extended the familiar analogy that Charles I seemed the greater victim. The House of Lords and its more Whiggish bishops had enough. They debated whether to have the sermon burned by the common hangman but finally proclaimed that "there are several expressions that give just Scandal and Offence to all Christian People." The Lords required that Binckes be disciplined by his bishop in Lichfield. Either house also could withhold its thanks and request to publish after a sermon, as it did to Charles Trimnell, bishop of Norwich, in 1712 and to Samuel Croxall in 1730. Croxall's sermon to the Commons imprudently and frequently labeled Walpole a bad adviser to George II and a "screen."[12]

As the sermons moved through time, they also offered subtle but important visual and verbal nuances. The commissioning group could order its thanks, its thanks and request to print, call it an excellent sermon, or withhold comment and request but allow the offender to publish his own sermon and explain the fuss. The title page could call Charles the holy blessed martyr, or the blessed martyr, or the royal martyr and grieve for his horrid and execrable murder, or his murder, or none of the above. That page could be outlined by a black border or by a black double-lined empty frame or conventionally printed without a frame. The text itself regularly could lament the martyr's unprecedented death by unprecedented enemies of God. It could lament the regicide and extol Charles I's monarchic, religious, and personal virtues, or not. It could, more radically, blame his folly, which induced his death by overzealous, or even properly acting, patriots. It could even ignore him, his name, and the punishment inflicted on him, as did, among others, Joseph Butler, bishop of Bristol and then Durham, before the Lords in 1741.[13]

In spite of such glitches, replies, and subtleties, the most vocal choristers among available thirtieth of January sermonizers generally sang what the Establishment wanted or was willing to hear and what it would punish for not hearing. Hence, however little we have, the sermons and responses to them indicate clear cultural directions. As a generalization, and with the usual caveats regarding overlap and subjective interpretation, the sermons from the early Restoration to the later eighteenth century fall into five loose categories: rigorous High Church sermons that excoriated Dissenters and Whigs and sanctified Charles I and the union of church and state; High Church or higher church sermons with moderating voices; more Whiggish sermons that argued for toleration of Dissenters, amelioration of High Church anger in the sermons, and perhaps even elimination or major modification of the thirtieth of January sermons themselves; more abusive dissenting or lower church sermons that became the mirror image of High Church rage, except that now the ugly traitorous villains were the High Church rascals and even Charles I himself, whose tyranny rather than his religion caused the rebellion; and finally sermons that were essentially indifferent to Charles I and the regicide and largely considered the nature of government. We indeed have relatively few extant thirtieth of January sermons, and there certainly were exceptions to their general movement. That direction, however, is clear: like the culture in which the sermons existed, they gradually became Whiggish, temperate, Erastian, irenic, sometimes even civil, but also sometimes revolutionary.

The sermons are remarkable repositories for the works of major literary and theological figures. All of these thoughtful and learned men needed to commemorate a terrible act in a terrible time that necessarily and daily moved further from its original impressions and relevance. How did darkness move into "enlightenment," and why? The first step is to see how the first generation of sermons commemorated what in 1710 high-flying Luke Milbourne called *"The Solemn Day of Fasting and Humiliation for the Execrable Murder of CHARLES the Martyr, of blessed Memory."*[14]

The High Church Response and the Beginning of Change

The law of 12 Car. 2, c. 30, 6–9 epitomized royalist ideology and rejection of budding contract theory. It outlined the wretched deeds by the "Fanatical Rage of a Few Miscreants." It also expressed loyalty by the assembled Lords and Commons, who protest and abominate the regicide. They ask his Majesty to declare "that by the undoubted and fundamental Laws of this Kingdom, neither the Peers of this Realm, nor the Commons, nor both together in Parliament or out of Parliament, nor the People collectively or representatively, nor any other Persons whatsoever, ever had, have, hath, or ought to have, any coercive Power over the Persons of the Kings of this Realm." They further beseech that 30 January "shall be for ever hereafter set apart to be kept and observed" in all the churches and chapels in England, Ireland, Wales, Berwick upon Tweed, Jersey, Guernsey, and all other royal dominions. The anniversary day shall be one "of Fasting and Humiliation, to implore the Mercy of God, that neither the Guilt of that Sacred and Innocent Blood, nor those other Sins by which God was provoked to deliver up both us and our King into the Hands of cruel and unreasonable Men, may at any Time hereafter be visited upon us or our Posterity." By legal definition, then, the people lack "coercive power" over their monarch, and the thirtieth of January sermons must "be for ever" observed. From the High Church and Tory point of view, the secular law had the force of holy writ in defense of "the Sacred Person and Life of our said late Sovereign and your Majesty's most Royal Father."[15] They would do whatever they could to ensure that its letter and its intellectual backing were followed.

The early High Church response to these sermons thus was both simple and complex; it was unsurprisingly royalist, patriotic, and theocratic. No bishop, no king, and no king, no bishop, were both tautology and ideology. For Robert South, those who attacked the king also would "crucify Christianity." Thomas Sprat's 1678 sermon urged that the blood of the "Martyr'd King" was the "perpetual Seed, both of the Church, and Monarchy of England." In 1702 John Williams, bishop of Chichester, told the House of Lords what they already knew. In their system, the church and state are so intermingled that the "Church blesses and obeys the State; and the State defends the Church, and supports the Religion of it." When thus ordered, they so "mutually establish each other" that, in words his audience surely knew came from Jesus to Peter in Matthew 16:18, "the Gates of Hell shall never be able to prevail against them." Nothing apparently had changed when Pawlet St. John preached before Queen Anne in 1712. "The Religion and the Loyalty of a Christian are inseparable." It was "dangerous to divide, 'tis impossible to oppose them, without destroying our Obedience" and becoming either a traitor to the state or an apostate to the church.[16]

The logic was clear. Since the unity of Crown and church was divinely ordained, the monarch was divinely ordained. Conventional high flyers, non-jurors, and Jesuits all amplified that received truth regarding the divine right of kings. South concludes his sermon with the observation that it is "God by whom Kings reign and . . . by whom their Thrones are establish'd, and their Blood reveng'd." A few years later Joseph Glanvill added that "Kings wear Gods Image and Authority" and that a king was "God's living Image." The deprived bishop William Sheridan epitomized one, surely illogical and blasphemous implication of regicide: "To Kill a Man, is but to deface the Image of God, but to kill a King is to murder God himself." Philo Basileus insisted that Charles I was "God's immediate Vicegerent." Accordingly, "the Affront done" to Charles was "done to God also whom he represented." Edward Scarisbrike, SJ, read a sermon to the oddly daring or perhaps thoughtless James II at his royal chapel at Whitehall in the fateful year 1688. He would not have been permitted so to speak before either the Commons or Lords. No doubt James agreed that his father's death "struck at the *Divinity* of Power, as well as the *Administration* of it." The "*Sacred Image of God* . . . is stamped upon *Sovereignty*." It followed that nonresistance and passive obedience to God's anointed were necessary. God placed James on the throne: "Who then shall dare to Oppose You?" No one should physically or verbally so dare, for "the *Reviling of a Prince* is a foul step towards the *Beheading* of him."[17] James kept his head but lost his crown to his older Anglican daughter and her Dutch Calvinist husband.

By the end of 1688 that uncomprehending exiled monarch was Louis XIV's client and pawn.

The more dreadful "foul step" of course happened in 1649, the event the thirtieth of January sermons annually commemorated. At first they painted Charles as a saint as much as a monarch. Edward Pelling put the commonplace this way in 1679: When that perfect example of God's surrogate was murdered, "with him the breath of our Nostrils was taken away, the Joy of the Earth, the Beauty of Sion, the Fountain of Law, and the Father of the Church; and all Order, Peace, and Religion followed him, and was buried with him in the same Grave." Thomas Mangey later told the Commons "how gradually doth the King grow into the Saint, and while his Body is on Earth, how much is his Conversation in Heaven."[18]

The murder of a divinely appointed saintly monarch is dreadful. The nonjuror William Sheridan begins his sermon "Of the Martyrdom of King Charles I" with a rhetorical question on this day of "great Lamentation, and the deepest expressions of Sadness." He asks whether he should "accent every Syllable with a Sob, and entertain you with no other Discourse upon these words [from Judges 9:19–20], than Sighs and Tears." For Thomas Sprat, however, the question and the answer were simultaneous. He must stop his sermon before the Commons in 1678 because "I can go no farther. For this [scene of Charles' execution] can scarce be spoken without Tears: and Tears will not become a Death so triumphant."[19]

Regicides who evoked tears deserved severe punishment, both to themselves and to their posterity, at least unto the third and fourth generations. This severity might deter them and the many lingering like-minded brutes from comparable actions they again sought to inflict upon a lax monarch and church. "What has been may be" Luke Milbourne and many others knew as declarative rather than subjunctive. Robert South was more than willing "to drop the blackest Ink, and the bitterest Gall upon the Fact" of regicide. That "is not Satyr but Propriety." Edward Pelling's 1679 sermon invited Charles II to use "God's Sword" to avenge the terrible deed. George Smalridge sees no value in the putative moderation that only masks rebellion. He would have shared Philo Basileus' objections to "canting hypocritical Exhortations to Moderation" against those who desire "a truly Christian Warmth and Zeal" toward them. Smalridge thus describes these dangerous frauds in "lively Colours" and brands "the Memories of Wicked Men with lasting Marks of disgrace." Indeed, he demands, is it not "Blame-worthy to be Cool, dispassionate, upon so provoking an Occasion?" As we have seen, Milbourne used words to wound his adversaries, who in a typical catalog he characterizes as "Schismatics, Hereticks, Papists, Fornicaters, Adulterers, Rebels, Renegadoes." The change of order in the church and state lead to an "Inundation of Tyranny, Heresy, Superstition, Blasphemy, and worse than Paganism." Such villains, we remember, would extirpate and "depopulate the Universe" if possible. No wonder that in 1708 Milbourne bluntly gave both a title and a wish to that year's sermon: *The utter Extirpation of Tyrants and their Families*.[20]

These tyrants hoped to destroy the Anglican Church together with its Anglican monarch and his very memory as models of the best religion within the best religion, what Francis Browne called "the purest and most Primitive Church of Christ, that was then, or is this Day." Milbourne adds that the Church of England is "the strongest bulwark of the whole Reformation," a sanctuary for the persecuted, and the home of "the most Learned Reformed Divines in Christendom." Purity and sanctuary nonetheless were in danger of pollution. For South, "the only thing that does now cement and confirm the Church of England, is the Blood of this blessed Saint." Remove the sanctified blood, and the building collapses. William Tilly, of High Christ Church College, Oxford, delivered his sermon in 1704. The Oxford auditors would have known and lamented his allusion to Samuel 4:11 regarding the danger to their church: "The Ark of God is almost in the Enemies Camp."[21]

God's enemies sought to undermine the bases of monarchic supremacy and of the thirtieth of January sermons as legally established. Robert Moss quoted relevant passages regarding the fundamental laws that prohibit Parliament, the people, or any individual from ever having or properly seeking *"to have any Coercive Power over the Persons of the Kings of this Realm."* Since this same law established the thirtieth of January sermon, abolition of it hints at abolition of monarchy. If so, " 'twill be high time for the Queen, and all Crown'd Heads to look about them," Henry Gandy warns.[22]

Anyone who argued against monarchic superiority thus doubted and challenged the fundamental laws of the kingdom. By 1679 Edward Pelling was among those who abominated such ominous stuff. Some terrible Machiavels or Hobbists "have declared . . . that The King is King by Law, that Government is not Jure Divino, but that the Country-Swain hath as good a Title to his Cottage as the King hath to his Crown." Fiddlesticks. That confuses Magna Charta with scripture. "It is impossible to shew by the strength of any Philosophy, that Government can be derived but from God alone." It is irreligious to make such an attempt. Pawlet St. John, chaplain to George Hooper Bishop of Bath and Wells, preached his own thirtieth of January sermon before Queen Anne in 1712. Like his colleagues, he is appalled by the growing Whiggish, Lockean concept of resistance to a presumed illicit monarch. He is incensed by the term "The Duty of Resistance," which is "A Sound not heard before by English Ears, or in a Christian Country!"[23] In this world turned upside down, Christian England was populated by un-Christian and un-English men.

Such men sought to impose an alien form of thought and government upon the monarch's native subjects. Some sources of the alien were just across the Channel. Francis Turner identified "Old Voet that abominable Divinity Professor at Utrecht" as one who preached the moral innocence of regicide and left "Sanguinary stains" upon his students' minds. Henry Gandy complained that "we never had a Toleration of any sort, by Act of Parliament, till the time of William and Mary." Milbourne's post-1688 observation enlarges on the ominous leveling "Dutch way." Now, he laments, "all Religion is almost lost in the Toleration of all Religions," heresy abounds, and "the poor Apostolick Church of ENGLAND [is] betrayed by her own false Children." Corruption of the true English to the false Dutch was further enhanced by three sternly anti-Charles and anti–thirtieth of January pamphlets. These were by parliamentary Major General Edmund Ludlow and were published in "Amsterdam." Yet worse, French and Spanish Jesuits have taught that "the Original of all Power is from the People; that lawful Princes are accountable to, punishable and deposable by their own Subjects." This shocking deviation from law was in turn "transferr'd into the Writings of our Knox's, Buchanan's, Milton's, Sidney's, Lock's, and the like Agents of Darkness." Their principles are fit only to "Ruin Kingdoms and Common-wealths, to overturn Churches, to extirpate Christianity," Milbourne laments.[24]

These recognitions and fears of change were among the familiar topoi in High Church thirtieth of January sermons and sympathetic commentary upon them. The present generation seemed to justify, glorify, and teach regicide. The "Fanatic Schools, and ... Country Academies" propagated and perpetuated "the Guilt of the Blood that was shed this day," Francis Turner complained as early as 1685. A few years later Richard Hollingworth feared that the "Good Old Cause was now revived ... upon its Legs again" and about to ravage monarchy and episcopacy. Robert Moss joined those who stigmatized the putative Calves' Head Club for its annual mockery and joyous celebration of the regicide: "And what means it at last, that there is so much earnest Wishing and Urging to have the Day abolish'd?" An unsigned attack upon William Stephens' anti-Carolean sermon in 1700 saw a troubled answer to that question: to do away with those sermons is "no less Treasonable than his [Charles I's] Murder."[25]

This commentator probably would have shared the Tory High Church view that Whigs had joined Dissenters and latitudinarians to insult deity and to break the mingled church-state constitution. In 1711 William King crudely put it this way regarding attacks on Henry Sacheverell: a Whig clergyman "breaks the most solemn Sacramental Oaths, he betrays his Trust, he gives up the Cause of God, and the Church." A woodcut broadside that year more concisely claimed that "Whigs and Traytors all agreed / To make our Royal Monarch bleed." In 1715, *Popery and*

Schism Equally Dangerous to the Church of England insists that the Dissenters were created and manipulated by Jesuits and other papists. They were responsible for the blood they again wished to flow. Abrogating the thirtieth of January sermons would diminish "the Rights both of the Crown and Church." By 1730 William Newton looked back upon the career of White Kennett and made plain what being thought a Whig clergyman could mean. After publication in 1708 of Kennett's sermon for the Duke of Devonshire's funeral, "he was now stampt for a Whig-Writer; which was as bad as the being a Republican, and a Presbyterian; and that was worse than the being a Papist."[26]

Such readers were so troubled because, as in Stephens' case, the sermon was preached before the House of Commons, at Saint Margaret's Church in Westminster. However controversial Stephens indeed was, the sermon seemed to have a dangerous kind of official government sanction. Robert Moss thus asked why "even under the Shelter of the highest Authority, we cannot be permitted to Solemnize the Day in Confessions and Deprecations . . . without being indecently ridicul'd, and scandalously traduc'd."[27] Moss' question had two points: the thirtieth of January sermon apparently had been softened or even attacked with Parliament's approval; when they more cordially sheltered loyalist sermons, these too were mocked and savaged.

Moss could not acknowledge the possible accuracy of the ridicule, but he nonetheless was correct on both counts. Henry Gandy also attacked White Kennett's Whiggish and compassionate sermon in 1704. He was appalled by its apparent attempt to blame Charles I for the civil war: that effort by a "Church-Man and an Arch-Deacon . . . makes all good Men stand amaz'd!" Philo Basileus was among those who complained that Richard West's thirtieth of January sermon darkened "the Memory of the best of Kings" and of monarchy itself. Astoundingly, a son "of the Church of England" spoke from the Commons' own church with such "seeming Authority."[28] Decay, dissolution, and alienation seemed everywhere, and traditional English virtue, nowhere.

High Churchmen were correct about one of their more abusive complaints as well: that lower church Whigs were friendly toward the Dissenters and even softened the odium of the regicide. This "association," as Charles Leslie more ominously claimed, was between "those call'd *Moderate*-Church-Man with the Modern-*Whigs* and *Fanaticks*: to *Undermine* and Blow-up the present Church and Government."[29] For example, William Baker was warden of Whiggish Wadham College, Oxford, chaplain in ordinary to King George, bishop of Bangor in 1723, and bishop of Norwich in 1727. He addressed the House of Commons on Monday, 30 January 1721, arguing on behalf of amelioration and benevolent obliteration of differences: let "the Injuries themselves be forgotten, and the Memory of them, as soon as possible, be Abolish'd." Given errors on either side, it is hard "to determine, whether the Principles of Resistance in some Cases, or those of Absolute and Unlimited Obedience, did most contribute to the Distractions and Desolation that ensued." In the same year, Benjamin Hoadly addressed the upper house, also urged amelioration, but asked for greater balance in assessing blame. He refused to accept unjustly harsh treatment to "One Side only, and to clear the Other of every thing that looks like Guilt." Infamous usurpers should be condemned, but "the Memory of True Patriots may not be cursed" for their sake.[30]

Zealous and once confident High Churchmen thought themselves challenged on all fronts and in all places, including in both houses of Parliament and in the sermons addressed to them. Memory of regicide was to be abolished. Regicides had become "True Patriots." Divine right, passive obedience and nonresistance, an indefeasible hereditary Crown, the unified church and state, a received social order, regicide as national guilt, permanent punishment for assassins and their families, exclusion of Dissenters from recognition and power, and the authority and privileges of their national Church—all these presumed certainties were being discussed, negotiated, and even rejected in favor of the "people" as powerful arbiters of government and monarchy. The undoubted fundamental laws of the kingdom were doubted, no longer fundamental, and perhaps no longer laws. Especially after Dutch William's Act of Toleration in 1689, those laws seemed hostile to the religious kingdom the higher churchmen once knew and now was slipping from them.

Samuel Colby's 1709 lament reflects those concerns. He is troubled by increasing hostility and indifference to the thirtieth of January sermons:

> Some are for having this day blotted out of our Kalandar: and by the little Observation of it, it is so in effect; our Churches so thin, that in many there is scarce a Congregation, and in some no Sermon; some Ministers will not, and others pretend they dare not speak their Minds; and a third sort are for smoothing the matter, for fear of exasperating a Party, or being thought High-flyers; or High-Church: But they may as well speak plain, as not thinking it the best way to Preferment at this time.[31]

How did "this time" and "the best way to Preferment" so evolve during the half-century from 1660 to 1709 and beyond? Part of that evolutionary period clearly overlaps with the rage and fear induced by Defoe's *Shortest Way* in 1702. There nonetheless was an already growing reluctance to accept or reward the memorial sermons' fury. That reluctance and often rejection mark major changes in eighteenth-century Britain's religious, moral, political, and intellectual life. The changes were both difficult and the result of long and unpleasant battles. Henry Sacheverell and many other High Church loyalists knew that defenders of God's dispensation for God's king, church, and nation should use all the verbal and often physical weapons at their disposal. One High Church certainty, for example, was that the magistrate's coercive arm was available for the church's coercive arm. Luke Milbourne surely expected help in order utterly to extirpate tyrants and their families. Robert Moss gladly castigated "Defenders of so wicked a Cause," but they "deserve another sort of Castigation than what belongs to my Office."[32] The altitudinarians had not yet grasped that some of their own colleagues were losing spirit for their cause or, as Colby argued, sought secular preferment rather than spiritual perfection. Change was coming within the High Church ranks. Even the more extreme among them saw that their skillful and numerous enemies used their own weapons against them and were growing in political and religious power.

Higher Church and Moderate Responses to the High Church Response

The movement away from the High Church's outrage was enhanced by at least three factors within its own approximate group, including the more temperate Whigs. Anglican "moderate" men, after all, overwhelmingly shared the High Church assumption that the despicable sin of regicide stained the nation then and now, but they nodded toward amelioration and reduction of strife. William Fleetwood was a Whig but was sufficiently temperate to be admired by Queen Anne and by Thomas Hearne. As early as 1699 Fleetwood lamented the regicide in familiar terms, but he recognized that the sermons were "more for the Use, Instruction, and Advantage of the living Subject, than for the Praise and Honour of the dead King." We know that John Williams, bishop of Chichester, believed in the power of the unified church and state and in Charles I as the preeminent Anglican monarch and pious man. Williams nonetheless avoids Binckes' excess and makes plain that however great Charles "was in Quality or Sufferings, yet from him let us Look to one greater, one greater than all the Potentates of the Earth." Henry Brydges preached before Queen Anne in 1709. Though the regicides' national crime struck both church and state, he neither blames the entire nation nor sees Dissenters lurking in the wings with sharpened axes ready to be bloodied again. Edward Waddington, bishop of Chichester, was a fervent Whig who nonetheless held many High Church values. He disliked the Act of Toleration, insisted that the regicide demanded vengeance upon the perpetrators and the nation, and opposed the "false Appearance of Charity" toward them. He also asked that fellow subjects not "load the Innocent either then or now, with a Guilt they did or do abhor, and thereby to raise Heats and Dissentions among our selves." To do so violated prudent government policy; it was un-British and un-Christian.[33]

Gilbert Burnet's radical change from 1674 to 1681 had already suggested the pace of the amelioration process and the willingness to soften High Church rigor. On 6 December 1674 Burnet read his sermon *Subjection For Conscience-sake Asserted*. It exalted conscience and also insisted that proper conscience would not allow "through it one thought contrary to the Peace of the Society." Conscience, deity, religion, and monarchic stability are a single concept. Hence one is "highly criminal, who would question the King's Title to the Crown, or offer to void his Right" as the usurping, atheist, criminal "Insulting Hectors" did and might now do. Shortly thereafter, Burnet delivered his sermon *The Royal Martyr Lamented*.[34] The penultimate word indeed regularly echoes throughout his sermon. It condemns the national crime (p. 5) and the unprecedented "barbarous Regicide" (p. 33); it recognizes the "Divine displeasure" inflicted on England (pp. 43–44); and of course it bemoans the destruction of a divinely ordained monarch, whose murder leaves "guilt upon the whole Nation, which therefore must be expiated with a publick universal Repentance" (p. 32). The sins of the father are passed to the children. Burnet's two loyalist sermons could have been presented by many High Church Anglicans in the 1670s.

That was not the case in 1681, when Burnet delivered his *Sermon Preached before the Aldermen of the City of London* and virtually repudiated his earlier views. The biblical text itself was unusual for such a sermon—Zechariah 8:19, in which Zechariah the prophet priest returns to Jerusalem with the exiles from Babylon. *Zechariah* in Hebrew means "Yahweh remembers," and what he remembers or reminds his people of through the prophet is the larger divine moral law of mingled recollection and joy that the worst is past. This portion of the book responds to whether deep mourning for destruction of Jerusalem should continue. The Lord of Hosts calls for fasts in the fourth, fifth, seventh, and tenth months, after which in the House of Judah—for Burnet clearly an emblem of England—there shall be "Joy and gladness and cheerful Feasts; therefore love the Truth and Peace." Burnet joins Zechariah and immediately signals that the time of grief and mourning should end. He also promptly signals that though the "horrid and unexampled" crime of the day must be detested, it should now "be buried in oblivion" (p. 1). Here is a paragraph that later is cited warmly in *King Charles I. No Such Saint, Martyr, or Good Protestant as Commonly Reputed* (1698)[35] and to which Samuel Colby alluded in 1709. Burnet wishes that the thirtieth of January sermon could be abolished:

> I acknowledge it were better if we could have Job's wish, That this day should perish, that darkness and the shadow of death should . . . not see the dawning of the day, nor should the light shine upon it. It were better to strike it out of our Kalendar,

and to make our January determine at the 29th, and add these remaining days to February. (P. 2)

Perhaps after so long a period of mourning, the sin has been "expiated, and the land purged from the defilement of it" (p. 2).

This but begins Burnet's startling reversal. As consistent with his text, he asks whether the mournful days should not "be converted to days of joy and gladness" (p. 4). Should mourning still continue after thirty-two years? Should the anniversary "be forever observed?" (p. 5). He directly challenges the wording of Charles II's law creating a day of fasting and humiliation on the sermon day. Burnet's answer to those questions clearly is no. No again is the word when Burnet turns to the traditional praise of Charles I's many saintlike virtues: "the performing this as it ought to be, I confess, is a task above my strength," especially since so many before him have done that so well (p. 7).[36] He thus returns to the substance of his text, asks that all grow more temperate, that his own churchmen "should abate of their stiffness" in matters indifferent, and that they "consider things better without any heat and animosity." They will love peace when they can "bring our minds to live peaceably with those that differ from us, and have perhaps . . . really wronged us" (p. 24). That is the way "to love the Truth and Peace," protect the Protestant religion (p. 28), and evoke union within its varied groups. In such a case the effects of sad mourning will dissipate, and "our days of Fasting shall be turned into solemn and chearful Feasts" (p. 29).[37] Burnet's bravely irenic sermon stiffened the spines both of some resisting High Churchmen, who continued their stern rhetoric, and of Dissenters and Whigs, who cited it as an authority. His lesson needed repeating and often was rejected, but it may also have helped slightly to lower high-flying sermons and to induce caution in times of danger and stress.

In 1715 William Shorey told the Lord Mayor and Aldermen that there now was such a "Spirit of Bitterness and Animosity as threatens us with Civil Rage. For God's sake let us grow wise at the Expence of our Fathers." The Atterbury trial in 1723 further tarnished High Churchmen's credentials as loyal upholders of national virtue and further enhanced the need for accommodation. Peter Foulkes, of Christ Church, Oxford, delivered his sermons in Exeter. He lamented the earlier rebellion but did not refer to Charles as holy, blessed, or a martyr. He was a "Magistrate," a head of state and part of the "Regular Establishments" that provide for all the people.[38]

Such developments, however, were not only functions of dynastic stability, lower church attacks, and pleas for High Church accommodation and reduced "stiffness." Burnet was a naturalized Dutch subject, an adviser to William III, and his chaplain when he crossed the Channel to initiate the Revolution on 5 November

1688. Burnet translated Gaspar Fagal's *Declaration* of William's benign intentions from Dutch to English, and preached the royal coronation sermon on 11 April 1689. His authority grew yet further when William appointed him to the bishopric of Salisbury on Easter Day in 1689. His earlier, 1681 sermon was only one blow to a still formidable adversary for whom Burnet exemplified latitudinarian and then Williamite danger. As some evidence presented already suggests, the changes also were responses to vigorous and regular replies by the vigorously and regularly attacked lower church Anglican moderates and Dissenters. Neither group accepted that it was a diabolical regicide. Through accident or art, over time they gradually settled upon seven general, specific, and sometimes overlapping strategies.

Raising the Decibels in a Lowered Church

Numerous commentators argued that the generation of regicides was long dead. Surely it was time to bury hatred and to abandon an essentially un-Christian misreading of the Bible. The sins of the fathers were not passed to the children unto the third and fourth generations, none of whom could have known about or approved great-grandpaternal depravity. Nor indeed was the sin national or a function of dissent. As even Lord Clarendon admitted, only a small number of unrepresentative Independents were responsible for the horrible act, which the larger Presbyterian body condemned. We must not equate the many innocent with the guilty few. The Dissenters have been impressively loyal since 1660 and deserve respect, forgiveness, and inclusion. The state should end or at least redefine the sermons that kindle animosity, inflame the populace, and endanger the nation. These and other sometimes temperate and sometimes angry arguments often were repeated, often responded to by the thirtieth of January sermonizers, and in turn often blasted as archaic bigotry. In 1746 George Coade, for example, insisted that as a group the Presbyterians of 1649 had done everything possible to protect the king. Why brutally distort history to make a brutally false point?

> What Sort of Mortals must those Vicars, Curates, Doctors, and Dignitaries be, that pass Sentence of Damnation, every 30th of January, on those Ministers and their Brethren, for killing this very King, whom, with so much Boldness, Truth, and Courage, they laboured to save? Strange and surprizing Infatuation, egregious Ignorance and Baseness, which no Age or History can parallel![39]

Another strategy in this campaign was to label the High Church rhetoric harmful to the Church of England and to the nation it pretended loyally to serve.

Its both spoken and unspoken corollary, and a third strategy, was to urge that such activity was inconsistent with the humble and peaceful Christianity the Anglican Church sought to represent. Daniel Defoe thus urged that its sermons should seek "to compose our Differences by Words of Moderation, or shew... Inclination to Peace."[40] Like Defoe at his sternest, several presumed victims of High Church anger used some of their tormentors' harsh language.

A common complaint regarding angry High Church sermons was their instigation of violence against Dissenters and others on what opponents often called "THE MADDING DAY." In 1689 "A Protestant and True Englishman" objected that their "horrid Oaths, Cursing, Imprecations, Blasphemies and Uncleannesses... dispose Nations to Subversion and Extirpation." A few years later, D. J. complained that the harsh sermon mode poisoned the people with lies and horrid expressions. "Contrary to all Christianity, it effectually keeps up perpetual Animosities, Wraths, Feuds, and Divisions." The frequency of hostile thirtieth of January sermons had diminished by midcentury, but enough seem to have been read to raise Dissenters' concerns. Such a clergyman in Yorkshire fretted that "when the Clergy make it their business to dress one part of the Nation in the skins of wild beasts, it is equally natural to suppose the other part, if they have it in their power, will hunt them down and destroy them—and such have been (generally speaking) the blessed fruits of that Anniversary Day."[41]

There were several specific events in support of the broadly general complaints, as in *Observations or Reflections* (1709) on John Agate's "*virulent Sermon preached at Exeter.*" The observer notes that after a sermon a mob of two hundred "having their High-Church Blood rais'd" followed a dissenting minister to "the Streets as he went Home, shouting at him in a barbarous manner." Those brutal sermons included what John Wyng called the "Language of Hell." Their "unchristian, and blasphemous Expressions" were as "void of Coherence as Charity or Christianity" and kindled the people into "Rage and Inveteracy." Michael Hutchinson thus soon saw a "lamentable Sight" when "Men come reeking hot from Prayers and Sermons, to vent their Spleen" against the first person who disagreed with them. Shortly thereafter, Thomas Gordon turned the image of madness against the "High-Church Lunaticks." After their "Phrenzy"-inducing sermon, the parishioners were ready to take one another "by the Throat; and... Knock one anothers Brains out." A different author framed the alternative argument consistent with Defoe's: sermons should "endeavour to compose our Differences by Words of Moderation, or shew... Inclination to Peace."[42]

The sermons' harshness did not stop Sir Richard Steele's 1715 wittily ironic but serious epitome of causation and modes of proceeding. At the end of January and early February, we are, in a more than ordinary manner, called upon, to knock one another on the Head, because our Forefathers, (and particularly the Forefathers of many of our Modern High-Church-Champions) happen'd to be Great Villains, above sixty Years ago: And this is thought an Excellent Topick, to be insisted upon, from Generation to Generation: Nay, it is esteemed by many to be seasonable all the Year round.[43]

Steele's parenthetical aside suggests a fourth way in which the High Church opponents reacted to the thirtieth of January sermons. As we know from various responses, those self-styled patriots were in fact labeled traitors in thought and often in deed. This was part of a larger exercise in hoisting the High Church on its own petard, of using its terminology against it. The High Church regarded Dissenters and lower church Whigs as factions and as agents of the papists, whose religion they encouraged. The Dissenters responded by insisting that the High Church was "govern'd by the narrow Principles of Biggotry and Faction." *Observations or Reflections* is among those works that portray such bigots as making it their business "to foment Divisions, to make Way again for Popery and Slavery, as they did formerly."[44]

We have already seen aspects of the familiar and damning counterclaim—disloyalty to the Crown, which the churchmen presumably preserved and protected. As *Observations or Reflections* knew, disloyalty extended to potential filicide. Before Queen Anne's accession, the "High-Church was for bringing back the late King [James II], with the Pretender, to execute her Majesty, and the late Prince George of Denmark, as Rebels, and had agreed to levy Troops of High-Flying Priests to hallow the Rebellion" (p. 1). By the end of the *Observations* the scarcely covert has become overt. The Tory High Church faction are "raging fanatical Miscreants" all too like "those who murder'd King Charles the I" (p. 2). Dissenters have become loyalists, and High Churchmen have become regicides.

Other observers used the thirtieth of January sermons as springboards for comparable screeds, especially concerning dynastic change and consequent Jacobite rebellion. The deceptive High Church was "Sowing the Seeds of Sedition," Defoe claimed in 1704, words later repeated by other Dissenters. These men were "against the Settlement of the Crown in the Protestant Line" and wanted only to "advance the Interest of their Beloved Prince at St. Germains." The traitorous High Church tried to kill William of Orange, Michael Hutchinson says in *Counterfeit Loyalty*. Indeed they regularly and without any justification gave "the most undeniable Testimonies, in writing and acting of their Disobedience and Disloyalty; nay, and of their Treason and Rebellion." John Wyng wrote a decade before Atterbury's trial for treason, but he already knew that such men are "a rotten Part" of the church they so often disturb. They were "no more loyal . . . to their

King, or obedient to the Laws of the Land, than they are dutiful to their God." James Peirce made a similar point in 1717. The disloyal higher Church of England has "more than equall'd all that the Presbyterians did" in the civil war.[45]

Anglican Whig and dissenting opponents thus embraced their own rhetorical excess. Richard Willis, Atterbury's enemy and bishop of Gloucester as he then was, blamed the High Church for its analogy of 1688 and 1649. This ecclesiastical perversion sought "to raise a Rebellion, and to set up a Popish Pretender to the Throne of his Majesty." Ralph Skerret addressed the Lord Mayor and Aldermen in 1716. He lamented that some rebels "pretend to be the Truest Sons" of the established church but really chatter about the church in danger to rouse "Deluded People into Open Rebellion" against the constitutional monarch. The legal term *rebellion* appeared again in Thomas Blennerhaysett's vehement sermon at Barwick Chapel. He turned the '15 into a bloody, criminal, diabolical, enslaving, evil, fanatical, hellish, oppressive, papist, plaguing, tyrannical rebellion on behalf of "that False Spirit of Popery, and Foul Fiend of Jacobitism." Blennerhaysett was chaplain to Lionel Cranfield Sackville, the Earl of Dorset and Middlesex, an avid Hanoverian, and Lord High Steward at George II's coronation. Blennerhaysett dedicated his sermon to the wealthy merchant-heir Sir Joseph Hodges, Bart. Those exalted men probably shared the chaplain's view of the High Churchmen and their angry thirtieth of January sermons: he always suspected that rousing the people with cries of church loyalty "was Really, and Secretly Design'd, for Some Prince" unknown to the British constitution. Indeed, "we have Found, All This, but too Sadly Verified . . . by . . . Real Facts."[46]

Atterbury's episcopal treason of course fed such outrage. William Crowe told Sir Peter Delmé, the Lord Mayor of London, how appalled he was by nominal Protestants who yet engaged in the "horrid design" of trying to remove British civil liberties. Crowe informed the assembled aldermen that it was "monstrous" and "abandoned . . . to form a CONSPIRACY" against George I, especially by "the avowed professors of passive obedience, and non-resistance." In 1725 John Waugh, bishop of Carlisle, addressed the House of Lords, in which the guilty and exiled Atterbury once sat as a spiritual peer. He asked a rhetorical question: are we not becoming sinful again and re-creating the earlier matrix of corruption? Like other human beings, priests and bishops knew the side on which their bread was buttered, and they were keen to keep the right side up. A few years after George II's ascent in 1727, Thomas Chubb noted that "the doctrine of passive-obedience and non-resistance has been preached and inculcated more sparingly" since the Hanoverians were "happily settled upon the British throne."[47]

Robert Clavering's address to the Lords in 1731 suggests a consequence of the second George's arrival. Clavering was bishop of Peterborough, a distinguished

Christian Hebraist, and a moderate canon of elevated Christ Church, Oxford. The title page of his published sermon lacks any mention of Charles I or his fate. Clavering acknowledges the earlier national vice and the violence and heinous crime against "this glorious Martyr." Nevertheless, Clavering urges distinctions of blame: general condemnation of Dissenters rejects "the true Spirit of Christianity." He concludes not only with praise of George II and Queen Caroline but with a prayer for their secure continuity on the throne and for "their illustrious Progeny," so different from the royal vacuum of heirs under William and Mary and Anne.[48] As many sermon writers on the thirtieth of January noted, the new line had ample issue to ensure its longevity. After 1715, 1723, and 1727 most higher church advocates, like their relatively dominant lower church brethren, could count the numbers and recognize dynastic reality. Most but not all.

George Coade later offered a theory of causation for such moral and political tergiversation during yet another rebellion, the '45. He responded to an imprudent thirtieth of January sermon by urging Charles I's "Absolute, Indefeasible, Hereditary Right," certainly as support for the marauding Charles Edward Stuart, so intent upon using Scottish Highland blood to restore a then Franco-Italian-Polish indefeasible English Stuart line. Coade knew that the preacher's "impious Doctrine" was "imbibed . . . at Oxford, forty Years ago" and never questioned: "But the present Age is given to reasoning."[49] Those reasoners decided to challenge an essential High Church assumption. In the process, they marked a major evolution in thinking about the relationships between the present and the past, the church and the state, and politics and religion.

State, Not Church

Talk about reason and politics enabled the fifth strategy: either to show that religious persecution was in fact a mask for political persecution or more fully to separate the religious from the political motive for rebellion. To do this, it was necessary to confront a given of High Church dogma: that the Dissenters of 1641–49 sought to extirpate episcopacy root and branch. Nonsense. As the argument developed, the Dissenters insisted that they only wanted the right to worship a common God in their own way. The Laudian, poorly advised, crypto-papist, and demonstrably tyrannical Charles I was the source of their troubles. Remove him and the nation would be back on the road to the proper English limited constitutional monarchy that Charles sought to destroy. At the frequent extremes, this argument was as shockingly crass as earlier High Church apparent desire utterly to extirpate Dissenters. In its more moderate form, it nonetheless attacked the presumed High Church reverence for the stiff forms on which Charles I insisted and that exemplified the stiff forms of his politics.

Benjamin's brother John Hoadly was a loyal Walpole Whig, a chaplain in ordinary to George I, and upon the death of William King in 1730, the archbishop of Dublin. On 30 January 1718 he preached before the House of Commons, from whom he received thanks and an order to print his sermon. Hoadly's effort received two London and one Dublin edition, which Jonathan Swift may at least have known and by which he could not have been pleased.[50] Hoadly laments the party rancor during the sermons' existence and the un-Christian "Pride and Contention" they have evoked. His moderation does not extend to Charles I, whose faults he blames and whose High Church insistence on ceremony and ritual he calls "the greatest Encroachment on Liberty possible" and an affront to "Conscience and Religion" (p. 11). Such improper behavior depends upon force and violates religious and civil rights:

> There is nothing plainer in the Gospel, than that Sincerity and godly Simplicity is our proper Rejoycing before our Judge; and that our Union to Christ our Head, and to one another, consists in an Union of Faith and Love, and not in an Outward Conformity of Worship. So that to compel Men to this Outward Conformity, either by using them as Schismaticks from the Body of Christ, or as unfit and dangerous Members of the Civil Society, is not just either in Politicks or Christianity. (Pp. 12–13)

Hoadly also defends the resistance to James II in Lockean terms: "It is lawful and honourable, to defend the Liberties of a Nation against any that shall attempt to destroy them; and to do what ever is necessary to that Defence; . . . Liberty, without such a Power of defending it, is nothing but a Word" (p. 27). William of Orange is one of Hoadly's heroes (p. 25), but the greatest hero is George I. Culpable High Churchmen rebelled "against Oaths, and Principles, and Obligations" to their just and protective monarch. These churchmen claim to abhor disloyalty but "commit Rebellion" (p. 28). For John Hoadly, and indeed, as we know, for many lower church Anglicans after the accession of George I, the indefensible sedition was on behalf of "James III" in 1715, with which the High Church often seemed sympathetic.

Hoadly's relative moderation was not a uniform response. One expects a pamphlet by a Major General Ludlow to label the entire Stuart line as tyrannical, certainly including Charles I. We recall that White Kennett's *Compassionate Enquiry into the Causes of the Civil War* (London, 1704) caused instant controversy. The published sermon asked for healing of breaches, charity, and meekness to secure the church. Though Kennett deplored the regicide, he virtually justified the rebellion of 1641 as self-defense against Charles and his "Tyranny and Oppression"

(p. 11). Henry Gandy thought the sermon "an Invective against Charles I, or, A Justification of his Murderers." The author of *Remarks* on that sermon called it "a wicked Palliation" of regicide worthy of "*Milton, or Toland.*" Daniel Defoe nonetheless praised it, while opposing James II and the destructive passive obedience and non-resistance he, and by implication Charles I, sought. Dissenters and other Protestants more wisely "unite themselves in this, To defend the Act of the Settlement of the Crown, in the Protestant Line."[51]

Other harsh anti-Caroleans shared affection for that settlement and regularly justified the political rebellion behind it. The unsigned *Presbyterians Not Guilty of the Murther of King Charles I* (London, 1713) defends coreligionists, while reorienting the blame for regicide: "The Civil War was occasion'd by the Arbitrary Measures, which the High-Church Party put K. Charles the Ist upon; that 'twas they also who chiefly hinder'd his Majesty from coming to an Accommodation with the Parliament, which wou'd have prevented his Murther, and the Subversion of the Monarchy" (p. 22). Thomas Bradbury adds that the 30th of January celebrates "an Overthrow of Tyranny." Samuel Wright also agreed that the rebellion was not about religion, but about "Matters of State, and of the Civil Government." John Wyng's *Reasons Humbly offer'd to the Parliament for Abrogating the Observation of the Thirtieth of January* (1715) acknowledges High Church encouragement of Charles' "pernicious and illegal Practices," but essentially Charles was executed for "Matters of State," not religion (pp. 32–33). James Anderson's Presbyterian thirtieth of January sermon in 1715 described the several political "just Causes of War" to keep England "from impending Ruin." John Withers' *Vindication of the Dissenters* (1719) insists that the civil war was a "Civil, not a Religious Account."[52]

At its extremes, Hoadly's "whatever is necessary" argument justified regicide as an act of political self-defense. We know that was an argument with which Richard West agreed, and for which the House of Commons censured him just eleven years earlier. An "Independent" in 1749 shared both these views. He accepted that Charles' infamous reign required the people to resist him; he was no longer a king, but only a tyrant whom it was proper to depose or to kill. Charles "has unking'd himself." The so-called rebels, Caleb Fleming tells us in another work, were Protestant patriots whose task was completed "under the immortal WILLIAM." Charles' death thus was good and largely prevented "the utter ruin and desolation of his people." This view was commonplace by 1759. John Ross then told the Commons that patriots, who alas went too far, resisted the tyrant Charles I. He "began the attack on the constitution, and invaded the most sacred and inviolable rights of his people."[53] Ross was given the Commons' thanks, asked to print his sermon, and did so without a title-page border of any sort. For some commentators, Charles' regicide was transmogrified into suicide.

George Coade flirted with that transfer. He answered rather than wrote a thirtieth of January sermon, to whose High Church author he gave a bluntly educational Lockean discourse on resistance.[54] By the middle of the eighteenth century, indeed, the third generation of commentators had lost their horror of 30 January 1649. It was another historical event clouded by other historical events that buried the individual beneath the political movement. Coade thus speaks about Charles I as a politically depraved monarch no longer behaving like a proper English king bound by law. Since he virtually "unkings himself," he "may then not only be resisted, but even deposed, by his injured People. Lineal Succession, and Hereditary Right, have no Foundation in Nature" (p. 34). Hence "Tyranny is not Government" (p. 36). By government Coade means "the Parliamentary Establishment" (p. 76), which all Dissenters proudly supported in 1714 "for the Parliamentary Succession of the Crown in the HOUSE of HANOVER" (p. 80). Whether or not the latest Stuart pretender is a legitimate offspring is irrelevant, for absolute hereditary right is irrelevant, "wicked and profane." Instead, Coade insists upon the "present Parliamentary Succession of the Crown, with which are connected Religion, Laws, Liberty, and Independency" (p. 81). The High Church regarded its version of Protestantism as the best and as best exemplified in Charles the martyr. Coade and many other "moderates" thought their version of Protestantism "the most Pure Religion and the best Constitution in the Universe" because of the Act of Toleration and protective laws passed by "Our Glorious Deliverer" (pp. 87, 86). He also established an essentially Erastian church controlled by the monarch, "from whom alone all Ecclesiastical Power is derived" (p. 115).

By about midcentury, then, the newly evolved orthodoxy had established William of Orange, Parliament, and its legal rather than inherited succession as a secular trinity. These views crossed the Atlantic to a dour grouchy little city named Boston, to whose tea party its inhabitants later rudely refused to invite George III. In 1750 Jonathan Mayhew read his own thirtieth of January sermon in the West Meeting House and roundly demystified the mystery of Charles I's undeserved saintship and martyrdom. The absolute, arbitrary, despotic, oppressive, unconstitutional, uncontrollable, unjust tyrant Charles I forced not rebellion "but a most righteous and glorious stand . . . in defence of the natural and legal rights of the people, against the unnatural and illegal encroachments of arbitrary power."[55]

Indeed, the transformative "progress" of the thirtieth of January sermon gets better, or worse, as one's perspective dictates. Oxford High Church Thomas Nowell delivered his sermon to the Commons on Thursday, 30 January 1772. By then that house had more pressing business to transact. The four Members and the Speaker in residence voted the Commons' perfunctory thanks and request for publication. The no doubt pleased and ambitious Nowell then became the troubled and depressed Nowell. Once the sermon was in print, outraged readers saw that he had reverted to a version of the divine right of kings: Britain was a socially stable society in which the magistrate was to punish deviants on God's behalf; church and state were necessarily interdependent or chaos would ensue; the Members who disobeyed George III were like Israelites disloyal to God and to Moses when he returned from Mount Sinai with the Ten Commandments; George III himself was wonderfully like the blameless holy blessed martyr. These immodest proposals were not persuasive. The sermon soon was reprinted with anonymous *Critical Remarks* that were scarcely veiled in their rage toward the clergyman and his monarch. George III is "compared to the holy martyr, to the wretched monarch who suffered and deserved the block. . . . yet, notwithstanding this disparity, there is certainly a resemblance between his present majesty and the martyr, but to the misfortune of this nation, not in the most essential point." On Tuesday, 25 February, the House of Commons voted to expunge "out of their Journals these Thanks." The motion carried by 152 to 41. That was an end to Nowell's ecclesiastical preferment.[56]

These sermons now have come almost full circle. Much of the rage is on the Dissenters' side against Charles I and the High Church. For Mayhew as for his British contemporary Coade, the message seems to be, "We exterminated the brute, and not a moment too soon." For the author of the *Critical Remarks*, whether a Dissenter, a republican, a revolutionary American, or an otherwise loyal disgruntled subject, the message might as well be, "We did it before, and we can do it again." The "people" have become the arbiter of what constitutes a proper monarch. What constituted the "people" of course was another matter, and subject to another evolution in politics that reflected a cognate evolution in religion.

God's Hand, William's Hand, and the Divine Right of Government

These changes in reasoning suggest the sixth Whig, lower church, and dissenting strategy: substitution of 1688 and the Act of Toleration for 1662 and the law creating the thirtieth of January sermons in perpetuity. The god of that law was replaced by a deity more acceptable to evolving politics. This strategy elevated William to the sacred level the High Church hitherto claimed for its own sainted monarch. It also anticipated Burke's later argument that 1688 restored the true English constitution. Burke's conservative Whiggery was indebted to three earlier generations of ancestral polemicists still fighting for a place in the English mainstream. They would do so in part by enlarging on Defoe's practice when praising William's settlement—substitute secular parliamentary for divine monarchic supremacy.

Even the secular, however, came trailing bright clouds. Coade's familiar term *Glorious* for William of Orange was mild in comparison with terms by others, who used his deification against High Church royalism. Like other Dissenters and lower church Whigs, Defoe regarded William as the new agent of salvation. He also reversed Charles I's saintlike role in the higher church sermons. The final sentence below answers Bishop John Williams' use of Jesus' words to Peter as Williams' sign that higher church and royal state are as one:

> The Revolution in Eighty-Eight was the immediate Effect of the over-ruling Hand of GOD; his all-powerful Arm was most visibly seen in that Transaction, above and beyond the Expectation of the Wisest of Men, neither do I think, that the Prince of Orange himself did suppose it would fall as it did; No, It was GOD's immediate Hand, therefore it will stand, and the Gates of Hell shall never be able to over-turn it.[57]

William Stoughton's 1709 political, contract-based sermon in Dublin caused gastric upset for Swift and others. Though many in his audience would have agreed in spirit, they may have fretted about his hagiographic description of William of Orange as "Design'd and Fram'd by Providence" to free the English people from their oppressors—namely, the last of the destructive line of the male Stuarts. The author behind the 1710 *High-Church Politicks* was angry at zealots like Luke Milbourne and other of "the Devil's Commentators." The more angelic sort knew that in 1688 "the miraculous Hand of Heaven . . . saved us." Caleb Fleming later added that "the hand of God was visible in the revolution by William."[58] Perhaps it was the same hand of God that also permanently altered the British conception of government.

The deified William was cognate with a seventh lower church and dissenting strategy related to the thirtieth of January sermons: the divine right of kings gradually becomes the divine right of government, and often of the governors sitting in front of the clergyman addressing them in the Lords or Commons. Whether an unconscious or, as I think, a conscious decision, the Church of England, the spiritual and temporal lords, and representatives in the Commons had reached an approximate, if not unanimous, consensus: the time for armed rebellion or dynastic change was over. The Hanoverians were about as good as they could get and had numerous offspring, who promised stability. The '15 showed Jacobite martial intentions and incompetence; the Atterbury trial embarrassed the Anglican establishment and nourished its enemies; the '45 showed French collusion in British affairs; the lingering Catholic, European, Stuart line had lost its claim on British sympathy; the theological, political, and intellectual climate had moved away from late seventeenth- and earlier eighteenth-century High Church positions; and by the mid- and later eighteenth century the High Church itself was considerably lower than its altitudinarian ancestors. As the Methodist Great Awakening would make clear, this series of incremental evolutionary events had created a revolution that transcended even 1688.

Few doubted that government of some sort was part of God's design for humanity. According to the clergymen as well, God's design included obedience to the higher powers, as expressed in Romans 13:1–2, with damnation for those who disobeyed proper regal or legislative mandates. John Scott exemplified the first alternative in his sermon presented in 1685 but published posthumously in 1704 and expressing familiar divine-right theory. We should honor our "Princes and Governours," reverence their authority, assist them against their enemies, render tribute, and cheerfully submit to their commands. If we cannot, he continues, we must meekly suffer the consequences without disturbing the government, resisting its author, "or endeavouring to repel their Force with Force." The monarch's will is God's will. He commands us through him and his government "and stamps their Injunctions with his own Authority." Royal governance is divine governance on earth: "we are obliged to bow down as to the Divine Image which they bear about them."[59]

This was replaced by variations on a theme of divine right of different kinds of government, of course with the assumption that the British choice of limited constitutional monarchy was the wisest choice by the wisest people. In 1716 Ralph Skerret bluntly stated that "Government of every Kind by its Original Institution is the Ordinance of God," but the successive administrators of that government "he hath left Entirely to the Choice and Determination of Humane Wisdom." In Britain, the higher powers are not exclusively royal, but "are King, Lords and Commons. With these the Legislative Authority of the Nation is lodg'd."[60] Law, Parliament, acts, statutes, and shared power have replaced God's acts through a chosen monarch as his voice.

Such sermon writers thus recognized the empirical and experimental nature of government. By 1740 Thomas Herring, bishop of Bangor and then archbishop of Canterbury (1743), had dismissed all omnibus theories of government, whether based on patriarchy, contract, conquest, divinity, or merit. All had taken place in different parts of the world, but the royal form of government generally was chosen and generally excelled—as subjects found "that it is, when duly limited, the most natural and the wisest Model." Benjamin Hoadly would call that wise, limited British constitution "Sacred."[61]

Numerous writers thus agreed: "the divine right of government" required subordination to it and embodied itself in evolving legislation, with important consequences for Britain. Richard Willis, bishop of Gloucester, told the Lords that "it is the clear Law of our Country, that the King and Parliament may, for wise

Reasons, alter the Succession of the Crown." John Disney in Nottingham shared that view: the "Titles of Princes are determined by humane Laws." The divine right of government is indeed biblical; the divine right of succession is not. "God has left it to the Laws of every Nation . . . to determine who shall reign over them." Skerret in turn knows that the "Arbitrary Will of the Sovereign" has become "a dead Letter" for making or repealing law. The king is supreme in the political system, but as a part, not the whole, of the legislative process. As Edward Littleton made plain to the Commons, a subject's rights thus were established by the constitution's laws and not by the monarch's whims.[62] Two official thirtieth of January sermons, for 1729 and 1730, suggest the breadth of agreement, or at least the two houses' desire to hear that there was such agreement. Edward Young's sermon to the Commons in 1729 was called *An Apology for Princes, or The Reverence due to Government*.[63] He expanded it with a fifty-four-page discussion of the nature of benign monarchy, a concept not consistent with Charles I, but with the ideal monarch, whose glory is independent of lineage (p. 5). It depends instead upon personal traits that reflect and support religious values in public and in private. Young typically is reverential before his parliamentary betters. Both agree that they represent the "people," that the "Supreme Law is the Peoples Welfare," and that a monarch's "Supreme Dignity" is to be bound by that law as made by their representatives (p. 14). Accordingly, he dedicates the pamphlet and sermon to those representatives themselves. Whatever Young's affection for monarchy, he knows that the Members before him had great power: "An Apology for Princes may depend on Your Loyalty for Protection; and the Reverence for Government, is a Reverence for You," he tells the body that invited him to speak, thanked him, and asked that he print the sermon, which some of them may have heard, though they had not read the expansion appended (sig A2^r, italics and roman type reversed).

One year later, William Bradshaw, bishop of Bristol, spoke before the more exalted lords spiritual and temporal.[64] Like most of his and Young's colleagues in that effort, theology was subject to largely Whig politics. Bradshaw praises Charles I as much as he can and laments the civil war and regicide, but he also laments the "deplorable Calamities" thereafter "until it pleased God wonderfully to restore our Constitution in Church and State, and happily to settle it upon its antient Foundation" (p. 10). The line of lamentable male Stuarts is part of a calamitous history that William and his successors ended. Given the present dispensation, we have a duty to obey the deserving, legitimate, properly constrained present royal government. God has ordained "the Institution of Government" (p. 5), and God must be obeyed. Nonetheless, Bradshaw regularly refers to "Governours and Magistrates" (p. 26) rather than to the king. Perhaps that is because God has not ordained a specific kind of government: "this is left to the Wisdom and Care of Men; and we find by History and Experience, that such Forms and Models have been variously agreed on, and settled in the several Parts of the World, as men thought would best suit with their Conveniency and Interest" (p. 16). The appropriate levels of obedience also "are to be learnt from Human Laws" (p. 26). Those laws made by Bradshaw's government are so exemplary that he is "persuaded, no Government upon Earth . . . has a better Claim upon this Account" to the obedience and affection of its subjects (p. 28).

The Whig bias in such sermons was made yet clearer in a sermon other than on 30 January. Edward Arrowsmith spoke to London's aldermen on 11 June 1735, the anniversary of George II's accession. Like Arrowsmith's winter colleagues also concerned with Romans 13:1, he knew that "the Divine *Right of Governors or Government*" did not denote one divinely appointed family divinely instructed in a particular administrative form. Such decisions regarding humans should be made by humans concerned with the nation's place, time, and people. Having rhetorically banished the absolutist Stuarts, Arrowsmith nonetheless enshrines the demand for obedience to the Hanoverians, to whom Britons should "quietly" acquiesce and submit.[65]

The culmination of this ongoing movement, indeed orthodoxy, is made clear in a late eighteenth-century thirtieth of January sermon by Bishop Samuel Horsley, himself called a "High Church Prophet." The text is the familiar Romans 13:1, "Let every soul be subject unto the higher powers."[66] By 1793 the long displaced Presbyterian enemy had become the French republican threat, its values, and its assertion that return to a state of nature would purge the evils of civilization's inept efforts to govern itself. No, Horsley insists. God ordained government, and government requires obedience and subordination. That now received truth, however, also rejects the previous High Church amalgam of divine right, passive obedience, and nonresistance. Horsley prefers the British monarchic system, but it has no special sanctity. God has made all legitimate government a "divine institution." Nor does he believe in

> that exploded notion, that all or any of the present sovereigns of the earth hold their sovereignty, by virtue of such immediate or implied nomination on the part of God, of themselves personally, or of the stocks from which they are descended, as might confer an endless indefeasible right upon the posterity of the persons named. . . . [A]ll the particular forms of Government, which now exist, are the work of human policy. (Pp. 7–8)

Horsley rejects those views because he regards 1688 as the divine basis of the present British monarchy: "At the glorious epoch of the Revolution, the famous

Act of Settlement was the means, which Providence employed to place the British Sceptre in the hands, which now wield it. That statute is confessedly the sole foundation of the Sovereign's title" (p. 10). Horsley also embraces a Lockean view of dynastic change. The "great law of self-preservation, inherent in the body politic," empowers a society to change its leader, to appoint "by the consent of the Majority, for themselves and their posterity, a new head" (p. 9). In such a case, the people act "primarily from the will of God" to restore a functioning civil society, as England did in William's great providential intervention of 1688 (p. 10). There is no "pretended Divine right to the inheritance of the Crown" (p. 12). In a delightfully shocking observation by a High Church prophet, Horsley cites "Hoadly's Defence of Hooker" as evidence for kings' holding "power by human right only" (p. 12n). The High Church has used the Erastian, Whig, Low Church bishop as an argument on authority. That not only is evolution; after nearly one hundred years it is redefinition of what *High Church* means. The new form surely would have sent Charles Leslie, Luke Milbourne, and Henry Sacheverell into fits of rage, but the process typifies how a living organism changes in order to adapt to changing circumstances and indeed to survive.

Retrospective

One need only recall the thirtieth of January sermon that authorized Carolean law to note the massive changes that had begun as early as the 1680s and were completed less than a century thereafter. The law that once excoriated the people's attempt to gain coercive power over the monarch had become a dead letter. The sermons themselves often retained High Church anger and, if one believes the Dissenters and Whigs, abusive language that encouraged short-term brutality and long-term extermination. On balance, however, the season of Defoe's *Shortest Way with the Dissenters* was at the least in decline and more probably over. For example, by 1770 the French traveler Pierre Jean Grosley was astonished by London's "constant proofs of the mutual toleration" among all sects. They seem to be guided by the belief that "all, who believe the same God" are brothers. "The church of England baptizes all that offer, marries all, buries all . . . without disturbing the public tranquillity by impertinent enquiries: it considers conscience, as depending immediately upon God: it makes itself all things to all men."[67]

By analogy, eighteenth-century Britons had looked into the heart of darkness and did not like what they saw. They decided to step back from the brink and to preserve the Marlovian myths of a functioning system in an often bumbling limited monarchy with an often uncomprehending but reasonably tolerant established church, Parliament, and people. Indeed, if the church and state were more or less separated, that was acceptable as well. Once Tom Thumb's sufferings were comparable to Charles I's sufferings, the royal martyr lacked the power to evoke grief and rage. Such movements clearly are not the end of the story, and not even its middle. Church and state had at least two more major kinds of trauma with which to deal. The first was the implication for British politics and theology of Louis XIV's revocation of the Edict of Nantes in 1685, the Augustinian theology behind it, and the extension and ultimate rejection of key parts of that theology in eighteenth-century Britain. This complex of views was epitomized in sermons and commentary on Luke 14:23, "Compel them to come in." Changes of interpretation begin during the Restoration period and both magnify and solidify thereafter. These changes had significant implications for the development of eighteenth-century British thought and for the men of letters who functioned within it. Yet again, the severity of religious culture evokes an evolutionary backlash of moderation. Compulsion becomes moral and religious suasion.

NOTES

1. See Andrew Lacey, *The Cult of King Charles the Martyr* (London: Boydell Press, 2003), pp. 134–35. Lacey's admirable study is the most thorough of those concerning the thirtieth of January sermons. For further discussion, see Helen W. Randall, "The Rise and Fall of a Martyrology: Sermons on Charles the First," *Huntington Library Quarterly* 10 (1946–47): 135–67, and Louis Landa's comment on it in *Philological Quarterly* 27 (1948): 128. See also Byron S. Stewart, "The Cult of the Royal Martyr," *Church History* 38 (1969): 175–87; Edward W. Rosenheim Jr., "Swift and the Martyred Monarch," in "From Chaucer to Gibbon: Essays in Memory of Curt A. Zimansky," ed. William Kupersmith, special issue, *Philological Quarterly* 54 (1975): 178–94; J. P. Kenyon, *Revolution Principles: The Politics of Party, 1689–1720* (Cambridge: Cambridge University Press, 1977), pp. 69–80, 88–89, 133–34; S. J. Connolly, "Swift and Protestant Ireland: Images and Reality," in *Locating Swift: Essays from Dublin on the 250th Anniversary of the Death of Jonathan Swift, 1667–1745*, ed. Aileen Douglas, Patrick Kelly, and Ian Campbell Ross (Dublin: Four Courts Press, 1998), pp. 28–46; Andrew Lacey, "The Office for King Charles the Martyr in the Book of Common Prayer, 1662–1685," *Journal of Ecclesiastical History* 53 (2002): 510–26; and S. J. Connolly, "The Church of Ireland and the Royal Martyr: Regicide and Revolution in Anglican Political Thought c. 1660–c. 1745," *Journal of Ecclesiastical History* 54 (2003): 484–506. There are several relevant essays in *The Royal Image: Representations of Charles I*, ed. T. N. Corns (Cambridge: Cambridge University Press, 1999): Lois Potter, "The Royal Martyr in the Restoration: National Grief and National Sin," pp. 240–62; Laura Lunger Knoppers, "Reviving the Martyr King: Charles I as Jacobite Icon," pp. 262–87; and Kevin Sharpe, "The Royal Image: An Afterword," pp. 288–309. See also Howard D. Weinbrot, "Swift's Thirtieth of January Sermon: Politics, the Pulpit, and the Choice of Strife," in *Papers from the Fifth Münster Symposium on Jonathan Swift*, ed Herman J. Real (Munich: Wilhelm

Fink Verlag, 2008), pp. 223–42, and Weinbrot "The Thirtieth of January Sermon: Swift, Johnson, Sterne, and the Evolution of Culture," *Eighteenth-Century Life* 34 (2010): 29–55.

2. This is the estimate by Frank O'Gorman in *The Long Eighteenth Century: British Political and Social History, 1688–1832* (London: Arnold, 1997), pp. 6, 137. Julian Hoppit says that "there were about 12,000 [Anglican clergymen] serving some 9,500 parishes." *Land of Liberty? England 1689–1727* (Oxford: Oxford University Press, 2000), p. 210. In either case, however, the high figure surely overstates the number of functioning churches for such services. As O'Gorman observes, even in 1743 "only half the parishes in Nottinghamshire and Yorkshire had a resident priest," and low stipends "bred pluralism and non-residence" (p. 167). Even if there were only half a million thirtieth of January sermons read in the first century, that remains a staggering number, with a staggeringly small proportion available to us.

3. Francis Turner, *A Sermon Preached before the King on The 30th of January, 1684/5. Being the Fast Day for the Martyrdom of King Charles the First of Blessed Memory* (London, 1685), p. 26. For a clergyman rereading his own sermon, see John Jenings, *The Case of King Charles before the Regicides at Westminster* (London, 1711): "This Sermon was preach'd, two Years ago, at the Parish-Church of Great Gransden . . . and this Morning at Gamlingay, and again at Great Gransden in the Afternoon" (p. 3). See also Addison's *Spectator*, No. 106 (1711), in which Sir Roger de Coverly gives his country clergyman a collection of sermons that includes both higher and lower church examples. He reads a different sermon on each different Sunday. In all likelihood such a collection would have included at least one thirtieth of January sermon. See *The Spectator*, ed. Donald F. Bond (Oxford: Clarendon Press, 1965), 1:441–42.

4. For William Stephens, see *A Sermon Preach'd before the Honourable House of Commons, January 30, 1699/1700: Being an Anniversary Sermon for the Day* (London, 1700).

5. Stephen Taylor rightly notes that the absence of Members of Parliament or peers "is to miss the point. The prestige of Parliament meant that these were the most visible pulpits in the country, and official sermons delivered from them were guaranteed a large sale. The same was true, albeit on a smaller scale, of sermons preached before the Lord Mayor of London." See Taylor, "The Clergy at the Courts of George I and II," in *Monarchy and Religion: The Transformation of Royal Culture in Eighteenth-Century Europe*, ed. Michael Schaich (Oxford: Oxford University Press, 2007), p. 141.

6. Thomas Bradbury, *The Lawfulness of Resisting Tyrants, Argued from the History of David, And in Defence of the Revolution, Nov. 5. 1713. With some Remarks on Mr. Luke Milbourn's Preface and Sermon* (London, 1714), sig. A3^r, italics and roman type reversed.

7. John Henley, *Light in a Candlestick, to all that are in the House: Or, The Impartial Churchman, Considering the Celebrated Discourses on the 30th of January. . . . Wherein, With a just Praise of their Merits, Respect to their Characters, and Deference to the Church* (London, 1730), pp. 26 (Method), 28 (Justice). Henley's title page singles out for discussion "*Dr. Trap's Notion of visiting the Sins of the Fathers on the Children.*"

8. Edward Cobden, *Discourses and Essays, In Prose and Verse* (London, 1757), p. 327, in a paragraph among "Poems on Several Occasions."

9. Richard West, *A Sermon Preach'd before the Honourable House of Commons . . . On Monday, Jan. 30, 1709/10* (London, 1710). The comment is on the copy at Huntington Library shelf mark 487796. West's detractors probably objected to Whiggish lines like: "Certainly Men may be taught to abhor *Rebellion* without being told, that they have not so

much as a *Right* to preserve the *Society* from Destruction, should their Governours prove so unnatural as to attempt it" (p. 19). Such sentiments should not have been a surprise. West attacked Atterbury's high-pitched polemic to restore Convocation as parallel to Parliament (1707) and wrote *The True Character of a Church-Man.... Together with the Character of a Low Church Man* (London, 1702). His *Sermon Preach'd in The Cathedral Church in Winchester, at the Assizes Held there, July 23, 1707* (London, 1707) included these words: "Surely a Man may be a very good Subject, without allowing himself to be a Slave; or that he is obliged at the Will, or to gratifie the Humour of any one whatsoever, to be led like an Ox to the Slaughter" (p. 13). For Philo Basileus, see *Remarks On Dr. West's Sermon, Before the Honourable House of Commons, On the 30th of January 1709–10. In A Letter to the Doctor* (London, 1710), p. 2.

10. Luke Milbourne's many virulent sermons were attacked in the unsigned *High-Church Politicks: Or the Abuse of the 30th of January Consider'd. With Remarks on Mr. Luke Milbourne's Railing Sermons, and on the Observation of that Day*, sometimes attributed to Daniel Defoe (London, 1710). The angry author makes clear that "to call them Sermons, would be an Affront to Religion" (sig. A2^r). For Francis Hare, see *A Sermon Preached before the House of Lords ... Upon Monday, January 31, 1731* (London, 1731), with its black border in honor of the *"Day of the Martyrdom of King Charles the First."* It started a small pamphlet war, one contribution to which was Thomas Gordon, *An Examination of the Facts and Reasonings in the Lord Bishop of Chichester's Sermon Preached before the House of Lords* (London, 1732). William Berriman's *The Regard had by Providence to Prosperous Iniquities ... on Tuesday January 30, 1732/3* (London, 1733) was answered by an unidentified Protestant Dissenter in *Remarks on Some Passages in a Sermon before the Lord-Mayor ... by the Rev. Dr. Berryman* (London, 1733). Thomas Pickering's *Sermon Preach'd before the ... Lord Mayor ... on Tuesday, January the 30th, 1749–50* (London, 1750) was answered by Caleb Fleming as Rusticus in *The Devout Laugh. Or Half an Hour's Amusement to a Citizen of London, From Dr. Pickering's Sermon At St. Paul's* (London, 1750). For Samuel Horsley, see *A Sermon, Preached Before the Lords Spiritual and Temporal ... On Wednesday, January 30, 1793* (London, 1793), for which see below. Though the title page notes the *"Martyrdom of King Charles the First,"* it lacks a border of lamentation.

11. Henry Gandy, *Some Remarks, Or Short Strictures, upon a Compassionate Enquiry into the Causes of the Civil War. In a Sermon Preach'd ... By White Kennet* (London, 1704), pp. 32 (wisest), 3 (savours, Invective), 4 (Scandal). Gandy notes Kennett's defensiveness and insistence that he has not materially altered anything in the written version of the sermon, which Gandy regards as a lie. Ralph Skerret, *The Subjects Duty to the Higher Powers. Set forth in a Sermon Preach'd before the Right Honourable The Lord Mayor, The Aldermen, and the Citizens of London, In the Cathedral Church of St. Paul, On Munday the 30th of January, 1715* (London, 1716), sig. A3^r.

12. For William Binckes, see *A Sermon Preach'd on January the 30th. 1701/2.... Before the Reverend Clergy of the Lower House of Convocation* (London, 1702). He wonders "whether either the Prayers of our Saviour on the Cross, or of our Royal Martyr on the Scaffold, and in his Closet" obtained forgiveness for the murderers: they did not so obtain (pp. 15–16). See above, chapter 2 at n. 49, regarding Defoe's possible allusion to this sermon. The Lords responded with its *Resolution and Proceeding of the Right Honourable the Lords Spiritual & Temporal In Parliament Assembled, On Saturday the Sixteenth of May, 1702*. Upon a

Pamphlet, Intituled, Animadversions upon the Two last Thirtieth of January Sermons; One Preached to the Honourable House of Commons. The other to the Lower House of Convocation: In a Letter. As also upon a Book, Intituled, A Sermon Preach'd on January the Thirtieth, 1701/2 . . . before the Reverend Clergy of the Lower House of Convocation By W. Binckes, D. D. (London, 1702), p. 7. Binckes attempted to defend himself in the unsigned *Explanation Of some Passages in Dr. Binckes's Sermon Preached before the Lower House of Convocation, January the 30th, 1701/2* (London, 1702). He appended part of a 1649 sermon, *The Martyrdom of King Charles: Or, His Conformity with Christ in His Sufferings.* The conflict between orientations in 1649 and 1702 suggests the gradual changes in attitude toward the thirtieth of January sermons. Charles Trimnell, *A Sermon Preach'd before the Lords Spiritual and Temporal . . . On the 30th of January, 1711/12* (London, 1712); Samuel Croxall, *A Sermon Preach'd before the Honourable House of Commons . . . On Friday January xxx. 1729* (London, 1730), pp. 6, 13–16, 18–20.

13. Joseph Butler, *A Sermon Preached before the House of Lords . . . on Friday, Jan. 30, 1740–41* (London, 1741).

14. This is from the title page of Milbourne's *Measures of Resistance To The Higher Powers, So far as becomes a Christian: In A Sermon, Preach'd on January the 30th, 1709/10*, 4th ed. (London, 1710).

15. *The Statutes at Large From the First Year of King James the First* (London, 1770), 3:201, checked against a London 1677 edition in black letter. The law was known and cited by sermonizers. See Andrew Snape, *A Sermon Preach'd Before the Right Honourable the Lord-Mayor, The Aldermen and Citizens of London . . . on Monday the 30th of Jan. 1709/10* (London, 1710). The law recognizes "this *Essential Prerogative*, as antecedently inherent in the Crown" (p. 20 in a large-type edition of the sermon).

16. Robert South, *A Sermon Preach'd before King Charles II, on the Fast (Appointed Jan. 30.) For the Execrable Murder of his Royal Father. . . . Now first Printed* (1663; London, [1705]), p. 23; South attacks Milton on p. 22. Thomas Sprat, *A Sermon Preached before the Honourable House of Commons . . . January 30th 1677/78* (London, 1678), p. 16 (perpetual). John Williams, *The Case of Martyrdom Consider'd. In a Sermon Preached before the House of Lords. . . . January 30th. 1701* (London, 1702), pp. 14–15; Pawlett St. John, *A Sermon Preach'd before the Queen, at St. James's Chapel, On Wednesday, January 30. 1711–12* (London, 1712), p. 6.

17. South, *Sermon Preach'd before King Charles II*, p. 28; Joseph Glanvill, *Some Discourses, Sermons and Remains of the Reverend Mr. Jos. Glanvil*, ed. Anthony Horneck (London, 1681), p. 156; William Sheridan, *Several Discourses. . . . All Preach'd on Particular Occasions before the State in the Cathedral of St. Patrick's, and Christ Church, Dublin* (London, 1704), p. 380 in "On the Martyrdom of King Charles I." This was familiar High Church divine right theory. Basileus, *Remarks On Dr. West's Sermon*, p. 4; Scarisbrike (or Scarsbrick), *Catholick Loyalty: Upon the Subject of Government and Obedience. Delivered in a Sermon, Before the King and Queen, In his Majesties Chapel-Royal at White-Hall, On the Thirtieth of January, 1687* (London, 1688), p. 72 (struck), 9 (Sacred), 11 (Who), 22 (Reviling). Wounding his honor "is only a slyer way of striking him to the *Heart*" (p. 22). Scarisbrike also invokes the Virgin Mary (p. 5) and urges the legitimacy of the royal infant, so challenged by both Whig and Tory Anglicans. He concludes with *"In Nomine Patris"* (p. 24). Queen Mary indeed could have said "In nomine patris," but from a very different point of view.

18. Edward Pelling, *A Sermon Preached On the Thirtieth of January, 1678/9. Being the Anniversary Of the Martyrdom of King Charles the First, of Blessed Memory* (London, 1679),

p. 2. Pelling wrote other thirtieth of January sermons wholly supporting the divine right of kings and lamenting the regicide by diabolical agents who want to repeat the deed. See his *David and the Amalekite Upon the Death of Saul. A Sermon Preached on Jan. 30 1682* (London, 1683) and *A Sermon Preacht On January 30th. 1683. In Westminster Abby* (London, 1684). Thomas Mangey, *The Providential Sufferings of good Men. Set forth in a Sermon Preached before the Honourable House of Commons . . . On the 30th Day of January, 1719* (London, 1720), p. 21.

19. Sheridan, *Several Discourses*, pp. 355–56; Sprat, *A Sermon Preached*, p. 33.

20. Luke Milbourne, *The Utter Extirpation of Tyrants and their Families. A Sermon Preached at St. Ethelburga's, Jan. 30. 1707–8* (London, [1708]), p. 17; South, *Sermon Preach'd before King Charles II*, p. 8; Pelling, *A Sermon Preach'd* (1679), p. 11; Basileus, *Remarks on Dr. West's Sermon*, pp. 8 (canting), 4 (Warmth); George Smalridge, *A Sermon Preach'd before the . . . Alderman . . . January 31, 1708/9* (London, 1709), pp. 14 (moderation), 11 (lively), 13 (Memories), 8 (Blame-worthy). Milbourne collected his annual thirtieth of January sermons, with separate title pages and pagination, in *The Royal Martyr Lamented in Fourteen Sermons, Preached on the Thirtieth of January. Wherein the Rights of Monarchy are occasionally asserted; and the Republican Schemes, which have been of late advanc'd by H----y, B----y, the B----p of B----r, & c, are largely consider'd and confuted* (London, [1724]). For the schismatics, heretics, et al., see Milbourne, *The People not the Original of Civil Power Prov'd from God's Word . . . . January 30. 1706/7* (London, 1710), p. 3. For inundation and tyranny, see Milbourne, *The Danger of Changes in Church or State; Or, The Fatal Doom of such as love them and their Associates. In a Sermon Preach'd January 31, 1714/15* (London, [1715]), p. 2. For depopulation, see Milbourne, *Utter Extirpation of Tyrants*, p. 19. The topic is from parts of Isaiah 14:20–21 and includes: "Prepare Slaughter for his Children for the Iniquity of their Fathers; that they do not Rise nor Possess the Land." This is the tradition out of which Henry Sacheverell comes, and to which Daniel Defoe responds in *The Shortest Way with the Dissenters: Or Proposals for the Establishment of the Church* (London, 1702).

21. Francis Browne, *A Sermon Preach'd before the Right Honourable the Lord Mayor, and the Aldermen, and Citizens of London . . . On Friday, January 30. 1712–13* (London, 1713), p. 16; Milbourne, *Utter Extirpation of Tyrants*, p. 5; South, *Sermon Preach'd before King Charles II*, p. 9; William Tilly, *A Sermon Preach'd before the University of Oxford . . . Jan. 31, 1703/4, the Fast Day for the Execrable Murder of King Charles the Martyr* (London, 1704), p. 28.

22. Robert Moss, *A Sermon Preach'd before the House of Commons . . . On Thursday, Jan. 30, 1706/7* (London, 1707), p. 22; Henry Gandy, *Some Remarks, Or Short Strictures*, p. 13.

23. Pelling, *A Sermon Preached* (1679), pp. 5 (The King), 9 (Philosophy); St. John, *A Sermon Preach'd before the Queen*, p. 12.

24. Turner, *Sermon Preached before the King*, p. 22. He is referring to Gjisbert Voet, or Gisbertius Voetius, 1589–1676, a Dutch Reform theologian. I suspect that Voet is a surrogate for William of Orange. Gandy, *Some Remarks, Or Short Strictures*, p. 12; Luke Milbourne, *Royal and Innocent Blood expiated: Or, God justified in punishing a wicked People. In a Sermon Preach'd at the Parish-Church of St. Ethelburga's* (London, 1720), p. 33; Milbourne, *Utter Extirpation of Tyrants*, pp. 18–19.

25. Turner, *Sermon Preached before the King*, pp. 22–23; Richard Hollingworth, *A Second Defence of King Charles I., by Way of Reply to an Infamous Libel, called, Ludlow's Letter to Dr. Hollingworth* (London, 1692), sig. A3^r; Moss, *A Sermon Preach'd*, p. 28; A Gentleman,

Reflections upon Mr. Stephens's Sermon, Preach'd before the Honourable House of Commons . . . January the 30th, 1699/1700 by a Gentleman Who Took the Said Sermon in Shorthand (London, [1700]), p. 14. For William Stephens, only a BD, see *A Sermon Preach'd Before the Honourable House of Commons, January 30, 1702/1703. Being an Anniversary Sermon for the Day* (London, 1703). Unlike most such sermons published early in the century, it lacks a black border. Unlike other such sermons I have seen for that period, it mentions neither Charles I nor the occasion. The sermon was an act of defiance and was published without the thanks or approval of the House of Commons. Stephens argues that the Church of England should not force others into its confession, that government is a construct of the people, not of God, and that governments thus may vary (pp. 9–10, 14–16). As the controversy makes plain, it was met with severe parliamentary and nonparliamentary scoldings. Though it then was ahead of its time, its sentiments would be acceptable shortly and into the next decade.

26. [William King], *A Vindication Of the Reverend Dr. Henry Sacheverell, From the False, Scandalous and Malicious Aspersions Cast upon Him in a late Infamous Pamphlet, Entitled The Modern Fanatick. . . . In a Dialogue between a Tory and a Whig* (London, 1711), pp. 97–98; *The Royal Monarch: Or, The Bloody Tragedy of King Charles the First* (London, 1711); [Philo Britannus], *Popery and Schism Equally Dangerous to the Church of England, As by Law Establish'd* (London, 1715), p. xxi, italics and roman type reversed; William Newton, *The Life of the Right Reverend Dr. White Kennett, Late Lord Bishop of Peterborough* (London, 1730), p. 36.

27. Moss, *A Sermon Preach'd*, p. 28.

28. Gandy, *Some Remarks, Or Short Strictures*, p. 11; Basileus, *Remarks On Dr. West's Sermon*, pp. 2 (Memory), 8 (son), 2 (seeming).

29. Charles Leslie, *A Vindication of the Royal Martyr King Charles I. From the Irish Massacre In the Year 1641. . . . Being a Case of Present Concern*, 3rd ed. (London, 1704), sig. a1^v, with the title page regarded as 1r. Italicized words were in black letter in Leslie's text.

30. William Baker, *A Sermon Preach'd before the Honourable House of Commons . . . On Monday, January 30. 1720*, 2nd ed. (London, [1721]), pp. 7 (Injuries), 9 (determine); Benjamin Hoadly, *A Sermon Preach'd before the Lords Spiritual and Temporal . . . On Monday January 30, 1720–21* (London, [1721]), pp. 7–8.

31. Samuel Colby, *A Sermon Preach'd on the Anniversary Fast, for the Martyrdom of King Charles I. With a particular application to the Clergy of the Church of England, to avoid all manner of Divisions amongst themselves, as the only means to prevent all designs of the Enemy ever more succeeding in the subversion of Church and State, as by Law establish'd* (London, 1709), pp. 12–13.

32. Moss, *A Sermon Preach'd*, p. 18. See the discussion of Defoe's response to Sacheverell and fears of violence in chapter 2, above, and see chapter 4 for further discussion of the church and state as supportive agents in violence.

33. William Fleetwood, "Sermon IV. Preach'd at St. Paul's Cathedral, January 30. 1698/9. Before the Right Honourable the Lord-Mayor and Court of Aldermen," in *Seventeen Sermons Preach'd upon several Occasions* (London, 1717), pp. 99–100; John Williams, *The Case of Martyrdom Considered*, p. 22; Henry Brydges, *A Sermon Preach'd before the Queen, at St. James's Chapel on Monday, January 31, 1708/09* (London, 1709), pp. 11–16; Edward Waddington, *A Sermon Preach'd before the Lords Spiritual and Temporal . . . On Thursday, January 30, 1728/9* (London, 1729), pp. 29 (false), 31 (load).

34. Gilbert Burnet, *Subjection for Conscience-sake Asserted: In a Sermon Preached at Covent-Garden-Church the Sixth of December, 1674* (London, 1675), p. 3 (hereafter cited parenthetically in the text); Burnet, *The Royal Martyr Lamented, in a Sermon Preached at the Savoy, On King Charles the Martyr's Day 1674/5* (London, 1675). The sermons were collected in *The Royal Martyr, and the Dutiful Subject, in Two Sermons* (London, 1675).

35. D. J., *King Charles I, No Such Saint, Martyr, or Good Protestant as Commonly Reputed* (London, 1698), pp. 24–25.

36. Others copied Burnet's tactful and tactical retreat from praise of Charles I. William Fleetwood uses it in his sermon of 1696, reprinted in 1708. He observes that Charles I's virtues are so well known "that I need not enlarge upon them." *A Sermon Preach'd Before the Lords . . . January the 30th. 1695/6* (London, 1708), p. 13. White Kennett avoided such praise with a respectful negative: "Should I attempt to enumerate his Virtues, and recommend his Example, the time would fail." See his *Sermon Preach'd before the Honourable House of Commons . . . January XXX, 1705/6* (London, 1706), p. 16. Burnet was active in William's campaign to assume the English Crown and to induce comprehension. See the first volume of Bishop Burnet's *History of his Own Times* (London, 1724) for the elaboration of his roles. The *History* was a Whig answer to Clarendon. Sir Charles Firth's "Burnet as Historian" remains helpful. See Firth, *Essays Historical and Literary* (Oxford: Clarendon Press, 1938), pp. 174–209. Swift was not amused by Burnet, whose *History* he briefly discussed and amply annotated. See *The Prose Works of Jonathan Swift*, vol. 5, *Miscellaneous and Autobiographical Pieces Fragments and Marginalia*, ed. Herbert Davis (Oxford: Basil Blackwell, 1962), pp. 183–84, 266–94 (hereafter cited as *PW* by volume, title, and editor). Swift was almost as troubled by Burnet's apparently low style as by his low and Whig politics, which favored Presbyterians and Scots.

37. Burnet exemplifies this good advice in the preface to his *Relation Of the Death Of the Primitive Persecutors. Written Originally in Latin by L. C. F. Lactantius. . . . To which he hath made a large Preface concerning Persecution* (Amsterdam, 1687). "Impatience of Spirit" makes us seek to tyrannize over others and to hate those who do not adhere to our beliefs. To "strike at Persecution in its root, [reformers] must begin here, and endeavour to soften men, especially towards those who differ from them in matters of Religion" (p. 11); see also pp. 20–23.

38. William Shorey, *A Sermon Preach'd before the Rt Honble the Lord-Mayor, Aldermen, and Citizens of London . . . On Monday, January xxxi. 1715* (London, 1715), p. 24; Peter Foulkes, *A Sermon Preached in the Cathedral Church of St. Peter in Exeter, On Wednesday, Jan. 30. 1722–3* (Exon, 1723), pp. 14 (Magistrate), 24 (Regular).

39. George Coade, *A Letter to a Clergyman, Relating to his Sermon on the 30th of January. . . . By a Lover of Truth, who wishes the perpetual Peace and Prosperity of Great-Britain* (London, 1746), p. 74. The popular *Letter* was reprinted in London in 1747, 1749, 1760, 1766 (with "An Epitaph on Bigotry" in Latin and English by John Reynolds), and 1776. There was a "Fourth Edition" in New York, 1773. Swift offers a concise list of ongoing objections to the sermons at the beginning of his own such sermon at St. Patrick's in 1726. See Swift, *PW* 9, *Irish Tracts 1720–1723 . . . And Sermons*, ed. Herbert Davis and Louis Landa (Oxford: Basil Blackwell, 1963), pp. 219–20.

40. D. F. [Daniel Defoe?], *Moderation Maintain'd, In Defence of a Compassionate Enquiry Into the Causes of the Civil War, &c. In a Sermon Preached by White Kennett, D. D.* (London, 1704), p. 2.

41. *Madding Day* was a familiar term. See Edmund Ludlow, *Truth Brought to Light: Or, The Gross Forgeries of Dr. Hollingworth, in his Pamphlet Intituled, The Character of King Charles the First* (London, 1693), p. 12; A Protestant and True Englishman, *The Mystery of Iniquity Working in the Dividing of Protestants, in Order to the Subverting of Religion and our Laws for Almost the Space of 30 Years last past, plainly laid open* (London, 1689), p. 21; D. J., *King Charles I, No Such Saint*, p. 26; William Graham, *A Letter to the Right Reverend the Lord Bishop [Pearce] of Bangor; Occasioned by his Lordship's Sermon . . . before the House of Lords, January 30, 1749 [1750]* (London, 1750), p. 20.

42. *The Observations or Reflections On a virulent Sermon preached at Exeter, on the 31st of January last, with a Vindication of those now called Whigs and Dissenters, from having any hand in the Murder of King Charles the I.* (Edinburgh, 1709), p. 1 of the broadside; John Wyng, *Reasons Humbly offer'd to the Parliament for Abrogating the Observation of the Thirtieth of January*, 2nd ed. (London, 1715), pp. 36 (Language), 17 (unchristian), 37 (void), 38 (Rage); Michael Hutchinson, *Counterfeit Loyalty Displayed: Or, A Parallel Between Antient and Modern Pharisaism* (London, [1717?]), p. 13; [Thomas Gordon], *A Political Dissertation Upon Bull-Baiting and Evening Lectures. With Occasional Meditations on the 30th of January* (London, 1718), pp. 30 (Lunaticks, Phrenzy), 19 (Throat); D. F. [Defoe?], *Moderation Maintain'd*, p. 2.

43. Richard Steele, *An Account Of the State of the Roman-Catholick Religion Throughout the World* (London, 1715), pp. xxx–xxxi.

44. [Defoe?], *High-Church Politicks*, p. 3; *Observations or Reflections*, p. 1.

45. D. F. [Defoe?], *Moderation Maintain'd*, sig. A2^r, with the title page as A1^r (Sowing), p. 21 (against, advance). The Protestant Dissenter who wrote *Remarks On some Passages in a Sermon . . . by the Rev. Dr. Berryman* used the same phrase regarding sown seeds of sedition on p. 6; Hutchinson, *Counterfeit Loyalty Displayed*, pp. 10–11; Wyng, *Reasons Humbly offer'd*, p. 14; James Peirce, "The Curse causeless. A Sermon Preach'd at Exon, Jan. 30, 1716/17," in *Fifteen Sermons on Several Occasions. . . . By the late . . . Mr. James Peirce of Exon* (London, 1728), p. 104. Peirce prefaces his sermon by explaining that he disapproved of the rationale for the sermon; he delivered it only because "it was my turn to preach." He writes to vindicate Dissenters "at a time when we were every where insulted and abus'd" (p. 90). Of course tracts and sermons other than those on the thirtieth of January savaged the High Church's hypocrisy and treason, as with its presumed support for the Jacobites during the Sacheverell dustup and the invasion of 1715. See John Toland, *The Jacobitism, Perjury, and Popery of High-Church Priests* (London, 1710), passim, with references to abusive thirtieth of January sermons on pp. 6–7 and defense of loyal Benjamin Hoadly on pp. 7–8; Thomas Pyle, *The Wisdom of a Government in distributing Punishment or Mercy to State-Criminals* (London, 1716), pp. 20–21; and Pyle, *The Heinous Sin and Danger of Prevarication with God and the Government* (London, 1716), pp. 6–7, 16 by implication. These last texts are part of a movement in which law, the constitution, and Hanoverian compliance with Parliament, church, and people replace divine right.

46. Richard Willis, *A Sermon Preached before the House of Lords . . . On the 30th of January, 1715/16* (London, 1716), p. 11; Skerret, *Subjects Duty to the Higher Powers*, pp. 29 (pretend), 26 (Deluded); Thomas Blennerhaysett, *Legal Obedience, in Opposition to Unlimited; The Subjects Necessary Duty, and Prince's Best Security. A Sermon Preached January the 30th, 1715/16* (London, 1716), pp. 27 (False), 28 (Really, Found).

47. William Crowe, *The Duty of promoting the Publick Peace. A Sermon, Preached before the Right Honorable the Lord Mayor . . . on Thursday January 30. 1723–4*, 2nd ed. (London, 1724), p. 24; John Waugh, *A Sermon Preached before the Lords . . . Jan. 30, 1724* (London, 1725), p. 28; Thomas Chubb, *An Enquiry Concerning the Grounds and Reasons, Or What those principles are, on which two of our Anniversary Solemnities are founded—30 January and 5 November* (London, 1732), p. 12.

48. Robert Clavering, *A Sermon Preach'd before the Lords Spiritual and Temporal . . . On Saturday, January xxx. 1730* (London, 1731), pp. 16 (glorious), 21 (true), 23 (illustrious).

49. Coade, *A Letter to a Clergyman*, pp. 76 (Absolute), 77–78 (impious, imbibed, present).

50. John Hoadly, *A Sermon Preach'd before the Honourable House of Commons . . . On June 30. 1717–18*, 2nd ed. (London, 1718), p. 6 (hereafter cited parenthetically in the text). The verso of the title page includes the formulaic language that accompanies many other sermons: the thanks of the House for his sermon, a request that it be printed, and notification by the appropriate agents of the House of Commons. As I have suggested, not all these sermons were given such thanks or a request to print. The Huntington Library's copy of Hoadly's sermon has a telling annotation, though not in the same hand as that on the copy of Richard West's sermon (n. 9 above). It responds favorably to Hoadly's negative judgments of James II, for whom "Nothing short of Abdication" was appropriate. See Huntington Library, shelf mark 246783, p. 27 of Hoadly's sermon. The generally traditional thanks also could be modified in a positive way. Edward Chandler was bishop of Coventry and Lichfield in 1718, before becoming bishop of Durham in 1730. The House of Lords asked that he be thanked for his "very Excellent SERMON preach'd before this House Yesterday," on 30 January 1718, quotation located on the verso of the title page. *A Sermon Preach'd Before the Lords Spiritual and Temporal in Parliament Assembled in the Abbey-Church of Westminster the 30th of January 1717/18* (London, 1718).

Swift, perhaps reluctantly, made his peace with John Hoadly. For Swift and Hoadly, see Irvin Ehrenpreis, *Swift: The Man, His Works, and the Age: Volume III. Dean Swift* (Cambridge, MA: Harvard University Press, 1983), pp. 654–55, 792–93, 899. John Gay wrote to Swift regarding Hoadly on 3 July 1730, and Swift responded on 10 November. See *The Correspondence of Jonathan Swift*, ed. David Woolley, 4 vols. (Frankfurt am Main: Peter Lang, 1999–2007), 3:318–19, and 334: "I thank you for offering me the neighborhood of another Hoadly, I have enough of one; he lives within 20 yards of me, our gardens joyn, but I never see him except upon business."

51. Gandy, *Some Remarks, Or Short Strictures*, p. 3; N. N. [Samuel Grascome (Grascombe)?], *Remarks on a Sermon, Preach'd January the 31st 1703/4 by White Kennett* ([London, 1704]), pp. 2, 3; D. F. [Defoe?], *Moderation Maintain'd*, p. 24.

52. Bradbury, *Lawfulness of Resisting Tyrants*, p. 25; Samuel Wright, *The Mischievous Consequences of Publick Strife and Envy. A Sermon Preach'd at Black-Fryars, on the XXXIst of January, 1713/14* (London, 1714), p. 13; James Anderson, *No King-Killers. A Sermon Preach'd in Swallow-street, St. James's on January 30. 1714/15* (London, 1715), p. 14; John Withers, *A Vindication of the Dissenters From the Charge of Rebellion, And being the Authors of our Civil Wars*, 2nd ed. (London, 1719), p. 7.

53. *A Discourse on Government and Religion, Calculated for the Meridian of the Thirtieth of January. By an Independent* (London, [1749?]), p. 11; Rusticus [Fleming], *Devout Laugh,*

pp. 8 (William), 6 (utter ruin); John Ross, *A Sermon Preached before the Honourable House of Commons ... Upon Tuesday the 30th of January 1759* (London, 1759), p. 7.

54. Coade, *A Letter to a Clergyman*, p. 38 (hereafter cited parenthetically in the text).

55. Jonathan Mayhew, *A Discourse concerning Unlimited Submission and Non-Resistance to the Higher Powers: With some Reflections on the Resistance made to King Charles I* (Boston, 1750), p. 44. By midcentury such clergymen and political theorists were pushing on an open door. I have found little evidence to suggest that any serious thinker then was urging unlimited submission and nonresistance. As we have seen, the Commons authorized, listened to, and asked that moderate, rather than radical, Lockean political sermons be presented to it and be published.

56. *Critical Remarks on Dr. Nowel's Sermon, Preached on Thursday, January 30, 1772, Before the House of Commons; To which is annexed, The Sermon complete. Printed with the Approbation of the Speaker, At the Expence of a Member* (London, 1772), pp. 6 (compared); for the revised motion of the House, in italics, see 23n. James J. Caudle's *ODNB* entry on Nowell is helpful regarding Nowell as anti-Methodist polemicist as well as Oxford churchman.

57. D. F. [Defoe?], *Moderation Maintain'd*, pp. 22–23.

58. William Stoughton, *A Sermon Preach'd before the State in Christ-Church in Dublin on Monday January 31, 1708/9* (London, 1709), p. 18. Archbishop King wrote to Swift on 10 February 1709. Though King was unable to hear the sermon that "gave great offence. . . . If the representation I have of it be true, I am sure I should have suspended him, if it had cost me both my reputation and interest." The sermon later was burned by the common hangman. See Swift, *Correspondence*, ed. Woolley, vol. 1 (1999), p. 234. See also Swift's comment from London on 26 March (1:249), in which Stoughton seems nevertheless to be prospering. On 10 November, King tells Swift that the sermon was burned (1:393). [Defoe?], *High-Church Politicks*, p. 17. Caleb Fleming, *A Fund Raising for the Italian Gentleman: or, A Magazine Filling on the Scheme of Frugality* (London, 1750), p. 16.

59. John Scott, "Sermon VI. On Rom. xiii. I," in *Sermons Upon Several Occasions* (London, 1704), pp. 219–20 (Princes, endeavouring, stamps), 234 (obliged).

60. Skerret, *Subjects Duty to the Higher Powers*, pp. 11 (Government), 13 (Entirely), 18 (King).

61. Thomas Herring, *A Sermon Preached before the House of Lords ... on Wednesday, Jan. 30, 1739–40* (London, 1740), p. 8; Benjamin Hoadly, *A Sermon Preach'd*, p. 31.

62. Willis, *A Sermon Preached before the House of Lords*, p. 34; John Disney, *A Sermon Preach'd at St. Maries in Nottingham, January the ... 30th, 1722* (Nottingham and London, [1723]), p. 24; Skerret, *Subjects Duty to the Higher Powers*, p. 8; Edward Littleton, *A Sermon Preach'd before the Honourable House of Commons ... on Saturday, January xxx. 1730* (London, 1731), p. 10.

63. Edward Young, *An Apology for Princes, or The Reverence due to Government. A Sermon Preached ... January the 30th, 1728/9* (London, 1729) (hereafter cited parenthetically in the text).

64. William Bradshaw, *A Sermon Preach'd before the Lords Spiritual and Temporal ... On Friday, January 30. 1729/30* (London, 1730) (hereafter cited parenthetically in the text).

65. Edward Arrowsmith, *The Reasonableness and Origin of Government, and what ought to be the Behaviour of every Christian subject. A Sermon ... at the Cathedral Church of St. Paul* (London, 1735), pp. 10–11. For fuller discussion of the concept of such government, see

Gerd Mischler, "English Political Sermons 1714–1742: A Case Study in the Theory of 'Divine Right of Governors' and the Ideology of Order," *British Journal for Eighteenth-Century Studies* 24 (2001): 33–61. The topic has been broadly discussed by James J. Caudle in "Measures of Allegiance: Sermon Culture and the Creation of a Public Discourse of Obedience and Resistance in Georgian Britain, 1714–1760" (PhD diss., Yale University, 1996).

66. Samuel Horsley, *A Sermon, Preached Before the Lords Spiritual and Temporal* (see n. 10 above) (hereafter cited parenthetically in the text). The Baptist minister Robert Hall attacked Horsley's sermon as a venomous, malicious, polluting, repugnant, diabolical effort by "the apologist of tyranny" to resurrect the divine right, passive obedience, and nonresistance that Horsley explicitly repudiated. The pamphlet is a tribute to the violence of partisan discourse in the French revolutionary period. See Hall, *An Apology for the Freedom of the Press, and for General Liberty. To which are Prefixed Remarks On Bishop Horsley's Sermon* (London, 1793), pp. iii–xvi, quotation from p. xii. For Horsley's larger career, see F. C. Mather, *High Church Prophet: Bishop Samuel Horsley (1733–1806)* (Oxford: Clarendon Press, 1992).

67. Pierre Jean Grosley, originally *Londres* (Lausanne [i.e., Paris], 1770), here *A Tour to London; Or, New Observations on England, and its Inhabitants*, trans. Thomas Nugent (London, 1772), 2:25 (constant, believe), 27 (church). The translator notes that Grosley was criticized for errors and asked that they be corrected for the 1772 version (1:viii–ix). The passage on religion was unchanged.

CHAPTER FOUR

"Compel Them to Come In," Luke 14:23

From Persuasion to Persecution; Against Augustinian Compulsion

In 1679 Vincent Alsop defended Saint Augustine from attacks by Hugo Grotius and other presumed impertinents. Such men must be vastly overconfident to "hope with one puff of contemptuous breath to blow away that fair heap of Repute, that that Fathers Name has gathered in so many Centuries." In fact, the "Papists with incredible zeal have struggled for him; the Protestants have tooth and nail wrestled to draw him into their Tents, all parties have ambitiously courted his suffrage." Alsop overstates for at least one major case, but even those who disagreed with Augustine recognized his vast shadow. There is no one, Herbert Croft says, "to whom I could more readily submit than to St. *Austin*, a Person of wonderful sharpness in understanding."[1]

The wonders of that understanding nonetheless long would cause grave danger to those dissenting from their national church. Augustine's several attacks upon the Donatists, an early North African schismatic sect, were key documents in the history of persecution. The Donatists claimed that the bishops who surrendered holy books to Diocletian's demands had sullied the church, from which it must separate. Thereafter the Emperor Constantine issued numerous decrees against the Donatists, many of whom were executed and many of whose churches and lands later were seized as penalty for exclusion from the recently established Roman Church. A fringe, sometimes terrorist group of martyrdom-seeking Circumcellions fought fire with fire, thus increasing hostilities and suggesting schism within schism. By 405 and 411 new imperial edicts increased penalties. Hitherto, Augustine had argued that persuasion was the appropriate way to change the mind and to lead wanderers back to the faith. By the earlier fourth century he had recanted and argued on the value of fear and force to make conversion effective. The civil magistrate became the severe and sometimes fatal ecclesiastical agent.

Donatist and *Circumcellion* thus became familiar terms and object lessons in the dangers of schism. As the *Glossographia Anglicana Nova* put it in 1707, the

Donatists were "a Sect of Hereticks, so call'd from *Donatus* Bishop of *Carthage*, the first Broacher of the Heresy." The more rigid among them were called Circumcellions, and the moderates, Rogatists. They regarded the African church as the only true church, and they were Arians: "the Son in the Trinity was less than the Father, and the Holy Ghost less than the Son." Ephraim Chambers' *Cyclopædia* (1728) points out that the Donatist schismatics were condemned in councils both in Rome and in Arles. Emperor Constantine "decreed exile, and even death" against them; there were later "laws for their banishment"; and "Theodosius, and Honorius, condemned them to grievous mulcts."[2]

Accusations against later British Dissenters that evoked this history thus came trailing storm clouds seeded by Augustine's epistles, what now are called 93 and 185. When in 1703 John Sage likened Presbyterians to Donatists, a troubled George Meldrum replied that all Presbyterians behaved "in a peaceable orderly way, tho this Author callumniously accuse us, as having behaved ... Carnally and Circumcellian-like." Several years later the author of *Light out of Darkness* complained that it was absurd to regard his people as heretics, for they had "never separated from the Truth" as had the Donatists and Circumcellions.[3] Given such nerves, Restoration Dissenters and lower church Anglicans must have been more than usually concerned when Augustine's epistle to the Donatist bishop Vincentius appeared in English with its formidable title, *The Judgment of the Learned and Pious St. Augustine, concerning Penal Lawes against Conventicles, and for Unity in Religion. Deliver'd in His 48th Epistle to Vincentius* (1670).

The translator tells the reader what he already is likely to have known, namely "the Great Esteem, which this Holy and Learned *Prelate* hath alwayes had in the *Church* of *Christ*" and especially among the reformed. Those who have written against the Church of England cannot charge Augustine with bias, for he died long before the present argument regarding dissent and unity. His words are the more adaptable since, we hear in a virtual précis of Augustine's doctrine, laws made by Christian monarchs in his own time "against CONVENTICLES and FACTIOUS ASSEMBLIES" moved entire cities into the true Christian fold. He thus finally agreed that the civil magistrate should forcefully serve the monarch and God. Those who differed needed to respect Augustine's authority and execute the laws against schism on behalf of church and state. Augustine, the disinterested, authoritative, learned, pious agent of the established church, knew that the Crown served God through God's church, whose unity denoted a unified state.[4] The text itself reinforces the reader's desired reaction.

The several assumptions on which Augustine's epistle rests clearly include the union of church and state. Perhaps even more important, since God is king of kings, the state is subordinate to the church. It therefore follows that "the Kings of the Earth serve *Christ* by making LAWES for Christ" (p. 13). Those laws must be good, effective, and well executed. They are good because "the *Light* of *Truth* may expel the *Darkness* of *Error*" (p. 3) and, in words surely dear to Henry Sacheverell and his associates, it is "better to love with *Severity*, than to deceive with *Lenity*" (p. 4). The power of "wholesome Discipline" (p. 5) is necessary to awake the spiritually lethargic from their sleep, that "they may Awaken to *Salvation*." These good laws are effective, since fear, terror, and the pains of "*Temporal Punishments*" are useful to "break the *Bonds* of *Evil Custome*" (p. 4). Moderation and suasion against the Donatists did not work, and so they were "Compel'd to that which is good" (p. 10). This was not persecution but "a love to heal" (p. 5). After all, there are times when the sufferer is unjust and "he [is] Just who afflicts" (p. 7). The laws were well executed. They brought numerous "Converts, through the fear ... of the Emperour's Lawes, made by *Constantine*, and continued even to our present Emperour." Legal force and fear converted stubborn Donatists. Many who longed to return were grateful, and one could scarcely "believe them ever to have been guilty" (p. 11). Such effective "Terror of Temporal Powers" abolished Donatist conventicles, "by which LAW the Memory of *Hereticks* and *Schismaticks* was Destroyed" (p. 13). Augustine reminds Vincentius of the biblical basis of the ideology of secular coercion for spiritual purposes: "Think you that no man ought to be Compell'd to Goodness? when you read how the Father of the Family sent out his Servants to Compel them to come in whom they found, *Luke* 17 [i.e., 14]. 23?" (p. 4). Many indeed so thought.

Revocation of the Edict of Nantes: Response and Rage

Reverence for Augustine all too handsomely supported the schemes of both the seventeenth-century Gallican church and its agent and patron, his Most Christian Majesty Louis XIV. France would be wholly Catholic, without the corrupting intrusion of the pretended reformed church fathered by the heretic Calvin. Antoine Arnaud stressed his and his church's "grande veneration" for Augustine. All the fathers were excellent guides to conduct, but one could not doubt that Augustine "a porté à plus haut point de perfection cette divine Philosophie." In 1686 a putative abbé made plain one implication of a specific Augustinian influence. He told a correspondent who had fled to England to read the incomparable epistles "du Docteur de la Grace, le grand S. Augustin." He then would abandon his complaints regarding the great, pious, charitable "grand Roi de la terre" and convert as he should.[5] The great king's final triumph of course was thanks to the revoked Edict of Nantes on 18 October 1685 and the years of preparation for it. Dragoons marched through France intimidating Protestants, destroying their churches, homes, and, too often, the recalcitrant nonconformists themselves. The dragoons thus restored church unity on the king's behalf.

Louis so ordered with the church's urging and compliance. His revocation was translated in 1686 as *An Edict of the French King, Prohibiting all Publick Exercise of the Pretended Reformed Religion in his Kingdom. Wherein he Recalls, and totally Annuls the perpetual and irrevocable Edict of Nantes [1598]; full of most gracious Concessions to Protestants* (London). The second edition appeared in the same year and laid out royal revisionist history. Both Louis' grandfather and father indeed signed edicts granting privileges to the pretended reformed religion. That was necessary for the unsettled wartimes when Protestants were powerful. Royal ancestors nonetheless always intended to unify the state's religion, as the present peace now permitted. This was "Our Intention ever since we came to the Crown" (p. 4). Louis thus revoked all previous edicts, "declaring them null and void, as if they had never been Enacted; together with all the Concessions granted in them" (p. 5).

Accordingly, (1) All Protestant churches within French dominions are to "be forthwith demolished." (2) No French subjects may convene in any private homes for purposes of worship. (3) Lords of all ranks are forbidden to hold worship on pains "of Confiscation of Body and Goods." (4) All Protestant ministers must either convert or leave the country within fifteen days and are forbidden to preach or exercise any ministerial function "upon pain of being sent to the Galleys" (p. 5). (5) Those ministers who do convert, and their widowed wives so long as they continue Catholic, will be exempt "from Payments and Quartering of Souldiers." These converts also will receive one-third more than the normal minister's pay, and half of that pension shall go to their widows so long as they remain single. (6) Should the ministers seek to become doctors in law, the three-year study requirement will be void, and upon passing their examination as doctor, they need pay only one-half of the usual dues. (7) No school may instruct any children of the pretended reformed religion, nor teach anything that might seem favorable to it. (8) All children of that religion must be baptized in parish churches or the parents will be fined "500. Livres or more, as it shall happen." All such children shall be educated and brought up in the Catholic religion (p. 6). (9) "For a mark of our Clemency" all those Protestant subjects who have left the country but return in four months may resume their possessions and estates; those who do not return within that time will have their goods confiscated (p. 7). (10) Protestants, their families, and their goods are forbidden to leave the country "upon Penalty of the Gally for Men, and of Confiscation of Body and Goods for Women" (p. 7). (11) Those who have converted but relapsed shall be punished. Those who have not yet converted may stay in the country until "it shall Please God to enlighten them," but they may not practice their religion, "upon forfeiture above specified of Body and Goods" (p. 7). All counselors, judges, and the like, as well as their subordinates, are to read and post the edict "even in Vacation time, and the same keep punctually, without contrevening or suffering the same to be contrevened; for such is Our Will and Pleasure" (p. 8).

The new unity of religion was broadly praised across France, including by the Immortals within Louis XIV's Académie Française. It sponsored a contest concerning the revocation and awarded a prize to Jesuit-educated Bernard le Bovier de Fontenelle, nephew of the great Corneille dramatists. Houdar de la Motte, a later mortal Immortal Académie colleague, wrote an "Eloge funebre de Louis Le Grand, protecteur de l'Académie Française" (1715). He praised Louis for crushing the monster from hell and restoring the church's authority.[6]

The 1686 edition of Louis Maimbourg's *Histoire du calvinisme* (originally 1682) illustrates some of the further intellectual and moral consequences of such approbation. Maimbourg celebrates his monarch's "incomparable pieté," his wise generosity to the church, and his glorification of the kingdom "en rétablissant la religion par la ruine de l'hérésie." God surely will recognize Louis with "tout la glorie & tout le bonheur qu'on peut souhaiter."[7] Maimbourg's frontispiece to the *Histoire* embodies the nation's and its institutions' delight in the dramatic triumph of light over darkness. A male Calvin ineffectually huddles behind an open ragged folio book labeled "JOANNIS CALVINI Institutiones Relig. Christi." The female Gallican church stands in triumph over him. Her powerful left arm holds an unlabeled, closed folio book, probably the Bible, that rejects heretical incursions by Calvin or other individuals and on which shines the emblem of the Sun King, emblazoned on her classically draped breast. The rays and smoke of the illuminated torch in her raised right arm highlight the truth, as another symbol of the Sun King looks down from an elevated pedestal. We also see the quivering, close-eyed Calvin and the altar behind and above him, which holds a symbol of the lamb of Christ on a pedestal flanked by ecclesiastical figures: one, to the viewer's left and the participants' right, apparently wears the papal triregnum, or triple hat, and the other, to his left, wears an episcopal miter. Above the church's striking figure, a large obelisk labeled "Histoire du Calvinisme" crumbles and is invaded by weeds and plant limbs, while the title itself remains clear and unsullied. The union of church and state appropriately demolishes the unseeing Calvin. Throughout the *Histoire*, advocates of his pretended reformed religion are heretics, false wise men, hypocrites, seducers, seduced, disloyal subjects, insolent, divisive apostates, conspirators, dangerous schismatics, and horribly cruel to defenders of the true religion ("Sommaire des livres," sigs. ii^r–iii^r).

Maimbourg later laments the appalling attempted genocide of the Saint Bartholomew's Day Massacre in 1572. He praises Jean Hennuyer, bishop of Lizieux, for disobeying the royal lieutenant's order that he kill all the Huguenots in the city. The apparent sympathy, however, soon becomes a comment on tactics rather than on ends: The Protestant holocaust was an ineffectual way to eliminate Calvinism. On the contrary, it made the survivors more deeply rooted, powerful, and formidable than ever. They spread to Switzerland, Germany, Poland, Sweden, Denmark, and England. They now urge war against God's religion "avec plus de force et encore plus de rage que jamais" (pp. 433–34).

The new *Histoire* concludes with an allusion that was not possible in 1682 and hence was not in that earlier edition. There, Maimbourg was encouraged by the decline of Protestantism in France, whose ravages and religion he wished soon would be utterly eliminated. He hoped that France would be bound by the same law, the same monarch, and the same faith. By 1686 "j'espere que nous le serons" has become reality.[8] In 1686 he thus adds the argument on approving authority, the text that Saint Augustine cites as justification for empowering the civil magistrate with the state's punitive arms. It may induce fear, pain, deprivation, or worse, in order to cleanse the soul, prepare it for the true church, and eliminate sacrilegious schism. God reserved the glory of uprooting heresy for Louis le Grand. He wisely destroyed Protestant churches, forced Catholic baptism of children of mixed marriages, and limited the power of Protestant justices. He also promoted selected, loyal Protestants to elevated court positions. As a result, a great many Protestants daily abjure their heresy. Less pliant Protestants are constrained to change "selon l'Evangile, d'entrer dans la salle du grand festin de Jesus-Christ où ils sont invitez." All this wise, just, and mellow royal method converted multitudes "sans bruit, sans éclat, sans tumult" and succeeded where Louis's predecessors' resort to war had failed. He compelled the Huguenots to come in—"selon l'Evangile"—so that France enjoyed one king and one religion, "l'Eglise Catholique, Apostolique & Romaine" (pp. 447–48). From 1682 to 1686 the future tense and hope have become the mingled past and present tense and reality. "J'espere" for the future yields to "voyons-nous," what we see today (p. 447). Maimbourg and so many celebrants like him on either side of the Channel are proudly in debt to Augustine. Le Grand Roi and le grand Saint Augustine are cognate regarding religious compulsion.

Needless to say, this and comparable Augustinian celebrations of unity by annihilation were shocking within French and British Protestant circles. For many, royal duplicity, the use of royal arms to enforce private religious belief, and the revocation itself sadly recalled the sadly remembered horrors of the Saint Bartholomew's Day massacres in 1572. As Gilbert Burnet's unsigned *Relation of the Massacres* put it in 1678, "All Protestants did every where abhor it, and hold the remembrance of it still in detestation." Those Protestants regarded the massacre and the revocation as shared qualities of French and Catholic modes of behavior. A Huguenot put it this way in 1682: the *"English* naturally hate the *French,* and find new reason to hate them in the rigorous Proceedings of the Catholicks of *France* against" fellow Protestants.[9] The Jacobite invasion of 1715 was broadly thought to be supported by French and Catholic interests. About then British clergymen thus regularly used sermons on Luke 14:23 to demonstrate the ravages of Continental compulsion on their Protestant brethren. In 1716 Peter Needham told his Cambridge audience about the violent papist conduct, as in "St. *Bartholomew's* in *France* . . . or the late *Persecutions* in *France,* and the daily Triumphs of the *Inquisition* in *Portugal* and *Spain.*" One year later Bishop Ralph Lambert addressed Christ Church, Dublin, to memorialize Protestant losses in the 1641 Irish rebellion. He remarks on "some Hundred Thousands of *Protestants* . . . in . . . the Southern Parts of *France*" recently murdered. He also notes "the memorable *Massacre* of *Paris,* [which] bears some Resemblance of this Day." Thomas Lucas soon returned to Luke and the traditional complaints of papist compulsion: "Witness the *Parisian* Massacre in 1572," and "Witness the late Dragooning in *France,* the Inquisition in *Spain, Portugal* and *Italy.*"[10]

Huguenots were the most immediate victims and of course fed this fire in texts promptly translated and eagerly, if angrily, read. The English *Edict of the French King* soon was followed in the same volume by *"A short Account of the Violent Proceedings, and unheard-of Cruelties"* inflicted on the Protestants of Montaubon (p. 10). It in turn was followed by *"A Letter sent from* Bourdeaux" to the same effect (p. 17), after which we see yet another *"Extract of a* Letter" with further *"Cruel and Barbarous"* acts against French Protestants (p. 27). The abundance and the geographical spread effectively suggest nationwide persecution. We read of soldiers destroying, appropriating, or selling Protestants' goods cheaply for their own benefit. They capture, beat, starve, humiliate, confiscate, forcibly convert, and coerce blasphemy and abjuration within conversion. These dragoons "are the very Emissaries of Hell" (p. 14). Never, we read in the *"Violent Proceedings,"* was "any Persecution, upon pretence of Religion, carried on to that pitch, and with that Politick Malice and Cruelty that this hath been" (p. 15). Worse and worse. As the Edict decreed, Protestants were prohibited from leaving the country "upon pain of Confiscation of Goods, of the Gally, of the Lash, and perpetual Imprisonment" (p. 16).

Jean Claude's *Account of the Persecutions and Oppressions of the French Protestants* (Paris and London, 1686) also chronicles the sad consequences of the revoked Edict of Nantes. Huguenots were ravaged by their monarch and his dragoons, so intellectually and wrongly justified by Augustine's interpretation of Luke 14:23's *compelle intrare* against the Donatists (p. 45): "Terror and Dread marched before them" (p. 18). They obeyed their marching orders. Claude demonstrates the endless horror of their acts to force conversion: "Amidst a thousand hideous Cries, and a thousand Blasphemies, they hung Men and Women by the Hair or Feet, on the Roofs of the Chamber, or Chimney Hooks, and smoakt them with Whisps of Wet Hay, till they were no longer able to bear it" (p. 19).[11]

The most important writer within the Huguenot diaspora resistance was Pierre Bayle, and especially in his two-volume *Commentaire philosophique sur ces paroles de Jésus-Christ, Contrain-les d'entrer; ou l'on prouve . . . . qu'il n'y a rien de plus abominable que de faire des conversions par la contrainte . . . Traduit de l'Anglois du Sieur Jean Fox de Bruggs par M. J. F* (Amsterdam, 1686–88). Its unflinching French title alludes to growing French and English Protestant emphasis on toleration. That title also was softened for its English two-volume translation: *A Philosophical Commentary on These Words of the Gospel, Luke XIV. 23. Compel them to come in, that my House may be full*. Its translator notes that Bayle chose the nominal *John Fox* because his book's reasoning "resembl'd that Depth and strenuous Abstraction, which distinguishes the Writers of *England*."[12] It nonetheless regularly makes the same points as did its French original.

Bayle had good personal reasons vigorously to resent the consequences of dragooning, the revocation, and the church's validation of persecution with Augustine's authority. In 1675 Bayle was appointed professor of philosophy at the Protestant academy in Sedan. Louis XIV abolished it in 1681. While holding a comparable chair as an exile in Rotterdam, Bayle published his reply to Maimbourg's *Histoire du calvinisme*, the *Critique générale* (1682). In March of 1683 it was burned by the common hangman in Paris. French authorities were unable to seize and imprison Pierre in Rotterdam, so they captured his only living relative, his brother Jacob. He died in prison on 12 November 1685.

Bayle's response in the *Commentaire philosophique* was scarcely only personal. His title makes plain that he has a specific target for a specific interpretation of a specific text. Part 1 refutes the literal interpretation of "Compel them to come in." Part 2 raises and answers objections to his refutation. Part 3 minutely analyzes and denigrates "those Letters of St. AUSTIN which are usually alledged for the compelling of Hereticks, and particularly to justify the Persecution in France." Part 4 is a supplement that considers the logical consequence of allowing one religion to persecute another. In such a case, heretics should "have as much Right to persecute the Orthodox, as the Orthodox them" ([1:I])—a version of the *lex talionis* that Defoe would adopt.

The long work is roughly unified by Bayle's insistence that reason must guide theology. Reason cannot justify persecution so inconsistent with real Christianity; the free private conscience is the proper guide to human religious behavior. Toleration is the only logical, moral, and prudential way to keep peace and to avoid a war of all against all. Otherwise, each sect and religion will think itself the true religion and will seek to persecute its persecutors when it has power. Without toleration, "we shou'd see a continual War between People of the same Country, either in the Streets or in the open Field, or between Nations of different Opinions; so that Christianity wou'd be a mere Hell upon Earth to all who lov'd Peace, or who happen'd to be the weaker side" (1:144). This must "occasion a Concatenation of Insult, Cruelty, Sacrilege, and Hypocrisy" (2:440). Bayle finds it especially appalling, indeed "what looks most monstrous in the whole Affair," that approbation of bloody persecuting laws has been approved "by Prelates, Councils, Popes, and most of the private Doctors" (2:750). One expects monarchs to abuse their power and to be generally depraved: "we are accustom'd to this, and don't wonder at it" (2:751). We do not expect "the most Venerable Part of the Christian Church" to encourage and applaud "so mad a Doctrine as that which authorizes the punishing of those" whose conscience forbids them to convert (2:751–52). Bayle has little doubt regarding the moral worth of Augustine's doctrine of compulsion as practiced in Louis XIV's France. It "is a Heresy in Morality, a practical and most pestilential Heresy, and which, with the Crimes it produces, does more than ballance any mere speculative Falshood" (2:753).

Bayle thus regularly abuses Augustine, whom he regards as a dull, dangerous, and corrupt polemicist with an appalling influence on France and its Protestant minority. As "the great Apologist for Persecution" (2:676) he is scandalous, disingenuous, duplicitous, zealous, malicious, and an inciter of violent hooliganism on behalf "of the booted Apostles of *France*" (2:381). Ever since France infatuated itself with the persecuting spirit, it has had "the Lord knows how many Parasites, mercenary Scriblers, bigotted Flatterers" compiling all the ancient Roman laws against Donatists and other sects. They were egged on by "some of the Fathers of the Church: particularly St. *Austin*, who has written the Apology of Persecution with more Intenseness of Thought, than *Tertullian* that of the Christian Religion" (1:220–21).

Bayle reserves his heaviest fire for the second volume and its dedicated section on Augustine's abundant aberrations. I consider one section in his refutation of Augustine, a portion of his epistle to Vincentius that also was well known in England and in France. Augustine says that he is even more a lover of peace than when he was a young man in Carthage, but the Donatists are so restless that he knows *"that it's fit to restrain 'em by the Authority of the Powers ordain'd by God."* Bayle will have none of this scurvy, dishonest, pitiful, artificial, and fallacious argument, worthy of a dishonest gambler trying to hide "the true state of the Question." Augustine gives the impression that restlessness is the reason for invoking the state's secular arm against the Donatists. In fact, they were peaceably ensconced in their homes. Augustine really wanted the law to force all heretics, "even the most meek and inoffensive," into his church. He does not know "how to write and reason solidly" (2:372–73). Of course the law protects the innocent against oppression and theft, but that was not Augustine's motive or intention. He wanted only to punish the Donatists "in case they persisted in their Opinions" (2:373). He is resolved "to extinguish the Sect, to condemn 'em to these Punishments unless they return to the Catholic Church" (2:374).

The Donatists clearly are a surrogate for Huguenots, and Constantine's laws are clearly a surrogate for Louis XIV's laws and dragoons. Law, we hear in lines just short of Swiftian anger and irony, should function against disturbers of domestic tranquility, against

> only those who scour the Country, plunder Villages and Towns, and rob upon the Highway; they who stir up Seditions in a City; they who smite and buffet their Neighbor, as soon as they have got an advantage of him; in a word, they who won't suffer their Fellow-Citizens to live in the full and peaceable Enjoyment of all their Rights, Privileges, and Property. (2:376)

Bayle inevitably concludes that such conduct is alien to Christianity, reason, and humanity, "insomuch as St. *Austin*'s undertaking the Defence of it is scandalous to the last degree" (2:378).

The title page of the English version says that it is *"Translated from the French of Mr. Bayle, Author of the Great Critical and Historical Dictionary."* That *Dictionary* elaborates upon swipes against other saintly un-Christian persecutors and is part of the international attack upon the church fathers, their disciples, and their authority. The *Commentary* calls Gregory I both a time-server who fathered Louis Maimbourg's anti-toleration histories and a great flatterer rather than the truly "Great" with which he was anointed by his church (1:25, 2:435). He also was all too much in the Augustinian tradition. He approves "the constraining of heretics to return to the church" through *"Compelle intrare* . . . by a rigorous treatment of the obstinate." Bayle's annotated "Reflections," in the sense of harsh criticism, are stern on unthinking solipsist Gregory, that virtual sceptic who used "to turn the rules of morality like a nose of wax." He is allied with Augustine regarding persecution: "Those who propose this alternative, condemn it as a tyrannical action, wherever they are exposed to it themselves; as evident sign, that they only judge of the justice of an action by the rule of their interest." Moreover, if one followed the Augustinian-Gregorian counsel, the church "would have a greater power than is exercised by the most despotic princes. . . . She might punish as a capital crime the change of some ideas." Bayle is aware of Gregory's association with Augustinian cruelty. He not only refers the reader to his own *Philosophical*

Commentary but also reiterates one of its main points regarding violent compulsions for religion: "it is morally impossible but that sovereigns, who authorize them, must be put upon unjust and base measures."[13]

Across the Channel, High Church Anglicans recognized and reinforced Huguenot anger at French compulsion. They nonetheless also sought to differentiate themselves from improper French persecution, presumably unlike their own proper acts of Augustinian tough love. The Restoration church in fact so acted both before and after the French experiences of dragooning and revocation. Such churchmen regarded Protestant schismatics as dangers to their blessedly renewed Christian royal nation. Matthew Hole put it this way in still "High" 1702: divine authority has decreed "Christians *to be of one mind.*" Since those who prosper through division wrongly think otherwise, he seeks to persuade these "Sons of Discord" and "Deceivers" to enter the fold as the Apostle Peter decreed.[14] To be sure, there were variations within the higher church's attitudes toward Augustinian compulsion. On balance, however, most dismissed charges of persecution; compulsion was the right approach by the right religion toward the wrong beliefs in church and state. They had enough of schismatics' antimonarchic dissent, rejected comprehension, and in Augustine found an ally of apparent supreme authority. We recall the 1670 commentator and translator of *The Judgment of the Learned and Pious St. Augustine.* The modern author noted Augustine's great esteem in the church, his final insistence upon effective secular power to serve God's ends in the early fifth century, and the precedent for his own age. Augustine's example should "incourage *AUTHORITY* to persist steadfast in the *EXECUTION* of such *LAWS*, which have in all Ages been so Advantageous to the *Peace* and *Quiet* of *CHURCH* and *STATE*" (A2^{r-v}, italics and roman type reversed).[15]

Many ecclesiastics accommodated and encouraged that view. Along the way they also accommodated both Luke 14:23 and their own history to the history of Augustine's conflict with the schismatic Donatists. For Benjamin Laney, bishop of Ely, failure "to punish them that transgress were to proclaim perpetual *Jubilee*, and set open all prison doors." God has ordained magisterial punishment here and hereafter for disobedience: "For our Saviour in the *Parable* . . . commanded his servants to *Compel them to come in.*" Samuel Parker was comparably troubled. He hoped to stop the spreading "Infection," to encourage "Authority . . . to restrain the Insolence" of Dissenters and atheists. As with the Donatists, faction and sects breed other factions and sects. The solution is clear: there are only some hundred "ignorant and seditious preachers; against whom . . . the severity of the Laws" should be leveled. This soon would "reduce the people to a quiet and peaceable temper" and eliminate schism.[16]

Francis Turner was a relative moderate. For him, in 1676, the magistrate might indeed force open the eyes of a schismatic who blindly refused to see the truth: "this may be done without *dashing* out his brains with a Club." Like the turbulent Donatists, such men should be forced "into our Churches" to hear a proper statement of the proper church's cause. A few years later William Sherlock abandoned Turner's moderate moderation in favor of necessary violence. The magistrate's sword indeed may be vindictive. He acts on behalf of the monarch, who acts on behalf of God "to execute wrath upon him that doth evil."[17]

Thomas Long comparably insists on the magistrate's divine right to force religious cohesion. He even more dramatically supports it with Augustine's example of the wholesome severities that caused the Donatists to come in. Long's *Character of a Separatist* (1677) assumes that mutually supportive church and state are as one. Hence those who "withdraw from the communion of the Church, were professed enemies to the King." When the church loses a congregant the king gains an enemy. Such withdrawal ends "all charitable Opinions, and amicable conversation" toward the separatists. As Augustine rightly argued regarding the Donatists, ministers of the gospel should apply to the minister of the law to force the schismatics back to political and religious truth and unity. No wonder when in 1684 Long delivered a sermon titled *The Original of War* he said that it was "high time to *search out* those Sacrilegious *Achans* and disobedient *Jonahs* that have raised such *Storm*, and *Wars* among us."[18]

Long's *History of the Donatists* (1677) is the fullest English discussion of that group's denigration by Augustine and its analogy with English dissent. The book indeed is fairly punctuated with allusions to its sanctified supporting authority, whose work "the Church of GOD doth now injoy."[19] Augustine knew that the Donatists' schism would lead to atheism and shake "the Foundations of the Church" (p. 42). Donatists thus were heretical Arians (p. 39), violent (p. 44), diabolical (p. 46), instruments of Satan (p. 52), and vandals of Catholic churches and Bibles (p. 56); they excluded themselves from what they knew to be religious truth (p. 57) and misinterpreted the Bible to serve their own schismatic purposes (pp. 58–59). They corrupted almost all the Eastern churches (p. 43) and "did with the more violence prosecute their good old cause" at home (p. 44). The emperor Constantine properly suppressed them and "the Church had a Prospect of Peace and Unity" (p. 51).

An allusion to the "good old cause" makes even clearer the already clear analogy of North African fourth-century Donatists and seventeenth-century English Dissenters. These moderns are not the offspring of primitive Christians but are "acted and animated by the spirit of *Donatus*," to whose "Race" they belong (sig. A3ʳ). They wrongly claim persecution, but in fact they exactly reenacted "every

Scene of that horrid Tragedy" in Africa and indeed "over-acted in the Church of *England*." No one can deny that those who destroyed the established church and its monarch "were the most natural off-spring of those *Donatists*" who vexed Constantine, ravaged the churches, and fostered "the present Sectaries" who diligently follow Donatist practices and continue to bring confusion to the nation (sig. A3ᵛ).

The answer to modern dissent is the same as the answer to ancient dissent that Augustine so well explained. As in Luke 14:23, heretics or schismatics should "be constrained to the Lords Vineyard, by the Power which the Church hath received, ever since Kings received the Christian Faith." They should not fret about being driven by force; they really are driven to where their souls will find "true food, and rest" (p. 127). He who refuses obedience to such benign "Laws made for the truth, deserves a great punishment: See [Augustine] *Epistle* 50" (p. 127). Execution of strict laws restrained the "insolency of the Faction" and established a general "unity and peace . . . in the Church" (p. 149). Force in God's name is neither persecution nor denial of conscience. It is an Augustinian encouragement by fear that allows truth to be heard and received. Long's views were both familiar and soon under siege.

Contexts Changed and Augustine Charged

The national churches on either side of the Channel thus exercised power in what the excluded thought variously brutal persecution. The Church of England now was tarred with a French brush and needed to make distinctions. As the argument goes, it is the true Church of Christ; French papists are the true church of the Antichrist. The Church of England is established by law and has always supported the monarch; Dissenters are beyond the law and have always subverted the monarch. This attempt persuaded few who were not already persuaded. In 1718, for example, Thomas Lucas knew that Jesus detested "that exterminating Spirit." He also knew that there are High Churchmen who "exclaim against external Compulsion in the Papists, but yet have not been free from it themselves." Many of these anti-Romanists have "not been backward . . . to oppress and persecute their innocent Neighbours." Such men rage against George I for protecting Dissenters. Lucas had many allies, including Charles Chauncy across the Atlantic. He too later argues that the High Church was behaving all too like its papist adversary: "The Method of *secular Discipline*" is especially common among tyrannizing clergy who fine, whip, hang, or burn those with a different religious conscience and practice. "The *Right of Private Judgment*" trumps any power of the stirred-up "*civil Magistrates*."[20]

Moderate higher churchmen, latitudinarians, and especially Dissenters thus quarreled with the High Church's *"secular Discipline."* We know that one part of the argument was spurred by effectively communicated French Protestant outrage regarding dragooning and the consequences of the revocation. As with Pierre Bayle's powerful example, this became part of a broadly based attack upon Augustine's moral and theological authority and on the church fathers in general. In 1728, for example, Thomas Gordon added a preface to a partial translation of Jean Barbayrac's hostile *Traité de la morale des pères de l'église*. Gordon denigrates the fathers' importance, relevance, and Christian decency. This turbulent, proud, self-contradictory group, we hear, regularly denounced one another, praised villains, lacked common sense, and scarcely can guide modern behavior. They are largely and deservedly unread. There is little to learn from them, and "they who know much of them, are only esteem'd by such as know little of any Thing." Nothing is more "insolent and dishonest" than to tell us to read the Bible with their guidance. They "were so very ignorant of them, that they almost constantly understood them in every Sense, but the true Sense."[21]

The second and more domestic part of the argument also was a consequence of the first. Namely, Augustine was wrong to say that compulsion in Luke 14:23 denoted the magistrate's sword on behalf of the monarch's will, which embodied God's will. Augustine's divinely anointed monarch was God's ally and a servant of his church. Divine-right theory in Britain, however, was under increasing pressure and was bound to crack. Whatever contract theory's early vilification, it made significant inroads as more Whiggish if aristocratic sources of power emerged in both the Commons and the Lords. James II would pay dearly for blindness to those trends.

One aspect of the trend was gradually increasing Erastianism. Bishop Hoadly was an effect, not a cause, of the fissure between church and state. The church becomes the junior partner, controlled by secular interests often indifferent to matters of the spirit. The Quaker Francis Bugg's *De Christiana Libertate* (1682) argued that since Christ's government "is wholly Spiritual," it cannot "clash with any humane power, because that is the Boundery of it." The anonymous translator of a French lament for the Huguenot eradication from France regarded the High Church as a persecutor because it elevated itself above the state. Its "asserting the Authority of the Church of *England* to be superior to that of the State, is no better than Popery" and too like the French clerical argument against toleration. Thomas Gordon uttered familiar Whig dogma in 1733: The layman's law makes and can unmake a priest. The British constitution recognizes only what the law permits. Parliament could wipe out all priests tomorrow and create new priests the next day if it wished. No "Priests are above the Law and the Laity." The rise of Methodism enhanced the rise of Erastianism. Richard Finch put it this way in 1740: the Act of Toleration came not "from the church, but the state, because inconsistent with the common temper of [High Church Anglican] clergymen."[22] After 1688, and upon the Hanoverian accession, what Jesus and the Apostles would do was less immediate than what ministers like Walpole and the Commons would do. Magistrates had enough business confronting bloody-minded Britons without hauling many thousands of Dissenters off to jail. Given the hostility to a standing army, there were few troops available or perhaps even willing to compel Dissenters to come in. When individuals seemed disloyal or threatening, the law took action, but even Defoe suffered only the soon profitable pillory, soon emerged from bankruptcy, and soon became a government agent in his own right.

Political historians normally regard the 1710 Sacheverell trial for high crimes and misdemeanors as a political embarrassment to Whigs and moderate Tories. Sacheverell apparently both affirmed indefeasible divine right on behalf of the Pretender and attacked William's revolution and Queen Anne's legitimacy. His skillful defense produced a slight penalty and High Church rejoicing, but his outrages nonetheless evoked persuasive counter-outrage, as in Defoe's earlier *Shortest Way with the Dissenters* (1702). Defoe and his muse Sacheverell revealed the uglier side of Altitudinarian zeal. Sacheverell mentioned neither Augustine nor the forced conversion of the Donatists, but he clearly was in that tradition. Defoe of course made plain that such high-flyers gladly would have seen Britain free of Dissenters. This might have been through mass coerced conversions, as with Donatists and Huguenots; mass expulsions, as in Louis XIV's France; or mass murder in God's name, as in the Saint Bartholomew's Day Massacre.[23] In 1718 the Dissenter Thomas Lucas alluded to Sacheverell's virulent *Perils of False Brethren both in Church and State* (1709). Lucas scolded those high Anglicans, who in turn scolded "Men of Temper and Clemency" and banished them from the fold of true Protestant Christians: "They are look'd upon as false Brethren, as Dissenters in disguise, secret Enemies to the Church, and not fit to be trusted with the Management of her Affairs. But 'tis strange that Cruelty and Uncharitableness must be the distinguishing Mark of a true Churchman."[24] So far as many could see, in the earlier eighteenth century Anglican persecution and Gallican persecution were both cognate and attached to biblical interpretation—here, Luke 14:23's "Compel them to come in" to the master's feast.

As we have seen, the evolutionary process of amelioration significantly changed the history of the thirtieth of January sermons. This happened in part thanks to fatigue with often ineffectual rage, the passage of time, the end of a mourning process, and perhaps especially with dynastic change. Such was the case with response to Augustinian force of arms to induce change of heart. A Curate of London put it this way in 1739:

> Since the Accession of the Present Royal Family, this Part of the World has been quieter, with respect to Religion, than at any Time for so long a Period together: I mean, Men have carry'd on their Debates upon Religious Subject, without having been liable to those Terrors, or coercive Operations, that in former times were exerted against those who happen'd to differ with the Majority.[25]

Whether, for the time being, politics changed theology, theology changed politics, or yes and yes, is for wiser heads than mine to determine. We can determine that the politics of theology inverted the Augustinian and French concepts of "coercive Operations" in religious commitment.

Happy Had His Works Not Been Preserved

Commentators could offer reasonably respectful correction of a church father, but correction nonetheless. In 1669 John Crump glossed *The Parable of the Great Supper* and its key line. Compulsion may be either magisterial or ministerial. "St. Augustine useth this for the Magistrate's compelling his subjects to the worship of God; but this cannot be so meant here," for the commission is to the minister. That commission is disciplinary and applies to those who already are within the church and need correction. It cannot apply to the parable in Luke, whose guests are outside of the church. Such compulsion therefore must be doctrinal. Compel by "the strength of argument, and the force of perswasion" that overcomes the reluctant soul. This distinction became part of regular discourse concerning Luke, as in Matthew Poole's late seventeenth-century *Annotations Upon the Holy Bible*, and by Ralph Erskine in 1739. For Poole, Christ spoke to "the Ministers of the Gospel," who neither then nor ever had magisterial power. For Erskine as for Crump, "It is not a magisterial, but a ministerial Compulsion." The ministers had "no Civil Power committed to them." Though Peter Needham does not so distinguish, he insists that Augustine and his followers "very improperly" used the text to justify violence and were "mistaken ... both in the Sense and Application of this passage of Scripture."[26]

Marginally respectful engagement was too laced with anger long to flourish. The dominant attitude toward Augustine on Luke became harsh and, as in Pierre Bayle, often rude and damning. The father and Father of persecution was increasingly alien to a post-William age. Growing numbers of British subjects then would celebrate their partial, if often resisted, vilified but transforming Act of Toleration, against which they also often set the horrors of French persecution.

Such celebrants had friends on both sides of the Channel and on both sides of the Irish Sea. They joined the international Protestant quarrel with Augustinian moral and theological authority.

Augustine, after all, suffered the dual burden of being resolutely papist and, we have seen, the modern intellectual authority for persecution of presumed heretics in Catholic countries. Complaints regarding repressive conversion by blood, confiscation, expulsion, fire, galley, jail, perjury, racks, slaughter, terror, and torture unsurprisingly evoked the intellectual source of such aberration. Peter Needham in 1716 lamented Augustine's misreading of the Gospel and excoriated the consequences. This was the "Foundation" of "that abominable super-structure of Perjury and Blood so often and so zealously employed for the Conversion of Hereticks." Matthew Clarke was comparably outraged by papists, who "justify themselves in these inhumane proceedings" by distorting the text. They became both absurd and trifling "for compelling mens consciences by outward force in the matters of religion." In the year of Francis Atterbury's trial, the dissenting minister William Sheppard urged his parishioners to embrace Christian love and charity. Sheppard adapted Bayle on Luke 14:23 and scolded both the High Church and Augustine for violating those virtues by compulsion, persecution, and even inquisition. Augustine himself "was so carried away both from reason and scripture." He was sophistical, childish, persecuting, and brought "a great blot upon his memory, as to the defect both of his wisdom and temper." He also enabled the "butcherly proceedings . . . to vindicate" the revocation of the Edict of Nantes and "all its horrid consequences." When by midcentury Andrew Gordon in Aberdeen described the horrors of punitive conversion, he did not need overtly to cite Augustine on Luke 14:23. The power of association and a later footnote to Pierre Bayle's *Commentaire philosophique* did the job for him. The biblical words have been twisted into un-Christian meaning and "used as a divine Warrant to *burn the Bodies* of Men, because they would not make *Shipwreck of their Souls*."[27]

Perhaps the most damning British remarks, however, came from what may be called the Church over the Waters. In 1685 Gilbert Burnet feared that James II's religious and political policies would harm both England and its national church. He voluntarily removed himself to Europe and finally to Holland and the more religiously and politically sympathetic ear of William of Orange, whose chaplain he would become as William crossed the Channel in 1688: "When he found I was in my opinion for toleration, he said, that was all he would ever desire to bring us to, for quieting our contentions at home."[28] While on the Continent he also saw what he called "that dismal tragedy, which was at this time acted in *France*." It was "one of the most violent persecutions that is to be found in history." Like others, he predicted its repetition in England under James II, when a spurious Declaration of Indulgence would empower "Popery . . . till it should be strong enough to set on a general persecution."[29]

Persecution indeed is the key term and concept with which Burnet is concerned. He adds *"a large Preface concerning Persecution"* to his translation of Lactantius' *Relation Of the Death of the Primitive Persecutors* (1687) for its Amsterdam publication. The preface reappears in the following, fateful year in London as *The Case of Compulsion In Matters of Religion Stated*. Burnet makes plain that in Augustine's case sanctity was not synonymous with probity. "All Persecution," Burnet begins, "rises out of an impatience of Spirit, which makes a man less able to bear Contradiction." Men are tyrannical by nature and seek to subdue others by strength of reasoning. They have "an implacable hatred to all that do not render themselves to their Reasons" and think themselves affronted by refusal to submit. To arrest this destructive zeal, one must "endeavour to soften men, especially toward those who differ from them in matters of Religion."[30] Augustine thus appears within a context of un-Christian hatred, irrational offense toward those with whom he disagrees, impatience, and tyranny in need of softening. He exemplified that severity in his attitude toward the Donatists. They long were unruly, and laws against them finally were executed with such rigor that even Augustine and other bishops interceded with the magistrates to urge restraint. Though he condemned the excess "in some particulars, he set himself to justify severity in General, when it was imployed upon the account of Religion." This immoderate conduct wrongly distanced him from colleagues like Tertulian, Cyprian, and Lactantius, whose wisdom "in a great measure [he] forgot" (pp. 10–11).

Augustine's overheated imagination and allegorizing bent reflect his human impatience. He brought "together a vast number of proofs for every cause that he undertook; without troubling himself to examine critically what the true meaning of those Passages might be." His excessive reasoning was off the mark, and his rhetoric was too full and "uncorrected." Hence "it is no wonder to find that Passage in our Saviour in the Parable, *Compel them to enter in*, with some other Places misapplied on this occasion" (p. 11).

Hostile Augustine thinks poorly, writes poorly, and interprets poorly. Those influenced by him must be equally erroneous. "With that Father the Learning of the *Western Church* fell very low." He was the most read of the church fathers, but that was a destructive popularity: "Men that knew not how to reason themselves, contented themselves with that lazy and cheap way of copying from him, and of depending on his Authority" (p. 11). Such dependence helped to induce revocation of the Edict of Nantes and the terror, death, expulsion, and general violence that Protestant Europe so remembered. Burnet's investigation of the human and the

Augustinian heart of the matter found cardiac corruption and a morally corrupt posterity.

Burnet's essay began its life in Amsterdam. A comparable, even angrier effort began in Dublin several years later. Edward Synge came from a distinguished Church of Ireland family. His father became archbishop of Tuam, and his younger brother, bishop of Killaloe. Edward himself would be translated to the bishopric first of Confert, then of Cloyne, and finally of Ferns and Leighlin. The prominent family had its own burial vault in Saint Patrick's Cathedral, Dublin. On 23 October 1725 Synge addressed the Irish House of Commons in a sermon titled *The Case of Toleration consider'd*. It is in the familiar tradition of the occasional sermon, in which theology is subordinate to politics, here the conflict between Protestant rulers within a mistrusted Catholic majority. It is made more complex by Synge's thoughtful consideration of the private right to worship and the public's right to security. The sermon's title also points us toward its main issue: to what degree may either a church or a state persecute those who are not of the national religion?

Synge mistrusts and dislikes the ambitious, resentful, and often disloyal many believers in "the *Romish* Religion." They always have "shewn themselves Enemies to the Establish'd Government, as well Civil as Religious."[31] The wise legislature thus has passed laws designed to weaken them and to control their power. What right, however, does either the church or state have to compel them to come into the Anglican Church, "To *reform* and bring them back to a right Faith and Mind"? (p. 6). If they do not so reform, should they be severely punished with "*wholesome Severities*"? (p. 4). Those who argue in the affirmative base their argument on Augustine and the power of the divinely appointed church. Synge virtually paraphrases the relevant portion of Augustine's letter to Vincentius while also adapting it to the French experience:

> To prove the Right of punishing Corporally in order to *Reformation*, they insist often on the Words of the Text, *Compel them to come in*, which they, following the Authority of St. *Austin*, explain so, as to favour the greatest Severities, Fines Imprisonment, Dragooning, Banishment, every thing but Death. (Pp. 6–7)

The divine office requires their "power of Coercion," the severities are useful and necessary to make the violent schismatics see reason, and they are equally useful "in converting Numbers who have been in Error, and bringing them back to the bosom of the Catholick Church." Those who are incorrigible may have "Capital Punishments" properly inflicted on them (p. 7). Synge is demonstrably troubled, and perhaps doubly so because "in this Doctrine several Protestants have unhappily agreed" with the Augustinian-Catholic view. The more extreme among the extremists "have even maintained a *Coercive Power* over the Prince, if he refuses to extirpate a *false Religion*." Some Protestant churches may argue regarding who is a heretic, but they are too willing to kill "those who refuse to believe them, or believe the opposite Doctrines." Hence, "concerning the use of Force in Matters of Religion, they do in all Points agree with those of the Church of *Rome*" (p. 8).

This prebendary of Saint Patrick's and chaplain to the Lord Lieutenant—John, baron as he then was, Carteret—rejects such notions, whether based on Augustinian priestly, Hobbesian civil, or Sachevrellian High Church power to compel. Like Bayle, whose arguments Synge adapts, he knows that justifying Protestant extirpation of Catholics authorizes Catholic extirpation of Protestants or Muslim extirpation of Christians. Synge again labels the source of such dangerous folly: "To say with St. *Austin* and the Church of *Rome*, that 'tis Lawful for the *Church* to persecute *Hereticks*, but that it is not so for *Hereticks* to persecute the *Church*," or that the magistrate of the true church may persecute the false church, but not vice versa, "is plainly absurd" (p. 16). The authority of the church fathers is irrelevant, but if it were relevant, the oldest and the best did not support such stuff. Synge isolates Augustine as the chief perpetrator of a horrid doctrine. Its argument on force is not supported in the text, by the fathers prior to Augustine, or by biblical analogies. "Compel them to come in" evidently means "*strong and vehement Perswasions* and other endeavours" that might lead the recalcitrant to Christian belief (p. 19).

Synge offers an essential and familiar distinction regarding coexisting Catholics and Protestants. All those whose religious principles "have no Tendency to hurt the Publick, have a Right to a *Toleration*." They may worship God according to their conscience "without any *Encouragement* from the Civil Government on the one Hand, or *Fear of Infliction of Punishment*" on the other (p. 21). Assuming that Catholics are good subjects, they have both a legal and a practical right to toleration. The church's power is spiritual. It may excommunicate. It may not inflict temporal punishment (p. 20). Augustine, the persecuting Church of Rome, and the persecuting churches of England or of Ireland are ominously wrong.

Some of Synge's readers were not amused by his harsh characterization of Augustine and of toleration elastic enough to include Catholics. A nominal Weaver was abusive, and the author of *An Excellent New Song, To a good Old Tune* ([Dublin], 1726) was both abusive and obscene. Stephen Radcliffe's *Letter To the Reverend Mr. Edward Synge* (1725) was more thoughtful but clearly was outraged by each part of Synge's approach. The sermon was especially offensive when delivered to commemorate the Irish Rebellion, in which papists sought "the utter Extermination of our Religion and Government."[32] Radcliffe knows that toleration for Catholics is suicidal, that Augustine's way was preferable, that it was approved in other biblical passages and by other fathers before him, and that *compel* indeed meant "force." Augustine was an *"ancient and venerable Father,"* insults to whom could only please the Church of Rome. He certainly was not absurd (p. 11). One should not mimic "the *Romish Church*, [with] the utmost and greatest Severities, yet certainly moderate and wholesome Restraints are necessary, and justifiable." Augustine was in the mainstream, and Synge was high and dry: "sure in no Sense, or Construction of the Words, was *compel them to come in*, ever made use of by any Author, to signify, indulge, or tolerate them" (p. 13). Christian, that is, Anglican, magistrates rightly say that if you do not choose to come in, God has authorized us "to reduce you to such Difficulties and Straits, as may *compel* you to come in, and worship God after the manner he has prescribed in his Word" (p. 14).

Synge in turn thought that Radcliffe, like his patristic guide, was all wet. Synge's long reply again associates Augustine and *"moderate and wholesome Restraints"* with Louis XIV's brutality against Huguenots.[33] Look at the French apologists for those acts and "you'll scarce find one, who does not urge the Authority of St. *Austin*, both in favour of these Cruelties, and of that Exposition which 'twas for their purpose to give of this Text" (p. 18). Synge reiterates several of his earlier points regarding Augustinian and Catholic misinterpretation of Luke 14:23 as "the main Support of a false and destructive Opinion," whose "Deformity" he exposed (p. 10). Alas, "That St. *Austin* was an Advocate for Persecution, this is too notorious to need much Proof" (p. 15). Such advocacy "has been Employ'd to the Ruin of Thousands of innocent Men" (p. 19). In an outburst consistent with Bayle and worthy of Voltaire, Synge excoriates both Augustine and his enabler Radcliffe:

> I think it had been in the whole, happy for the Christian World, that his Works had not been preserv'd; because all the Good which his best Writings have done or will do to the End of the World, is vastly over-ballanc'd by the Mischief he has already occasion'd, by this one wrong Opinion of the Lawfulness of Persecution, on Account of Errors in Religion. And so I have for the present done with St. *Austin*, and with his and your Exposition of the Text. (P. 20)

If the eighteenth century was Augustinian, as regards persecution it was an Augustine red in tooth and claw. In such a case, most British clergymen would as soon have been vegetarians. Many also would have seconded the anti-Augustinian author of an attack upon Thomas Sherlock's vindication of the Test Act: his arguments were "nothing but the old decay'd Foundations on which false Zeal erected her Slaughter-house many Ages since."[34] The more benign interpretation of "Compel them to come in" was closer to Synge's, was rooted in seventeenth-century biblical commentary that was enhanced during the eighteenth century, became orthodox, and would reflect a multifaceted eighteenth-century evolutionary and educational process. Britons learned that toleration was difficult and dangerous but that intolerance was more difficult and more dangerous. Persuasion had to replace coercion.

Persuade Them to Come In

Dozens of sermons and commentators from the mid-seventeenth to the later eighteenth century confirm that compulsion in Luke 14:23 can only mean Christian ministerial love. It is exercised through persuasion and the promise of sublime happiness in salvation. Even relatively moderate High Churchmen shared this view. Henry Hammond's 1653 paraphrase, for example, characterizes Luke's call to heathens and sinners, who were "importunately woo'd to come to that feast." Matthew Hole's *Practical Discourses* (1714–16) agrees that penalties "may be useful in many Cases, and in some necessary" to bring the reluctant into the feast; but compulsion "by Persuasion" is more desirable.[35]

The most vocal and numerous members of the chorus were the increasingly powerful Latitudinarians and Dissenters. Daniel Whitby assumed several religious postures during his career, but he was predominantly a Latitudinarian Whig. His *Paraphrase and Commentary on the New Testament* (1700) both dismisses the Augustinian version and urges friendly concern in the act of compulsion: "How vainly these Words are brought, to prove that Men may be compelled by the secular Arm to embrace the true Faith." A host does not invite a dinner guest by force, "but only by the Importunity of Persuasion." One compels "not only by Example, but by Exhortation" on behalf "of God's great Power to make the *Gentiles* believe." Nicholas Brady shared Jacobite and High Church sympathies until his perhaps opportunistic conversion to William's political and religious dispensation. His sermon on Luke 14:23 shows no such fluctuation. Like Whitby before him, Brady defines his own position by contrast with Augustine's and his followers'. Compulsion cannot mean corporal force or violence: "some, I know, have wrested this Text, to patronize it by that unchristian Practice of making Converts with Fire and Faggot." No: "the Force which he used was that of Argument and Persuasion." These are the only methods by which "we must compel the Irreligious to come in." The learned Whig Peter Needham both agrees and blames Augustine and his successors for violation of moral truth. Physical compulsion violates Christianity, reason, and human decency. It leads to "the horrid Effects and Consequences that may, and in a great measure must, attend it."[36]

Dissenters of various sorts were especially keen to reject the monarch's and the magistrate's limits upon conscience and freedom of practice. John Owen left the Church of England in favor of independent Presbyterian principles, which he preached and practiced on Oliver Cromwell's behalf. After the Restoration, he wrote works like *Indulgence and Toleration Considered* (1667), which argued for toleration in the face of High Church resurgence. Like others thereafter, Owen confronted Samuel Parker's demands for unity at whatever cost. Owen's *Insolence and Impudence triumphant* (1669) labels Parker as savage, cruel, and profane: he incites "the Magistrates to the utter Extirpation of Phanaticks; telling them its much safer *to tolerate Open Debaucheries, than Liberty of Conscience.* Urging far severer Laws against Nonconformists." Parker lacks both Christian and ministerial love.[37] As with the thirtieth of January sermons, Dissenters believed that the higher the church, the higher the danger not merely to their version of Christianity but also to the very concept of Christ as loving, universal savior.

Owen the Presbyterian was joined by a heterogeneous group that included Baptists, Quakers, and freethinking laymen more concerned with politics than with theology. Their shared views included hostility to Roman Catholicism, to coercion through Spanish racks, French dragoons, or episcopal establishment restraints upon liberty of conscience, and to the imposition of the church's business upon the state. Luke 14:23 fit these concerns.

The Baptist Benjamin Keach, for example, urged that the evangelist could not mean physical force: "Our Lord never taught any *Spanish* Conversion, nor *French* Conversion; not to Dragoon them, or by inhumane Cruelties, to compel them against their Consciences; No," he says with words that often appear, "this is of the Devil, and not of Christ." A few years later the Quaker Thomas Ellwood reinforced and enlarged upon the spirit of Keach's familiar remarks. Of course violence was utterly inappropriate, since there must be *"kind Invitations"* to a feast. From a practical point of view, those lolling about in highways and hedges did not need to "be *dragged by force,* or *driven by Blows to a good Supper.*" Ellwood was more threatening than his literal-minded approach suggests. He used a relativist, antigovernment, and antipapist logical tactic. If it was right to compel men to the Good, who was to say what the Good was? Those being compelled were not likely to accept the goodness of what they refused to do because they thought it was Bad. If the compellers determined the Good, then even the Bad might be defined as Good, and those compelled might be forced to receive the Bad as Good. Go higher than the magistrate to the Christian monarch, a term with which all European princes anoint themselves, and we are in a dreadful ethical drama several of whose ugly acts already have played themselves out. If every Christian prince may, and indeed, as in charity to others' souls,

> ought to compel Men to that which he judges good, what hinders then but he, whose Ancestors received from *Rome* the Title of, *Most Christian King,* and who

professeth himself a *Son of the Church of* Rome, lawfully *may*, yea *must* (according to this Position) both as his *own Duty*, and as an Act of *necessary Charity* to their Souls, compel all *Protestants* in his Dominions to the *Romish* Religion, which he judges good? Thus, Reader, thou seest the horrid Consequences of this false and *Antichristian* Position.[38]

The Church of England's attempt forcefully to convert Dissenters implicitly justified the Edict of Nantes' revocation and compelled conversion of brother Protestants. In fact, neither the monarch nor the monarch's agents had the right to impose their religion upon peaceful subjects. A fellow Quaker, Richard Claridge, put it this way when discussing Luke in about 1726: it is "a most unreasonable Thing to constrain a Man by Pecuniary or Corporal Penalties, to worship in a Way that is against his own Judgment and Conscience, and an Abomination in the Sight of God." Gospel worship "should be Voluntary" and not subject to magisterial violence.[39] Quakers were among the several Protestant sects glad to affirm or swear loyalty to the crown and glad to be left alone to worship without the established church's established coercion.

They were joined by hostile lay commentators pleased to savage the trinity of the Anglican High Church, its Gallican papist neighbor, and its parent Church of Rome. Matthew Tindal's "Of the Powers of the Magistrate, and the Rights of Mankind, in Matters of Religion" does not overtly mention Luke 14:23. That long essay in *Four Discourses* (1709) nonetheless is based on responses to it and to Augustine as paterfamilias of magisterial power in religion.[40] Defenders of any persecution, Tindal says, enable all persecution, including that directed toward themselves. Any argument they frame to justify force on their own behalf is easily marshaled to justify force on another persecuting religion's behalf: "As we find the loose Harangues of St.* *Austin* upon that Subject are urg'd by the Patrons of Persecution, of what Sect or Denomination soever" (p. 158). The asterisk asks us to "*See Mr.* Bayle's *Philosophical Commentary on those Words of the Gospel,* Compel 'em to come in, *lately* [1708] *publish'd in English,* Vol. 2d" (p. 158n). Like Bayle, but without his religious belief, Tindal excoriates the spirit of persecutors who are diabolical (p. 166), induce hypocrisy (p. 188), and confuse carnal with spiritual Christian weapons (p. 188). Persecutors will turn brutal crimes into "religious and vertuous Actions," so that "'twou'd be an Act of Piety and Vertue to make use of pious Frauds to calumniate, to lye, to bear false Witness, to murder, to assassinate even the Magistrate himself" (p. 164).

We recall Ammianus Marcellinus' *Res gestae libri XXXI*. Julian there knows "from experience that no wild beasts are such enemies to mankind as are most of the Christians in their deadly hatred of one another."[41] Whether or not Tindal had that passage in mind, he shares its sentiments regarding the sadly metamorphic powers of persecution: Anti-Christian persecution "has transform'd the mild and sociable Nature of Man into greater Ferocity than that of Wolves and Tigers." Men who merely followed their consciences will resent persecution to them as individuals and to their entire sect. They must therefore regard such overlords as "their mortal Enemys," for they attack without provocation and "endeavour to force 'em to ruin themselves eternally." Victims are likely in turn to persecute their tormentors should they have the chance. Men gradually "arrive to the height of Fury, Rage and Madness" and break the ties of Christianity and of humanity. The consequences and conflict are terrible for society and its members, who so powerfully provoke "endless Discords, Hatreds, Factions, Wars, Massacres." They nonetheless regularly mouth "the Good of the Church and Salvation of Souls" and forget that love and charity are necessary for Christ's disciples and for Christianity. Yet worse, they "tempt Men to make themselves miserable hereafter, to avoid being so here." Persecutors force their victims either to "continue all their Lives under Persecution, (which who can support?) or else buy their temporal Quiet, with the loss of their Eternal Happiness" (p. 156).

This is not mere anger. It is rage addressed to the consequences of Augustine's "loose Harangues" for collective and individual humanity. As we have seen, that paternal saint's shade suffered more severe attacks upon his legacy, and from sources that could not be dismissed as the rant of a freethinker trying to justify his self-exclusion from the true church. By 1727, and throughout the century, few British clergymen of any denomination would have disagreed with Matthew Clarke's more benign reading of Luke 14:23. Compulsion there means "a rational moral Perswasion," and not external force and its Roman-French "fire and faggot, jayls and galleys." Thanks to a loving benevolent God, man is a free agent capable of reason and understanding, "and therefore beating out his brains can never be the way to bring him to his senses."[42]

Adopt Men From All the Nations of the Earth: Equiano's Conversion

We see the developed orthodoxy of compulsion as Christian love, spiritual engagement, and conversion in Olaudah Equiano's *Interesting Narrative* (1789). By then, the wisdom of the French Jansenist Le Père Pasquier Quesnel, the English Dissenter Isaac Watts, and the founding Methodist John Wesley, among others, had been absorbed into the debate. For Quesnel, Luke 14:23 meant, "Lord, draw to you our rebellious Hearts, do to us that Violence which does not force nor necessitate our Wills, but delivers forces and cures them." For Watts on the same text,

Christ's place within the hall was sweet, awe inspiring, the home of "everlasting Love," and the "Food for dying Souls":

> 'Twas the same Love that spred the Feast,
> That sweetly forc'd us in,
> Else we had still refus'd to tast,
> And perish'd in our Sin.

For Wesley, "Compel them to come in" had to mean "With all the Violence of Love, and the Force of GOD's Word. Such compulsion, and such only, in Matters of Religion, was used by *Christ* and his Apostles."[43]

These remarks and the numerous comparable sermons emphasize "such *Goodness*" through "an invitation of men to a *Feast*" of salvation.[44] That is Equiano's experience. He grieves about his own sinful life and begs for God's mercy, time to repent, and a cleansing place beyond his wicked sailors' lodging. Fortunately, he meets "an old sea-faring man" who proclaims "the love of Christ" with remarkable clarity (p. 183). He then is joined by a dissenting minister, probably either a lay preacher or an ordained Methodist who has withdrawn from the Church of England. The minister recognizes Equiano's Anglican places of worship and invites the "churchman" to a love feast at his chapel that evening. The scene enacts Luke 14:23, in which the master's servant calls sinners from the highways and the hedges and lovingly compels them to join the feast. Equiano indeed mentions *feast* four times and *banquet* once (pp. 183–84). The chapel is "filled with people" whose prayers and songs nourish Equiano's soul: "my heart was attracted, and my affections were enlarged. . . . I was entirely overcome, and wished to live and die thus" (p. 184).

The congregants soon add real food to the dissenting Protestant spiritual feast. The meal is not a lord's supper of bread and wine, appropriate for either the Roman or the Anglican Church. Instead, the minister and his flock share "neat baskets full of buns" and "water out of different mugs." Equiano acknowledges both the ceremony's novelty and its antiquity. He had never before seen such "Christian fellowship," which was like "what I had read in the Holy Scriptures of the primitive Christians, who loved each and broke bread." The soul feast leaves him with a desire "to win Heaven, if possible" (p. 184). Here is Quesnel's divine forcing and curing of the heart, Watts' "Love that spreads the Feast," Wesley's "Force of GOD's Word," Samuel Clarke's belief that the persuasive Gospel will "adopt Men from all the Nations of the Earth," and Matthew Clarke's insistence upon showing and sharing benefits. He notes "the happiness of those that are enabled to comply with this call, and accept the invitation, that is given to this feast."[45]

Equiano's brief conversion narrative mirrors the larger conversion interpretation of Luke 14:23. It moves from a slightly ameliorated *exterminate the brutes* with the magistrate's laws or swords to an emphatic *reform the sinners with the Bible's love*. That conversion in turn mirrors a broader British conversion. The century moves from Augustinian repression, so well exemplified in Louis XIV's revocation of the Edict of Nantes, to the Anglican High Church's variously successful coercive attempts to eliminate occasional conformity, but without France's bloody dragooning, and then to practical extensions of the Act of Toleration. Some consequences of such theological and intellectual change even included a movement to eliminate Quaker tithing, frontal attacks upon Augustine's moral authority, and the consequent redefinition of "Compel them to come in." The journey was scarcely so neat, consecutive, or, even granting Bayle's extensive French and Synge's briefer Irish outbursts, apparently anodyne as this summary suggests. There was plenty of heavy weather along the way, but Equiano's later eighteenth-century experience with Protestant Dissenters was made possible by more than one hundred years of evolutionary changes. These combined changes finally produced an intellectual, moral, theological, and political revolution that helped to produce a new national consensus. Methodists were included in this ongoing process of reconsidering the nature of humanity and humanity's response to its own capacity for evil, so well expressed in the turmoil of religious and political disruption. Methodism's birth, experience of turmoil, and gradual acceptance closely parallel comparable movements in the thirtieth of January sermon and Luke 14:23. Its growing pains also were comparably painful.

NOTES

1. [Vincent Alsop], *Melius Inquirendum. Or A Sober Inquiry Into the Reasonings of the Serious Inquiry: Wherein The Inquirers Cavils against the Principles, his Calumnies against the Preachings and Practices of the Non-Conformists Are Examined and Refelled, And St. Augustine, the Synod of Dort, and the Articles of the Church of England in the Quinquarticular points, vindicated* (London, 1679), p. 49. Alsop was a Presbyterian, and his style often suggests irony rather than explicit meaning. He responds to John Goodman's *A Serious and Compassionate Inquiry Into the Causes of the present Neglect and Contempt of the Protestant Religion and Church of England*, 3rd ed. (London, 1675). Goodman is tactful but nonetheless insists that the way to induce peace and respect is for Dissenters to abandon scruples and join the Church of England. [Herbert Croft], *The Naked truth. Or, The True State of the Primitive Church. By an Humble Moderator* ([London], 1675), p. 13.

I gratefully acknowledge my debt to Mark Goldie in this chapter. See his "The Theory of Religious Intolerance in Restoration England," in *From Persecution to Toleration: The Glorious Revolution and Religion in England*, ed. Ole Peter Grell, Jonathan I. Israel, and Nicholas

"Compel Them to Come In," Luke 14:23   171

Tyacke (Oxford: Clarendon Press, 1991), pp. 331–68. He begins with a sad truth: "Restoration England was a persecuting society" (p. 331). He adds that "it is difficult for the modern liberal mind to grasp that intolerance was ever anything other than the product of unthinking bigotry" (p. 332). He hopes to show the theological basis of Restoration, perhaps really later seventeenth-century High Church, arguments on persecution. "Thinking bigotry," however, is scarcely preferable to "unthinking bigotry."

2. *Glossographia Anglicana Nova: Or, A Dictionary, Interpreting Such Hard Words of whatever Language, as are at present used in the English Tongue* (London, 1707), s.v. "Donatists"; Ephraim Chambers, *Cyclopædia: Or, An Universal Dictionary of Arts and Sciences*, 4th ed. (London, 1741), s.v. "Donatists." Standard church histories discuss these sects, but see also Brent D. Shaw, "Who Were the Circumcellions?" and W. H. C. Frend, "From Donatists Opposition to Byzantine Loyalism: The Cult of Martyrs in North Africa 350–650," in *Vandals, Romans and Berbers: New Perspectives on Late Antique North Africa*, ed. A. H. Merrills (Aldershot, Hants, UK: Ashgate, 2004), pp. 227–58 and 259–70, respectively.

3. George Meldrum, in his *Sermon Preached in the New Church of Edinburgh, on Sabbath, May 16, 1703* (Edinburgh, 1703), was especially harsh on schism in church and state; see pp. 10–14. [John Sage], *A Brief Examination Of some Things in Mr. Meldrum's Sermon Preach'd May 16. Against Toleration To Those of the Episcopal Perswasion. In a Letter to a Friend* ([Edinburgh?], 1703), e.g., pp. 6–8. For Meldrum's reply to another attack, see *A Defence of the Vindication Of Mr. Meldrum's Sermon Against a Second Assault of the Examiner* (Edinburgh, 1704), pp. 26–27. *Light out of Darkness: Or, A Dialogue Between Mr. Currie and a Country-Man* (Edinburgh, 1741), p. 10. Early Methodists also were accused of being Donatists. See *A Short History of the Donatists. With an Appendix, In which The proud and Hypocritical Pharisee and Schismatical Donatists are compared with the Rev. Mr. George Whitefield and the Methodists* (London, 1741), pp. vii, 23–24. Augustine, we read, was pleased that, thanks to severe laws against the Donatists, his city of Hippo "was as much united in *Catholic Unity*, as if there had never been a Schism in that Place" (p. 24).

4. *The Judgment of the Learned and Pious St. Augustine, concerning Penal Lawes against Conventicles, and for Unity in Religion. Deliver'd in His 48th Epistle to Vincentius* (London, 1670), sig. A2^{r-v} (hereafter cited parenthetically in the text). An anonymous British Whig author characterized the French union of church and state in unflattering terms that reflect upon Augustine and other persecutors. That malign arrangement, he says, also suggests the aims of the Anglican High Church: from 1614, the French "King and Clergy have proceeded by Concert and Combination, *the King to sacrifice the Protestants to the Clergy, the Clergy to sacrifice the Liberties of the Nation to the King*." See *An Account Of the Conduct of the Roman-Catholick Clergy and Zealots of France, From the First Toleration of the Protestants, to Their Expulsion* (London, 1710), p. 132; see also pp. 133–34.

5. Antoine Arnaud, *Traduction du livre des Augustin des moeurs de l'eglise catholique* (Paris, 1720), sig. iiij^{r-v}; [Pierre Bayle], *Ce que c'est que la France toute catholique, sous le regne de Louis le Grand* ([Saint-Omer?], 1686), p. 4. The work comprises three parts: (1) a French abbé writes to a Huguenot woman who has fled to London; (2) a violent letter to the abbé by another Protestant refugee; and (3) the response by the abbé, from which I quote. The angry Huguenot tells the abbé that using force "selon la maxime de l'Evangile, *contrain les d'entrer*, en commençant par le Roi" has caused "mille meurtres, désolations, & guerres

civiles," among other horrid aberrations (p. 101). See also Bayle's larger response in the *Commentaire philosophique* within.

6. For Fontenelle and the contest, see Jules Chavannes, "Le protestantisme français et l'Académie française," *Bulletin de la société de l'histoire protestantisme français* 4 (1856): 607. The prize poems are reprinted in *Pieces de poësie, qu on remporté le prix de l'Académie, 1671–1747* (Paris, 1747). Neither the content nor the style do much credit to the Académie's judgment. I have not been able to locate Fontenelle's effort. Houdar de la Motte, *Reflexions sur la critique. . . . Avec plusieurs autres ouvrages*, 2nd ed. (Paris, 1716), p. xxx of new pagination. André Dacier, like his distinguished wife, Anne le Fèvre Dacier, a recent convert to Catholicism, also warmly praised Louis XIV as God's minister who made his people happy by removing them from a hereditary error and turning their darkness to light. See his initiation discourse in *Recueil des harangues prononcé par messieurs de l'Académie française dans leurs receptions . . . depuis l'establissement de l'Académie jusqu'à présent* (Paris, 1698), pp. 732–40. Geoffrey Adams' *Huguenots and French Opinion, 1685–1787: The Enlightenment Debate on Toleration* (Waterloo, ON: Wilfred Laurier University Press, 1991) is useful on such matters; see esp. pp. 19–33. The French intellectual elite welcomed the revocation and regarded it as a way to flatter Louis XIV, regain court favor, and improve their careers (p. 30).

7. Louis Maimbourg, *Histoire du calvinisme* (Paris, 1686), sig. eii^{r-v} (hereafter cited parenthetically in the text). The work evoked significant response from offended Protestants and their Dutch publishing arms. See esp. Pierre Bayle, *Critique générale de l'Histoire du calvinisme de M. Maimbourg* ([Amsterdam], 1682); Jean Rou, *Remarques sur l'Histoire du calvinisme de M. Maimbourg* (The Hague, 1682); and Pierre Jurieu, *Histoire du calvinisme & celle du papisme mises en parallèle . . . contre un libelle intitulé, l'Histoire du Calvinisme par M. Maimbourg* (Rotterdam, 1683). There is of course abundant secondary literature upon Bayle, French Protestantism, and the revocation of the Edict of Nantes. Among other texts, see Elisabeth Labrousse's two-volume *Pierre Bayle* (The Hague: M. Nijhoff, 1963–64), translated by Denys Potts as *Bayle* (Oxford: Oxford University Press, 1983); Walter Rex, *Essays on Pierre Bayle and Religious Controversy* (The Hague: M. Nijhoff, 1965); Elizabeth Israels Perry, *From Theology to History: French Religious Controversy and the Revocation of the Edict of Nantes* (The Hague: M. Nijhoff, 1973); Elisabeth Labrousse, *Essai sur la révocation de l'Edit de Nantes* (Geneva: Labor et Fides; Paris: Payot, 1985); Gerald Cerny, *Theology, Politics, and Letters at the Crossroads of European Civilization: Jacques Basnage and the Baylean Huguenot Refugees in the Dutch Republic* (The Hague: M. Nijhoff, 1987); John Kilcullen, *Sincerity and Truth: Essays on Arnauld, Bayle, and Toleration* (Oxford: Clarendon Press, 1988); Michelle Magdelaine, Maria-Cristina Pitassi, Ruth Whelan, and Antony McKenna, eds., *De l'humanisme aux Lumières: Bayle et le protestantisme: mélanges en l'honneur d' Elisabeth Labrousse* (Paris: Universitas; Oxford: Voltaire Foundation, 1996); Thomas Lennon, *Reading Bayle* (Toronto: University of Toronto Press, 1999); and Ruth Whelan and Carol Baxter, eds., *Toleration and Religious Identity: The Edict of Nantes and its Implication in France, Britain and Ireland* (Dublin: Four Courts, 2003).

8. Louis Maimbourg, *Histoire du calvinisme*, new ed. (Paris, 1682), p. 505.

9. [Gilbert Burnet], "A Relation of the Massacres of the Protestants, begun in Paris, and carried on over all France, in the Year 1572," (1678), in [Gilbert Burnet], *A Vindication of the Ordinations of the Church of England*, 2nd ed. (London, 1728), 1:31, also reprinted in

volume 1 of Burnet's *Collection of Several Tracts and Discourses Written in the Years 1677 to 1704* (London, 1704); a Huguenot on English hostility to France, *The Last Efforts of Afflicted Innocence: Being an account of the Persecution of the Protestants of France*, trans. William Vaughn (London, 1682), p. 31.

10. Peter Needham, *A Sermon Preached before the University of Cambridge, Upon the 25*th *of January, 1715/16, Being the Day of St. Paul's Conversion* (Cambridge, 1716), p. 17; Ralph Lambert, Bishop of Dromore, *A Sermon Preach'd in Christ's-Church Dublin, On Wednesday October 23'd 1717. Being the Anniversary of Commemoration of the Happy Deliverance from the Irish Rebellion and Massacre in 1641* (Dublin, 1717), p. 15; Thomas Lucas, *Christian Compulsion not Persecution. A Sermon Preach'd at Trowbridge . . . November the 5th, 1718* (London, 1718), pp. 29–30. See also *A Seasonable Warning to Protestants; From the Cruelty and Treachery of the Parisian Massacre, August the 24th. 1572. Wherein the Snares laid for the Innocent are Detected, and Posterity Cautioned not to Believe* (London, 1680). The pamphlet addresses itself to the apparently parallel Irish rebellion of 1641 and its consequent Catholic wolves preying upon and devouring Protestant sheep (p. 6). Dragooning, the revocation itself, its consequence, and an assumption that the "civil magistrate" should enforce religious belief were behind much of John Locke's *Letter concerning Toleration* (1689). Here are two examples among many: if God wished to enforce Christianity by force, he would have done it with "Armies of heavenly Legions" and not by means of "any Son of the Church, how potent soever, with all his Dragoons"; God has never "given any such [secular, coercive] Authority to one Man over another, as to compel any one to his Religion." See the *Letter* in *The Works of John Locke Esq;* (London, 1714), 2:234.

11. For a comparable work, see the translation of the first two parts of [Elie Benoist], *Histoire de l'Édit de Nantes* (Delft, 1693–95), as *The History Of the Famous Edict of Nantes: Containing an Account of all the Persecutions, That have been in France From its First Publication to the Present Time*, trans. Cooke (London, 1694). The title page and its facing permission stress publication "*With her Majesties Royal Priviledge*" in black letter. Jean Claude's work was republished with a long English preface as *A Short Account Of the Complaints and Cruel Persecutions of the Protestants In the Kingdom of France. With A Useful and Politick Preface, and also an Account of the Torments the French Protestants endure Aboard the Galleys*, trans. [Hilary Reneu] (London, 1708). The preface is predictably anti-Augustinian, anti-revocation, and of course hostile to its prior and consequent violence. According to the English writer, the French tried to get the 1686 copy burned and the translator and printer fined, imprisoned, and ruined (p. 1). He also reiterates the familiar belief that " 'Twas at the same time that Preparations were making in order to put the same Methods in practice against the *Protestants* in *England*, where the Pope kept openly a Nuncio besides several Monks and Jesuits" (pp. 1–2). See also n. 29 below.

12. Pierre Bayle, *Philosophical Commentary on These Words of the Gospel, Luke XIV. 23. Compel them to come in, that my House may be full* (London, 1708), 1:iii, italics and roman type reversed. Bayle of course was answered, as in Philippe Naudé, whose ample title makes clear its tone: *Refutation du "Commentaire philosophique"; ou, Solution generale et renversement de tous les sophismes que l'auteur y employ, à dessein d'établir en tous lieux une tolérance sans bornes, pour l'exercise public de toutes les erreurs et les hérésies dont l'esprit humain peut estre capable* (Berlin, 1718). The English *Philosophical Commentary* has been partially translated by Amie Goodman Tannenbaum as *Pierre Bayle's Philosophical Commentary:*

A Modern Translation and Critical Interpretation (New York: Peter Lang, 1987). The 1708 text, with slight modifications but geared to the original English pages, has been helpfully reprinted as *Philosophical Commentary*, ed. John Kilcullen and Candran Kukathas (Indianapolis, IN: Liberty Fund, 2005).

13. Pierre Bayle, *The Dictionary Historical and Critical of Mr Peter Bayle*, ed. Pierre des Maizeaux, 2nd ed. (London, 1734–38), 3:222n[H] (turn), 220n[E] (propose). Bayle makes a similar point in the entry for Mahomet, and a more positive point regarding Milton's toleration. Augustine was guilty of comparable or worse solipsism: "by righteous Laws, St. Austin understands Laws in favor of his own Party; and by Good, he understands whatever's conformable to his own Ideas; as by Evil he understands what's repugnant to 'em." This makes it impossible either to be enlightened or to end persecution. *Philosophical Commentary*, 2:460. *Gregory* in its various numbers would become an odious name in the history of persecution and of papal abuse of power. See the Reverend J. Baker, *The History of the Inquisition, As it subsists in the Kingdoms of Spain, Portugal, &c.* (London, 1734), with several deservedly stern comments on Gregory IX, XI, XIII, and XV. Gregory IX, for example, "gave a famous Instance of his Tyranny and Injustice" by using threats of inquisitorial means to Ezelinus and threats of poverty to his children to force Ezelinus into submission (p. 10).

14. Matthew Hole, *The Danger of Divisions, Together with the Benefit of Unanimity: In a Sermon Preach'd at Bridgewater, On Monday, September XXIX. . . . I Pet. iii. 8. Be ye all of one Mind* (London, 1702), pp. 2–3. Regular reiteration of the demand suggests the difficulty of its implementation. On either side of the Channel the established church almost always defined unity as the Dissenters' surrender to its greater wisdom and piety. Dissenters generally returned the compliment with insults thought appropriate for the occasion. The first three chapters above outline some of the consequent verbal brutality on each side.

15. Perhaps the sternest argument on punishment appeared earlier than the approximate limits of this chapter. See William Prynne, *The Sword of Christian Magistracy Supported: Or a Vindication of the Christian Magistrates Authority under the Gospell, To punish Idolatry, Apostacy, Heresie, Blasphemy, and obstinate Schism, with Corporall, and in some Cases with Capital Punishment* (London, 1647, 1653).

16. Benjamin Laney, *Five Sermons, Preached before His Majesty at Whitehall* (London, 1669), p. 85; [Samuel Parker], *A Discourse of Ecclesiastical Politie: Wherein The Authority of the Civil Magistrate Over the Conscience of Subjects in Matters of External Religion is Asserted*, 3rd ed. (London, 1671), pp. xxxii (Infection), xxxv (Authority), 253 (ignorant).

17. [Francis Turner], *Animadversions Upon a Late Pamphlet, Entituled The Naked Truth, or The True State of the Primitive Church*, 2nd ed. (London, 1676), pp. 12 (dashing), 14–15 (our Churches); William Sherlock, *The Case of Resistance of the Supreme Powers Stated and Resolved According to the Doctrine of the Holy Scriptures* (London, 1684), p. 127.

18. Thomas Long, *The Character of a Separatist: Or, Sensuality the Ground of Separation. To which is Added, The Pharisees Lesson. . . . And an Examination of Mr. Hales Treatise of Schism* (London, 1677), sigs. a4^{r-v} (withdraw, charitable), b2^v (Donatists); Long, *The Original of War: Or, The Causes of Rebellion. A Sermon Preached in the Castle of Exon, On the 15th of January, 1683* (London, 1684), p. 12. See also Long, *The Case of Persecution, Charg'd on the Church of England, Consider'd and Discharg'd, In order to her Justification, and a Desired Union of Protestant Dissenters* (London, 1689), esp. pp. 6–7: Augustine and the Church of

England functioned as physicians guiding Dissenters toward health and unity and not as persecutors.

19. Thomas Long, *The History of the Donatists* (London, 1677), p. 38 (hereafter cited parenthetically in the text).

20. Lucas, *Christian Compulsion not Persecution*, pp. 11 (exterminating), 32 (exclaim, backward), 34 (rage against George I); Charles Chauncy, *The only Compulsion proper to be made Use of in the Affairs of Conscience and Religion* (Boston, 1739), p. 14.

21. Jean Barbayrac, *Traité de la morale des pères de l'église: Où en défendant un Article de la Preface sur Puffendorf, contre l'apologie de la morale des pères de P. Cellier* (Amsterdam, 1728). Barbayrac skewers Augustine on pp. xxxvi–xxxviii and discusses other aspects of toleration, the Donatists, and Augustine on pp. 300–310. We see Franco-English cross-fertilization regarding the dangers of persecution when he refers both to Pierre Bayle and to Locke on toleration (p. 307n8). For Thomas Gordon, who immediately proclaims his Whig sympathies, see *The Spirit of the Ecclesiasticks Of all Sects and Ages, As to the Doctrines of Morality, And more particularly the Spirit of the Ancient Fathers of the Church, Examin'd, by Mons. Barbeyrac, Professor of Laws and History in the University of Lausanne. Translated from the French by a Gentleman of Gray's-Inn. With a Preface by the Author of the Independent-Whig* (London, 1722), sig. A2^v, in italics. Gordon also refers favorably to Jean Daillé's *"of the Use of the Fathers"* (sig. A4^v). His *Traité de l'employ des saincts Pères pour le jugement des différendes qui sont aujourd'hui en la religion* (at least 1632, 1656, 1686) was Englished in both 1651 and 1675 (London) as *A Treatise concerning the Right Use of the Fathers, In the Decision of the Controversies that are at this day in Religion. Written in French by John Daille, Minister of the Gospel in the Reformed Church at Paris*, trans. Thomas Smith. Voltaire adds his own outrage regarding Augustine and the fathers in *Questions sur l'encyclopédie* (1770); see *Oeuvres completes de Voltaire* ([Paris?], 1784), 42:214–20. Voltaire's tone in the *Questions* generally is amused cynicism and civilized superiority to the subjects he condescends to consider. The entry on Augustine, "le persecuteur" (42:214), however, is demonstrably angry, especially regarding predestination and grace for the select few and unbaptized infants designed for hell.

22. Francis Bugg, *De Christiana Libertate, Or, Liberty of Conscience Upon it's true and proper grounds Asserted and Vindicated* (London, 1682), p. 32. This was reprinted in 1719 as *Equal Liberty of Conscience Asserted: Or, the Power of the Christian Magistrate in Religion, Consider'd*; see p. 25 for this quotation. The entire text argues for limits upon government control of religion. *An Account of the Conduct of the Roman-Catholick Clergy and Zealots of France*, sig. A3^v, italics and roman type reversed. A Layman [Thomas Gordon], *A Sermon Preached before the Learned Society of Lincoln's Inn, On January 30 1732. From Job xxiv. 30. That the Hypocrite reign not, lest the People be ensnared* (London, 1733), p. 37. The lay sermon is avidly against Augustine, the church, Charles I, Laud, Tories, Atterbury, and French persecution. It is of course warmly Whig and Hanoverian. For Finch, see him as the pseudonymous T. S——Y, *A Letter to the Rev. Dr. Trapp: Occasioned by A Late Pamphlet, Entituled, The True Spirit of the Methodists, &c. Supposed to be written by the Doctor himself* (London, 1740), p. 67.

23. We recall Daniel Defoe's *Lex Talionis: Or, An Enquiry into the Most Proper Ways to Prevent the Persecution of the Protestants in France* (London, 1698), which argued by analogy with ancient Roman law: Europe was divided into papist and Protestant states; "it seems

justifiable ... that while the one part commit Hostilities and Depredations on the other, the injur'd Party shall have a Right of Retaliation on any Member of the same Body, of what Nation or Government soever they shall be, where the Power is properly put into their Hands" (p. 10). Defoe clearly includes French behavior in his concept (pp. 12, 13–14). It was promptly translated into French as *Lex Talionis, La Loi du Talion. Ou Moyen juste & infallible pour arrêter le Cours de la Cruelle & Barbare Persecution des Protestans de France.... Traduit de l'Anglois. A Londres, Par Pierre de la Verité.* The British Library says that the imprint is "fictitious" and attributes the close translation to "[Daniel Defoe?]." Defoe's arguments are consistent with Pierre Bayle's logical extension of potential Protestant persecution of Catholics, or of any one religion against any other should it regain power. See, for example, Bayle's summary in the *Philosophical Commentary*, 2:677–79, 682–83. Bayle laments that under such circumstances, "the greater the Zeal of Christians is, the more they'l ravage the World, and lay wast Towns and Countrys, in hopes of making Converts." Pagan nations would be correct to resist "the Attempts of such Convertists, by destroying 'em off the Face of the Earth like so many wild Beasts" (2:683).

24. Lucas, *Christian Compulsion not Persecution*, p. 34. Hostile allusions to Sacheverell's *False Brethren* was a regular trope in Whig attacks. See A Layman [Gordon], *A Sermon Preached*: High Churchmen are so keen on Charles I that "they treat as Monsters and false Brethren, all impartial Clergymen" (p. 54).

25. A Curate of London, *A Short Preservative Against the Doctrines Reviv'd by Mr. Whitefield and his Adherents. Being a Supplement to the Bp. of London's late Pastoral Letter* (London, 1739), pp. 7–8. See also Robert Seagrave, *The True Protestant: A Dissertation Shewing The Necessity of asserting the Principles of Liberty in their full Extent* (London, 1746), p. 43: "Bigotry, has evidently lost Ground; and Liberty is more understood and esteemed daily. Possibly Providence has reserved for the HOUSE of HANOVER, the Honour of bringing this great Article to its Perfection." See also p. 48; and thereafter George Campbell, *The Character of a Minister of the Gospel as a Teacher and Pattern* (Aberdeen, 1752), pp. 58–59: the ugly spirit of persecution "is almost, if not altogether extinct" in Britain. Butchery, torment, and using "fire and sword" in "the cause of holiness" has been replaced by *"spiritual weapons."* This would become a commonplace, as in James Creighton, *A Letter, Addressed to Mr. Samuel Bradburn, Containing, Some Strictures On His Pamphlet, Entitled: "The Question; Are the Methodists Dissenters?"* (London, 1793), p. 14: "persecution has not been encouraged by the Hanoverian family." Seagrave and his Methodist colleagues were slightly more optimistic than the situation allowed. See the lament that Whitefield's influence had not been legally checked by the law at once and the hope that it could be checked now. Methodists were as dangerous as the Dissenters of 1641: *A Compleat Account of the Conduct Of that eminent Enthusiast Mr. Whitefield.... Together with Some Remarks on Mr. W's Journals* (London, 1739), pp. 10–11. See also the parodic version of the state's *compelle intrare* in *The Mock Preacher: A Satyrico-Comical-Allegorical Farce. As it was Acted to a Crowded Audience At Kennington-Common, And many other Theaters. With the Humours of the Mob* (London, 1739), pp. 20–21. For example, according to one participant, "It is ... necessary the temporal Sword should interfere, if Reason will not. The Church, in all Ages, has had recourse to the State in time of Danger.... A Protestant Inquisition would be of infinite Service for the Punishment of all those who dare oppose the true Orthodox Faith." He wishes that Queen Anne again were on the throne: "Had she liv'd, the *Convocation* would

have taken these Affairs in hand." See chapter 5 below for further discussion of changes in attitudes toward Methodism.

26. John Crump, *The Parable of the Great Supper Opened. Wherein is set forth the fulness of Gospel-provision* (London, 1669), pp. 326–27; Matthew Poole, *Annotations Upon the Holy Bible Volume II. Being a Continuation of Mr. Pool's Work by certain Judicious and Learned Divines* (London, 1685), 2: sig. Aa1^{r-v}; Ralph Erskine, *Gospel-Compulsion: Or, Ministerial Power and Authority. A Sermon Preached at The Ordination of Mr. John Hunter to the Pastoral Office* (Edinburgh, 1739), p. 15. Poole's collaborators reject any notion of "Swords or Staves, or Whips, or pecuniary mulcts to inforce" the use of reason and persuasion. Erskine adds that the compulsion is spiritual (p. 16) and evangelical (p. 17). Like other non-Anglicans and Anglican moderates, he regards High Church "compelling of *Mens Consciences*" as offensive: "As for Example, in the Business of the sacramental Test, you shall be fined, imprisoned, ruined in your Estate, if you take not the Lord's Supper: No such Compulsion is here intended. Ministers are not *Lords over God's Heritage*" (pp. 15–16). Needham, *Sermon Preached before the University of Cambridge*, p. 1. Needham quickly became angry at the persecutors and "what they call salutary Force and wholesome Severities for the good of Souls," which only lead to "Perjury and Blood" (p. 2).

27. Needham, *Sermon Preached before the University of Cambridge*, p. 2. He later added that "our modern Persecutors . . . justify and recommend all the brutal Outrage and Barbarity, that Flesh and Blood can undergo on this side the grave" (p. 7). Matthew Clarke, *Sermons upon Several Occasions; By the Reverend Mr. Matthew Clarke: Some of which were never before publish'd. To which are added, Some Memoirs of his Life, and the Sermon preach'd at his Funeral, [By] Daniel Neal. M. A.* (London, 1727), p. 343; William Sheppard, *An Essay on Love and Charity: Wherein Our Saviour's new commandment is seasonably urged upon the professors of Christianity* (London, 1723), pp. 87–88, and see also pp. 31, 40, 81–86, 91; Alexander Gordon, *A Sermon Preached at the Assizes at Aberdeen, October 3. 1749* (Edinburgh, 1750), p. 6. Gordon cites Bayle's *Commentaire philosophique* in p. 18n. The word *compel* also evoked associations with French dragooning and with Augustine. William Wishart so demonstrates in his unsigned *Principles of Liberty of Conscience Stated and Defended: In a Letter to a Friend by GWITMARPSCHELDON* (Edinburgh, 1739): "the Use of Force to deter a Man from one kind of religious Profession, and compel him to another" hinders rather than encourages impartial inquiry (p. 8). Wishart refers to Augustine in p. 26n. "Until *Augustine*" no church father had urged that the civil magistrate use corporal punishment and force to eliminate heresy. Whether "his Reasons as to this Point be convincing, let any impartial Man read his *Epistle 50*, and determine." Wishart's entire essay answers No.

28. See Gilbert Burnet, *Bishop Burnet's History of His Own Time. Vol. I. From the Restoration of King Charles II. To the Settlement of King William and Queen Mary at the Revolution* (London, 1724), p. 776, for Burnet as chaplain, though he stresses his importance throughout the long chapter on James II; the quotation is from p. 691.

29. Burnet, *History*, pp. 655 (dismal), 659 (one of), 702 (Popery); for further discussion of the revocation of the Edict of Nantes and its violent persecution of Huguenots, see pp. 655–87. Burnet was scarcely alone in fearing that James would translate Louis XIV's persecution to Britain. See [Pierre Jurieu], *A Defence of Their Majesties King William and Queen Mary* (London, 1689): James was so allied with Louis and so "zealously bent on the

same courses" that many thought he "would in time, push on things to such an issue, (to take effect in his own or his Successours days, whom he was setting up) as has already fallen out in *France*. They were afraid of it, I say, and they had reason" (p. 42). See also p. 50 on the Saint Bartholomew's Day Massacre, and n. 11 above, the preface to Claude's 1708 *Short Account Of the Complaints, and Cruel Persecutions of the Protestants In . . . France*, p. 2.

30. Gilbert Burnet, *The Case of Compulsion In Matters of Religion Stated. By G. B. Addressed to the Serious Consideration of the Members of the Church of England, in this present Juncture. Licensed August 21. 1688* (London, 1688), p. 1 (hereafter cited parenthetically in the text). Burnet also is more concerned with Anglican persecution than with Roman or French persecution.

31. Edward Synge, *The Case of Toleration consider'd with Respect both to Religion and Civil Government, In a Sermon Preach'd in St. Andrew's Dublin, Before the Honourable House of Commons; On Saturday, the 23rd of October, 1725. Being the Anniversary of The Irish Rebellion*, 2nd ed. (Dublin, 1726), p. 1 (hereafter cited parenthetically in the text). The occasion of the sermon made it especially moving for its Irish Protestant audience. The sermon was known in Britain. See [Wishart], *Principles of Liberty of Conscience*, p. 8n, where he is quoted as "a learned and worthy Author on this Argument." Swift had a characteristically uncertain relationship with Synge, whom he recommended for a bishopric but by whom he seemed otherwise unimpressed. See Synge's letter to Swift of 18 September 1738 in *The Correspondence of Jonathan Swift*, vol. 4, ed. David Woolley (Frankfurt am Main: Peter Lang, 2007), pp. 540–41, and vol. 5, *The Correspondence of Jonathan Swift*, ed. Harold Williams (Oxford: Clarendon Press, 1965), pp. 124–25 and esp. p. 124n1.

32. Stephen Radcliffe, *A Letter To the Reverend Mr. Edward Synge, Prebendary of St. Patrick's, Occasion'd by a Late Sermon Preach'd in St. Andrew's, Dublin, Before the Honourable House of Commons* (Dublin, 1725), p. 4 (hereafter cited parenthetically in the text). Synge also was answered by the probably pseudonymous R. M. Weaver, and without a bookseller's name on the title page: *A Letter To the Revd. Stephen Radcliffe, Vicar of Naas* (Dublin, 1725). Weaver refers to Swift's *Tale of a Tub*, "a famous Treatise" (p. 6 and n). I am indebted to James Woolley for bringing Weaver and the raucously vulgar *Excellent New Song* to my attention.

33. Edward Synge, *A Vindication of a Sermon Preach'd before the Honourable House of Commons of Ireland. . . . In which the Question concerning Toleration, particularly of Popery under certain Conditions and Limitations is farther consider'd, and the Mistakes and Weak Reasonings about it are laid open. In Answer to the Rev^d. Mr. Radcliffe's Letter* (Dublin, 1726), p. 6 (hereafter cited parenthetically in the text).

34. *Doctor Sherlock's Vindication of the Corporation and Test Acts Considered. With a Short Appendix concerning Persecution from Mr. Bayle's Philosophical Commentary, Upon those Famous Words of the Gospel. Compel them to come in* (London, 1718), p. 19. The author attacks Thomas Sherlock's *Vindication of the Corporation and Test Acts. In Answer to the Bishop of Bangor's Reasons for the Repeal of them* (London, 1718).

35. Henry Hammond, *A Paraphrase, and Annotations Upon all the Books of The New Testament, Briefly Explaining all the Difficult Places thereof*, 11th ed. (London, 1702), p. 211; Matthew Hole, in part of *Practical Discourses on All the Parts and Offices of the Liturgy of the Church of England* (London, 1714–16), *Practical Discourses Upon All the Collects, Epistles, and Gospels, to be us'd thro-out the Year*, 4 (1716): 126, with new pagination in part 2.

Hole agrees that the "Force of Reason" can carry a benign message more deeply than a sword. He also insists that where reason does not work, the listeners "may be driven by Laws and Punishments.... for holy things may not be given to Dogs" (4:126–27). This is one of the relatively mediating positions between overt violence and overt persuasion.

36. Daniel Whitby, *A Paraphrase and Commentary on the New Testament*, 5th ed. (London, 1727), 1:421; Nicholas Brady, *Several Sermons, Chiefly upon Practical Subjects, Many of which were preached before Her Present Majesty, when Princess of Wales* (London, 1730), 3:39. See also Samuel Clarke (1675–1729), *Sermons on the Following Subjects: Viz. Against Persecution for Religion* (London, 1731), 7:1. Needham, *Sermon Preached before the University of Cambridge*, p. 11.

37. The British Library catalog has a question mark regarding John Owen's authorship. EEBO lists the author as Anonymous. See *Insolence and Impudence triumphant; Envy and Fury enthron'd: The Mirrour of Malice and Madness, In a late Treatise, Entituled, A Discourse of Ecclesiastical Polity* (London, 1669), sig. A3^r, italics and roman type reversed. Owen's(?) preface "To the Conscientious READER; Whether *Conformist* or *Nonconformist*" laments but understands the royal and ecclesiastical efforts to induce "a rigorous Uniformity" after earlier disruption. "But men are fallible; nor can we expect our Senators should be Prophets. It hath been since understood that 'tis impossible to reconcile the different Apprehensions of Mankind in Religious Affairs; and that external Force in matters of Conscience, may make Hypocrites, but few Converts; Differences have not been lessened, but rather improved" (sig. A2^r, in italics). John Humfrey's *Authority of Magistrate about Religion Discussed* (London, 1672) also consistently lambastes Parker, while granting the magistrate's authority to compel external action but not conscience; see, for example, pp. 86–88, 95–96, 126–33. Andrew Marvell joined the debate in, among other places, *The Rehearsal Transpros'd: Or Animadversions upon a Late Book, Intituled A Preface Shewing What Grounds there are of Fears and Jealousies of Popery*, 2nd ed. (London, 1672). Parker expanded upon the argument on magisterial compulsion in *A Discourse of Ecclesiastical Politie: Wherein the Authority of the Civil Magistrate over the Consciences of Subjects in Matters of External Religion is Asserted*, 3rd ed. (London, 1671). The title suggests that he wished to displace or at least to modify Richard Hooker's own founding and more liberal document concerning the Anglican Church, *Of the Lawes of Ecclesiastical Polities* (London, 1593).

38. Benjamin Keach, *Gospel-Mysteries Unveil'd: Or, An Exposition of the Parables, and Express Similitudes of our Lord and Saviour Jesus Christ* (London, 1701), 2:81; Thomas Ellwood, *The Foundation of Tythes Shaken*, 2nd ed. (London, 1720), pp. 364 (kind, dragged), 366–67 (compel, Good). It is consistent with Bayle's arguments. *The Foundation* originally was published in 1678, as a response to Thomas Comber, *The Right of Tithes re-asserted* (London, 1680). There was another response in 1682, *An Historical Vindication of the Divine Right of Tithes* (London). Ellwood's second edition was part of an effort to allow Quakers to avoid legally mandated tithing.

39. Richard Claridge, *The Life and Posthumous Works of Richard Claridge, Being Memoirs and Manuscripts Relating to His Experiences and Progress in Religion.... Collected by Joseph Besse* (London, 1726), pp. 501 (unreasonable), 502 (Voluntary). Here as in so many other eighteenth-century examples, Locke's *Letter concerning Toleration* provides the intellectual and philosophical frame of argument. See n. 10 above.

40. Matthew Tindal, *Four Discourses on the Following Subjects* (London, 1709) (hereafter cited parenthetically in the text).

41. *Ammianus Mercellinus . . . II: History*, trans. John C. Rolfe (London: William Heinemann; Cambridge, MA: Harvard University Press, 1963), p. 203, 22.5, with the Latin on p. 202: "nullas infestas hominibus bestias, ut sunt sibi ferales plerique Christianorum expertum." Compare Locke on *Toleration*: Turks "silently stand by, and laugh to see with what inhuman Cruelty Christians thus rage against Christians" (Locke, *Works*, 2:238).

42. Matthew Clarke, *Sermons upon Several Occasions*, pp. 343 (rational, fire), 345 (therefore). Clarke's observations essentially were repeated by Zachary Pearce, bishop of Rochester, in his *Commentary with Notes, on the four Evangelists and the Acts of the Apostles*, ed. John Derby (London, 1777), 1:392–93: compel does not "here mean that any outward force should be used. . . . nothing but his commanding or persuading them to do it can be reasonably understood." Samuel Johnson wrote Derby's dedication to George III.

43. For Equiano, see *The Interesting Narrative of the Life of Olaudah Equiano, or Gustavus Vassa, The African. Written by Himself*, in *Olaudah Equiano: The Interesting Narrative and Other Writings*, ed. Vincent Carretta (New York: Penguin Books, 2003) (hereafter cited parenthetically in the text). Equiano would have seconded Whitefield's remark in his *Continuation Of the Reverend Mr. Whitefield's Journal, During the Time he was detained in England by the Embargo* (London, 1739), p. 10: his opponents "say, it is not regular our going out into the Highways and Hedges, and compelling poor Sinners to come in," but God has so designed the Methodist mission. For Pasquier Quesnel, see *Moral Reflections Upon the Gospel of St. Luke. . . . Translated from the French* ([London?], 1707), 1:275, from *Le Nouveau Testament en François: Avec des Réflexions morales sur . . . l'Evangile selon Saint Luc* (Brussels, 1702); Isaac Watts, *Hymns and Spiritual Songs. In Three Books* (London, 1707), pp. 195–96; John Wesley, *Explanatory Notes upon the New Testament*, 2nd ed. (London, 1757), p. 187n. Quesnel was accused of sedition by the Gallican church. See [Jacques Philippe], *Quesnel seditieux et heretique dans les reflexions sur le nouveau testament* (Brussels, 1705). The bishops *"d'un grand merite"* forbad the reading of such pernicious Jansenism.

44. Samuel Clarke, *Sermons on the Following Subjects*, 7:4.

45. See Samuel Clarke, *A Paraphrase On the Four Evangelists. . . . Together With Critical Notes on the more difficult Passages* (1701–2) 4th ed. (London, 1722), 2:158, and more broadly, Matthew Clarke, *Sermons upon Several Occasions*, with three sermons under the heading "The Gospel Invitation." The love feast Equiano describes is consistent with the ones that Nathaniel Lancaster characterized in his Methodist mock epic *Methodism Triumphant, Or, The Decisive Battle Between the Old Serpent and the Modern Saint* (London, 1767). The meetings are spiritual, not carnal, guided by faith, grace, zeal, and new births:

> And when indulging in the Feast of love,
> They eat—they drink—then sing an Hymn, and pray;
> From the abundance of the inward Heart,
> Breaks forth their Diction, sweetly intermix'd
> With Scripture-phrases—those mellifluent Sounds,
> Which charm, which edify the Hearer's Soul. (P. 66)

CHAPTER FIVE

Methodism

From Antagonist to Relation

In 1765 John Wesley offered a brief *History of Methodism* in order to rectify "the various Accounts which have been given," many of which were "far remote from Truth." He hoped to replace such often wilful misapprehensions with what he called "a bare *Relation* of a Series of naked Facts."[1] The Methodists began at Oxford in November of 1729 when John and Charles Wesley, William Morgan of Christ Church, and Robert Kirkham of Merton joined to study the Greek testament. Other students from their own and from other colleges asked to join them, as did Pembroke's George Whitefield in 1735. Thanks to the "exact Regularity" of their lives and studies, they were called Methodists and soon "were known all over the University." Wesley makes plain that they were deeply loyal to their spiritual and secular institutions, to the Church of England and to Oxford. They were in particular bound by the Bible, "it being their one Desire and Design to be downright *Bible Christians*: Taking the Bible, as interpreted by the primitive Church and our own, for their whole and sole Rule" (p. 5). Consequently, they were criticized for being *"righteous overmuch"* and too scrupulous in attending to the Church of England's rubrics and canons and the university's statutes. They also were thought to be literalists regarding the Bible: "if they were right, *few* indeed would *be saved"* (pp. 5–6).

In October of 1735, John, Charles, and Benjamin Ingham left England to preach to Native Americans in Georgia. The other Methodists stayed at Oxford, continued to meet and study, later were ordained in the Anglican Church, and left the university. In 1738 Whitefield also went to Georgia to assist Wesley, who had in fact already departed for England. Whitefield there joined with the colonial Methodists, and they "resolved to be *Bible-Christians* at all Events, and wherever they were, to preach with all their Might, plain, old, Bible-Christianity" (p. 6). In the process, they determined that "Justification by Faith was the doctrine of the Church, as well as of the Bible." Their doctrine implied that we are naturally *"dead in Sin"* and *"Children of Wrath"* (p. 7); that we are justified only by faith; and that faith produces inward and outward holiness. They preached these doctrines regularly, drew large congregations, and as a group were identified as Methodists.

By March of 1741 Whitefield had returned to England and exacerbated the first of several schisms within Methodist practice. That already was in process thanks to Whitefield's harsh response to Wesley's sermon on free grace.[2] The Wesleyans believed in universal redemption. Whitefield believed in particular redemption, that is, though Wesley does not so indicate, the Calvinist doctrine of predestination as written in article 17 of the Church of England's Thirty-Nine Articles. Wesley's broader concept allowed for a more generous divine dispensation and for the possibility of human "perfection" in this world by means of faith-induced inner holiness.[3] Wesley's people continued to think of themselves as Church of England men. Whitefield and others who had broken away continued to berate the church, its clergy, and its apparent deviation from articles sworn to as the word of God. So began Oxford Methodism, and so began a new Protestant dispensation that permanently altered the face of religion in Britain and in much of the world. Methodism was indeed "the most astonishing eruption in the eighteenth-century history of religion."[4] Oxford was the first to react to the holy and methodical young men increasingly present in its midst. That reaction was alarming for both sides.

The Spreading *Fog*

On 9 December 1732 *Fog's Weekly Journal* published a letter from an Oxonian troubled by the Methodists, who "have occasioned no small Stir" in his city.[5] They are a throwback to the gloomy Puritans of yesteryear, are absurdly and perpetually melancholic, and are so devout that they alienate normal folk who wish to enjoy normal life and normal religion. Such excesses include rising at four every morning and spending "two Hours a Day in singing of Psalms and Hymns." They regard anyone who fails to behave as they do as violating "an indispensable Duty requisite to the Being of a Christian." These sexually licentious hypocrites wilfully exclude themselves from "the Judgment of other Persons."

The correspondent is concerned that Methodists will have a "very fatal Consequence" for religion. As the allusion to earlier Puritans suggests, he also is concerned that the new Methodists are like the old revolutionary Presbyterians. Their immoralities recall those of "the Sect of the Neighbouring Nation, which agreed in several Particulars with them." What is barely coded soon becomes overt. The Oxonian recognizes "Enthusiastick Madness and superstitious Scruples." The Methodists are like those "who, with the Author of the Tale of a Tub, suppose the Innovators in Religion to be Persons, whose natural Reason hath suffered great Revolutions." Here indeed is a new sect of madmen and fools. The writer's attitude toward these deviant innovators is clear in his hostile reference to Origen as a pattern for Methodists and for what he hopes will eliminate them. Origen believed that the self-castration he practiced would allow him greater spiritual focus. If the Methodists do not know how to do that, perhaps a physician can do it for them. The remedy of castration fortunately excluded, the Oxonian's complaints and accusations would echo through much of the early and mid-eighteenth century.[6]

The most serious accusation, of course, was that the Methodists were versions of earlier fanatical, enthusiast, antimonarchic, and anti-episcopal Dissenters. These concerns were enlarged by the publication of George Whitefield's journals in 1738–39 and John Wesley's in 1740. To more traditional Anglicans, these memoirs characterized self-important and self-anointing saints who proclaimed divine inspiration and denigrated the Anglican Church and its hierarchy, to which they claimed obedience.[7] James Bate put it this way after Whitefield defended himself against Bishop Edmund Gibson's concerned but temperate pastoral letter to his London diocese: all the expressions Gibson cited were "pick'd out of your Journals, where you speak of yourself or your own Actions, [as] Instances of your claiming either some *extraordinary Gift*, or some *extraordinary Influence* of the Spirit."[8] The Methodists regularly were referred to as schismatics, and so, like the Oxonian, their adversaries adapted some of the language and tactics of an earlier conflict with defilers of the church as the body of Christ. The author of *A Short History of the Donatists* (1741) makes plain that Whitefield is the old fanatic in a new garb. Like his ancestors, he dubs himself and his followers saints and is a proud hypocrite upon whom Augustine's corrective wrath should be exercised.[9]

Joseph Trapp long had been a High Church warrior. He too perhaps naturally saw the Methodists as heirs to the root-and-branch barbarians seeking to rise again. Whitefield, still technically Church of England, fit the bill as the ambitious apparent Dissenter busy *"magnifying himself,* as if he were another St. *Paul."* In so doing, the enthusiasts profane, blaspheme, and make "their own Case parallel with that of the Apostles" and even of Jesus. These factious men are enemies to the church and clergy, whom they *"maliciously traduce."* No wonder that when Trapp wrote about the *Danger of being Righteous over-much* he saw "nothing but a Revival of the old Fanaticism in the last Century," with its lunacy and brutality "committed *in the Name of the Lord."*[10]

Others sounded similar alarms. The author of *A Compleat Account* (1739) comparably evoked "the History of former Times" and the great disturbances that came from small matters by these "bold Movers of Sedition." Consequently, the troubles "at last over-turn'd the Constitution, and ruin'd the Nation." There was "too great a Similitude" between then and now. Yet worse, "the present *Enthusiasts* have made much quicker Progress" than their ancestors and have madly and vainly laid paving stones for Jesuits. Like the perpetrator of the Donatists' revival, this author urged the Church of England to use the civil magistrate to stop Whitefield's hordes and impose Anglican discipline—if it was not already too late.[11] Here again is High Church concern with 1649 redivivus, with need for Augustinian compulsion of dissidents and—worse and worse—with enemies inside the Anglican confession. Perhaps the arguments that had seemed to be won on behalf of ameliorative evolution really were lost. At the least, they needed to be argued again.

John Wilder joined those many who regarded Methodism as a return to religious and political disorder. In *The Trial of the Spirits* (1739) he told his Oxford parish that the enthusiasts would start a war and perhaps reduce the "Church and State, to Anarchy and Confusion," as in the last century. The unsigned *Enthusiasm no Novelty* (1739) evoked traditional High Church rhetoric against Dissenters, who, in a familiar phrase, then as now *"pour'd forth a Deluge of Misery and Confusion"* that overflowed the country. In other familiar images, Henry Stebbing thought the Methodists mad, and a Country Curate saw them as latter-day Puritans who have perpetually sown "the Seeds of Dissention among us." Other resurrected metaphors included careless sparks that "have kindled Fires, which Floods of repentant Tears and the Blood of Thousands were never able to quench."[12]

Such attacks extended well into the mid-eighteenth century. Methodist numbers and power increased, and it seemed to many that the Church of England's power was proportionally decreased. Methodists apparently still kindled "the schismatic coals of sedition" and like their fanatical forbears were determined to destroy "the *Church* of England." In 1759 the energetic polemicist John Free complained that the national church was as isolated as *"a Lodge in a Garden of Cucumbers."* The nation's established religion "demands some *immediate* Effort for it's Preservation." The enthusiasts, he says elsewhere, "propagate a dangerous Sort of *Atheism*, and talk *Blasphemy*." Free even recycles Sacheverell on Dissenters: Methodists are "False Brethren."[13]

For some, Britain again was in a world where all men were mad and one knew not whom to trust. The Methodist incursion, however, was more complex than the analogy with 1641 and the rhetoric of lunacy, propagation, floods, fires, seeds, and false brethren suggest. The other objections nonetheless were substantial and fell into two rough and roughly overlapping secular and theological classes.

Attacks upon Methodists were demonstrably class based and demonstrably by a frightened, endangered elite. The clerical world should belong to the properly educated, to gentlemen who could meld with the ancient universities and participate in the systems and patronage associated with them. Some reasoning behind this view was based upon orthodoxy: clergymen should have the same clerical training and beliefs in order to avoid discord. In 1702 High Church William

Binckes thus urged that all men looking toward the ministry "shall be trained up in the same Notions of things, and . . . in the same Schools and Universities." Joseph Trapp put the matter bluntly regarding socially gauche religious zeal: be careful neither to do nor to say "any Thing *Contrary* to *Decency*, and *good Manners*; or what is called *good Breeding*" among the politely educated.[14]

The Tory-educated Wesley brothers from Christ Church and Whitefield from Pembroke were Oxford men, but all three found that methodical religious worship distanced them from Oxford's ignored obligations. Whitefield the lowly servitor recounted his persecution as a Methodist who followed university rules. Each term began with a sacrament, at which all and "especially the Seniors, are, by Statute, obliged to be present," yet "Harlot" Oxford was so corrupt that few masters and "no under Graduates (but the Methodists) attended upon it." This sense that demonstrative worship was vulgar extended to Methodist association with the impoverished nonuniversity underclass. Pembroke's master scolded Whitefield for visiting them and once threatened to expel him if he "visited the Poor again." Wesley also insisted upon Oxford's spiritual corruption. His sermon at St. Mary's in 1744 made plain that Oxford lacked Christianity and that its residents refused to accept God's wisdom through him. Hence, in the words of Psalms 119:126, "*It is time for thee,* LORD, *to lay to thine Hand!*" for, in a line implied but not spoken, "they have destroyed the law."[15]

The Methodists of course benevolently continued their charitable vein, and their opponents continued to berate them for disruption of a nominally functioning class system. One argument was that evangelicals were driving artisans and laborers from their divinely appointed tasks. For Henry Stebbing, conventicles were perhaps acceptable "*provided* Men keep themselves within their proper Bounds." Transgression deserved a sterner response and a reminder of why laborers were laborers. Stebbing affectionately, he says, tells Methodists that they should "honestly and diligently attend" to their stations and callings. They thereby serve themselves, their families, the public, and God. Not to do so is inexcusable, as it is for those who desert their crafts and even their country. Remain "in whatever Way or Rank Providence has placed you." John Green later was not sure that either God or Stebbing had it right. Methodists' "low and groveling minds" could not move from material to spiritual objects. Hence it was dangerous "to raise in the vulgar too high notions of their favour and interest in heaven." The uppity tapster Whitefield needed to learn that lesson and to apply it to himself. His foolishness would be better "in your blue apron and snuffers" than in the academic "scholarlike and respectable garb, which you now wear."[16]

Methodists thus were neither to abandon the loom for the Bible nor think themselves worthy of a university place. This last issue became notorious in 1768, when Methodists, Oxford, and its class system briefly took center stage in an unpleasant little melodrama: six students at St. Edmund's Hall then were tried, convicted, and expelled. Their crimes included being overtly Methodist and thus presumably violating university mores and Church of England regulations. Equally important, they were convicted of being really quite awfully, shockingly, terribly the wrong sort to be at university in the first place. This would not do. Rather than allow the students to remove themselves from the St. Edmund's rolls, the university paraded them together with the vice chancellor and other officers in full academic regalia. They gathered the accused students together, and "commandment was given that the young men should be brought forth." All this mimicked a "high court of justice, and formally expelling them in the house of God" inflicted maximum emotional distress.[17]

The charges made clear that whatever their presumed limitations in learning, on social grounds alone at least three of the students should not have been admitted, because they were "bred to trades." James Matthew was a weaver, Thomas Jones a barber, and Joseph Shipman a drapier. Oxford's Dr. Thomas Nowell denied that their menial trades were the chief reason for expulsion, but he nonetheless asked, "What business had they here? They had no occasion to come to the University for instruction or degrees, to apply for orders." Since Mr. Jones makes a good periwig, he may "get his bread by his proper profession," as could his laboring colleagues the weaver and the tapster. Sir Richard Hill had it right when he replied to Nowell: "You say, that the having been bred to trades would not have been objected against the young Men, had they made any progress in their studies afterwards.—Then why was this brought as a particular article of accusation?"[18] The answer was in Nowell's question: "What business had they here?"

The list of offenses against Methodists in general also included accusations of financial fiddling. The Anglican clergy were state employees whose livelihood was protected by law and by the civil magistrate, as with mandated tithes. Methodists excluded themselves from that system, had to raise their own money, and were vulnerable to charges of being spiritual pickpockets. As John Green wrote to Whitefield, you had "not chosen to put yourself in a situation to claim any legal dues from your hearers." John Free regarded Methodist attacks upon Anglican clergy as a national offense: "we are the LEGAL *Servants of the State*, and as such ought not to be *injured*." The author of *The Progress of Methodism* (1743) saw that Whitefield and the Wesleys wanted more than the saving of souls: they called upon their constituents "To contribute, out of their Store, / To pious Uses, (*somewhat more!*)" for a church in England or an orphanage in Georgia: "Good Shepherds always take that Care, / To fold their Sheep as well as shear."[19] Many of these and other charges were reiterated in the ample satiric literature regularly inflicted upon Methodists.

Few such efforts were amusing. Many were unsigned. Most were intended both to stiffen the spines of the politely rational and to be hurtful toward their victims. These works included *The Accomplished Methodist* (1739), *The Mock Preacher: A Satyrico-Comical-Allegorical Farce* (1739), *Trick upon Trick: Or Methodism Displayed. A Farce* (1743), *The Progress of Methodism in Bristol: Or, The Methodist Unmask'd* (1743), *Harlequin Methodist. To the Tune of An Old Woman Cloathed in Grey* (1750), Samuel Foote's *The Minor: A Comedy* and *The Epilogue to The Minor, Or, A Methodist Sermon* (1760), *The Amorous Humours and Audacious Adventures of One W * * * * * * * d* (1760?), and Evan Lloyd's elegiac and troubled *The Methodist* (1766). In at least one case the anti-Methodists produced a long and occasionally comic poem that also characterized several of the charges against the title character.

By 1767 the Anglican clergyman Nathaniel Lancaster had published his unsigned mock epic *Methodism Triumphant, Or, The Decisive Battle Between the Old Serpent and the Modern Saint*. Both the *Monthly* and the *Critical Review* scolded this effort, which they thought should have been in Hudibrastics.[20] Lancaster nonetheless sometimes wittily assembled many of the complaints against Wesley in particular and Methodism in general. He also put Methodist defenses in Wesley's mouth, and in weirdly outrageous language. The reviewers' allusion to Butler taps two other concepts: on the one hand, the Methodists were like the rebellious Presbyterians; on the other, they were "defeated" and could safely be mocked. As we shall see, that was hardly the case for the vibrant and growing Methodist numbers, whatever Lancaster's excesses in deploying his comic muse.

The poem often allows Lancaster to tap and invert epic devices. *Methodism Triumphant* includes an argument to each of its five books, bathetically heightened Miltonic blank verse, magical intrusion of the gods—here the unnamed Countess of Huntingdon—and a martial hero who triumphs against the Great Adversary. The poem borrows from mock-scholarly, biblical, and Wesleyan devices, like his journals and other works that annotate much of the text. Lancaster always refers to him as W----y. Given the obvious references and Wesley's own fame, fear of litigation seems unlikely. The device suggests the Old Testament prohibition against graven images, in which even God becomes G-d, as Wesley seems to be. He speaks "like a God!—And like a God he acts" (p. 7). His burning, active, boundless, fierce "wonder-working Faith—/Ecstatic Fervors—High-fermented Joys—/Visions and Dreams, and copious floods of Grace" define his supernatural character, no doubt with a nod toward the grape and Bedlam (p. 8). Lancaster the ordained Anglican minister could not have missed his own omission of references to Jesus. In the comic heresy W----y becomes the spiritualized Augustus born to bring Saturnian times. Nor could Lancaster have missed his own Wesleyan parody. It combines a Harrowing of Hell (Acts 2:27, 36) with the sea giving up its dead, from the Book of Common Prayer's Burial of the Dead. In this visit to the underworld Wesley walks beneath the water, marches under the ocean, and uses his wet hand to retrieve numerous lost souls who hope to return to spiritual life and solid soil. This task would have been impossible for the tepid, polite, rational Church of England cleric "Who will not shock sweet Delicacy's ear, / To save ten thousand Souls from Death and Hell" (p. 30). Reason cannot evoke "a Second Birth" as passion can (pp. 36–37).

Toward the end of the poem Wesley has preached to thousands, saved and reborn thousands, produced the sweetest fruit from the sick stock of original sin, and communicated his wisdom to North America, as in this pithy couplet: "Thus qualified from Pole to Pole I fly; / And now to Christians, now to Iroquois" (p. 63). By then he is ready to confront Satan, who hopes to "raise up The Dead in Sin" (p. 84) and indeed is using Wesley "for my Substitute" (p. 125). Or so he foolishly thinks, and so Wesley bravely denies.

Wesley arms himself with the Bible and his journals, each of which dutifully wards off the devil's blows. That diabolical miscreant then mischievously transforms himself into an apparently innocent babe who places a hand grenade within Wesley's robes, blows him into tiny bits, and gloats like a Greek warrior over a fallen Trojan. Not so fast. The benign Countess of Huntingdon so restores him that now there is "Health to his Navel—Marrow to his Bones" (p. 133). Wesley throws his journals into the air, and they fall upon the devil's horns. The violent mock-heroic consequences recall Swift's *Battle of the Books* (1704): the journals "Batter'd his Skull, and squash'd his igneous Brains" (p. 134). Wesley chops off Satan's cloven hooves and seizes the moment as limping Satan is vulnerable to the ultimate insult: "With a Jerk, beyond Angelic Strength" Wesley pulls off the devil's tail and tosses it into the air as "surest Proof, that METHODISM springs, / With all her Tenets, from an Heav'nly Source" (p. 137). Thanks to that source, "The Final Blow is struck!—The Tail—The Tail" is gone (p. 137). Hornless, hoofless, tailless, humiliated Satan roars, yells, can no longer sting mankind, and is carried away in disgrace to his "gloomy Realms," whose gates then are closed forever (p. 139). Lancaster implicitly makes plain that the secular and theological overlapped in Methodist practice, as they did in Anglican attacks and vigorous Methodist defenses.

Reforming the Reformation? Reforming Reform?

With appropriate exceptions, then, Methodists often were thought undereducated, self-deluding, and self-important enthusiasts, redolent of 1641, dangerous Puritanism, and schism. "I was almost led into a Perswasion of your being a rigid

Dissenter." It also "rather seems a Vindication of the Dissenters," one commentator said upon reading Robert Seagrave's response to Trapp's anti-Methodist sermons.[21] Aside from such often repeated fears, major Anglican concerns regarding germane theological issues included the nature of Methodist preaching, the nature of the congregants, and the venues at which the preaching often took place. There also were significant reservations regarding the ordained Wesley and Whitefield, and even more significant reservations regarding lay Methodist preachers, whom the universities often did not educate and the established church often neither trained nor ordained. Bishop Gibson's pastoral letter to his London diocese was a typical Church of England plea for a via media, here between enthusiasm and indifference. It also included an episcopal defense of institutional and hierarchic modes of proceeding. Religion must have order and regularity in its services and in its representatives in the pulpit, those "appointed within particular Bounds and Districts." Without these, "nothing can follow but Disorder and Confusion" as in "the Time of our Forefathers."[22]

Bounds and regularity, however, were uncongenial for evolving Methodist conduct. Anglican ministers on each side of the Atlantic thus had begun to bar Methodists from their pulpits. Both their evangelical method and their message went beyond the pale. Henry Stebbing lamented the decline from the first group of strict and regular Methodists, who adhered to "the Rules of our Church" and kept "within these Bounds." They understood "that Religion is a sober, reasonable Service, a Work of the Understanding and Judgement, as well as of the Heart and Affections." These sensible men soon changed. They rudely berated their Anglican brethren, preached "intricate and dangerous Doctrines," further attacked the clergy, claimed *"Divine Communications,* and *Directions,"* and ignored friendly and theologically sound attempts to return them to orthodoxy. It thus was necessary to banish them from respectable churches, which nonetheless did not dissuade certain deviants from seizing "a Pulpit or two without Leave." Yet worse, they defied ecclesiastical laws that specified sanctified churches as places of worship and "exercised their Ministry in Fields and Commons, and other unlicensed Places." Another defender of Trapp more sternly insisted that impatient strangers who usurped legitimate pulpits were un-Christian, broke "through every Fence of *Duty* and *Decency,"* and wrongly preached justification by faith alone.[23]

Those illicit, fenceless places of worship, we hear, were magnets for licentious preaching to foolish lower-class hordes. John Green characterized what seemed to him the madness of crowds encouraged by the madness of Whitefield. His harangues induced "a constant number of groaners, sighers, tumblers and convulsionists" who succumb to pastoral enthusiasm:

These occasionally break out into such a dreadful concert of screams, howlings and lamentations, as surprizes and shocks the sober part of your audience.... You are reported to use on these occasions some strange expressions, which, accompanied with a loud tone of voice, vehement gesture, wild looks, and that terrible relievo which is sometimes given to the cheeks and eyes of a field-preacher, must strongly operate on weak minds, and strike terror into an ignorant and unexperienced multitude.

Yet worse, another author knew, that multitude often included swarming prostitutes who "make Merchandize there as at a Country-Fair." They may even have included women who were allowed to preach. Charles Chauncy was outraged by "the suffering, much more the encouraging WOMEN, yea, GIRLS to speak in the assemblies" as female lay exhorters when such conduct was expressly forbidden.[24] These comments of course encouraged attacks upon presumed Methodist hypocrisy and sexual predation.

The need for clergymen and authors to repeat their attacks suggests that they scarcely dented Methodism's increasingly solid armor. It was reinforced by forceful defense and refusal to accept certain premises of Anglican apologetics. Religion was not a function of rational discourse and inquiry; it was a function of immediate divine intercession. The light within transcended the light of reason and did not denote deleterious enthusiasm. Whitefield's response to Bishop Gibson's pastoral letter insisted that "your Lordship's Definition of *Enthusiasm*, when examined, does not convey any ill Idea at all." His own "immediate Impulses" were delivered by God and thus were well grounded.[25] A cleric's good manners were a sign of superficial polish that removed him from the immediacy of God's gift and produced what William Law calls the *"cold Neglect, to say no worse"* that now afflicted worship. Scripture, not a licensed preacher, is the best guide. One need not be polite to erroneous, indifferent, pluralist, lazy, spoiled establishment clergymen. These blind shepherds cannot protect their sheep, do not represent true Christianity, and are neither "properly the Church it's self" nor "the *only* valid Communion wherein Persons can possibly be sav'd!"[26] Learning was not necessary for a clergyman; after all, the Apostles were humble men like the fishermen Peter and Andrew. Archbishop Tillotson was learned, and he knew no more about Christianity than did Mohammed. God did not bless the rich with his gift of new birth more than he blessed the many more poor, women, and children, who, Humphry Clinker would reiterate in 1771, were equally deserving of God's grace.

The formidable William Law defended Methodists, outlined their beliefs, and challenged *Fog*'s hostile Oxonian. Law emphasizes continuity, inclusion, and differences from 1641; he hopes that these virtuous men will continue to reform "a vicious World" long after their scoffing opponents are dead and forgotten. The properly instructed Oxonian will find that Methodists do not establish new doctrines, but only seek to follow those already recorded in Gospel and conform to it. They "govern themselves by *such Methods* as they find prescribed to them in common with *all Christians*, and not which they themselves prescribe and impose on one another, as several new Sects have done with great *Singularity* and *Affectation*."[27] For Law, Methodists are not schismatics but part of an ancient Christian community.

Methodist defense also included attacks upon the present Church of England, with which it developed a symbiotic relationship. The Wesleyan Methodist Richard Finch was as capable as *Fog*'s Oxonian of alluding to Swift's history of the church in the corrupting world. Unlike the Oxonian, though, he transformed Swift's proto-Anglican Martin into the persecuting Catholic Peter, who needs reform. Finch knows that the Church of England rejects spontaneous prayer in favor of a composed official liturgy. Such absolutism is absolute nonsense: "These authorities, are much the same as those brought in the *Tale of a Tub*, by Lord *Peter*, in behalf of Transubstantiation, whereto I refer the reader."[28]

Calvinist Methodists were especially keen on a new reformation based upon Genevan principles within the Thirty-Nine Articles. In so arguing, they too reversed the process in which their Anglican adversaries borrowed the anti-Dissenter language of deluge and broken fences. Like Finch, these Methodists adapted early eighteenth-century rhetoric in which Dissenters called the Church of England the intolerant enemy who needed both correction and constraint. Like Finch as well, Robert Seagrave regards the established church as fanatical and papist. He uses the outsider's familiar language of resentment toward spiritual exclusivism. Popery embodies "an asserting of *Infallibility* to one Sett of Men, and what is Fanaticism, but Persons being Obstinate in their own Way, *reviling, despising,* and *persecuting* (had they Power) all who differ from them?"[29]

The Methodists amplified this resentment in several ways. One essential Calvinist argument was based upon the Thirty-Nine Articles' belief in justification by faith, predestination, and perseverance in God's judgment of those whom he has predestined, as in articles 9, 10, and especially 17. These Reformation tenets rested upon Reformation authority. Jonathan Warne was among those who responded harshly to Joseph Trapp's claims that Methodists were overrighteous enthusiasts. Warne in turn insisted that Trapp was a schismatic "who departs from, and banters the *Doctrine of Assurance*," which once had been so important within the reformed church but "began to decline" under Charles I and Archbishop Laud. These and other "doctrines are now unfashionable with the polite, letter-learned Men of these Times." As Warne says elsewhere, hypocritical Anglican clergymen subscribe the truth of the Thirty-Nine Articles. Once in a secure living, "they take upon them to put another Sense on the Articles, than the Compilers ever meant."[30]

Others also lamented the new and celebrated the old sense. In 1768 the Oxford High Churchman Thomas Nowell and Sir Richard Hill engaged in a theological exchange regarding what Hill insisted was deficient orthodox Anglican theology. Hill defied Nowell "to find one Divine of any note, from the Reformation to CHARLES the first, who embraced your opinions about free-will, justification, and the Spirit's influence." When Sir Richard finds arguments on his own behalf, he reverts to Edward VI, James I, and the Synod of Dort (1618–19) for "the sense of our Reformers, and of the original, pure, primitive Church of *England*." These, alas, now are regarded as absurd. A putative enlightened faction "has since prevailed towards the overthrow of the Church." In so writing, Sir Richard joined Jonathan Warne, Robert Seagrave, and a Lover of Truth. They long had insisted that the Church of England had *"Turn'd Dissenter at Last,"* that it *"properly so call'd, is not now existing,"* and that anti-Methodist Joseph Trapp should be *"Vindicated from the Imputation of Being a Christian."*[31]

Methodist pleas for a return to Reformation theology indeed were early and consistent. By 1731 a troubled evangelical insisted that the deist threat required restoration of the "Old Divinity." He means "that Scheme in Religion, which ascribes Human Salvation to *supernatural Assistance*; being the Scheme of the Protestant Reformation, contain'd in the Church-Articles, and constantly taught by the Body of Divines, till the present Century." Modern divines have become Arian and wrongly depend upon inadequate reason as a guide. A few years later Robert Seagrave lamented establishment ministers' politely tepid but destructive preaching. They have allowed natural religion "to shut out Reveal'd Religion, and *supersede* the GOSPEL." Jonathan Warne soon praised several dissenting groups, like Baptists and Presbyterians as paradoxical supports of the true Church of England. Unlike the present establishment, they preached and wrote about the importance of "original Sin, Free-will" and the like. Shortly thereafter, Warne thanked Whitefield for preaching doctrines *"which are almost lost, and exploded by a Great Part"* of the Anglican clergy. Richard Finch would put much of this into ironic praise of Joseph Trapp. He preaches "the *modern Gospel*, not that which JESUS CHRIST taught," which long has been laid aside in favor of the new one "which you and many of your *Brethren* preach." The powerful modern clergy have so ignored the true Bible and the true Thirty-Nine Articles that they have as little to do with religion as "the *Histories* of *Tom Thumb*, and *Jack the Giant Killer*, or any romance whatever." Robert Seagrave epitomized many of these objections in 1740:

"The original Foundation of our Church was Calvinism." The Church of England now has "substituted in its Room a mere moral one, [and] it is effectually another Object."[32]

That other object responded in two ways. In one, it said No, we are not enemies of our own Church. As usual in such polemics, it turned the already turned rhetoric upon its adversary. Charles Chauncy was among those who knew that Methodists were imagination-crazed enthusiasts and "not therefore capable of being argued with; you had as good reason with the wind."[33] All the heat to the contrary, however, the church slowly followed the trend in rejecting the magistrate's arms as an extension of its power. There was indeed persecution of Methodists, especially in their early days. This normally was by individuals and groups rather than by the state's fire, faggot, and royally dispatched armed troops, sent, no doubt, with lovingly Christian orders to exterminate, exile, or forcibly convert the heretic false brethren.

Granting the usual exceptions in human conduct, responses to Methodists followed this approximate pattern: physical violence became verbal violence, which became theological and then political debate. In that process, Wesleyan Methodists sometimes joined the latitudinarian Anglican Church. This coalition either could repudiate the Reformation's Augustinian roots, on which Calvinists insisted, or, in the Church of England's second response, more temperately say that even the Reformation was not as Calvinist as its critics claimed. This confrontation forced the Church of England's substantial changes into the open as it moved, figuratively speaking, from the darker High Church Genevan Tudors and Stuarts to the lighter and lower church Canterbury Hanoverians. As in other instances of evolutionary eighteenth-century culture, the softening impulse eventually triumphed—if only after substantial defections from traditional Anglican worship even by the middling and some higher classes. In its characteristic way, the Church of England also lurched resolutely toward the center of the road. Instead of becoming roadkill, it became its own counterreformation to the Methodist reformation.

At least two important scriptural interpretations contributed to these Methodist contexts. One concerned the ongoing debates regarding original sin. Putative Arians, Socinians, deists, freethinkers, and even some lower church Whigs urged that one could not be guilty of a sin committed perhaps some fifty-five hundred years earlier. This concept was consistent with the argument of those seeking to mitigate High Church fury against Dissenters. All of their subsequent generations should not be held accountable for the root-and-branch destruction of monarchy and episcopacy by their ancestors. By simple extension, if the loyal Presbyterians of 1702 were not guilty of the regicide of 1649, it was equally true that Christians of 1702 were not guilty of Adam's disobedience in 5,552.[34] John Scott dedicated his anti-Methodist *Fine Picture of Enthusiasm* (1744) to Edmund Gibson, bishop of London. Scott made plain that he regarded those spiritual enthusiasts as propagating absurd and monstrous notions regarding the influence of Adam's sin upon consequent humanity,

> as if *all* Men were looked upon by God as guilty of their *first Parent*'s Crime, and as deserving *Death, eternal Death* for it; and that Man is *so* depraved by Reason thereof, that he has neither *Power* nor *Will* to do any Thing acceptable to his Maker.— *On the Contrary*, the *Sensual Enthusiast* will not admit of any Manner of Alteration, even in the *outward* Condition of Man.[35]

Neither High Church Anglicans nor Calvinist Methodists were pleased by such apparent revisionism. William Delaune clearly states the doctrinal importance of original sin: it is so weighty and important "a Fundamental Article of the Christian Faith" that God sent His son to compensate for our corruption. Anthony William Boehm, chaplain to Prince George of Denmark, drew the appropriate inference: "To put asunder these great and cardinal Principles, is to break the whole Order of our Salvation." He thus warned listeners of his sermon that Pelagians and others "will hardly allow any Taint of *Original* Corruption" or communication of Adam's sin to his posterity. Nonetheless, that sin muddied all of the human stream. "St. *Austin* is the first . . . who gives this Sin the Name of *Original* Sin."[36]

Matters were indeed worse than Boehm thought. By 1719 Samuel Clarke had joined those who urged reconsideration of the words of the "first Reformers" if those words were based on human and not scriptural authority, as with original sin and predestination. Consequently, these terms now are by most men understood . . . in a Sense which it is not very certain the Compilers originally intended." Henry Heywood later negatively enlarged Boehm's identification of Saint Augustine as the originator, not merely of the name, but of the concept, without biblical grounding. Here again is an evolutionary process consistent with other theological trends. Augustine fabricated both the homicidal interpretation of Luke 14:23 and the concept of permanent human depravity. Each wants rejecting. As Heywood insists, Augustine and Jerome were destructive innovators whose singularity the Apostles would have rejected, who abandoned their own and the early church's views, and who wrongly introduced "new Opinions in the West." Most church ancients "abhorred and abominated such Conceits as the *Calvinists* have vented on these Points." Anti-Augustinianism and anti–original sin solidified throughout the eighteenth century, crossed the Atlantic, and evoked controversy in the New England colonies. Samuel Webster's *A Winter Evening's Conversation Upon the Doctrine of Original Sin, Between a Minister and three of his Neighbours accidentally met together* (1757) proclaims that "one St. *Augustine*" invented the irrational and irreligious concept of original sin. When writing their Articles, the English reformed churchmen paid "more regard to St. *Augustine* than to the *Bible*, and so they were formed upon that plan." Wise men resisted them from the start, and now "almost all the clergy of the Church of *England* profess to have given up those *Augustine* doctrines, and to be on the other side [of] the question." Both a Lover of the Gospel in London and Nicholas Manners in York later also agreed that original sin was not in the Bible. George Dyer was among those who made overt that the undesirable term and concept were the products of that "frail saint" who generated his theory, not from the Bible, but by "his own passions as well as by his dispute with Pelagius and Celestius."[37]

Denial of original sin had theologically traumatic implications. A kindly London curate nonetheless scolded "the Absurdity of the Modern Doctrine" of universal corruption and the consequent need for universal regeneration. That was contrary to scripture and to the beauty of little children leading us. It also was clear evidence that God neither knew nor inculcated "this Romantic Doctrine of the Universal Turpitude of our Nature; or of any of the Cruel and Injurious Consequences drawn from it." Richard Finch was equally blunt and theologically astounding: Jesus blessed all and cleansed all; "properly speaking, there is now existing no such thing as Original Sin, nor is any one, strictly speaking, born a sinner." Such remarks could not have surprised either Joseph Priestley as a Gospel Lover or Nicholas Manners. Both believed that the sacrifice purged any notion of original sin. For Priestley, not to believe this means that "then hath Christ died, and the gospel been published in vain."[38]

These views denote a major change in Anglican and in some dissenting points of view. The change was even sharper regarding article 17 of the Thirty-Nine Articles, which concerned the always controversial theory of predestination. High Church Anglicans and Methodist Calvinists agreed that it was central to proper Reformation Christianity. In so arguing, the Whitefield Methodists also embraced an ever more alien or at least distant concept. Even the controversial lower church bishop Gilbert Burnet cited official Church of England policy regarding the Thirty-Nine Articles. According to the thirty-sixth canon, the clergyman must willingly submit to and preach the Articles "and *acknowledge all and every Article to be agreeable to the Word of God*." He also must "read the Articles in the Church, with a Declaration of his *Unfeigned Assent to them*. These things appear to be very plain."[39] It should also be plain that deviation from the Articles was deviation from God's word—unless, that is, from the nominal Reformation to the nominal Enlightenment powerful and generally lower church Anglican theologians had redefined their concept of God as well as of individual articles. Within this process, conflicts with Methodist and with lingering High Church Calvinists were inevitable and often unpleasant, as they discussed conflicting versions of a benevolent God.

As in other cases, Bishop Burnet was a central player in this drama. He also was centrally concerned with the Anglican confession as inclusive rather than exclusive. Accordingly, we recall, his *Exposition of the Thirty-Nine Articles* (1699) troubled High Church Anglicans. He sought to avoid disputes about words, to reduce argument, and to bring "men to a better understanding of one another and to a mutual Forbearance in these matters" (p. vi). Burnet claimed not to take sides in disputes concerning interpretations of scripture in general and of the Thirty-Nine Articles in particular. He was especially concerned with article 17, on predestination, and especially clear on explaining his new method. He states "the Arguments of all sides with so much Fairness" that his own opinion is invisible (p. vi). Religious controversialists invariably think themselves right and their adversaries wrong. Efforts to unify them are useless "Projects." The only sensible approach is impartially to lay out the strengths and weaknesses of each side as explained by "wise and good Men: Here is a Foundation laid for Charity" (p. vii). Yet more, Burnet immediately acknowledged and encouraged a major change in the Anglican response to Saint Augustine. The Articles had not been much explicated, because they seemed "so plain a Transcript of St. *Austin*'s Doctrine," but now "the far greater Number" of Anglican divines are "of a different Opinion" (p. 1). Burnet extends the implication of his remarks when discussing Augustine on predestination in the key seventeenth article. Yes, as with "St. *Austin*'s Doctrine," those who wrote the article probably meant that men are damned unless predestined to have been saved, but "since they have not said it, those who subscribe the Articles do not seem to be bound to any thing, that is not expressed in them." For Burnet, most Anglican clergymen now "may subscribe this Article without renouncing their Opinion as to this matter" (p. 168). After all, the church itself "has not been peremptory" and "a Latitude has been left to different Opinions" (p. 170).

Burnet's views are representative rather than innovative. Thomas Bennet's *Directions For Studying . . . Divinity* (1715) is stark. Like commentators on original sin, he finds no scriptural basis for absolute predestination. If that were the required meaning, he "could not subscribe to the Use of the Liturgy." Like Burnet, he believes that since the church does not dictate belief on that score, those who so believe may do so, but he "will not be bound to do the same." A Cambridge man later tells his Oxford compatriot to believe that latitude of interpretation is preferable to the limited meaning of the words, even if the church so believed. Implicitly like Burnet, he asks: if the church designed limited belief, "why did she not so express her self?"[40]

John Veneer and Edward Welchman offered a partial answer to the Cambridge author. At one point we read that indeed the article only asserts the grace of election and is silent on the severity of reprobation. Welchman nonetheless urges the reader to stop and to restrain his curiosity at the brink of predestination, that "profound Abyss" whose depths there is no reason for a young man to plumb. It is even less proper for preachers to "trouble their Auditors about these deep Mysteries: They should rather set forth God's Promises in general Terms, as they are propos'd in the Holy Scriptures, and as it is our Duty to embrace them." Veneer makes his own views known in other editions. Why should we understand article 17 "in the most harsh and severe Sense, when the Words do not, of Necessity, import any such Meaning?"[41] Bluntly, predestination is worth neither contemplating nor preaching. It may in fact be incomprehensible.

Many other clergymen within the Church of England also expanded upon Bishop Burnet's latitude. Some commentators even dismissed the Thirty-Nine Articles as either secondary or antique relics. Charles Chauncy, in Boston, told his flock to adhere to the Bible as their "great rule of judgement." The combination of scripture and reason, and not the unmentioned Articles, is a proper guide. John Scott was yet more overt and punitive when he distinguished between the Articles and Christianity. Calvinists' only support for predestination is their presumed adherence to the relevant articles. Never mind. They are not consistent with one another, do not embody "the Doctrines of *pure Christianity*," and are "irreconcilable with the Doctrine of the *New Testament*." Yes, clergymen subscribe the Articles, but their chief concern is their flock. They are "the *Ministers of Jesus Christ*" and therefore should preach "the *Doctrine of Jesus*" rather than the Articles "of such a *Civil Constitution*." Even High Church John Free urged latitude of interpretation when it suited his anti-Methodist purposes: no one should preach against the Thirty-Nine Articles, since those indeed describe God's attributes. Nonetheless, some are more important than others, and ecclesiastical authorities have "a Liberty of Interpretation" to reconcile presumed inconsistencies.[42]

As I have suggested, on this score Calvinist Methodists and High Church Anglicans were of one mind regarding innovations that threatened the foundations of orthodox belief. We know that William Binckes so argued on behalf of the Lower Convocation's censure of Burnet and, by implication, those who followed what they thought his nearly heretical mode of proceeding. The *Exposition* offended "the Generality of the Clergy." Burnet's method is not neutral; it is prejudicial to Anglican belief. Religious words are not subject to various interpretation; they are defined by what the church says is authentic and orthodox. Binckes isolated an issue that in different ways was urgent both to lower church Anglicans and to Calvinist Methodists. We know his insistence that if a new sense of the Thirty-Nine Articles differs from the established church's "Doctrine and Practice . . . it is in effect to frame new Articles of Religion, and bids fair for putting the Reformation upon a new foot, or at least does change the Boundaries, and alters the Terms of Communion." The latitude that Burnet encouraged could render subscription to the Articles "altogether insignificant" and "more effectually open a way to *Comprehension* than any thing that hath yet been thought of." Given Burnet's emphasis on latitude, one can subscribe an article and not believe in its stated words. The church, however, expressly declares "that such as subscribe to the Articles, should agree in the things therein contain'd."[43] For Binckes and for so much of the Lower Convocation, the bishop of Sarum undermined God's word, Augustine's recording of it, and the Church of England's hitherto reliable implementation of such truths. Binckes correctly thought that a new moderate theology would evoke a new reformation. In 1702 he could not be aware that there would be two reformations: the latitudinarian Church of England against its own origins, and the Methodists, especially the Calvinists, against that reformation on behalf of a return to origins. These men and women were as firmly opposed to comprehension as was Binckes, if for different reasons. However one parses those reasons, the newer Anglican concept of God remained essential. It rejected Augustinian predestination as firmly as it rejected Augustinian persecution based on his reading of Luke 14:23.

Like the Methodists, the lower Church of England ably defended itself with articulate and tireless apologists. They well understood the nature of their changes or reinterpretations of Reformation principles. They also proudly knew and proudly proclaimed that their concept of God was not compatible with the notion of a God who inexplicably damned almost all of humanity. As we have seen, in the often startling process they even challenged Augustine's basic concept of original sin, a challenge in which some Wesleyan Methodists, if not Wesley himself, were pleased to join. This revisionism in turn was part of the gradual perhaps sentimentalizing of traditional religion that finally led to an ecclesiastical "man of feeling," well exemplified in Sterne's seventh sermon, "Vindication of Human Nature." Long before then, however, Edward Young was a chaplain in ordinary to George II and dedicated his *Vindication of Providence* (1737) to Queen Caroline. He there affirms an increasingly Whiggish divinity alien to Whitefield's darker views: God did not create a world of gloom and doom, but one in which joy and legitimate pleasure were omnipresent. He both enabled and enjoined man "to be Happy."[44] Young's compatriots sought to help in that process.

Indeed, by 1737 Young had voiced the lower church Anglican establishment's position. It could be stern, but, all things considered, it was reasonably muted in the face of the Calvinist Methodist challenge. We know that a curate of London made plain one reason for that relatively irenic tone: Since the Hanoverian accession, "this Part of the World has been quieter, with respect to Religion, than at any time for so long a period together." Britons now debate religious issues "without being liable to those Terrors, or coercive Operations" that hitherto victimized those who differed "with the Majority. . . . Long, very long, may this be thy Boast, O happy *Britain*! favorite Isle." This happy man's respectful letter in 1739 is confident that the Gospel represents God "as the kind and beneficent Father of All Men." He could not have been the creator of "the fruitful wild Fancies of Dark, Imaginative Men."[45]

Others not quite so calm as the courtly curate were nonetheless equally insistent on God's universal rather than selective benevolence, favored by Calvinists. Their chorus was large, and their voices often basso profundo, as they angrily proclaimed love. Ebenezer Hewlett told Whitefield that he and his cohorts ignored "the first Principles of Religion," namely, that God judges us by our works and that God is not partial but universal in his love, for which mankind loves him in his perfection. Such a God could not design the bulk of humanity for damnation and become an appalling felon: "Is not this murdering mens SOULS by thousands?" John Wilder draws the relevant conclusion from that sort of question. If Calvinist predestination is true, "How is the God of all Mercy and Goodness, the God of Love, Comfort, and Joy, turned into a Cruel and Tyrannical Being, that delights not to save, but to destroy Mankind!" John Scott equally rejects the apparent Calvinist angry God who would turn mankind against him for damning so many to "everlasting Misery!" That is not God as one who "*equally desires the Happiness of all*" but a God who is "*injurious* and *hateful*." The Wesleyan Methodist Richard Finch joined his lower church Anglican friends in this view. The Calvinists make God abominably wicked, and a "great part of mankind unjustly and wretchedly miserable."[46]

Evan Lloyd's *The Methodist* in 1766 presents perhaps the most moving and troubled response to this aspect of Calvinist theology. He apologizes for his anger but anathematizes the fraudulent rotten saints who disfigure reason, truth, and both Jesus and God, whom they make

> A *Tyrant-God* of Cruelty!
> As if thy *right Hand* did contain
> Only an Universe of Pain,
> *Hell* and *Damnation* in thy *Left*,
> Of ev'ry gracious Gift bereft,
> Hence raining Floods of Grief and Woes,
> On those that never were thy Foes,

Ordaining Torments for the doom
Of Infants, yet within the Womb. (P. 50)

Lloyd's almost tactile heat testifies to at least three major developments in the history of eighteenth-century Methodism: the anger that the Calvinist theory of predestination could evoke; the power of what I have called the Anglican counter-reformation in the face of the Methodist new reformation; and the symbiotic relationship between the Church of England and its Methodist brethren, some of whom insisted that they too were loyal sons of the national church. John Wesley so insisted throughout his life.

Grudging Acceptance

We should neither exaggerate the progress of "toleration" nor gloss over the ongoing dislike, disagreement, and in many cases downright hatred of Methodists in the eighteenth century and beyond. Many still shared the view expressed in Joseph Trapp's catalog title: *The True Spirit of the Methodists, and their Allies (Whether other Enthusiasts, Papists, Deists, Quakers, or Atheists) Fully Laid Open* (1740). For the like-minded, the church still was in danger and still needed men like John Free to savage Methodists. In 1758 he tells his parishioners that those false brethren "who decry their lawful Teachers, do sometimes *avowedly*, and always *virtually* oppose their lawful Governors." In one text of 1759 he knows that their *"Pernicious* PRINCIPLES" endanger the nation, induce atheism, and should bring Wesley to the whipping post or the pillory. In the same year he again labels them "as dangerous to *any* STATE, and particularly our *own Constitution.*" These *"Hellhounds"* threaten to subvert the Church of England and are seditious potential revolutionaries. They induce "downright *Atheism*," he says elsewhere, dissolve society, and perpetuate "a Sort of *Treason*" that should be controlled by the magistrate.[47] The wholesome severities of Luke 14:23 were in retreat but fought vigorous rear-guard action. In 1760 as in 1706 hatred sought excuses rather than reasons.

That much being said, however, a version of acceptance, change, or at the least a change of kinds of attack upon Methodists clearly had taken place from the late 1730s to the late 1790s. One reason was well expressed in the London curate's remark that post-Hanoverian religious toleration had raised the tone of disagreement. That trend increased as the century increased. In 1793 Samuel Bradburn asked a once burning question: are the Methodists Dissenters? He begins with symbolically declarative sentences. Had he raised the question two hundred years earlier, it would have been "of great importance to those whom it concerned, as life or death might have been the consequence of the decision. At present, blessed be the Lord, it is but of little moment." When James Creighton responded to Bradburn he confirmed that "persecution has not been encouraged by the Hanoverian family."⁴⁸

One key reason that the Hanoverians did not encourage persecution was that the Methodists regularly expressed their loyalty to the nation in general and to the reigning dynasty in particular. As early as 1740 Robert Seagrave argued that a legal church establishment was harmful to the state and increased rather than decreased disruption. Many British subjects nevertheless wanted few rights for nonconformists. The "present Royal Family must never expect to become their real Admiration." Seagrave soon put the argument more positively. From George I forward, "high-flying Principles received a Check, and Liberty revived.... Bigotry, has evidently lost Ground; and Liberty is more understood and esteemed daily." Providence may have reserved for Britain the honor of bringing liberty "to its Perfection." Wesley himself proclaimed his love for England "as that Part of the World, and *the Church* as that Part of *England*, to which all we who are born and have been brought up therein, owe our first and chief Regard." He urged fellow Methodists to attend Anglican services, avoid dissenting meeting houses, and, if ministers, avoid dissenting modes of preaching. Methodists soon extended their loyalty to the third George. In 1760 Martin Madan twice expressed Methodist affection for the Crown. At first he insisted that Whitefield's preaching of virtue had so moralized the common people that if there were a rebellion, twenty thousand Methodists would band together "to repel the invaders of their king and country." Shortly thereafter he exhorted his parishioners to lament the sad death of George II, "of ever-blessed memory." Since George III inherited his grandfather's virtues, Madan advised Methodists to maintain their laudable and "remarkable loyalty and veneration for your sovereign." Madan expressed a familiar British conservative assumption that soon enlarged within Methodist circles: "Without a respectful submission to the royal authority, the ends of government can never be answered."⁴⁹

Hanoverian indifference to High Church demands, the increasing lower church dominance, and demonstrable Methodist loyalty were important factors in their assimilation, or their diminished exclusion, as the case may be. In addition, however, the growing Methodist numbers reduced rather than enhanced national fear. There were indeed ugly riots and persecutions aplenty, theatrical and poetic attacks and mockery, and consequent ongoing denigration. Britain nonetheless suffered neither an armed nor an unarmed Methodist putsch. No Methodist troops in tartans or Methodist Scots wrote recipes for human haggis during the '45. Methodists were becoming increasingly important in trade, and as the 1768 Methodist expulsions from Oxford made plain, they remained sufficiently ambitious for themselves and their cause to seek university degrees. The church to which they aspired while at university had become ever more Erastian and less troubled by arguments once potentially fatal regarding whether matters were indifferent or essential—like crossing, the wearing of a surplice, or kneeling before the altar. On an equally important scale Madan, if perhaps with overstatement, correctly observed that Methodist attention to the underclass had improved the quality and safety of public life. Circa 1740, he said, "the bulk of the common people" throughout the kingdom had regularly engaged in "murders and robberies in the streets and highways." Now the situation has mended, and "the lower class of people are reduc'd to a regularity and good behaviour, that is not to be paralleled in the inhabitants of any great nation upon earth."[50]

These and other reasons had clear implications for Methodism's place in the eighteenth century. Granting predictable exceptions, as in the case of John Free, hostility began to change its face. There were fewer analogies with 1641, revolutionary Puritanism, and regicide. For the most part, Methodism no longer seemed a threat to episcopacy or to the state. Crown and Protestant church, however defined, still were cognate. Anglican ongoing skirmishes with Methodists overwhelmingly were about doctrine, like the relevance of Calvinism and the conflict of faith and works. Methodist loyalty no longer was questioned and soon would be loudly proclaimed. One could still properly hate that Other, but increasingly and dramatically it was about whether Methodists endangered Christian souls, rather than whether they endangered the dynasty or the miter.

We see the stark change from 1714 to 1766 in the difference between two roughly similar, violent biblical allusions. The Independent minister Thomas Bradbury preached during the decades of Sacheverell-like High Church attempts to limit comprehension and to demonize Dissenters. In a sermon read shortly after George I's accession, Bradbury alludes to Psalms 18:42 and calls upon the new monarch to behave like divinely inspired David and pulverize God's enemies—here the High Church. Beat them *"as fine as Dust before the Wind . . . cast them out as Dirt in the Streets."* For Bradbury, as for religious polemicists of almost all persuasions, power required religion and religion required power, often through the magistrate's arms. Evan Lloyd later used Matthew 21:44 with comparable violence, but to a different source of power. In that parable, a master lets out his vineyard to husbandmen, whom he later asks to return the fruits of his vines. The husbandmen fear that the master will replace them, and so they beat or kill all of his messengers, including the master's own son. Jesus as speaker draws the appropriate conclusion, in which a stone once rejected from a building becomes its foundation: "And whosoever shall fall on this stone shall be broken; but on whom it shall fall, it will grind him to powder."

For Lloyd, the request is not that the magistrate root out this cursed race because it threatens the church and state. Instead, he asks God to do that job, because the Methodists endanger the human in the world, not the church in the world:

> Root, root from *Earth*, those baneful weeds,
> That choak *Religion's wholesome Seeds*!
> Give them the headlong Winds to bear,
> And scatter in a desert Air!
> Grind them to Powder, that no more
> They sprout and grow as heretofore!

Lloyd is in an exterminating mood. As in many other such outbursts, though, he mentions neither church nor state, religious conformity nor nonconformity, High Church nor Low. As major evolution in the thirtieth of January sermons demonstrated, regicide, 1641, and dynastic change had diminished evocative power. Lloyd's anger is a function of perceived abuse of God's mercy and love and man's obligation to put these into earthly practice: "Thy boundless *Goodness* they blaspheme!" God's teaching proceeds "By *friendly Arguments*." Calvinist Methodists apparently proceed by inducing "Floods of Grief and Woes, / On those that never were thy Foes."[51] Lloyd is as angry as Bradbury or as a comparable Sacheverell. The source of the anger is the Methodists' presumed malign betrayal of humanity rather than of the monarch or the archbishop of Canterbury.

The change marks another dramatic evolution in the half-century from Defoe to Lloyd and Smollett and from Swift (b. 1667) to Johnson (b. 1709). Methodists indeed were not yet fully integrated into British culture, but they had been integrated as conventional objects of secular political attack. Their leader was labeled a scoundrel who would have turned free Britons into slaves of George III and his surely satanic ministry. The example of John Wesley, America, and Samuel Johnson illustrates this event.

Johnson's *Taxation No Tyranny* appeared in 1775. Though unsigned, it was promptly recognized and promptly vilified. The perpetrator of *The Pamphlet, Entitled "Taxation No Tyranny," Candidly Considered* knew that unpatriotic, Jacobite Johnson refused to support the Crown regarding the Falkland Islands, was an enemy to the constitution, and sought "to oppress and enslave a free people." His "policy, almost freezes the blood in our veins—and our natures shrink back with horrour." The warmer man behind another *Answer to . . . Taxation no Tyranny* had better circulation but nonetheless proclaimed that Johnson sought "to ripen tumult to anarchy, and dissatisfaction to rebellion." He would create "waste and extirpation." Even less abusive commentators knew that Johnson was the unfortunate author.⁵² These unfair and severe attacks addressed themselves both to Johnson and to the king and his ministers.

John Wesley walked blithely and blindly into a clearly labeled minefield. His *Calm Address to our American Colonies* (1775) filched Johnson's central arguments and much of his wording without acknowledging his source. For example, the American colonists had no rights other than those granted by the Crown's charter and by Parliament, in which governing power properly resided. The large majority of British subjects in the mother country cannot vote but nonetheless are dutiful subjects. Almost all consent to law is passive, since even voters have not voted for almost all of the laws under which they live. Ancestors of the American colonists could not vote on their own taxes, so the colonists have not given up anything. Denial of the right to tax denotes denial of other civil or criminal laws. Unlike Johnson, however, Wesley concludes with an exhortation to fear God and honor the king. Both Wesley's royalism and his plagiarism promptly were so labeled and abused by Augustus Toplady, for whom the *Calm Address* is "a Bundle of Lilliputian Shafts picked and STOLEN out of Dr. *Johnson's* Pin-cushion." Toplady uses ten pages of double columns to show Johnson on one side and Wesley as clone on the other. Wesley flatters the Crown and steals from Johnson in hopes of a pension and of becoming a bishop at large, or an English bishop, or even the first American bishop.⁵³

Others also scolded Wesley for that plagiarism and more than scolded him for the ideas within his *Calm Address*. By then pro-Americans already had made Johnson a political antichrist, so attacks upon him were amplified by attacks upon Wesley. The blunt political theorist behind *A Constitutional Answer to the Rev. Mr. John Wesley's Calm Address* (1775) bruised the "disingenuous" and "insidious" author and eulogized the invaluable British political achievement. His typographical aids help those unable to decode his subtlety: "Blush, if ye can, ye JOHNSONS and WESLEYS, who are endeavouring . . . to perswade men, that they are inevitably born SLAVES." Caleb Evans knew that the plagiarist really hoped to revive "*hereditary indefeasible* right" and to restore the Stuarts. *Fallacy Detected* (1775) insists that Wesley's allies the Tories, Jacobites, and papists are anti-American and pro-ministerial. Beneath the calm exterior, Wesley himself seeks to "consign the noble spirited Americans to the utmost rigour of tory despotism and cruelty." A Lover of Truth and the British Constitution also wades into the political ebb tide's fetid backwater. Wesley is an advocate of divine right, endorses the politics of Charles I and James II, favors arbitrary power, and is an ignorant "Friend to Popery . . . to *France* and *Spain*, to *Rome* and the *Pretender*." No wonder, then, that he is "a greater Enemy to the *Constitution* of these Kingdoms, than any one that I know is to the King or kingly Government." He and his followers have nearly arrived to a "Pitch of Madness." The equally intemperate Patrick Bull gored Wesley, whose pamphlet he found worthy of Father Petre, James II's Jesuit adviser: He surely planned to turn good Anglican Britons into slaves, no doubt wearing wooden shoes crafted in part by Johnson. Would the minister of peace Wesley have sought, we hear in words redolent of some response to Defoe's *Shortest Way with the Dissenters*, "to kindle the torch of war, and to foment a civil dissension?" Was he really a hypocrite with black "designs that lurked within a deceitful heart"? Presumably he was, for Wesley wrote the *Calm Address* "to usher in *despotism*."[54]

Wesley continued to be abused for his pro-ministerial views and as usual defended them as best he could. In a new edition of the *Calm Address* he tells the reader that he once had a different view but that after he read *Taxation No Tyranny* he changed his mind, adapted its arguments, and anticipated the brutal treatment he received: "but let it be, so I may in any degree serve my King and Country." Both should know that the "designing men, the Ahitophels are in England."[55] Like John Dryden long before him, John Wesley now alerts his monarch and fellow subjects to the political danger from within, but certainly not from the supportive messenger. That political service indeed is my point as we return to the Lover of Truth's untrue comment that Wesley and his followers "are arrived nearer to the Pitch of Madness, than any People that I know."[56] The truthteller is talking about political, not religious, followers and madness, with which Wesley and his people once were accused. His readers of course knew that the Reverend Mr. Wesley was the preeminent founder of the Methodist movement, but affiliation plays a small role in the attacks. He has become yet another placeseeker, political miscreant, and ally of various Tory stock-figure villains, including Samuel Johnson, who regularly were displayed in the Whigs' cabinet of horrors.

In 1775 few rational Britons could have feared a Jacobite attempt to restore the Stuarts. The desicated alcoholic Charles Edward Louis Philip Casimir long had been banished from France and domiciled in Rome, the city of his birth and supporter of his Catholic faith. France, Spain, and the papacy regarded him as the "Count of Albany" rather than as the royal Charles III he preferred to be. As the author of *A Reply to an Appeal from the Protestant Association* (1780) said a few years later, "It is well known, the Pretender has lost all influence with the Court of Rome."[57] Charles' brother Henry Benedict Stuart, nominal Cardinal York and Duke of York in the Jacobite succession, was the last legitimate Stuart claimant to the British Crown. Upon Charles Edward's death in 1788 he also was styled and ignored as "King Henry IX." He was baptized by Pope Benedict XIII on 6 March 1725. By 1775 he had been archbishop of Corinth (1758) and cardinal-bishop of Frascati (1761), with further dignities in the Catholic hierarchy to follow. Aside from rumors of his homosexuality, and thus reduced likelihood of producing an heir, he was a demonstrably improbable cause for which British Catholics were likely to fight. Neither Stuarts nor civil war for their sclerotic dynasty were risks worth taking at home or abroad. The charge of Jacobitism was traditional partisan mudslinging sadly made easier by Wesley's foolish plagiarism, association with JOHNSON, and with the ethic of political SLAVERY he no doubt shared with WESLEY.

Several of Wesley's detractors indeed found him as religiously virtuous as politically vicious, for like other British polemicists, they had learned to compartmentalize, to separate the secular from the theological. Wesley's acceptably generic Protestant Christianity then replaced his unacceptably schismatic Methodist Christianity. By later in John's life he in fact was on good terms with the Anglican Church and had been invited to preach from its pulpits. The *Constitutional Answer* thus observes that its author has seen Wesley "with pleasure, in the character of a *Christian Minister*" who did "some good in the moral world." He regrets that Wesley now is "a *Court Sycophant*, doing much more harmful mischief in the political world." Caleb Evans knows that multitudes follow Wesley and hopes that he will be steadier and more consistent as "*Divine*, than . . . as *Politician*." The Lover of Truth rejoices in Wesley's religious success and hopes he continues his role "in awakening Sinners, and turning them from Darkness to Light, and from the Power of Satan to GOD." A work like the *Calm Address* shows that Wesley must repent. Patrick Bull aggressively asks: "Has he left preaching, which was his province, for politicks, which were not?"[58] The clergyman who once seemed the proud self-created saint seeking to reform the Church of England had become the placeseeker willing to barter freedom for a potential bishopric within that still unreformed church. Here was assimilation all too familiar to political discourse of any time.

An exchange in 1796 further suggests Methodism's generally benevolent, if noisy, intrusion into the mainstream of British Protestant ecclesiastical life. The Reverend John Gardiner's *Brief Reflections on the Eloquence of the Pulpit* (London, 1796) laments that the Church of England's sermons have become tiresome, overly rational, and at the least no longer attract congregants. That was scarcely the case for the Methodists. Whatever the nonsense of their doctrines, they so zealously and sincerely pronounce them "that the populace cannot resist the force of their impressions." They suspend their reason and become Methodist converts—less to the religion than "to the efficacious and persuasive manner in which these doctrines are delivered." Gardiner draws a visually painful conclusion: "Hence our Churches are deserted, and Conventicles are crowded" (pp. 56–57).

Gardiner's *Reflections* also belabored those too many British subjects who supported France rather than Britain in the revolutionary wars. He was answered by the anonymous author of *A Letter to the Rev. John Gardiner*, who spared few adjectives against the presumably wretched friend to tyranny—with the exception of his limited praise of Methodists, upon which the answerer enlarged. He quoted lines just after David Hartley said that the way to check Methodist irregularities is for the Church of England "to adopt their Zeal, and Concern for lost Souls." The Methodists in turn should respect their superiors, avoid "spiritual Selfishness," attachment to "particular Phrases and Tenets," and sour dissension, and instead become peacemakers and "be called the children of God." The author of the *Letter* added, however, that Hartley's comments now were largely outdated. This is due to "the indefatigable exertions, and wise regulations of that wonderful man JOHN WESLEY," whose memory he so admired.[59] The *Letter* writer's religion is not clear from his text. If he was an Anglican, respect for Wesley indicates respectful acceptance of the once Methodist Other. If he was a Methodist, acknowledgment of corrected errors indicates respectful acceptance of the previous Anglican Other. Citation of Wesley as opposed to Whitefield comparably suggests the triumph of the Methodist persuasion closer to the Church of England's establishment theology. Perhaps Wesley himself had it right when on 26 January 1777, after preaching at Anglican All Hallows Church in London, he comments: "How is this? Do I 'yet please men'? Is the offence of the cross ceased? It seems, after being a scandalous near fifty years, I am at length growing into an honourable man!"[60]

Neither amusing inclusion by political condemnation nor Anglican happy envy of persuasive sermons was the final word regarding eighteenth-century attitudes toward Methodists. Class divisions remained even for the upwardly mobile; the Church of England remained the seat of religious power; affirming the Thirty-Nine Articles remained a requirement for university admission; and students remained ignorant or indifferent regarding them in "Harlot" Oxford. As we shall see, political and religious rage would fatally return in 1780. Nonetheless, for the most part, and only that, later in the century Methodists profited from an ameliorative evolution in a softened political, religious, and dynastic realm. They also profited from a shift in attacks upon them—from their presumed affiliation with revolutionary Puritans to an attack upon Whitefield's apparently harsh theology. Perhaps as a culmination of this progress, they also received the characteristic British right to be branded as fools, traitors, villains, tyrants, Jesuits, hypocrites, Jacobites, absolutists, and various other kinds of monsters that one's benighted political opponents must be. Smollett's last novel exemplifies that trend toward an idiosyncratic kind of inclusion, but with a great novelist's evocation of the human ability to change, both by his characters and by himself.

Humphry Clinker: Joining the Family

Religion is a demonstrably important aspect of *Humphry Clinker* (1771). It plays a comic variation on *A Tale of a Tub*'s version of different churches in the world.

Swift is troubled by the collapse of unity. Smollett more or less accepts it as a fact of modern religious life. Matt Bramble as the gentry Church of England embodies the rational religion that the Anglican Church then embraced. The lawyer Mr. Mcklewhimmen embodies the dissenting Presbyterian self-importance, self-involvement, and hypocritical absorption of divine incursions into daily life. During a fire he knocks down all those in his way, because "charity begins at hame!"[61] When he is asked why in spite of the fire he placed a portmanteau on his shoulder, he replies that his good angel placed it there to protect him from the blows to his head (p. 172). These really were the blows of an angry clergyman's crutch when Mcklewhimmen knocked him down in a violent rush down the hall. Thereafter, Lismahago's grandfather was "one of the original covenanters," but he himself now seems to be a freethinker (pp. 187, 191).

The freethinker characterizes French Jesuit attempts to convert the Miami Native Americans as exercises in false theology by false thinkers unable to explain putative mysteries and revelations. According to Miami lights, these missionaries were indeed heretical to claim that God allowed his only son and equal to enter a woman's body, be born human, and be tortured and executed as a criminal. They were shocked when told that thereafter God allowed humans regularly to re-create "God himself, to swallow, digest, revive, and multiply him *ad infinitum*, by the help of a little flour and water." Like High Church Jonathan Swift, the Miami sachems regard transubstantiation as an abuse of reason and rational religion. They convict the French Jesuits of "blasphemy and sedition" and satisfy their desire for martyrdom (p. 191). The Methodist portions of *Humphry Clinker* are far more substantial in quantity and in quality, but they are part of the generally harsh estimate of religion at work in the novel. I say "generally," since one of the key themes of Smollett's novel is metamorphosis, which includes both our view and Matt Bramble's view of Humphry's Methodism. For example, Smollett notably chooses to portray the Jesuits' fatal failed mission to the Miamis, whereas both Wesley and Whitefield also were missionaries and returned home intact.

Such metamorphosis indeed extends to Smollett's own view of Methodism. Frances Brooke praised his *Critical Review*'s anti-Methodist bias.[62] In the fourth volume of his *Continuation of the History of England* (1768) Smollett labeled Methodism a ridiculous, schismatic, fanatical, irrational, enthusiastic infection of the lower classes. It was spread by the Wesleys and Whitefield, who preyed upon "Weak minds" and purses throughout the nation and the colonies. Too many "were seduced by the delusions of a superstition stiled Methodism, raised upon the affectation of superior sanctity, and maintained by pretensions to divine illumination." Nothing could be clearer regarding these hindrances to the "progress of reason, and free cultivation of the human mind."[63] *Humphry Clinker* itself, however, tells at the least a more benevolent tale, one consistent with the work of Smollett's less hostile final years than with his aggressive youth and middle years. Matt Bramble, after all, comes to love his illegitimate son and welcomes him to his home, his estate, his family, and his church. Along the way, the novel also makes clear that the presumably rational Anglican confession can be rationalized to justify sycophancy and potential murder.

The central Methodist theme of *Humphry Clinker* begins with two apparently interpolated tales that Jerry Melford relates to his Oxford chum Sir Watkin Phillips. Each appears shortly before Humphry does, each vividly contrasts with his later behavior, and each reflects badly upon the dominant English-Anglican culture as viewed by Moderate Scottish Presbyterian Smollett.

The first episode is the sort that angers Matt Bramble, for whom "ingratitude makes his teeth chatter" (p. 65), as well it might in the Paunceford-Serle tale. Paunceford had suffered adversity and poverty until Fortune and Mr. Serle's patronage raised him to a higher financial and social eminence. Fortune alas did not raise him to proper acknowledgment of those who helped him in adversity. He both ignores and gratuitously insults Serle, while allowing others to think that he gratefully repays his emotional and financial debts. Serle now lives in marginally genteel poverty, while indifferent Paunceford lives in palatial splendor.

The Eastgate-Prankley episode is both more dangerous and more demonstrably corrupting. Eastgate was "on the foundation" as a poor scholarship student at Queen's (p. 70). He attaches himself to George Prankley, a wealthy gentleman commoner at Oxford's most Establishment college, Christ Church. Prankley was to have the gift of a handsome ecclesiastical living, whose present incumbent soon would go to his reward. Eastgate flatters his potential donor, tolerates his insults, and follows him to Bath when he celebrates his enrichment and freedom from college. Prankley also publicly insults Eastgate and then further humiliates and betrays him by bestowing the living on another clergyman. The supplicant's patience and timidity turn to anger; the men squabble; Prankley challenges Eastgate to a duel; pistols will be fired at dawn. Prankley's frightened bluster before the pending combat nonetheless well epitomizes the episode's ethical vulgarity: "it ill became a clergyman to be concerned in quarrels and blood-shed" (p. 71). Eastgate compounds the error. He has sullied his clerical calling with self-promoting affected subordination, to which he adds secular and social intrusion on his nominal religion of peace. He demands a gentleman's right to violate the laws of God and man and to blow Eastgate's brains out in the name of personal honor. He will defend his religious order "even at the expence of my heart's blood; and surely it can be no crime to put out of the world a profligate wretch, without any sense of principle, morality, or religion" (p. 71)—words that apply to himself as well. In the event, Anglican ministerial hectoring works; Prankley wilts and withdraws, presents the living to Eastgate, and leaves Bath in disgrace.

Smollett clearly characterized troubling ingratitude in Serle and troubling abuse of religion in the Oxford-educated, ordained Anglican priest Eastgate. As poor men seeking to move upward through native ability, they, and Eastgate in particular, are rough analogues to Humphry. In contrast, he later fights only with a cudgel and then in defense of his budding love for Win Jenkins and against the servant fop Dutton. Humphry's response to Dutton's challenge implicitly comments upon Eastgate's immoral morality: Clinker will not falsely claim the gentlemen's privilege "to kill one another when they fall out; moreover, I would not have his blood upon my conscience for ten thousand times the profit or satisfaction I should get by his death" (p. 203). Eastgate is a conscienceless religious reprobate willing to murder for gain. Gratitude and sound religious principles that effect positive actions, as in the later prison sermon, blend in Humphry from almost the first time that we see him. Indeed, Humphry's growth and change and his relationship to the Bramble clan approximate the larger pattern of growth and change within the Methodist movement and the larger British conformist culture.

Though Humphry cannot know this, one of his chief early functions is a form of exorcism. Matt tells his friend and correspondent Dr. Lewes that he himself is "obliged to truckle to a domestic dæmon," his sister, Tabby, whose snarling character is well exemplified in her dog, Chowder (p. 74). When the Bramble carriage overturns, the distressed animal makes a meal of Matt's leg and the footman's finger. He promptly damns "the nasty son of a bitch, and them he belongs to" and is as promptly sacked when he demands that the dog be killed (p. 76). That footman is replaced by a sickly, shabby country lad who accidentally splits his britches and displays his bare bottom when riding postilion before Tabby, for whom poverty and illness are no excuse. She demands that Matt dismiss the impudent rascal. Matt does so after finding that Humphry is an honest and honorable young man who in the last six months has spent all of his little money on doctors. Matt has a physician friend who consistently helps him; Humphry is alone. Part of the scene anticipates Matt's second freeing, or expediting, of Humphry in London. "Heark ye, Clinker, you are a most notorious offender—You stand convicted of sickness, hunger, wretchedness, and want." Since Matt is not in the criminal-punishing business, he liberates and cures Humphry of his illness and isolation with the powerful magic of a golden guinea and compassion. Humphry "had the fever and ague these six months" (p. 80). With the generous separation benefit he redeems some of his clothing from pawn and becomes both smartly dressed and a good and grateful servant very unlike Paunceford. Matt "had been so good to him, that... he would follow him to the world's end, and serve him all the days of his life without fee or reward" (p. 81).

Like the previous footman, however, Humphry is willing to kill Chowder, except that in his case he will do so apparently at Tabby's own request. He is a clumsy server, pours custard on her shoulder, steps back onto Chowder and forces the dog's pained loud howl. For demon Tabby, though, Humphry's act was part of a conspiracy against her, for whom Chowder was surrogate. "Here it is: kill it at once; and then you'll be satisfied," she shouts (p. 82). Literal-minded Humphry is keen to please, seizes a knife, and promises to kill him neatly at a ditch in the roadside, for which he receives a box on the ear that sends him reeling. Like Matt, who used the word *family* in a sense he could not then understand, Tabby bases an ultimatum on the bond of blood relations: "You shall part with that rascal or me, upon the spot, without farther loss of time; and the world shall see whether you have more regard for your own flesh and blood, or for a beggarly foundling, taken from the dunghill" (p. 85).

Matt, enraged at the injustice, substitutes his own ultimatum: "Either discard your four-footed favourite, or give me leave to bid you eternally adieu—For I am determined, that he and I shall live no longer under the same roof." Matt reestablishes the patriarchal order that Tabby now accepts: "It is your prerogative to command, and my duty to obey," she admits (p. 85). Confrontation leads to reconciliation within two family units: the immediate one of brother and sister and the yet undiscovered distant one of father and illegitimate son. Had Matt surrendered to demonic demands, he might later not have been rescued by Humphry when the carriage overturned in the water. Of course he also never would have known that Humphry was the product of his youthful intemperance. Matt indeed inadvertently has shown regard for his own flesh and blood.

Smollett later elevates the scene's importance. The profligate Mrs. Baynard refuses to acknowledge her husband's request that they live within their moderate means. Her rejection insincerely mimics Tabby's sincere words: "It is your prerogative to command, and my duty to obey" (p. 277). The consequence is a dysfunctional family in which children die or are badly raised, the estate, finances, and farm are ruined, and only Mrs. Baynard's death and Matt's later intercession return normalcy. Humphry serves as conciliator and initiator of a *concordia discors*, as isolated, exploited, emotionally undisciplined Mr. Baynard cannot. In addition, by the end of the novel Lydia Melford has grown from a romantic postadolescent all agog at the great world that is not her provincial boarding school. Like her brother, she has matured and come to love her uncle Matt and to mistrust her aunt Tabitha, whose predatory husband-hunting conduct Lydia rejects as a female role model. She does not overreact when the thirteen-year-old young Baynard boy tries to steal a kiss, but she punches him soundly when he puts his hand in her bosom (p. 284). Once Wilson reappears, we see that her judgment of men in fact is reliable. Lydia no longer is a flighty girl, but a sensible young woman who also welcomes virtuous but illegitimate Humphry into her family. Hence, when she speaks about the basis of his conduct her words have special authority. His presence when Matt nearly drowned was not chance: "Providence really seems to have placed [Humphry] near him for the necessity of this occasion." Lydia is not superstitious when she says that he acted beyond "common fidelity—Was it not the voice of nature that loudly called upon him to save the life of his own father?" (p. 320). Providence was helped along far earlier, when Matt listened to his own voice of nature and helped and defended the indigent young man, who in turn reacted with the gratitude that united him to his then only surrogate father.

Methodist Humphry thus embodies the gratitude that Paunceford lacks and the reconciliation that those interpolated characters lack. As we soon see, Humphry also has sounder religious principles than Eastgate, the rational, homicidal university-trained Anglican priest. Indeed, it is hard to resist the suspicion that Smollett is contrasting "Harlot" Oxford Anglican Eastgate with the saintlike Humphry, a Methodist conceived in Oxford. Once Humphry arrives in London, he finds large numbers of the poor and others willing to hear him preach God's word—in the streets, without a licence, clerical garb, or examinations in theology and the learned languages. Here is one of the scenes in which the sophisticated, wealthy, reasonable Anglican religion meets the Methodist social upstart, whose preaching threatens the social distinctions that Matt requires for subordination.

Matt, Jery, and Mr. Barton have just left an amusing visit to the royal court and to the displaced Duke of Newcastle. They see Humphry outside on a stool before "a crowd of laqueys and chairmen . . . with his hat in one hand, and a paper in the other, in the act of holding forth to the people" (p. 97). Matt soon finds that Humphry was urging his fellow servants to avoid swearing. He expects to succeed by convincing them that he has their best interests at heart and that the "sin and folly" of swearing "affords neither profit nor pleasure." Matt is twice taken aback. He "changed colour" because his own practice includes swearing and because elimination of swearing among the lower classes will make their language too like that of their betters. Humphry again tactfully and handsomely corrects Matt: at least the servants no longer will be offensive, and more importantly, "at the day of judgment, there will be no distinction of persons."[64] Even Tabby is impressed with this "sober civilized fellow . . . and, she believed, a good Christian into the bargain" (p. 98). Humphry's first overt appearance as a Methodist, then, lays out four basic principles of his religious movement: it is aimed at the lower classes, whom it seeks to improve; it nonetheless is egalitarian; it affects the upper classes' conduct and judgment; and it is especially congenial to women.

We see these and other Methodist elements in a second episode. The novel plots Humphry's modest but real rise in the social scale, which also is consistent with his rise in the religious scale. Humphry had bought and studied John Wesley's sermons, but he confirms and enriches his faith presumably upon hearing Wesley preach. Alluding to Wesley removes Humphry from Whitefield's dark predestinations and from Calvinist attacks upon the Church of England as insufficiently reformed Protestant. This in turn allows him more successfully to persuade others (p. 136).[65] Accordingly, Matt and Jery find Humphry preaching at a large Methodist meeting near Longacre. Now he not only addresses a socially homogenous lower-class group but has preached a proper sermon before a socially diverse audience. He sings a Wesley psalm "with peculiar graces," and his audience includes "all the females of our family," that is, Lady Griskin, Tabby, Win Jenkins, and Lydia accompanied by her nonce suitor, Mr. Barton, "and all of them joined in the psalmody, with strong marks of devotion" (p. 134). We find a sermon by a footman, a handsome psalm handsomely sung, an audience with many well-born women and gentlemen, and demonstrable devotion. Smollett has either denied or transformed the commonplace that Methodists are sexually licentious reprobates who prey upon women. Instead, respectful Humphry elevates the women of varied ages and social groups. Indeed, he later protects Win Jenkins and punishes Dutton, who would sexually or socially exploit her. Humphry also gladly marries the woman he loves, though Matt and Tabby think that he should marry someone more appropriate for his new family (pp. 329, 330).

Smollett further enhances the typical reaction from establishment figures, while also showing that Methodist Humphry both holds his own in argument and maintains his secular role without abandoning his religious role. For example, Humphry's more exalted sermon audience is distressed upon being discovered—perhaps because of lower-class associations, perhaps because of their own emotional responses. Ever-improving Lydia thinks that there could be "no harm in hearing a pious discourse, even if it came from a footman," especially since she was properly chaperoned by her aunt (p. 134). Matt reassures her but also makes plain to Clinker that he must leave Matt's service if he wishes to serve God: "I am unworthy to have an apostle in my service," Matt insists. Humphry in turn urges his loyalty to Matt as well as to God, whose spirit he feels. Foolishness. That is "an admonition of the devil," Matt passionately says to the "blockhead" before him, who has no "right . . . to set up for a reformer." Humphry respectfully rejects the class-consciousness behind Matt's remarks by insisting that God's grace shines upon the humble poor and ignorant as well as the wealthy and the learned. Foolishness again. "I will have no light in my family but what pays the king's taxes, unless it be the light of reason, which you don't pretend to follow" (p. 135). Matt has abandoned his first, noncondemning role as benevolent liberator and curer of illness. He now needs curing by means of Humphry's mind and soul.

Matt uses *reason* in its largely secular rather than theological sense. His reason is not the God-given inner sense that leads to revelation, faith, and, broadly, religious light. Such reason is the manners and mores of the Establishment squirearchy, with land, power, and seats in Parliament. We recall that Joseph Trapp long ago delivered his anti-Methodist Oxford sermon *The Nature, Usefulness, and Regulation of Religious Zeal*. He there characterized proper Anglican priests' behavior: they should speak and behave with "*Decency, . . . good Manners;* or *. . . good Breeding.*"[66] Humphry's religion dismisses that worldly mode in favor of an evangelical guide to the next, spiritual world. He knows that sermons should not have "a dangerous Politeness." He also intuitively knows what Pembroke College's Thomas Griffith preached in 1756: unaided human reason is unreliable. "In truth, Reason consider'd in this manner will scarcely differ from Taste, or Opinion, which every single man claims as his indisputable Right."[67] So viewed, for all Matt's gentry role, he embodies the enthusiast's "indisputable Right" of private judgment. Humphry embodies the values shared by the temporal and spiritual worlds.

Here is one of the two crises in this scene. Matt once had decided to take newly accoutered Humphry into his "family" but now will exclude him. It seems that either Matt or Humphry must relent and that either secular or spiritual forces must triumph. This seems especially so when Humphry dismisses worldly reason as no more "than a farthing candle to the sun at noon" (p. 135). Matt reverts to familiar anti-Methodist insults and denounces Humphry as either a hypocrite or a mad fanatical enthusiast, neither of whom should be in his service. Methodists like Richard Finch were well able to use such reason in their own defense. Uneducated Humphry also is intuitively clever enough to understand how to deal with a hypothetical syllogism. He is not a hypocrite; therefore he must be mad. A poor madman deserves Matt's support and healthful doctoring. Given Matt's basic decency, the plea works, "provided he would mind the business of his place, without running after the new-light of methodism" (p. 136).

Just as it seems that a sensible compromise has worked, Smollett gives us a second crisis and a second way to confirm Matt's bond with Humphry and Humphry's with Matt. Tabby seeks to redefine Providence, Humphry's "place," and the nature of Methodism when she offers him a position in her service.

Humphry again tactfully negotiates these turbulent waters, praises Tabby's religious zeal and voice, but recalls earlier words and reaffirms his love and loyalty to Matt: "I will follow you to the world's end, if you don't think me too far gone to be out of confinement" (p. 136). Humphry shows more than his enduring gratitude to his deliverer. He also shows his perhaps unconscious estimate of genuine religious fervor. Matt's consequent inquiries demonstrate that Lady Griskin was the chief mover of the visit to the Methodist chapel and that she "only made use of Clinker as tool, subservient" to her own design, which was to ensnare Mr. Barton as Tabby's suitor by also ensnaring him into Methodism (p. 137). Moreover, Humphry's conduct refutes one of the familiar attacks upon Methodists: that their zealous religious worship drew them from their proper social roles. Humphry knows better, and knows as well that his religion and his temperament demand gratitude to his earthly as well as his divine father. Equally impressive, however, neither Humphry nor Matt fears or invokes the state's power to impose the Church of England's version of "reason." The Anglican Church no longer used Luke 14:23 to compel apparent deviants to come in. Robert Seagrave was among those Methodists who so insisted and who enjoyed that benefit of a changing society. "No prudent *State* will make it's self the mere Executioner of *Other's Resentments*." Denying "the Liberty, our selves should be apt to plead for" is both a great vanity and a great evil. As Richard Finch said shortly thereafter, "We have learned to mind the priest less, and God and our own consciences more than in time past. The civil power is now become very untractable to the priest's will."[68]

Smollett has splendidly exemplified the strengths and weaknesses of Methodism as then perceived: it was largely the voice of the poor and of women but was beginning to engage the higher classes; it depended more upon evangelicalism, with emotional and lovely song, than on Anglican theology, which had largely jettisoned or redefined the harsher numbers of the Thirty-Nine Articles, which seemed more like Geneva than Canterbury; it was able to confront the learned Establishment religion, with its honest zeal, while also maintaining its adherents' temporal roles in society; but it also was subject to hypocrites, false zeal, and manipulation. Swift's *Tale of a Tub* long ago had chronicled the dubious progress of the church in the world. The Methodist version of that church was subject to its own abuses, deceits, and human limitations.

We see more of the movement's strengths and weakness when Humphry is falsely imprisoned for the hanging crime of highway robbery. Throughout, Humphry has exemplified the virtuous behavior that Martin Madan attributed to Methodist reform of the raucous poor. Humphry nonetheless is a dreadful witness in his own defense: "God forbid, that I should call myself innocent, while my conscience is burthened with sin," he laments to puzzled Matt

(p. 144). He and Jery soon work to free Humphry from prison, again to his unspeakable joy. He also evokes a keyword that recalls wealthy Anglican Paunceford's ethical amnesia: "My poor heart is bursting with gratitude to you and my dear—dear—generous—noble benefactor" (p. 146). Humphry's jailer is as keen to see the amusingly diabolical Humphry exorcised: "Here has been nothing but canting and praying since the fellow entered the place." With no alcohol sold, the inmates "get drunk with nothing but your damned religion. . . . I believe as how your man deals with the devil" (p. 147). Like other newly devout women in the prison, however, the jailer's wife more properly sees Humphry as "a saint in trouble" and as a necessary force "in every gaol in England" (p. 147).

Smollett again gives us a sermon scene, one in which that jailer's wife and daughter enlarge the crowd of the poor. Jenkins, the Bramble housemaid, Tabby, and Lady Griskin become observers. Now, however, there is no hint of hypocrisy, deceitful courtship, or Anglican Eastgate's intimidation and bartering of self-respect for ecclesiastical preferment. Indeed, the scene validates Richard Finch's remark regarding the relationship of the ancient Apostles to the modern Methodists: "They did not study or understand languages, but were most of them *unlearned* and *ignorant Men*, and full as obstinate and troublesome then, as any of our *Methodists*, or other *Sectaries* are at this day."[69] Matt almost rejected Humphry as a false apostle. Now, Jery Melford both anoints him with Establishment approval and makes clear that the imprisoned auditors recognize Humphry's virtually apostolic quality:

> I never saw any thing so strongly picturesque as this congregation of felons clanking their chains, in the midst of whom stood orator Clinker, expatiating, in a transport of fervor, on the torments of hell, denounced in scripture against evildoers, comprehending murderers, robbers, thieves, and whoremongers. . . . As for Mrs. Winifred Jenkins, she was in tears, overwhelmed with sorrow, but whether for her own sins, or the misfortune of Clinker, I cannot pretend to say. The other females seemed to listen with a mixture of wonder and devotion. (P. 147)[70]

When Humphry finally is freed, the entire family, once at odds with one another and with Humphry, welcome him home. They embrace both his amiable manner and "his talents of preaching, praying, and singing psalms, which he has exercised with such effect, that even Tabby respects him as a chosen vessel." Matt and the others know that there is nothing "like affectation or hypocrisy in this excess of religion" (p. 150).

As with Humphry's first sermon, both the preacher and his audience are remarkable for what they do not do. We remember that in 1760 John Green characterized an apparently typical Methodist meeting: Its pastoral harangue induced "a constant number of groaners, sighers, tumblers and convulsionists." They shockingly sometimes broke into "a dreadful concert of screams, howlings and lamentations." He ascribes these either to fanaticism or to the oratory, loud voice, strange expressions, and "terrible relievo . . . of a field-preacher" at work on the "weak minds" of "an ignorant and unexperienced multitude."[71] Those visual and verbal excesses disappear when the preacher moves to a smaller, internal venue. Matt is passionate but scarcely howling. Moreover, though much of Humphry's audience indeed is naive, it includes the educated and sophisticated Bramble group and the jailer's wife, whose sympathy and good judgment we trust. In spite of the prisoner's clanking chains, Jery also transforms the scene into a version of the fashionable picturesque. Here, however, we see a gritty interior urban landscape rather than Gilpin's later views of the Anglo-Welsh River Wye. The internal prison scene to the contrary, Humphry's consequent fate suggests that, perhaps following the Countess of Huntingdon's example, Methodism has begun to go upscale.[72]

Near the end of the novel, Humphry saves Matt from drowning and discovers that he is Matt's illegitimate son. Matt has in effect been reborn and returned to health thanks to his Methodist bye-blow. His early physical constipation mirrored an emotional constipation, to which Humphry has so ably ministered and which again makes plain that Humphry assumes a healing role. Humphry's illegitimacy, though, also functions as a mingled corrective and rebuke to Matt. His affair with "Dorothy Twyford . . . bar-keeper at the Angel at Chippenham" surely was not angelic and produced Humphry, one of "the sins of my youth [that] rise up in judgment against me" (p. 305). Matt had hoped to do a version of the right thing by acknowledging and supporting his illegitimate child, but he had no intention of marrying beneath him or of turning sex into love. Humphry turns love into sex and rejects his father's social and sexual norm regarding courtship. Matt discourages Humphry from marrying Win Jenkins, who now is socially beneath him. The loyal Methodist nonetheless is faithful to his beloved, who Matt predicts will join Humphry to provide "a whole litter of his progeny at Brambletonhall" (p. 329). Anglican gentry-class exploitation surrenders to Methodist class loyalty, of course, as well as human decency. The single illegitimate child by the bachelor surrenders to the numerous progeny of married love.

The relationship between Matt and Humphry also suggests a metaphor for the relationship between the Church of England and Methodism as offshoots of the same family. Matt hopes to bring his newly named son into his church's physical space. For now he will supervise the family farm and its animals, but Matt approves of Dr. Lewes' observation regarding Humphry as the parish vestry clerk: "I make no doubt but Matthew Loyd is well enough qualified for the office"

(p. 335). That office literally is in an Anglican church, where Anglican vestments are stored and where Humphry/Matthew would tend to the vestry's temporal accounts. The vestry room also serves as a meeting place for the specific church's religious society.[73] The Anglican establishment remains paramount. It is the home of patriarchal Matthew Bramble, who generously doles out benefits to his dependents and now is keen to "provide for my son Loyd" (p. 335). The first two evangelical Methodist generations soon would soften, or perhaps harden, into their own respectably hierarchic and sedate establishment. Churches and ordained ministers would replace the inner, egalitarian spirit that enabled the humble to preach to the humble. *Humphry Clinker* thus gets it about right. Methodism shows its loyalty, diminishes as a presumed threat to the nation and its episcopal parent, and for the time being remains allied with it as a cognate confession. So far from being a threat to the Establishment rural gentry, Methodist Humphry supports it, probably will join it, and only respectfully challenges its interpretive theology. The Methodists' benevolently intrusive God and the Anglicans' benevolently withdrawn God find themselves compatible.

Smollett's novel of reconciliation has joined England, Wales, and Scotland as variously civilized parts of the United Kingdom, to which expatriates like Lieutenant Lismahago should return rather than leave to settle in barbarous North America.[74] The novel also reconciles the several members of the Bramble/Lloyd family, the Dennison/Wilson family, the remnants of the Baynard family, and the Church of England and the Wesleyan Methodists. Smollett leaves superstitious French Jesuit missionaries and Presbyterian hypocrites out of the mix and beyond the pale. *Humphry Clinker* is not quite Smollett's *Tempest*, but his Methodist readers could be forgiven for thinking so. They themselves now were fast becoming welcome or at the least acceptable threads in the rich cultural fabric being woven in evolving later eighteenth-century Britain. Whether that evolution would progress or regress toward its earlier, shortest ways and bloody flags remained to be seen.

NOTES

1. John Wesley, *A Short History of Methodism* (London, 1765), pp. [3]–4 (hereafter cited parenthetically in the text). The group Wesley describes would be called the "holy club."

2. See John Wesley, *Free Grace. A Sermon Preach'd at Bristol. By John Wesley, M. A. Fellow of Lincoln-College, Oxford* (London, 1740); and George Whitefield, *Free Grace indeed! A Letter To the Reverend Mr. John Wesley, Relating to His Sermon Against Absolute Election; Published under the Title of Free Grace* (London, 1741): "To hear the Whispers of the Enemy, reviving from the Mouth, and Pen, of the Reverend and learned Mr. Wesley, gives

me Room to apprehend, That there is none, in Time, can plead Exemption from sinning" (p. [3]).

3. One of Wesley's coreligionists characterized "perfection" as "the arriving to that Degree of Faith, or that State of Union with Christ wherein all evil Tempers, and Desires, together with all Opposition to the Will of God, are done away, and all that is in us becomes Holiness unto the Lord: Or it is the loving God with all the Heart, and Soul, and Mind, and Strength, and in our Neighbour as ourselves according to our present Capacity." See *A Treatise on Christian Perfection. In Two Parts. By an Unworthy Member of Jesus Christ* (London, 1767), p. 11. The title page does not list a publisher, and as the introduction makes clear, it was published as an act of public piety. For further discussion of Wesley and "perfection," see Henry D. Rack, *Reasonable Enthusiast: John Wesley and the Rise of Methodism* (Philadelphia: Trinity Press International, 1989), pp. 381–93; and esp. Harald Gustaf Åke Lindström, *Wesley and Sanctification: A Study in the Doctrine of Salvation* (London: Epworth Press, 1950). Wesley later changed his mind regarding humans' ability to gain "perfection." The Wesley-Whitefield split had been anticipated about one hundred years earlier with the Baptists' split between General, or Arminian, Baptists and Particular, or Calvinist, Baptists, that is, between the possibilities of salvation for all through Christ and salvation only for the few elect. See Andrew W. Bradstock, *Radical Religion in Cromwell's England* (London: I. B. Tauris, 2011), pp. 8–12, 19–22.

4. Jim Smyth, *The Making of the United Kingdom, 1660–1800* (Harlow, UK: Longman Pearson Education, 2001), p. 183. Studies of Methodism are so extensive that I can only list a few of the books and articles that I found most useful, some of which I have included at other relevant places in the notes. Students of Methodism who seek fuller bibliographies, in this case to 1988, should see volume 4 of *A History of the Methodist Church in Great Britain*, ed. Rupert Davies, A. Raymond George, and Gordon Rupp (London: Epworth Press, 1988). The three narrative volumes of this major work appeared, respectively, in 1965, 1978, and 1983. David Hempton's bibliography in *Methodism: Empire of the Spirit* (New Haven, CT: Yale University Press, 2005) is extremely valuable as well. For others, see Elie Halévy, two articles in the *Revue de Paris*, 1906, translated as *The Birth of Methodism in England*, trans. Bernard Semmel (Chicago: University of Chicago Press, 1971); E. P. Thompson, *The Making of the English Working Class* (London: Victor Gollancz, 1963); Bernard Semmel, *The Methodist Revolution* (New York: Basic Books, 1973); Michael R. Watts, *The Dissenters*, vol. 1, *From the Reformation to the French Revolution* (Oxford: Clarendon Press, 1978); David Hempton, *Methodism and Politics in British Society, 1750–1850* (Stanford, CA: Stanford University Press, 1984); John Munsey Turner, *Conflict and Reconciliation: Studies in Methodism and Ecumenism in England, 1740–1982* (London: Epworth Press, 1985); Gordon Rupp, *Religion in England, 1688–1791* (Oxford: Clarendon Press, 1986); Henry Abelove, *The Evangelist of Desire: John Wesley and the Methodists* (Stanford, CA: Stanford University Press, 1990); James E. Bradley, *Religion, Revolution, and English Radicalism: Nonconformity in Eighteenth-Century Politics and Society* (Cambridge: Cambridge University Press, 1990); Isobel Rivers, *Reason, Grace, and Sentiment: A Study of the Language of Religion and Ethics in England, 1660–1780*, vol. 1, *Whichcote to Wesley* (Cambridge: Cambridge University Press, 1991); Richard P. Hertzenrater, *Wesley and the People Called Methodists* (Nashville: Abingdon Press, 1995); David Hempton, *The Religion of the People: Methodism Popular Religion, c. 1750–1900* (London: Routledge, 1996); Hempton, *Religion*

and Political Culture in Britain and Ireland: From the Glorious Revolution to the Decline of Empire (Cambridge: Cambridge University Press, 1996); John Kent, *Wesley and the Wesleyans* (Cambridge: Cambridge University Press, 2002); and Misty Anderson, *Enthusiastic Methods: Methodism in the Eighteenth-Century British Imagination* (Baltimore: Johns Hopkins University Press, 2012), a book that, sadly, appeared too late for me to consider its findings. Among the many valuable articles, see W. R. Ward, "Power and Piety: The Origins of Religious Revival in the Early Eighteenth Century," *Bulletin of the John Rylands University Library of Manchester* 63 (1980): 231–52; and John D. Walsh, "'Methodism' and the Origins of English-Speaking Evangelicalism," in *Evangelicalism: Comparative Studies of Popular Protestantism in North America, the British Isles, and Beyond, 1700–1990*, ed. Mark S. Noll, David W. Bebbington, and George A. Rawlyk (New York: Oxford University Press, 1991). There are several illuminating contextual essays in two collections: *From Persecution to Toleration: The Glorious Revolution and Religion in England*, ed. Ole Peter Grell, Jonathan I. Israel, and Nicholas Tyacke (Oxford: Clarendon Press, 1991); and esp. *The Church of England, c. 1689–c. 1833: From Toleration to Tractarianism*, ed. John Walsh, Colin Haydon, and Stephen Taylor (Cambridge: Cambridge University Press, 1993). These lists could be quadrupled and still be inadequate for the subject.

5. The letter in *Fog's Weekly Journal* appeared on the first page, recto and verso, and was dated 5 November 1732.

6. Allusions to potential establishment violence against Methodists were not unusual, and indeed often the violence became real. For another such allusion, see James Bate, *Methodism Displayed; Or Remarks Upon Mr. Whitefield's Answer, To the Bishop of London's Last Pastoral Letter* (London, [1739]): what if you prophesy "that you shall come Home with your Head miserably broke at Night; and particularly by some Body cloathed in Red?" (p. 34).

7. As John Wesley made clear in the *History*, and as we shall see, both Wesleys proclaimed deep loyalty to the Church of England, from which they refused to separate. See John Wesley, *Reasons against Separating from the Church of England* (London, 1758), with later reprints.

8. Bate, *Methodism Displayed*, p. 16; see also pp. 27–28, 33. George Whitefield, *The Rev. Mr. Whitefield's Answer to the Bishop of London's Last Pastoral Letter* (London, 1739), corrects Gibson's theology, history, and rhetoric and urges him not to be angry in the face of Whitefield's own "Gentleness and Humility!" (p. 6). It concludes with his "hearty Prayers for your Lordship's temporal and eternal Welfare" (p. 27). A sceptic might doubt Whitefield's sincerity. Gibson's letter reached a third edition within its first year of publication. See Edmund Gibson, *The Bishop of London's Pastoral Letter To the People of his Diocese; Especially those of the two great Cities of London and Westminster: By way of Caution, Against Lukewarmness on one hand, and Enthusiasm on the other*, 3rd ed. (London, 1739), as on pp. 16, 22, and others. Bishop Gibson was among the many devout Anglicans troubled and offended by the Methodist, especially Whitefieldian, attacks upon its clergy. These fell "little short of that of our Saviour against the Scribes and Pharisees" and with thundering authority: "But I hope it is very far from the Truth. . . . To call it a *rash* Censure, is by far too gentle" (p. 40). Whitefield was not so persuaded. Both Whitefield and Wesley already had published numerous sermons and theological works, but the journals allowed an apparent window into their modes of thought. Whitefield's journals in particular provided Henry Fielding with typographical and character cues for *Shamela* (1741). For one of the overt attacks, see

Remarks on the Continuation of Mr. Whitefield's Journal. Pointing out the Many Direct Inconsistencies, Gross Absurdities, and Enthusiastick Notions Therein Contained. . . . By the Reverend Mr. J. B. Curate of N—th—t (London, 1739). For the journals, see Wesley, *Extract of the Rev. Mr. John Wesley's Journal from his Embarking for Georgia To his Return to London* (Bristol, 1739); Wesley, *An Extract of the Rev. Mr. John Wesley's Journal From February 1. 1737–38. To his Return from Germany* (London, 1740); Whitefield, *A Continuation Of the Reverend Mr. Whitefield's Journal, From His Arrival at London, To His Departure from thence on his Way to Georgia* (London, 1739); and Whitefield, *A Continuation Of the Reverend Mr. Whitefield's Journal, During the Time he was detained in England by the Embargo* (London, 1739). The increase in non-evangelical Anglican anger seems related to the increase in such publications.

9. *A Short History of the Donatists. With an Appendix, In Which The proud and Hypocritical Pharisee and Schismatical Donatist are compared with the Rev. Mr. George Whitefield and the Methodists* (London, 1741), pp. 50, 23–24. For further discussion of Augustine and the Donatists, see chapter 4 above.

10. Joseph Trapp, *The True Spirit of the Methodists, And Their Allies, (Whether other Enthusiasts, Papists, Deists, or Atheists) fully laid open; In an Answer To Six, of the Seven Pamphlets . . . Lately publish'd against Dr. Trapp's Sermons upon Being Righteous over-much. By which it appears, that the said Pamphlets united make up one of the greatest Curiosities that even This curious Age has produced* (London, 1740), pp. 31 (magnifying), 28 (own Case), 24 (maliciously); Trapp, *The Nature, Folly, Sin, and Danger Of being Righteous over-much; With a particular View to the Doctrines and Practices Of certain Modern Enthusiasts. Being the Substance of Four Discourses Lately Preached in the Parish-Churches of Christ-Church, and St. Lawrence Jewry, London; and St. Martin's in the Fields, Westminster*, 3rd ed. (London, 1739), p. 42. Trapp responds to Whitefield's *Folly and Danger of being Not Righteous enough. A Sermon Preached at Kennington Common, Moorfields, and Blackheath* (London, 1739). Whitefield is as keen to note these locations as to include his credentials on the title page: *By GEORGE WHITEFIELD, A.B. of Pembroke College* OXFORD. Like other main-line Anglicans, Trapp also laments the Methodist Calvinist emphasis, to which many, including John Wesley, objected. The multiple editions of works by Gibson, Trapp, and others suggest the serious concern with which the Methodist "reformation" was greeted.

11. *A Compleat Account of the Conduct of that eminent Enthusiast Mr. Whitefield. . . . Together with Some Remarks on Mr. W's Journals* (London, 1739), pp. 10–11. See p. 12 for the desire to have had Methodists checked by the state's authority, and see nn. 13, 47, and 67 below for another call for the civil magistrate's authority in religion.

12. John Wilder, *The Trial of the Spirits: or, a Caution against Enthusiasm, or Religious Delusion. In a Sermon preached before the University of Oxford, August 5th. 1739* (Oxford, 1739), p. 21. Wilder also calls for "the Governours" of church and state to "Restrain and put a Stop to the Proceedings of These Spiritual Champions, lest they prevail, and *lay her Honour in the Dust*" (p. 22). *Enthusiasm no Novelty: Or, the Spirit of the Methodists In the Year 1641 and 1642* (London, 1739), p. iii; this author extends the metaphor, since his country is one *"subject to dangerous Inundations"* thanks to *"the Overflowings of the* private Spirit" (pp. iii–iv). Henry Stebbing, *A Caution against Religious Delusion. A Sermon on the New Birth: Occasioned by the Pretensions of the Methodists* (London, 1739), p. 16. A Country Curate, *Observations on the Reverend Mr. Whitefield's Answer to the Bishop of London's Last Pastoral Letter* (London, 1739), pp. 43 (Seeds), 44 (Fires).

13. Samuel Bowden, "The Mechanic Inspir'd: Or, The Methodist's Welcome to *Frome. A Ballad*," in his *Poems on Various Subjects; With Some Essays in Prose* (Bath, 1754), p. 213 (schismatic); A Layman of the Church of England, *A Letter to the Rev. Mr. George Whitefield, Containing some Remarks on His Letter To the Rev. Dr. Durell, Vice-Chancellor of Oxford, Wherein it is proved, That the Growth of Methodism hath arisen by the Neglect of the Parochial Clergy and Church Officers* (London, 1769), p. 13 (Church); John Free, *Dr. Free's Remarks, Upon Mr. Jones's Letter* (London, 1759), pp. iv (Lodge), 53 (demands); Free, *Dr. Free's Edition of the Rev. Mr. John Wesley's First Penny Letter* (London, 1759), p. 32 (propagate); Free, *Rules for the Discovery of false Prophets: Or the Dangerous Impositions of the People called Methodists detected at the Bar of Scripture and Reason. A Sermon Preached before the University At St. Mary's in Oxford, On Whitsunday, 1758*, 2nd ed. (London, 1758), p. vii (False Brethren). Free there also reverts to earlier language when he fears that Methodists seek to attack the constitution and to change "the whole *System*, both of our *Ecclesiastical* and *civil* Polity" (p. 3). For another use of, or complaint, regarding Sacheverell's relevance, see Robert Seagrave, *An Answer to the Reverend Dr. Trapp's four Sermons against Mr. Whitefield. Shewing The Sin and Folly of being Angry Over-Much* (London, 1739), p. 13; and [Richard Finch], *A Congratulatory Letter to the R$^{evd.}$ Dr. Trapp: Occasioned by his Four Sermons against Enthusiasm. . . . By T. S—Y, Esq;* (London, 1739). Finch ironically tries to clear the path for "persecution, or the use of such *wholesome Severities* which Dr. *Sacheverell* has long ago recommended, and the present time and state of things seem to require." He alludes to Spain and France as putative benevolent models of such severities: "in proportion as force has prevailed, peace has abounded" (p. 9). He may also be alluding to Defoe's *Shortest Way with the Dissenters*.

14. [William Binckes], *A Prefatory Discourse To An Examination Of A late Book, Entituled An Exposition Of The Thirty Nine Articles of the Church of England, by Gilbert, Bishop of Sarum. . . . By a Presbyter of the Church of England* (London, 1702), pp. 9–10; Joseph Trapp, *The Nature, Usefulness and Regulation of Religious Zeal. A Sermon Preached at St. Mary's Oxon, Before the Honourable Mr. Justice Fortescue Aland, and Mr. Baron Thompson; and before the University of Oxford: At the Assizes held there, on Thursday Aug. 2d, 1739. . . . Publish'd at the Desire of the Judges and the Vice-Chancellor* (London, 1739), p. 24. Trapp's full title makes plain why good breeding was a touchstone of good religion. His sermons were attacked by Methodists, including Robert Seagrave in his often harsh *Answer To The Reverend Dr. Trapp's four Sermons*. One anonymous author based his objections to Seagrave on class grounds. See *Observations and Remarks on Mr. Seagrave's Conduct and Writings. In Which His Answer to the Rev. Dr. Trapp's Four Sermons is more particularly considered* (London, 1739): "A Clergyman is generally esteem'd as a Gentleman and a Scholar of genteel Education and good Learning." Seagrave's bad manners to Trapp level him with "The Man who rubs your Shoes" and "He who sweeps your Door." The paragraph ends with an implicit threat as well as a social scolding: "The Reflections may be of some Service to you, consult your own Welfare and learn to pity yourself" and your "want of Breeding" (p. 18). Charles Chauncy in Boston had a similar reaction, as itinerant Methodists had begun to make converts in the colonies. He urged a "reasonable and solid religion." See Chauncy's *Enthusiasm described and caution'd against. A Sermon Preach'd at the Old Brick Meeting-House in Boston the Lord's Day after Commencement, 1742* (Boston, [1742]), p. 22.

15. George Whitefield, *The Full Account of the Life and Dealings of God With the Reverend Mr. George Whitefield, A. B. Late of Pembroke-College, Oxford* (London, [1747?]), p. 20. See also Whitefield's *Continuation of the Reverend Mr. Whitefield's Journal at Oxford ... to his Departure ... to Georgia* (London, 1739), p. 85, on Oxford's spiritual corruption, and *A Continuation Of the Reverend Mr. Whitefield's Journal, From a few Days after his Return to Georgia To his Arrival at Falmouth* (London, 1741) as an example of "the more things change, the more they stay the same." The little college in Cambridge, Massachusetts, was as bad as its British cousins: "Tutors neglect to pray with and examine the Hearts of their Pupils. Discipline is at too low an Ebb. Bad Books are become fashionable amongst them. *Tillotson* and *Clarke* are read instead of *Sheppard, Stoddard*, and such like evangelical Writers" (pp. 28–29). For Wesley, see *Scriptural Christianity: A Sermon Preached August 24, 1744 at St. Mary's Church in Oxford, Before the University*, 2nd ed. ([Bristol], 1744), pp. 22–24 (not Christian), 29 (it is time). This is from the latter part of the sermon, which Wesley prints because of *"the false and scurrilous Accounts of it which have been published, almost in every Corner of the Nation"* (sig. A2^r). Tillotson's legacy has been well considered by Jacob M. Blosser in "John Tillotson's Latitudinarian Legacy: Orthodoxy, Heterodoxy, and the Pursuit of Happiness," *Anglican and Episcopal History* 80 (2011): 142–73; nn. 3, 4, 5, 17, and 47 offer especially full bibliographic information concerning latitudinarianism, the eighteenth-century Anglican Church, and several modern arguments regarding these topics.

16. Stebbing, *Caution against Religious Delusion*, p. 19 (provided); A. B. [Stebbing], *An Earnest and Affectionate Address To the People called Methodists*, 2nd ed. (London, 1745), pp. 41–42 (honestly). It is unlikely that Stebbing feared an anti-Hanoverian Methodist putsch on behalf of the Jacobites in 1745. As a rule, Methodists were loyal Hanoverians who were grateful for the Georgian relative toleration not likely to be practiced under Charles Edward Stuart. As we shall see, Wesley later entered the American colonial fray on George III's behalf and paid a dear price. For John Green, under the pseudonym Academicus, see *The Principles and Practices of the Methodists Farther considered; In a Letter To the Reverend Mr. George Whitefield* (London, 1760), p. 24 (low, raise), and *Principles and Practices of the Methodists* (Cambridge, 1761), p. 6 (blue apron).

17. Sir Richard Hill describes the scene in his unsigned *Goliath Slain: Being a Reply To the Revered Dr. Nowell's Answer to Pietas Oxoniensis* (London, 1768), pp. 15 (commandment), 42 (high court). The final pages of this book include the several newspaper reports on the controversy. Hill wrote, and also did not sign, *Pietas Oxoniensis: Or, A Full and Impartial Account of the Expulsion of Six Students from St. Edmund's Hall, Oxford ... By a Master of Arts of the University of Oxford*, 2nd ed. (London, 1768). Hill was a devout evangelical Methodist who also thought himself a loyal Church of England man. Whitefield defended the students in his *Letter to the Reverend Dr Durell, Vice Chancellor of the University of Oxford; Occasioned By a late Expulsion of Six Students from Edmund Hall* (London, 1768). Among other places, he was abused in the unsigned *Remarks upon the Rev. Mr. Whitefield's Letter* (London, 1768). S. L. Ollard discusses the events and compiles a bibliography in *The Six Students of St. Edmund Hall Expelled from the University of Oxford in 1768* (London: A. R. Mowbray & Co., 1911). He is demonstrably and understandably on the Methodist students' side. This and other relevant matters concerning the Methodists are discussed in Rupp's *Religion in England, 1688–1791*, pp. 476–78, within the larger context of "The People Called Methodists," pp. 389–453.

18. [Hill], *Goliath Slain*, p. 39 (bred to trades); Thomas Nowell, *An Answer To A Pamphlet Entitled Pietas Oxoniensis, In a Letter to the Author. The Second Edition, With large Additions, and a Postscript occasioned by the Reply of the Same Author* (Oxford, 1769), pp. 46 (What business), 57–58 (bread). Hill replies in *Goliath Slain*, p. 39.

19. Academicus [Green], *Principles and Practices of the Methodists* (1761), p. 67; John Free, *Dr. Free's Edition of the Rev. Mr. John Wesley's Second Letter* (London, 1759), p. 24; *The Progress of Methodism in Bristol: Or, The Methodist Unmask'd. . . . By an Impartial Hand* (London, 1743), p. 8. The charge was familiar.

20. For comments on Lancaster's poem, see *Monthly Review* 37 (1767): 394–95; and *Critical Review* 24 (1767): 66–67. Neither reader was amused, and both regarded the Methodists as fanatics. The *Monthly*'s reviewer uncharacteristically is not identified in Benjamin Christie Nangle's *The Monthly Review: First Series 1749–1789* (Oxford: Clarendon Press, 1934). Albert M. Lyles considers Lancaster and many other anti-Methodist satires in his *Methodism Mocked: The Satiric Reaction to Methodism in the Eighteenth Century* (London: Epworth Press, 1960). I more fully consider *Humphry Clinker* in the final section of this chapter.

21. *Observations and Remarks on Mr. Seagrave's Conduct*, pp. 4 (almost), 6 (Vindication). See also p. 33, in which Whitefield "is in Practice a Dissenter" who has renounced "the Liturgy of the Church of *England*" and has chosen to "pray *extempore* in his own Words."

22. Gibson, *Bishop of London's Pastoral Letter*, p. 29.

23. A. B. [Stebbing], *Earnest and Affectionate Address*, pp. 34–35 (Rules, Bounds, pulpits), 26 (Religion), 35 (exercised). For the image of usurpation and breaking of fences, see *An Earnest Appeal To the Publick: On Occasion of Mr. Whitefield's Extraordinary Answer To the Pastoral Letter of the Lord Bishop of London. Intended To Vindicate his Lordship from the Extravagant Charges and Mean Evasions Contained in the said Pretended Answer* (London, 1739), p. 20. The writer is convinced that "the *Quakers* and *other Dissenters* openly support" Whitefield (p. 19). For a comparable colonial exercise in expulsion, see Chauncy, *Enthusiasm described and caution'd against*, p. 12; and [Nathanel Eells], *A Letter to the Second Church and Congregation in Scituate. Written by their Rev. Pastor. Shewing some Reasons why he doth not invite the Rev. Mr. George Whitefield into his Pulpit* (Boston, 1745). The pamphlet also mentions "the Rev. Rector and Tutors of *Yale-College* in *New-Haven* . . . in their Declaration against the Rev. Mr. *George Whitefield*, his Principles and Designs, in a Letter to him" (p. 14).

24. Academicus [Green], *Principles and Practices of the Methodists* (1760), pp. 28–29; *Observations and Remarks on Mr. Seagrave's Conduct*, p. 19; Chauncy, *Enthusiasm described and caution'd against*, p. 13. Chauncy amplifies the Methodist facial and vocal mannerisms during sermons. For example, they are so seized by imagination that, as with the Quakers of old, sometimes "it affects their bodies, throws them into convulsions and distortions, into quakings and tremblings," and of course "strangely loosens their tongues, and gives them such an energy, as well as fluency and volubility in speaking" (p. 4). Paul Goring relates Methodist preaching to the bodily actions both like and unlike those appropriate for sensibility. See *The Rhetoric of Sensibility in Eighteenth-Century Culture* (Cambridge: Cambridge University Press, 2005), pp. 60–90.

When dealing with Methodist preaching, however, one must remember that field preaching had large audiences stretched over large areas. Urban outdoor preaching competed with noise, wanderers, and other distractions. *Humphry Clinker*'s prison sermon, in contrast, though fervid and passionate, apparently lacks the quaking, trembling, and grimace often associated with oration to masses. See the discussion of Humphry in prison, below.

25. Whitefield, *The Rev. Mr. Whitefield's Answer*, pp. 10–11.

26. William Law, *The Oxford Methodists: Being an Account of some Young Gentlemen in That City, in Derision so called; Setting forth their Rise and Designs. With Some Occasional Remarks on A Letter inserted in Fog's Journal of December 9th, 1732* [No. 214], *relating to them*, 2nd ed. (London, 1738), p. ii. This edition is addressed to George Whitefield; the first edition, in 1733, lacked this epistle. Seagrave, *Answer to the Reverend Dr. Trapp's four Sermons*, p. 13.

27. Law, *Oxford Methodists*, p. 19. He later adds that Methodists seek to revive primitive Christianity and "a *Revival* of that good old Way which was practised by the best People of the first Ages" as directed by Jesus (p. 26). This is consistent with the argument on Methodist reformation.

28. T. S——Y [Richard Finch], *A Defence of a Congratulatory Letter To The Reverend Dr. Trapp, &c. In a Reply to a late Pamphlet, Intitutled, Quakero-Methodism, &c. by James Bate. . . . Where His Calumnies, Misrepresentations, and False Reasonings are clearly Demonstrated, To Which is prefix'd, A previous Letter to the Bishop of London* (London, 1740), p. 41.

29. Seagrave, *Answer to the Reverend Dr. Trapp's four Sermons*, p. 14.

30. Jonathan Warne, *Dr. Trapp Try'd, and Cast; and allow'd to the 10th of May next to Recant. Being Some Remarks On a Late Book, Intitled, The Nature, Folly, Sin, and Danger, of Being Righteous over-much: The Second Edition, with a Postscript in Vindication of Mr. Whitefield* (London, 1739), pp. 16 (departs), 42 (Doctrines). Warne also laments that such Anglican schismatics long have been trying to discredit the orthodox doctrines they have subscribed: "O shameful Impiety! To subscribe to *Calvinistical* Articles, and preach up *Arminian* Doctrines" (p. 17). Warne makes similar points in his *Arminianism, The Back-Door to Popery* (London, 1739). Each fire-breathing side would have roasted its adversaries out of pure Christian love.

31. [Hill], *Goliath Slain*, p. 89 (find one); [Hill], *Pietas Oxoniensis*, pp. 61 (Edward), 68–69 (James I, Synod), 61 (Reformers), 69 (prevailed); Jonathan Warne, *The Church of England Turn'd Dissenter at Last: Or, The Generality of her Clergy have forsaken the Most Material Doctrines of the Common Prayer* (London, 1737); Robert Seagrave, *Observations Upon the Conduct of the Clergy. Shewing That the Church of England, properly so call'd, is not now existing*, 3rd ed. (London, 1740); Lover of Truth, *Doctor Trapp Vindicated from the Imputation of Being a Christian. Occasioned by a Pamphlet of that Reverend Author against the Methodists, Intitled, the Nature, Folly, Sin, and Danger of being Righteous over-much* (London, 1739); [Jonathan Warne], *An Attempt to Promote True Love and Unity Between the Church of England and the Dissenters . . . By setting down the Thirty-Nine Articles of the aforesaid Church in one Column, and Articles of Faith of the Dissenters in another* (London, 1741), p. viii, in italics. Warne's title is irenic. His preface is martial.

32. [Jonathan Warne], *A Remonstrance Address'd To the Clergy. Shewing where the Charge of Deism (without returning to the Old Divinity) will necessarily terminate. By a Friend of the Clergy* (London, 1731), pp. 4 (Old Divinity, Scheme), 5–6 (inadequate reason). He fears that overdependence upon reason will replace revelation. Paullinus [Robert Seagrave], *A Letter to the People of England. Occasion'd by the Falling away of the Clergy from the Doctrine of Perfection* (London, 1735), p. 5; see also Seagrave, *Six Sermons Upon the Manner of Salvation. Being the Substance of Christianity* (London, 1737), sermon 5, p. 65. Warne,

Arminianism, The Back-Door to Popery, p. iv; Warne, *The Dreadful Degeneracy of a Great Part of the Clergy*. . . . *To which is prefix'd A Letter to the Reverend Mr. George Whitefield* (London, 1739), sig. A1^r; [Finch], *Congratulatory Letter to the R*$^{evd.}$ *Dr. Trapp*, pp. 3 (modern), 5 (Histories). Like many other Methodists, Finch regularly accuses the Church of England of being a persecuting church; see pp. 4, 7–10. He alludes to France as an oppressive model in which "force has prevailed, [and religious] peace has abounded" (p. 9). Seagrave, *Observations Upon the Conduct of the Clergy*, p. 32. The subtitle is germane: *With an Essay Towards Real Protestant Establishment*.

33. We note one such remark in Seagrave, *Answer To the Reverend Dr. Trapp's four Sermons*, p. 14; Chauncy, *Enthusiasm described and caution'd against*, p. 5.

34. For the dates, see Thomas Burnet, *The Theory of the Earth: Containing an Account of the Original of the Earth, and of All the General Changes Which it hath already Undergone* (London, 1684), p. 2. Burnet writes that it is "now more than Five Thousand Years since our World was made" (p. 7); Noah's flood was about sixteen hundred years "after the Earth was made, and inhabited" (pp. 8–9). Burnet's original Latin edition was *Telluris theoria sacra* (London, 1681). Burnet is among the many who criticized St. Augustine, here for his ignorance of the nature of creation: he interposed "in a controversie where his Talent did not lie" (sig. a1^v).

35. John Scott, *A Fine Picture of Enthusiasm, Chiefly Drawn by Dr. John Scott, Formerly Rector of St. Giles's in the Fields, wherein The Danger of the Passions Leading in Religion is strongly described. To which is added An Application of the Subject to the Modern Methodists, Exposing the Principles and Practices of all such.* . . . *Dedicated to the Bishop of London* (London, 1744), pp. 29–30. Freethinking Voltaire would have agreed with his Anglican colleague regarding Augustine and the folly of original sin. The *Dictionnaire philosophique* (1764), often reprinted, generally is clever, dismissive, ironic, and smarmy. In the case of "Original (Peché)," it is angry regarding Augustine's invention of this concept "digne de la tête chaude & romanesque d'un africain débauché & repentant." *Oeuvres completes de Voltaire* ([Paris?], 1784), 42:214; see 38:144–46 on Augustine and 42:213–20 on original sin. Note also that for Voltaire "ce système tomba malgré le nom de son auteur" (42:220).

36. William Delaune, *Of Original Sin. A Sermon Preach'd before the Right Honourable the Mayor and Aldermen, at the Cathedral-church of St. Paul* (London, 1713), pp. 18–19; Anthony William Boehm, originally Anton Wilhelm Böehm, *Several Discourses upon Tracts For Promoting the Common Interest of True Christians . . . III. The Doctrine of Original Sin* (London, 1717), pp. 87 (asunder), 86 (hardly), 89 (Austin).

37. Samuel Clarke, *The Scripture-Doctrine of the Trinity. In Three Parts* (London, 1712), pp. xx–xxii (human and not scriptural authority), 444 (most men). Henry Heywood, *Defence of Dr. Whitby's Treatise of Original Sin, And of the Translator's Introduction, Against the Late Attempts of Mr. John Gill* (London, 1740), p. 12; see also pp. 13, 32–34. [Samuel Webster], *A Winter Evening's Conversation Upon the Doctrine of Original Sin, Between a Minister and three of his Neighbours accidentally met together. Wherein the Notion of our having sinned in Adam, and being on that Account only liable to Eternal Damnation, is proved to be unscriptural, irrational, and of dangerous Tendency* (Boston, 1757), pp. 23–24. This was reprinted in New Haven, Connecticut, in 1757. The Huntington Library's Boston copy, shelf mark 149409, includes sympathetic annotation. The signature of T. Foxcroft is upper right, but the annotations are not likely to be his. He was one of the signatories to Peter Clark's reply

in 1758, *The Scripture-Doctrine of Original Sin, stated and defended in a Summer Morning's Conversation, between a Minister and a Neighbour* (Boston, 1758). John Taylor's anti–original sin *Scripture-Doctrine of Original Sin Proposed to Free and Candid Examination* (London, 1740) went into a fourth edition by 1767. It too became part of the transatlantic debate. Samuel Niles replied in *The true Scripture-Doctrine of Original Sin stated and defended. In the way of Remarks on a late Piece Intitled "The Scripture-Doctrine of Original Sin proposed to free and candid Examination"* (Boston, 1757). Each side assumed that it was joined by the proper and virtuous religion. Gospel Lover [Joseph Priestley], *A Familiar Illustration of Certain Passages of Scripture* (London, 1785), pp. 10–13; Nicholas Manners, *An Attempt To set the Doctrine of Original Sin in a Right Light* (York, 1785), p. 150; George Dyer, *An Inquiry into the Nature of Subscription to the Thirty-Nine Articles* ([London?, 1790?]), pp. 98, 302, arguing on Saint Augustine as intellectually "frail."

Protestants in France were subject to Franco-Augustinian *compelle intrare*, for which see chapter 4 above. They thus shared and anticipated hostility to Augustine as an argument on authority. Their concerns crossed the Channel, as in Jean Daillé, *A Treatise concerning the Right Use of the Fathers, In the Decision of the Controversies that are at this day in Religion. Written in French by John Daille, Minister of the Gospel in the Reformed Church at Paris*, trans. Thomas Smith (London, 1651; 1675 ed. quoted below). Book 2 has new pagination. See "the Judgment... of S. *Augustine*, and of S. *Hierome*, (the two most eminent Persons in the Western Church) touching this Particular": that their words replaced the Bible (p. 26; see also p. 37). This is Thomas Smith's translation of *Traité de l'employ des saincts Pères pour le jugement des différendes qui sont aujourd'hui en la religion* (Geneva, 1632, and other editions). A manuscript note on the Huntington Library's 1651 edition, shelf mark 319828, reads: "Not a true Translation."

38. A Curate of London, *A Short Preservative Against the Doctrines Reviv'd by Mr. Whitefield and his Adherents. Being a Supplement to the Bp. of London's late Pastoral Letter* (London, 1739), p. 25; S——Y [Finch], *Defence of a Congratulatory Letter*, p. 26; Manners, *Attempt To set the Doctrine of Original Sin*, pp. 18–19; Gospel Lover [Priestley], *Familiar Illustration*, p. 13.

39. Gilbert Burnet, *An Exposition of the Thirty-Nine Articles of the Church of England*, 3rd ed. (London, 1705), p. 8 (hereafter cited parenthetically in the text).

40. Thomas Bennet, *Directions For Studying I. A General System or Body of Divinity. II. The Thirty nine Articles of Religion*, 2nd ed. (London, 1715), p. 94; Phileleutherus Cantabrigiensis, *An Essay On Imposing and Subscribing Articles of Religion.... In a Letter to Phileleutherus Oxoniensis* (London, 1719), pp. 48–49.

41. Edward Welchman, *The Thirty-nine Articles of the Church of England, Illustrated with Notes, and Confirmed by Texts of the Holy Scripture, And Testimonies of the Primitive Fathers.... Written in Latin by the Rev. Mr. Archdeacon Welchman, And now Translated into English*, 6th ed. (London, 1774), p. 43. For the Latin, see *XXXIX Articuli Ecclesiae Anglicanae* (Oxford, 1718), for example, p. 20: "Praedestinationis enim doctrina est profunda quaedam Abyssus, in qua scrutanda Juniorum animos occupari parum expedit." John Veneer, *An Exposition on the Thirty Nine Articles of the Church of England: Founded On the Holy Scriptures, and the Fathers of the Three First Centuries*, 2nd ed. (London, 1730), 1:360.

42. Chauncy, *Enthusiasm described and caution'd against*, p. 17; Scott, *Fine Picture of Enthusiasm*, p. 26; Free, *Dr. Free's Edition of the Rev. Mr. John Wesley's First Penny Letter*, pp. 40 (No one), 35 (Liberty).

43. [Binckes], *Prefatory Discourse To An Examination of a late Book, Entituled An Exposition of the Thirty Nine Articles*, pp. 1 (Generality), 5 (Doctrine), 3 (altogether, effectually), 11 (such as subscribe). Throughout, Binckes argues that Burnet's latitude of interpretation encourages the discord that the Articles were designed to avoid. God is the "God of Order; *not the Author of Confusion, but of Peace*" (p. 9). See also chapter 2 above at nn. 33, 34.

44. Edward Young, *A Vindication of Providence: Or, A True Estimate of Human Life. In Which The Passions are considered in a New Light*, 5th ed. (London, 1737), sig. A2^v. Young tells Queen Caroline that such gloom is an erroneous "Reflection on Providence" (sig. A2^r). The *locus classicus* for study of this movement remains R. S. Crane's 1934 essay "The Genealogy of the 'Man of Feeling,'" reprinted in Crane, *The Idea of the Humanities and Other Essays Critical and Historical* (Chicago: University of Chicago Press, 1967), 1:188–213. For Sterne, see The Florida Edition of the Works of Laurence Sterne, vol. 4, *The Sermons of Laurence Sterne*, ed. Melvyn New (Gainesville: University of Florida Press, 1996), pp. 65–73. Contrast Swift's *Verses on the Death of Dr. Swift* (London, 1733–39). Sterne begins his first sermon with, "The Great Pursuit of man is after happiness" (p. 3).

45. Curate of London, *Short Preservative Against the Doctrines Reviv'd by Mr. Whitefield*, pp. 7 (Part, without), 8 (Majority), 27 (kind), 28 (fruitful).

46. Ebenezer Hewlett, *Mr. Whitefield's Chatechise. Being an Explanation of the Doctrine of the Methodists. . . . In a Letter to Mr. Seagrave* (London, 1739), pp. iii (first), 14 (not partial), 13 (not design), 11 (murdering); Wilder, *Trial of the Spirits*, p. 16; Scott, *Fine Picture of Enthusiasm*, p. 18; S——Y [Finch], *Defence of a Congratulatory Letter*, p. 24.

47. Free, *Rules for the Discovery of false Prophets*, pp. vii (false brethren), 2–3 (lawful Teachers); Free, *Dr. Free's Edition of the Rev. Mr. John Wesley's First Penny Letter*, pp. 20 (Pernicious), 25 (whipping); Free, *Dr. Free's Edition of the Rev. Mr. John Wesley's Second Letter*, pp. 21 (dangerous), 27 (Hell-hounds), 29 (subvert), 31 (seditious), 32 (revolutionaries); Free, *A Display of the Bad Principles of the Methodists in certain Articles Proposed to the Serious Consideration of the Worshipful Company of Salters in London*, 2nd ed. (London, 1759), pp. 9 (downright), 10 (Sort of, magistrate).

48. Samuel Bradburn, *The Question, Are the Methodists Dissenters? Fairly Examined to Remove Prejudice, Prevent Bigotry, and Promote Brotherly Love* ([Liverpool?], 1792), p. [3]; James Creighton, *A Letter Addressed to Mr. Samuel Bradburn, Containing, Some Strictures On His Pamphlet, Entitled: "The Question; Are the Methodists Dissenters?"* (London, 1793), p. 14.

49. Seagrave, *Observations Upon the Conduct of the Clergy*, pp. 57 (disruption), 47 (Admiration); Seagrave, *The True Protestant: A Dissertation Shewing The Necessity of asserting the Principles of Liberty in their full Extent* (London, 1746), pp. 42–43 (high-flying, Perfection). See also Seagrave's *Remarks Upon the Bishop Of London's Pastoral Letter. In Vindication of Mr. Whitefield, and His Particular Doctrines*, 2nd ed. (London, 1739). He argues that "*Protestant Liberty*, and *Protestant religious Truths*, are closely linked together, and together must *stand* or *fall*" (p. 34). As usual, Seagrave insists that such principles are Reformation Calvinist principles that the Church of England explains away, and thus makes itself a dissenting church. John Wesley, *Reasons against A Separation from the Church of England. . . . With Hymns for the Preachers among the Methodist (so called), By Charles Wesley* (London, 1760), pp. 7 (Part), 11 (attend Anglican services), 9–10 (avoid dissenting). For Martin Madan, see [Madan], *Christian and Critical Remarks On a Droll, or Interlude, called The Minor. Now acting by a Company of Stage Players in the Hay-Market; and Said to be Acted by*

Authority. In Which The Blasphemy, Falsehood, and Scurrility of that Piece is properly considered, answered, and exposed (London, 1760), p. 9; [Madan], *An Exhortatory Address to the Brethren in the Faith of Christ* (London, 1760), pp. 15 (ever-blessed), 17 (remarkable, Without). Methodist affirmation of loyalty parallels Presbyterian affirmation of loyalty and repudiation of regicide.

50. [Madan], *Christian and Critical Remarks*, pp. 7–8.

51. Thomas Bradbury, *The True Happiness of a Good Government: Explain'd in a Sermon on the Fifth of November, 1714*, 2nd ed. (London, 1714), p. 6. The fifth of November was the anniversary of the failed Gunpowder Plot and the landing of William of Orange. Evan Lloyd, *The Methodist* (London, 1766), pp. 53 (Root), 51 (boundless, friendly), 50 (Floods).

52. *The Pamphlet, Entitled "Taxation No Tyranny," Candidly Considered, and It's Arguments, and Pernicious Doctrines, Exposed and Refuted* (London, [1775]), pp. 6 (Falkland), 7 (oppress), 25 (policy); however late in the day, Johnson is labeled a Jacobite on pp. 6, 8, 17, 23, 68. *Answer to a Pamphlet, Entitled Taxation no Tyranny. Addressed to the Author, and to Persons in Power* (London, 1775), p. 62. Several others hurl relatively small missiles: *A Defence of the Resolutions and Address of the American Congress, in Reply to Taxation no Tyranny* (London, [1775]), pp. 9, 15; *Tyranny Unmasked: An Answer to a Late Pamphlet, Entitled Taxation no Tyranny* (London, 1775), p. 10; *A Letter to the Rev. Dr. Price. By the Author of The Defence of the American Congress, in Reply to Taxation no Tyranny* (London, 1776), p. 16. Johnson collected his four political tracts of the 1770s under his name in 1776. The two best introductions to Johnson's politics remain Donald Greene's *Politics of Samuel Johnson* (New Haven, CT: Yale University Press, 1960) and Greene's standard text and commentary, The Yale Edition of the Works of Samuel Johnson, vol. 10, *Political Writings*, ed. Greene (New Haven, CT: Yale University Press, 1977). See also John Cannon, *Samuel Johnson and the Politics of Hanoverian England* (Oxford: Clarendon Press, 1994); and some of my own essays: Howard D. Weinbrot, *Aspects of Samuel Johnson: Essays on His Arts, Mind, Afterlife, and Politics* (Newark: University of Delaware Press, 2005). Several of these essays deal with the inadequacy of the notion that Johnson was a Jacobite.

53. [Augustus Toplady], *An Old Fox Tarr'd and Feather'd. Occasioned by What is Called Mr. John Wesley's Calm Address to our American Colonys* (London, 1775), pp. 19 (Bundle), 5 (Bishop at large). He also calls Wesley "a methodist Weather-cock" (p. 3) and a shameless thief and liar who deserves to be tarred and feathered (pp. 19–20). For further discussion of Wesley and America, see Allan Raymond, "'I Love God and Honour the King': John Wesley and the American Revolution," *Church History* 45 (1976): 31–28. Raymond discusses two interesting possibilities: that Wesley wrote the *Calm Address* at the ministerial urging of Lord North, who then had some 100,000 printed and distributed; and, as an overt conjecture I do not find plausible, that Johnson may have given Wesley permission to adapt and abridge *Taxation no Tyranny* so that it could be widely distributed. For further discussion of the relationship, see Henry Abelove, "John Wesley's Plagiarism of Samuel Johnson and Its Contemporary Reception," *Huntington Library Quarterly* 59 (1996): 73–79.

54. *A Constitutional Answer to the Rev. Mr. John Wesley's Calm Address to the American Colonies* (London, 1775), pp. 14 (disingenuous), 9 (insidious), 7 (Blush), with repeated references to Johnson on pp. 4, 6, 7, 14, 16, 21. Both wicked men sought to deceive good Britons "out of their birth-right, and persuade them they are slaves" (p. 21). One can only rejoice that Johnson and Wesley were such poor orators. Americanus [Caleb Evans], *A Letter to the*

Rev. Mr. John Wesley, Occasioned by his Calm Address to the American Colonies. A New Edition. To which are prefixed, Some Observations on the Rev. Mr. Wesley's late Reply (London, 1775), p. 24; *Fallacy Detected: In a Letter to the Rev. Mr. John Wesley. . . . and His "Calm Address to the AMERICANS"* ([London?], 1775), p. 36; A Lover of Truth and the British Constitution, *A Letter to the Rev. Mr. John Wesley; On his Calm Address to the American Colonies: Wherein is Shewn, That his Arguments are inconclusive; His Principles arbitrary; and that His Assertions are without Foundation* ([Manchester], 1755), pp. 16 (Friend), 6 (Enemy, Pitch). The author adds that this believer in divine right's "Reasonings are inconclusive, your Principles unconstitutional, and your Assertions Falshoods" (p. 14). Patrick Bull, *A Wolf in Sheep's Cloathing: or, An Old Jesuit Unmasked. Containing an Account of the Wonderful Apparition of Father Petre's Ghost, In the Form of the Rev. John Wesley. With Some Conjectures concerning the Secret Causes that Moved him to Appear at this Very Critical Juncture* (Dublin and London, [1775]), pp. 11 (kindle, designs), 21 (usher). The quotations above are selections. The abuse is commonplace. For a defense, see John Fletcher, *A Vindication of the Rev. Mr. Wesley's "Calm Address To Our American Colonies:" In some Letters To Mr. Caleb Evans* (London, [1775?]). Evans was equally energetic in his reply to Fletcher's reply: Evans, *A Reply to the Rev. Mr. Fletcher's Vindication of Mr. Wesley's Calm Address* (Bristol, 1776). Evans almost uniformly focuses on Fletcher's politics, which he deplores, rather than on his Methodist religion, which, though different from his own Calvinist Baptist, he respects (p. 90). For another example of a political attack on Wesley that couples him with Johnson, see Joseph Towers' discontent with Wesley's approval of the government's actions in the Wilkes' affair in *A Letter to the Rev. Mr. John Wesley; In Answer to His late Pamphlet, Entitled "Free Thoughts on the Present State of Public Affairs"* (London, 1771), p. 13. Like his colleagues cited below, Towers distinguishes between Wesley's sphere as praised clergyman and his sphere as blamed politician (pp. 56–57).

55. John Wesley, *A Calm Address to our American Colonies . . . A New Edition, Corrected, and Enlarged* (London, [1775]), pp. [iii] (King), 17–18 (designing). Wesley does not acknowledge the extent of his borrowings from Johnson. The pamphlet concludes with a plea for peace and the putting away of sin, which cannot "be thoroughly removed, till we fear God and honour the King" (p. 18).

56. Lover of Truth and the British Constitution, *Letter to the Rev. Mr. John Wesley*, p. 6.

57. *A Reply to an Appeal from the Protestant Association to the People of Great Britain* (London, 1780), p. 4.

58. *Constitutional Answer*, p. 22; Americanus [Evans], *Letter to the Rev. Mr. John Wesley*, p. 24; A Lover of Truth and the British Constitution, *Letter to the Rev. Mr. John Wesley*, p. 15; Bull, *Wolf in Sheep's Cloathing*, p. 10. For Charles Wesley on John's relative acceptance in the Church of England, see William Gibson, *The Church of England, 1688–1832: Unity and Accord* (London: Routledge, 2001), p. 206, together with Gibson's "Altitudinarian Equivocation: George Smalridge's Churchmanship," in *Religious Identities in Britain: 1660–1832*, ed. Gibson and Robert G. Ingram (Aldershot, Hants, UK: Ashgate, 2005), pp. 43–59. For another, related point of view regarding change and continuity, see Robert G. Ingram, *Religion, Reform and Modernity in the Eighteenth Century: Thomas Secker and the Church of England* (Woodbridge, Suffolk, UK: Boydell Press, 2007). For other helpful scholarship on Wesley's relationship to the established church, see Frank Baker, *John Wesley and the Church of England* (Nashville: Abingdon Press, 1970); W. M. Jacob, "John Wesley and the

Church of England, 1736–40," *Journal of the John Rylands University Library of Manchester* 85 (2003): 73–98; Jeremy Gregory, "'In the Church I will live and die': John Wesley, the Church of England, and Methodism," in Gibson and Ingram, *Religious Identities*, pp. 147–78; and Geordan Hammond, "High Church Anglican Influences on John Wesley's Conception of Primitive Christianity, 1732–1735," *Anglican and Episcopal History* 75 (2009): 174–207. For Wesley's invitations to preach in Anglican churches, see The Bicentennial Edition of the Works of John Wesley, *The Works of John Wesley*, vol. 23, *Journal and Diaries*, ed. W. Reginald Ward and Richard Heitzenrater (Nashville: Abingdon Press, 1995): 36 (10 November 1776, St. Vedan's Church, London); 41 (28 January 1776, morning and afternoon at All Hallows Church, London); 44–45 (St. Werburgh's Church, Bristol); 45 (St. Ewen's Church, Bristol).

59. For David Hartley, see *Observations on Man* (London, 1749), 2:452–53 and quoted in *A Letter to the Rev. John Gardiner . . . Occasioned by the Brief Reflections on the Eloquence of the Pulpit* (London, 1796), p. 46n, in which the author also comments regarding Wesley.

60. Wesley, *Works*, 23:41.

61. The Works of Tobias Smollett, *The Expedition of Humphry Clinker*, intro. and notes by Thomas R. Preston, ed. O. M. Brack Jr. (Athens: University of Georgia Press, 1990), p. 170 (hereafter cited parenthetically in the text). Brett C. McInelly cites this passage and the agitated response in Wesley's *Journal*. See McInelly, "Redeeming Religion: Wesleyan and Calvinistic Methodism in *Humphry Clinker*," *Journal of the John Rylands University Library of Manchester* 85 (2003): 285–86, and the article itself, 285–96. Numbers 2 and 3 of this *Journal* include several other valuable essays on Wesley and Methodist contexts.

I have also found variously helpful the following studies regarding *Humphry Clinker*: On Methodism, Byron Gassman, "Religious Attitudes in the World of *Humphry Clinker*," *BYU Studies* 6 (1964–65): 65–72; and Claude-Jean Bertrand, "Humphry Clinker, a 'so-called Methodist,'" *Recherches anglaises et américaines* 47 (1969): 189–202. For *Clinker* as a novel, see esp. Paul Gabriel Boucé, *The Novels of Tobias Smollett*, trans. Boucé and Antonia White (London: Longman, 1976), pp. 191–251, on Methodism pp. 229–30; Jerry C. Beasley, *Tobias Smollett: Novelist* (Athens: University of Georgia Press, 1998), pp. 184–225, on Methodism, pp. 193, 213; Eric Rothstein, *Systems of Order and Inquiry in Later Eighteenth-Century Fiction* (Berkeley: University of California Press, 1975), pp. 109–53, on Methodism, pp. 133–34, 147–49. The list of course is selective. Several other studies concern the novel's structure, social contexts, travel, class structure, sympathy, and feeling.

62. See Thomas Preston's edition of Smollett's *Expedition of Humphry Clinker*, p. 387n6. John Sekora made a comparable point regarding the *Critical Review*'s attitude toward Methodists in *Luxury: The Concept in Western Thought, Eden to Smollett* (Baltimore: Johns Hopkins University Press, 1977), pp. 185–87.

63. Tobias Smollett, *Continuation of the Complete History of England. Volume the Fourth* (London, 1768), pp. 121–22.

64. Cleansing of working-class language and swearing was one of the social reforms that Wesley introduced and that filtered up to the gentry. As one example see his brief *Swear not at all, Saith the Lord God of Heaven and Earth* ([London?, 1744?]).

65. Thomas Preston believes that the text's reference to "Mr. W——'s" preaching is to Whitefield's (Smollett, *The Expedition of Humphry Clinker*, p. 388n13), given Humphry's attendance at the Tabernacle. He follows Lewis M. Knapp, ed., *The Expedition of Humphry*

Clinker (London: Oxford University Press, 1966), p. 364n139. Ross identifies Mr. W—— as Wesley, whose more benevolent, rational, and works-oriented Methodism Smollett would have found at the least less alienating. See *The Expedition of Humphry Clinker*, ed. Ross (Baltimore: Penguin Books, 1967), p. 402n50. Wesley appears twice in the Preston edition, on pp. 201 and 231, while Whitefield does not appear. Even in the prison sermon Humphry's Methodism largely is uplifting rather than Calvinist predestinarian. Whitefield left for America in September of 1769 and died on 30 September 1770 in Newburyport, Massachusetts. In about 1770 Wesley was again in the news regarding perfectionism and Calvinism. He clearly was closer to the British and to the London public than Whitefield.

66. Trapp, *Nature, Usefulness and Regulation of Religious Zeal*, p. 24.

67. Paullinus [Seagrave], *Letter to the People of England*, p. 5 (dangerous Politeness); Thomas Griffith, *The Use and Extent of Reason in Matters of Religion. A Sermon Preached before the University of Oxford, at St. Mary's. . . . Published at the Request of the Vice-Chancellor and Heads of Houses* (Oxford, 1756), p. 5. Griffith was a fellow of Pembroke; Johnson and Whitefield were undergraduates at approximately the same time.

68. Seagrave, *Answer to the Reverend Dr. Trapp's four Sermons*, p. 30; S——Y [Finch], *Defence of a Congratulatory Letter*, p. 150. This optimism, however, did not stop Methodist opponents from hoping to use the state's arm against its putative enemies. See Free, *Display of the Bad Principles of the Methodists*: Methodist principles and practices lead to atheism; the state is justly offended by such doctrines and their consequences. "*Atheism* has been deemed a *capital* Crime, and Atheists in some Countries have been put to Death, as Persons very dangerous to a State, at least in the Opinion of those who govern it" (p. 9). Free was the Methodists' persistent enemy.

69. [Finch], *Congratulatory Letter to the R$^{evd.}$ Dr. Trapp*, p. 4. Finch makes a similar point in his *Seasonable Advice To A Young Clergyman; In A Letter from A Gentleman in the Country, To His Kinsman in London, Just enter'd into Orders* (London, 1740), pp. 10–11. These and comparable remarks countered the Church of England's argument that languages and learning were necessary for ordained clergymen, all of whom were to have a university education.

70. Visiting and comforting of prisoners characterized Methodists' behavior from their earliest days at Oxford in 1729. See Law, *Oxford Methodists*, pp. 3–5, 8, 16, 20, 24, 28.

71. Academicus [Green], *Principles and Practices of the Methodists* (1760), pp. 28–29. Nathaniel Lancaster's anti-Methodist satire pretended to regard such behavior and its "Groans and Shrieks, and Agonies" as a sign of God's grace and of the irrelevance of reason as a guide. See his *Methodism Triumphant, Or, The Decisive Battle Between the Old Serpent and the Modern Saint* (London, 1767), pp. 36–37. Church of England clergymen often complained of such disorderly and enthusiastic Methodist meetings. See, for example, *Compleat Account of the Conduct of that eminent Enthusiast Mr. Whitefield*, pp. 9–10; [George Lavington, Bishop of Exeter], *The Enthusiasm of Methodists and Papists Compared* (London, 1754), sigs. 3^v–4^r, p. 11; Charles Chauncy, *A Letter from a Gentleman in Boston, to Mr. George Wishart, One of the Ministers of Edinburgh, Concerning the State of Religion in New England* (Edinburgh, 1742), p. 13; Free, *Display of the Bad Principles of the Methodists*, p. 6. The list is selective.

72. In addition, the presbyter John Wesley referred to himself as a "scriptural episcopos." The American Methodist Church, once freed from its Anglican parent, adopted an

administrative episcopal system. At its inception it was not bound by diocesan boundaries, and it did not claim apostolic succession for ordination; for Methodists succession meant permanent preaching of the Gospel. See, for example, *The Methodist Episcopal Church and the Protestant Episcopal Church Compared in a Dialogue between Rev. Mr. Smith a Travelling Preacher, and Rev. Mr. Townley, a Rector of —— Parish* (Philadelphia, 1844). The topic seemed especially compelling for nineteenth-century American Methodist historians. For other works pertaining to Methodism in America, see John H. Wigger, *Taking Heaven by Storm: Methodism and the Rise of Popular Christianity in America* (New York: Oxford University Press, 1998); Dee Andrews, *The Methodists and Revolutionary America, 1760–1800* (Princeton, NJ: Princeton University Press, 2000); and Russell E. Richey and Thomas Edward Frank, *Episcopacy in the Methodist Tradition: Perspectives and Proposals* (Nashville: Abingdon Press, 2004). David Hempton has handsomely chronicled Methodism's various fortunes. See his *Methodism: Empire of the Spirit* (n. 4 above).

73. See the anti-Methodist tract by A Layman of the Church of England, *Letter to the Rev. Mr. George Whitefield, Containing some Remarks on His Letter to the Rev. Dr. Durell*, p. 9: as a young man the layman "was a member of a religious society at the Vestry Room of St. Michaels Church, Crooked-Lane London, which consisted of above one hundred, most of them young men, and at that time there were many such societies in and about London."

74. For discussion of this synthesizing effect in the novel, see Howard D. Weinbrot, *Britannia's Issue: The Rise of British Literature from Dryden to Ossian* (Cambridge: Cambridge University Press, 1993), pp. 512–16. Alex Wetmore has suggested synthetic qualities in Smollett, Hume, and Smith, among others. See "Sympathy Machines: Men of Feeling and the Automaton," *Eighteenth-Century Studies* 43 (2009): 37–54.

PART THREE

EVOLUTIONARY REVERSION

The Gordon Riots, Return to Rage, and Reinventing a Cure

CHAPTER SIX

Déjà Vu All Over Again?

The Gordon Riots; Bedlam Revisited, Restoration of Order, and a Trial on Trial

Surely now God was in his heaven and all was right with the world. The heaven could have been that of the established but moderate High or Low Church, altitudinarian or latitudinarian, Wesleyan or Whitefield Methodist, Presbyterian or other Dissenter. Even deists might be welcome. By the later eighteenth century, characterization of Whigs as evil false brethren seemed a barely audible echo of yesteryear. After all, the Whigs of varied sorts, including Whigs in Tory clothing, were in control; successfully rebellious Americans excepted, the empire flourished; and the traditional French enemy seemed contained and limited in much of North America, if not on the Continent. The accusatory rage of the thirtieth of January sermons largely had spent itself amid accommodation to a stable Hanoverian dynasty with ample heirs and spares. Religious compulsion shifted from force to the suasion of love. In spite of the *Protestant Magazine*'s incandescent anti-Catholicism, it puffed its religion as "too just and generous to *compel*."[1] Methodists, and until the French Revolution Dissenters, generally were absolved of seditious schism, though not of being oddly wrongheaded and noisy. They had navigated into significant streams of British life as respectable and often revered members of the spiritual and secular worlds. Whatever the abusive political sloganeering, as toward Wesley and Johnson, no sensible person feared a Stuart-Jacobite threat. There was no support for a Stuart claimant when George III assumed the throne in 1760. The exiled alcoholic Charles Edward (1720–1788) in Italy was scarcely bonnie or capable of mounting an invasion or of persuading France or Spain again to encourage his folly. He lacked male issue and was denied the courtesy title of King Charles III by Pope Clement XII, who recognized a lost cause. Upon Charles' death in 1788 his brother Henry Benedict Maria Clement Thomas Francis Xavier Stuart (1725–1807), Cardinal Duke of York, styled himself Henry IX. He nonetheless had no interest in or hopes of obtaining the crown that his pope acknowledged belonged to George III and that Henry never could attain without an impossible foreign invasion and unwinnable civil war. Indeed by 1800 he was receiving annual pension support of four thousand pounds from the generous Hanoverian monarch. Britain had far more troubling rivals than those in a movement essentially dead on Culloden's fields.

Neither individuals nor cultures are perfect. Bloody-minded Britons must have their fun; imperial adventures had their misadventures; satire and the deservedly satirized never disappeared. Human tribalism often defines nontribal members as somehow deviant and dangerous. On balance, though, educated Britons thought their nation had evolved into an enlightened model of general benevolence. They were a polite and commercial people, a polite and aristocratic people, a polite and religiously and politically tolerant people. What could go wrong in this imaginary bliss if Parliament wisely legislated within the era's gentle temper and liberal spirit? A great deal. It was not supposed to be that way.

Repeal, No Popery, and the Gordon Riots: Destruction and the Puritan Redivivus

On 14 May 1778 Sir George Savile moved a bill to repeal certain penalties and restrictions upon British Roman Catholics passed under William III. These laws once were necessary, but now, within a stable and benign Protestant succession, "men of humanity could not avoid lamenting" severity inconsistent with Protestant generosity and national interest. William's acts perpetuated ancient discord and victimized subjects who long had demonstrated their loyalty. They deserved to "share in the common interest" and, in a key term, "were rendered incapable of forming any part of the common union of defense." That is, Catholics could join the British military. The bill repealed only the most onerous of the laws but nonetheless encouraged "the safety, and the good consequences . . . likely to attend this liberal procedure of Parliament." As a sensible precaution and sign of good faith, Sir George included a loyalty oath to bind the Catholics "to the support of the civil government."[2]

The *Annual Register* knew that the bill removed "great and grievous penalties": life imprisonment of a conventional Catholic priest or a Jesuit who taught students or officiated in religious services; forfeiture of property by those Catholics educated abroad and whose estates then could be seized by the closest Protestant heir, thus allowing a son to confiscate his father's lands; and the inability of Catholics to purchase and hold property. Some of the penalties no longer were necessary; the laws rarely were enforced, but they might be and rendered humane judges powerless; the laws always were "a disgrace to humanity." They must be repealed in so liberal an era in which "little was to be apprehended from these people." The *Register* chronicled Parliament's happy response: "The motion was received with universal approbation, and a bill was accordingly brought in and passed without a single negative." Many fellow Britons "were relieved from the pressure, of some of the most intolerable of those grievances under which they had long laboured" (*AR* 1778, 191). As a loyal, once troubled, and now grateful Roman Catholic subject said in praise of the monarch, the Parliament, and Sir George, "LIBERTY shall reward the Hand, which nobly dared unfetter the last remaining Shackles of her servile Chain."[3]

Out of other doors, however, the bill evoked numerous negatives, massive public unrest, and a clear sense that the elites had consulted themselves rather than history and the public on so important an issue. This was especially true in Scotland. The London Parliament hoped that the repeal would apply to the north as well, but the Kirk and its allies sternly objected and fostered a vigorous anti-repeal campaign whose violence surprised and annoyed South Britons. As an English commentator complained, those tumults were "an unlooked for event in this enlightened and liberal age."[4] The compiler of Scotland's *Short View of the Statutes at Present in Force . . . Against Popery* (1779) had no patience for such self-congratulation. He lamented "encouragements given to Popery in England" and urged that Scotland not follow suit:

> Shall we be silent? Have we already forgotten the days of our *forefathers*, and the sufferings which they endured from the hand of Papists? Can we, without uneasiness for *ourselves*, again receive these instruments of cruelty into our bosom? And are we altogether unconcerned for what may be the fate of generations *yet unborn*? No surely. Though we are degenerate, we are not come to this.[5]

John Erskine was among the many who had not come to that. His *Considerations On the Spirit of Popery, and The intended Bill for the relief of Papists in Scotland* (Edinburgh, 1778) embodies Scottish and much consequent English response. The spirit and major points of his objections were repeated and enlarged upon in both north and south Britain well into the 1790s. Erskine favors liberty of conscience. Differences in religious practice should be tolerated even if, like Catholicism, the other religion is "subversive of Bible Christianity." A sect that uses fear and violence to deny all other sects' religious and civil rights, however, is unacceptable. Its advocates in power will "tolerate no religion save their own." It is "blind or distracted moderation" to permit a bigoted group to increase in size and danger. The House of Commons thought itself benevolent and sensible. The Protestant resisters thought them wilfully self-deluded or worse. Fraud is at the heart of Catholics' practice; their oaths are not credible, for they are loyal to Mother Church and not to God or to the secular state, to which they swear false allegiance. Papists are docile now, but their future conduct is unpredictable. The chained lion is no threat, but can one conclude that he will not devour us "when set at liberty?" (p. 8). The way in which the bill was passed suggests neither intellectual openness nor "a fair and free discussion" of so urgent a question.

Erskine is troubled by the bill's implicit authorization of new Catholic soldiers. Yes, we require a larger military against a common enemy, but be careful to guard "against a lesser danger by exposing ourselves to a greater." Their zeal may turn their arms against us; their Protestant comrades may not trust them and may fight poorly or perhaps panic. Even if all this is wrong, such alarming "indulgence to men hitherto accounted bitter enemies of our constitution . . . may hurt rather than forward exertions against our ambitious neighbours" (p. 22). We need to avoid "fool-hardy experiments" in which we arm our enemy (p. 23). Be prudent, and do not malign skeptical Protestants, who only seek protection from papists and their long history of sanguine persecution. The Scottish people should "use their constitutional right of petitioning the legislature against every measure which they apprehend hazard to their lives, their liberty, their religion" (p. 41).

The British Parliament regarded, or said it regarded, repeal as wisely humane. The Protestant opposition regarded the repeal as foolishly suicidal. In the event, a combination of petitions, riots, and the Protestant Association soon led by Lord George Gordon rejected repeal of the law in Scotland and later attempted to do the same in England. Many Britons, and especially the Scots, praised his patriotic and religious efforts. As one correspondent put it, Lord George's conduct in the last session of Parliament "cannot be sufficiently admired: in him may be observed every duty of a senator united."[6]

Many more in the south were less admiring by far. Suicide and homicide now seemed more than metaphors. Britain might be returning to Sacheverell's aggressive religious world—or even what Ammianus Marcellinus long ago saw and lamented: "No savage beasts are so noisom and hurtful to men, as Christians are to themselves, and for the most part of them mortall and deadly."[7] The Scottish aggressive model nonetheless was a congenial import for English Protestant polemicists and tacticians. They too agreed that liberty of conscience was essential and that religious rights depended upon civil rights. Remove one, and you remove the other. Protestants regularly were taught that Catholics in power had perpetrated such removals and would do so again if given the chance.

Much of the established church and its Dissenters indeed believed that popery was superstitious, idolatrous, tyrannical, arbitrary, and a past, present, and future assault upon the national religion and government. Like Erskine in the north, English Protestants believed that the pope advised his coreligionists not to keep faith with heretics; oaths were useless. The pope absolved the murderers of heretics, including regicides; all Catholic subjects were suspect. The pope controlled any Catholic monarch he installed; Catholic politics meant despotism and slavery. The Saint Bartholomew's Day Massacre (1572), revocation of the Edict of Nantes (1685), and the Spanish, Portuguese, and Italian inquisitions were regular signs of the regular practice of papal blood lust. Such lumber provided enough kindling for a conflagration that needed only a skillful arsonist to set the match. Lord George Gordon was pleased to comply.

Lord George was the third son of the Scottish Duke of Gordon and raised as a strict Calvinist Presbyterian. He became the celebrated voice of No Popery riots, whose consequences nearly were catastrophic for London and Britain. On 2 June 1780 he led at least 40,000 angry Protestants with symbolic blue cockades in their hats and assembled them in Saint George's fields. They divided into four groups, with Lord George "in the centre of the Scotch [division], who were distinguished by martial music." They marched on Parliament with a massive roll of some 120,000 signed petitions, demanded repeal of the new law, and gradually became rowdy as vagabonds, or "unprincipled lawless banditti," joined them and further darkened the group's mingled dark and carnival tone. They abused several grandees and bishops, aggressively tapped passers-by for money, imbibed large quantities of alcohol, and hectored anyone not wearing the blue cockade that identified their ideological bent. When they burst their way into the House of Commons' lobby, some members "with difficulty saved their lives." Parliament thought itself under siege and in "a truly perilous situation."[8] London soon became a war zone amidst war ruins. Lord George nominally led the massive group, which soon was infected by mobs interested more in destruction and plunder than in popery and more in its own actions than in his guidance. He became irrelevant for most of his followers; his adversaries regarded him as a throwback to an earlier time and a different war in a Puritan past. Perhaps British culture had largely evolved in a positive and tolerant way. Perhaps also that progress either was reversible or merely a parallel, rather exclusive national path. The next few years would help to suggest which path was taken.

The intellectual posture of the Protestant Association was consistent with the Puritan paradigm. Presbyterian and Independent ancestors vilified and then beheaded Archbishop Laud, captured and then beheaded Charles I, later contributed to James II's forced exile, and celebrated William III and his Act of Toleration. Eighteenth-century Protestants resurrected some of these ancestral roles but shifted their anger to Catholics in general and to the administration of George III in particular, which for many became Carolus and Jacobus redux. The Protestants' Presbyterian Calvinist bias was explicit and explicitly seen. They emphasized "the *right of private judgment*" even more than their establishment colleagues. They more consistently invoked John Knox and Calvin as intellectual mentors, and they insisted on personal guidance by personal angels, who magically were not considered papist. Maria De Fleury, for example, knew that Lord George's own "celestial guards" would "shield him from impending ills" in prison and in trial. They scoffed at *"lukewarm Protestants,"* enjoyed spirited, energetic, preaching against sin rather than for "morality," and, we shall see, looked toward Scotland as a model of successful protest and upright Calvinism.[9]

Early in June of 1780, however, much of London was reduced to rubble and burned-out buildings. The panic of mob rule threatened to spread, destabilize the nation, and diminish international standing based upon economic and military strength. As Samuel Johnson wrote to an alarmed Mrs. Thrale on 12 June 1780, "The history of the last week would fill You with amazement, it is without any modern example." Boswell later added that Gordon's No Popery riots were "the most horrid series of outrage that ever disgraced a civilized country." Thomas Holcroft described an apocalyptic scene during the height of the riots.[10] These were caused for several reasons: repeal of the anti-Catholic laws; licentious anger by thousands of often adolescent drunken hooligans fuming against their betters; generalized rage regarding the elites' indifference to them; hostility to the Quebec Act and the American war; and sheer unbridled human fury, in which all men become mad for whatever reason all men become mad. For Holcroft, all aspects "of universal anarchy, and approaching desolation, seemed to be accumulating." Neither sleep nor rest was possible; "the streets were swarming with people, and uproar, confusion, and terror reigned in every part" of London (p. 23). If the mob had sacked the Bank of England, "nothing less than national bankruptcy and destruction could have ensued." Since "the very existence of the empire" was at stake, survival depended upon "the exertion of Government." It failed until George III removed control of the military from hapless civil to royal authority that allowed officers' discretion to fire as the situation warranted. The troubling and controversial act ended "this dark and diabolical business" (p. 49). As another commentator put it, without such action they would have seen "the wreck of liberty, the ruin of fam'd Britannia."[11]

The horrors continued until the troops killed at least 236 and wounded some 500 more. Other estimates range as high as 700 dead, including the many who died from the fires they set, the buildings they collapsed, and the alcohol they devoured. Twenty-five later were hanged, almost all of them under the age of eighteen and many far younger, indeed children. By the time the rioters were subdued, property damage was massive, prisons were burned down, prisoners freed and then recaptured, native Catholic residences and foreign Catholic embassies in which Catholic Londoners worshiped were destroyed, and the homes of Parliament's movers and shakers of the repeal were moved and shaken to the ground. Even the redcoats' restoration of order fed fears of ministerial collusion in permitting and then crushing the outburst for political purposes. Horace Walpole thought that the government action was designed to destroy opposition to the American war. The court and ministry sought to "unite *all* the military and militia, and all under one standard," as it has.[12]

Lord George had found that it was easier to raise a mob than to control it. He later was arrested for "constructive treason," transported to the Tower with the largest number of soldiers "ever remembered to guard a state prisoner," tried on a capital charge, and acquitted.[13] He nonetheless spent much of the rest of his life in prison, where he effectually held court. His visitors among the Great and the Good included the Duke of York and John Wesley. Gordon comforted other prisoners with food, talk, and music and wrote numerous letters and pamphlets on various subjects to various recipients in various but often prophetic and scolding tones. He died of jail fever—typhus—on 1 November 1793 at the age of forty-two. As we shall see, as a cosmic irony the icon of rigorous Protestant Calvinism lost his Christian faith, in 1787 converted to orthodox Polish Judaism, and hoped to ally the Jews with Protestants against a common Catholic enemy. He was circumcised, dressed in traditional Polish Jewish costume, wore traditional prayer items, grew a long beard, and called himself Yisrael bar Avraham Gordon, Israel son of Abraham. While in prison he meticulously observed Jewish religious and culinary ceremonies, wrote and spoke in Hebrew when appropriate, and arranged matters so that he could worship on the Jewish Sabbath. Of course he was mocked and ridiculed. He later apparently was not offered, and may have been denied, Jewish burial, probably on prudential grounds. Of course, also, he failed to deliver his new people to their promised land.[14]

Lord George clearly had many allies before, during, and after the riots he induced and that the justifiably appalled elites could not or would not understand. The commentators who helped the cause used religious discourse familiar to readers some three generations earlier, but still part of much Protestant thought and language. The angry past now seemed more alive than dead. It returned trailing clouds of bigotry-tinged gore.

Renovating the Language of Cultural Regress

Such apparently retrograde brutality was unnerving. Enlightened Britons had persuaded themselves that theirs was a deservedly earned post–William Hanoverian birthright, one that Sir George Savile used to justify repeal of the anti-Catholic laws. Edward Gibbon thought that the Gordon Riots embodied "a dark and diabolical fanaticism, which I had supposed to be extinct." He had ample company in that view. The author of *Observations on "An Appeal From the Protestant Association"* (1780) acknowledges the blood spilled in the seventeenth century, yet "the disposition of the present age is much altered. An increased humanity must be allowed us." Whatever the allowance, the authors of the *Protestant Appeal* have not "kept pace with the general improvement" (p. 35). After all, John Newton claimed, Britain's Georgian world offered "unrestrained liberty" of religious worship. Arthur O'Leary, in Dublin, was angry regarding the contrast between what the Gordon Riots showed and what the age should have been. Amiable religion now abjures "frantic fanaticism, banished from all the quarters of Europe." Perhaps not. Fanaticism after all has "found shelter among" the Protestant associators and with "calamitous evils."[15]

To be sure, the Gordon Riots could not have happened if the pleasing dreams that modern virtue largely displaced ancient vice were real. Such dreams and dreamers wilfully overlooked the fears that both the established and dissenting confessions nurtured regarding presumably malicious Catholicism. A Scottish commentator in 1781 Edinburgh ticked off an impressive list of luminaries who wanted Catholics restrained, a list to which he soon added Addison: "A Russell—A Sydney—a Newton—a Swift—a Bolingbroke—a Tillotson—a Locke—have, in ages as *enlightened* as the present, avowed and supported this doctrine." The *Protestant Magazine*'s contributor for June of 1782 insisted that preaching against popery was commonplace: witness "Archbishop Tillotson, and every divine of the last and present age . . . and he did not know a clergyman of the Church of England . . . from whom he had not heard at some time or other, similar discourse" that popery was dangerous tyranny and must not be allowed to increase. The author of *Strictures on a Pamphlet* (1782), on behalf of loyal English Catholics, was so influenced. He adheres to the Church of England "upon principle, and from conviction," and he knows that English Catholics are as knavish now as ever. Bishop Sherlock had it right: Britain's worst fear is "the prevailing power of Popery." It seeks to ruin the state and the Protestant religion. John Butler, bishop of Oxford, confirmed that commonplace in his thirtieth of January sermon to the House of Lords in 1787. He so spoke because he rightly assumed that the peers and other bishops agreed. The regicides sent the rest of Charles I's "family into exile, where they actually and largely imbibed the obnoxious principles of religion and government imputed to him, and became unfit to fill his throne."[16]

Such concerns indeed long had been mainstream in British Protestant polemic and literature. John Milton's "In quintum Novembris" (1625) characterizes the devil and the pope plotting to blow up Parliament and King James. *Aereopagitica* (1644) is keen on a free press, but not for papists. The popes censored presumed heresy and "any subject that was not to their palate," which they either prohibited or sent to "a new Purgatory of an Index." In an essay printed in 1673 Milton joined his voice to the many "who exhorted the People to beware the growth of this Romish Weed."[17] Swift's *Tale of a Tub* (1704) remained well known in part because it embodied a traditional portrait of Catholic political and spiritual dogmatism. In 1780 *The Protestant Packet* received a mock complaint regarding that "hellish book" and its "dreadfully blasphemous" characterization of Peter's papal infallibility (*PP*, p. 138). Shortly thereafter the *Protestant Magazine* echoed either the letter or the spirit of another traditional Protestant and Swiftian *Tale* attack. The pope and his daringly wicked clergy "keep the Scriptures locked up in an unknown tongue, from all the millions of the common people" (*PM* 1 [1781]: 13–14). The ever-popular *Gulliver's Travels* (1726) reminded readers that the Portuguese sea captain Don Pedro had to shield Protestant Gulliver from the Inquisition (4.11). Sterne's more recent and friendly *Tristram Shandy* (1759–67) transcribed a horrendous Catholic excommunication curse, Yorick's anti-Catholic sermon on conscience, and poor Corporal Trim's lament regarding his brother's fourteen-year imprisonment by the Portuguese Inquisition (3.11, 2.17). John Baillie, in Newcastle, thus was merely affirming a Church of England received truth: Spain and Portugal embody the "true genius of Popery." It maintains its "same ignorance and bloody bigotry as in the darker ages." Alderman Frederick Bull confirmed that connection between elite propaganda and popular response when he addressed the Commons on 7 June 1780. Such language resonated throughout those troubled times. During the '45, Anglican bishops and clergy were "indefatigable in warning the people to beware of Popery," a false religion "which had deluged Europe in blood," sought to banish George II, and is today what it was then. Yet now that clergy represents the Catholics and their horrors as "perfectly harmless, and deserving of our countenance and support!" No wonder that in 1780 as well a defender of the Catholic amelioration law both acknowledged and lamented the numerous angry "pastoral instructions" that are "anathemas and defamatory libels" that disgrace those putative teachers of Christianity.[18] In 1780 the protesting Protestants thus were mimicking the values, rhetoric, and generations of pastoral instructions by the established and the major dissenting churches. By then it was too late to transmogrify recent Anglican rage into present Protestant stoicism. The elites felt no obligation to consult and persuade those other than themselves regarding so radical a change of course.

Here was a downside of the "divine right of government" as it had developed and been manifest in the progress of the thirtieth of January sermons. If the government itself is "divine," those external to government, and certainly the overwhelming majority of Britons who cannot vote, are political heretics who can be ignored. Few of Sir George Savile's parliamentary colleagues would admit this similarity, but the elites of 1778 had adapted apparently long-moribund High Tory views of the "people," views indeed that would be overt in Lord George's trial for constructive treason in 1781. We recall Mary Astell's *Impartial Enquiry Into the Causes of Rebellion and Civil War in this Kingdom* (London, 1701). She made clear that "the People have no Authority over their own Lives." Those "who place the Supreme Power originally in the People" foster rebellion (pp. 48–49). By 1710 Francis Atterbury's *Voice of the People, No Voice of God* added that "the People" not only were a false god but uttered "the Cry of Hell" (p. 6). In 1780 both the elites and the nation would pay dearly for such mingled indifference and hostility.

The Protestants' robustly hostile language in turn also evoked earlier eighteenth-century heated discourse. We recall that the dominant but threatened High Church attacked its lower church, Whigs, Dissenters, and other putative false brethren: they will rise to kill again; they are a torrent of vice; they will undermine the Church and state; they are like wild animals, who would destroy humanity if possible. Later eighteenth-century Protestants repeated but varied that language. They generally targeted what seemed a growing Catholic power block authorized by a monarch, ministers, and Parliament who must have taken leave of their senses. Or worse. John Baillie spoke for and with many concerned anti-Catholic Protestants in the 1780s: If papists had the power, they would force us to worship as they do or "burn us alive," as "a thousand years of dreadful experience have demonstrated." Moreover, "Say, can they ever from their purpose shrink, / Till the Most High shall give them blood to drink?" Much of that ensanguined beverage was produced in America and its cruel "aceldema, this field of blood."[19]

There were of course dire consequences from papal wolves, locusts, and other dangerous beasts. John Wesley put it bluntly regarding Catholics in what may have been a theological pun: "A Protestant ought not to trust you, any more than he would trust a wild Bull."[20] In a related but different old metaphor in a new context, they seek to "lay the ax to the root of our dearest privileges and most sacred rights" (*PM* 3 [1783]: 11). These evildoers not only hope to extirpate Protestantism and its advocates. They once made a handsome start both in that direction and against the large portion of the human race that the papacy found unacceptable. Many readers in 1780 thought these troubling numbers troublingly credible. Between 1540 and 1570 papists had murdered 900,000 European Protestants, including 23 barons, 148 earls, and 39 princes. Within a four-year period the Inquisition killed 150,000. During the fourteen hundred years of the papacy, its agents killed upwards of 50,000,000, or about 35,714 persons per year (*PM* 1 [1781]: 70–71).

We again immediately recall the language of annihilation in the fiercely metaphoric exchanges of some eighty years before the Gordon Riots. Henry Sacheverell's

Political Union (1702) urged that Dissenters be held in check by Augustinian "wholesome severities." These might be an occasional hanging of ringleaders *pour encourager les autres*, exile, or forced conversion for their own good. Sacheverell and other High Churchmen knew that if Dissenters were not rigidly constrained, they once more would rise and seek to root out monarchy and episcopacy. Get them or they will get us. That also was later eighteenth-century Protestant language, but as spoken and written by Dissenters, often evangelical lower church Anglicans, and probably Methodists of Gordon's Protestant Association. For these writers, properly constrained papists "become good subjects; and ought laws, whose wholesome severities hath produced such salutary effects, to have been essentially changed, or virtually repealed?"[21]

Alas, given the dreadful consequences of the repeal, the salutary became the mortuary. "The mischief was done, before the design was made known; and ... before it could be prevented" (*PM* 3 [1783]: 16). Thomas Bell's *Standard of the Spirit* (1780) was dedicated to Lord George, who had so successfully helped Scotland reject the anti-Catholic laws. Bell's *Standard* enlarges and reorganizes several of his sermons, many of whose themes overlap. They also embrace the earlier High Church language of frightened opposition to threatening forces. The Catholic enemy rushed in with heretical doctrine, idolatrous worship, and tyrannical government. It induced "a flood of infidelity, error, immorality." In some cases, with an often repeated image, the flood was "a torrent" of wickedness or of corruption or iniquity roaring through the land. A "deluge of Popery" had overspread England before William's revolution and his anti-Catholic laws.[22]

As the papacy's apparent murder of millions makes plain, the floods' deadly work also was done by an advancing army's siege engineers. Catholics not only regularly work to sap the foundation of Protestantism. If permitted to educate Protestant children, they also will "undermine the very foundation of our constitution, in church and state." There again must be someone willing to stand in the gap or stand in the breach and resist the torrent, flood, army, sappers. To do this, one must have a sustainable bulwark, which the repeal maliciously sought to destroy. Fortunately, the good English jury that acquitted Lord George remains the bulwark of national liberty, as the Protestant Association remains the "bulwark of these favour'd lands."[23] Hell and Rome nonetheless plan "to pull the sacred building down." Eternal vigilance and the union of all British reformed churches are necessary to rebuild the true church's "Protestant bulwarks so lately broken down."[24] Without such protection, there would be a horrid deluge of destructive blood, so pleasing to thirsty papist wolves.

Sometimes the Protestants' language appropriated comparably familiar images, as with *fence* and cognate terms that papists violated. We again hear words that long had been available in religious polemic seeking to protect the Church of England from ominous Dissenters and now focused on Catholics. Henry Sacheverell abhorred internal enemies to the established church, who hoped to "have Taken down its Fence, and Remov'd Its *Land-Marks*" in order to debauch and subvert its doctrines, discipline, and "the Only Support of the *Protestant* Religion in the World." Thereafter, the Presbyterian Benjamin Bennet was one of the Protestant Association's favorite authors. His *Memorial of the Reformation* (1717) laments that James II so trampled "the Fence of Law" that a desperate people petitioned William and Mary for succor. William Graham urges that since papists are wolves, when "legal fences decay . . . they need to be speedily restored." Edmund Burke, a chief mover of the repeal, was scolded for his unprecedented alterations of governmental forms, which "break down the great fence of British liberty."[25]

The *Protestant Magazine* added striking visual form and overt causation when it explained its unsubtle frontispiece and its role as symbolic protector of the true faith. Religion on its throne is supported by the pillars of the Protestant Associations of England and of Scotland. It receives "from an Angel a book open, *The Protestant Magazine*." Lord George stands before the throne "holding a Banner, with the motto, *Protestant Interest and House of Hanover*, generously engaging to support the true Religion." Behind him "the Fence which formerly stopped the inroads of Popery in these kingdoms, being broken down, the Pope is advancing hastily, leading the beast with seven heads and ten horns, with an intention to over throw Religion's throne. While the eye of Providence surveys the whole."[26] Protestantism is saved by a divinely delivered book, the surrogate for scripture, on which the religion relies. The book, however, is the collected wisdom of a collected secular body of Protestant writers uniformly resisting the advancing pope. They in turn require powerful secular patrons—the throne and especially aristocratic Lord George as the Association's voice and standard-bearer. He is the respectful male before an adored and holy female. The intrusive invading pope leads an animal who reflects his own malign inner state that also is a perverted sexual threat to Religion.

The explanation darkly reworks Win Jenkins' comic observation about the difference between Welsh and Scottish Gaelic in *Humphry Clinker* (1771): the language is the same, "but the words are different."[27] Such pillars in the Sacheverell era would have been episcopacy and monarchy; Catholics were evil, but the invading menace was more likely to have been John Knox than the pope. This, then, was not déjà vu all over again but a major shift in power relations within British Protestant confessions that presented the nation with a new set of problems. The High Church had lost as much power as the lower church had gained. At least as important, evangelical Anglicans, Methodists, Dissenters of various sorts, and Scottish Presbyterians demanded and received more authority, if from their points of view not nearly enough. The terrible Gordon Riots themselves suggest that these groups did not know how to manage their public, or street, power. The major shift, though, was demonstrable in the event, in rhetoric regarding it, in the Protestants' acknowledged affiliations, and in their sense of causation.

Church, State, and Political Causation

We see the word *Protestant* almost everywhere in the large literature before, during, and after the 1780 riots. It is a generic term, not a synonym for the established church and certainly not for the shards of the lingering and much changed High Church. Its earlier defenders' call to arms was "the Church in Danger." The later Protestant call to arms was "the religion in danger." One writer claims that about two-thirds of those who signed the petition to reverse the repeal belonged to the Church of England. If improbably so, they were likely to be evangelicals who still aligned themselves with a church with which they often differed. A mock-biblical commentator characterized the mob as, among others, Presbyterians, Anabaptists, Seceders, Independents, Antinomians, Muggletonians, Moravians, and Sandemanians, but not Quakers, who refused to disgrace their hats with blue cockades. The absence of Anglicans is not accidental.[28]

Several other writers typically invite the Church of England to join them in protest. The Protestant Association, for example, asks all coreligionists cordially to "unite, and strenuously exert themselves on this important occasion." The dissenting *Protestant Packet* is praised for its efforts on behalf "of every *denomination of Protestants.*" Its anti-Catholic works "must be of the greatest utility to Protestants of all ranks and characters." The *Protestant Magazine* wants Protestant writers to stop defaming one another and helping papists to divide and conquer. Thomas Lewis O'Beirne, though, rejected that offer and praised the established church for divorcing itself from the rabble who signed petitions. Among some forty thousand we did not "find more than *one* archdeacon, reprobated in this by all his brethren, and few *very few* of the inferior clergy, notorious for methodism, with Westley [sic] at their head." As for the rest, they were fanatical Methodists, "the very dregs of the people" who populated the tabernacles, and "the scum of the Scotch fanatics whom that nation has thrown out in such numbers."[29]

In more cases, provocative publications made overt their bias against the established church. Lord George was part of a Protestant deputation to the Earl of Shelburne. The committee wrote *Sketches* of that unsuccessful effort to engage him on its anti-repeal side. Its Association readers must be told "that the majority of their Deputation being Scotsmen," the majority of their argument also had

Presbyterian principles. That was not by design but because the "backwardness of the church of England clergymen . . . deprived the Scots priests of their assistance." As the *Protestant Packet* knew, friends of arbitrary power were the *"cavaliers, high churchmen, Jacobites* and *modern Tories,"* who even eulogized the "diabolical, popish, persecuting spirit" of the deservedly beheaded Archbishop Laud. The *Packet* warned that Toryism again was rising and noted the "alarming truth" that the Crown and the Anglican Church sought "to establish episcopacy" in the American colonies. William Graham's *False Prophets Unmasked* (1780) berated the self-destructive Anglican Church. It foolishly sought "the good opinion of Rome" and kept "the whole plan of Antichristian hierarchy," except for papal supremacy and other "whorish ceremonies of the Mother of Harlots." It nonetheless was subject to the depredations of "the Arch-Wolf and his Accomplices in rapine."[30]

Such language predicts another term familiar from seventeenth-century attacks on the Church of England. The perpetrating poet of *The Fall of Romish Babylon* put on tattered singing robes to denigrate "gaudy forms" and impure theology: "Prelate!—A Pope is but another name; / 'Tis the same thing!—their doctrine is the same." We shall see that activists generally were opposed to the American war. In contrast, a Church of England *Prayer to be Used . . . . In Times of War and Tumults* (1781) belatedly asked all Britons in all Anglican churches to pray that God turns "the Hearts of his rebellious Subjects in *America*" toward loyalty and away from "unhappy Divisions." There clearly was an unhappy division between such a view and that of the Protestant Association. There also clearly was good reason for the putative Jeremiah Trist's remark in 1790: Dissenters could not be branded with the "whole charge" of those evil events, of which they nonetheless were the "original and chief cause" and which they "promoted and conducted."[31]

The Association rejected halfway measures when Lord George addressed it on 29 May 1780. He then addressed a key word to the large crowd that he would lead to Westminster a few days later, but not if they "were too lukewarm to join him in all hazards" on behalf of their nation and religion. "He was not a lukewarm man himself," and if all they wanted was "mock debate and idle opposition, they might get another leader." John Baillie adapted the negative term and its connotation of tepid devotion to truth. He was among those who thought pro-repeal congregants *"lukewarm Protestants"* naively dreaming that Rome no longer was dangerous. In fact, its tenets burst the human ties "by which mankind are connected." The 1780 High Church surely was neither Cavalier nor Jacobite. For many non-Establishment Protestants it was too cool and detached, too apparently reasonable, to see the hot reality of its neo-papist actions or the glory of Lord George's acquittal. William Augustus Clarke celebrated the triumph with a thanksgiving sermon that also celebrated the joyous side of Puritanism. Fervent prayers in his church put him "in mind of the puritan days" when parishioners were free, bold, and "importunate at a Throne of Grace." Clarke could only guess that Puritanism was so vibrant "according to what is said concerning those times." He surely knew that such "solemn work of prayer" to "the great and eternal JEHOVAH" was scarcely lukewarm.[32]

The political and religious Establishment seemed oblivious, if not hostile, to the passions and needs of so significant a part of their constituency. David Fairer has shrewdly characterized Edmund Burke's typical mode of proceeding in political theory. We there "encounter national character that has been shaped by recalcitrant human experience rather than by the legislation of the powerful." The Protestant Association thought that the opposite now was the case. Burke and his powerful parliamentary friends legislated without consulting their electors', much less the non-electors', "human experience." Burke in fact had been prescient regarding motives for popular discontent. On 8 October 1777 he wrote to Charles James Fox: "People crushed by law, have no hopes but from power. If laws are their enemies, they will be enemies to laws; and those who have ... nothing to lose, will always be dangerous more or less"—more so, of course, for Gordon's people.[33] It hardly mattered that most of the forty thousand in the streets were not among the approximately 5 percent of adult males who could vote. They could petition and if necessary become extremely unpleasant as a secondary form of voting. Their legislators had behaved more like Norman rulers than British subjects dependent upon and accountable to other British subjects for their actions. The House of Lords and its bishops did not have a voting constituency to whom they must answer, but they too were constitutionally obliged to receive petitions and respectfully debate proposed issues. Instead, all three groups behaved as if the Protestants were an affliction to be vilified rather than what they thought themselves, namely, a wrongly aggrieved body that sought redress, reflected the ancient views of the elites and the established church, and were not paid even the appearance of shared deliberation. Horace Walpole and William Mason characterized the elites' belief that their wise judgment should be wisely imposed. On 12 July 1780 William Mason so wrote to Walpole: "Amongst all my acquaintances I know not above two besides yourself who agreed with me from the first, of the impropriety of introducing that bill which was the cause of the tumult."[34]

Both houses of Parliament, then, seemed blind and deaf to the fear that popery was rising and threatening the nation and its civil and religious rights. This consultive apathy was as much class hostility as reasoned judgment. There were several "new men," military, and commercial sorts in government, but the Members, lords, and bishops overwhelmingly were from the higher and educated classes. Many of them regarded a seat in the Commons as personal property, as did Lord George, for whom a seat was purchased when he was twenty-two. The

Members had country homes to which they wanted to adjourn rather than stay in London and go on about tiresome legislation and petitions. Squabbling among the lords or the Members of Parliament could become heated. In many cases, though, they exchanged favors, compromised, and found nuance and gray areas amidst the civilized discourse and gift exchange of the privileged in an enclosed environment. They were habituated to speaking with one another rather than, occasionally, to purchasable voters or the more or less powerless, who, they knew, surely deserved to be more or less powerless.

The Protestant Association was guided by a duke's son, but it was drawn from the lower or middling classes. Its values were not subject to compromise. because it knew that Truth was not gray, that the Mosaic law was not a series of parliamentary actions open to debate and vote, but commandments. Bishops represented prelatic hierarchy, not Jesus. The bigwigs had the power, but the Protestants had the crowd, the booze, and the well-lubricated barbers to disorder those wigs and the heads beneath them. The Protestants also knew that they were dealing with their superiors, who in turn knew that they were dealing with their inferiors and behaved accordingly. The conflict was lethal. Five grievances thus often motivated polemical Protestant discourse of the 1780s, for whose writers their government had become an enemy. They did not see isolated incidents, but parts of a wicked "train of circumstances" that threatened the Protestant religion and the British national character (*PM* 2 [1782]: 15).

One repeated complaint was that repeal was a secretive and hurried act in a "thin" house at the end of a session that merely dismissed counterarguments. The Members caballed among themselves and voted to go home rather than to have a thoughtful discussion of a monumental revision of British law. The author of *Strictures on a Pamphlet* complained that "this Act was so suddenly introduced, and so hastily passed, before the sense of the nation at large could be obtained, or any opposition against it." The legislature was "in a great degree unacquainted with the general sentiments" of its people and maliciously or wrongly insisted on staying that way. An outraged nation then exercised the "fundamental principal" of British law, circulated petitions "throughout the kingdom," and presented them to Parliament "from every corner of the land" and "with numerous signatures from every county, city, and corporation; and from other respectable bodies of people." Instead of respectful consideration, as the petitioners were massed outside of the House of Commons, both Horse Guards and Foot Guards were called to clear the way for the Members. From the Protestant Association's point of view, the government began hostilities against its own people's rights of assembly and petition.[35]

Nothing worked. The petitions' and petitioners' concern and, they thought, inherent gravity were insulted and rejected by indifferent and ultimately pernicious elites. Their "unaccountable partiality" refused to ease laws against Dissenters, while tolerating papists and even abusing one of their own. As *A Defence of the Protestant Association* said, yes, a large body of British subjects assembled before Parliament. That was necessary because they had presented thirteen petitions on "behalf of the ancient laws of this kingdom," not by noise and numbers but by means of a "Right Honourable Member, according to the laws of the House, and conceived in the most decent and respectful terms." The assembled multitude, in short, assembled for two reasons. As Alderman Bull told the House of Commons on 7 June 1781, the Crown's "baneful influence" ensured that the petitions would be "spurned at and trampled upon." Since the House also doubted "the *real existence*" of the petitions with so many signatures, the Association resolved to give "their representatives *occular demonstration* of their *reality*" by delivering them directly to the House.[36] The reality soon turned into a waking nightmare.

The Protestant defender laments that the voices of the people in fact were "wantonly" ignored and provoked "resentment" that Parliament condemned. He then more bluntly suggests causation and consequences: "when great men take . . . liberties, the vulgar will quickly claim the same, especially if they are drunk." *The Sense of the People* (1780) uses familiar language to attack Edmund Burke's role in the controversy. It reiterates that the real provocateur is an insulated arbitrary government that enlarges its power and shrinks the people's rights. The sense of the people cannot nullify their own Parliament as "the constitutional bulwark of their rights, a parliament of their own choice." They surely would not then place that confidence "in self-appointed committees, and junto of men assuming unprecedented and unauthorized power to alter the form of government, to break down the great fence of their liberties . . . and to establish a new and unheard of supremacy over King, Lords, and Commons."[37]

The intentional usurpation of power altered government, destroyed protective fences, threatened William III's bulwark of Protestant protective legislation, and ignored his 1689 codification of the right to petition the Crown and its legislators. Benjamin Bennet's well-known *Memorial of the Reformation* stressed what he and much of the British nation believed: William was "the incomparable Hero" and "the Deliverer of *Britain*, of *Europe*, and the Ornament and Defence of the Protestant Religion thro' the World." Hence "the Glorious Year of Eighty Eight should never be forgotten by *English* Men and Protestants." The heroic liberator knew that he was engaged in a religious war and acted accordingly. The *Protestant Magazine* recognized that for William the revolution's work was "incomplete and defenceless." His antipopery laws were "pieces of defensive artillery" designed to make the Protestant fortress "more strong and impregnable." Unilateral disarmament endangers both Revolution principles and the Hanoverian succession. *The*

Fall of Romish Babylon comparably emphasized that William the Deliverer freed the nation from Stuart tyranny and popery, brought light, smiles, peace, bliss, pure religion, Brunswick, and "GEORGE's sacred name." The inferences are clear: changing William's laws abrogates the revolution, totters the Protestant succession, and returns slavery, darkness, and a religious dunciad in which universal darkness buries all. Well might the Protestant Association "tremble" for its posterity, considering "the fatal consequences that will probably result from" repeal of the statute.[38]

William made the world safe for Protestantism. Lord North's administration was making the world safe for popery and tyranny. George III addressed both houses of Parliament on 22 June 1774 and gave his royal assent to the Quebec Act. It was, he said, "founded on the clearest principles of justice and humanity" and would quiet his Canadian subjects' minds and promote their happiness. The bill in fact was contentious from the moment the House of Commons sent it to the House of Lords after apparently little discussion by the fatigued and diminished Commons, in which most peers had "retired into the country."[39]

The House of Commons and especially the opposition there and in the House of Lords were alarmed. The bill established Catholicism as British Quebec's religion, denied the right of habeas corpus and jury trial, and created a royally appointed legislative council instead of popular elections. The movers argued that the former subjects of French absolutism neither wanted nor understood political freedom. The Quebec Act ceded vast new territories to the Canadians, marginalized Protestants residing there, and placed approximately today's Ohio Valley and upper midwestern America in Catholic hands. There "were great altercations" in the Commons and "very warm" conflicts regarding a Catholic establishment. Many Britons feared that the ministry sought to create "an arbitrary government in one colony . . . in order to extend by degrees that model of ruling to all the others." Many Americans in turn feared that a large hostile territory of former enemies would both block their own westward growth and force them into the "abject vassalage" they fought alongside the mother country to eliminate. The *Annual Register* thought this parliamentary session perhaps as important as "any . . . since the revolution."[40] So far from inducing peace or disheartening the restless Americans, the session fostered a revolution very different from that in 1688. Protestants on both sides of the Atlantic felt betrayed. Britons who objected to the expansion of episcopacy to the colonies could scarcely sanction the expansion of popery to the colonies. Here was another part of the sequence of events that so troubled the Protestant coalition. Its allies made their feelings known at both ordinary and aristocratic levels.

John Jay Stevenson dismissed the notion that the Quebec Act was about religion: It was a crude attempt to intimidate the "refractory" colonies. It also fostered their rebellion and saw them join "our natural enemies for the destruction of their parent state." So far as the *Protestant Magazine* saw, the unnatural act mirrored the British government's other unnatural acts, indeed the "train of circumstances" that suggested dark conspiracy rather than mere folly. The wisdom of the Quebec Act's giving "legal support" to a religion "subversive of the British constitution and the Reformation . . . is at the least very doubtful" and deepened the American conflict. Doubt soon became near certainty. Whether or not the consequent bloody events were divine retribution, the act certainly was "the beginning of many evils." These included Protestants' loss of trust in their government, as popery in Canada now "was not only tolerated, but *established*" by a "Bill founded in *despotism* and *tyranny*." The faithless representatives would gradually encourage Catholicism "till it should acquire a strength that might be dangerous." The *Protestant Magazine* praised and extensively quoted Sir Joseph Mawbey in the Commons. He opposed "all the train of *mistakes* if not *wicked* measures" that caused the war, "beggared the country, and lost AMERICA."[41]

A repeal movement in the House of Lords made plain that such views were scarcely limited to Protestant zealots. Charles Pratt was well connected, an old Etonian, a King's College, Cambridge, graduate and fellow, a former Member of Parliament, attorney general, and Lord Chancellor, and first Earl Camden. In April of 1794 he was buried in his thirteenth-century Church of England parish church at Seal, Kent. On 17 May 1775 he presented a long and impassioned argument urging repeal of the law; his motion was defeated, 88 to 28. Camden was convinced that the Quebec Act was designed to "prevent the further progress of freedom and the protestant religion in America." It sought "to secure a popish Canadian army to subdue and oppress the Protestant British colonies in America."[42] Almost one-fourth of his lordly colleagues apparently agreed with at least some of those remarks.

Hostility to the Quebec Act was part of larger Protestant hostility to the American war. The sternest part of that anger stemmed from the contrast between "establishing" popery in Canada and fighting Protestants in America, a sin that indeed provoked divine and secular punishment. Britons long expected to fight Irish, Scottish, and Continental Catholics. Dissenters and many lower church Protestants had accepted the ugly but, they thought, necessary civil war of the 1640s. The 1688 bloodless revolution replaced that unpleasant event as the proper mode of protecting Protestants from religious uprisings. Unlike Cromwell in 1641, William's revolution seemed permanent rather than a troubled twenty-year hiatus. The American war shattered that apparently amiable paradigm.

Since the Americans had large contingents of Methodists, Presbyterians, and other Dissenters, war against them seemed like a royal and episcopal putsch against true Protestants. This was especially alarming since one reason to repeal the anti-Catholic laws was to increase the military pool by several thousands, including Scottish and Irish Catholics. Alarmed commentators feared that many papists then would cross the Atlantic to fight Protestant British subjects. The author of *Strictures on a Pamphlet* thus notes Lord George's alarm regarding papist "eagerness and joy . . . to contribute their mite in support of an unhappy civil war against Protestant America." War was terrible under any circumstances; it was worse "when kindled within a nation and among the subjects of the same empire." The *Protestant Packet* believed that Britain was being mocked by popish nations for its "fruitless civil war, against her own Protestant subjects." War was worse still when fought within the same family. That war was a sign of God's displeasure with British sins and with violation of the "connection between us and the *Americans*," a connection "founded in relation . . . [and] closely cemented by mutual interest, to be so suddenly broken." *Moderation Unmasked* (1780) perhaps recalls Swift on Marlborough. The non-moderate speaker mourned that "*America* has overflowed with Blood; the Catalogue of Human Sorrow has been exhausted. . . . Let Widows and Orphans speak." If not for the American war, John Short complained, "we should now have been a happy People."[43]

Part of that unhappiness was a function of lost confidence in George III and his administration. The vindicator of the Protestant Association flatly stated that among all political groups, "none are to be regarded with a more jealous eye than those who style themselves '*The King's Friends.*'" The badly advised king himself was not a friend to his nation. "The baleful influence of the Crown" authorized Parliament to ignore the Protestant petitions.[44]

Some Protestant anger thus stemmed from impatience with George III's ministry, the "Counsellors" who did the wrong that the monarch putatively could not do. *Moderation Unmasked* complains that the ministry has shown "themselves cruel and determined Enemies of Freedom wherever it exists." The *Protestant Magazine* comparably knew that repeal of William's laws was "part of a deep-laid *ministerial* plan" to destroy liberty and create a despotic government with Papist aid. The administration "was hated; their measures universally condemned," and political and religious disorder now was "extremely dangerous." As well it should be, a defender of the Protestant Association insists: "Real Protestants suspect that some secret Popish influence prevails at court." Such "friends" and influential ministers misguided their monarch, harmed the nation, allowed useless and sycophantic royal placemen, and encouraged arbitrary power, tyranny, despotism, and the near establishment of popery. They fostered the locusts, wolves, bulls and alien armies who would destroy British youth, drink and bathe in their blood, undermine the foundation of Protestantism, and sap the once constitutionally protected civil rights consistent with Protestant freedom. This continuing return to far earlier fears and language did not arise from mere government bad judgment, but from "a settled, uniform plan, pursued with steadiness and vigour" to shed "seas of Protestant blood."[45]

For Protestant activists, here was an orchestrated train or plan of malign events. These included rapid parliamentary action that ignored widespread constitutional petitions for reconsideration and repealed laws wisely installed by the great deliverer William III. The Quebec Act established popery in North America, where new Catholic recruits would gladly follow orders to kill Protestants seeking their birthright of British liberty. Loss of faith in government from the Crown to the Lords to the Commons to the established church bred self-justifying alienation and further radicalism. Rejection of deference both contributed to the riots and was among the several postmortem responses to them. What had seemed an almost century-long ameliorative evolution was disintegrating. Religiously and politically fanned fire had returned both as metaphor and as fact; rage literally had ravaged bodies of stone, flesh, and law, as well as the inner spirit of a nation. How could restoration of moral and evolutionary order take place, if at all?

Strategies of Defense and Alternative Responses

The rioters destroyed buildings, lives, and, as Thomas Holcroft put it, "every thing that is dear to society, or to Englishmen." Hair shirts, jeremiads, and suspicion thus were understandable. John Newton saw such collapse as part of God's anger against a sinful people who must relent, "stand in the breach," and reform lest they perish. The author of *Fanaticism and Treason* was among the several who attributed the ruin to dark political causes. Incinerating the Bank of England would have bankrupted the country, forced Britons into "either democratical or foreign slavery," and eternally blotted British annals. The author alludes to a sad and heroic event. John Dunning defended the legal chambers at Lincoln's Fields like "Leonidas in the narrow pass of his own Themopylae." In this case, he succeeded, but readers knew that Leonidas finally was overwhelmed by massive Persian numbers and by a traitor within the Spartan ranks. Gordon's rioters were not merely "a sett of deluded fanatics," as Burke thought, but "grand traitors to our country" and part of a "deep laid cabal to dissolve the constitution" in league with France, Spain, and America. The consequences would be tragic: "*Delinda est Carthago* was the word."[46]

Others enlarged upon the rioters' frightening "democratical" aspects. Felix McCarthy was hostile to Lord George, his cause, and his collaboration with the rabble, "the very dregs of the earth." *The World As It Goes* (1781) anthologizes poetic passages that comment upon contemporary events. Shakespeare and Dryden provide images of disorder, and Dryden images of madness: "The captain and the rabble issued out" as "lords of anarchy; / Chaos of power." Samuel Johnson made plain that only King George's soldiers liberated from incompetent magistrates had saved London "from calamities, such as a rabble's government must naturally produce."[47]

The Protestants themselves offered more affirmative responses. At times they would defend their patron on some of the same grounds that were used to defend the Protestant Association. Upon Lord George's death, Robert Hawes wrote a sometimes moving *Acrostical Tribute of Respect* (1793) to the memory of what the initial letters of his first fourteen lines spelled as Lover and Friend who "meant no harm." Gordon was a good and well-born man whom Hawes often visited in his prison. He there found that the Jewish convert possessed Christian virtues. Hawes knew that Lord George hoped to bring the Jews into the Christian fold but was blocked by his contemporaries' inadequate Christian love. After all, Christ himself was Jewish. Blending the laws of Moses and of Jesus would make "England the first free Theatre of Praise."[48]

Those Protestants closer to the events shared Hawes' more optimistic notion regarding Lord George's conduct and its consequences. They clearly were on the defensive but were vocal, undaunted, and skillful in their manifold strategies. One was to distinguish between the tragic consequences, which they lamented, and the justness of their cause, which they celebrated. Yes, Maria De Fleury said, there were riots and flames—sent from hell and not from the Protestant associators: "Reason, Truth, and Providence, / Unite to prove their innocence." That was why a British jury, presumably as a sign of the true Protestant and not alien nation, acquitted Lord George "'Mid the applause of Earth and Heav'n." A Man of Ross manfully raged against perpetually endangering, encroaching, and numerically increasing papists, who sought to demolish and undermine Protestantism. In such a case, it was necessary for the Protestants to associate as they did in order to prune religion's "rotten branches." Unfortunately, "a few banditti mingled with a great concourse of well-disposed men" and caused the damage for which the Protestants were wrongly blamed. They sought only to restore Protestant strength before popery and "artful men" stifled their "last expiring grasp." Indeed, as the author of *Strictures on a Pamphlet* said, the mob included wily papists, who destroyed the Sardinian chapel and Newgate "to bring an odium and a stigma on the Protestant Association." The *Protestant Magazine* was among those who agreed that papist "lurking incendiaries" joined other foreign enemies to discredit the cause so clearly improving for Britain. Perhaps a few Protestants had been no better than they should be and pulled down houses, but they were not at fault. "If ignorant drunken Protestants are driven to desperate acts of violence, who is to blame for it?" Certainly not those men who were there to petition and who were slighted by their betters. No. The real rioters were those who began "*to pull down* the sacred fences of the revolution establishment."[49]

This last remark suggests how regularly the Protestants stressed that they had done nothing wrong. They exercised a proper constitutional right to petition their legislature with "a legal and peaceable" method. Denial of such a right also denies Britain's essential character, threatens the future, and feeds the view that a wicked ministerial faction seeks to establish arbitrary power. In contrast, the Protestants were "zealously attached to the PROTESTANT FAITH and our HAPPY CONSTITUTION." They were determined to take lawful steps "to transmit those invaluable blessings . . . pure and inviolate, to our latest posterity." The bandits and brigands who committed the outrages were neither part of the Protestant design nor in many cases even Protestant. Indeed, the *Strictures* insists, not one person among the many thousands who signed and urged the repeal-petition "was found amongst the persons either tried, or executed, or slain: and not one of the persons who were tried or executed, were ever at any meeting of the Association. . . . None were ever found amongst the dead; none were ever missing." The Association had no "evil intentions whatever," and no member "could be charged with the least unbecoming behaviour, after the most scrupulous inquiry."[50]

There were, though, papists among those groups. Spanish arms, French guile, and the hellish tools of the Antichrist came from Rome, Babylon, or even the corrupt encouragers of popery in the ministry and court. One important post-Riot function of the Protestant polemicists indeed was to keep such thoughts alive, to stiffen the spine of believers who might have been chastened by the national disaster. Many individual publications did such bucking-up before and after the fact. *The Fall of Romish Babylon* celebrated Lord George, "who brought salvation nigh. / For Babylon, now fall'n, shall rise no more!" Journals like the *Protestant Packet* in Newcastle and its successor the *Protestant Magazine* in London had to cope when Babylon seemed still to babel. The *Magazine* regularly reprinted horror stories regarding the permanent character of individual and general bloody Catholicism. It never can offer Protestant religious and civil freedoms, which it always tries to destroy, as it tries to destroy anyone who does not surrender himself to Mother Church. Such publications traced the papacy from its infancy through its growth, through its great triumphs of serial murders, which it managed and enjoyed. We are reminded of the Saint Bartholomew's Day Massacre in

1572, the revocation of the Edict of Nantes in 1685, the bloody Irish Catholic rebellion of 1641, Queen Mary's fatal persecutions of Protestants in England between 1555 and 1559, the various inquisitions, burnings at the stake, roastings on a spit, and the like amusements. The *Protestant Magazine* so regularly supplied such supportive documents and engravings that one reader politely asked for a more instructive alternative. He enjoys those images of "the cruelties of Papists, in massacreing their fellow creatures for thinking different from themselves. These are very proper, and very useful." For variety, perhaps the editor could add "plates of some of the most striking pieces of history from the Old and New Testament."[51] The editor was not persuaded.

The most ominous of the Protestants' strategies was to recall and reinforce their power and their potential to change the dynasty and the political system. Loyalty to GEORGE and to the sacred Hanoverian succession was a staple of their rhetoric. In most cases it was genuine. In others it was a mask for angry radicalism and republicanism. In yet other cases, loyalty was discarded in favor of brute populist strength that alluded directly to the horrid regicide in 1649 or to the forced royal emigration in 1688 as warnings. Listen to us and be proper Protestants. Or else. *The Fall of Romish Babylon,* for example, ends with confidence that popish locusts never will reach British shores again amid Protestant peace and bliss. Nonetheless, "Be wise, enthroned Monarchs of the earth." You will last "whilst thou still maintain's MESSIAH's laws."[52] In 1780 as in 1641, Protestant zealots' loyalty to God trumped loyalty to a misguided and blasphemous Crown. Along the way, the polemicists adapted earlier apocalyptic language. As this warning suggests, they also adapted earlier physically ominous language, with Lord George as the sharp edge of a threatening ax. The Protestants had the power of the mob, of chaos, and the evocation of regicide or of revolution, which Britons wrongly thought long buried in dusty rolls and books.

What to do? Would there be a Hanoverian version of Stuart Bloody Assizes with quartered corpses lining the roads? Or could the genie be put back into the bottle after all the blood, flames, angry rhetoric, destruction, arrests, and hangings? Perhaps, to each question, but the literate public at least had a good if often troubling try and perhaps a better one than their government. In the process, each side implicitly asked and partially answered some essential questions. For example, How does the nation begin to heal itself after such trauma? How does the nation thereby seek to minimize rage and maximize efforts to return to "normal" and to a version of civilization? There were several answers, including celebration, inquiry, political debate, rallying around the flag, and efforts to prevent such an atrocity from happening again. In short, Britons sought to use their enlightened minds in order to mend their darkened hearts.

"What Is to Depose the Sword?": The Return to Order; Debate, Arrest, Trial, and Consequences

After several days of destruction even the tender-hearted were ready for redcoats and red blood. On 9 June, Frances Burney in Bath wrote to Charles Burney in London. She has heard that the military has "made much slaughter ... amongst the mob." Death indeed is troubling, but "never, I am sure, can any set of wretches less deserve quarter or pity," for "they were too outrageous & powerful for civil power." Hester Thrale later told Frances that the dispersed Parliament would reconvene for "the hanging Lord George Gordon ... — he is to be hanged sure enough." Samuel Johnson was less sanguinary and more hopeful about the restoration of royal and quotidian order, if at much cost. On 10 June 1780 he assured Mrs. Thrale that "Government now acts again with its proper force; and we are all again under the protection of the King and the Laws." On 14 June he praised the monarch and ministers, who finally "put the soldiers into motion, and saved the town from calamities."[53]

Horace Walpole, though, raised a concern that troubled much of the political and chattering classes. He acknowledged that the "dreadful overture" of the riots was gone but another kind of danger was not: "The sword reigns at present, and so saved the capital! What is to depose the sword?" That urgent post-Gordon Riots anxiety was part of a complex larger issue. Should limited martial law have been imposed? To what degree indeed could it be limited and civil law restored? The king wisely promised that all those arrested would be tried in civil courts, but legal niceties could be irrelevant before long-suffering and long-harangued soldiers. On some occasions they made good use of nearby lampposts for bad rioters; the North Hampshire militia fired on and sank a boat carrying plundered coins from the Black Friars' Bridge tollgate, presumably at the cost of the boaters' lives; the same militia threw several of the rioters over the balustrades and into the Thames, again to their death; the Horse Guards killed several and slashed many among an aggressive crowd at Fleet Bridge; armed redcoats now seemed everywhere and evoked traditional British fears of a standing army at the monarch's command. What did the need for such law say about the British nation? Edmund Burke gave an unpleasant answer. His house was among those the soldiers occupied in order to save: "Savile House, Rockingham House—Devonshire House to be turned into Garrisons! Oh tempora!" Long-serving distinguished legislators were "obliged to put ourselves under military protection for our houses and our persons!"[54]

Such emotional distress nonetheless was kin to cerebral argument, exchange, and the painful process of healing in the face of rabble, rubble, and hundreds who lay dead from their own depredations and from the redcoats' swords, bullets, and bayonets. London called on the army because it lacked an effective police force. Thomas Holcroft noted that the mob encircled a group of constables, "broke their staffs, and converted them into brands, which they hurled about whenever the fire, which was spreading very fast, had not caught." True lovers of their country must think seriously of establishing a proper constabulary, "which shall enable them to defend themselves without the aid of powers which may, sometime, be turned to their destruction." David Williams comparably feared that martial law was an unconstitutional response to an unconstitutional assembly. The state might have been overthrown in June unless that was "prevented by a power whose protection must be purchased at a price to which nothing on earth is an equivalent." An apparently benign creature "seldom shews its fangs until it be too late to escape them." Williams needs to resolve a painful paradox: the army's role in the riots "was an *act of prerogative, unconstitutional* and *illegal*, though perfectly seasonable and beneficial."[55] The answer is to create armed local associations with police powers to disperse and control dangerous assembly.

One schadenfreude response to the destruction was mischievous gratitude. Elizabeth Robinson Montagu would have mollified the rabble by putting "blue flags and no popery . . . on my houses." In the event, the "madly wicked" Lord George did the state a service by bringing to the gallows those who "would have levelled" the courts, palaces, and Parliament. Ravaged private homes and public prisons were a small price to pay for Gordon's violent excesses, which nonetheless effectually "cured the epidemical democratick madness. The word petition now obtains nowhere, the word association cannot assemble a dozen people. We are coming to our right senses."[56]

Few were so grateful. Fears of chaos surfaced in much other discussion of the need for an effective nonmilitary police force. Like Williams, many Britons both acknowledged and feared the army's role in restoring order. First, it was necessary to distinguish British police from the autocratic French system of surveillance and arrest. As Richard Brinsley Sheridan acknowledged when proposing his own Westminster bill, "The term *police* . . . was unknown to the language of our law." He nonetheless would use it in hopes of creating such a force to protect civil liberty and the constitution. Even a modified motion failed. The year 1785 also saw both the failed London and Westminster Police Bill and Sir William Blizard's possible solution to the problem: a police department supplemented by a civilian militia under parliamentary control. He remembered that during the Gordon Riots there were nearly twelve thousand troops in London and that they had remained camped in St. James's and Hyde Parks until August. About one thousand still guarded the Bank of England. Such an armed body too easily could become a royal, or more probably "aristocratical, tyranny" to destroy British liberties. The Bank precedent might then "afford a pretext for making a GARRISON of *every* PUBLIC OFFICE" and thus do by stealth what overt violence could not achieve.[57]

As Blizard made plain, the alternatives to police should not be the potentially destructive army or what Holcroft called "universal anarchy." There were two prerequisites before the troops could fire and disperse the vast mobs. The civil magistrate must read the Riot Act to a threatening group. If the group did not disband within the specified period of time, the magistrate could give the order to shoot. The magistrates, however, probably were sympathetic to No Popery, feared for their lives and homes, and neither read the act nor ordered gunfire. Johnson shared George III's view that the timid and negligent "Magistrates had not done their duty."[58] The void later could be filled only by royal permission for officers to commence firing at their own discretion. The issue concerned civil rights, civilian versus royal authority, the limits of tolerance in the face of violence and perhaps sedition, and the nature of a society that finally turned to arms to save itself.

The author of *Fanaticism and Treason* had no qualms about the Riot Act or its consequences. It was right to read it. It was right to call in the troops. It was right to put down the frenzy. It should have been done earlier. It was not an "excuse for extending the royal prerogative." Mrs. Piozzi's longer view in her *Retrospection* (1801) reinforced what she thought the benign, indeed grateful, view of most Londoners. The king's "intrepid coolness saved the state. He put the town in peace, preserved the Bank and records of the Tower, and when exertion of prerogative alone could have preserved tranquility among us, his care was chiefly employed to shorten the time, and the necessity for such exertion." Sir William Jones' response was slightly different. He too "admitted the necessity," while lamenting the "consequences" of deploying royal troops. Given the magistrate's difficult role, the aggressive job should belong to a body of well-trained men serving under the sheriff of each county. They were to be called out to suppress riots or insurrections against any social or political group. His scheme avoids the dangers of a standing army or of the Crown's using its troops for nefarious purposes. Allan Ramsay was comparably troubled by the "whimsical" Riot Act, offense against which wrongly was made a capital crime and which he reduced to absurdity. The act must be read to twelve or more men assembled for more than one hour. It does not apply to eleven men assembled for fifty-nine minutes. They have not committed a crime unless they had been ordered to disperse before the hour began. Even so, they are not guilty until a magistrate pronounces "a certain form of words, read from a certain paper called a *proclamation*." This statutory process violated common sense and could "equally make it a felony to eat buttered peas." Ramsay's solution balanced firm response with protection of civil rights. First, banish the idea that there was conflict between liberty and the military. Return the law to its pre–George I wording. Allow a *"military officer"* to read the Riot Act after the Parliament so authorized. Such a process removes both royal autocracy and mischief and the rabble's democracy and mischief.[59]

For others, like A Man of Ross, invoking the Riot Act and the military were offenses against the Protestant Association's legal actions. Its loyal members defended their civil and religious rights as they assembled before Parliament. Britons may bear arms and petition their government. The greater danger is a royally manipulated army that could invade an Englishman's home and assemblies. Accordingly, the civil magistrate must control the soldiery during public disruption. Philonomos was not part of the Protestant Association, but he agreed with A Man of Ross' essential premise: royal military power can subvert the constitution and "rarely, if ever" should be managed by any but the civil magistrate. The state must withhold such power from the Crown and improve the magistrate's education and public responsibility. Use of troops requires "infinite caution, to prevent its recoiling upon those who should be its masters."[60]

Several troubled but often sympathetic commentators shared those basic points of view regarding the army freed from civil authority. The puritanical rioters and their Cromwellian urge for destruction were worse than the threat to civil rights, but that threat was real and terrible nonetheless. Holcroft's *Plain and Succinct Narrative* again strikes a thoughtful balance between what was necessary, what was desirable, and what martial conduct could become. We recall that he believed "the very existence of the empire" was at stake and that national survival depended upon "the exertion of government" (p. 33). London was at once saddened and relieved by the 7 June royal proclamation of near martial law. The government wisely issued broadsides affirming that all prisoners would be tried by civil courts; the troops generally conducted themselves with restraint, but "they had discretionary power to bayonet or shoot"—among other forms of armed response that we know they used. The possibility of being "but one hour under control of a Military Force, was humiliating, derogatory, and alarming" (p. 41). Here indeed was both an insult to the national character and awareness "that the Constitution was endangered" (p. 42). George III sought to minimize that danger. He continued to assure his subjects that such exertion was his necessary obligation on their behalf, that the war powers had been "intrusted to Me by Parliament," and that he continues to respect "the Principles of our Excellent Constitution in Church and State."[61]

These acts of cerebration, concern with future options, and discussion of the monarch's role in the constitution extended to the highest social and governmental levels. The *New Annual Register* well chronicled George III's visit and speech to the House of Lords on 19 June 1780. He received the thanks of both houses and explained that he was obliged by his duty and affection for his people to suppress the dangerous "rebellious insurrections" with the military force that Parliament entrusted to him. The opposition Whig Charles Lennox, Duke of Richmond, raised a significant and marginally respectful objection. Surely some of his Majesty's ministers should assure the lords that the martial law was "defensible only upon the ground of necessity . . . and that what was illegally done, on the ground of necessity, would be cured by an act of indemnity." William Murray, the Earl of Mansfield and Lord Chief Justice, rose to rebut the notion that his Majesty had violated his Majesty's own laws: All British subjects are required to help stop crime wherever perpetrated. Soldiers thus share their fellow Britons' inherent right to make arrests to deter felony. Most lords were too polite to condemn this novel theory of the relationship of the king's soldiers to his other subjects. Neither the Duke of Richmond nor the literate public were so shy. Many thought Mansfield demonstrably un-British. The idea of blending soldiers "with the common subjects of the state, and giving persons of their description a right of judging on its most important occurrences, would have filled our ancestors with horror." As indeed it filled Willoughby Bertie, Earl of Abingdon, with the horror and anger he expressed in 1782 when debating the marriage law he thought both unnatural and destructive. Such folly was too typical of a government run by "a thumper of lawbooks, and a retailer of words." Abingdon then even less subtly pointed to his target. The unnamed but obvious Mansfield supported the administration's catastrophic American policy and "has made us believe that every common soldier in England, for the purposes of suppressing riots, is a justice of the peace."[62]

Mansfield's unapologetic apology for royal action persuaded few, but many nonetheless accepted that such action was preferable to chaos and flames. Others saw that action as a mask for despotism or at least for political control. *The Protestant Association, Written In the Midst of the Tumults, June 1780* stated the case.[63] This long, energetic, and angry tetrameter couplet poem characterized the anarchic rioters as diabolical Cromwellian "Saints of Forty-One" and "Rebels, Regicides, and Traitors" (pp. 3, 4). Such "Devil's slaves" merely "smile to see the troops draw nigher / With no authority to fire" (pp. 6, 7)—until they attempt to burn and loot the Bank of England and are "answer'd by a guard within," who so repulses them that "on heaps they lie" (p. 10). The monarch himself is divinely inspired "in the gap to stand" and to dispatch troops against the Achitophel, Catiline, and Franklin–inspired Luciferians (pp. 19, 21). George III and not the putative "patriots" saves the nation (p. 23)—parts of which deny the danger, withhold gratitude, and insist that he acts for private and tyrannical motives. He acts "Only to rob us of our freedom / Debar us of our native right" to defend ourselves. The author well captures City paranoia and fears of absolutism, as in the probable allusions to Louis

XIV's dragoons, who forced Protestant conversion to Catholicism, and Charles XII of Sweden, who invaded Denmark, Norway, Saxony, Poland, and Russia:

> Unless the King his troops withdraw,
> He means to rule by martial law,
> And for our most unfeign'd affection
> Dragoon us into tame subjection,
> At last to change the constitution;
> By military execution
> Accomplish his despotic plan,
> And as the Swedish Monarch reign. (Pp. 26–27)

No, the poet insists. Now is the time for loyal unity and "not a spirit of opposition" (p. 28), denial of danger, or false patriotism in the face of "So mild, and merciful, and just" a king (p. 29).

Some others were pleased with the tepid ameliorative laws but complained about the perpetual deprivation of Catholic rights and the violent anarchy the riots produced and reflected. This terrible case of appalling options in an appalling situation of course produced rage against Lord George both from Catholics and from non-Association Protestants. Presumably liberal and enlightened Britain had not lost its capacity for outrage toward outrage. Joseph Berington movingly put the case for Catholic anger and for integration of that "oppressed and injured people." The "boasted excellencies of the British constitution are nothing to me, who am deprived of the common rights of humanity." Dangerous deprivation creates "a restless desire of changes and revolutions. My situation cannot be worse, and it may be mended." Berington so complained in his *State and Behaviour of English Catholics, From The Reformation to the Year 1780* (London, 1780). The gravamen of his argument was that the few Catholics in England were not a threat, were loyal subjects, and deserved liberation from intolerable derision. Even the repeal of a few of William III's anti-Catholic laws was "but a little relief" (pp. 134–35).

Berington generally proceeded by means of positive examples. Other Catholics were more direct. His *State and Behaviour* naturally drew Protestant rebukes, which in turn drew rebukes from Berington's fellow Catholics. They and others knew whom to blame for the death and destruction to life, property, and perhaps Protestantism itself. One author directly addressed the Protestant Association. He too insists that Catholics are good and loyal subjects, as perhaps Lord George is not. He tells "My Lord" that events in 1780 "have done more injury" to Protestantism than any wound since its creation. The remark is staggering in its anger, which must include the Saint Bartholomew's Day massacre and regicide, among other horrors. This author essentially banishes Lord George from the religion he pretends to serve. Its genius "is humane and liberal; in your hands it is cruel and intolerant." Gordon deplores religious peace, which "would stab enthusiasm to the heart." In a question that is at once despairing and frightening, Berington asks: "Will the voice of malevolence never be silenced?" This terrible man is worse than the Portuguese Inquisition and, in familiar but expanded language, would "extirpate the religion of Christ." Both Arthur O'Leary's and Felix McCarthy's sorrowful fury thus was linguistically commonplace. Gordon seeks "a crusade for the extirpation of infidels," O'Leary complains. He is a disgrace to himself and his family, has a wicked mind, and is thought "more than contemptible by all parties," McCarthy argues.[64]

Protestants with such views were likely to be from the established church, from London, where the ravages were so painful, or at the least were moderates troubled by what they thought Scottish covenant excess. Some such writers took the high ground. "A Protestant" defended the repeal on Lockean grounds of individual human freedom and the consequent exile of persecution. The "boundless and universal freedom in Religion, is the doctrine of reason." Another writer is less exuberant but comparably open to religious freedom. He insists that "popery is no *crime* in the eyes of any good protestant." In earlier days all religions engaged in terror tactics. The Protestant Association must accommodate itself to the general improvement and modern "increased humanity" that seemed to have passed it by. Joseph Priestley agreed. Protestantism diminishes itself by its appeal to the civil power and makes Catholics "our enemies by becoming theirs." He more than implies that the maker of enemies is an enemy. *Fanaticism and Treason* had no patience for such polite rebuke for someone with "the dark designs of modern Cromwells." These men, Gordon to be sure, must be punished "according to their deserts." *The Flames of Newgate* also played upon Gordon as Cromwell. There now is a new ministry run by "Lord HUDIBRAS" Gordon as the "lawless multitude crowd at his heels." Religion is their excuse for malicious "seraphic zeal" to burn and demolish. "Their heav'nly souls play hell about the town." Lord George is neither epic hero nor savior of Protestantism.[65] The Hudibras analogy evokes that mock-heroic wretch's intellectual and religious ethic of pike, gun, infallible artillery, orthodoxy induced by violence, civil war, and regicide as elements of reform. It also reiterates Britain's fears of its malign inheritance of religious and political rage and outrage.

Manasseh Dawes provides further evidence of the evolved Anglican response to the Gordon Riots. That Whig, pro-American barrister, politically Lockean member of the established church, insisted that the riots were un-Christian, un-Protestant, and un-English. He reaffirmed that the apparent values of the Catholic Relief Act of 1778 were right and proper. The riots were "a disgrace to humanity" by "pretended protestants." They were "servile enthusiasts" and fanatical vagrants" whose wrath and vengeance sought, in familiar terms, "to undermine the superstructure of religious toleration" too typical of their opponents. Their riots failed to criminalize toleration; "religion and toleration are now free," and the only intolerance is the magistrate's lingering ability to punish those not of the established church. In short, for Dawes and many others seeking to heal the nation, the Gordon Riots were an uncharacteristic moral blight upon the English people. The Catholic Relief Act of 1778 itself had it right and was the proper voice of the people: the rioters "were considered by the legislature, to their wisdom be it spoken, as idle and disorderly persecutors . . . destitute of all religion."[66]

Britons thus tried to deal with the Gordon Riots, their aftermath, and evolutionary regress in several ways. The need for an effective police force was urgent. Some thought the chaos was beneficial, for it destroyed a political case for "democracy" and showed the rabble's true colors. The absence of police nonetheless evoked not only a martial response but a potential violation of the constitution that endangered liberty. This in turn promoted serious concern with civil rights—of the Protestants' preserved right to petition government and the Catholics' right to enjoy the liberties of loyal British subjects. Britons returned to their familiar bloody-minded squabbles with authority: the Lords, Commons, press, and individuals questioned their monarch, his administration, and the basis of their constitution. The nation tried to cope by arguing about what had gone wrong and how to correct it; by confronting the painful paradox of odious but necessary solutions to odious but unnecessary anarchy; by using their heads instead of their rifles, bayonets, and sabers.

Those in power chose two other ways as well. One was to try many and to hang enough to remind others that the rope remained an option. The second way was to put Gordon on trial for his life. Mrs. Thrale surely was among the many in London who expected him to hang. Gordon thus became the villain-in-chief and the focus of deserved anger at the ineffective manipulator of a vast mob led by Hudibras redivivus. Here was the apparent Dissenter at it again, endangering the nation's ability to survive and prosper in a difficult world. Gordon himself thus was subject to verbal blows and knocks—both by the public and, more ominously, by the state, which sought to do to him what he had done to it. One further way in which Britain tried to deal with the riots thus was to destroy the rioters' presumed master. Neither side could claim much light amidst the darkness.

The Trial of Lord George Gordon for Treason, 1781

There clearly was demonstrable anger toward Lord George, his mobs, his religion, and his associates. In the nature of things, there also were defenses of him and those associates, that remained powerful for many years. The arguments for and against, however, soon took a more ordered, mannered, and grim form. A trial codifies and regularizes hostility. It is how advanced societies disguise vengeance and turn it into legal punishment, not from an individual but from an official body, like the state, or the Crown, or the people, or the nation, and its representatives obliged to follow specified procedures. It also is the way in which those societies manage and justify their own anger with an often fictitious possible escape. An apparently neutral body evaluates the evidences for and against the accused and may render a verdict of not guilty, or innocent, or not proven, as local practice prescribes. The sides have the right to attack or to defend before a jury, judge, or judges obliged, the rationale goes, only to blind justice. Few in 1781 thus seemed troubled that the trial's chief justice was Lord Mansfield, whose home, art, books, and legal library the mob had destroyed. He was known for his severity, for his justification of soldiers as judges of felony, and for views that were hostile to the defendant, some of whose evidence he misrepresented to the jury.[67] Lord George's trial for constructive treason was part of that apparently benign process that, depending upon one's point of view, became a proper mess, the triumph of victimized virtue, or perhaps even a Machiavellian ploy to make the best of a very bad job indeed.

The Crown, Parliament, and the ministry, after all, had put themselves in painful binds from the start of the riots. They may unwisely have chosen to let the rabble roar for a couple of days to let off steam and then ignored them as rabble letting off steam. Lord George himself refused to be bought off. They could have arrested him once he took command or seemed in command, but that would have made him a martyr, enhanced his already vast attraction, and increased the violence. They also would have created political troubles with a powerful Scottish family still supporting its unruly cadet and, Johnson amusingly reported based on London's fears, perhaps ready to send seventy thousand men with the Dukes of Gordon and Argyle "and eat us, and hang us, or drown us." Once the depredations were contained, they belatedly arrested Lord George on a capital charge. After all, as one writer said, Gordon "usurped patriotism on purpose to usurp empire."[68]

As a duke's son he would escape the full horror of the punishment for treason: being drawn to the gallows, hanged, and removed from the noose while still alive; then disemboweled, with the gore shown to him; after which came beheading and quartering, with those parts displayed on pikes, probably in London. He might merely be hanged by the neck until dead. In such a case the more than forty thousand whom Lord George rallied when breathing might become more dangerous than ever, Scotland and the Duke of Gordon would take such punishment as a national insult, and rumors of a Scottish invasion would cause panic, as the ruins from the first week in June remained visible. The Gordon clan would have many colleagues in disruption. As one contemporary put it, if an English jury found him guilty, "it is hardly possible to believe that those men who have been guided all along by the phrenzy of enthusiasm, will submit without clamour to a punishment which they conceive to be unmerited."[69] George III would be in the painful position either of signing the death warrant for George II's godson, pardoning a Presbyterian aristocrat who generated vast mischief, or, on the Atterbury paradigm, perhaps exiling a traitor, as I suspect he would have done, but nonetheless without silencing Gordon's voice or removing his pen. Gordon was young and healthy. Unlike Atterbury, he would not die reasonably soon and might be a perpetual thorn on a French rose. Given one bad alternative after another, it seems to me possible, if not likely, that the Crown purposefully avoided the conflict by making a good show in a bad loss.

Some parliamentary commentators expressed doubts about the nature of the charges and thus the Crown's strategy. Richard Brinsley Sheridan, in the House of Commons, for example, later pointed out that all other prisoners were charged with felony, but that Lord George was accused of treason. Thus "war was levied against the King by *one* man; [and] . . . Lord George was himself at once a *General* and an *Army*." The foolish charge contributed to the not-guilty verdict. The royal court, though, probably was at the least relieved that it did not have to choose among unpleasant options, and no doubt regarded Gordon's arrest and humiliation as ways to silence him. The judicial court staged a vigorous but defective prosecution that excellent defense attorneys sought to demolish, in part by insisting that Lord George was correct regarding dangerous popery. The government might, wrongly again, hope that Lord George's difficulties would sufficiently intimidate him into surly or respectful retreat. However all that might be, on 5 February 1781 Lord George was acquitted after a twenty-one-hour trial for constructive treason, whose outcome rebuked the government. Many Britons thought the trial a test both of Lord George's faith and of God's justice. For John Wesley, "the Supreme Ruler of events rescued [Gordon] out of their unhallowed hands, [and] set him upon a rock, and established his going," as God did for David in Psalms 27:5 and 40:1–3.[70] The trial showed that Lord George then had a better understanding of his nation's character and biases than did his accusers.

Gordon's first appearance at the King's Bench alarmed him. He complained that the doors at the Westminster court were closed, thus denying entry to those who might wish to hear the proceedings—presumably many of his supporters. Moreover, his prior long incarceration limited his ability to prepare a case, caused personal hardship, and continued public anger. He was surprised at the "vast numbers of jurors" in the jury pool, for this deprived him of certain challenge rights beyond the twenty he was allowed. The prosecutors also had consulted many exalted judges to help their case against him and had brought witnesses from Scotland "to prove he knew not" what, since the English court had no jurisdiction in Scotland. The indictment ignored the law requiring treason cases to cite an overt act, and so he could not offer specific evidence against a specific charge. Gordon hoped both that the court therefore would help him when appropriate and that he could receive a fair trial from the judges "seated on the bench ... clad in their August robes of ermine" and presided over by Lord Mansfield. He assured Gordon that he would so guarantee.[71]

The indictment regularly repeated its general charges. When John Wesley saw it, he was "aghast! What a shocking insult upon truth and common sense? But it is the usual *form*. The more is the shame. Why will not the Parliament remove this scandal from our nation?"[72] Wesley was moved not only by what he thought improper attribution of motives. According to the Crown, Lord George lacked the fear of God. He was "seduced by the instigation of the devil" into withdrawing his love for his lawful monarch, the duty of his allegiance to whom he did not weigh.[73] He wickedly devised and intended to disturb England's "peace and public tranquility." Most ominously, during that intended disruption he led more than five hundred persons "armed and arrayed in a warlike manner ... with colours flying, and with swords, clubs, bludgeons, staves, and other weapons, as well offensive as defensive." They were "unlawfully, maliciously, and traitorously assembled and gathered together" in order to "ordain, prepare, and levy public war against" the lawful king (pp. 217–18). Mr. Norton, one of the Crown's seven prosecuting attorneys, then explained two urgent aspects of the case for constructive treason and for the irrelevance of Gordon's British followers, for whom the law should not have mattered. Lord George had raised war against the Crown "to effect by force an alteration of the established law ... or the reformation of grievances, real or imaginary, in which the insurgents have no particular or special interest" (p. 219). Those insurgents were like a large trained army engaged in "dreadful outrages and conflagrations," chiefly the responsibility of Lord George himself. So malign an offender "has not often appeared in a court of justice" (p. 220). This was not merely the Crown versus Lord George. It was the Crown versus the devil, imaginary grievances, and insurgents falsely claiming interest in the British law by which they were governed.

Most of the defense portion of the trial was handsomely conducted by the eminent senior attorney, Lloyd Kenyon. He yielded to his junior colleague, Thomas Erskine, for a long speech that was praised and reprinted as a separate text and was regarded as the decisive demolition of the Crown's indictment of constructive treason and a potential death penalty for the leader of the mob.

Erskine rejected that charge and insisted on the still novel theory of intention. The consequences in June of 1780 were dreadful, but the defendant should be judged based on his intention, not on an undesired outcome. Lord George and the Protestant Association engaged in a benign and constitutionally protected act of petitioning their legislature. Lord George issued several printed exhortations urging his Association to be peaceful and to resist the unauthorized ruffians who performed all of the destructive acts. The witnesses against him were impeached liars, or had muddled and hearsay recollections of muddled words that they may or may not have heard or that Lord George may or may not have said. In contrast, exonerating witnesses were reliable, truthful, and so numerous that calling them would be endless.

So far so good. The Crown clearly had bungled, as it had from the start of the riots. The jury's prompt verdict of not guilty, however, must also have been based on far more than the defense's well-presented rebuttal and its own adherence to the plain sense of the law: it also was based on views shared with Erskine and with Lord George. In effect, Erskine's peroration convinced the jury that Gordon was innocent, because they were exonerating Gordon's, Erskine's, and their own prejudices, shared, they knew, by heaven and by other true Christians: "KENYON arose, and behold the guardian angel of Lord George, even Ithuriel touched his tongue."[74]

Erskine's vision of the ancestral past is very like that of the *Protestant Magazine*. He presents a series of bloody stories in which papist monarchs were evil arbiters of treason and in which "tumults and riots" paralleled the events of June 1780 and were "on a footing with armed rebellion." The always demonized old Queen Mary exemplified such legal horrors, by then extended to Protestants because they were Protestants. William III's anti-Catholic laws thus were necessary not only to protect the state from its internal enemies; the security of the House of Hanover required such help against "the machinations of these very papists, who are now so highly in favour."[75] The papists undermined the secular and spiritual state on whose behalf William III had so well legislated. Erskine is astounded to hear the attorney general vilify those "wise regulations of our patriot ancestors." They were then and they are now "regulations to which this country owes its freedom, and his Majesty his crown." He is obliged to secure "that religion which these acts were made to repress" (p. 84). Here are familiar Protestant Association assumptions and grievances, including the fears that popery would be tolerated in Britain and highly favored at St. James's. It should not be, for many reasons, one of which is that the papists themselves joined with other ruffians, ignored Lord George's pleas for peace, and became violent (p. 111).

Such behavior was radically unlike the Association's behavior. The multitude was not armed or hostile and certainly was not engaged in acts of war against the monarch to whom they were loyal (p. 76). Erskine regularly stresses that they were presenting a lawful petition and always lacked weapons. Moreover, in words that could have been drawn from many defensive Protestant polemics, "out of forty-four thousand persons who signed the petition . . . not one . . . was to be found among those who were convicted, tried, or even apprehended on suspicion" (p. 114). We again hear the drumbeat of Association rhetoric when Erskine insists that repeal of the laws themselves was a rushed job that ignored or at the least was indifferent to the will of the people. The bill was presented by distinguished legislators, but, he says, "without fear of contradiction, . . . it was sudden and unexpected." It "passed with uncommon precipitation, considering the magnitude of the object." There was no discussion and "the heads of the church, the constitutional guardians of the national religion, were not consulted upon it." The "many sincere Protestants" were properly alarmed because their religious and civil liberties were in danger (p. 85). By implication, and contrary to Mr. Justice Norton's indictment, the petitioners had both "particular" and "special interest" in laws affecting their spiritual and secular lives.

Erskine suggests that the blame for the riots had at least two further sources. In so doing he makes clear that the legal Establishment was aware of the national discussion of the riots' causes and cures. One source, he says adapting a familiar complaint, was the absence both of government and of police. Instead, London saw the "shameful indolence of our magistrates," who sanctioned drunkenness and destruction (p. 112). He also implies that the fault lay not with the Protestant Association but with Parliament's own improper legislative conduct. Gordon's jury heard both orthodox Protestant Association self-defense—that the Association reflected near-unanimous British opinion—and that the real lawbreaker was Parliament. On this view, Lord George was the man who stood in the breach to defend the constitution. The jurors should admonish their legislators and join him. Erskine also rejects the Crown's argument that the people had no business arguing on behalf of their own laws. In fact, Parliament is a small minority, in this case making bad law that the people "unanimously" deny.

> It is the duty of Parliament to listen to the voice of the people, for they are the servants of the people; and when the constitution of church or state is unanimously believed, whether truly or falsely, to be in danger, I hope there will never be wanting men, notwithstanding the proceedings of to-day, to desire the people to persevere and be firm. (P. 92)

The energetic speech combined several effective elements. Erskine explained the law, drew upon eminent interpreters like Blackstone, and used persistent and popular Protestant rhetoric, much of which still was believed by most mainstream

Anglicans. Erskine thus cleverly orchestrated the jury's own biases, which he presented as his own and the nation's, if not those of the bigwigs on the bench. His near-final remark sums up the conclusion that many Britons outside of the elites and apparently liberal and tolerant government shared: "Since Lord George Gordon stands clear of every hostile act or purpose against the legislature of his country, or the properties of his fellow-subjects; since the whole tenor of his conduct repels the belief of the traitorous purpose charged by the indictment, my task is finished" (p. 114).

Of course it was not finished. The attorney general, James Wallace, presented the facts and the law. The violent mode of mass petitioning, for example, was illegal; Lord George's regular toing and froing during the House of Commons' frenzied discussions clearly incited the mob's further hostility. Erskine and Gordon were troubled by the cool refutation and thereafter by Mansfield's jury instructions. These approximated a directed verdict of guilty by that chief justice, so highly placed in the government, so warm an apologist for the king's actions, and so firm an assurer that Gordon would receive a fair trial.

Mansfield's definitive remarks express the unanimous judgment of his colleagues on the bench. The prosecution, he says, insists that the crowd aimed "by force and violence, to compel the Legislature to repeal a law." If so, "without any doubt I tell you . . . that . . . it is High-Treason." What applied to the crowd applies equally to the individual who convened it, whether or not he joined them and was personally violent. "Whosoever incites, advises, encourages, or is any way aiding to such a multitude so assembled with such intent . . . is equally principal with those who act, and guilty of High-Treason." Mansfield the administration peer also added editorial comment regarding Sir George Savile's law that inspired the riots. It did not, as claimed, tolerate popery; it eliminated a few penalties and left many others; some harsher penalties were responses to James II, and others were added in spite of William III's better judgment. The law itself thus could not be considered as part of the trial: complaints about it "raise the blind spirit of fanaticism, or enthusiasm, in the minds of a deluded multitude." Mansfield blended judicial with political fiat: "nothing can be so dishonorable to government, as to be forced to make or to repeal by an armed multitude, any law." As for the constitutional right to petition one's legislators, the bench again unanimously agreed that "the attending a petition to the House of Commons by more than ten persons is criminal and illegal."[76]

The jury then needed to decide only two issues, on both of which Mansfield's views and the Crown's views were clear: Did the crowd assemble with the intention of violently forcing a repeal of Sir George Savile's law? If not, the jurors should acquit at once. If yes, they should determine whether the defendant encouraged and promoted the insurrection. Better to remind and surely to guide the jury, Mansfield catalogued parts of the prosecution's case: Lord George assembled the people in order to bring them to the House; he met them in St. George's Fields; he spoke with them from the Commons' lobby; he wore their blue cockade; other parts of his conduct must have "had the same intention."[77] Given such directions, it surely seemed to Thomas Erskine and Lord George Gordon that the jury would answer yes to the first question, regarding the crowd, and guilty to the second question, regarding Gordon's guilt. The jury nonetheless rejected the Crown's arguments, Mansfield's directions, Savile's law, and the proceedings by which it had evolved. After withdrawal and a thirty-minute discussion, the jury returned with a verdict of not guilty. The single decision meant refusal to accept that the crowd had tried violently to force repeal of the law.

The verdict thwarted the Crown. It also apparently surprised Gordon and Erskine, who "sinks into the arms of his late client unable to support the torrent of joy, too great for humanity." As a mock-biblical author observed, the joy spread to the auditors, a rainbow seemed to grace Gordon's head, God's thunder approved, the devils were exiled back to hell, and *"Babylon, the mother of Harlots is fallen."*[78] Those many auditors applauded. The defeated were chagrined. They had just witnessed both jury nullification and the humiliation of the elites by those who were regarded as too insignificant and ignorant to be consulted regarding their laws. The *Gazetteer and New Daily Advertiser* for 7 February did not hear God's thunder, but it did hear thunderous human approval. It was indeed "impossible, by any words language can afford, to convey an adequate idea of the extreme joy that seized every one upon hearing the verdict announced." Apprehension turned to joy, the good news was like a bolt of lightning that flashed throughout the court "and threw the multitude into shouts of applause that shook the very place." The news spread to Scotland with comparable results.[79]

The joy continued and spread from the crammed courtroom to a crammed tavern when the Protestant Association invited some three hundred sympathetic celebrants with the "greatest signs of joy . . . in every face." The company of course featured Lord George and his ducal family, "together with the Jury, Counsel, and Sollicitors" as well as other "most respectable friends to the Protestant interest; among whom were several noblemen, members of parliament, clergymen, and Ministers of different denominations." The Crown and ministry may have thought Lord George a broken man, but in fact he was energized, validated, and reinforced. Here was a triumph that seemed to be celebrated on both sides of Hadrian's Wall, by the high and the low, by members of the House of Commons who once had refused to repeal Sir George Savile's Act, and by a broad cross section of Protestant sects. Surely this supported Lord George's indignant remark to the jury when it proclaimed its verdict: "Gentlemen, it has been a wicked and infamous prosecution."[80] Now he again would be free to proclaim his society's outrages.

Perhaps not quite. As we shall see, the government bided its time and waited until Lord George again gave it an opportunity to remove danger from its flanks. The Crown, its courts, and its established church then disgraced themselves, but in 1787, and with subversive Lord George's own help, they got the job done. That secular trinity used reasons of state legally to destroy the man they could neither silence nor control. Lord George clearly was an obsessional religious bigot. Many of his other values nonetheless embodied the best of the "enlightened" modern state that Parliament claimed to represent. One of his chief crimes was to demonstrate the hypocrisy of the people, who would and did kill him. Lord George Gordon won this legal and cultural battle but lost the war. What I have called the ameliorative evolutionary process was at the least on hold.

NOTES

1. *The Protestant Magazine; Or, Christian Treasury. Designed to Encourage A Perfect Knowledge of the Protestant Religion* 1 (1781): 75 (hereafter cited in the notes and parenthetically in the text as *PM*). The editor adds that Protestants are "often too indolent, even to *persuade.*" The *Magazine* intends to rectify that apparent problem. Wesley acknowledged the Methodists' relative assimilation and movement away from earlier mob violence. In 1781 he compared the present persecution of the anti-Catholic Protestants with "the treatment formerly given to the Methodists" during their love feasts. See John Wesley, *A Letter to the Printer of the Public Advertiser, Occasioned By the late Act, passed in favour of Popery* (London, 1781), pp. 16–17.

2. *The Annual Register, or A View of the History, Politics, and Literature, For the Year 1778* (London, 1779), pp. 189–90 (hereafter cited parenthetically in the text as *AR* by year).

3. *A Letter to Sir George Saville, Bart. Upon the Allegiance of a British Subject Occasioned by His late Bill in Parliament in Favour of the Roman Catholics of this Kingdom* (London, 1778), p. [3].

4. *A Survey of the Proceedings in the House of Commons, on the Petition of the Roman Catholics in Edinburgh and Glasgow, and of the Debates which took Place on that Affair* (London, 1779), p. [i]. The editor quotes Lord George's contribution: the ameliorative law should not pass in Scotland "because the constitutions of the two churches of England and Scotland were exceedingly different; the religion of the church of England, his lordship observed, was a *tolerant* religion, but that of Scotland *intolerant*" (p. 24). The editor also quotes Lord Frederick Campbell, who opposed compensation for Scottish Catholics' destroyed property: those wretches "had even dared to offer a regiment of Papists for his Majesty's service, which in other words was only wanting to have arms put into their hands, and have the power of doing mischief" (p. 26). "Mr. Burke replied to his Lordship, and with some warmth" (p. 27).

5. *A Short View of the Statutes at Present in Force in Scotland Against Popery: The Nature of the Bill Proposed to be Brought Into Parliament for Repealing these Statutes: and Some Remarks showing the Propriety and Necessity of opposing such Repeal. With a few Hints on the Constitutional and Prudent Mode of Opposition* (Edinburgh, 1779), pp. [3]–4. Scottish and English anti-Catholicism of course was rampant. For two examples, see *The Scots Demonstrations of Their Abhorrence of Popery with all its Adherents* ([Edinburgh?, 1679?]) and the more extreme *Reasons Humbly Offer'd for a Law to Enact the Castration, or Gelding of Popish Ecclesiastics, As the Best Way to Prevent the Growth of Popery in England* (London, 1700). The several Scottish objections were compiled in *Scotland's Opposition to the Popish Bill: A Collection of All the Declarations and Resolutions; Published by the Different Counties. . . . for preventing the Growth of Popery* (Edinburgh, 1780). There was a second printing of *Reasons Humbly Offer'd* in 1700, without *Gelding* in the title. For broader scholarly studies, see Colin Mark Haydon, *Anti-Catholicism in Eighteenth-Century England, c. 1714–c. 1780* (Manchester: Manchester University Press, 1993); and Claire Haynes, *Pictures and Popery: Art and Religion in England, 1660–1760* (Aldershot, Hants, UK: Ashgate, 2006).

6. *The Edinburgh Eighth-Day Magazine, or, Scots Town and Country Intelligencer* (Edinburgh, 1779), p. 286, by an unnamed correspondent from London, 29 October 1779. The volume is warmly dedicated to Gordon (pp. [iii]–iv) and includes several laudatory references and quotations from his letters to Protestant Associations.

7. For aspects of the Scottish response, see Eugene Charlton Black, "The Tumultuous Petitioners: The Protestant Association in Scotland, 1778–1780," *Review of Politics* 25 (1963): 183–211; and Black, *The Association: British Extraparliamentary Organization, 1769–1793* (Cambridge, MA: Harvard University Press, 1963), pp. 147–73. For Ammianus' *Res gestae divi augusti*, see *The Roman Historie. Containing such Acts and occurrents as passed under Constantius, Iulianus, Iovianus, Valentinianus, and Valens, Emperours*, trans Philemon Holland (London, 1609), p. 193, at the end of 22.3. See chapter 1 above, n. 7, for the modern Latin text.

8. Robert Watson, *The Life of Lord George Gordon: With A Philosophical Review of His Political Conduct* (London, 1795), pp. 20–22. Watson claims that Gordon was "followed by more than Sixty Thousand men. The whole city was amazed" (p. 20).

9. *The Protestant Packet, Or; British monitor. Designed for the Use and Entertainment of Every Denomination of Protestants in Great Britain* (Newcastle upon Tyne, 1780), pp. 57 (right), 165 (Knox) (hereafter cited in the notes and parenthetically in the text as *PP*); *PM* 2 (1782): 23 (Calvin); Maria De Fleury, *Poems Occasioned by the Confinement and Acquittal of The Right Honourable Lord George Gordon, President of the Protestant Association* (London, 1781), p. 8; John Baillie, *The Nature and Fatal Influence of Popery upon Civil Society. A Sermon Preached Before the Committee of the Protestant Association* (Newcastle, 1780), p. 23 (lukewarm). *The Protestant Packet*'s targeting of all British Protestants was an attempt to meld the Church of England with its more Calvinist coreligionists. The tactic was marginally successful at best. Though the term *lukewarm* must have been in general circulation, it also came from Lord George himself. See n. 13 below.

10. Samuel Johnson, *The Letters of Samuel Johnson*, ed. Bruce Redford (Princeton, NJ: Princeton University Press, 1992–94), 3:271; James Boswell, *Boswell's Life of Johnson Together with Boswell's Journal of a Tour to the Hebrides*, ed. George Birkbeck Hill, rev. L. F. Powell (Oxford: Clarendon Press, 1934–50), 3:427; Thomas Holcroft, *A Plain and Succinct*

Narrative of the Late Riots and Disturbances in the Cities of London and Westminster and Borough of Southwark (London, 1780) (hereafter cited parenthetically in the text).

There are two older but still useful books on the Gordon Riots: John Paul de Castro, *The Gordon Riots* (London: H. Milford and Oxford University Press, 1926); and Christopher Hibbert, *King Mob: The Story of Lord George Gordon and the Riots of 1780* (1958; reprint, Thrupp Stroud, Gloucestershire, UK: Sutton, 2004). George Rudé contributed several useful articles and books, some of whose conclusions have been challenged but all of which set the riots in the context of crowds, mobs, and group behavior: "The Gordon Riots: A Study of the Riots and their Victims," *Transactions of the Royal Society*, 5th ser., 6 (1956): 93–114; "The London 'Mob' of the Eighteenth Century," *Historical Journal* 2 (1959): 1–18; *The Crowd in History: A Study of Popular Disturbances in France and England, 1730–1848* (New York: Wiley, 1964); *Paris and London in the Eighteenth Century* (New York: Viking, 1971); and *Hanoverian London, 1714–1808* (Berkeley: University of California Press, 1971). Two more recent studies include those by the Tory politician and Member of Parliament Sir Ian Gilmour, *Riot, Risings and Revolution: Governance and Violence in Eighteenth-Century England* (London: Pimlico, 1993), in which see esp. pp. 342–70, 371–90; and Nicholas Rogers, *Crowds, Culture, and Politics in Georgian England* (Oxford: Clarendon Press, 1998), pp. 152–75. Rogers discusses two of the many images that describe events and attitudes in the riots. His figure 2, "A Priest at his Private Devotions" (p. 173), shows "a tonsured George [III] praying before a Catholic altar while county and Protestant petitions lie scattered on a latrine floor." For other illustrations of the riots, see Richard Wendorf, *London, June 1780* (Cambridge, MA: The Johnsonians, 2010); and Ronald Paulson, *The Art of Riot in England and America* ([Baltimore]: Owlworks, 2010). The most recent contribution is *The Gordon Riots: Politics, Culture and Insurrection in Late Eighteenth-Century Britain*, ed Ian Heywood and John Seed (Cambridge: Cambridge University Press, 2012). Unfortunately, it appeared too late for me to consider its findings.

11. *A Syllabus of Lucubrations: With a Dedication to Five Illustrious Men* (London, 1780), p. 2. The author laments "this very awful period—this most dangerous and most horrible of all possible conjunctures, public or private." It was the worst crisis "ever known or heard of" (p. [1]). For Lord George's role, see pp. 7–16, largely in Scots dialect for "Geordy" (pp. 9–10). A Highland Colonel Campbell tells Lord George that his "wanton, wicked, and ill tim'd [hostility], only serves to disgrace and injure the kingdom." It will "draw the contemp o' gude men, an' the curse o' *Gode* upon a' it's members!" (p. 14).

12. For these numbers of dead and wounded, see Stanley H. Palmer, *Police and Protest in England and Ireland, 1780–1850* (Cambridge: Cambridge University Press, 1988), pp. 85 and 630n8; and Frank McLynn, *Crime and Punishment in Eighteenth-Century England* (Oxford: Oxford University Press, 1991), p. 236. The totals vary from source to source and from 250 to 850 dead. McLynn cites 300 rioters killed by their own folly or by soldiers, 75 dead thereafter from gunshots, 210 further bodies found, and 25 hanged. His numbers come from *The New Annual Register, or General Repository of History, Politics, and Literature, For the Year 1780* (London, 1781), pp. 262–63. Horace Walpole to William Mason, 29 June 1780, in The Yale Edition of Horace Walpole's Correspondence, ed. W. S. Lewis, vol. 29, *Horace Walpole's Correspondence with William Mason. II*, ed. W. S. Lewis et al. (New Haven, CT: Yale University Press, 1955), p. 63 (hereafter cited as YEW by volume, title, and editor).

13. William Vincent [Thomas Holcroft?], *A Narrative of the Proceedings of Lord Geo. Gordon, and the Persons Assembled under the Denomination of the Protestant Association* (London, 1780), p. 48. Vincent/[Holcroft?] quotes Gordon's speech to his followers. He twice rejects the concept of "lukewarm" Protestants and will not lead mere talkers in "idle opposition" when their country and conscience need them (p. 2).

14. For Gordon and Judaism, see Israel Solomons, "Lord George Gordon's Conversion to Judaism," *Jewish Historical Society of England. Transactions* 7 (1911–14): 222–71; Yirmeyanu Bindman, *Lord George Gordon* (New York: CIS Publications, 1992); and David Katz, *The Jews in the History of England, 1485–1850* (Oxford: Oxford University Press, 1994). Edmund Burke was a prime mover of the 1778 Catholic Relief Act and thus verbally assaulted Gordon and his new religion. Gordon's philo-Semitism and revolutionary fervor and results in part motivated Burke's anti-Semitism and his anti–French Revolution rhetoric and fear. See Iain McCalman, "Mad Lord George and Madame La Motte: Riot and Sexuality in the Genesis of Burke's *Reflections on the Revolution in France*," *Journal of British Studies* 35 (1996): 343–67; F. P. Lock, *Edmund Burke: Volume I, 1730–1784* (Oxford: Clarendon Press, 1998); and Franz De Bruyn, "Anti-Semitism, Millenarianism, and Radical Dissent in Edmund Burke's *Reflections on the Revolution in France*," *Eighteenth-Century Studies* 34 (2001): 577–600. For other verbal abuse of Gordon's Judaism, see *The Christian Turned Jew. Being the most Remarkable Life and Adventures of Lord G. G. With the Letter sent to him by a certain Great Lady, since his Confinement* (London, [1790?]); and The Reverend Mr. Bradshaw as an Ecclesiastic, *A Scourge for Dissenters; Or, Non-Conformity Unmasked. . . . With Animadversions on Dr. Price's Sermon . . . at the Old Jury* (London, 1790), p. 51. The obituary in the *Gentleman's Magazine* 63 (1793): 1056 reports Lord George's dismay regarding his exclusion from Jewish burial rites: "His last moments were additionally embittered by the knowledge that he could not be buried amongst the Jews whose religion he sometime since embraced, and to which he was warmly attached. His remains were interred on the 9th with the utmost privacy, in a vault in St. James's burying-ground on the Hampstead Road." Excommunication forbad burial in Christian sacred ground, but whether Gordon indeed was fully excommunicated remains uncertain. See chapter 7 below.

15. Edward Gibbon to his mother, Dorothea Gibbon, 27 June 1780, in *The Letters of Edward Gibbon*, ed. J. E. Norton (London: Cassell & Co., 1958), 2:245; see also 242 and 243. Gibbon thought that such fanaticism was more widespread in Britain than in any other European country. *Observations on "An Appeal From the Protestant Association, To the People of Great Britain"* (London, 1780), p. 35. He responds to *An Appeal from the Protestant Association to the People of Great Britain; concerning . . . the Act of Parliament in Favour of the Papists*, new ed. (London, 1780). The author adapts the language of the earlier eighteenth century: Papists wanted "to root out heretics" and destroy them *"root and branch"* (p. 6). John Newton, *The Guilt and Danger of such a Nation as this! A Sermon Preached in the Parish of St. Mary, Westminster* (London, 1781), p. 12; Arthur O'Leary, "Remarks," on John Wesley's Letter concerning Roman Catholics, in O'Leary's *Miscellaneous Tracts*, 2nd ed. (Dublin, 1781), p. 267.

16. Scottish Commentator, "Appendix: Reasons against repealing the Statutes enacted to suppress the growth of Popery" (in italics), in *The Trial of Lord George Gordon, for High Treason, at the Bar of the Court of King's Bench, On Monday, February 5th, 1781* (Edinburgh, 1781), pp. [187], 190 (for Addison). All these men "have abhorred its [Catholicism's] enslaving

principles." *PM* 2:15; *Strictures on a Pamphlet, Entitled, "The State and Behaviour of England's Catholics, From the Reformation to the Year 1780"* (London, 1782), pp. 11 (upon), 17n (prevailing); John Butler, *A Sermon Preached Before the House of Lords at the Abby Church, Westminster, on Tuesday, January 30, 1787* (London, 1787), p. 14. Butler's title page notes Charles I's "MARTYRDOM" but lacks a black mourning border or the earlier terms *holy* and *blessed*. The text is the familiar Proverbs 17:14, "The beginning of strife is as when one letteth out water." Butler is appalled by the regicide but will not enter "into the allegations of either side" (p. 11).

17. John Milton, *A Complete Collection of the Historical, Political, and Miscellaneous Works of John Milton* (London, 1738): *Areopagitica*, 1:144; the 1673 text "Of True Religion, Heresy, Schism, Toleration, and what best Reasons may be us'd against the Growth of Popery," 2:122.

18. The *Protestant Magazine* printed a version of Erenustus' excommunication curse of heretics, which it thought had been invented by the devil: 1 (1781): 51–53. Baillie, *Nature and Fateful Influence of Popery*, p. 16. Frederick Bull, in *Trial of Lord George Gordon*, pp. 198–99. The publisher wanted the trial's record and its verdict of not guilty widely circulated—"PRICE ONLY SIXPENCE." *A Reply to an Appeal from the Protestant Association to the People of Great Britain* (London, 1780), p. 28.

19. Baillie, *Nature and Fatal Influence of Popery*, p. 36 (burn); [A Protestant], *The Fall of Romish Babylon Anticipated. A Poem; in Three Parts. . . . Inscribed to the Right Honourable Lord George Gordon* (London, 1780), p. 38 (Say); Samuel Stennett, *National Calamities the Effect of Divine Displeasure. A Sermon Preached in Little Wild-Street . . . February 21, 1781* (London, [1781]), p. 10. De Fleury also is among those who cite the Aceldema. See "An Irregular Ode" in her *Poems*, p. 12.

20. Wesley, *Letter to the Printer of the Public Advertiser*, p. 20. See also *A Warning to English Protestants, On Occasion of the present more than ordinary Growth of Popery* (London, 1780) for a compilation of presumed papist horrors. In contrast, see *Observations on "An Appeal From the Protestant Association, To the People of Great Britain,"* which significantly modifies such rage.

21. Henry Sacheverell, *The Political Union. A Discourse Shewing the Dependance of Religion in General: And of the English Monarchy on the Church of England In Particular* (Oxford, 1702), p. 19; *Appeal from the Protestant Association*, p. 27. The term *wholesome severities* had indeed become familiar in such religious discourse. John Fellows used it in *The Protestant Alarm; or Popish Cruelty fully Displayed* (London, 1778), p. 264, and in *A Fair and Impartial Enquiry into the Rise . . . of the Church of Rome* (London, 1779), p. 264: these "are really infernal cruelties"; Calvinus Minor, Scoto-Britannus [Archibald Bruce], *Free Thought on the Toleration of Popery* (Edinburgh, 1780), p. 274, in which a restored Catholic tyranny will again martyr Protestants; Benjamin Bennet, *A View of the Whole System of Popery* (London, 1781), p. 297. Alternatively, Benjamin Choyce Sowden, in *Universal Toleration recommended. A Sermon* (London, [1780]), p. 4, laments that such severities had been and still were practiced by Protestant churches.

22. Thomas Bell, *The Standard of the Spirit lifted up Against the Enemy coming in like a Flood. Being the Substance of Several Sermons Preached from Isa. lix.19. On the Late Alarming Progress of Popery* (Glasgow, 1780), pp. xiv (infidelity), 18 (torrent), 22 (corruption), 97 (iniquity), 29 (roaring), iii, 272 (William). The pope is *"drunken with the blood of the saints"* (pp. ix, 71, 72, 87). See also pp. 117 and 230, as well as nn. 23 and 24 below, for the protec-

tive "bulwark" against such torrents. Charles Chandler asked Sir George Savile how he could sponsor "that *curs'd Bill,* / At once to *tolerate all ill,* / *Protestant blood* again to spill?" *Ancient and Modern Popery, Compared and Considered. A Poem. . . . Dedicated by Permission to . . . Ld George Gordon* (London, [1780]), p. 20. Chandler warmly praises Lord George on pp. 20–22.

23. Maria De Fleury, *Unrighteous Abuse Detected and Chastised, or, A Vindication of Innocence and Integrity, Being an Answer to a Virulent Poem, Intituled, The Protestant Association*, 2nd ed. (London, 1781), pp. 8 (jury), 5 (bulwark); see also her *Poems*, p. 24. *PM* 3 (1783): 17 (undermine); 1 (1781): 6 (remains).

24. *PM* 1 (1781): 26 (pull); 2: (1782): 33 (Protestant). For other uses of *bulwark*, see *PM* 1 (1780): 8, 57 and 3 (1783): 7, 268; and Bell, *Standard of the Spirit*, pp. 117, 230. The list easily could be expanded.

25. Henry Sacheverell, *Political Union*, p. 49; Benjamin Bennet, *The Memorial of the Reformation (Chiefly in England) and of Britain's Deliverances from Popery and Arbitrary'Power, Since that Time, to the Year,* MDCCXIX, 2nd ed. (London, 1721), p. 411; William Graham, *False Prophets Unmasked. A Sermon Preached, and now Published At The Behest of the Protestant Association* (Newcastle upon Tyne, 1780), p. 54; *The Sense of the People: A Letter to Edmund Burke, Esq. On His Intended Motion in the House of Commons* (London, 1780), p. 27. The same page notes that Burke threatens "the constitutional bulwark" of the people's rights.

26. *PM* 1 (1781): 21. See also Baillie, *Nature and Fatal Influence of Popery*. "The prophecies of *Daniel*" show that the Roman church is the Antichrist in a new government: "Seven heads are interpreted by the Angel to signify seven mountains, and seven kings, chap. xvii, 9, 10. Hence we may sufficiently understand, that by this beast was meant a *Roman* government" (pp. 3–4).

27. The Works of Tobias Smollett, *The Expedition of Humphry Clinker*, intro. and notes by Thomas R. Preston, ed. O M Brack Jr. (Athens: University of Georgia Press, 1990), p. 252, Win Jenkins to Mary Jones, 7 September.

28. *PM* 1 (1781): 53–54 (two-thirds); *The Third Book of the Chronicles of London, For 1780. A New Translation, With Notes Critical and Elucidatory. . . . Written in Arabic, by an Oriental Sage, in the Time of the Jewish Captivity: and Translated literally into English as far as the Idiom of the Language would admit* (London, 1781), p. 8. The translator's preface is signed Zaphaphpaniah Zerubbabel. It is not clear whether the names are subtle clues to the author's identity or are geared to the Gordon Riots, described within. Zaphnath-Paaneah was the name Pharaoh gave to Joseph when he elevated him to grand vizier, or prime minister (Exodus 41:45). Zerubbabel, stranger in Babylon, appears at several place in the Old Testament, but especially in Haggai 1:1. He was a descendant of David, head of the tribe of Judah, and shepherded some 42,360 Israelites out of Babylon and to Jerusalem. They helped to rebuild the Temple circa 522.

29. *Appeal from the Protestant Association*, p. 44 (unite); *PM* 3 (1783): 15 (defaming); *PP*, pp. 62 (every), 103 (must), 62 (of every); [Thomas Lewis O'Beirne], *Considerations on the Late Disturbances. By a Consistent Whig* (London, 1780), p. 13. The *Protestant Magazine* also estimated that the remaining one-third of non-Anglicans in the crowd was made up of Presbyterians, other Dissenters, and even a few Catholics who feared that "if Papists could once prevail, our whole system of Government would be overturned" (1 [1781]: 54).

30. [Protestant Association], *Sketches of a Conference with the Earl of Shelburne* (London, [1782]), p. 17, in italics; *PP*, pp. 145–46 (cavaliers), 195 (alarming); Graham, *False Prophets Unmasked*, p. 52.

31. [A Protestant], *Fall of Romish Babylon*, p. 38; *Prayer to be Used Every Day next after the Prayer In Time of War and Tumults* (London, 1781), p. 4; Jeremiah Trist [pseud.?], *Historical Memoirs of Religious Dissension; Addressed to the Seventeenth Parliament of Great Britain* (London, 1790), pp. 58n–59n.

32. Vincent [Holcroft?], *Narrative of the Proceedings of Lord Geo. Gordon*, p. 2; Baillie, *Nature and Fatal Influence of Popery*, pp. 19 (lukewarm), 20 (mankind); William Augustus Clarke, *Innocence in eminent Lustre, and Malevolence confounded, A Thanksgiving Sermon on the Happy and Honourable Deliverance of Lord George Gordon*, 3rd ed. (London, 1781), pp. 29–30.

33. David Fairer, *Organising Poetry: The Coleridge Circle, 1790–1798* (Oxford: Oxford University Press, 2009), p. 121; Edmund Burke, *The Correspondence of Edmund Burke: Volume III*, ed. George H. Guttridge (Cambridge: Cambridge University Press; Chicago: University of Chicago Press, 1961), p. 387, concerning Irish affairs.

34. Walpole, YEW, vol. 29, *Horace Walpole's Correspondence with William Mason. II*, p. 66.

35. *Strictures on a Pamphlet*, p. 44; *PM* 1 (1781): 228 (great); *The Associators Vindicated; and the Protesters Answered* (London, 1780), p. 11 (fundamental); *PM* 1 (1781): 228 (throughout); *Appeal from the Protestant Association*, pp. 43–44 (throughout, often repeated, as on pp. 6, 24), 44 (every, numerous); McLynn, *Crime and Punishment*, p. 233 (Horse Guards).

36. *PM* 1 (1781): 180 (unaccountable); *Defence of the Protestant Association. Or An Attempt to show that the fifty thousand Petitioners to Parliament . . . were not Chargeable with . . . Outrages . . . London, June 1780* (Glasgow, 1780), p. 17 (behalf, noise, Right); *Trial of Lord George Gordon*, pp. 198 (baneful, spurned), vii (real, representatives).

37. *Defence of the Protestant Association*, pp. 17 (wantonly, resentment), 31 (when great); *Sense of the People*, pp. 26–27.

38. Bennet, *Memorial of the Reformation*, p. 412; *PM* 1 (1781): 79 (incomplete), 86 (Revolution); [A Protestant], *Fall of Romish Babylon*, pp. 27–28; *Appeal from the Protestant Association*, pp. 1 (tremble), 35 (fatal).

39. *The Annual Register, or A View of the History, Politics, and Literature, For the Year 1774*, 2nd ed. (London, 1778), pp. 262 (founded), 74 (retired). The remark, however, should be modified by the attempt at repeal, as per Lord Camden's remarks quoted below.

40. *Annual Register . . . For the Year 1774*, pp. 75 (great) 77 (warm), 76 (arbitrary), 77 (abject), 78 (any . . . since). For a valuable discussion of Anglican expansion into the recalcitrant colonies, see Rowan Strong, *Anglicanism and the British Empire, c. 1700–1850* (Oxford: Oxford University Press, 2007), pp. 41–118.

41. A Lay Dissenter [John Jay Stevenson], *A Letter to a Dissenting Minister, Containing Remarks on the late Act for the Relief of his Majesty's Subjects professing the Popish Religion* (London, 1780), p. [1]; *PM* 2 (1782): 15 (train; *PM* 1 (1781); 179 (legal, subversive), 180 (beginning); *PM* 2 (1783): 16 (was, Bill).

42. *The Parliamentary Register; Or, History of the Proceedings and Debates of the House of Lords* (London, 1775), 2:133–39 for Camden's arguments, 2:134 for the quotation. Hostility to the Quebec Act, to Catholicism, and to France were staples of Whig opposition to the North administration's policies.

43. Palmer, *Police and Protest*, p. 84; see Robert Kent Donovan's valuable "The Military Origins of the Roman Catholic Relief Program of 1778," *Historical Journal* 28 (1985): 79–102, pp. 100–101 for Gordon and his belief that Catholic relief was less an act of impiety than of despotism; *Strictures on a Pamphlet*, p. 42; Stennett, *National Calamities*, p. 7 (kindled); *PP*, p. 103; Newton, *Guilt and Danger*, p. 26 (connection); *Moderation Unmasked; or, the Conduct of the Majority Impartially Considered* (Dublin, 1780), p. 8; A Devonian [John Short], *The Rights and Principles of an Englishman Considered and Asserted* (Exeter, 1780), p. 17.

44. *Associators Vindicated*, p. 31 (none); *PM* 1 (1781): 173 (baleful).

45. *Moderation Unmasked*, p. 62; *PM* 1 (1781): 172 (part), 2 (1782): 20 (hated), quoting a speech by Sir Joseph Mawbey to the Commons; *Defence of the Protestant Association*, p. 29 (Real); *PP*, p. 167 (settled).

46. Holcroft, *Plain and Succinct Narrative*, p. 26; Newton, *Guilt and Danger*, p. 31; [A Real Friend to Religion and to Britain], *Fanaticism and Treason: Or, A Dispassionate History of the Rise, Progress, and Suppression of the Rebellious Insurrections In June of 1780* (London, 1780), pp. 55 (either), 75 (Leonidas), 85 (sett, grand), 80 (deep laid), 86 (Delinda). The Newberry Library's copy includes a title-page note in an apparently contemporary hand: "Herbert Croft Junr Esqr." I have not been able to verify this, and the book is not included in the 1,547 lots in the sale of Croft's library for debt, though it could be among the many "Other" unnamed tracts. Thomas King, *Books. A Catalogue of the Library of the Rev. Herbert Croft* ([London, 1797]).

47. Felix McCarthy, *A Serious Answer to Lord George Gordon's Letters to the Earl of Shelbourne . . . and . . . the Salvation of the State* ([London], 1780), p. 14, and see also p. 56; McCarthy, ed., *The World As It Goes: Exemplified in the Characters of Nations . . . Selected from the Most Distinguished Poets from Chaucer to Churchill* (London, 1781), pp. 10 (Shakespeare, Dryden), 38 (Dryden, captain); Johnson, *Letters*, 3:275.

48. Robert Hawes, *An Acrostical Tribute of Respect, To the Memory of the Late Right Honourable Lord George Gordon, Who died in Newgate, November 1. 1793. In Which are Introduced Some Prophetic Ideas Relative to the Call of the Jews* (London, [1793]), pp. 3 (Lover), 4 (meant, England). Hawes was keen on the acrostic as a literary form. He also continued his interest in Judaic prophesy in the broadside *A Letter from a Citizen in London to his Friend in the Country* ([London, 1793]).

49. De Fleury, *Unrighteous Abuse*, pp. 7–8; A Man of Ross, *A Defence of the Protestant Association, And Others, In Two Letters* (London, 1780), pp. 5–6 (endangering), 20 (rotten), 9 (banditti), 5 (artful), 7 (last); *Strictures on a Pamphlet*, pp. 62 (destroyed), 65 (bring); *PM* 1 (1781): 8, with which *Strictures on a Pamphlet*, p. 63, among other sources, agrees; *Defence of the Protestant Association*, p. 30. The French soon would be comparably suspicious of British mischievous doings in the early phases of the Revolution. See Alfred Cobban, "British Secret Service in France, 1784–92," in *Aspects of the French Revolution* (New York: W. W. Norton & Company, 1968), pp. 192–227.

50. *Defence of the Protestant Association*, p. 8 (legal); *Strictures on a Pamphlet*, pp. 34–35 (zealously), 67–68 (was found), 32, 35 (transmit); *Defence of the Protestant Association*, p. 34 (no evil). For other examples of the commonplace, see *Strictures on a Pamphlet*, p. 57; and De Fleury, *Unrighteous Abuse*, pp. 9–10.

51. [A Protestant], *Fall of Romish Babylon*, p. 40; *PM* 2 (1782): 266.

52. [A Protestant], *Fall of Romish Babylon*, p. 40.

53. Frances Burney, *The Early Journals and Letters of Fanny Burney: Volume IV. The Streatham Years. Part II. 1780–1781*, ed. Betty Rizzo (Montreal, ON: McGill-Queens University Press, 2003), p. 176; Johnson, *Letters*, 3:271 (Government), 274 (put). On military deaths, see Holcroft's *Plain and Succinct Narrative*, p. 41 and n; and Palmer, *Police and Protest*, p. 87.

54. Horace Walpole, YEW, vol. 33, *Correspondence with the Countess of Upper Ossory*, ed. W. S. Lewis et al. (1965), p. 194. Walpole feared that "other swords may be lifted up" in continued turmoil or even civil war. *The Correspondence of Edmund Burke: Volume IV*, ed. John A. Woods (1963), p. 247. Walpole was at least as gloomy as Burke regarding the causes and effects of the Gordon Riots. Both de Castro and Hibbert usefully describe the debates, uncertainties, concerns, and conduct regarding martial law and, indeed, whether the many troops and militia from distant areas would follow their orders. See de Castro, *Gordon Riots*, pp. 170–80, and Hibbert, *King Mob*, pp. 99–107. For actions of the North Hampshire militia, see *The Newgate Calendar; Comprising Interesting Memoirs of the Most Notorious Characters*, ed. Andrew Knapp and William Baldwin (London, 1825), 3:106. The editors add that the "number of persons killed by the military in these riots is unknown; various calculations have ben made, from one hundred to one thousand." They guess that about five hundred were so killed (p. 104; see also p. 106).

55. Holcroft, *Plain and Succinct Narrative*, p. 27; [David Williams], *A Plan of Association on Constitutional Principles, For the Parishes, Tithings, Hundreds, and Counties of Great Britain; By which the Outrages of Mobs, and the Necessity of a Military Government Will be Prevented* (London, 1780), pp. 19 (unless), 33–34 (seldom), 62 (act).

56. Mrs. Montagu *"Queen of the Blues": Her Letters and Friendships from 1762 to 1800*, ed. Reginald Blunt (London: Constable & Co., 1923), 2:89 (blue flags, to Mrs. Vesey, 10 June 1780), 92 (madly, to her sister, 16 June), 92 (levelled, to her sister, 25 July), 92 (cured, to Leonard Smelt, 24 July). Mrs Montagu of course made plain that greasy mechanics were part of the anarchic democratic madness for which the gallows were proper places of arrival and departure.

There is a large body of research concerning the law, the police, and the relationships between them. Histories include Sir Leon Radzinowicz's magisterial *History of English Criminal Law and its Administration from 1750*, esp. vol. 1, *The Movement for Reform, 1750–1833* (New York: Macmillan Company, 1948), esp. pp. 399–493. John Baker outlines some of the essential modes of proceeding in trials in "Criminal Courts and Proceedings at Common Law, 1550–1800," in *Crime in England, 1550–1800*, ed. J. S. Cockburn (Princeton, NJ: Princeton University Press, 1977), pp. 15–48; see p. 43 for the growth in leniency regarding hangings. John M. Beattie deals with such proceedings at greater length in *Crimes and the Courts in England, 1660–1800* (Princeton, NJ: Princeton University Press, 1986). See also Peter King, *Crime, Justice, and Discretion in England, 1740–1820* (Oxford: Oxford University Press, 2000).

Studies of the history of policing complement and partially overlap with studies of the law. See T. A. Critchley, *A History of Police in England and Wales, 900–1966* (London: Constable, 1967); Clive Emsley, *Crime and Society in England, 1750–1900* (London: Longman, 1987); Douglas Hay and Francis Snyder, eds., *Policing and Protection in Britain, 1750–1850* (Oxford: Clarendon Press, 1989); and John M. Beattie, *Policing and Punishment in London, 1660–1750: Urban Crime and the Limits of Terror* (Oxford: Oxford University Press, 2001). A productive controversy percolated in 1975 with *Albion's Fatal Tree: Crime and Society in*

Eighteenth-Century England, ed. Douglas Hay, Peter Linebaugh, et al. (London: Allen Lane, 1975). This collection and several other books and trends in the history of legal scholarship were well discussed by Joanna Innes and John Styles in "The Crime Wave: Recent Writing on Crime and Criminal Justice in Eighteenth-Century England," *Journal of British Studies* 25 (1986): 380–435, but without discussion of "public order and policing" (p. 380). At this writing the eighteenth-century volume of the *Oxford History of the Laws of England* has not yet appeared. I cite other works in relevant notes herein.

57. Richard Brinsley Sheridan, in the *London Courant and Westminster Chronicle*, 6 March 1781. See also the *Morning Chronicle and London Advertiser*, the *Morning Post and Daily Advertiser*, and the *Public Advertiser* for the same day. The extensive reporting suggests the importance of the issue. Sheridan was especially concerned with the breadth of the royal decree: the anarchy was largely in London and relatively nearby areas, but the martial law extended to the entire country. Sir William Blizard, *Desultory Reflections on Police: With An Essay on the Means of Preventing Crime* (London, 1785), p. 55; see pp. v–vi, 2, 42, and 55–56 for alternatives to martial law. William Pitt supported the London and Westminster Police Bill but acknowledged that his failure was in part the result of his poor preparation. A reduced version passed in June of 1792, in part because of new riots in Birmingham. See Jennifer Mori, *William Pitt and the French Revolution, 1785–1795* (New York: St. Martin's Press, 1997), p. 92. The difference between French and British policing was noticed by the French visitor Piere Jean Grosley; see his *Tour to London Or, New Observations on England, and its Inhabitants*, trans. Thomas Nugent (London, 1772), 1:48–49. For example, most policing was run from the feeble offices of the justice of the peace: "it has no spies in its retinue, nor those offices of covert and secret correspondencies, which it looks upon with the same evil eye as the best Roman emperors did upon informers" (1:48).

58. Holcroft, *Plain and Succinct Narrative*, p. 33; Johnson, *Letters*, 3:269.

59. [A Real Friend to Religion and to Britain], *Fanaticism and Treason*, p. 69. Hester Lynch Thrale Piozzi regarded the Gordon Riots as a major historical event. See her *Retrospection: Or A Review of the Most Striking and Important Events, Characters, Situations, and Their Consequences, which the Last Eighteen Hundred Years Have Presented to the View of Mankind* (London, 1801), 2:478. William Jones, *An Inquiry into the Legal Mode of Suppressing Riots. With a Constitutional Plan of Future Defence* (London, 1782), pp. 9 (admitted, consequences), 17, 37–40 (advantages of his scheme). A Dilettante in Law and Politics [Allan Ramsay], *Observations upon the Riot Act, With an Attempt Towards the Amendment of it* (London, 1781), pp. 6 (whimsical), 9 (certain), 8 (equally), [28] (military), 29–31 (expansion of his plan).

60. A Man of Ross, *Defence of the Protestant Association*, pp. 23–36, for the broader discussion of Protestant rights and martial law's danger; [Philonomos], *The Liberty of the Subject, and Dignity of the Crown, Maintained and Secured Without the Application of a Military Unconstitutional Force* (London, [1780?]), pp. 41 (potential subversion), 5 (rarely), 59–60 (withhold power from the Crown), 41 (infinite). This reprinted *The Right Method Of Maintaining Security in Person and Property To all the Subjects of Great-Britain* (London, 1751).

61. For army and Horse Guards actions, see Walpole to Mason, 9 June 1780, in YEW, vol. 29, *Horace Walpole's Correspondence with William Mason. II*, p. 58. See also *His Majesty's Most Gracious Speech to Both the Houses of Parliament, On Monday, June 19, 1780* (London, 1780), p. 1. This sedate proclamation contrasts with a broadside warning the peaceable

to stay home and away from the "many Acts of Treason and Rebellion": *Whereas a great Number of Disorderly Persons have Assembled Themselves in a Riotous and Tumultuous Manner* ([London?, 1780?]).

62. *New Annual Register . . . For the Year 1780*, pp. 174 (Duke of Richmond), 175 (popular outcry, ancestral horror); *The Parliamentary Register; or History of the Proceedings and Debates of the House of Lords* (London, 1782), p. 403 (Earl of Abingdon).

63. *The Protestant Association, Written In the Midst of the Tumults, June 1780* (London, 1781) (hereafter cited parenthetically in the text). The pamphlet consists of the four-canto poem "The Protestant Association" (pp. [3]-21), an "Address to the City. Written in June, 1780" (pp. 22–30), and a "Second Address to the City, Written in June, 1780" (pp. 31–34). The mob is so blind to reality that it verbally attacks John Wesley, "to Papists kind, / Who wrote against them for a blind, / Himself a Papist still in heart, / He and his followers shall smart" (p. 11). The author may seek to discredit the familiar notion that the mobs were heavily Methodist. "In the gap to stand" alludes to Ezekiel 22:30. Isaiah 6:8 also is germane. Horace Walpole thought that the Court encouraged the insurrection in order to suppress it and "unite *all* the military and militia, and all under one standard" (Walpole to Mason, 29 June 1780, in YEW, vol. 29, *Horace Walpole's Correspondence with William Mason. II*, p. 63). For another relevant, but dreary and pompous blank verse, poem see *A Poem, Occasioned by the Late Calamities of England; in Particular, Those on the Sixth and Seventh of June 1780* (London, 1780). David Edwards' sermon appeals to civilians and soldiers alike to show Christian mercy and love to all, certainly including Catholics and their property. *Doing Violence to the Persons and Property of Men, Opposite to the Gospel of Christ, A Sermon Preached At Ipswich, Suffolk, June 11th, 1780; Occasioned by the Late Insurrections in London* (London, [1780?]). Edwards probably is a Dissenter.

64. *An Address to the President of the Protestant Association* (London, 1782), pp. 16 (have done), 17 (humane), 59 (would stab), 62 (will), 69 (extirpate); O'Leary, "Remarks on the Foregoing Letter and Defence" (n. 15 above), p. 223; McCarthy, *Serious Answer*, p. 46.

65. A Protestant, *A Defence of the Act of Parliament Lately Passed for the Relief of Roman Catholics* (London, 1780), p. 15; this *Defence* was dated 16 December 1779, before the June riots in 1780. *Observations on "An Appeal From the Protestant Association,"* pp. 10 (popery), 35 (increased). A Lover of Peace and Truth [Joseph Priestley], *A Free Address to Those Who Have Petitioned for the Repeal of the late Act of Parliament, in Favour of the Roman Catholics* (London, 1780), p. 12. [A Real Friend to Religion and to Britain], *Fanaticism and Treason*, pp. 47 (dark), 65 (according); *The Flames of Newgate; Or, The New Ministry* (London, 1782), pp. 61 (lawless), 66 (seraphic), 63 (heav'nly).

66. Manasseh Dawes, *An Essay on Crimes and Punishments, with a View of, and Commentary upon Beccaria, Rousseau, Voltaire, Montesquieu, Fielding, and Blackstone* (London, 1782), pp. 233–34.

67. See Peter Linebaugh, *The London Hanged: Crime and Civil Society in the Eighteenth Century* (London: Allen Lane, 1991), on Mansfield, p. 360. The attack upon Mansfield's home was "an attack upon the leading exponent of British imperialism" (p. 358). The soldiers arriving after the fact killed several of the rioters. Thanks to Linebaugh for pointing to Francis Grose, *A Classical Dictionary of the Vulgar Tongue*, 2nd ed. (London, 1788): "The chevaux de frize round the top of the wall of the King's Bench Prison" were known as Lord Mansfield's teeth. The French term originally denoted a portable frame with spikes to deter

infantry; by extension, it became the fixed spikes or glass and other obstructions atop a defensive wall. Linebaugh discusses the burning of Newgate and Mansfield's role in Gordon's trial on pp. 357–60. For charges that Mansfield misrepresented evidence against Gordon, see the *London Courant and Westminster Chronicle* for 9 and 14 February 1781. John Oldham is far more respectful of Mansfield's achievements. See his *English Common Law in the Age of Mansfield* (Chapel Hill: University of North Carolina Press, 2004).

68. Johnson, *Letters*, 3:274, 12 June 1780; John King, *Thoughts on the Difficulties and Distresses in which the Peace of 1783 Has Involved the People of England. . . . Addressed to the Right Hon. Charles James Fox* (London, 1783), p. 7.

69. *The History of the Right Honourable Lord George Gordon. To which is added, Several of His Speeches in Parliament, and his Most Remarkable Letters To the Eighty-five Societies* (Edinburgh, 1780), p. 10. Such fears surely were behind the large force that conducted Lord George to the Tower on 9 June. That "remarkably strong guard, [was] said to be far the most numerous that ever escorted a state prisoner" (p. 10).

70. For Richard Brinsley Sheridan, see the *Morning Chronicle*, 6 March 1781, from his speech in the House of Commons on behalf of a motion to establish a Westminster police force. In the same exchange, both the solicitor general and the attorney general defended their strategy and Lord Mansfield's interpretation of the law. John Wesley as quoted in *Pulpit Eloquence On Characters and Principles of the most Popular Preachers Of each denomination in the Metropolis and its Environs* (London, 1782), p. 56.

71. For the number of juror-challenges, see Beattie, *Crime and the Courts in England*, p. 340. I quote the proceedings from "*The Trial of* George Gordon, Esq; . . . *on Monday, Feb. 5, 1781*," in *The Annual Register . . . For the Year 1781* (London, 1782), here p. 164 (hereafter this number is cited parenthetically in the text). For the well-dressed judges, see the *Third Book of the Chronicles of London*'s mock-biblical sequel, *The Fourth Book of the Chronicles; or The Second Book of Gordon. To which are added, The Chapters of Donnellan . . . Written Originally in Arabic, by an Oriental Sage, in the Time of the Jewish Captivity: and Translated literally into English as far as the Idiom of the Language would admit* (London, 1781), p. 7. Like the *Third Chronicle*, this pamphlet was "Printed for the Translator." He is confident that the Devil was behind the trial, but on the day of Gordon's acquittal "religion and true liberty triumphed over error and slavery, when the righteous rejoiced, and the wicked were covered with confusion" (p. [1]).

72. John Wesley, *An Extract From the Rev. Mr. John Wesley's Journal, From August 9, 1779, to August 26, 1782. XIX* (London, 1786), p. 42. This section includes Gordon's second request that Wesley visit. He spent an hour with Gordon in the Tower, discussed "Popery and Religion," was impressed with the prisoner's knowledge of the *Bible*, his good nature, and the many books he had at hand. Wesley "cannot but hope, his confinement will take a right turn, and prove a lasting blessing to him" (p. 42).

73. The French, almost certainly Huguenot émigré author of *A Petition Written With an intention that it should be presented to the House of Lords, concerning Freedom in Religion* (London, 1781) believes that the splendid Gordon correctly denigrated intolerant and murderous Catholicism and that the trial was absurd. He has special fun with the nonsense that Gordon had been seduced by the devil (pp. xiii–xviii). *Seduce* suggests a female devil, but "Great Britain swarms with beautiful women. This is a great affront put upon the British Ladies" (p. xviii).

74. *Fourth Book of the Chronicles*, p. 11.

75. Thomas Erskine, *Mr. Erskine's Speech at the Trial of Lord George Gordon in the Court of King's Bench On Monday, February 5, 1781* (London, 1781), p. 73 (hereafter cited parenthetically in the text). Christopher Hibbert observes that like his father, the Earl of Buchan, Erskine was a devout and anti-Catholic Presbyterian. When in the navy, he preached sermons to his men rather than joining fellow ensigns in drink. Hibbert, *King Mob*, p. 147.

76. *The Trial of George Gordon, Esquire, Commonly Called Lord George Gordon, for High Treason, at the Bar of the Court of King's Bench, On Monday, February 5th, 1781. Taken in Short-Hand by Joseph Gurney* (London, 1781), pp. 63–64.

77. *Trial of George Gordon*, p. 65. Lord Mansfield then withdrew, whether because of understandable fatigue and indisposition or because of either confidence or fear concerning the verdict.

78. *Fourth Book of the Chronicles*, p. 17. The biblical and epic machinery of course is the author's own invention; the joy of the auditors and readers near and far is not. The Scottish compiler of *The Trial of Lord George Gordon* (n. 16 above), for example, was among those who felt that "thus under divine providence was this extraordinary and important trial brought to a happy issue" (p. 186).

79. For the joyous response, see the *Gazetteer and New Daily Advertiser*, 7 February 1781. For Scotland's joy, see the *Morning Chronicle and London Advertiser*, 24 February 1781.

80. For the dinner with three hundred at the London Tavern, see *London Courant and Westminster Chronicle*, 16 March 1781, and a shorter form in the *Whitehall Evening Post*, 15–17 March, and the *Public Advertiser*, 16 March. For Gordon to the jury, see *Gazetteer and New Daily Advertiser*, 7 February, for which a juror reprimanded him and for which he apologized.

CHAPTER SEVEN

A Very Near Thing

State Terrorism, the Fury of the Aggrieved, and Incompatibility with the Safety of Millions

Let us assume that sometime in the 1780s we met a man of ducal family, great privilege, intelligence, and energy. He is a strict Calvinist and, given his background, well may think himself among the elect. Though a younger son and not rich, he could have used his name and connections to attract a wealthy bride, join rank to affluence, and live a life of leisure. Alternatively, he might have used his ties to rise in the military or, if he preferred less sanguine warfare, perpetually be elected to a safe seat in the House of Commons and make speeches. If he was prudent, he then might receive a government place, wait for his older brothers to break their necks while jumping five-barred fences, inherit a vast fortune, and later assume a place in the House of Lords, where he might again make speeches, but never to ears impolite.

Instead, even while holding a seat in the House of Commons, this young man seeks a life of extra-governmental political action. He rallies the faithful, wins some victories, but then makes a proper mess of everything. He is obliquely responsible for hundreds of deaths, national panic, vast expense, and much devastation. He is tried for the capital offense of treason and found not guilty. Though still bigoted against Catholics, he hopes to atone for the fatal consequences of his riots. He might do so with retreat into mournful passivity or gracious acceptance. He chooses activist politics instead. He believes passionately in liberty and already has withdrawn from his Majesty's navy, hostile to colonists who should be as free as their British brethren. He insists that if British soldiers enlist for a set period of time and for a set task, they should not then be sold to a company in a distant land and used as mercenaries for private profit. He also believes that his nation's brutal policies of capital punishment or transportation to the ends of the world for trivial offenses violate human decency and God's laws. He is appalled by slavery and works diligently to ensure that black Africans are not living commodities for white Britons. He equally thinks that the queen of a great nation should not collaborate in theft or persecute opponents and that if she does, she may be so labeled in a free press. He insists that Jewish subjects in Britain, France, Germany, and Poland should have their own civil and religious rights.[1] Put all these presumably benevolent views together, and surely we have met a man who embodies an enlightened eighteenth-century aristocrat, one whose virtues might at least in part balance his past sins. Surely as well, at least a significant portion of his nation and its rulers must love him and protect his rights as firmly as they protect their own. His evolving enlightenment should foster theirs.

Neither scenario of course applies to the lives that Lord George Gordon embodied. He died delirious and ravaged by typhus on the felon's side of Newgate Prison on 1 November 1793. He abandoned his Presbyterian religion, could not be buried by his new Jewish friends, and was a pariah for the establishments that regarded him as a plague in need of terminal cure. Though he was found not guilty of constructive treason, he continued to feed his government's fears with the liberating and lacerating views in his several post-trial publications.

That complex later career was extraordinary. In one sense, it was literally self-destructive. The Crown remembered his leadership of the ghastly riots and thought him a threat to its stability. Someone who could muster forty thousand men for one purpose might do so for another. The crowd's exercise of its violent logic urged an attack upon the Bank of England, one of the centers of its hatred to the indifferent elite, as it was the center of British commercial strength. Had the Bank fallen, the nation might have fallen. The Protestant Association remained powerful. The North administration had alienated many Britons. America was gone with French help. France itself temporarily was at rest but soon would be in its revolutionary throws, which spread republicanism and blood throughout its nation and the Continent. The English Channel might protect Britain from naval invasions, but not from intellectual and political invasions. Lord George Gordon would become an enemy of the state and indeed the Church of England, which by extension he grudgingly and only implicitly defended in 1780. How could everything have gone so wrong? Why did church and state decide that Lord George Gordon had to die? Britain tried to mend itself after its earlier riots. Along the way, those in power decided that such mending included removal of a presumed threat to its stability. The *Gentleman's Magazine* obituary in 1793 acknowledged the episode's political contexts, from the apparent waging of war against George III to the regicide of Louis XVI:

> With respect to the alleged cause of his first confinement, a recent melancholy event induces us to be silent. With respect to the severity of his [1787] sentence, and the bail demanded for his liberation, we are also silent. Those, however, in whose memory the riots of 1780 are yet fresh, when they consider the present state of po-

litical speculation, and weigh the character, genius, and talents of Lord George, must in candour admit, that such a person could not well be at large without some degree of hazard to the good order of society.²

The "good order of society," or the less anodyne "reasons of state," required that Lord George either be permanently incarcerated or killed, especially given "the present state of political speculation." That is, British Jacobins sympathetic to the French Revolution perhaps could be mobilized by Lord George if he were free to create an ominous fifth column. In the event, and as his jailers must have expected, Newgate did the job for them. The government based its actions on the fears we have already seen and others that we shall see. Most immediately, in 1780 he seemed a throwback to Scottish Presbyterian revolutionaries. Horace Walpole was scarcely alone when he said of Lord George's ancestry: "What a nation is Scotland, in every reign engendering traitors to the state, and false and pernicious to the kings that favour it the most."³ The state tried to reason with the favored Lord George and failed. It then decided to do to him what his followers had done to London. He was, after all, a Scot, a traitor, and even worse than a Dissenter. In the Gordon Riots we saw the "people's" evolution regressing. In the later Gordon trials, we see British secular and ecclesiastical justice regressing.

A River Too Far

Gordon's northern exposures noticeably alarmed observers. One English author knew that Scotland and the Scots were behind "us at least a century; the oblique rays of benevolence, like those of the Sun, have not yet warmed their hearts, or brought their imagination to maturity." They need the "genial warmth" emanating from George III's throne. The troubled Joseph Berington knew that rabid Lord George would never be among "real English Protestants." That could only happen if the Thames could "run northward, and mix his placid stream with the chilling waters of the Tweed." On this view, proper Protestants south of Hadrian's Wall were mild and tolerant of religious difference. Affiliation with Scotland and with Presbyterians thus caused grave concern. Felix McCarthy was angered by Gordon's *"true old covenant principles,"* their disrespect to the monarch, and their friendship for "the *true Presbyterian interest.*" Like Cromwell, Gordon sought "the total subversion of the constitution and government." England now had better security against such treachery, for which there would be "certain destruction"—of Lord George, not King George.⁴ The remark was prophetic.

Both the Protestant Association and its detractors also recognized Lord George as a throwback to another generation and another mode of thought and action.

Thomas Holcroft expanded McCarthy's covenant analogy on the basis of Lord George's bearing and political bias. Holcroft saw a man with "the manners and air of a modern Puritan; his figure is tall and meagre, his hair strait and his dress plain." His simple but inflammatory writings "might rather have been expected from the famous William Prynne, than from a noble Commoner in this philosophic age."[5] Lord George was too like the pugnacious, avidly Presbyterian enemy of Laud and the episcopal establishment.

Fanaticism and Treason yet further turned the physical into the political. The author knew that, yes, Protestant religious energy in 1780 was like that of Cromwell under Charles I.[6] The clear implications emerged when Lord George addressed a large body of rabble shortly after his mother's death. Had matters been slightly more unsettled, "it was a moment for a Cromwell, with the waving of his hand, to have overturned an empire." Lord George was a tool of foreign forces who sought to overthrow the ministry or perhaps the country (p. 27). That suggests the days of Charles I, when Cromwell subverted the constitution and enshrined tyranny (p. 47). *Fanaticism's* author argues that it was worse in June of 1780 than in those distant days when the public knew what to expect: "Now, no one could set bounds to his fears" (p. 60). Now "universal bankruptcy and ruin" could approach (p. 55). As the Cromwell analogy suggests, dynastic change, or worse, also seemed possible. For some Protestants, King George should be deposed and then replaced with "so firm a friend to religion as Lord George." He would abolish the nobility and "reduce all his subjects to one happy level" (p. 87). *The Flames of Newgate* thus drew on a familiar tradition in 1782. Its Hudibrastics liken Cromwell, and by implication Lord George, to Satan: "High thron'd in glory, with tyrannic blood, / His hands still smear'd, the Great Protector stood." Only Cromwell "Cur'd the King's evil on the BRITISH Throne."[7]

The period between late February of 1781 and late 1786 nonetheless was golden and non-satanic for Lord George. Though often excoriated by the "enlightened" public, he was lionized by those who cared for him and for whom he cared—the Protestant Association, its allies among the dispossessed, anti-Catholics in general, and certainly even the jurors, ministers, and solicitors who attended his massive post-trial celebration. He did not learn discretion from the riots or from his consequent near-death experience. He indeed seemed to become yet more impregnable. As Felix McCarthy put it, Lord George now believed "that there is no power in the community competent to your punishment." He churned out aggressive polemics against various kinds of evils, whether Catholic, legal, or social. He demanded audiences with George III and the Prince of Wales to argue Scotland's anti-Catholic position. He was increasingly sympathetic to the poor everywhere around him and increasingly hostile to the Georgian monarchy. The gist of all this, he later wrote to the Hanoverian minister Baron de Alvensleben, was a nation so "grievously imposed on, deluded, and nearly betrayed out of their Constitutional Liberties" that civil war was possible. Gordon ended this angry letter when he was "interrupted by a visit from Doctor Dowlin, from Cork, touching the conduct of the Admiralty Court towards him."[8]

Gordon held the North administration especially responsible for the catastrophic and immoral American policy and defeat. On 13 April 1778 in the House of Commons he even invoked a biblical analogy with Ezekiel 33:11 that threatened Lord North's life. The prophet assures desperate Israel that though its cities may fall, God's loving mercy will spare individuals who repent. Gordon obliterates mercy and becomes the prophet speaking truth to malicious power. Along the way he implicitly suggests why various British administrations, and Lord North's in particular, might find Gordon's virtues more dangerous than helpful:

> I sincerely wish him to save his country and his own life. I exhort him to call off his butchers and ravagers from the Colonies; to retire with the rest of his Majesty's evil advisers from the public government, and make way for honest and wiser Counsellors; to turn from his wickedness and live; it is not yet too late to repent.[9]

Nor was post-acquittal Lord George timid about reminding monarch and ministers that he had aligned himself with Britain's armed forces. On 3 September 1781 he asked Lord North to arrange an interview with George III, to whom Gordon would present *Scotland's Opposition to the Popish Bill*. The highly respectable Scots, Gordon says, number "about 20,000 men, including the train of artillery at Woolwich, and the best part of all the regiments of horse and foot-guards." Graciously complimenting them on their wisdom "in opposing the Popery Bill" would be "judicious, and in season."[10] Just six months after being acquitted on the capital crime of treason, Lord George implied that he could subvert Scottish royal artillery and Horse and Foot Guards—that is, those in London as Praetorian Guards to protect the Crown. Neither George III nor the Prince of Wales would see such a man with such a request.

These years also were the time of what many thought yet another sign of madness when in 1787 Lord George converted to orthodox Polish Judaism and rigorously engaged in its rights and rituals. He thereby deprived himself of any possible power in the state or any chance of release when imprisoned.[11] As the attack upon Lord North shows, Old Testament rhetoric and ways of thinking were congenial to Gordon, as in some ways they were congenial to Dissenters generally. By early 1787, then, Lord George seemed to have threatened his monarch with military insurrection and certainly tried to intimidate the Crown on behalf of the Protestant Association. He berated the monarch, the monarchy, and those who administered its justice and its martial conduct. He did so not only as a member of a powerful northern aristocratic family but as a convert to a still alien religion. Yisrael bar Avraham Gordon was a traitor to his class, perhaps a traitor to king and country, and could rally large numbers of potentially dangerous partisans who opposed government policies. Gordon's remark to the many who asked for and received his help was telling: he was "still dreaded by their proud Rulers" when he resisted "oppression and injustice." Felix McCarthy again drew what he and others thought an accurate inference: Lord George desired "to create a dangerous unrivalled influence among the most contemptible gross, and abandoned parts of the community." He must be dealt with severely. If he does not repent and instead re-creates the 1780s chaos, "it will be then too late, when you are involved in their consequences."[12] He needed to be put away. It was not personal; just government business.

The Trials of Lord George Gordon, 1786–1787, and Excommunication

The troubled Crown and much of the public found an ally in the Church of England. The Gordon phenomenon largely was a dissenting movement that perhaps included evangelical Anglicans, but very few higher or lower established church congregants. That church indeed was nearly as threatened by unleashed violence as was the Bank of England. In the event, the church nearly proclaimed the equivalent of royal martial law and street justice against Lord George. It also apparently used the pulpit as a less obvious weapon.

The church was covertly overt with subtler modes of attack beyond the power of its ecclesiastical court and archepiscopal authority. William Paley's 1777 Carlisle sermon on 2 Peter 31:15–16 was reprinted as a third edition in 1787 London. Its title indicates its relevance for the climate in which Gordon was tried: *Caution Recommended in the Use and Application of Scriptural Language*. In 1787 John Butler, the bishop of Oxford, read a thirtieth of January sermon to the House of Lords in which he evoked the familiar words of Proverbs 17:14 before a sympathetic audience: "THE BEGINNING OF STRIFE IS AS WHEN ONE LETTETH OUT WATER." Butler's ostensible topic and time line concern the regicide in 1649. Most in 1787, however, probably heard the Gordon Riots as part of Butler's subtext: history teaches "that the fittest instruments of public confusion were . . . bodies of men acting without reflexion, without advice, incited and united merely by the irrational motives of anger, hatred, malice, or, at the best, blind party-zeal."[13] Even 136 years after the tragic regicide, Butler's audience saw that confusion, anger, hatred, malice, and blindness led not only to London in flames but also to deracination of monarchy and episcopacy.

In fact, in May of 1786 the church took steps to avert such actions by its presumed antagonist: it exercised its power potentially to sentence Lord George to the equivalent of life imprisonment, without benefit of trial or jury. The established church surely colluded with the Crown to eliminate Lord George body and soul. Since the ecclesiastical court lacks the power to arrest, it sends a sealed writ to the Court of Chancery, from whence it is sent to the King's Bench, where it is opened and delivered to the sheriff.[14] We may reasonably assume that this church-state alliance was an alternative to the earlier failed treason trial, which left Lord George as a public danger. Hence on 5 May 1786 the Church of England exercised its authority enumerated in article 33 of its Thirty-Nine Articles: it excommunicated Lord George, probably for contumacy, when he refused to testify in an ecclesiastical trial regarding the estate of the dissenting clergyman Thomas Wilson. News of the judgment rapidly spread from London to the provinces and made clear that it could terminate in termination:

> Lord Geo. Gordon was this day excommunicated in the parish of St. Mary-le-Bonne. The excommunication was very long, and took near a quarter of an hour to read it. Several of Lord George's friends came up from the city to hear it. Lord George Gordon went in the afternoon to the clerk of the parish to obtain a copy of it for his own defence, but was informed that one of the officers of the Spiritual Court had waited in the church till it was read, and carried it back with him to the Spiritual Court, and that the clergyman who had read it had it not ten minutes in his possession. In 40 days the King will be applied to for a writ *de excommunicato capiendo*, when his Lordship will be imprisoned in Newgate without any trial or jury, till he complies with the Archbishop's authority, and then the Archbishop will present another petition to the King *de excommunicato deliberando*.—The refusal of his Lordship from religious scruples, to give evidence in a cause now pending in Doctors Commons, has occasioned the above event.[15]

Gordon retaliated with a witty, if ineffectual, insult: "to expel him from a society to which he never belonged, was an absurdity worthy of an *Arch-Bishop*."[16] Lord George, among others, did not know, or was not told, that the ecclesiastical court's secrecy invalidated its excommunication: "if the spiritual court . . . refuse a copy of the libel, a prohibition shall go, with a clause to absolve and deliver the party injured." The humiliation nonetheless provided elite culture with new opportunities for denigration and intimidation. On 29 May 1786 the *Morning Herald* used the excommunication as an analogy for a recently failed Italian opera. Thomas Townshend, Lord Sydney, a member of the Privy Council, sent a royal messenger to Gordon with an abusive letter labeling him a madman whom Sydney threatened to murder. The law courts ignored Gordon's appeal for protection.[17]

Such actions naturally added to Gordon's understandable concern. His arch response to the excommunication masked the anxiety revealed in a letter to Robert Jenner, a proctor in the spiritual court. Gordon tactfully, if mendaciously, praises Jenner's tenderness, understanding, and forbearance and hopes that the archbishop will "yet refrain from proceeding to extremities." He asks to be warned "in the technical terms of the Court, of all the different punishments that will follow" from his refusal to appear at the trial. Jenner's disheartening reply, written on 5 May, nods to Lord George's rank, claims that he would accommodate him if possible, but insists that his client's interest comes first. In the usual terms, if Lord George does not comply, the excommunication will be read on the following Sunday; if he refuses to testify within forty days, the spiritual court will apply to the Crown for a writ of *excommunicato capiendo*; thereafter the temporal court will imprison him "till you comply with the order of the Court." As Calvinus Minor, in Edinburgh, put it, that legal action would violate the subject's rights enumerated in the Magna Charta and habeas corpus. Given such an arbitrary, illegal popish law, "deliverance [is] but by death or submission." Here indeed seemed a grotesque resurrection of compulsion to come in, but to moral capitulation or temporal death, not spiritual life. Lord George soon removed himself to Scotland, where prudence, family, and the Kirk no doubt limited such action until such time as he returned to London. Sir James Fitzjames Stephen far later epitomized an appropriate response to such excommunication: he could not "understand how people submitted to it so long as they did."[18]

On 22 November Jenner again threatened Gordon with archepiscopal action: Gordon had been in contempt of the ecclesiastical court for six months, and it was time to seek royal and judicial approval for his arrest. One does not know whether by then the fuss had blown over, whether Jenner was uninformed or enjoyed threatening his social betters, or whether the public was misinformed. However that may be, the *European Magazine* buried this discreet notice in its Monthly Chronicle for July 1786: "The Ecclesiastical Court has dropped the proceedings against Lord George Gordon."[19]

Or perhaps not, for Lord George thought himself excommunicated. On 24 January 1787 he told the court that he was "*homus et legalis homus* [a free and lawful man neither outlawed nor denied civil rights] and entitled to all the privileges of other subjects, notwithstanding he was excommunicated." Lord George thus enjoyed the possibility of bail, which he sought in 1793. As Calvinus Minor knew, and as Giles Jacob and Blackstone wrote, imprisonment through excommunication did not permit bail.[20] Given the contradictions, three hypotheses suggest themselves. The least likely is that the church realized the danger of its action and withdrew its writ, but somehow the news never reached Lord George. More probably, it presented the writ and the king chose not to sign the petition of *excommunicato capiendo* for sensible reasons of state, including avoidance of grief with the Duke of Gordon and Scotland. More probably still, the *excommunicato*, also called a *significavit*, included limits on punishment. Assuming that Gordon was excommunicated for contumacy, that nominal sin was not among the several causes of excommunication, like idolatry, refusal to baptize a child, usury, or simony, for which both excommunication and punishment were required. Absent such sins, "it has been adjudged, where a person has been excommunicated and, none of those causes were contained in the *significavit*, that the person excommunicated should be discharged of the penalties, but not of the excommunication." The intimidation nonetheless must have been impressive. So was some public response.

Gordon's friends surely would have agreed with the *Public Advertiser*'s complaints for 3 June 1786, complaints that support the hypothesis that the church was acting on the government's behalf: "Oh! what a happy triumph to Ministry!—What a degradation in the Protestant Interest!—What a humiliation to the family of Gordon!" That family included Lord George's angry, sympathetic, and troubled sister the Countess of Westmoreland. Like her other relations, she had not heard of the excommunication or of the pending imprisonment in Newgate until the last few days. This "alarming piece of news" was "artfully . . . concealed" within ministerial publications.

Philo Veritas joined Calvinus Minor in reflecting the response of the many Britons as puzzled and troubled as he was by the earlier ecclesiastical event. On 18 June 1786 Veritas elaborated on the benign fiction that they were living in an "enlighten'd age, when prejudices are in a great measure professedly banish'd from the minds of men in general."[21] The exalted archbishop of Canterbury, Veritas ironically claims, then could not be motivated by prejudice or personal pique. His Grace surely knows that the hateful ecclesiastical court has excommunicated the noble, loyal, Protestant Lord George "for no other crime than disobedience to the mandate of that court." This must spread "universal discontent throughout the united kingdoms" and render those courts even more odious than usual. After all, now is a time when men boast of "universal toleration" (pp. 5–6). No. That aberration must be the court's and not his Grace's fault. Lord George refused to testify before a body whose authority opposes God's word and the British constitution. Anglican excommunication of a Scottish Presbyterian is absurd, but there is a graver issue: "it is the perpetual imprisonment consequent thereon, which gives it all its weight" (p. 7). Veritas has an answer to this alienating abuse of power. Excommunication and imprisonment are not official until the king signs the writ that sends Lord George to Newgate. The brave, wise, loyal, honest, god-fearing, liberal, disinterested, public-spirited archbishop is titular head of the ecclesiastical court. He should urge the gracious monarch not to sign the writ. This would "endear your Grace to the hearts of thousands" (pp. 9–10).

Philo Veritas was not alone in finding excommunication of non-Anglicans more than a puzzlement. The Reverend John Roe, of Calverton, threatened revolution and regicide in hopes of reclaiming his wife, who had been excommunicated and imprisoned.[22] In the case of Gordon, though, the church almost certainly colluded with the Crown to ensure that Lord George left Newgate only in a casket. Like the faulty treason trial, excommunication frightened, embarrassed, and troubled Lord George, while leaving him free, vocal, and presumably dangerous. Excommunication in fact littered the coal mine with dead canaries to whom Gordon paid too little attention. Given another chance, the state would protect itself through and with the temporal law. There would be no more blunders.

The Trials of Lord George Gordon, 1786–1787: Libeling France and Britain

Gordon had two judicial charges against him in June of 1787, a libel against Marie Antoinette and a libel against the British judges and their courts. That system signaled its hostility even before the trial began. Gordon objected that preparing for one trial made it impossible to prepare for the other unless he was given more time. The court also had placed the trial for which he was unprepared first on the calendar. Judge Buller dismissed the argument as irrelevant and beyond his ability to fix. Moreover, the initial indictment banished Lord George's identity and social station, to which he sternly objected. He was served under the name George Gordon, "without any addition whatever, which was an error." The action gave the Earl of Mansfield and Pepper Arden, Esquire, their titles, and he had as good a right to his as they did to theirs, "or even George Guelph himself"—that is, George William Frederick Guelph, King George III of England in the Hanoverian succession. If the court did not call "upon him by his right name and additions, he would not answer; and bowing respectfully to the Bench and Bar, [he] retired."[23]

Lord George was not able to turn his back on the trials themselves. The ostensible reason for the charge regarding Marie Antoinette was that he had endangered the amity the Anglo-French commercial treaty of 1786–87 was designed to foster. On 24 August 1786 his unsigned notice in the *Public Advertiser* complained that "even in this free country," so different from "an arbitrary kingdom," the French queen's circle persecuted and defamed the Comte de Cagliostro.[24] He had wisely counseled the queen's enemy Cardinal de Rohan, presumably regarding the affair of the diamond necklace, "which has never been properly explained to the public in France." Gordon alludes to "the Queen's faction" but never names Marie Antoinette herself. Considering traditional cross-border insults, much less the often vicious slanging of political and royal opponents in the United Kingdom itself, Gordon's comments were mild. The British government nonetheless claimed that the "evil-minded" mischievous Gordon endangered international harmony and required punishment. The Crown would "secure the peace of the Country by taking from you the power (at least for a time) of disturbing its tranquillity."[25] The charge of course was nonsense.

Some trade began early in the difficult Anglo-French negotiations. The same *Public Advertiser*, on 24 August 1786, for example, bluntly stated that the discussions were "by no means brought to a conclusion" and remained in "a very crude and imperfect state. . . . The truth is, that the business advanced very slowly." There probably would not be much action before Christmas. After a breakthrough, an initial draft of the treaty was signed at Versailles on 26 September 1786. William Pitt brought the bill to the House of Commons on 12 February 1787 for its successful ratification, well after which the final treaty was signed at Versailles on 31 August 1787.[26] Lord George was tried some two months before the treaty officially became law. Whether or not his tepid insults were fair or accurate, they scarcely endangered or impeded commerce or either nation's silent harmony and tense tranquillity. The Crown, however, designed to endanger, indeed destroy, Lord George's tranquillity. He was tried on 6 and 13 June 1787, almost seven years to the day after the terrors of 2–8 June 1780, about which the prosecuting attorney general, Richard Pepper Arden, made sure to inform any forgetful juror.

Loosely, the treaty reduced tariffs on French goods, like wine and silks, and English manufactures of various sorts. Each side hoped to profit from diminution of untaxed smuggling; lower prices meant higher sales and profits for individuals and for the respective treasuries; French markets would compensate for Britain's loss of the American colonies; British markets would compensate for the French loss of India and North America. As Pitt told the House of Commons, "France gains as we extend our market for her produce. We gain as she extends her market for our manufactures." Britain had the better of the deal. "France opens to us a market of above twenty millions. We open to her only a market of eight millions." Pitt hoped to replace a mercantile beggar-thy-neighbor ethic with one of mutually advantageous freer trade in which Britain gained more than France. In May of 1786 the *Yorkshire Magazine* reported that "every thing in France is at this time in the English taste; the rage for boots and leather breeches is so general, that the genius of the people seems altered, and jockeyship appears to take place of gallantry."[27]

Pitt's strong positive vote for the treaty nonetheless faced almost one-third negatives: 248 ays and 118 nays. If there were to be criminal penalties for insulting France, many of those voters and others in the political class would be indicted for virulent attacks upon the Great Satan across the Channel. One commentator knew that French food would replace English food and French foppery would replace English manhood: "Your ploughman, your sailors, are by necessity or inclination dwindled into manufacturers . . . and the greatness of Britain is no more." Another troubled patriot shared that concern regarding the wiley and wicked French. They were trying to separate Britain from the Austrian Empire, alienate her from her true Protestant allies like the Dutch and Germans, and detach Ireland from the United Kingdom. The few would be enriched at the cost of the many. None of his readers "can tolerate the idea of France being friendly to England in *any* one point of view whatever." Nor indeed should they allow the already infected upper classes to spread corrupt French values to sturdy Britons, who irretrievably would become "half Frenchmen" before they saw their error. British men would become as effeminate, and the women as shameless, as their French mentors. A French commentator thus accurately read much of the British public's mood regarding the pending commercial treaty: the English newspapers, he says, are always full of remarks that try to prove the treaty's danger for England. Even the bill's allies agreed that a commercial treaty with France "should create a general alarm." Anglicanus was tentative regarding success: the "much cavilled at, and so much abused [treaty], will perhaps lay the foundation" of peace between the two great nations.[28]

Pitt's own speech to the Commons acknowledged such abuse. Yes, the treaty "has been represented as subversive of the whole of the commercial and political system of this kingdom." It might "be attended with the most dangerous and destructive consequences." Pitt tactfully refutes, or at least answers, those charges, but along the way he unwittingly also refutes part of the charge that Lord George "unjustly, wickedly, maliciously and scandalously" libeled Marie Antoinette. Unless that libel was punished, it would "interrupt, disturb, and destroy the friendship, good-will, peace, harmony, and concord" between France and England. Aside from a lack of evidence for such a charge, friendship was a secondary and distant element in a hardheaded, long-negotiated commercial and agricultural treaty. Pitt indeed hoped that mutual enrichment and mutual dependence would diminish threats to peace, but he scarcely proposed a utopian fiction. Yes, he argued, there might be some improvement in relations; the measure could not be "a pledge of perpetual peace, but it tends to put off the season of hostility." There can be good commerce in good times "without destroying our power of going to war." Martial Britons will be Britons still; winter follows summer as war follows peace; Anglo-French combat is as regular as the seasons. The charge that Lord George was an evil enemy to peace thus was an obvious fabrication. Even Pepper Arden could not believe that Frenchmen in English boots would not try to kill Englishmen with French wine stains on their French silk shirts. The charge was payback for Gordon's bellicose behavior toward the ministry regarding the American war, for the riots, for the Crown's inability or reluctance to put him away in 1780 and 1781, and for his consequent antigovernment activism. As a Mr. Thompson put it in 1786, "Every one remembers the riots in London." The "every one" extended to interested French readers as well. In 1786 they were told that Gordon exemplified British monstrous abuse of a free press, that he was a seditious libertine without principles, dressed in fanatic gear, and had committed "les désordres les plus graves" with impunity.[29]

The *Public Advertiser* for 24 August 1786 suggests a further reason that the ministry newly sought to rid itself of Lord George: he again seemed to threaten the state and had virtually declared his disloyalty. The paragraphs immediately below the putative libel include Gordon's answer to an earlier comment in the *Advertiser*. Since Wilkes was well received at court, perhaps Lord George might be as well; if so, he would speak on behalf of the Protestant Association, and "at the time of conferring dignities . . . his lordship will be created at least a peer." In short, it looked as if Lord George had capitulated to power and prestige. Under the voice of a "Reply from Authority" Lord George insists that the Protestant Association is "not preparing a congratulatory Address to his Majesty." Mr. Wilkes certainly was no precedent for Lord George, who long ago was offered an exalted civil office, command of a Highland regiment, and command of a seventy-four-gun ship of the line as implicit rewards for silence. He refused each because "the petitions of the people who trusted in him, were not complied with." Moreover, in key words, he rejected such commissions because "he could not take the oaths of allegiance and abjuration." That stunning response was a gauntlet thrown before the Hanoverian dynasty, to whom Scottish Lord George no longer could swear the loyalty those oaths required. The Oath of Allegiance proclaimed, "That I will be faithful and bear true Allegiance to His Majesty King *George*." The Oath of Abjuration proclaimed, "I . . . do truly and sincerely acknowledge, profess, testify, and declare in my Conscience, before God and all the World, That our Sovereign Lord King *George* is lawful and rightful King of this Realm, and all his Majesty's Dominions thereunto belonging. And I solemnly and sincerely declare" that the so-called James III is not king of the realm and that the oath taker will report any treasonous activity "to his Majesty, and his Successors." The Jacobite moment was long past. The republican moment might be now, perhaps with Lord George as Protector. He could not take a Georgian loyalty oath "upon the true Faith of a

Christian." In a letter to Dublin, he promises to support increased Scottish Calvinist emigration to Ireland, after which "down with Kings, Bishops, and Peers; and huzza for a Republic." Once he is free, he tells his recipients in the Corporation, "I will fly with haste to join you, and larger cities than Dublin have felt the effects of my antipapistic zeal ere now."[30]

The power of those oaths had waned since the first two Georges' more tenuous reigns, but Nicholas Carter's sermon *The Obligations of an Oath, and particularly of the Oaths of Allegiance, Supremacy, and Abjuration* (1716) remained emotive and accurate. The Oath of Allegiance supposed that the person receiving the oath deserved allegiance and that the person swearing was "well satisfied in his Conscience of the Authority of the Imposer." No one should take the Oath of Abjuration who was "doubtful of the King's Title, or shall be wanting in any part of natural Allegiance" to him.[31] As an adolescent army ensign in 1759 and a naval lieutenant in 1772, Lord George must have so sworn. As a thirty-five-year-old, publicly accused of tergiversation, he virtually declared himself "doubtful of the King's Title."

Yet worse, immediately next to Gordon's apparent disloyalty in the *Public Advertiser* was a letter of support and gratitude from a Highland association drawn from eight counties. Lord George is "to a very considerable degree" the friend and supporter of those "who stand in need of supply." As a sign of respect to one who is "so great a friend to societies and the public in general," the Highlanders elected their officers on Lord George's birthday, 25 December. Here again was an obvious reminder that Lord George had significant and potentially dangerous Scottish allies, a fear yet further reinforced when in 1783 he successfully intervened on behalf of an Athol Highland regiment that refused deployment to the East Indies to protect private slaveholding estates. The ministry either had embarrassed itself by failing to convict Gordon for treason in 1781 or had miscalculated the results of perhaps designed or accidental loss. It could not try him again on the same charge, for after the Norman invasion *autrefois acquit* had become "a universal maxim of the common law of England."[32] The *Public Advertiser's* relevant page offered that government both a threat and an opportunity, which it exploited. It further protected itself by adding another, equally factitious charge as a fail-safe mechanism.

According to the Crown, Gordon libeled British judges and their administration of law when in 1787 he published *The Prisoners' Petition to the Right Hon. Lord George Gordon, to Preserve Their Lives and Liberties, and Prevent Their Banishment to Botany Bay*. The ferociously brilliant *Prisoners' Petition* could not be mistaken for the work of criminals guilty merely of petty crime and conventional felonies. Gordon cites Athelstan, Sir Henry Spellman (both p. 11), Sir Thomas

More, the marquis de Beccaria, Puffendorf, and Sir Matthew Hale (all pp. 12–13), who, like the Old Testament God, know that only the taking of life demands that the law take life. Lesser and often insignificant crimes deserve neither the pending banishment to alien and tyrannical Botany Bay nor "the Hangman and the scaffolding of the New Drop . . . already prepared for our execution" (p. 10).[33]

The *Petition*'s dominant mode of proceeding reflects Gordon's intense study of the Old Testament, whose rhythms, historical settings, and prophetic tones and metaphors he handsomely adapts. He says of the brutal British law and its judges, "These are they who have devoured Jacob, their sins are as scarlet, the peoples blood they have shed like water" (p. 13). The prisoners are the ancient Israelites, and Gordon is the Moses demanding their freedom from those who "blaspheme with Pharaoh, saying, who is the Lord, that we should obey his voice to let Israel go? We know not the Lord, neither will we let Israel go" (p. 12). The prophet speaks truth to power: "Be wise now therefore, O ye Kings; be instructed, ye Judges of the earth. A true Law hath the Almighty given to his people, by the hand of Moses, his servant, the faithful in his house" (p. 21). Gordon's reader surely knew the consequences of Pharaoh's disobedience.

Though Gordon alludes to Matthew 5:18, he regards the Ten Commandments as already available and the Crown as a danger to them: "Kings shall not add therefore nor diminish from it" by jot or tittle. The prisoners "have reason to cry aloud from our dungeons and prison-ships in defense of our lives and liberties" (p. 8), destroyed by violation of God's law. The prisoners appeal to God by evoking Matthew 23:27, in which the Pharisees are like whited sepulchres, beautiful without but unclean and dead within: "How long, O Lord, shall these whited walls of council, who sit to judge the people after the law, command us to be hanged, contrary to the law" (pp. 9–10). Gordon quotes Genesis 9:6 to call up God's judgment of such illicit purveyors of death: "Whoso sheddeth man's blood shall his blood be shed; for in the image of God made he man" (p. 10).

Nonetheless, behind all this rage is Gordon's insistence that British law not only violates God's law. It also violates the powerful contemporary and pan-European movements toward prison and penal reform, as well as the 1778 enlightened Catholic amelioration laws, to which Gordon and his followers so objected. In "this advanced period of the world when many kingdoms and commonwealths affect holiness unto the Lord, and profess to take hold . . . of all languages of the nations, even to take hold of the skirt of him that is a Jew" and accept him as joined with God, even now the British law turns its back upon mercy (p. 8). It is "just as if the kingdoms and commonwealths, at this advanced aera, were still aliens from the commonwealth of Israel, and strangers from the covenants of promise" (p. 9). Gordon does more than "libel" the British legal system; he calls its bluff. He implicitly makes clear that the pieties of 1778 were hypocritical boastings that masked the desire to fill "the streets of our city... with a stream of blood" (p. 9). The nominal prisoners conclude as they began, by entreating Lord George to intervene on their behalf "with the King, and the Rulers" to save them from death and often fatal transportation (p. 22). King and rulers chose instead to add Lord George to the ranks of those prisoners.

The attack on Gordon for seeking prison reform indeed was doubly pernicious. It not only removed Lady Justice's blindfold the better to raise her sword against the state's presumed enemy. It also was an attack upon Parliament's own halting progress in alleviating the inhumane and often fatal state of British prisons. From at least midcentury numerous British and Continental commentators sought to infuse good sense and human decency into treatment of real and presumed criminals. John Howard's epochal *State of the Prisons in England and Wales* (1777) depicts a world of horrors: prisoners forced to subsist on a daily small loaf of bread and bad water, without heat, light, beds, sanitation, separation of the sexes or of debtors from felons. The system demanded generally unpayable fees for everything, including acquittal or pardon, in order to be freed. Those sentenced to transportation but pardoned often languished in prison because they lacked funds for their exit charges (p. 289). Vermin, frequent and deadly jail fever, and appalling odors were everywhere. Howard chose to ride horseback forty miles per day during his tours because after his prison visits the smell of his clothing in an enclosed carriage was intolerable. So far from being indicted for libeling British justice, Howard was elected a fellow of the Royal Society and given the thanks of the House of Commons, before whom he testified in 1774.[34]

Howard there urged the need promptly to free prisoners who were acquitted, for the county to pay the fees, and for the Crown to improve prisoners' medical attention and general hygiene (14 Geo. 3, c. 20; 14 Geo. 3, c. 59; and later 19 Geo. 3, c. 74). "I saw many sick and dying," he reported (p. 192). The Whig pro-American Manasseh Dawes' omnibus title could also have included Samuel Johnson and Oliver Goldsmith: *An Essay on Crimes and Punishments, with a View of, and Commentary upon Beccaria, Rousseau, Voltaire, Montesquieu, Fielding, and Blackstone* (1782). Like Gordon, Dawes often argues that execution is appropriate only for murder (pp. 58, 63–64, 65–68, 75, 84). He lived his quiet life unmolested by the government. The Whig physician and clergyman John Jebb was a chief mover of the 1772 Feathers' Tavern Petition, which sought to eliminate subscription to the Thirty-Nine Articles. He was warmly pro-American, Unitarian, and near radical. His *Thoughts on the Constructing and Polity of Prisons, With Thoughts on their Improvement* (1786) uniformly chastises the "overwhelming evils, of such complicated unimaginable misery" in British prisons (p. v). He laments the "multitude of sanguinary laws" and the "crowds of capital sentences" that destroy potentially useful human beings (p. 105). He too was elected a fellow of the Royal Society (1779), and he died peacefully in his London home on 2 March 1786.

Even another unpleasant episode of intimidation was far from the level of state oppression represented by the Gordon trials. Josiah Dornford collected several of his essays in the *Morning Chronicle* under the title *Nine Letters to the Right Honourable the Lord Mayor and Aldermen of the City of London, on the State of the City Prisons* (1786). Dornford liberally quotes from and praises John Howard's book and points out that in spite of the new laws, nothing had been done to ameliorate the horrors of London's prisons. There still was all too familiar madness, vermin, starvation, filth, rags, cold, chains, exploitation, and, in the case of Elizabeth Gurney, among others, death through neglect of basic needs like edible food. The resentful magistrates subjected Dornford to a mock trial, in which they found him guilty of not proving his charge that prisoners had died for want, and so printed their judgment in the *Morning Chronicle*. Dornford nonetheless appended a vigorous defense at the end of his *Nine Letters*. He complained that they tried to crush him but said that he resisted: "It is well that it has happened in the mild reign of George the IIId.[35] The London magistrates indeed tried to "crush" Dornford, but through public opinion, not prosecution, incarceration, and death. Neither he nor his fellow prison reformists constituted enough of a threat. The case was demonstrably different with Lord George.

The Crown had two strategic choices for its prosecution. Giles Jacob's *New Law-Dictionary* (1729) includes three folio pages regarding libel, which cannot be justified by its truth. The greater the appearance of truth in a "malicious Invective, so much the more provoking it is." Libeling the king and state is especially actionable. Anyone selling such a book or "reflecting on the Government may be punished." A more "general Reflection on the Government is a *Libel*" even if no specific person is named. The law thus is clear: "the Contriver, Procurer, and Publisher of a *Libel* are Punishable by Fine, Imprisonment, Pillory or other corporal Punishment at the Discretion of the Court, according to the Heinousness of the Crime."[36] The law's longevity was well known. As the anonymous author of *A Satire. Also Imitation of the First Satire of Boileau* (1777) wrote, "Lawyers hold (we all love something new) / That libels are most *infamous* when *true*" (p. 6). Gordon's publisher, Thomas Wilkins, published the *Petition*, also was tried and found guilty, but was released after a short prison stay. For Gordon, though, seeking a reduction in capital crimes would be regarded as seditious and heinous enough for serious punishment.

Since the Crown could not grant the truth of Gordon's charges, it chose a less embarrassing tack: the *Petition* was false and defamatory, lessened respect for the monarch and his law, and inflamed the prisoners and the populace. The prosecutor's information repeated much of the *Petition*'s main points and words. It also insisted that the pamphlet was a "false, wicked, malicious, scandalous, and seditious libel." It was knowingly written by "a wicked, malicious, seditious, and ill-disposed person . . . greatly disaffected to our . . . lord the king, and to the laws and constitution of this realm."[37] The accused devised and contrived "to stir up and excite tumults, discontents, insurrections, and seditions, as well in divers of his said majesty's gaols in this kingdom." He insinuated and caused it "to be believed" that so many laws "punishable with death, were made contrary to the law of God and the rightful power of the king and parliament." As the *State Trials* records, such actions produce "a general disaffection amongst his said majesty's subjects towards the administration of justice" and evoke their "general ill-will, contempt, and hatred" (22:177). Thus viewed, Lord George's short pamphlet imperiled the monarch, his judiciary, and even his church. It attempted to dissociate the secular head of the Church of England from the laws of God, which, Lord George argued, that monarch's own law's desecrated. Of course there were many who criticized the appalling bloody code by which some three hundred were hanged in the years 1784–87.[38] Gordon was special because he had the acknowledged power "to stir up and excite tumults" in London and in many prisons throughout the kingdom. He set "the evil example of all others in the like case" and attacked "the king, his crown and dignity" (22:178). "Every one remembers the riots in London" indeed.

Some of these claims may have been technically correct, but as with the "libel" of Marie Antoinette, they were surrogates for the charge's underlying basis. The attorney general began his case by citing the 1780 riots and reminded the jurors of "the horrid tendency which this publication bears upon the face of it. It is but seven years ago since the three great gaols of this kingdom were sapped to their foundation, and every prisoner set at liberty." Lord George immediately objected that "this has nothing to do with the present charge." Pepper Arden brushed the comment aside and repeated his warning:

> All I say is, that the history of that time would have taught any man (I mean not to apply it particularly) to be extremely cautious of any kind of publication which would, in any degree, lead to the repetition of the same outrages. This publication has for its object the very same attempt; this gross libel carries upon the face of it the language of holy writ; and the scriptures of God are made use of to induce the people of this country to resist its laws. (22:184)

In a context enhanced by the Church of England's efforts, jurors were likely to have been predisposed to think ill of Lord George. He was an instrument of public confusion and thus guilty of a previous, as well as present, punishable crime. Men of property would have been troubled by reductions in the death penalty for theft and the apparent innovation that fatal blood should only be drawn from those who had drawn fatal blood. The attorney general confirmed their bias regarding so outrageous, dangerous, and insulting a tendency in their merciful nation. He had three barbed arrows in his quiver.

Consider, he says regarding one, that "the reason why executions are more frequent in England than elsewhere is, because the laws are milder. We know nothing of tortures; God forbid we ever should practise them." Criminals are convicted only on the basis of evidence and in cases for which "it is hardly possible to suppose a conviction where innocence can exist" (22:185). The remark applied to Lord George as much as to those awaiting execution for the theft of property worth twelve pence. The second argument sadly recalls Henry Sacheverell's thoughts regarding the shortest way with Dissenters in 1702 and yet again reminds us that "evolution" regularly takes a winding road. The attorney general suggests exile or annihilation of Lord George and those who, like him, questioned the justice or legality of English law. Any man who "can entertain the ideas that this noble lord . . . does, I am sure he is not a fit subject for this kingdom; I believe for no other upon the face of the earth." No government could exist, he adds as a third point, if his views "were admitted to be disseminated among the people" (22:187). The government is strong enough to oppose such attempts and to ensure the nation's prosperity. The Crown's ideological justifications, in short, are that it kills but does not torture, with the assumption that life imprisonment in deadly typhus-prone Newgate or transportation to Botany Bay was not torture; it should banish or destroy those who oppose hanging or other harsh punishments for theft of insignificant sums; and it should prohibit the dissemination of views that urge amelioration of English law.[39]

The jurors were predisposed to accept the attorney general's mode of proceeding, as well as his broader assumptions and justifications. He was not obliged to prove any of his inflammatory statements, nor was he judicially stopped from making them when they were not germane. The court assumed the charges to be true and assumed Gordon to be guilty. To affirm that guilt, the court needed only to show that Lord George wrote the work in question, that it was published, and that it was disseminated. The Crown's argument thus could be fatuous, superficial, and successful: (1) Lord George pretended that the letter was written by convicts, but he really wrote it himself. (2) He went to Newgate and tried to gain entry in order to speak with, and no doubt to agitate, the prisoners sentenced to death or transportation. Mr. John Pitt, the turnkey, properly denied such entrance. (3) Lord George dispatched his footman with several pamphlets, which he gave to

Mr. Pitt, who in turn gave one to the sheriff, who brought it to the attorney general's attention. (4) The attorney general did his duty and brought Lord George to trial "for so seditious an attempt" (22:186). (5) Lord George sent two men to attempt to deliver the pamphlets to prisoners in Newgate. When that failed, they disseminated the pamphlets in the streets and to anyone apparently about to enter Newgate. (6) Mr. Pitt visited Lord George, who admitted having sent the initial set of pamphlets with his footman. (7) Mr. Pitt asked Lord George to identify those who disseminated the pamphlets before the prison and remonstrated with him for his behavior. Lord George "did then that which God forbid he should do now, and I hope he will not now attempt it; he justified what he had done, and insisted he had a right to make this address to the prisoners, which he is now called upon to answer for" (22:186). The rest of the case then rested upon Pitt's verification of the details and authentication of Lord George's admission that he had written and distributed the pamphlet. The solicitor general's examination of John Pitt confirmed all that and more.

God did not forbid Lord George from justifying what he had done. Given his limited financial resources, he generally acted in his own defense and was destined to do poorly. Perhaps he knew that the verdict was inevitable. Perhaps, instead, given his elevated status and after the trial of 1781, he thought himself invulnerable. Perhaps he sought the confrontation and expected to win. John Pitt quoted him responding to the "sad piece of work about these pamphlets. . . . 'Don't you mind it; I am ready for them, let them begin as soon as they will'" (22:188). Lord George's cross-examination failed in part because, like Thomas Erskine in 1781, he hoped to convince the court and the jury that libel was determined by intention. He asked Pitt whether there was "any conversation I ever had with you to stir up the prisoners to any violence of conduct"? Gordon was concerned only with reforming the government, not with inciting the prisoners. "Let them go on. I am ready for them. . . . did not relate to the prisoners you see?" Pitt did not take the irrelevant bait: "I can't tell what it related to" (22:189).

Gordon's long peroration immediately seemed ineffectual. One spectator said that it "was delivered in a desultory manner" and was composed of heterogeneous matter. The defense also included sensible observations that had no positive legal result. Informed Britons would have noted the difference from the rising attorney Erskine's successful defense in 1781. He shared Lord George's and the jury's prejudices, which he confirmed and manipulated. He amplified their own views regarding the Crown's inept witnesses. He played upon the difficulty of hearing specific words in a large noisy crowd. He had the contrasting hard evidence of Lord George's own broadsides urging restraint. He had his own energetic professional presentation. In contrast, by 1787 Lord George represented himself and had to confront the inference that no one else would represent him. Indeed, Erskine now was part of an imposing group of well-connected attorneys ranged against him: the attorney general, the solicitor general, and Messrs. Erskine, Bearcroft, Baldwin, and Law. As the *European Magazine* noted, "On the other side Lord George Gordon stood alone, and pleaded his *poverty* as an excuse for having neither Advocate nor Solicitor."[40] The prosecutors were elaborately dressed in their legal finery, ermine, big wigs, and implicit iconography of state power and wealth. The depleted aristocrat Gordon stood alone. The visual rhetoric made the power imbalance clear and predicted an already predictable outcome. Lord George nevertheless refused to acknowledge that having meant well was irrelevant before the law.

His long presentation embodied his case and his last efforts at freedom. It began with a personal anecdote of causation as recorded in the *State Trials*. Gordon had turned to the laws of theft when one of his servants stole eighteen pence and begged to be forgiven and not dismissed as a thief subject to hanging. Lord George contrasted British law with God's Old Testament law, in which only those who had taken life had their lives taken. He found that other countries were not as severe and that even sympathetic British judges were bound by the hanging laws' constraints. Judge Gould tearfully urged him to write his thoughts. As a result, Gordon spoke to Sheriff le Mesurier, sought permission to visit the prisoners, and was refused when he identified himself. He returned home, recorded his views regarding capital punishment, and now swears that malice, scandal, and disaffection "were not in my heart at all." He did not intend "to subvert order in the country," since the attorney general and the government themselves "have drawn up a bill to alter the law . . . as much as I could wish." The king himself stated that observing God's law is necessary and that it blesses the nation. "God's law should be over the whole world." Nor, Gordon insists, did he visit the prison to stir up the inmates or to see them prior to execution; he only sent word to Mr. Pitt and his associate. Lord George himself had no connection with the prisoners (22:198–99).

Gordon also sees judicial misconduct. The presumed libel upon Marie Antoinette was sixteen months old; the presumed libel upon the British legal system was ten months old; there was no conventional grand-jury indictment; and he was denied the right to call his own witnesses. The entire libel proceedings were conducted *"ex officio* . . . only upon the information of the attorney-general" (22:200). The court has "winked at" such abuse, which resembles the trials without jury by the military in Botany Bay. So far as the defendant could see, the illicit proceedings mimicked martial law for a transported felon.

Lord George claims good intentions, no contact with the prisoners, but corrupt judicial contact with him. He finally realizes that these are not helpful for the sour pickle in which he finds himself. He fears that his defense will not persuade his judge or prosecutor and thus not be communicated to the jury.

> I have heard, that you hold this doctrine, this pernicious doctrine, that the jury are not the judges whether the libel is scandalous, false, and seditious, but that the jury are only to judge whether the facts are proved or not: that does not relate to my case; I only give Mr. Justice Buller this opportunity in his charge to the jury, to say whether the jury are not also the judges whether the libel is false, scandalous, and seditious, or whether the jury are merely confined to say whether the facts stated are proved or not. (22:202–3)

From Gordon's and indeed from Thomas Erskine's and many other jurists' point of view, the Crown is obliged to show that Gordon maliciously stirred up the prisoners and interfered with transportation to Botany Bay. He did neither, and he characterized himself as in the increasingly main stream of thought regarding the excesses of capital punishment and the nature of libel trials. Malice cannot be assumed. It must be proven.

Gordon badly fails to make his case before a court and jury that already knew its verdict. He is increasingly isolated as the peroration continues. He lacks his books and cannot show that the Bible supports the claim that God's law has been violated. He was not allowed to subpoena his witnesses. A letter regarding his intention had been forged at the king's direction. He was followed everywhere. The Crown tried "to make me a publisher in a seditious manner." He had not visited the prisoners or had malicious intentions. He wanted only the ameliorative biblical justice toward which the king and Parliament already were moving (22:206).

Mr. Justice Buller paid all this no mind. The jury was to consider only the two matters of fact that the Crown's information alleged: (1) did the defendant write and compose or print and publish the libel? and (2) has the Crown shown that the prisoners in various jails were either to be transported to Botany Bay or to be executed? The final jury instruction was as clear as the immediate verdict: if the offense has been proven, you find the defendant guilty; if not, you acquit. "The jury immediately pronounced the defendant Guilty" (22:209).

Aftermath: Flight, Conversion, and Sentence

Since the Crown delayed the sentencing phase of the trial, Lord George absconded to Amsterdam, where he wrongly thought he could be safe. On a perhaps symbolic 4 July 1787 he wrote an angry and moving letter to his antagonist Pepper Arden, to whom he regularly referred by his mother's family name. Pepper was attacking his social superior; he was a mere spice, an accoutrement, and not a threatening attorney general. The work's partial title is *A Letter from the Right Hon. Lord George Gordon to the Attorney General of England, in which the Motives of his Lordship's Public Conduct from the Beginning of the memorable Year 1780 to the present Time, Are Vindicated Upon Principles of Religion, Morality, and sound Policy*. Gordon there attempts to justify more than seven years of political activity and is especially indignant regarding the rigged charges in his recent trial. His virtual appeal of the case refutes the conceptual and factual bases of the Crown's complaint—which no longer could be reheard.

The putative "greatest cordiality and friendship" between the kings of England and France was absurd on the face of it as, he could have said, opposing speeches in Parliament made clear. Gordon himself "took a retrospective glance at the many mischiefs done by Lewis the Sixteenth to George the Third, in the course of the late war" and concluded that no two men could be more opposite. After a long list of French insults and triumphs over England, Gordon proclaims: "How often did those two great men brand each other with the most vindictive epithets, and with charges of the most heinous and atrocious nature" (pp. 24–25). The monarch who caused so much British blood to flow, who helped to steal America and other British colonies in Asia, Africa, and Europe—such a man could not "in moral possibility" be George III's friend (pp. 25–26). This charge, like its mate, "was not supported by the evidence of a single fact, or the concurrence of a single circumstance" (p. 24).

Gordon also returns to the consternation regarding capital punishment that he ineffectually offered at his trial. Now, however, he transforms it into a deeply disturbing picture of the post-riot hangings, for which he was partly responsible. The passages are redolent of his grief and human outrage at the state's moral outrages. How, he wonders, could it be libel to object to hanging a child wearing a discarded cloak whose owner she did not know, for whose theft she was not responsible, and who in any case had no understanding of the law? The heartbreaking passage concludes with Gordon's differentiation between what is legal and what is just, what is a lawyer's cold fact for hanging and what is a feeling man's burning disgust. The passage makes clear that the out-of-control rioting rabble has been replaced by the elites' out-of-control rioting legal system. Twenty-one were hanged as a result of the riots; seventeen of these were under the age of eighteen, and three were under fifteen:

> I shall never sufficiently lament the execution of two beautiful females, scarcely arrived at the age of puberty; and so innocent, that to the last moment, they could not be made to understand *why* they were deprived of life! I shall never sufficiently lament

the scandalous exhibition . . . where an infant boy, whose weight being insufficient, was strangled by the strength of ruffians. I can never forget the untimely death of another unhappy *infant girl*, convicted upon the evidence of being seen giddily dancing with an old cloak of Lady Mansfield about her shoulders. Those, Mr. Attorney, are facts, which however trifling, familiar, and necessary to a lawyer, I shall never reflect on but with grief and horror. (P. 12)[41]

Lord George was arrested in Amsterdam, where he had settled in the Jewish quarter and furthered his Jewish education. When his identity was revealed, he was deported back to Britain under Dutch guard. He then removed himself to Birmingham's Jewish community, was circumcised, and formally converted to Judaism. He lived quietly in Birmingham until he again was discovered and, only after the Jewish Sabbath on Saturday, forcibly returned to London and King's Bench prison. There "the disguise and oddity of his figure are so remarkable as almost to defy the recollection of those who formerly knew his Lordship." When sentenced on 8 January 1788, he was dressed like an orthodox Polish Jewish congregant, which made him appear as sartorially incoherent as his defense presentation seemed conceptually incoherent. He seemed "a very grotesque figure, being wrapped up in a great coat, his hair lank as usual, his beard about three inches long, extending under his chin and throat from ear to ear, and differing from the colour of his hair." Gordon now had to pay a £500 fine, post £10,000 as security for fourteen years of good behavior, together with two further sureties of £2,500 each, for which others were bonds on his behalf.[42]

The sentencing itself generated repeated insults. Justice Ashurst addressed both Lord George and Thomas Wilkins, the printer of Gordon's pamphlet, concerning the prisoners awaiting transportation to Botany Bay. George III soon pardoned Wilkins, but since Gordon was a repeat and apparently uneducable offender, he had no such luck. He was guilty of "low, scurrilous and indecent abuse." His paragraph in the *Public Advertiser* was "calculated most daringly to asperse the character of Her Most Christian Majesty the Queen of France, by imputing to her great tyranny and oppression." Such stuff, "written with malevolence and wicked intention," endangered the "peace and tranquility" between the two nations. Less enlightened nations not graced with British freedom and liberty of the press might think that Lord George spoke for the government rather than as an individual.[43]

The sentencing continued to ignore the ancient and ongoing hostility between the two nations, made worse by French aid to rebel Americans. Sir James Harris spoke for many when in 1786 he told Pitt what he and other Britons long knew: the untrustworthy French are "an ambitious and restless rival power . . . whose enmity we have the most to apprehend." Harris also told Sir Robert Murray Keith that France sought allies, "the object of which is the Destruction of England." Indeed, as one historian has put it, "from 1787 onwards . . . a resumption of hostilities was regarded as likely."[44]

The court pretended to believe Prime Minister Pitt's naive, or fabricated, notion that the commercial treaty would bring at least temporary peace and prosperity to both nations. Aside from Bordeaux's vintners, protectionist French merchants were either suspicious or sternly hostile. Arthur Young reported from Lisle: "The cry here for a war with England amazed me." The chief of many reasons for war with Britain was "the commercial treaty, which is execrated here, as the most fatal stroke to their manufactures they ever experienced."[45] The court's apparently wilful ignorance of predictable response and its own pretense were explained by Justice Ashurst's stark sentence: Lord George must be removed because "it is in the power of the Law to take from evil-minded men the ability of doing mischief, and to restrain them of that liberty which they so grossly abuse."[46] The mischief clearly did not relate to a paragraph regarding France and Marie Antoinette. By 1788 Britain was understandably concerned regarding a possible violent dynastic change in the nation that sought at the least Britain's significant diminution. That mischief related instead to a dangerous man who would not otherwise be silenced and who might repeat the outrages of 1780. Whatever the excuse, Lord George must not be allowed to do that again. The enormous penalties would amount to a death sentence.

Some lamented but many applauded the obvious severity and its outcome, presumably well deserved for a worse than Dissenter. The *New Annual Register* for 1788 was pleased that Lord George "was now suffering in his Jewish gabardine." One nominal poet parodied Burke, rejoicing that "we have him safe in jail" and "there we'll keep him fast" and penalize the alien's bad manners: "We'll teach the *Rabbin* to call whore." *The Christian Turned Jew* gleefully played upon Gordon's new dietary restrictions: "So forward my Lord, since to Newgate you're taken, / You may find it hard to save your own bacon." Burke's vulgar and unworthy remarks found him oddly in agreement with Tom Paine. His view of the rights of man did not extend to a lunatic properly incarcerated in a bedlam called Newgate. Paine knew that the libel was an excuse, not a fact. "It was a madman that libelled—and that is sufficient apology; and it afforded an opportunity for confining him, which was the thing that was wished for."[47]

The prison rigors continued in spite of the sentence's termination. On 28 January 1793 he returned to the court with two poor Jewish tradesmen willing to stand as his bondsmen, but the court rejected their insufficient funds. Lord George no longer was the elegant, handsomely dressed aristocrat of his 1781 trial, in which he was defended by the cream of senior and rising attorneys. He no longer even was the defeated Lord George passionately arguing for amelioration of the bloody code that hanged pubescent girls and strangled boys for insignificant thefts they did not know they had committed. He was instead the odd outsider accompanied by other odd outsiders. Lord George

> was brought from Newgate into the court of King's Bench, accompanied by the keeper, two men as his bail, and several Jews. He had a large slouched hat on his head, and a beard of enormous length. He was ordered to take off his hat, which he refused. The court directed the cryer to take it off, which he did accordingly. Lord George desired the court to take notice, that his hat had been taken off by violence.[48]

He fruitlessly urges Jewish writers as authorities for his covered head. When that fails, he replaces the hat with "a white cap . . . and tied a handkerchief over it" in the Jewish way, appropriate for Yisrael Avraham George Gordon. Lloyd Kenyon, his defense attorney in 1781, adds that "if I had been in the Court, I should have directed your hat to be taken off." When the judge denies bail, "lord George was remanded, till he could procure better bail." The defendant acknowledged the unspoken subtext: "the Court really intended imprisonment for life when they demanded such excuses and unprecedented bail," which all knew meant a death sentence. John Howard stated the obvious in 1777 and repeated it in 1784: many more prisoners than the 678 executed between 1749 and 1772 were killed by jail fever. "This frequent effect of confinement in prisons seems generally understood." Charles Dickens later observed that the French sought "warmly to procure his release—which I think they might have done, but for Lord Grenville" and almost certainly with Pitt's concurrence.[49] Reformist and radical groups were in full throat. The London Corresponding Society was founded in 1792. The king issued his Royal Proclamation Against Seditious Writing in May and in December indicted Tom Paine, found him guilty of treason, and allowed him to escape to France. Neither Crown nor ministry wanted to see Lord George in the streets rallying domestic Jacobins.

Gordon behaved nobly in Newgate, where he purchased a private room and relieved the grief of other prisoners with food, talk, and music. He received exalted guests as if he were being visited at a ducal levee, wrote many letters and pamphlets on behalf of causes he held dear, and ineffectually sought French diplomatic help to secure his release from prison. He held Jewish services on Saturday with a minyan of ten fellow Polish Jewish worshipers. He wrote about the Old Testament as the basis for the British Test, Corporation, and Settlement acts. He deserved P. W. Hall's compliment that "a virtuous Jew is better than a profane Christian." To the degree possible, he tried to atone for the horrors of June 1780 that he had instigated. He nonetheless became more radicalized in prison and was not moved by the death of Marie Antoinette. He already had written successfully on behalf of the Athol Highlanders, who were wrongly being sent to protect the East India Company, were willing to mutiny if forced to go, and instead were rightly demobilized. In November of 1784 he also rallied English Protestant sailors to go to war on behalf of the Dutch against the Catholic Austrian Empire.[50] He thereby yet again showed himself a continuing and dangerous force able to mobilize soldiers in his debt and sailors to his aggressive wishes.

We recall that as late as 1792 he boasted of helping Scottish Presbyterians to replace Irish Catholics in Dublin; that city also could feel "the effects of my anti-papistic zeal." His government would not allow that possibility. Britain, at deadly war with the France supposedly its dear friend and trading partner, turned to more important matters. After so many traumatic events, so much destruction and death regarding Lord George's influence, after so much violation of judicial equity and Christian mercy by the Church of England, the ominous Lord George succumbed to jail fever and received one sentence in the *European Magazine*'s Monthly Obituary for 1793: "In Newgate, aged 41, the Hon. George Gordon, brother of the present and third son of the late duke of Gordon, commonly called by courtesy lord George Gordon." I suspect that the Jewish community feared persecution if it allowed him to be buried in its cemetery, probably at Mile End. He was interred with virtual secrecy in a vault in St. James's burial grounds on the Hampstead Road. As yet another cosmic irony or insult, St. James's was an Anglican church from which he had been excommunicated.[51]

Some were elegiac rather than triumphant. Henry Redhead Yorke put it movingly regarding the hopeless in those "monstrous caverns": Lord George was "doomed in the full vigour of his days, to count a life of imprisonment, and to slide gradually into the mansions of death." Charles Pigott knew that the human body was not capable of lasting long "against the tainted air and complicated horrors of Newgate." He thus was troubled by Gordon's legal persecution and the illicit and unconstitutional bail. "He died through the rigour of his imprisonment." The *New Annual Register* for 1793 recorded his death in a sentence even less adorned than that in the *European Magazine*: "Nov. 1. In Newgate, lord George Gordon."[52] His ghost would have to wait until 1795 to be resurrected by another passionate believer.

True Colors: Robert Watson's *Life of Lord George Gordon*

The radical republicanism sometimes present in Gordon's and in dissenting Protestant rhetoric is writ large in Robert Watson's later *Life of Lord George Gordon* (1795). Watson was Lord George's secretary prior to and during the turmoil. He wrote the *Life* while in prison for fomenting riots against the Militia Act in 1794. A domestic and international opposition career brought him many wounds but neither friends nor money. He garotted himself in 1838, before he could read Dickens' characterization of him as the manipulative, unlovely Gashford in *Barnaby Rudge* (1841).

Watson's *Life* of Gordon is a vibrant document inspired by mingled revolutionary fervor and anger at social injustice. It also accurately perceived the government's intentions regarding Lord George. Having failed to arrest or contain him early in the troubles, it compounded its error by later charging him with treason and waging war against the Crown, for which he was acquitted. The Crown later corrected its error with the unyielding penalties we have seen. We recall the *Gentleman's Magazine*'s sharp tack away from judgment, which in fact became a judgment on the British legal system: "With respect to the severity of his sentence, and the bail demanded for his liberation, we are silent." The *Gentleman's Magazine*, Watson, and Gordon himself had it right. As Watson said, "It was easy to foresee that it [persecution] would never terminate but with the life of the noble democrat," an event in which the Church of England tried to participate.[53]

In ways, Watson's French Revolutionary–era *Life* is a compendium of the charges and strategies we have seen from about 1778 to 1782. His language often adapts the Protestants' own adaptation of High Church and other earlier eighteenth-century verbal fervors. Lord George's mode of truth, for example, was "like a rapid torrent" (p. 3); he knew that the "*slaves*" of rejoined church and state would "deluge the world with blood" (p. 89); the Protestants formed a "national bulwark" to defend British religion (p. 13). The American war "sullied the character of Britons," led to massive and unpayable debts and taxes (p. 9), and saw British swords "reeking with the blood of their murdered brethren"—that is, of fellow Protestants (p. 45).

Moreover, repeal of the anti-Catholic laws rewarded the papists' "attachment to arbitrary power" and their contributions to the American war (p. 9). The repeal itself was "hurried through the House" the better to find new troops and supplies to prosecute "an unhappy civil war" (p. 10). Parliament so rushed because it wanted the people neither to know it nor discuss it: "the mischief was done before their eyes were opened" (p. 14). Scotland became the model for England's attempt to void the repeal. The Scots' legal petition to government for reconsideration was received with "studied neglect," which induced riots, destruction, and potential insurrections. All these were stopped only by Lord George's intervention and by the government's capitulation (pp. 10–12). The English Dissenters, rather than the established church, saw this success and formed their own Association, with Lord George as president. He himself was opposed to mobs, rioting, and destruction, all induced by French agents, who encouraged the infiltrating bandits, and papists, who did the dirty work (pp. 22, 29). The ministry allowed the upheavals in order to discredit the Protestant Association (p. 22), which was pristine regarding such violence: no Association members were arrested, killed, or hanged (p. 27). The ministry and government, whether Tory or Whig, cared only for their own power and benefits rather than for "the happiness of the people" (p. 69), to whose freedom they were and are hostile (pp. 4, 22).

Watson raised the decibels, but much of his *Life* of Gordon sings the Protestants' earlier song, as well as Thomas Erskine's persuasive defense of Gordon in 1781. Much else, however, makes overt and enlarges the Protestants' sometimes sub rosa darker, ominous tones. By 1795 America of course was lost. The Bastille had fallen. The French Revolution was in full sanguine bloom. The Terror had guillotined many thousands, who no doubt preferred to keep a good head on their bad shoulders. New constitutions were being formulated in France and the United States and perhaps were contemplated even on the British side of the Channel. Minds had become concentrated indeed. The Protestants of 1780 urged their loyalty to the House of Hanover and to the principles of limited constitutional monarchy enshrined in 1688. They thus often disguised or diminished their republicanism. Watson strips the veil and more fully places radical politics within the Protestant Association's scheme in general and Lord George's scheme in particular.

Some motivation is vengeance—if not by the Protestants, certainly for Watson. The associators themselves caused no damage, but they should have, and in any case they enjoyed their tormentors' pain. "For many days a dreadful vengeance threatened the guilty city." That was good and proper. "The great Law-lords" who cruelly punished "their unfortunate fellow creatures" now suffered "just retribution" or flight (pp. 21–22). The government had best not unleash its own *"Church and King mobs,"* for once the "long oppressed"—like the Protestants—took arms, "they generally turn them against the Authors of their misfortune" (p. 51n*). By 1795 Watson had a terrifying and clear analogy with such a rebellion in France. Nature designed us to be happy. The malicious union of church and state has made us the miserable slaves of those who delight in blood, slaughter, and human gore. Then on 14 July 1789 "the pillars of superstition were shaken . . . and the thunderbolt of reason hurled despotism from its throne." This pleased Lord George, who was wrongly suffering in Newgate, his British version of the Bastille (pp. 90–91). The incendiary scheme might well have been part of his own plan. If not, so far as Watson could see, it deserved to be.

Lord George, we read, was keen on Quakers, but not on their passivity toward tyrants (p. 58). The aggressive rather than accommodating urge characterized Watson's Gordon. He could have ordered Pitt's house to be torn down, but tactically desisted so as not to give the government an excuse to intervene (p. 51). Lord George refused Catholic Lord Petre's attempt to coax him out of the Association's presidency. A different leader might have been personally ambitious enough to start a civil war (p. 16). In each case the scarcely unspoken message is that Lord George could destroy the homes of enemies or create insurrection if he so wished. Then as now, those enemies should be careful and comply. Gordon himself encouraged the awareness that dynastic change could become regicide. He insisted that there was "a window at Whitehall that kings should often think of" and that they should contemplate the platform at which Charles I was beheaded.[54]

Gordon threatened a less fatal outcome. There were serious consequences to George III's disloyal establishment of popery, which threatened British political and religious freedom. At Lord George's trial, William Hay testified that Gordon spent much time reading the penal laws of Charles II, William and Mary, and George II, after which he observed of George III: "That by his Majesty's giving his assent to the Quebec law, and the late act tolerating the Roman Catholics in England, his Counsellors had brought him to that pass or situation in which James II was after his abdication." George III had violated his coronation oath and must be held accountable.[55] Two of what we may call monarchic moments suggest Watson's view of Gordon's true radicalism.

In one, Gordon has an audience with George III in St. James's but is demonstrably in charge and demonstrably threatening. He promptly "bolted the door very deliberately and in a solemn tone" reminded his monarch that the Stuarts had been banished "for encouraging Popery and arbitrary power." Gordon then "requested that he would order his ministers to support the Protestant Petitions." King George says that he had nothing to do with that act, and Gordon contradicts him: he gave "his royal assent to it." One of the royally appointed judges also corresponded with a Catholic bishop "for the diabolical purpose of arming the Papists against the Colonies in America." Blather about enlightenment coming from the legislature and from establishment pulpits was false and base. Gordon continues to hector the king, who continues to evade his questions and affirms only that "he was a Protestant" (p. 19). By the end of the episode, Lord George has locked King George's door, threatened him with deposition and exile, and in effect called him a liar. Gordon also insisted that the royal legal bench and established church were engaged in seditious activities and were arming enemies against their own distant brothers. Assuming that Watson's tale is true, the great wonder is that even though Lord George was a powerful duke's son, he was not promptly arrested for *lèse majesté*.

Lord George's second Watsonian brush with royal power was epistolary. On 23 August 1791 he wrote to M. le President Abbé Gregoire, of the French National

Assembly's Committee of Reports. He advises Gregoire regarding what the French government should do to the captured Louis XVI and the royal government he represents. As we have seen, some of Watson's text refurbishes familiar Protestant Association language, and some abandons the Association's real or posed loyalty on behalf of radical republicanism. The Association, however, regularly affirmed its good Whiggish principles and loyalty to the Williamite revolution. That confirmed the Protestantism and anti-Catholicism that the current administration had foolishly diminished. Watson's Lord George would have nothing to do with such a tactic. His startling position recalls the republican option contemplated in 1688.

What to do with Louis now? France is in the same situation that England was in when it rid itself of the tyrant James II. It had then wrongly continued monarchy "upon the sinful scheme the English fell into ... of making a stranger, a foreigner, a Prince of Orange, a King over them." Instead of the post–Charles II corrupt politics, the French should declare "your independence of Louis XVI, upon the model of the United States of America, throwing off the house of Hanover." Louis XVI is as much a traitor as James II, "and his bringing back to Paris, puts him now exactly in the predicament of Charles I. when brought back from Windsor to London, for high treason and perjury" (p. 115). Bluntly, Louis XVI must be executed. The National Convention tried him for treason, found him guilty, and guillotined him on 21 January 1793, nine days before the thirtieth of January on which Charles I was beheaded. Whether or not Lord George was pleased by the approximate dates, he must have been pleased with the event, with which he apparently had been threatening his own monarch.

Watson's Lord George was heroic, charismatic, brave, intelligent, stoical, self-composed, freedom-loving, and "one of the most extraordinary persons of the age" (p. [1]). He also was destructive, self-destructive, self-important, self-deluded, perhaps variously demented, and certainly the representative of political change based upon extraparliamentary coercive mass action. There were indeed changes afoot in British politics. Watson's Gordon saw them this way: "the Despots of the Earth perceive the change, they dread their fate and tremble" (p. 3). Whether or not George III was trembling, the British government and its people chose their own ways of healing and of compromise. In some cases that process was perversely aided by malign, if self-protective, repression, as with Lord George and more overt Jacobin movements in Britain.

Power always seeks to preserve itself in ways other than polite or even rude exchange. That is why the state and its church, so far as they were able, combined in morally, politically, and legally malign ways to put Lord George away for good in death as in life. To avoid pilgrimage to the martyr's tomb, he was quietly buried in as inconspicuous a place as minimal discretion toward a ducal family would allow. We remember George Santayana's long familiar commonplace: those who forget the past are condemned to repeat it. In 1787 the British church and state remembered the 1780 past, ignored justice, and refused to allow its entrepreneur of mobs to repeat it.

After a few years Lord George also was buried, or almost barred, from literature.[56] Once the French Revolution entered its aggressively invasive martial phase, Britons had more pressing threats of revolution with which to contend. Gordon's cause abandoned him and rendered him irrelevant. Horace Walpole looked back upon the riots and lamented, "A capital blazing and held in terror for a week by so contemptible a rabble, will not tell well in story!"[57] Even Charles Dickens' story could not raise Gordon very far into Victorian prominence. He was made irrelevant again and scarcely even the hero of his own riots. One way in which evolution works is to ignore or discard its past and its errors so that it can improve the future. The dinosaurs "live" only in film, in museums, and as pet lizards. In *Barnaby Rudge* Lord George played second fiddle to a crow.

NOTES

1. Gordon writes on behalf of European Jews in *Copy of a Letter from the Right Honourable Lord George Gordon to E. Lindo, Esq. And the Portuguese, and N. Salomon, Esq.* (London, 1783), and in *To W. Smith, Esq. M. P. Chairman of the Meeting in Support of the People of Poland, at the London Tavern* (London, 1792). He attacks slavery in *House of Commons! Extract of a Letter, dated Thursday the 26th of April, 1792, from George Gordon, In Newgate, to Henry Addington, the Speaker of the House of Commons, on the Subject under Consideration* ([London, 1792]); even Wilberforce is too timid and inferior to the Quakers. See the discussion within for the *Prisoners' Petition to the Right Hon. Lord George Gordon, to Preserve Their Lives and Liberties, and Prevent Their Banishment to Botany Bay* (London, 1787) and the *Athol Highlanders* (1793).

2. *Gentleman's Magazine* 63 (1793): 1056.

3. Horace Walpole, The Yale Edition of Horace Walpole's Correspondence, ed. W. S. Lewis, vol. 25, *Sir Horace Mann and Sir Horace Mann the Younger. IX*, ed. W. S. Lewis et al. (New Haven, CT: Yale University Press, 1971), p. 62 (hereafter cited as YEW by volume, title, and editor).

4. *A Reply to an Appeal from the Protestant Association to the People of Great Britain* (London, 1780), p. 19 (century, genial); *An Address to the President of the Protestant Association* (London, 1782), p. 59; Felix McCarthy, *A Serious Answer to Lord George Gordon's Letters to the Earl of Shelbourne . . . and . . . the Salvation of the State* ([London], 1780), pp. 33 (true), 53 (total), 54 (certain).

5. Thomas Holcroft, *A Plain and Succinct Narrative of the Late Riots and Disturbances in the Cities of London and Westminster and Borough of Southwark* (London, 1780), p. 11. One

aspect of the Anglo-Scottish turmoil during the civil war anticipated a key error in the years 1778–80. In 1637 Charles I and Archbishop Laud attempted to bring the Church of Scotland into the Church of England by means of a shared Book of Common Prayer and a Book of Canons to replace John Knox's *Book of Discipline*. Monarch and archbishop consulted with neither the Kirk nor the Scottish parliament, a tactical error all too like the government's indifference to its populace prior to the Gordon Riots and their grave results. The earlier Scottish outrage at such disrespect induced the Presbyterian Covenant of 1638 and the Solemn League and Covenant in 1643–44, designed to help Charles I fight the threat of Irish Catholic troops. The collapse of the royalist cause and apparent Scottish self-serving never were forgotten south of Hadrian's Wall. For a fuller discussion, see David Stevenson, *The Scottish Revolution, 1637–1644: The Triumph of the Covenanters* (New York: St. Martin's Press, 1977).

6. [A Real Friend to Religion and to Britain], *Fanaticism and Treason: Or, A Dispassionate History of the Rise, Progress, and Suppression of the Rebellious Insurrections In June 1780* (London, 1780), pp. 3–4 (hereafter cited parenthetically in the text).

7. *The Flames of Newgate; Or, The New Ministry* (London, 1782), pp. 3 (High), 2 (Cur'd).

8. McCarthy, *Serious Answer*, p. 57; George Gordon, *A Letter from Lord George Gordon in Newgate to Baron de Alvensleben, Minister from Hanover, Grosvenor Square* (London, 1792), pp. 2 (grievously), 8 (interrupted).

9. *The Beauties of the British Senate: Taken from the Debates of the Lords and Commons, From . . . Walpole, to . . . Pitt* (London, 1786), 1:82. The remarks are included in the "Attack" section and, according to the title page, were among the "MOST IMPORTANT AND TRULY INTERESTING" speeches during that period. By 1783 Gordon seems already to have been more than usually attracted to Old Testament history and theology, as with *Innocence Vindicated and the Intrigues of Popery and its Abettors displayed. . . . Part I*, 2nd ed. (London, 1783): he performed his actions in 1780 "to promote the glory of the God of Israel, and the people" (p. 8; see also p. 9). In *Innocence Vindicated. . . . Part II*, 2nd ed. (London, 1783), Gordon likened himself to Moses, and George III to Pharaoh (pp. 17–18).

10. Copy of a letter from Gordon to Lord North, 3 September 1781, as in "Appendix to the Chronicle," *The Annual Register, or A View of the History, Politics, and Literature for the Year 1781* (London, 1782), p. 245. Gordon also wrote to Lord Southampton, the Prince of Wales' groom of the stole, seeking an interview with the prince for a comparable purpose. In each case the answer was no. On 14 September Lord George tried to deliver his book to the monarch at St. James's, but without royal permission. He was refused. He appeared at the royal levee without the book and was told that his Majesty "did not think proper to admit Lord Geo. Gordon into his presence, to present *any* book announced by *such* a letter" to Lord North (p. 246).

11. In spite of modest movement toward toleration, Jewish subjects often remained even further beyond the pale than Catholics. Elizabeth Sarah Villa-Real Gooch was among the many talented later eighteenth- and early nineteenth-century women of letters. She also was descended from a Portuguese Jewish father. She observed that "the Laws of England have sufficiently operated against me. . . . The Laws (the boast of Englishmen) have been exercised towards myself with severity, but without justice . . . and have proved a galling yoke of slavery, when they should have served as a barrier against injustice and oppression; and they have fully convinced me, that in this *Christian* Kingdom, as elsewhere, the

hydra of despotism rears his head unabashed if not swayed by a golden sceptre." See Villa-Real Gooch, *The Wanderings of the Imagination* (London, 1796), 1:9.

12. George Gordon, *The Memorial Which the Right Honourable Lord George Gordon... Has Written in the Prison of Newgate* ([London?, 1789?]), p. v; McCarthy, *Serious Answer*, pp. 16 (create), 58 (will be).

13. John Butler, *A Sermon Preached Before the House of Lords at the Abby Church, Westminster, on Tuesday, January 30, 1787* (London, 1787), p. 10. As with most published thirtieth of January sermons by then, the title page lacked a black border.

14. This information regarding excommunication comes from Giles Jacob and John Morgan, *A New Law'Dictionary: Containing the Interpretation and Definition of Words and Terms used in the Law*, 10th ed. (London, 1782), s.v. "excommunication." For Blackstone, below, see *Commentaries on the Laws of England*, 5th ed. (Oxford, 1773), 3:103 and esp. 4:199: excommunication "by writ *de excommunicato capiendo*" was among those crimes "clearly not admissible to bail by the justices." The excommunication documents remain undiscovered. I have not yet been able to find them at either the London Metropolitan Archives or the Lambeth Palace archives. Much of the non-written process is likely to have been done with episcopal and ministerial winks and nods. The germane royal Domestic Papers at Kew and the scattered documents of Bishop Lowth of London and Archbishop Moore of Canterbury remain unexplored regarding this matter.

15. The excommunication was anticipated and predicted in the *Public Advertiser* for 5 May 1786 in *Hendry v. Kidd*. The paragraph above is quoted from *Yorkshire Magazine* 1 (1786): 157. It appeared as well in the *General Evening Post* and the *London Chronicle* for 6 May 1786, the *Public Advertiser* for 8 May, and the *Gazette and New Daily Advertiser* for 9 May, no doubt among other places. The paragraph is virtually identical in all places. No wonder that on 23 November the *Public Advertiser* reported that "we have from Authority, that the Archbishop of Canterbury is going to proceed to the confinement of Lord George Gordon." Article 33 of the Thirty-Nine Articles is *"Of Excommunicate Persons, how they are to be avoided."* Such a person is to be treated as a "Heathen and Publican, until he be openly reconciled by Penance, and received into the Church by a Judge that hath Authority thereunto." Lord George of course hardly wished to be received into the Church of England. For the relevant ecclesiastical laws, see Edmund Gibson, *Codex juris ecclesiastici anglicani: Or, the Statutes, Constitutions, Canons, Rubricks and Articles, of the Church of England*, 2nd ed. (London, 1761), 2:1049–64, 1049 quoted above. Contumacy was so familiar an offense, especially regarding civil matters, that from Queen Elizabeth's reign forward the church sought to establish a separate and less severe category, *De contumace capiendo* instead of *De excommunicato capiendo*. This required an act of Parliament that apparently was not forthcoming. See *Codex juris ecclesiastici anglicani* 2:1049 n. d.1, and 1059n.

16. Robert Watson, *The Life of Lord George Gordon: With A Philosophical Review of His Political Conduct* (London, 1795), p. 67.

17. On excommunication, see Jacob and Morgan, *New Law-Dictionary*; on Italian opera, *Morning Herald*, 29 May 1786; on Lord Sydney, *Public Advertiser*, 18 May 1786.

18. George Gordon, *Public Advertiser*, 8 May 1786; Robert Jenner, *Public Advertiser*, 6 May 1786; Calvinus Minor, as a voice of the Protestant Association and perhaps by Archibald Bruce, *An Appeal from Scotland in which the Spiritual Court of the Church of England, is Demonstrated to be Opposite to the British Constitution, and a Part and Pillar of*

Popery (London, [1788]), pp. 17–18; Sir James Fitzjames Stephen, *A History of the Criminal Laws of England* (1883; reprint, New York: Burt Franklin, [1964]), 2:413. Stephen also thinks that Gordon's acquittal for constructive treason "was right" and that Gordon "was guilty of nothing more than hare-brained and criminal folly in leading unlawful assembly" (2:274). He does not consider Thomas Erskine's often inflammatory anti-Catholic peroration.

19. *European Magazine* 10 (1786): 63. As a sign of widespread interest in the case, the news was reported both in the *London Chronicle* and the *Whitehall Evening Post* on 21 November and in the *Public Advertiser* and the *Morning Herald* on 23 November.

20. Calvinus Minor, *Appeal from Scotland*, p. 18: "Persons who happen to incur their [tyrannical and resentful ecclesiastics'] displeasure [are] without bail." For Blackstone, see n. 14 above.

21. Philo Veritas, *A Letter to His Grace the Archbishop of Canterbury, Occasioned by the Excommunication of the Right Honourable Lord George Gordon* (London, [1786]), p. 3 (hereafter cited parenthetically in the text).

22. John Roe, *A Letter From the Rev. John Roe, Minister of the Protestant Dissenters at Calverton, near Nottingham. Concerning the Imprisonment of their Wives, for Life, for Nonconformity to the Church of England, by force of the Writ Excommunicato Capiendo. Addressed to the Rt. Hon. Ld. Geo^e Gordon, President of the Protestant Association* (Nottingham, 1789). The wives had been imprisoned for twenty-one months "in a loathsome stinking prison, bereft of their children and all their friends" (p. 6). The pamphlet's angry tone regularly is reinforced by biblical example and analogy. "Kings and all others, should beware of persecuting any in any wise, and especially beware of taking any man's wife from him, lest they die" (p. 13). A putative illicit marriage, however, was an offense subject to excommunication.

23. *European Magazine* 12 (1787): 74 (Buller); 11 (1787): 130 (without). On modern and even eighteenth-century standards these trials were malicious prosecution. See Douglas Hay, "Prosecution and Power: Malicious Prosecution in the English Courts, 1750–1850," in *Policing and Prosecution in Britain, 1750–1850*, ed. Douglas Hay and Francis Snyder (Oxford: Clarendon Press, 1989), pp. 343–95.

24. The putative Comte Alessandro de Cagliostro was the Italian charlatan Giuseppe Balsamo (1743–95), whom Goethe discusses in his *Italienische Reise (Italian Journey)*, of 1786–87, published in 1816–17. Cagliostro outlined his case and Gordon's English role in his *Lettre du comte de Cagliostro au peuple anglois, pour servir de suite à ses mémoires* ([London?], 1786), pp. 41–48. At least one person thought his meeting with Gordon detrimental to Cagliostro's fortunes. See Lucia (pseud.), *The Life of the Count Cagliostro. . . . Dedicated to Madame la Comtesse de Cagliostro* (London, 1787), pp. 97–101: "Every sincere well-wisher to the Count must lament his intimacy with a nobleman whose illfated enthusiasm has justly rendered him an object of universal censure" (p. 100). Throughout 1786, and occasionally beyond, the *Courier de l'Europe* waged a relentless war against Cagliostro as an Italian fraud, imposter, and imposer upon aristocracy.

25. *Appendix to the Trials of Lord George Gordon, and Thomas Wilkins, For Libels* ([London, 1788]), p. 5.

26. *Treaty of Navigation and Commerce Between His Britannick Majesty and The Most Christian King. Signed at Versailles, the 26th of September 1786* (London, 1786); William Pitt, *The Speech of the Right Honourable William Pitt, in the House of Commons, February 12, 1787* (London, 1787); *Convention Between His Britannick Majesty and The Most Christian King.*

Signed at Versailles, the 31st of August, 1787 (London, 1787). For discussion of the treaty, see W. O. Henderson, "The Anglo-French Commercial Treaty of 1786," *Economic History Review*, n.s., 10 (1975): 104–12; and Marie Donaghay, "The Best Laid Plans: French Execution of the Anglo-French Commercial Treaty of 1786," *European History Quarterly* 14 (1984): 401–22. Henderson's dates for ratification differ from the documents I cite within: signed, 26 September 1786; ratified, 10 November 1786; in force, May 1787. See his "Anglo-French Commercial Treaty," p. 108. Whichever figures one uses, Gordon's remarks in the *Public Advertiser* could not have affected the treaty, which Charles James Fox, among others, thought detrimental to British interests. The British version of the 1786 Treaty of Navigation in fact is less affectionate and friendly than the French version pretends to be. The British text opens with the factual "His Britannick Majesty, and his most Christian Majesty" (sig. A2^r); the French opens with "notre très-chere & très-amé Frère le Roi de la Grande *Bretagne.*" *Traité de navigation et de commerce entre la France et la Grande-Bretagne. Conclus à Versailles le 26 septembre 1786* (Paris, 1786), sig. Aij^r.

27. Pitt, *Speech of the Right Honourable William Pitt*, pp. 62–63, tally for and against the commercial treaty on p. 67; *Yorkshire Magazine* 1 (1786): 157.

28. *Observations on the Agricultural and Political Tendency of the Commercial Treaty* (London, 1787), p. 29 (ploughman); *Sentiments on the Interests of Great Britain. With Thoughts on the Politics of France, and on the Accession of the Elector of Hanover to the German League* (London, [1787]), pp. 18–19 (Austrian), 24, 25, 49 (Dutch and Germans), 78 (Ireland), 44 (tolerate), 76 (half Frenchmen); *Helps to A Right Decision Upon the Merits of the Late Treaty of Commerce with France. Addressed to the Members of both Houses of Parliament* (London, 1787), p. [3] (general alarm). The French remark appeared in the *Courier de l'Europe* 20, no. 49 (1786): 402: "Ce qu'il y a remarquable dans cette opposition, c'est que les feuilles Angloises, sont, tout à la fois, remplies de commentaires par lesqueles on essaie de prouver le danger de ce Traité pour l'Angleterre." The *Courier* regularly discussed, and favored, the treaty through much of 1786. Anglicanus, *The Necessity and Policy of the Commercial Treaty with France &c. Considered* (London, 1787), p. 61 (much cavilled). Further discussion of course was widespread. As one more example among many, see the *Morning Post and Daily Advertiser*, 20 November 1786, with "Gresham's" complaint regarding the "miserable subterfuges to which a malignant *faction* is driven in its opposition" to the treaty. See also Josiah Tucker, *A Brief Essay on the Advantages & Disadvantages which Respectively Attend France and Great Britain, With Regard to Trade*, 3rd ed. (1753; reprint, London, 1787); and [Dennis O'Bryen], *A View of the Treaty of Commerce with France: Signed at Versailles, September 20, 1786. By Mr. Eden* (London, 1787). The latter was answered by the unsigned *Short Vindication of the French Treaty* (London, 1787).

29. Pitt, *Speech of the Right Honourable William Pitt*, pp. 2 (represented, attended), 57 (pledge, without); *The whole Proceedings on the Trials of Two Informations Exhibited ex Officio by the King's Attorney General against George Gordon, Esq. . . . taken in Short Hand by Joseph Gurney* (London, 1787), pp. 71–72 (unjustly, interrupt); Mr. Thompson, *The Female Amazon, or A Genuine Accgunt [Account] of the Most Remarkable Adventures, and Complicated Intrigues, Displayed in the Life of the Celebrated and Notorious Miss Fanny Davies, the Borough Beauty* (London, 1786), p. 16. Fanny is an excellent thief and prospers during the Gordon Riots. For the French commentary, see M. de la Coste, *Voyages philosophique d'Angleterre, fait en 1783 et 1784* (London [Paris?], 1786), 2:68; see also 69–71, 231. Gordon is

part of "convocations séditieuses." He is "sans principes, libertin, et même crapuleux; mais fanatiques par costume" and exemplifies "l'abus monstreux de la liberté de la presse." De la Coste generally thinks little of English "freedom" or of the justice and penal system that removes such freedom.

30. I quote the oaths from Howard D. Weinbrot, "Johnson and Jacobitism Redux: Evidence, Interpretation, and Intellectual History," *Age of Johnson* 8 (1977): 115–16. For the Irish threat, see *A Letter from Lord George Gordon, to the Corporation of the City of Dublin* (Dublin, 1792), pp. 5 (down with Kings), 7 (fly with haste). Gordon also expressed his republicanism and his antipathy to Edmund Burke in, among other places, the 1792 *To W. Smith, Esq.* (n. 1 above). Gordon had long indicated that he rejected "insidious proposals" and bribes from the North administration. See *Innocence Vindicated.... Part II*, p. 28.

31. Nicholas Carter, *The Obligations of an Oath, and particularly of the Oaths of Allegiance, Supremacy, and Abjuration* (London, 1716), pp. 20–21. The topic remained lively for non-Anglicans. See *A Discourse Delivered in One of the Catholic Chapels, On the Propriety and Necessity of taking the Oath of Allegiance Tendered by Government* (Durham, 1778); and for Presbyterians, *A Copy of a Letter From a Friend, Concerning the Oath of Abjuration* (Edinburgh, 1773).

32. The episode's key moments in print were collected from 1783 news reports and reprinted ten years later, surely as a memorial to Lord George, as *Athol Highlanders. The Following Account is taken From the Public Newspapers, Published in 1783; And is sufficient to demonstrate that the Whole Force of Government Is incompetent to compel the Soldiers of a single Scots Regiment, To Surrender to their Officers, or any Body of Men whatever, Their Rights and Liberties* (London, 1793). The pamphlet begins with Gordon's letter to the Earl of Shelburne and the Highlanders' letter seeking help from Lord George. The episode also is recounted with anger at the ministry and ironic praise of King Geordie in *Six Excellent Songs* (Falkirk, 1783), pp. 2–5, "The Athol Highlanders." For rejection of double jeopardy, see Blackstone, *Commentaries on the Laws of England*, 4:335. John Prebble has a long and helpful discussion of the Athol affair in *Mutiny: Highland Regiments in Revolt, 1743–1804* (London: Secker & Warburg, 1975), pp. 225–59; see pp. 225–28 for the Atholmen and Gordon.

33. By 1787 the Botany Bay matter was known, and perhaps trivialized, in Hamburg, where it was proposed as a subject for a debating society: "Was Lord George Gordon justifiable in *justifying* his *calm* address to the new Colony of Botany Bay—and did he manifest his love of liberty in preferring a residence in Switzerland to St. George's Fields?" See *The English Lyceum, or, Choice of Pieces in Prose and in Verse Selected from the Best Periodical Papers, Magazin[e]s, Pamphlets and other British Publications*, ed. J. W. V. Archenholtz (Hamburg, 1787), 1:364. For other "Gordonia," see *Probationary Odes for the Laureateship*, ed. Sir John Hawkins (London, 1785), pp. xxxv–xxxvi, 108, in parody. The same volume has a parodic poem putatively by Pepper Arden (pp. 35–38).

34. John Howard, *The State of the Prisons in England and Wales, With Preliminary Observations, and An Account of Some Foreign Prisons* (Warrington, 1777), with a third edition in 1784. The dedication reads: "To the Honourable the House of Commons, In Gratitude for the Encouragement Which They Have Given To the Design And For the Honour The House Conferred On The Author, This Book is Respectfully Dedicated By Their Most Obedienct Servant." John Bender discussed prisons and prison reform in his *Imagining*

the *Penitentiary: Fiction and the Architecture of Mind in Eighteenth-Century England* (Chicago: University of Chicago Press, 1987).

35. Josiah Dornford, *Nine Letters to the Right Honourable the Lord Mayor and Aldermen of the City of London, on the State of the City Prisons; With Some Account of Eliz. Gurney, Thomas Trimer, and Robert May, Who "died for want of Care and the common Necessities of Life"* (London, [1786]), pp. 131, 130. In the same year Dornford also published his comparably troubled and troubling *Seven Letters to the Lords and Commons of Great Britain, upon the Impolicy, Inhumanity, and Injustice, of our Present Model of Arresting the Bodies of Debtors; Shewing the Inconsistency of it, with Magna Charta and a Free Constitution* (London, [1786]). He regrets that "no civilized government in Europe but Britain's will endure" such evil conditions and their consequences (p. 6).

36. Giles Jacob, *A New Law-Dictionary: Containing the Interpretation and Definition of Words and Terms used in the Law; and also the Whole Law, and the Practice thereof, Under all the Heads and Titles of the same*, 8th ed. (London, 1762). See also n. 14 above for the later Jacob-Morgan version, in 1782. I cite this text to suggest the longevity of the libel law's indifference to presumed truth.

37. *A Complete Collection of State Trials and Proceedings for High Treason and Other Crimes and Misdemeanors*, ed. Thomas Jones Howell (London, 1826), 22:176 (hereafter cited parenthetically in the text).

38. See Douglas Hay's valuable essay "The Laws of God and the Laws of Man: Lord George Gordon and the Death Penalty," in *Protest and Survival: Essays for E. P. Thompson*, ed. John Rule and Robert Malcolmson (London: Merlin Press, 1993). *Albion's Fatal Tree: Crime and Society in Eighteenth-Century England*, ed. Douglas Hay, Peter Linebaugh, et al. (London: A. Lane, 1975), includes several other sadly relevant essays.

39. This Sacheverell-like abuse was remembered by Gordon's allies. See P. W. Hall's clumsy but moving *Thoughts and Inquiry on the Principles and Tenor of the Revealed and Supreme Law*—of God that rejects capital punishment for theft or slavery of other humans (London, 1792), p. 168. Hall quotes the Crown's lines regarding its refusal to allow criticism of its laws and considers them a threat to the truths in the Bible, as well as to those who read it and base their lives upon it, like Lord George. See also p. 167, which demolishes the court's defense of British modest punishment: "meaning that we only hang men, as if death and murder were nothing, while that strangling method only was used." Hall was a participant in the rally's first and peaceful day; he knew that the later collapse of order had nothing to do with the Protestant Association (pp. 172–74, 175–77). Hall seeks Gordon's release and large compensation for his illegal incarceration and massive, unpayable fine. Hall regards Lord George as an Old Testament prophet like "Isaiah, Jeremiah, and Daniel" (p. 168). This antislavery and anti–capital punishment document needs to be considered in discussion of the Gordon Riots and their aftermath.

In addition to other studies cited in this chapter and in chapter 6 concerning the severity of eighteenth-century law, see Randall McGowen's analysis of the assize sermons and the justice there distributed: "'He Beareth Not the Sword in Vain': Religion and the Criminal Law in Eighteenth-Century England," *Eighteenth-Century Studies* 21 (1987–88): 192–211. Ministers regarded it as their sacred obligation to protect virtue and religion by making examples of malefactors. See also McGowen's "'Making Examples' and the Crisis of Punishment in Mid-Eighteenth-Century England," in *The British and Their Laws in the*

Eighteenth Century, ed. David Lemmings (Woodbridge, Suffolk, UK: Boydell Press, 2005), pp. 182–205. In exercising severity, the clergymen and magistrates were continuing the Restoration practice. Mark Goldie observes: "Many an assize sermon [during the Restoration] became a fruitful occasion for rhetorically yoking priest and magistrate together in a godly cause, the sword of the latter animated by the spiritual admonition of the former" against the "fanatic vermin" ravaging the land. See Goldie, "The Theory of Religious Intolerance in Restoration England," in *From Persecution to Toleration: The Glorious Revolution and Religion in England*, ed. Ole Peter Grell, Jonathan I. Israel, and Nicholas Tyacke (Oxford: Clarendon Press, 1991), p. 331.

40. *European Magazine* 11 (1787): 446 (delivered), 448 (other side).

41. Gordon uses *infant* loosely to mean young boys and girls. He nonetheless was not alone in being appalled by the hangings of children. On 6 July 1780 Horace Walpole told Sir Horace Mann that the condemned included a "woman, a black girl, and two or three escaped convicts." On 24 July he wrote that "dissatisfaction grows again . . . on the number of boys that have been executed for the riots, for the bulk of the criminals are so young, that half a dozen schoolmasters might have quashed the insurrection." Walpole, YEW, vol. 25, *Sir Horace Mann and Sir Horace Mann the Younger. IX*, pp. 67 and 75, respectively; for the ages of the children hanged, see 75n2.

42. Israel Solomons, "Lord George Gordon's Conversion to Judaism," in *The Jewish Historical Society of England: Transactions Sessions, 1911–1914* (London: Ballantyne, Hanson & Co., 1915); *Papers Read before the Jewish Historical Society of England, June 2, 1913* 7 (1911–14): 246 (disguise), quoting from Felix Farley's *Bristol Journal*, "Lord George Gordon turned Jew." Solomons' article remains a valuable contribution to Gordon's story. *European Magazine* 13 (1788): 140 (grotesque). Dominic Green is at work on a new life of Gordon, which is likely to include additional information on Gordon's conversion. For a preview, see Green, "George Gordon: A Biographical Reassessment," in The Gordon Riots: Politics, Culture and Insurrection in Late Eighteenth-Century Britain, ed. Ian Haywood and John Seed (Cambridge: Cambridge University Press, 2012), pp. 245–64.

43. *Appendix to the Trials of Lord George Gordon*, pp. 3 (low), 2 (calculated, written, peace), 5 (liberty of the press). Wilkins' royal pardon and Gordon's continued incarceration were reported in *European Review* 14 (1788): 176. See also 16 (1789): 280 for a copy of Gordon's letter to the French National Assembly requesting intervention on his behalf: he sought only French liberty and alleviation of tyranny and relied on the words of French subjects seeking his help. The Assembly accepted the letter without comment and relegated it to the archives.

44. For Harris to Pitt and to Keith, see Jeremy Black, *Natural and Necessary Enemies: Anglo-French Relations in the Eighteenth Century* (London: Duckworth, 1986), p. 70; the quotation regarding war is from p. 80.

45. Arthur Young, *Travels During the Years 1787, 1788, and 1789 Undertaken more particularly with a View of Ascertaining . . . the Kingdom of France* (Bury St. Edmunds, 1792), p. 73. Bordeaux and Guibry were more optimistic (pp. 42, 79); Amiens and Lyons, among other cities, were hostile or concerned (pp. 6, 262). The *Travels* appeared in French in 1793 and 1794 and in German in 1793–95. Young's distinction as an agricultural innovator made his observations especially valuable.

46. *Appendix to the Trials of Lord George Gordon*, p. 5.

47. *New Annual Register, or General Repository of History, Politics, and Literature, For the Year 1788* (London, 1789), p. 79; "Reflections on Reflections," in *An Asylum For Fugitive Pieces: In Prose and Verse, not in any other Collection*, comp. [John Almon], (London, 1793), p. 51, parodying Burke, for which see below; "A Copy of Verses," in *The Christian Turned Jew. Being the most Remarkable Life and Adventures of Lord G. G. With the Letter sent to him by a certain Great Lady, since his Confinement* (London, [1790?]), p. 8; Edmund Burke, *Reflections on the Revolution in France, and on the Proceedings of Certain Societies in London Relative to that Event* (London, 1790), p. 125: let Lord George in Newgate "meditate on his Thalmud . . . until some persons from your side of the water, to please your new Hebrew brethren, shall ransom him." Gordon the "Protestant Rabbin" might use the long-hoarded compound interest on thirty pieces of silver to purchase "the lands which are lately discovered to have been usurped by the Gallican church." Tom Paine, *The Rights of Man, Part I*, in *A Comparative Display of the Different Opinions of the Most Distinguished British Writers on the . . . French Revolution* (London, 1793), 1:202.

48. *The New Annual Register . . . For the Year 1793* (London, 1794), p. 5.

49. *New Annual Register . . . For the Year 1793*, p. 5 (white cap); Solomons, "Lord George Gordon's Conversion to Judaism," p. 214 (If I had); *New Annual Register . . . For the Year 1793*, p. 6 (lord George); Christopher Hibbert, *King Mob: The Story of Lord George Gordon and the Riots of 1780* (1958; reprint, Thrupp Stroud, Gloucestershire, UK: Sutton, 2004), p. 184. Hibbert speculates, accurately, I believe, that Lord George proudly refused to allow his wealthy family to pay his fines. He had already told his older brother, the duke, that he would not recant his opinions in exchange for freedom: to "sue for pardon was a confession of guilt" (p. 184n1). Howard, *State of the Prisons*, p. 16. The first edition, quoted, cites visits from the years 1773–74 as based on his own observations; the third edition, of 1784, adds 1775 as well (p. 8). In each case he refers to the "vast numbers who to my certain knowledge, some of them before my eyes, have perished in our Gaols" (p. 16); the third edition specifies "perished by the gaol fever," p. 8). For Dickens, see The Pilgrim Edition, *The Letters of Charles Dickens*, vol. 2, *1840–1841*, ed. Madeline House, Graham Storey, and Kathleen Tillotson (Oxford: Clarendon Press, 1969), p. 295, Dickens to John Forster, 3 June 1841. I have not been able to verify Dickens' conjecture, but William Wyndham, Lord Granville, was Pitt's foreign secretary in 1791 and of course part of the program to suppress radical activity. The *Courier de l'Europe* was published in London but also distributed in Paris. Throughout 1780–81 and 1786–87 it was almost uniformly hostile to Lord George, whom it regarded as a maniacal bigot and whose demise and humiliation it was glad to see. If the *Courier* reflected or attempted to influence official French views, Dickens' observation is suspect.

50. Hibbert, *King Mob*, p. 184 (Jewish services); Gordon, *Letter from Lord George Gordon in Newgate to Baron de Alvensleben*, p. 4 (Old Testament precedent). See also Gordon, *Memorial* (n. 12 above), pp. xi, xxv–xviii; Hall, *Thoughts and Inquiry*, p. 173, with p. 172 in defense of Gordon's and Christians' general affections for Jews; *Athol Highlanders*; Watson, *Life of Lord George Gordon*, pp. 45–52 (Dutch), with a characteristically harsh exchange with the ministry, here Pitt.

51. *European Magazine* 24 (1793): 407. The obituary also appeared in other places, as in the *New Annual Register . . . For the Year 1793*, Deaths, p. 60; see Solomons, "Lord George Gordon's Conversion to Judaism," p. 263. Excommunication denied one burial in sacred ground. If he was in fact excommunicated, he was not subject to its punishments.

52. Henry Redhead Yorke, *These are the Times that Try Men's Souls* ([1793]), pp. 32 (monstrous), 54–55 (doomed); Charles Pigott, *Persecution, The Case of Charles Pigott* (London, 1793), p. 41n (against, died); *New Annual Register . . . For the Year 1793*, p. 60.

53. Watson, *Life of Lord George Gordon*, p. 85, by Watson; pp. 131–32 by Gordon. He asks the court to accept his "sureties, unless the Court really intended imprisonment for life, when they demanded such excessive and unprecedented bail." He was correct. Hereafter cited parenthetically in the text.

54. As in John Paul de Castro, *The Gordon Riots* (London: H. Milford and Oxford University Press, 1926), p. 24.

55. *The Annual Register, or A View of the History, Politics, and Literature for the Year 1780* (London, 1781), p. 221. Lloyd Kenyon impeached this testimony as improbable (p. 227). On George III's violation of his coronation oath, see *The Protestant Magazine; Or, Christian Treasury. Designed to Encourage a Perfect Knowledge of the Protestant Religion* 1 (1781): 32, from the Crown's evidence in the trial transcript.

56. Carol Houlihan Flynn has discussed this curious cultural de-memorializing. See her "Whatever Happened to the Gordon Riots?" in *A Companion to the Eighteenth-Century English Novel and Culture*, ed. Paula R. Backscheider and Catharine Ingrassia (Oxford: Blackwell Publishing, 2005), pp. 459–80.

57. Walpole to Mann, 24 July 1780, in YEW, vol. 25, *Sir Horace Mann and Sir Horace Mann the Younger. IX*, p. 76.

CHAPTER EIGHT

Coping, Repairing, and Dickens' Barnaby Rudge

I began the chapters on the Gordon Riots with mingled caveats and questions. If the approximate direction of eighteenth-century British culture was toward amelioration and inclusion, how could the Gordon Riots have happened? Thereafter, how did the culture heal after such trauma? All answers to such questions remain tentative, tenuous, and aware of the abundant brutality in British racism, imperialism, and class conflict throughout the eighteenth and consequent centuries. These are among many sad exercises in human moral deficiency. Examples of what I take to be the dominant eighteenth-century evolutionary movement nonetheless also must be acknowledged.

How to Cope? The World after the Gordon Riots

In Denham's *Cooper's Hill* (1668) the king kills a hunted stag as an emblem of his power over man and nature. In Somerville's *The Chace* (1735) the king spares the weeping stag as an emblem both of his power over man and nature and of his recognition of vulnerability, of the sentimental bond between human and animal, and of the monarch's virtual *nolo prosequi*. Political power now includes benevolence. In about 1765 Samuel Johnson reported that when his mother lived in London there were two kinds of people, "those who gave the wall, and those who took it; the peaceable and the quarrelsome." Some aggressively seized the clean part of the street and forced others into the dirt. In contrast, "*now* it is fixed that every man keeps to the right; or, if one is taking the wall, another yields it; and it is never a dispute." Increased peaceful sharing of space was equally true for religion. In 1704 Ned Ward's *All Men Mad: Or, England A Great Bedlam* characterized lunacy in a collapsing world in which a once unified church and state have splintered. Dangerous Dissent has set "the Nation by the Ears." We know that by 1770, however, the French traveler Pierre Jean Grosley was astonished by London's "constant proofs of the mutual toleration amongst all sects." The Church of England "baptizes all that offer, marries all, buries all ... without disturbing the public tranquillity by impertinent enquiries: it considers conscience, as depending immediately upon God: it makes itself all things to all men." Pre–Gordon Riots Grosley could not predict the future but nevertheless acknowledged a then apparent cultural truth. That seeming truth also was behind Parliament's self-congratulatory Catholic amelioration in 1778. We also know that in 1793 Samuel Bradburn asked a once burning question: are the Methodists Dissenters? The answer was no, and the consequences of the question itself were radically different from such a question in, say, 1693: it once would have meant "life or death," but now it is "of little moment." Some of this blessing was the result of political change: William III encouraged toleration and appointed latitudinarian bishops; Queen Anne preserved but moderated the higher Church of England; whether by design, indifference, or ministers' manipulation, the first two Lutheran Hanoverians further solidified Whig government and latitude, which in turn supported the Whig government and the Hanoverian family.[1]

If the hypothesis of evolution as a modest version of moral progress is reasonable, the Gordon Riots are an emblem of a terrible but temporary reversion to a predatory world. They began, after all, in response to a dubiously motivated but still benign attempt to limit bigotry. The nation sought to heal itself in several variously wise but necessary ways. That it did so is suggested in Bradburn's confidence that questions regarding dissent had become "of little moment."

One mode of healing was what I have called cerebration, a discussion of causes, effects, and ways to avoid a future horror. That meant avoiding martial law by means of an effective police force able to establish order without soldiers' firing upon civilians. A cognate issue was energetic inquiry concerning the British constitution. If the military answered to civilian control, did the monarch in fact have the right to empower it for violent domestic duty? Whatever the answer to that question, it was necessary for order to be restored or the capital and the nation might have been crippled. The literate classes thus were forced to consider the nature of moral paradox and compromise, to understand the choice between more or less undesirable bad options, and to attempt to think and behave like thinking and morally behaving adults.

Other beneficial ways of dealing with the riots included rebuilding and acceptance of some military presence. Lord Mansfield's law library and notes could not be replaced, but Newgate could be. Acknowledgment of the essential value of the Bank of England allowed soldiers to be stationed there for almost the next two hundred years. Like the nascent police force, the fire department required improvement. The government also assumed the obligation of a national insurance company and compensated many of the commercial and some private establishments for their losses. By implication, Parliament admitted that it had not properly controlled the riots and that public money should respond to private loss. Responsibility was among the lessons learned.

Less amiable, if still deeply human, modes of coping also were important. After the mad "democratickal" riots, much of the populace rallied behind the government and the military. The legal system's disgraceful abuse of law was obliterated, as in the *Gentleman's Magazine*: "With respect to the severity of his [Gordon's] sentence, and the bail demanded for his liberation, we are silent."[2]

Such relative solidarity behind government and amnesia regarding civil rights would be helpful as the French Revolution, then imperial France, and then internal Jacobins threatened Britain's commercial success and political system. The Gordon Riots at the least contributed to Burke's hostility to the French Revolution: destruction of Newgate was too ominous a precursor of destruction of the Bastille. Once both the riots and Lord George were put down, Britain had more important matters to worry about. The diminished troubles faded from both popular imagination and literary representation. Horace Walpole recognized the brevity of attention span in the face of new grief. On 24 August 1780 he lamented to William Mason:

> The glorious campaigns in the two parks [the armies in St. James's and Hyde Parks] and the vengeance inflicted on a parcel of schoolboys and housemaids, who have been executed for performing a rebellion that was suckled for a week by the whole legislature and by the magistracy of London, are a little obscured already by the entire capture of our East and West Indian fleets by the Spanish squadron.[3]

What once had seemed to be London besieged by all the devils from hell now had become naughty schoolboys and housemaids behaving very badly indeed. The great British Parliament, once the mother of limited government, had become the nurse of unweaned, pubescent rascals. In the relatively short long run, much of Britain dealt with the Gordon Riots by ignoring them about as much as it ignored Gordon's death. The nation agreed to go forward and look forward. Lord George scarcely even pointed a moral or adorned a tale until Charles Dickens took him up and readers laid him down. Indeed, Dickens' *Barnaby Rudge* in 1841 was yet another way in which Britons dealt with the fading memory of the Gordon Riots: Gordon becomes a minor figure in tales of courtship, fathers and sons, a bastard child, a loving mother, her psychologically disabled child, and his magical crow.

Dickens' *Barnaby Rudge*: To Point a Moral but Not Adorn a Tale; The Victorian Retrospective and Punishment by Neglect

Lord George clearly was capable of grief because of the riots and their consequences, but he apparently lacked self-contempt. When negotiating with his past, he was as confident in the Hebrews' Old Testament God as he had been in the Christians' New Testament God. Certainty was a common denominator in each of his belief-sets, as it was in his nuance-free political life. The Calvinist-friendly Old Testament God was congenial for him in many ways. These included God's anger at malefactors, including his own chosen people; the threatening alarmist tones of his prophets; and their regular sense of the personal and national failures of those whom they harangued. Like those prophets, Lord George was most comfortable when uncomfortable, when bravely fighting the forces of internal and external evil. As in the Old Testament mode as well, he spoke truth to power—in the House of Commons, the ministry, and the royal court. Once imprisoned in Newgate, Gordon was handsomely kind to other inmates, held virtual salons, meticulously observed his new religion, and kept a sustained and sustaining correspondence with major political figures and events.

To such a man, being removed from the ranks of movers and shakers was also to be removed from life's active significance. Charles Dickens may have sensed this personal imperative when he conceived *Barnaby Rudge* in 1836 and in effect punished Gordon by making him a bit player in a long tragedy. The novel is historically interesting rather than aesthetically important. It is overly long, complex, and stuffed with extravagant coincidences and artificial devices as moral statements. The last of these is Barnaby's own in-the-nick-of-time reprieve from the gallows, a fictive ploy reminiscent by contrast of Gay's *Beggar's Opera* (1728).[4] Gay has fun with authors' satisfaction of readers' expectations or hopes, but Dickens regards Barnaby's salvation as right and proper in a riot-free brave new world.

Character and plotting generally in *Barnaby Rudge* are Dickensian in the bad sense and often are rigid rather than flexible. Barnaby of course is the wise lunatic protected by an idealized mother and a magical and vocal raven, whom most readers would have been pleased to see fly away. The father-and-son conflicts may as well have had a Shandyan finger in the margins saying, *nota bene*: here is discord that suggests national discord, so please attend carefully. Several characters might as well have worn signs that announced their obvious roles. The locksmith Gabriel Varden's would have read, "I am the sturdy key to preserving Olde England and can put the lock back on Newgate's gates." His preening, physically meager apprentice Simon Tappertit's sign would have read, "I parallel and reflect Lord George's true nature." Sim is a self-appointed captain of the reactionary group 'Prentice Knights. He hopes to lead his forces and turn back all technical advances. John Willet's Maypole Inn and pub sign would read, "I am Olde England destroyed by Olde Enthusiasm." Emma Haredale and Dolly Varden are too angelic, even if Dolly briefly tastes the nectar of girlish vanity. Edward Chester and Joe Willet, the upright, if now one-armed, inn boy gone for a soldier, are models of virtuously tiresome young gravitas. The effete but variously violent Chesterfieldian Sir John Chester regularly resorts to a golden toothpick that marks his character and is a Lilliputian version of the sword with which he tries to kill Haredale. As Emma's uncle and surrogate father, Haredale represents the virtuous Catholic community, unfairly stigmatized but bravely upholding familial values even at the price of protective violence. And so on.

In short, the characters in *Barnaby Rudge* are highly marked, immediately identifiable, and present as vivid, if one-dimensional, figures. All but one: Lord George Gordon himself, whose riots dominate the second half of the novel. Lord George appears largely as a spectral presence whom both the crowd and his agent Gashford manipulate. He dreams that he may be Jewish but remains Lord George, whose Calvinism Dickens largely ignores and places in "his Puritan's demeanour" as a subtle allusion rather than a demonstrated or discussed belief (p. 298). The strong out-of-control crowd led by strong out-of-control Hugh become the chief areas of interest. Lord George is not a key actor, because he is an excuse, not a reason. The key actors in the riots other than Hugh and Barnaby soon become the re-actors. These are Edward Chester and one-armed Joe Willet, conveniently back from the American war, which also cut off a limb of British territory. Together they save their true loves—Dolly, Emma, and their eighteenth-century but Victorian virtue.

Dickens in fact structures his return to order around two basic elements during a week of horror. Then "the worst passions of the worst men were . . . working in the dark, and the mantle of religion, assumed to cover the ugliest deformities, threatened to become the shroud of all that was good and peaceful in society" (p. 370). One response to such darkness is the individual's insistence on lighting a candle. Barnaby's mother, for example, lovingly protects her son and fruitlessly watches "for the dawn of mind" (p. 209). She herself is a moral dawn, whom Dickens uses to reject the purveyors of "gloom and austerity." One must remember "the sense of hope and pleasure which every glad return of day awakens in the breast"; "all the mirth and happiness" in Barnaby and, by extension, in the works "of Infinite benevolence"; and the "songs and cheerful sounds" that such joy evokes (p. 208). The preservation of joy and song nonetheless needs a stronger presence than a loving mother and a kind narrator. The novel shows why such additional secular power was necessary.

As a sometime journalist, Dickens drew much of his material for the Gordon Riots from eighteenth-century newspapers. He thus had numerous, often repetitive sources for his major themes and images. Perhaps his first job in this more grimly vital part of *Barnaby Rudge* was to make plain how ominous the riots were. We recall the repeated sermon text from Proverbs 17:14: "the beginning of strife is as when one letteth out water," a text that young Charles well may have heard either at the established church of his childhood or from his Baptist schoolmaster William Giles. The released water represented the torrents of rage that sapped foundations, broke hedges, and destroyed the fences that proclaimed borders or moral limits. Dickens adapts this simile. He regularly uses the wild sea as an emblem of the mob's oceanic, uncontrolled, turbulent rage—"terrible," "unreasonable," "cruel" (p. 429). Or it was "roaring and chafing like an angry sea" (p. 522; see also pp. 412, 413, 438, 558).

The dangerous sea drowns all beneath it, including order, decency, and restraint. The mob had "broken all bounds and set all law and government at defiance" (p. 420). "No authority restrained them" (p. 435). Only the law of the street was rigorously enforced: "The crowd was the law, and never was the law held in greater dread, or more implicitly obeyed" (p. 521). Such a world was "like nothing that we knew of, even in our dreams" (p. 539)—or nightmares. The mob destroys both Lord Mansfield's home and invaluable papers: "nothing could replace this loss, the great Law Library" (p. 551). The repetition of *no*, *nothing*, and *never* underlines the unprecedented nature of the events.

Destruction of Mansfield's repository of collected legal wisdom is not performed by rational human beings, but "by legions of devils" (p. 567) led by a "fiery devil . . . a flaming, furious devil" (p. 425). Those assembled demons reverse and destroy Christian proceedings. They take "some relics" of their destruction (p. 443), have "an infernal temple" (p. 450), and when they break into Newgate and spread turpentine on Warden Akerman's furniture, they perform an "infernal christening" (p. 533). Brutality of that sort produces "groans, plunder, fear, and ruin!" by barbarians and madmen (p. 450). Dickens sees both. The hostile mass "danced, and howled, and roared about these fires [they had set] till they were tired and were never for an instant checked" (p. 435). The "dark mass" of the mob was "shouting and whooping like savages" (p. 449). They howl, yell, and expect to sate their "senseless rage" (pp. 462, 539, 551), because they are indifferent to linguistic order and indeed are a mortal plague, a contagious infection spreading "a dread fever." No wonder that "society began to tremble at their ravings" (p. 438). Dickens uses his regular image of madness, not to characterize Lord George, as often was the case, but to characterize the crowd's "hideous madmen" in general, for the "whole great mass were mad" (pp. 419, 536). Had Bedlam been emptied onto the streets, its people would not have been as mad as those in the night frenzy (pp. 461–62).

Hugh in particular embodies frenzy. He is among those terrible madmen, indeed is their drunken leader, who has beaten and could kill those in his way, has burned buildings, and has stolen gold and silver (p. 434). He also places a weapon into hapless Barnaby's hands and characterizes himself as an Achilles ready to lead his Myrmidons. "Reach me my stick and belt," he orders Gashford, now Hugh's, rather than Lord George's, assistant. "Here! Lend a hand master. Fling this over my shoulder, and buckle it behind" (p. 441). We later find that Hugh, captain of destructive men, destroyer of civilization, is the illegitimate son of Sir John Chester. The knight has disinherited his son Edward for loving Catholic Emma Haredale and rejecting an arranged marriage with a well-fortuned Protestant woman. Hugh's literal violence amplifies Sir John's moral and emotional violence. Each in his way is an enemy of responsible behavior.

Dickens also uses Hugh as the physical foil to Lord George, the rapidly disappearing provocateur whose zeal initiated but could not control the tides of encroaching darkness. Lord George hears a concerned friend tell Barnaby to flee or the soldiers may arrest and hang him. No, Barnaby cries. "Gordon for ever! Let them come." Lord George echoes Barnaby and implies his own dim apprehension of reality: "Ay! . . . let them." Gordon also signals another connection and his self-delusion. There will be attacks on his power, his Scottish solemn league and covenant is not the entire British nation, and Hugh, not Gordon, leads Barnaby. Lord George is oblivious to such facts as he orates to Barnaby: "Let us see who will venture to attack a power like ours; the solemn league of a whole people. *This* a madman! You have said well, very well. I am proud to be the leader of such men as you" (p. 475).

Lord George finally is arrested and accompanied "to the Tower under the strongest guard ever known to enter its gates with a single prisoner." He is isolated, without any of the forty thousand followers he thought he commanded: "none were there. . . . and he whose weakness had been goaded and urged on by so many for their own purposes, was desolate and alone" (p. 614). The halting attempt to restore law and civilization was made possible by the strong guard obeying strong orders. That was Dickens' view of the proper action in *Barnaby Rudge*.

We know the anguish with which the version of royally proclaimed martial law was greeted in 1780. David Williams' *Plan of Association, on Constitutional Principles, for the Parishes, Tithing, Hundreds, and Counties of Great Britain* (1780) exemplifies such anguish. The combination of an inadequate police force and British degeneracy may have demanded the army's assistance during the riots, but this would enslave the Britons, who will "taste our misery in multiplied bitterness, while we have any recollection of our former situations."[5] It was a necessary horror, a threat to the constitution and the rule of civil and constitutional law. During the immediate aftermath of the Gordon Riots, Britons turned to complaint, the press, and cerebration on paper to reestablish a familiar world. They strengthened the frayed cultural bonds that unsheathed swords and fixed bayonets also could tear. The magic of distance and a happier outcome than feared changed all that. Dickens well may have reflected respect for British arms after Waterloo (1815) and Napoleon's demise. He also knew of the Duke of Wellington's prime ministerial championing of the Catholic Relief Act in 1829 and 1832. The true hero of *Barnaby Rudge*'s final long section thus is the army, whose efficiency and physical and moral order Dickens regularly admires. Without the redcoats the anarchic, ragged brutality of Hugh and thousands like him would have turned London into an ash heap and England into a bankrupt nation vulnerable before her enemies. Victorian Dickens looked back and unambiguously approved of Georgian martial actions. London then had seemed "invaded by a foreign army" and not just soldiers, but "demon heads and savage eyes . . . a bewildering horror," which Hugh exemplified (pp. 418, 419). He was "mad with liquor and excitement, and halloing them on like a demon" (p. 560). He was a leader among the "besiegers" of the Maypole (p. 460), which suffered a "dread invasion of the serenity and peace of night" (p. 457). He urged a "plan of attack" upon Newgate to free his arrested friends and all other inmates (p. 503). The horror the horror, the darkness, the fall into diabolical chaos, must be eliminated by color and order and a loyal army fit to repel invaders. Dickens saw redcoats and said jolly good.

Exemplary martial behavior begins with individual rather than regimental conduct. Hugh and many other Gordon followers have stormed the lobby of the House of Commons. They raucously assemble in front of the door to the visitors' gallery, before which Gordon updates the exasperated, violent crowd on Parliament's actions. As Gordon addresses them, two senior army officers make a brilliant surprise tactical move. General Henry Seymour Conway walks through the door; he insists that as a soldier he will protect the House's freedom and that its Members are armed and will "defend that pass [into the House] to the last," whatever the bloodshed. The nation is more important than kinship. Colonel Adam Gordon, Lord George's uncle, firmly tells his nephew that if anyone in the crowd "crosses the threshold of the House of Commons, I swear to run my sword that moment—not into his, but into your body" (p. 411). They then flank Lord George, take him by the arms, draw him back into the House, and lock and bar the door on the inside. The image makes clear that Lord George can be manhandled, removed by resolute strength, and coerced back to the confines of law, which nonetheless can destroy him as a result of his illicit conduct.

The maneuver nonetheless is a clever feint, a show of command and of force against superior numbers that buys time as it raises the stakes: "Have a care what you do" (p. 411). The "gallant and resolute" actions briefly stun the faltering, panicked, and confused crowd—until Gashford encourages Hugh to counterattack. He leads the crowds against the door of the "besieged" House, as those within "stood on the defensive" ready to shed their own and others' blood (p. 412).

Their attack halts when the crowd learns that a detachment of Horse and Foot Guards has assembled in the street. Dickens characterizes the crowd as both irrational animals and a school of fish in water. They pour out of the House "as impetuously as they had flocked in." The "whole stream" then turns as "the whole mass floated" into the street to confront the Guards. Two hostile armies seem to brace for a frontal attack. The difference between the two, however, is that lawless Hugh leads one, and a "commanding officer" leads the other. He is joined by a civil magistrate and a representative of the House of Commons. The Crown's agents are restrained by the civil law. Procedures must be followed. The magistrate reads the Riot Act, which demands, but does not evoke, dispersal. He then gives the order for the Guards' cavalry to charge. Even here, however, such a charge is tempered by a desire not to hurt, to take casualties rather than to give casualties, as with this rider who knows and follows his orders:

> he galloped here and there, exhorting the people to disperse; and although heavy stones were thrown at the men, and some were desperately cut and bruised, they had no orders but to make prisoners of such of the rioters as were the most active, and to drive the people back with the flat of their sabres. (Pp. 412–13)

Two riders are cut off as they see Hugh and Barnaby, who hurls his pole at an advancing soldier and promptly unseats him. Both Hugh and Barnaby then flee after this first skirmish among many, which will become more violent. The contrast, though, is immediate and clear. The army, whether in the House of Commons or in the streets, behaves both intelligently and gallantly and accepts commands designed to establish order and to minimize civilian loss. The crowds behave malignly, irrationally, and with hostile, angry leadership that recalls the violence of once restrained and now released rushing water.

Barnaby's later capture continues this pattern. A body of troops marches across a field in an "orderly and regular mode of advancing . . . as one man" (p. 476). They load their weapons and encircle the house in a single file. A private gentleman reads an arrest order; the officer thrice asks Barnaby to surrender; he fights "like a madman" (p. 478) and knocks down two of the troops but finally is himself knocked down, arrested, shackled, and marched off: "Tramp, tramp. Tramp, tramp. Heads erect, shoulders square, every man stepping in exact time—all so orderly and regular" (p. 480). The geometric images of circles, lines, and squares set against Barnaby's mad combat and rejection of order clearly also contrast the nature of the riots and the nature of the necessary restoration of order. Further martial activity continues comparable images. The regiments on duty were "in obedience to the orders" sent them (p. 520). Soldiers are posted at major places, including those the rioters tried to storm or destroy, like the houses of

Parliament, the law courts, and the Bank of England (p. 555). The Crown establishes martial law (p. 557), which allows threatened officers, rather than civil magistrates, to give the order to fire. The military thus roots out the remainder of the mob (p. 581) until "the disturbances were entirely quelled, and peace and order were restored to the affrighted city" and "the crowd was utterly routed" (pp. 604, 605).

As we have seen with the initial episode at the House of Commons, the military represents restraint as well as force. Dickens again stresses the importance of this coupling. When Barnaby is arrested, the officer in charge moves along smartly because he "was humanely anxious" to avoid a rescue attempt that "must lead to bloodshed and loss of life." If the civil magistrate ordered him to fire, many innocent civilians would be killed. The officer chooses "merciful prudence" and a "wise proceeding" (p. 480). That is true as well when a wounded soldier seeks to retaliate. Barnaby has been marched off to prison by troops in an "unbroken order" (p. 485). The crowds seek to free him, grow violent, and rush or throw stones at the few soldiers until one, badly hurt with a blow to the temple, "levelled his musket, but the officer struck it upwards with his sword, and ordered him on peril of his life to desist." Barnaby thus can be "fenced in," and the angry soldier is as restrained as the angry crowd (p. 486). Dickens must have known about the occasional military street justice in 1780. In 1841 he chose to banish it as inappropriate for his novelistic needs.

In the novel as in life, however, the Crown's subjects nonetheless feared that martial rioting could be as ominous as the crowd's. The next time there might not be an officer to raise an angry soldier's musket or an officer to stop hangings from lampposts. The Crown thus declares that "all the rioters in custody would be tried by a special commission in due course of law" (p. 606). The final triumph of martial law, in the novel at least, is to surrender to civil law. As Lord George's sad lament for the hanging of pubescent girls and the strangling of a young boy makes clear, that special commission was especially brutal. By then, Londoners overwhelmingly were happy just to have the bloody mess behind them. Let God look after the hanged as he would look after incarcerated Lord George for starting the mess in the first place and for complaining about the deaths he caused. The Crown would let neither its Hughs nor Lord George back onto the street to do any more damage. Evidence was evidence and did not lie, however uncomprehending the perpetrator might be.

I have said that Dickens' actors are at once flat and prominent. Like humors' characters, they have individual traits that announce and define them. That is not true of *Barnaby Rudge*'s narrator, however, who has an excellent sense of the complexities of moral and indeed of immoral life. He summarizes Lord George's behavior during his extended and fatal time in prison after he was abandoned by his church, his state, his followers, and perhaps his family. Dickens' great gifts included sympathy for the poor, whose plight he hoped to alleviate. He also celebrated those who relieved poverty in their immediate surroundings—like Lord George Gordon in Newgate:

> He had his mourners. The prisoners bemoaned his loss, and missed him; for though his means were not large his charity was great, and in bestowing alms among them he considered the necessities of all alike, and knew no distinction of sect or creed. There are wise men in the highways of the world who may learn something, even from this poor crazy Lord who died in Newgate. (P. 683)

Lord George's ultimate punishments included those inflicted upon him by his government, as well as those inflicted upon him by history. "The prisoners bemoaned his loss," but they were part of a small fraternity in a wretched episode that reflected badly upon Gordon, the established church, the Crown, and the rioting populace, led by the illegitimate son of an effete but dangerous knight of the realm and Member of Parliament. That is just one of the several acts of paternal betrayal in *Barnaby Rudge*. Dickens was scarcely a royalist, but his novel characterizes a model father, after all, one who resembles Haredale in his concern for the innocent and his willingness to protect them with his sword. That father is the controlled military that George III finally imposes upon the city and whose life-and-death authority he quickly removes.

There nevertheless were hundreds of deaths, immense damage, broad panic, and the sense that "demon heads and savage eyes . . . a bewildering horror" were again at work in the land. It took the military to preserve a civilization that was as threatened in 1780 as it had been in, say, 1708. There were demonstrable advances in toleration, political liberty, and, sometimes and halting, judicial restraint and modes of incarceration. The partners in danger changed their costumes somewhat. They nonetheless still were the melded forces of religion, politics, and the dark "bewildering horror" ever present within the human spirit. Lord George and so many others praised the thunderbolts of enlightenment and reason that the French Revolution promised. In the event, the thunderbolts projected the light from muskets, canon, and the flash of the guillotine. Some forty thousand died in the Terror, and some million or so in the different revolutionary and Napoleonic wars within a twenty-two-year span. In light of this, we might well ask, with Barnaby Rudge upon first entering London during the riots, when the city seemed populated by devils: "This flight and pursuit, this cruel burning and destroying, these dreadful cries and stunning noises, were they the good Lord's noble cause?" (p. 567). It was not biblical Sodom destroyed by an angry God. It was London in 1780, almost destroyed by itself.

In the event, the British government and its legal system agreed with Horace Mann regarding Lord George: "The existence of such a wretch is incompatible with the safety of millions."[6] *Barnaby Rudge* follows but modifies that counsel. It offers Lord George as a distant secondary wretch, from whom Britains' millions nonetheless are not safe. "His" riots are conducted by diabolical Myrmidons commanded by a mad bastard Achilles, supported by a sweetly naive and demented young man all too like a nation seeking a better paternal guide.

For many of the Great and the Good the end of Lord George indeed justified the means of his incarceration and death. After the larger means of martial law, Dickens would have agreed with Johnson's remark on 12 June 1780: "All danger here is apparently over.... When it is known that the Rioters are quelled in London, their Spirit will sink in every other place, and little more mischief will be done"—at least for the time being.[7] Evolutionary progress had a painfully won, if brief, return to a version of normalcy.

NOTES

1. Samuel Johnson, in James Boswell, *Boswell's Life of Johnson: Together with Boswell's Journal of a Tour to the Hebrides*, ed. George Birkbeck Hill, rev. L. F. Powell (Oxford: Clarendon Press, 1934–50), 1:110; [Edward Ward], *All Men Mad: Or, England A Great Bedlam. A Poem* (London, 1704), p. 19; Pierre Jean Grosley, originally *Londres* (Lausanne [i.e., Paris], 1770), here *A Tour to London; Or, New Observations on England, and its Inhabitants*, trans. Thomas Nugent (London, 1772), 2:25 (constant), 27 (baptizes). For Methodists, see Samuel Bradburn, *The Question, Are the Methodists Dissenters? Fairly Examined to Remove Prejudice, Prevent Bigotry, and Promote Brotherly Love* ([Liverpool?], 1792), p. [3]; and James Creighton, *A Letter Addressed to Mr. Samuel Bradburn, Containing, Some Strictures On His Pamphlet, Entitled: "The Question; Are the Methodists Dissenters?"* (London, 1793), p. 14, in which the author notes that the Hanoverians discouraged persecution. See chapter 5 above for fuller discussion of the Methodist movement and its place in Britain's religious evolutions.

2. *Gentleman's Magazine* 63 ([1793]): 1056.

3. Horace Walpole, The Yale Edition of Horace Walpole's Correspondence, ed. W. S. Lewis, vol. 29, *Horace Walpole's Correspondence with William Mason. II*, ed. W. S. Lewis et al. (New Haven, CT: Yale University Press, 1955), p. 75n (hereafter cited as YEW by volume, title, and editor). The Spanish captured sixty-three British ships.

4. Charles Dickens, *Barnaby Rudge*, ed. Gordon Spence (Harmondsworth, UK: Penguin, 1973), p. 662 (hereafter cited parenthetically in the text). Criticism of *Barnaby Rudge* is reasonably ample, but not as extensive as for Dickens' major novels. Even his sympathetic biographers long have had reservations, as with John Forster, who thought the tepid characterization of Lord George tiresome, and Edgar Johnson, who thought much of the bifurcated novel tiresome. See Forster's 1872 *The Life of Charles Dickens*, ed. J. W. T. Ley

(London: Cecil Palmer, 1928), pp. 168, 170, with pp. 164–72 for extended discussion of the novel; Johnson, *Charles Dickens: His Tragedy and Triumph* (New York: Simon & Schuster, 1952), 1:330, with pp. 329–37, 341–44, for the longer analysis. For more tolerant, or patient, critics in addition to Spence, above, see John Butt and Kathleen Tillotson, *Dickens at Work* (London: Methuen, 1957), pp. 76–89; Steven Marcus, *Dickens: from Pickwick to Dombey* (London: Chatto & Windus, 1965), pp. 169–212; Sylvère Monod, *Dickens the Novelist* (Norman: University of Oklahoma Press, 1968), pp. 186–94; Avrom Fleishman, *The English Historical Novel: Walter Scott to Virginia Woolf* (Baltimore: Johns Hopkins Press, 1971), pp. 102–26; Joseph Gold, *Charles Dickens: Radical Moralist* (Minneapolis: University of Minnesota Press, 1972), pp. 116–29; Myron Magnet, *Dickens and the Social Order* (Philadelphia: University of Pennsylvania Press, 1985), pp. 49–170; and Peter Ackroyd, *Dickens* (London: Sinclair-Stevenson, 1990), pp. 325–29. There are several useful articles and chapters as well: Thomas J. Rice, "The Politics of *Barnaby Rudge*," in *The Changing World of Charles Dickens*, ed. Robert Giddings (New York: Barnes & Noble, 1983), pp. 51–74; Steven Connor, "Space, Place and the Body of Riot in *Barnaby Rudge*," in *Charles Dickens*, ed. Connor (London: Longman, 1996), pp. 211–29; Iain Crawford, "Dickens, Classical Myth, and Representations of Social Order in *Barnaby Rudge*," *Dickensian* 93, no. 3 (1997): 185–97; and Mark Willis, "Charles Dickens and the Fictions of the Crowd," *Dickens Quarterly* 23, no. 2 (2006): 85–97. In the nature of things, critics contradict one another. Iain Crawford, for example, rightly reads *Barnaby Rudge* as "rhapsodic upon the virtues of military discipline" and thinks "the regular army the true hero of the hour" ("Dickens, Classical Myth," p. 187). John Glavin regards the army's action as "state brutality" in "Politics and *Barnaby Rudge*: Surrogation, Restoration and Revival," *Dickens Studies Annual* 30 (2001): 101. There is a useful bibliography of *Barnaby Rudge* studies to 1987 in Thomas J. Rice, *Barnaby Rudge: An Annotated Bibliography* (New York: Garland, 1987).

    5. [David Williams], *A Plan of Association on Constitutional Principles, For the Parishes, Tithings, Hundreds, and Counties of Great Britain; By which the Outrages of Mobs, and the Necessity of a Military Government Will be Prevented* (London, 1780), p. 20.

    6. Horace Walpole, YEW, vol. 25, *Sir Horace Mann and Sir Horace Mann the Younger. IX*, ed. W. S. Lewis, Warren Hunting Smith et al. (1971), *Sir Horace Mann and Sir Horace Mann the Younger*, 25:64.

    7. Samuel Johnson, *The Letters of Samuel Johnson*, ed. Bruce Redford (Princeton, NJ: Princeton University Press, 1992–94), 3:274.

Conclusion, Summary, Implications

A Brief Summary of a Long Book

This book began with discussions of the troubled residue of the civil war. Religious and political turmoil threatened the church, state, monarch, and monarchy. Nominally insular matters also were international matters, with at the least foreign links and causation. One familiar attack upon both Charles II and James II was that they had been educated in papist France and absorbed the many aberrations of that culture. Abdicated or exiled, but certainly dismissed, James returned to France as Louis XIV's client and, like his son, an invasion pawn. William III, of course, was demonstrably Dutch, and the first two Georges demonstrably German. One monarch took England into a long and expensive European war against the Bourbon dynasty. The other two took Britain into further long and expensive wars against those Bourbons, among others, on the Continent, in North America, and in more exotic climes.

The book ends with discussions of the troubled residue of what very nearly was a civil war that turned much of London into rubble. Religious and political turmoil again threatened the church, state, monarch, and monarchy. In spite of such apparent historical congruence, the worlds of, say, 1660 and 1780 were vastly different. We do not see déjà vu all over again so much as evolutionary conflict that becomes permanent revolution—but in which defeated guerrillas still do serious damage. There were allegations that French, Spanish, and American agents fomented the destructive No Popery riots, a notion based on fear and cultural paranoia rather than empirical evidence. For all the understandable outrage at class-based and poor government policies and at the enlightened elites' indifference to the largely disenfranchised rabble, the Gordon Riots were self-performed amputations of basic decency. The Crown's and the church's later responses to Lord George were homegrown, ugly abuses of power in which legal camouflage disguised legal murder.

However appalling that conduct, it also marked major changes in Britain's way of dealing with such ominous events. In the earlier cases, conflict and resolution focused largely on the monarch. Politics seemed like a chess game, designed to take the king with set moves by opposing knights, bishops, and perhaps the queen. The Exclusion Crisis, the death of Charles II, the short reign of James II, William's revolution of 1688, the reign of Queen Anne Stuart, who died without issue, and then the reigns of the Protestant German Georges—all these were dynastic concerns. Parliament and its relationship with the Crown clearly changed along the way, but it is not until the 1720s that one begins to speak about the prime-ministerial Walpole years and administration as gradual but significant replacements of royal with parliamentary, really House of Commons, power. The opposition to James II was different from the opposition to George II, which in turn was different from the opposition to George III.

In James II's case, religion was the central issue. That religion was assumed to be the arbitrary, un-English, tyrannical, wooden-shoe creating, slave-inducing agent of the pope, France, Spain, and Beelzebub thrown in for good measure. The man had to go. In George II's reign, administration corruption was the central issue. Walpole seemed to have absorbed royal authority and determined royal rewards, government places, and literary patronage. In spite of one incompetent and one dangerous Jacobite invasion, the Hanoverians were settled and biologically productive. The powerful monarch was constrained in part by the Commons' control of the purse, but the Crown was progressively, if subtly, diminished as the Commons grew in stature. In the case of the third and native-born George, the opposition centered on his attempt to renew royal power and, many thought, an American policy that threatened Protestant Britons' freedom as much as their Protestant American cousins' freedom. By about 1760 both the public and the Commons have been brought more firmly into public play, the geopolitical concerns have spread across the Atlantic, and Britain has become a world force with world troubles and obligations. Along the way, High Church bonds with the Crown, indeed the High Church itself, had been significantly weakened. Neither Dutch Calvinist nor German Lutheran monarchs were keen to place altitudinarian exclusionists and perhaps Jacobites on the episcopal bench or in the royal court. Detachment of the church's political power from the Crown's power was in part responsible for the developments I have chronicled in this book.

Restoration and early eighteenth-century political and religious rage made the world seem mad and could not be sustained in a civilized nation. The thirtieth of January sermons as read over a century saw restraint replace much of that rage and the divine right of government replace the divine right of kings, as the sermons themselves began to seem archaic and unnecessary. There was a comparable evolutionary interpretation of Luke 14:23, "Compel them to come in." Augustinian violent compulsion, so clear in Louis XIV's revocation of the Edict of Nantes in 1685, produces intense Huguenot response, High Church distancing from its own threats of physical compulsion, and a final insistence that now compulsion is Christian moral and religious suasion. Methodism moves from provincial Oxford to a world religion, no longer thought of as yet another dissenting sect, but a member of the Protestant Anglican family, however much it might be the poor relation, as in Smollett's *Humphry Clinker* (1771). Sir George Savile's Catholic Relief Bill of 1778 seemed to embrace and enlarge upon these changes in British culture's breadth of religious toleration, which even the French traveler Pierre Jean Grosley saw and admired in 1772. Both Grosley and Savile were wrong regarding large portions of the British public, who for generations had been told that Catholicism was, at the least, the devil's destructive and bloody tool. The evolutionary process was powerfully arrested in the 1780 Gordon Riots, which returned religious bigotry to the forefront and returned solid buildings to rubble. Anarchy seemed in charge of Riot as the soldiers on hand were restrained by frightened or anti-Catholic magistrates. Lord George's trial for constructive treason in 1781 began the state's sequence of misguided and finally fatal legal and ecclesiastical attacks upon the man they could not control, but could finally incarcerate and let die of the rampant jail fever that disgraced the British penal system. Britain tried bravely to heal itself after George III evoked controversial martial law. It contemplated options to the redcoats, discussed a police system, blamed Lord George, blamed George III, but accepted the necessity of moral compromise in the face of a possible disaster if the Bank of England were destroyed by the incendiary mobs. The evolutionary process obviously hit a bad bump in its road. It also tried to put itself back on track—one way of doing so Dickens characterized through that martial order as the true hero of *Barnaby Rudge* (1841).

The world thus was not so jolly a place as amelioration, acceptance, and adaptive inclusion suggests. Hanoverian toleration, or perhaps indifference, softened but could not remove religious tension. In 1737 Hildebrand Jacob reviewed what he regarded as regress. His poem *The Progress of Religion* concludes with a mournful series of questions regarding Christianity's inability to bring its promised peace and love to the world: "When shall our *Pride*, and dire *Dissentions* cease?" (p. 8). Certainly not by 1780—witness the sad episodes of Lord George Gordon and the Gordon Riots, whether in reality or in Dickens' version of them.

Throughout, I have related religion and literature, whether in sermons, poems, political or religious polemic, journalism, novels, or parliamentary and judicial reports. The texts demand broad contexts, some of which I hope to have supplied. Many of these texts were well sprinkled with insults and often threats but often as well came to acknowledge the value of conscience and respect for difference. This evolutionary process had numerous developments, trends, and quirks consistent with the metaphor of change, which can be both progressive and regressive. I have referred to these changes as ameliorative evolution, in which cultures use adaptive mechanisms in order to improve chances of survival and improvement. When they fail, they also lead to the slaughter and moral collapse in the sad Gordon episodes from 1780 to 1793. That was a failure worth avoiding in the future.

Illustrating Evolution

I have called these movements ameliorative evolutions, of a culture that made significant changes from 1660 to 1780. They also clearly could revert to the kind of moral barbarism, unintended consequences, human inability to foresee events, hubris, and reasons of state that scarcely mask vengeance. One stipulates inconsistency when discussing human actions. Such discussion and stipulation, however, do not negate change. In the civil war of the 1640s, Cromwell's army was the source and enforcer of power. In the almost civil war of 1780, George III's army was the last resort, and its power soon was returned to the civil courts. Given the eighteenth-century bloody legal code, that was a modest moral advance, but it was an attempted restraint upon men with guns and swords, and a restraint that soon also yielded to harmless paper wars and hot air.

Such examples easily can be multiplied.[1] I further illustrate this evolutionary process with only two brief and one extended example. The first relates to the movement from the throne to Parliament as sources of central power. The second concerns the changes from High Church rigor to lower church practicality concerning ritual and oaths. The third considers the major change in attitudes toward trade and money.

Dryden's *Absalom and Achitophel* (1681) begins and ends with David/Charles II's conduct. At first, he is an irresponsible monarch self-indulgently and destructively spreading his seminal seed. He rebels against proper monarchic restraint and in turn breeds the rebellion that torments him and the nation through his ambitious illegitimate son, Absalom, the Duke of Monmouth. The poem ends when David finally grasps the true nature of kingship, resolves the conflict between his roles as loving father and powerful monarch, and warns Absalom that his disloyal behavior threatens both his life and the nation's. As a result of David's peroration, "Th' Almighty, nodding, gave Consent; / And Peals of Thunder shook the Firmament."[2] Here is a true restoration of the true godlike monarch whom "willing Nations" acknowledge as "their Lawfull Lord" (line 1131). Dryden's emphasis throughout the poem is upon the relationship between monarch and rebellion, including the monarch's rebellion against sexual prudence and paternal control. Divine affirmative thunder suggests divine approbation of the legitimacy of the divine right of kings and of this king.

Parliament has its own helpful function in the poem. Its few loyal members stand in the breach to oppose extremists like Achitophel; Barzillai and his son are models for the wise union of aristocratic father and son; the best of the lot advise David that he must recognize the danger in which he has put the state and return to a proper royal role. Dryden nonetheless uses a key term, "band," which suggests parliamentary subordination: "their band was *Israel's* Tribes in small" (line 906). Parliament not only is a collection of tribal units, several of which have agendas alien to the monarch's and could unbind monarchy. The "band" also is small in several ways. The poem is not about how different levels of Parliament work or function; it is about how Parliament does or does not support a monarch, who is the center of value and upon whom the nation relies. *Ad exemplum regis* makes clear that the nation prospers as the monarch prospers. Divinity does not thunder for Sir John in the House of Commons or Lord John in the House of Lords. It thunders for the monarch external to such inferior government houses.

We need little further synopsis of the gradual movement from a dominant Stuart monarch, through the gradual reduction of such still impressive powers after 1688, to George III's evocation of a constitutional crisis when the Crown attempted to enliven its moribund authority. The outcome, of course, was hostile and not benign. The monarch and the monarchy clearly remained powerful as political and social forces, but public perception had changed regarding where wisdom and responsibility were best found. Samuel Johnson's "Life of Samuel Butler" (1779) epitomizes this change about a century after *Absalom and Achitophel*: "The wisdom of the nation is very reasonably supposed to reside in the parliament."[3] Reasonable supposition is based upon the public's experiences with an elected body of men whose wisdom has been tested through time. In this secular focus, the only thunder is likely to come from clamors of political debate in the House of Commons or canvassing for votes on the hustings. Such a view is not interested in the "Series of new time" (line 1028) that begins with David's restoration to his crown, himself, and his nation. Johnson celebrates the continuity of collective wisdom earned in the workaday political world. We see such evolution as well in attitudes toward the Bank of England.

William Whiston's *Memoirs of the Life and Writings* (1749–50) suggests another aspect of such evolution. He comments upon the parliamentary coercion his blind Leicester Presbyterian clergyman father experienced in 1657. An agent of "those at the helm" insists that either he sign the subscription or be recorded as a refuser in a black book to be shown to "those in authority." The compliant father is troubled by his surrender to coercion, understandably so in part, Whiston says, because until his father's death in 1685 "he kept the 30th of *January* . . . more solemnly, as a religious fast, than any other clergyman in *England*."⁴ By the second or third decade of the eighteenth century William embodied a different sort of Whiston. He himself became a Unitarian, after 1710 no longer was a practicing cleric, and refused to sign the Thirty-Nine Articles if that was a price of reinstatement or even of being archbishop of Canterbury (1:145–46). Others had far less interest in self-exclusion. He discusses the signing of articles necessary for preferment but in which one did not believe. *"We must not lose our usefulness for scruples,"* his adversarius replies (1:140). Whiston later laments that after much learning and effort a clergyman cannot hold a living or receive preferment without exercising "great prevarication" by signing the man-made Thirty-Nine Articles and other creeds (1:346–47). The clear denotation is that clergymen regularly so prevaricate, as did his friend the once zealously abstemious Mr. Rundle, who decided to join the established church, sign the Articles, and *"walk in the ways of darkness"* (1:233). Whether or not there was light in the darkness, such indifferent signing became commonplace as objections to predestination and original sin became commonplace. Methodists of the 1730s and 1740s would have agreed in blaming Mr. Rundle for compromising, as indeed the Church of England itself so acknowledged.

In one case I have cited, the central authority has moved from Crown to Parliament. In the other, ecclesiastical rigorism confronts ecclesiastical *laisser-faire* regarding oaths and articles. In another evolutionary case, trade and credit move from tenuous dream to the solidest of realities that must be preserved if British power is to be preserved.

In Addison's *Spectator*, No. 3 (1711), Mr. Spectator tells us about "one of my late Rambles, or rather Speculations" that takes him "into the great Hall where the Bank is kept." His "Speculation" embodies Johnson's first two definitions: "Examination by the eye; view," and "Examiner; spy."⁵ Addison introduces this urgent ocular espionage immediately after the two-essay introduction of his dramatis personae. The first proper exchange with his reader thus concerns the newly established British prosperity that is threatened by a competing force.

Mr. Spectator's rambling urban examinations also signal a radical change in his personal life, as in the nation's life. Addison already had delineated his main character's genealogy. His ancient gentry family owned a modest hereditary estate with the same property lines in 1066 as in 1711. Such ancestors were reliable stewards of land "delivered down from Father to Son whole and entire" without loss or gain for six hundred years (1:1). Mr. Spectator himself long had been a grave, distinguished, diligent, and quiet student at school and university, where he became learned in language and letters. He indeed was and is an outsider, claims to be politically neutral, and prefers the written to the vocal, except in his own club, to which we become surrogate members. Addison gives us an apparently perceptive, reliable, uncontentious representative of the best of old England's middling landed and educated classes—but with a major difference.

Two matters challenge this self-interested self-portrait. Mr. Spectator has, of course, left his inherited, geographically bounded and thus static estate. The limits of the land suggest limits to the growth of the mind and, we shall see, to the national wealth. Hence, upon his father's death—we note both the respect and the symbolic implications—Mr. Spectator travels abroad and attempts to quench his insatiable thirst for knowledge. The bounded gentleman farmer travels the apparently boundless world in search of "any thing new or strange" (1:2). Upon his return he finds London a microcosm of the greater world. He frequents Whig and Tory coffeehouses, listens to their denizens exchanging wisdom or gossip, reads the newspapers, attends the theater, passes for a merchant at the Royal Exchange and for a Jewish stockbroker at Jonathan's. He thus can seem "a Speculative statesman, Soldier, Merchant and Artizan," while viewing rather than participating in the complex world around him (1:4).

Mr. Spectator moves from a bounded ancient English estate to the larger Continental and then Eastern world. London thus is congenial as an emblem of Whiggish magnetic cosmopolitanism, essential for national wealth and greatness. For England to prosper, it must move from wealth based upon limited landholdings to wealth based upon expanding commerce, stocks, and international ventures: "Whenever I see a Cluster of People I always mix with them"(1:4), he says and implies that the same should be true of England.

In order for the nation to prosper along those lines, however, trade must be backed by a reliable system of credit supplied by a reliable bank, namely, the Bank of England. Addison then adds his dream vision of English life with and without the Bank William of Orange created in 1694. The vision shows that the concept, indeed the very existence, of such a bank is under attack by reactionary Jacobite forces intent on restoring the male Stuart dynasty by force of foreign or domestic arms if necessary. The Jacobite threat seeks both a new and malign restoration and an old and no longer wealth-producing system. It will abolish legitimate debts and in the process abolish the basis of fair commerce in which supplier, merchant, and customer profit. Such abolition would thereby return England to the "bounded" world that Mr. Spectator left in the country, often thought Jacobite enclaves. Addison's dream sequence shows the two alternatives that refute his claim of political neutrality. He characterizes what amounts to the alternatives of Whig/Anne Stuart urban and soon Hanoverian commerce, and wealth and Tory/Jacobite/James Stuart country impoverishment.

The dream takes him to the Bank's Great Hall, where he sees *"Publick Credit"* imaged as "a beautiful Virgin, seated on a Throne of Gold." The figure is so imaged in part to suggest the youth of the fragile seventeen-year-old Bank. The Virgin's health and color wax and wane as the news is good or bad for credit and commerce. Addison aligns Publick Credit with the Magna Charta and the Acts of Uniformity, Toleration, and Settlement. She is firmly planted in English history, which checks monarchic power, preserves the Protestant establishment within a moderate Church of England, and continues it by means of the Hanoverian succession. The Virgin is pleased "with such Acts of Parliament as had been made for the Establishment of publick Funds." Her actions denote adherence to law and prosperity, which are as fragile as she is. Addison represents the abundant prosperity in the "Throne of Gold" on which the Virgin, and by implication Queen Anne, sits (1:15–16). The massive bags of money behind her throne are arranged in a symbolic way that recalls Mr. Spectator's "Voyage to *Grand Cairo*" in his first essay (1:2): the gold "rose upon Pyramids on either side of her." Indeed, her secretaries have received letters from all around the world (1:16). Here is the Whig paradigm of a moderate Church of England and British government allied with commerce to spread and receive wealth securely based upon the credit supplied by the Bank of England.

The vision promptly is threatened with annihilation and obviation of the law and limits on which Publick Credit based national wealth. Six unspeakably "hideous Phantoms" break into the Great Hall, marching two by two in an awkward dance: Tyranny and Anarchy, Bigotry and Atheism, and "the Genius of a Common Wealth" with the armed Young Pretender, who threatens the Act of Settlement and legal credit. The fragile Lady faints, the bags of money are almost wholly emptied, the gold disappears. Since this is a dream, however, Addison is free to add a further corrective and predictive vision. Now, a second group of benignly paired dancers enter and restore wealth and order: Liberty and Monarchy, Moderation and Religion, and the future George I with "the Genius of *Great Britain*" (1:17). The consequences are immediate. The Lady revives, the useless shards of paper again transform into "Pyramids of Guineas," and Mr. Spectator awakes with a smile.

The allegory urges both the value of and danger to the Bank of England. Like the nation itself, it is threatened by an illicit, violent, and foreign force, supported in this case by France and Louis XIV. German Georg could become British George as French Jacques could not become British James. The triumph of credit is a triumph of proper expansion of foreign commerce supported by religious and monarchic moderation and true British values. Witness the repetition of the figure of "pyramids" and the contrast of "the Genius of a Common Wealth" and the

"Genius of *Great Britain*." We are equally impressed, though, with the need for argument, for Addison's warning about the alternative, the weakness of the Lady, and the dangers of the wrong monarch with the wrong international connections. The Bank of England remained in a parlous state, beset by violent domestic and foreign enemies. It may indeed have been merely a dream that the Bank could flourish with the nation and that George I could become the new protective sovereign.

Now contrast the Bank's 1711 tenuous foundation, need for intellectual and commercial defense, and dream salvation with the vastly different attitude toward the Bank later in the eighteenth century and during the Gordon Riots. By then the Bank of England had become a conceptual export. In 1760 Dublin a "Gentleman in Trade" urged that Ireland emulate Britain, whose "national bank . . . has fixed her credit upon a lasting and permanent foundation." Eleven years thereafter, one Cincinnatus added that the Bank was "the greatest commercial channel, and of the first credit in the world." By 1782 Gorges Edmond Howard alluded to, seconded, and expanded upon such observations. Every flourishing country has a national bank, but the Bank of England is above all others and is a model for an Irish counterpart. The English bank has established prosperity and a vast extension of commerce; it has reduced credit costs and enhanced liberal principles; and it is as firm as the nation itself. Even during potential calamity "it affords a sure asylum, and . . . the passing gale which disturbs the unpillared edifices of all private banks, serves but to firm the more this mighty rock which upholds the public prosperity, and whose plan and regulation has gained the confidence and credit of the world." Attempts to split the mighty rock threaten the wealth and stability both of Britain and of the larger commercial world. Thomas, Baron Lyttelton's iambic pentameters already had predicted that in 2199 an enervated Britain would collapse into literal, moral, and financial rubble. Perhaps with Addison's *Spectator* No. 3 in mind, he sees the place in which the Bank of England once stood, with its heaps of gold and both national and international prominence, now "Raz'd even with the dust." This poem, dated 21 March 1771 but published in 1780, surely resonated during the Gordon Riots and its aftermath.[6]

By then the Bank's established importance was reflected by its impressive changed physical presence. Its first venue was the Hall of the Mercers' Company in 1694. One year later it moved to the larger quarters of the Grocers' Company, in Princes' Street, which Addison refers to as the Hall. Between 1732 and 1734 George Sampson created an impressive purpose-built Bank building on Threadneedle Street. Between 1765 and 1782 Sir Robert Taylor then expanded that building both eastward and westward.[7] The westward expansion required that the Church of Saint Christopher-le-Stocks be both deconsecrated and demolished.

The church dated from 1282, was damaged in the Great Fire of 1666, and was rebuilt by Sir Christopher Wren in 1671. The symbolism of the Bank's displacing such an ancient church, rebuilt by so great an architect, must have been obvious. The Bank had outgrown mercers and grocers and become a pleasant tourist attraction. As the compiler of *The London Guide* (1782) put it, "The Bank, in its present improved state, will be worthy the visits of our Country Readers, who may have no other motive than to gratify their taste by the view of an elegant modern building." The promise of so important a building and the financial authority behind its Palladian facade thus had to be defended. Like the author of *Fanaticism and Treason* (1781), Cincinnatus knew that attacking the Bank of England was a "most daring outrage!" These savage proceedings were orchestrated by Bourbons in league with evil American rebels. A historian of Lord North's administration bluntly said that "the fate of the empire seemed to depend upon the torches of a ruthless banditti," who must not be allowed to prevail.[8]

Government had been "undecided, irresolute, timid" in the face of such an earthquake. The yet unalleviated threat and parliamentary dithering finally caused George III to call for martial law. The attorney general prosecuting Lord George for treason joined those who saw his actions as collusion with Britain's enemies, since the Bank had nothing to do with popery: "Other circumstances concurring, leave no doubt that greater designs than at first appeared were opening to the Public." The dire circumstances, joined to his Majesty's "anxious care, and extraordinary and unremitting exercises," brought thousands of troops and militia to the metropolis to "check the fury of the mob." The soldiery was instructed to protect three special venues, the Bank of England among them. Lord North's historian also knew that monarchic action finally evoked "that vengeance which had so long lingered." It was "the only means of saving the capital from destruction" but nonetheless threatened the British spirit of liberty. Never mind, another writer said regarding future plans. Yes, the army needed civilian rule, but the Bank itself should be guarded by "a Captain, Subaltern, and thirty Privates, completely armed and accoutred" and with plenty of ammunition nearby.[9] Once tranquility was restored by force, it could only be overturned by greater force. Commentators did their best to ensure that such a catastrophe would not happen again. The Bank picquet was not canceled until 1973.

Let us look briefly at the similarities and differences between attacks upon the Bank of England circa 1711 and those circa 1780. Addison's Bank of England is a promising experiment associated with and promoted by Whig politics and banking. Its emblem is a frail, virginal woman much in need of protection by British history, institutions, and a future German monarch whose invited reign is uncertain. The dream sequence itself suggests wish fulfillment rather than the stability of truth. Reality may not replicate visions of presumably benevolent abstractions engaged in presumably benevolent dance. This emblem of order and pattern is subject to the disorder of a Franco/Stuart invasion. The Bank's enemies are the nation's enemies: foreign, Catholic, Jacobites hostile to freedom, limited monarchy, and the fair basis of trade, of debts incurred and debts paid.

The Bank during the Gordon Riots no longer is an experiment, no longer a fainting female, and no longer subject to dream-world conventions. It is in a physical, not a phantom, place, or the relatively modest "Hall." It is not called up by a sympathetic writer in search of the sympathetic audience he hopes to create. Nonetheless, it requires protection, and if necessary "vengeance," against those who would betray it. That protection comes from the Crown in a hitherto stable state. The Crown calls armed forces from within and outside of London, establishes peace, and returns its legal authority to proper courts. Tents are pitched for some twenty thousand men in London's several parks and fields. The active monarch who protects the Bank is secure on the throne rather than, as in 1711, hundreds of miles away, still waiting for the present occupant of the throne to die and still not invited to visit his pending new nation. George III has established himself as "Farmer George" with proper heirs. He is scarcely like licentious Charles II, threatened by his own illegitimate son and his devious advisers, or like Queen Anne, whose misfortunes included seventeen pregnancies and no living offspring. Popery and radical Protestantism again are dangerous, but in ways different from in 1711. Parliament has clearly and foolishly misread or ignored the feelings and fears of its anxious populace and of the numerous dissenting and evangelical Protestants regarding Catholic relief. Both houses, though, unanimously voted to liberalize their anti-Catholic laws. They thereby made plain that from the government's point of view British Catholic subjects no longer were regarded as traitors waiting to replace George III with the latest papal puppet thirsting for Protestant blood. These subjects indeed are so loyal that in Parliament's judgment they can be trusted with arms to defend the nation.

We move from *Absalom and Achitophel*'s divine right of kings to Johnson's wise Parliament. We move from Addison's tenuous Bank of England under attack and in need of intellectual and dynastic defense to, for the sake of parallelism, Johnson's Bank of England as stable institution threatened from within the nation, royally and vigorously defended from within, and broadly regarded as the basis of British financial, imperial, and political freedom. George III acts on behalf of an unpopular, thoughtlessly passed but necessary expansion of religious toleration approved by both parliamentary houses.

I have used *evolution* in a quasi-Darwinian sense. How do living organisms change and develop characteristic traits that replace older with newer traits for newer circumstances? How, in short, does a culture, like the individual human beings who compose it, adapt to change? I have also used one of Johnson's pre-Darwinian but nonetheless germane *Dictionary* definitions of *evolution*: "The act of unrolling or unfolding," which may extend over several generations. I have focused in particular upon religious and political turmoil and events as markers to such evolutionary steps as portrayed in broadly defined literature from about 1660–1780. The later *Barnaby Rudge*, of course, concerns 1780. In the Darwinian sense, British culture evolved away from ancestral religious hatred and absolutism. In the Johnsonian sense, as noted from popular use, these were acts that unfolded over time. Both definitions suggest or imply improvement, an adaptive and sensible sorting out of difficulties. Appalling twentieth-century history makes plain that the evolution of organisms and of the moral sense are not congruent. Herbert Butterfield long ago reminded us of the uncertainties of putative Whig "progress," which is both "crooked and perverse."[10] The Gordon Riots sadly demonstrate that such perverse evolution was not a happy path toward genuine toleration in the eighteenth century. The forces of bigotry were violently triumphant for a week and indeed have never disappeared nor are likely to do so. After June 1780 the putative enlightened government used its court system to kill its real or apparent enemies, including several clueless children. In Lord George's case, wise Britons thought they knew, it was better for the state that a dangerous radical rot in jail and in his grave rather than lead a rabble army, orate in print, or scold in the Commons.

Two steps forward and one step back probably is as good an effort at unfolding as progress can suggest. George III supported repeal of the anti-Catholic laws in 1780 but refused to support further acts of liberation for Ireland in 1800–1801. That would violate his coronation oath to uphold the Anglican establishment as part of the British constitution. Nonetheless, within a generation the Catholic Relief Act of 1829 repealed both the Test Act of 1673 and the remaining penal laws against Catholics. Though flawed, its passage proceeded in ways significantly different from the fiasco of 1778–80. Top-down legislation yielded to long public and private political discussion, education of a reluctant populace, and major compromise that helped to avert, or postpone, a civil war. The House of Lords, led by the Duke of Wellington, followed the overwhelming approval by the House of Commons. As Richard W. Davis has observed, "Public opinion, or at least politicians' perception of it ... was fundamental to the transformation of the Lords' role." By then a French remark of 1793 had indeed been proven true regarding political England's obeisance to the public it had ignored a generation earlier: "Dans un pays comme l'Angleterre où l'opinion publique est toute puissante ... le gouvernement même ne pouroit pas lutter contre elle."[11]

Both houses also were aware that Ireland's peace and loyalty were in danger without such relief. Evolutionary adaptation in 1829 was a consequence of failure in 1780.

There were riots throughout the nineteenth century. Some were for food, some for religious venting, some because of disenfranchisement, some because of modern machinery, and some for something for some reason or some purpose, whatever that reason or purpose might be. Human hostility has not disappeared from hostile and restless humans. In Britain's case from 1660–1780, however, at least a portion of that rage was ameliorated, and a portion of the religious passion was separated from political passion. Each paramount endeavor in human activity began to take its own path, in which thorns among the roses were more visible and in many cases avoidable. The path was, is, and will be difficult, indeed perhaps in some cases fatally so. I hope to have chronicled a few of the early and painful steps upon it.

NOTES

1. The evolution of attitudes toward slavery, for example, clearly is voluminous. Some of the primary sources are admirably collected in the eight-volume *Slavery, Abolition and Emancipation: Writings in the British Romantic Period* (London: Pickering & Chatto, 1999), ed. Peter Kitson and Debbie Lee; see esp. vols. 2 and 3. Deidre Colman has considered the topic well in *Romantic Colonization and British Anti-Slavery* (Cambridge: Cambridge University Press, 2005). For a useful discussion of the different views on slavery by Johnson and Boswell, see James G. Basker, "Johnson and Slavery," in "Johnson after Three Centuries: New Light on Texts and Contexts," ed. Thomas A. Horrocks and Howard D. Weinbrot, special issue, *Harvard Library Bulletin* 20 (2009): 29–50.

2. The California Edition of the Works of John Dryden, vol. 2, *Poems, 1681–1684*, ed. H. T. Swedenberg Jr. and Vinton A. Dearing (Berkeley: University of California Press, 1972), p. 36, lines 1026–27 (hereafter cited parenthetically in the text).

3. Samuel Johnson, *The Lives of the Most Eminent English Poets*, ed. Roger Lonsdale (Oxford: Clarendon Press, 2006), 2:8. Given the lack of parliamentary wisdom before and during the Gordon Riots, Johnson here may be guilty of an uncharacteristic error and too rosy a view of human nature.

4. William Whiston, *Memoirs of the Life and Writings of Mr. William Whiston. Containing, Memoirs of Several of his Friends Also*, 2nd ed. (London, 1753), 1:5 (hereafter cited parenthetically in the text).

5. *The Spectator*, ed. Donald F. Bond (Oxford: Clarendon Press, 1965), 1:14 (hereafter cited parenthetically in the text); Samuel Johnson, *A Dictionary of the English Language* (London, 1755). Founding of the Bank of England, of course, was contentious. For two pamphlets in less than congenial dialogue, see H[umphrey] M[ackworth], *England's Glory, or, The Great Improvement of trade in General, by a Royal Bank or Office of Credit* (London,

1694); and *Some Observations by way of Answer, to a Pamphlet, Called England's Glory: or, The Royal Bank* (London, 1694).

6. A Gentleman in Trade, *Observations on, And a Short History of Irish Banks and Bankers* (Dublin, 1760), p. 38; Cincinnatus, *The Patriotic Mirror, or the Salvation of Great Britain in Embryo* (London, 1781), p. 49; Gorges Edmond Howard, *The Miscellaneous Works, in Verse and Prose, of Gorges Edmond Howard, Esq.* (Dublin, 1782), 3:ccxlvi–ccxlvii; [Thomas, Lord Lyttelton], "The State of England, In the Year 2199," in *Poems, by A Young Nobleman, of Distinguished Abilities, lately deceased; Particularly, The State of England, and The once flourishing City of London, In a Letter from an American Traveller . . . To A Friend settled in Boston* (London, 1780), p. 5, with the larger context on pp. 4–7.

7. For a history of the Bank of England's various incarnations, see David M. Abramson, *Building the Bank of England: Money, Architecture, Society, 1694–1942* (New Haven, CT: Yale University Press, 2005). For more general histories, see John H. Clapham, *The Banks of England: A History* (Cambridge: Cambridge University Press, 1945); and John Giuseppi, *The Bank of England: A History from its Foundation in 1694* (London: Evans Bros., 1966).

8. *The London Guide, Describing the Public and Private Buildings of London, Westminster, and Southwark* (London, 1782), p. 111; Cincinnatus, *Patriotic Mirror*, p. 49, responding to [A Real Friend to Religion and to Britain], *Fanaticism and Treason: Or, A Dispassionate History of the Rise, Progress, and Suppression, of the Rebellious Insurrections In June 1780*, 3rd ed. (London, 1781); [Lord North's historian], *History of Lord North's Administration, to the Dissolution of the Thirteenth Parliament of Great-Britain* (London, 1781), p. 382.

9. [A Real Friend to Religion and to Britain], *Fanaticism and Treason*, p. 29 (undecided); *The Trial of George Gordon, Esquire, commonly called Lord George Gordon, for High Treason, at the Bar of the Court of King's Bench, On Monday, February 5th, 1781. Taken in Short-Hand by Joseph Gurney* (London, 1781 [1782?]), p. 9 (Other, anxious, fury); *The New Annual Register, or General Depository of History, Politics, and Literature, For the Year 1780* (London, 1781), pp. 52–54 (soldiery, Bank of England); [Lord North's historian], *History of Lord North's Administration*, p. 382; [B.T., A Member of the Corporation], *A Plan for Rendering the Militia of London Useful and respectable, and For raising an effective and well-regulated Watch, Without subjecting the Citizens to additional Taxes or the Interposition of Parliament* (London, 1782), pp. 29–30 (Captain).

10. Herbert Butterfield, *The Whig Interpretation of History* (1931; reprint, New York: W. W. Norton & Co., 1965), p. 23.

11. Richard W. Davis, "The House of Lords, the Whigs and Catholic Emancipation, 1806–1829," *Parliamentary History* 18 (1999): 23. See also R. W. Linker, "The English Roman Catholics and Emancipation: The Politics of Persuasion," *Journal of Ecclesiastical History* 27 (1976): 151–80. Brian Jenkins includes a helpful "Bibliographic Essay" at the end of his *Era of Emancipation: British Government of Ireland, 1812–1830* (Kingston, ON: McGill-Queen's University Press, 1988), pp. 355–75. For the French remark, see *Courier de Londres*, no. 40 (22 November 1793).

INDEX

Abingdon, Willoughby Bertie, Earl of, 265
Académie Française, 148
Accomplished Methodist, The, 187
Act of Settlement, 125, 132, 350
Act of Toleration, 57, 126, 127, 158, 159, 170, 241, 350; and Anne, 82; and Defoe, 80; and Nottingham, 89; and Waddington, 116; and William III, 25, 40, 115
Act of Uniformity, 350
Addison, Joseph, 5, 26, 134n3, 348–53
Address to the President of the Protestant Association, An, 266–67
Agate, John, 120
Age of Wonders, The, 55
Alsop, J. D., 82
Alsop, Vincent, 144, 170n1
Altham, Roger, 61, 67, 94n28
Alvensleben, Baron de, 293
America, 14, 203, 204, 254–55, 265, 344
American war, 242, 243, 250, 255–56, 290, 293, 301, 311, 316
Ammianus Marcellinus, 27, 49n7, 167, 240
Anderson, James, 33, 38, 125
Anderson, John, 77–78
Anne, Queen of England, 25, 43, 81–82, 99n54, 116, 121, 344, 350; and Anglo-Dutch relations, 84; Beveridge on, 50n16; bishops appointed by, 10; and Brydges, 116; and Church of England, 331; and Clarendon, 32, 35; and Clavering, 123; death of, 26; and Defoe, 80, 81, 82, 85, 86, 87; and George III, 353; and Hickeringill, 31; and B. Hoadly, 24; and Nottingham, 89; and Rochester, 33, 34, 35–36, 47; and Sacheverell, 47, 68, 69, 158; and thirtieth of January sermons, 110, 112; and Trapp, 24

Answer to . . . Taxation no Tyranny, 203
Appeal from the City to the Country, An, 47–48
Arden, Richard Pepper, 299, 301, 306–7, 309, 310–11
Arians, 145, 155, 192, 193
Arnaud, Antoine, 146
Arrowsmith, Edward, 131
Ascham, Roger, 28, 29
Ashurst, Sir William Henry, 312, 313
Astell, Mary, 31, 32, 41, 42, 44, 45, 59, 87, 88; *A Fair Way with the Dissenters and their Patrons*, 77, 99n54; *An Impartial Enquiry*, 30, 39, 81, 99n54, 246; *Moderation Truly Stated*, 81, 99n54
Athol Highlanders, 302, 315, 325n32
Atterbury, Bishop Francis, 12, 39, 43, 45, 46, 52n29, 134–35n9, 270; and Defoe, 75, 76, 88; episcopal treason of, 122; exile of, 25–26; and Quakers, 24, 42; trial of, 25–26, 118, 121, 128, 160; *Voice of the People, No Voice of God*, 246
Augustine, St., Bishop of Hippo, 60, 89, 133, 144, 170, 171n3, 198, 344; and Bayle, 151, 152–53; and Burnet, 70, 196, 198, 226n34; and church and state, 145–46; criticism of, 157, 159–65, 167, 168, 170, 175n21; and Dissenters, 145; *Epistle to Vincentius*, 145–46, 152–53, 162; and France, 226–27n37; and High Church, 154; and Long, 155–56; and Louis XIV, 146, 150; and Maimbourg, 149; and Methodism, 183, 184; and original sin, 27, 194, 195, 198, 226n35; and Sacheverell, 158; and Sheppard, 160; and Voltaire, 226n35; and Wishart, 177n27

Baillie, John, 245, 246, 250
Baker, William, 30, 114–15

Bakewell, Robert, 3
Bank of England, 339; and Addison, 348, 349–51, 352–53; and Gordon Riots, 242, 257, 262, 263, 265, 290, 294, 345, 351, 353
Barbayrac, Jean, 157, 175n21
Barrington, John Shute, Viscount, 58
Basileus, Philo, 27, 107, 110, 111, 114
Bate, James, 183
Bayle, Jacob, 151
Bayle, Pierre, 157, 159, 170, 175n21; *Ce que c'est que la France toute catholique*, 171–72n5; *Commentaire philosophique*, 151, 160; *Critique générale*, 151–54; *The Dictionary Historical and Critical of Mr Peter Bayle*, 153, 174n13; *A Philosophical Commentary*, 151, 153–54, 173–74n12, 175–76n23; and Synge, 163, 164; and Tindal, 167
Bell, Thomas, 247
Bennet, Benjamin, 248, 253
Bennet, Thomas, 31, 42, 74, 196
Berington, Joseph, 266–67, 291
Berriman, William, 107, 135n10
Beveridge, Bishop William, 31, 50n16
Billa Vera, 66
Binckes, William, 70–71, 79, 95n34, 107–8, 116, 184–85, 197–98; *Explanation Of some Passages in Dr. Binckes's Sermon*, 135–36n12; *The Martyrdom of King Charles*, 135–36n12; *Prefatory Discourse To An Examination of a late Book*, 228n43; *A Sermon Preach'd on January the 30th. 1701/2*, 135–36n12
Birch, Peter, 45
bishops/episcopacy, 10, 28, 43, 108, 122, 251, 252, 344; and American colonies, 250, 254, 255–56; authority of, 28–29; and Dissenters, 60, 123, 183, 193, 247; under Elizabeth, 44; and George II, 122; and Gibson, 189; and Gordon, 292, 294, 296, 322n14; and Gordon Riots, 241, 244, 245, 251, 252; and Hollingworth, 113; and Maimbourg, 148; and Methodism, 193, 202, 218, 232–33n72; and Owen, 166; and Quakers, 30, 58; and Sacheverell, 67–68, 70, 248; under Stubbs, 55; and Swift, 100n57; and Toland, 58, 64, 100n57; and William III, 26, 41, 70, 82, 331
Bisset, William, 63, 65, 68, 86, 91n11, 97n45
Blackstone, Sir William, 273, 296
Blennerhaysett, Thomas, 122
Blizard, Sir William, 262–63

Boehm, Anthony William, 194
Book of Common Prayer, 105, 188
Boswell, James, 242
Bradburn, Samuel, 200–201, 331
Bradbury, Thomas, 38, 65, 86, 106, 125, 202, 203
Bradshaw, Bishop William, 106–7, 130–31
Brady, Nicholas, 165
Britannus, Philo, 27, 30
Brooke, Frances, 208
Browne, Francis, 112
Browne, Philip, 58
Brydges, Henry, 116
Buffon, Georges Louis Leclerc, comte de, 4
Bugg, Francis, 30, 37, 58, 91n11, 157
Bull, Frederick, 245, 253
Bull, Patrick, 204–5, 206
Burke, Edmund, 14, 127, 248, 251, 253, 279n14, 332; "An Essay Towards an History of the Laws of England ," 6–7; and Gordon, 279n14, 313, 325n30; and Gordon Riots, 257, 261, 332; *Reflections on the Revolution in France*, 328n47
Burkitt, William, 97–98n49
Burnet, Bishop Gilbert, 24, 42, 59, 64, 139n36, 160–61, 177–78n29, 197; and Binckes, 228n43; *The Case of Compulsion*, 161–62; *Exposition*, 69–71, 196, 197–98; and predestination, 195, 196; *Relation of the Massacres*, 149; *The Royal Martyr Lamented*, 117; *Sermon*, 117–18; *Subjection*, 117; and William III, 118–19
Burnet, Thomas, 5–6, 226n34
Burney, Charles, 261
Burney, Frances, 261
Butler, Bishop John, 244, 294
Butler, Bishop Joseph, 108
Butler, Samuel, 187
Butterfield, Sir Herbert, 10, 354

Cagliostro, Comte Alessandro de (Giuseppe Balsamo), 298–99, 323n24
Calvin, John, 146, 148, 241–42
Calvinism, 149, 182, 193, 199, 200, 202, 213, 231–32n65, 241–42, 333
Calvinists, 70, 194, 197, 199
Campbell, Lord Frederick, 276n4
Canada, 254, 255
Caroline of Ansbach, Queen of England, 123, 198
Carter, Nicholas, 302
Carteret, John, Baron, 163

Catholic Relief Act (1778), 243, 245, 247, 256, 257, 276n4, 331, 345; and Burke, 279n14; Dawes on, 267, 268; Gordon on, 303–4; and Gordon trial, 274, 275; and military pool, 256, 316; provisions of, 238–40; as rushed and ignoring will of people, 273, 316, 318. *See also* Roman Catholics

Catholic Relief Act (1829), 11, 337, 354

Cave, William, 45, 54n44

Chalmers, George, 66, 71–72

Chambers, Ephraim, 2–3, 145

Chapman, Richard, 93n19

Character of a Modern Tory, 57

Character of a Quaker, 43

Charles Edward Stuart (Young Pretender), 123, 205, 223n16, 237, 350

Charles I, King of England, 37, 39, 110, 116, 130, 133, 241, 244; and Clarendon, 32–33, 34, 35; execution of, 25, 26, 31, 105, 125–26; and Gordon, 292, 318, 319; Hickeringill on, 46; and limited constitutional monarchy, 123–24; and Presbyterians, 119; and Scotland, 320–21n5; and thirtieth of January sermons, 57, 89, 105, 107, 108, 109, 111, 114, 118; and Warne, 191; Withers on, 38

Charles II, King of England, 25, 26, 33, 58, 343, 344, 346, 353; and religious violence, 58, 64; and thirtieth of January sermons, 105, 111, 118

Chauncy, Charles, 156, 190, 193, 197, 224nn23, 24

Christian Turned Jew, The, 313

Chubb, Thomas, 122

church fathers, 28, 157, 163

Church of England, 12, 40, 44, 58, 66, 97–98n49, 167, 201; and Addison, 350; and Anne, 82, 331; and anti-Catholic laws, 249; authority of, 28–29; and Burnet, 69, 70; and Catholicism, 245; Cave on, 45; and Church of Scotland, 320–21n5; and Clarendon, 33, 34, 35, 36; and Crown, 31, 295, 298; and Defoe, 73, 79; and Finch, 225–26n32; and French church, 156–57; Gardiner on, 206; and Gordon, 267, 290, 294–98, 306, 316, 318, 322n15, 343; and Gordon Riots, 294; and Grosley, 330–31; and James II, 25; Lower Convocation, 197, 198; and Methodism, 181, 182, 183, 184–85, 186, 189, 191, 192, 193, 200, 207, 218, 220n7, 345, 348; *Prayer to be Used. . . . In Times of War and Tumults*, 250; and religious violence, 60, 62; and Roman Catholics, 30, 240; and Smollett, 208, 209, 213, 215, 217, 218; and thirtieth of January sermons, 110, 112; Thirty-Nine Articles, 182, 191, 192, 197–98, 207, 215, 304, 348; Thirty-Nine Articles (article 17), 195, 196, 197; and Wesley, 206. *See also* High Church; Low Church

Church of Ireland, 162

Church of Scotland, 320–21n5

Cincinnatus, 351, 352

Circumcellions, 144, 145

civil rights, 122, 262, 263–64, 268, 332

Clarendon, Edward Hyde, Earl of, 11, 32–36, 47, 59–60, 119

Claridge, Richard, 167

Clark, Peter, 226–27n37

Clarke, Matthew, 160, 168, 169, 180n42

Clarke, Samuel, 169, 194

Clarke, William Augustus, 250–51

Claude, Jean, 173n11; *Account*, 150–51

Clavering, Robert, 122–23

Clement XII, Pope, 237

Clerc, Jean le, *Account*, 32–33

Coade, George, 119, 123, 126, 127, 128

Cobden, Edward, 107

Colby, Samuel, 115, 116, 117

Collection of the Writings Of the Author of the True-Born Englishman, 78

Comber, Thomas, 179n38

Compleat Account, A, 183–84

Condorcet, Marie Jean Antoine Nicolas de Caritat, marquis de, 7–8

Constantine, Emperor and St., 58, 144, 145, 153, 155, 156

constitution, 35, 46, 62, 64, 113, 197, 203, 331; and Bradshaw, 130; and Burke, 127; and Catholics, 240, 247, 266; and Charles I as tyrant, 125, 126; and church and state, 157; and *A Compleat Account*, 183; and Erskine, 240; and Free, 200, 222n13; and Gordon Riots, 253, 255, 256–57, 259, 264, 268, 272, 273, 274; and B. Hoadly, 129; and Littleton, 130; and military, 262, 264; and monarchy, 9, 123–24, 129

Constitutional Answer to the Rev. Mr. John Wesley's Calm Address, A, 204, 206

Cotton, Thomas, 38, 40, 47

Coverly, Sir Roger de, 26

Creighton, James, 201

Critical Remarks on Dr. Nowel's Sermon, 127

Croft, Herbert, 144
Cromwell, Oliver, 24, 25, 26, 166, 255, 346; and Gordon, 291; and Gordon Riots, 264, 265, 267
Cromwell, Richard, 25
Crouch, Nathaniel, 79
Crowe, William, 37, 122
Crown, 33, 35, 204, 250, 253, 339, 344, 353; and Church of England, 31, 295, 298; and Gordon, 272, 290, 298–302, 307–8, 310, 311, 316, 343; and Parliament, 344, 346–47, 348. See also monarchy
Croxall, Samuel, 106–7, 108
Crump, John, 159
Cumyng, D., 26
Curate of London, 198–99
Cyprian (Thascius Caecilius Cyprianus, Bishop and Saint), 161

Daillé, Jean, 226–27n37
d'Alembert, Jean-Baptiste le Rond, 3
Darwin, Charles, 1
Darwin, Erasmus, 3–4
Davis, Richard W., 354
Dawes, Manasseh, 267–68, 304
Defence of the Protestant Association, A, 253
De Fleury, Maria, 242, 258
Defoe, Daniel, 43, 52n29, 57, 121, 127, 135n10, 158, 203; and Altham, 94n28; and Anne, 80, 81, 82, 85, 86, 87; and Bayle, 151; as character of own creation, 84–89; and Dissenters, 31, 72, 74, 77, 78, 79, 80–81, 84, 85, 87; and Harley, 82; irony of, 66, 67, 71–72, 73, 80, 81, 84; and Kennett, 125; and legion image, 43–44; and Moses, 73, 74, 75, 76; and Sacheverell, 69, 82, 158; sentenced to pillory, 72, 158; and thirtieth of January sermons, 120; and Wake, 68–69; and William III, 128; Works: *Bold Advice*, 66–67; "A Brief Explanation," 84–85, 86; "Challenge of Peace," 85; *The Consolidator*, 86; *The Experiment*, 85, 86, 100–101n62; *Friendly Epistle By Way of Reproof*, 86; *The High-Church Legion*, 43–44, 85; *Hymn to the Pillory*, 87; *Lay-Man's Sermon upon the Late Storm*, 85; *Legion's Memorial Presented to the Speaker of the House of Commons*, 72; *A Letter from A Gentleman At the Court of St. Germains*, 41; *A Letter to Mr. Bisset*, 97n45; *Lex Talionis*, 78, 85, 175–76n23; *Moderation Maintain'd*, 27, 31, 99n54, 128; *The Occasional Letter*, 31, 100–101n62; *The Paralel*, 85, 86; *The Present State of the Parties in Great Britain*, 87; *Review* essays, 88; *Robinson Crusoe*, 91n8; *Serious Reflections*, 67, 95n29; "The Shortest Way to Peace and Union," 85; *The Shortest Way with the Dissenters* (1702), 11, 66, 71–89, 115, 132, 205; *The True Born English-man*, 52n28; *True Collection. . . . Corrected by Himself*, 78; *True Collection*, 85, 86; *The Weakest go to the Wall*, 88
deism, 24, 42, 66, 192, 193, 237
Delaune, William, 194
Delmé, Sir Peter, 122
Denham, Sir John, *Cooper's Hill*, 330
Dennis, John, 30–31, 52n28, 65
Devonshire, William Cavendish, Duke of, 114
Dickens, Charles, 314, 328n49; *Barnaby Rudge*, 11, 14, 15, 316, 320, 332–40, 345, 354
Diderot, Denis, 3
Discourse on Government and Religion, A, 52n30, 55, 125
Disney, John, 130
Dissenters, 12, 30, 57, 174n14, 237, 255, 268, 281n29; and Act of Toleration, 25; and Augustine, 144, 145; and *Billa Vera*, 66; and Bisset, 97n45; and Brydges, 116; and Burnet, 118; and Charles II, 58; and church and state, 31; and civil war, 46; and Clarendon, 33; and Defoe, 31, 72, 74, 77, 78, 79, 80–81, 84, 85, 87; and Donatists, 155–56; and episcopacy, 44, 123; and Equiano, 170; and flood imagery, 37, 38; forced conversion of, 167; and High Church, 166, 193–94, 246, 247; and history, 45, 91n11; laws against, 253; and Leslie, 44, 56, 88; loyalty of, 119; and Mackworth, 92n12; and Methodism, 176n25, 183, 184, 189, 191, 200–201, 331; and Old Testament, 293; and Parliament, 126; and the people, 40; and persuasion, 165; polemics of, 30; power of, 248–49; and propagation, 42; and religious violence, 59, 60, 61, 62–63, 65, 67; and Rochester, 35; and Roman Catholics, 240; and Sacheverell, 68, 69, 71, 158, 247, 307; and thirtieth of January sermons, 107, 108, 113, 114, 120, 121, 127, 132; threat from, 29; Trapp on, 43; and Trist, 250; and Ward, 330; and Watson, 316; and William of Orange, 39; and Wotton, 89
divine right of government, 14, 127–32, 143n66, 245–46, 344

divine right of kings, 12, 14, 38, 52n30, 127, 128, 140n45, 157; and Dryden, 347, 353; and Fisher, 52n29; and High Church, 115; and Horsley, 131, 132; and Nowell, 127; and Pelling, 136–37n18; and Sacheverell, 56, 67–68, 158; and South, 110; and thirtieth of January sermons, 344; and Wesley, 204. *See also* monarchy
Dodwell, Henry, 28, 45
Donatists, 144, 145, 146, 150, 152, 154, 155–56, 161; and Methodism, 184; and Sacheverell, 158
Dornford, Josiah, 305, 326n35
Dorset, Lionel Cranfield Sackville, Earl of, 122
Drake, James, 82
Dryden, John, 4–5, 205, 258; *Absalom and Achitophel*, 9, 15, 346–47, 353; *The Hind and the Panther*, 26; "Lines on Milton," 5; *The Medall*, 9, 10; "The Original and Progress of Satire," 6; *Religio Laici*, 26
Dunning, John, 257
Dunton, John, 80
Dyche, Thomas, 2
Dyer, George, 195

E., S., *The Clamours of the Dissenters*, 31
Edict of Nantes, revocation of, 68, 77, 78, 167, 170, 241, 260; and Augustine, 133, 160, 161, 344–45; persecution through, 146–56; specifications of, 147–48
Edward VI, King of England, 192
Edwards, John, 55
Edwards, Johnathan, 46
Elizabeth I, Queen of England, 32, 44, 63
Ellwood, Thomas, 65, 166–67, 179n38
Encyclopaedia Britannica (1776), 4
Enthusiasm no Novelty, 184
Equiano, Olaudah, 168–70, 180n45
Erastianism, 31, 41, 88, 109, 126, 132, 157, 158, 202
Erskine, John, 239–40
Erskine, Ralph, 159, 177n26
Erskine, Thomas, 271–75, 308, 309, 310, 317, 322–23n18
Evans, Caleb, 204, 206, 229–30n54
evolution, 4–6, 9–10, 15, 345, 353–54; ameliorative, 184, 207, 257, 346–54; meaning of, 2–3; theory of, 1–2
Excellent New Song, An, 163
Exclusion Crisis, 25, 344
Eyre, Richard, 93n18

Fagal, Gaspar, 119
Fairer, David, 251
Fallacy Detected, 204
Fall of Romish Babylon, The, 250, 253–54, 259, 260
Fanaticism and Treason, 257, 263, 267, 292, 352
Fau[l]ts on both sides, 93–94n20
Feathers' Tavern Petition, 304
Fielding, Henry, 12–13; *A Dialogue Between the Devil, the Pope, and the Pretender*, 13; *Joseph Andrews*, 12; *Shamela*, 220n8; *Tom Jones*, 12; *True Patriot*, No. 25 (1746), 13
Fina, Ferdinand, 93n19
Finch, Richard, 158, 191, 192, 195, 199, 222n13, 225–26n32; and Smollett, 214, 215, 216
Fisher, Edward, *An Appeal to the Conscience*, 52n29
Flames of Newgate, The, 267, 292
Fleetwood, William, 26, 37, 116, 139n36
Fleming, Caleb, 125, 128, 135n10
Fletcher, John, 229–30n54
Fog's Weekly Journal, 182, 190, 191
Fontenelle, Bernard le Bovier de, 148
Foote, Samuel, *The Minor*, 187
For God or for Baal, 37
Foulkes, Peter, 118
Fox, Charles James, 251, 323–24n26
Fox with his Fire-brand, The, 80
France, 37, 46, 57, 63, 64, 146, 159, 170, 290; and Addison, 350; and Anglo-French commercial treaty, 298–301, 313; and Bank of England, 353; and Bayle, 152; and Charles II, 343; collusion in British affairs by, 128; commercial treaty with, 298–301, 323–24n26; containment of, 237; and Defoe, 77, 78; and Finch, 225–26n32; and Gallican church, 146, 148, 158; Gordon and relations with, 311, 312–13; as Great Satan, 14; and Horsley, 131; imperial, 332; and Jacobite invasion of 1715, 150; and James II, 343, 344; and Maimbourg, 149; and persecution, 166; police system in, 262; and Protestant Dutch, 83; Protestants in, 226–27n37; and Terror, 7, 8; war with, 88, 89, 315; and Watson, 317. *See also* Edict of Nantes, revocation of
Free, John, 184, 186, 197, 200, 202, 222n13, 232n68
French Revolution, 7, 8, 14, 237, 291, 317, 320, 332, 340

Gandy, Henry, 107, 112, 113, 114, 125, 135n11
Gardiner, John, 206
Gay, John, 333
Gentleman's Magazine, 316, 332
George, Prince of Denmark, 36, 82, 121
George I, King of England, 12, 26, 38, 58, 114, 124, 156, 201; accession of, 25; and Addison, 350; and Bradbury, 202; and Crowe, 122; and dynastic concerns, 344; and B. Hoadly, 124; and A. Pope, 41; and religious violence, 65; and war, 343; and Whig government, 331
George II, King of England, 108, 122–23, 131, 198, 270, 318, 344; and Methodism, 201; opposition to, 344; and war, 343; and Whig government, 331
George III, King of England, 126, 305, 312, 340, 344, 347, 353, 354; and America, 256, 344; and Bank of England, 353; and excommunication of Gordon, 295, 297–98; and Gordon, 290, 291, 292, 293, 318, 319, 321n10; and Gordon Riots, 242, 258, 261, 263, 264–65, 269, 346, 352; and Gordon trial, 270; and Henry Benedict Stuart, 237–38; and Louis XVI, 311; loyalty to, 260; and Methodism, 201, 203; and military, 331, 337, 340, 345, 346, 352; ministers of, 243, 256–57, 259; and Nowell, 127; opposition to, 344; and petitions, 256; Piozzi on, 263; and Protestants, 241; and Quebec Act, 254; and repeal of anti-Catholic laws, 318, 354; Royal Proclamation Against Seditious Writing, 314; and Stuarts, 237; visit and speech to House of Lords, 264–65
Gibbon, Edward, 243–44
Gibson, Bishop Edmund, 183, 189, 194, 220n8; *Reflexions Upon a Late Paper*, 95n34
Gildon, Charles, 101n65
Giles, William, 335
Gill, Abraham, 85, 86
Gilpin, William, 217
Gisbertius Voetius, 137n24
Glanvill, Joseph, 110
Glorious Revolution of 1688, 127, 129, 131–32, 158
Glossographia Anglicana Nova, 144–45
Godolphin, Sidney Godolphin, Earl of, 82, 83, 85
Goldie, Mark, 170–71n1
Goldsmith, Oliver, 304
Goodman, John, 170
Gordon, Andrew, 160
Gordon, Cosmo George, Duke of, 269, 297

Gordon, Lord George, 14, 240, 241, 242, 247, 249, 251, 256, 354; acquittal of, 250, 258, 270, 272, 275, 290; in Amsterdam, 310, 312; arrest of, 243, 270, 312; and Athol Highlanders, 302, 315, 325n132; as attempting to intimidate Crown, 293–94; and Bank of England, 352; and Bible, 303, 309, 310, 314, 321n9, 333; and bishops/episcopacy, 292, 294, 296, 322n14; and British Jacobins, 291; burial of, 243, 279n14, 290, 315, 319–20, 328n51; and Burke, 279n14, 313, 328n47; Catholic and Protestant rage against, 266; and Charles I, 292, 318, 319; and Church of England, 267, 290, 294–98, 306, 316, 318, 322n15, 343; and civil war, 293; complaints of at treason trial, 270–71; and courts, 276, 295, 297, 298, 302–10; criticism of, 266–67, 268; as Cromwell, 267; and Crown, 272, 290, 298–302, 307–8, 310, 311, 316, 343; Crown argument against, 271, 274–75; death of, 258, 290, 315, 332, 341; defense at trials for libel and treason, 308–10; and Dickens, 332–33, 334, 335, 336, 337, 339–40, 341; and English Protestant sailors, 315; and excommunication, 295–98, 322nn14, 15, 328n51; and George III, 270, 290, 291, 292, 293, 295, 297–98, 318, 319, 321n10; and Gordon Riot hangings, 311–12, 327n41, 339; as guilty of libel, 310; and Hall, 326n39; imprisonment of, 243, 270, 313–15, 328n49, 333, 339–40, 341; intention of, 272, 275; and James II, 319; and Judaism, 243, 279n14, 290, 293, 294, 312, 313, 314, 315, 333; and judicial misconduct, 309; and jury pool, 270–71; and legal system, 12, 316, 332, 341; *A Letter . . . to the Attorney General*, 310–12; letter to French National Assembly, 327n43; letter to Abbé Gregoire, 318–19; letter to Lord Southampton, 321n10; and Louis XVI, 319; loyalty of, 301–2; and McCarthy, 257; and Montagu, 262; and North administration, 293; obituaries of, 290–91, 315; polemics by, 292; *The Prisoners' Petition*, 302–4, 305–6, 307–8; and Protestant Association, 258, 272, 291–92, 301, 318; Protestant Association address of 29 May 1780, 250; and *The Protestant Magazine*, 248; as Puritan, 292; and Quakers, 317; and Quebec Act, 318; as Satan, 292; and Scotland's anti-Catholic position, 276n4, 292; Scottish allies of, 302; and Scottish military, 293; and Scottish Presbyterians, 315; sentencing of, 312,

332; silencing of, 270; as subversive of constitution and government, 291; Thrale on, 261; as threat to state, 301; as tool of foreign forces, 292; treason accusation against, 269, 270, 271–72; and trial for libel upon British legal system, 298, 302–10, 311; and trial for libel upon Marie Antoinette, 298–302, 306, 309, 312, 313; and trial for treason, 243, 246, 268–76, 302, 316, 345; tributes to, 258; Watson's biography of, 315–20; and Wesley, 287n72; witnesses for and against, 272
Gordon, Thomas, 43, 57, 120, 157, 175n21
Gordon Riots, 14, 15, 64, 241–44, 273, 320; and Bank of England, 351, 352, 353; and Burke, 332; causes of, 242; and Church of England, 294; and civil war, 343; and Condorcet, 8; and Crown, 290; Dawes on, 267–68; deaths from, 242, 278n12; destruction by, 242–43, 257, 261, 262, 264, 331–32; and Dickens, 334–41; and George III, 258, 346; Gibbon on, 243–44; and Gordon, 314–15; and Gordon's trial for libel, 299, 301, 306; and Gordon trial for treason, 272–73; hangings after, 242, 311–12, 327n41, 339; healing after, 331–32; losses compensated after, 331–32; and loss of faith in government, 257; and management of public, 249; and military, 242–43, 261–66, 268, 331, 332, 336, 345; and Parliament, 331–32; and Protestants, 258–59; and religious bigotry, 345; restoration of order after, 261–62; and toleration, 354; and Watson, 316–17
Graham, William, 248, 250
Grascome (Grascombe), Samuel, 29, 32, 34, 37, 56, 125
Green, John, 185, 186, 189, 216–17
Gregoire, Abbé Henri, 318–19
Gregory I, 153
Grenville, William Wyndham Grenville, Baron, 314
Griffith, Thomas, 214
Grosley, Pierre Jean, 132, 330–31, 345
Grotius, Hugo, 144
Gurney, Elizabeth, 305

Hall, P. W., 314, 326n39
Hall, Robert, 143n66
Hallam, Henry, 10–11, 19n20
Hammond, Henry, 97–98n49, 165
Hare, Francis, 107, 135n10

Harlequin Methodist, 187
Harris, John, 3
Harris, Sir James, 312–13
Hartley, David, 207
Hastings, Warren, 14
Hawes, Robert, 258
Hay, William, 318
Hearne, Thomas, 116
Henley, John "Orator," 106–7
Hennuyer, Jean, 148–49
Henry, Matthew, 76, 96n43
Henry Benedict Stuart, Cardinal, 205–6, 237–38
Herring, Thomas, 129
Hewlett, Ebenezer, 199
Heywood, Henry, 194
Hickeringill, Edmund, 24, 31, 38, 40–41, 43, 46, 50n16, 57, 65, 80, 90n7
Higden, Henry, 4–5
High Church, 12, 38, 57, 131, 154, 165, 195, 201, 248; and Anne, 82, 121; Beveridge on, 50n16; and *Billa Vera*, 66; and Bradbury, 202; and Burnet, 69, 118, 196; and church and state, 157; and Clarendon, 32, 33; and compulsion, 345; and Crown, 344; and Defoe, 71, 72, 73, 74, 76, 77, 79, 80, 81, 84, 85, 86, 87, 88; and Dennis, 30; and Dissenters, 43, 44, 123, 127, 166, 193–94, 246, 247; and episcopacy, 123; and Hickeringill, 31, 40, 43; and B. Hoadly, 124; and Jacobites, 250; and latitude, 29; and Licas, 156; and Low Church, 24, 26, 43, 246; and Methodism, 184–85; and occasional conformity, 170; and original sin, 27, 28, 194; and religious invective, 23, 24; and religious violence, 59, 60–61, 63, 64, 65, 67; and Rochester, 32, 35; and Sacheverell, 68, 158; and Sheppard, 160; and Smollett, 208; and Swift, 208; and Synge, 163; and thirtieth of January sermons, 107, 108, 109–16, 119, 120, 121, 122, 132; and Thirty-Nine Articles, 197; and Watson, 316; and Whigs, 46, 122, 246; and William III, 39, 41, 47, 128. *See also* Church of England
High-Church and the Doctor out of Breath, 31
High-Church Bully, The, 41
High Church Champion Pleading His Own Cause, The, 65
High-Church Politicks, 38, 43, 128, 135n10
Hill, Sir Richard, 186, 192, 223n17
Historical Vindication of the Divine Right of Tithes, An, 179n38

Hoadly, Archbishop John, 95n34, 124, 125, 141n50
Hoadly, Bishop Benjamin, 24, 40, 88, 115, 124, 129, 157
Hobbes, Thomas, 10, 55, 163
Hodges, Sir Joseph, Bart., 122
Holcroft, Thomas, 242, 257, 262, 263, 264, 292
Hole, Matthew, 154, 165, 178–79n35
Hollingworth, Richard, 113
Hooker, Richard, 179n37
Hooper, George, 112
Horace (Horatius Quintus Flaccus), 4–5, 6
Horsley, Bishop Samuel, 107, 131, 135n10
House of Commons, 66, 125, 158, 254, 293, 304, 344, 354; and anti-Catholic laws, 239, 252, 253; and Dickens, 337, 338, 339; and Gordon Riots, 241; and Gordon trial, 270, 275; and L'Estrange, 30; and Nowell, 126–27; and thirtieth of January sermons, 106, 108, 111; and Young, 130. *See also* Parliament
House of Lords, 66, 135–36n12, 251; and Catholic Relief Act (1829), 354; George III's visit and speech to, 264–65; and Quebec Act, 254, 255; and thirtieth of January sermons, 106, 107, 108, 110, 115. *See also* Parliament
Howard, Gorges Edmond, 351
Howard, John, 304, 305, 314
Hugh, James, *An Answer*, 100–101n62
Huguenots, 149, 150, 151, 153, 157, 158, 164, 345
Humfrey, John, 179n37
Hutchinson, Michael, 120, 121

Impartial Survey of Mr. De Foe's Singular Modesty and Veracity, An, 100n62
Ingham, Benjamin, 181
Inquisition, 241, 246, 260, 267
Ireland, 354, 355
Irish, 64
Irish House of Commons, 162
Irish Rebellion, 150, 163, 173n10, 260

J., D., *King Charles I*, 117, 120
Jacob, Giles, 296, 305
Jacob, Hildebrand, 345
Jacobins, 291, 319, 332
Jacobites, 12, 25–26, 67, 165, 237, 301, 349, 353; and Hanoverians, 344; and High Church, 250; invasion of, 58, 344; and invasion of 1715, 25, 38, 128, 150; and invasion of 1745, 13; and religious violence, 64; and Sacheverell, 47; and Wesley, 206
James Francis Edward (Old Pretender), 10, 25, 38, 46–47, 58, 63, 64, 89, 124, 158
James I, King of England, 72, 79, 192
James II, King of England, 10, 25, 38, 121, 157, 205, 319, 343; and anti-Catholic laws, 274; and Bennet, 248; and Burnet, 160–61, 177–78n29; and Defoe, 74, 125; and J. Hoadly, 124; and Louis XIV, 343; opposition to, 344; and Protestant Association, 241; and religious violence, 58, 64; and thirtieth of January sermons, 105; and Watson, 318; and William III, 39, 40, 47, 110–11
Jebb, John, *Thoughts*, 304–5
Jenkins, Win, 248
Jenner, Robert, 296
Jerome, St., 194
Jews, 62, 321n11. *See also* Gordon, Lord George
Johnson, Samuel, 14, 15, 203, 237, 258, 304, 330, 348; *Adventurer, No. 137*, 11; *Dictionary*, 10, 16, 69; and evolution, 2, 3, 354; and Gordon Riots, 242, 261, 263, 269, 341; on human life, 2; on hybridous, 4; on improvement, 5, 11; on James II, 10; "Life of Samuel Butler," 347; and Parliament, 353; preface to *Shakespeare*, 4; *Taxation No Tyranny*, 203–4, 205, 206; on time, 2; and West Indies, 79
Jones, Sir William, 263
Jones, Thomas, 186
Judgment of the Learned and Pious St. Augustine, The, 154
Justice and Necessity of Restraining the Clergy in their Preaching, 67

Keach, Benjamin, 166
Keith, Sir Robert Murray, 313
Kennett, Bishop White, 32, 43, 82, 99n54, 114, 135n11, 139n36; *A Compassionate Enquiry*, 34, 107, 124–25; *A Sermon*, 93n18
Kentish Petition, 44
Kenyon, Lloyd, 271, 272, 314
King, Archbishop William, 87–88, 113, 124, 142n58
Kirkham, Robert, 181
Knox, John, 40, 113, 241–42, 248, 320–21n5

Lactantius (Lucius Caecillianus Firmianus Lactantius), *Relation*, 161

Lambert, Ralph, 150
Lancaster, Nathaniel, 180n45, 187–88, 232n71
Laney, Bishop Benjamin, 154
latitudinarians, 12, 26, 28–29, 70, 82, 119, 165, 193; and religious violence, 61; and Sacheverell, 68, 69; and Savage, 31; and thirtieth of January sermons, 113; and William III, 331
Laud, Archbishop William, 33, 46, 47, 80, 123, 191, 241, 250, 320–21n5
Law, William, 190–91
Leslie, Charles, 12, 37, 42, 45, 57, 60, 132; *Cassandra*, 99n54; and Defoe, 43, 72, 73, 87, 88; on Locke, 55–56; *The New Association*, 44, 59, 96n38; *Now or Never*, 40; *The Principles of the Dissenters*, 39; and Quakers, 59, 90n4, 92n12; and religious conflict, 26–27, 60, 61, 65; *The Snake in the Grass*, 90n4, 91n11, 92n12; and thirtieth of January sermons, 114; *The Wolf Stript*, 44, 81
L'Estrange, Sir Roger, *Short Answer*, 29, 30, 37
Letter Out of the Country, A, 40
"Letter sent from Bourdeaux, A," 150
Letter to Sir George Saville, Bart, A, 239, 276n3
Letter to the Rev. John Gardiner, A, 206–7
Light out of Darkness, 145
Littleton, Edward, 130, 142n62
Lloyd, Evan, *The Methodist*, 187, 199–200, 202–3
Locke, John, 8, 40, 55–56, 106, 112, 113, 126, 267; and *Billa Vera*, 66; "Examination," 6; and J. Hoadly, 124; and Horsley, 132; *Letter concerning Toleration*, 76–77, 173n10, 179n39; on toleration, 175n21
London and Westminster Police Bill, 262, 285n57
London Corresponding Society, 314
London Guide, The, 352
Long, Thomas, 155–56
Louis XIV, King of France, 77, 83, 146, 150, 158, 177–78n29, 343, 350; and Bayle, 151, 152, 153; and Defoe, 78; *An Edict of the French King*, 147–48, 150; and Maimbourg, 148, 149; revocation of Edict of Nantes, 133, 170, 344–45; and Synge, 164; and William III, 25
Louis XVI, 290, 311, 319
Lover of Truth and the British Constitution, 204, 206
Low Church, 27, 37, 38, 47, 57, 64, 88, 247; and church and state, 31; and Defoe, 74; and Hickeringill, 40; and High Church, 24, 26, 246; and Methodists, 201; and original sin, 193; and the people, 40; polemics of, 30; power of, 248; and predestination, 198; and regicide, 119; and religious violence, 59, 63, 65; and thirtieth of January sermons, 107, 109, 114, 121. *See also* Church of England
Lucas, Thomas, 150, 156, 158
Ludlow, Major General Edmund, 57, 113, 124
Lyttelton, Thomas, Baron, 351

Mackworth, Humphrey, *Peace at Home*, 92n12
Madan, Martin, 201, 202, 215
Maimbourg, Louis, 148–49, 151, 153
Mangey, Thomas, 111
Mann, Sir Horace, 327n41, 341
Manners, Nicholas, 195
Man of Ross, A, 258, 264
Mansfield, William Murray, Lord Chief Justice and Earl of, 265, 269, 271, 274–75, 286–87n67, 287n70, 331, 335
Marie Antoinette, 298, 299, 300, 312, 313, 315
Marlborough, John Churchill, Duke of, 35, 82, 83, 88, 256
martial law, 14, 15, 265, 285n57, 331, 339, 341, 345; and constitution, 262, 336; and Gordon, 294, 309; and Gordon Riots, 261, 352. *See also* military
Marvell, Andrew, 179n37
Mary, Queen of Scots, 47, 58
Mary I, Queen of England, 260, 272
Mary II, Queen of England, 10, 25, 35–36, 39, 40, 113, 123, 248, 318
Mason, William, 251, 332
Matthew, James, 186
Mawbey, Sir Joseph, 255
Mayhew, Jonathan, 126, 127
McCarthy, Felix, 257, 267, 291, 292, 294
Meldrum, George, 145, 171n3
Methodists, 14, 170, 171n3, 181–218, 237, 247, 249; acceptance of, 200–207; American, 255; and Apostles, 183, 190, 194, 216; assimilation of, 276n1; as banned from pulpits, 189; and Bible, 193; Bradburn on, 331; and Calvinism, 221n10; Calvinist, 191, 193, 194, 195, 197; and Church of England, 181, 182, 183, 184–85, 186, 189, 191, 192, 193, 200, 207, 218, 220n7, 345, 348; and class, 184–86, 202, 207; congregants of, 189; and crime, 202; and Dissenters, 176n25, 200–201, 331; and Erastianism, 158; evangelical method of, 189; finances of, 186;

Methodists (continued)
and Free, 200; Gardiner on, 206; and Great Awakening, 129; and Law, 190–91; and Lloyd, 203; and loyalty, 218; loyalty of, 201, 202, 223n16; meetings of, 189–90, 216–17; and Oxford, 201; power of, 248; and preaching, 181, 182, 189, 190, 201, 206, 210, 213, 216–17, 224–25n24; and primitive Christianity, 191, 225n27; and prisons, 232n70; and Reformation's Augustinian roots, 193; and Reformation theology, 192; and sexuality, 182, 190, 213; and Smollett, 208–9, 210, 212–18; and trade, 201; Wesleyan, 193, 198; Whitefield, 195; and women, 190; zeal of, 206, 207

Miami Native Americans, 208

Milbourne, Luke, 12, 37–38, 39–40, 59, 88, 128, 132, 135n10; and history, 45; and legion image, 44; *Moderate Cabal*, 31; and sin, 27, 28; and thirtieth of January sermons, 106, 107, 109, 111–12, 113, 116; *The utter Extirpation of Tyrants*, 61–62, 93n18, 112

military, 3, 256, 316, 352, 353; and Dickens, 336–39, 340; and George III, 331, 337, 340, 345, 346, 352; and Gordon Riots, 242–43, 261–66, 268, 331, 332, 336, 345. *See also* martial law

militia, civilian, 262

Militia Act, 316

Milton, John, 40, 113, 174n13; *Aereopagitica*, 244–45; "In quintum Novembris," 244; "Of True Religion, Heresy, Schism, Toleration," 245; *Paradise Lost*, 5

Minor, Calvinus, 297

Mock Preacher, The, 187

Moderation and Loyalty of the Dissenters, The, 31–32

Moderation Unmasked, 256

monarchy, 30, 32, 37, 56, 73, 130, 350, 353; constitutional, 9, 123–24, 129, 317; as divinely ordained, 110; and divine supremacy, 127; and thirtieth of January sermons, 109, 110, 112. *See also* Crown; divine right of kings

Monmouth, James Scott, Duke of, 346

Montagu, Elizabeth Robinson, 262

Morgan, William, 181

Mortimer, John, 47, 63, 65

Morton, Charles, 74

Moss, Robert, 112, 113, 114, 116

Motte, Houdar de la, 148

Moult, John, 93n19

Mystery of Iniquity, 64

Naudé, Philippe, 173n12
Needham, Peter, 150, 159, 160, 165
Netherlands, 39, 40, 41, 52n28, 82–83, 84, 113
Newton, John, 244, 257
Newton, William, 31, 114
Niles, Samuel, 226–27n37
North, Frederick, Earl of Guilford, 254
North administration, 290, 293, 325n30
Norton, Mr., 271, 273
Nottingham, Daniel Finch, Earl of, 83, 84, 88, 89, 101n66
Novak, Maximillian, 72, 96n37
Nowell, Thomas, 126–27, 186, 192

Oaths of Abjuration and Allegiance, 301–2
O'Beirne, Thomas Lewis, 249
Observations on "An Appeal From the Protestant Association," 244, 267
Observations on the State of the Nation, 88
Observations or Reflections, 120, 121
occasional conformity, 27, 66, 170
Occasional Conformity Bill, 82, 88
Oldmixon, John, 33, 65
O'Leary, Arthur, 244, 267
Orford, Horace Walpole, Earl of, 243, 251, 261, 284n54, 286n63, 291, 320, 327n41, 332
original sin, 27–28, 193–95, 196, 226n35
Owen, Charles, 101n65
Owen, James, 39, 64
Owen, John, 165–66
Oxford, Robert Harley, Earl of, 82

Paine, Thomas, 313, 314
Paley, William, 294
Pamphlet, Entitled "Taxation No Tyranny," Candidly Considered, The, 203
Papists of all Sorts Working with the Dissenters of all Sorts, 54n44
Pardon, William, 2
Parker, Samuel, 48n1, 154, 166, 179n37
Parliament, 25, 38, 134n5, 157, 246, 262, 339, 350; and Clarendon, 32, 33; and class, 251–52; Coade on, 126; and Crowe, 37; and Crown, 344, 346–47, 348; and Erskine, 273; and Gordon Riots, 241, 242–43, 264–65, 269, 331–32, 353; and Gordon trial, 270; as ignoring petitions, 257; and Kennett, 34; and monarchy, 127; and occasional conformity, 41; and Occasional Conformity Bill, 88; and

penalties and restrictions on Roman Catholics, 238–40; and prison reform, 304; and repeal of anti-Catholic laws, 252, 316, 331; and Riot Act, 264; and Rochester, 35; and Roman Catholics, 251; and succession, 126; and thirtieth of January sermons, 105, 107, 112, 114, 115; Walpole on, 332; and Watson, 316. *See also* House of Commons; House of Lords

Patrick, Bishop Simon, 75
Paxton, Peter, 27–28, 42–43, 57–58
Pearce, Bishop Zachary, 180n42
Peirce, James, 122, 140n45
Pelling, Edward, 111, 112, 136–37n18
Penn, William, 24, 30, 58
people, the, 39, 113, 122, 127, 132, 137–38n25, 246, 273; and Charles I, 39–40, 125, 126; and Gordon Riots, 253, 268, 273; and thirtieth of January sermons, 109, 112, 132
Petre, Robert Edward, Baron, 318
Phillips, Edward, 71
Philonomos, 264
Pickering, Thomas, 107
Pickworth, Henry, 58
Pigott, Charles, 315
Piozzi, Hester Lynch Thrale, 242, 261, 263, 268
Pitt, John, 307, 308, 309
Pitt, William, 285n57, 299–300, 313, 314, 317–18
police, 15, 262, 263, 268, 273, 285n57, 331, 336, 345
Politicks of High-Church, The, 63
Poole, Matthew, 76, 96n43, 159, 177n26
Pope, Alexander, 4, 41, 248; *Dunciad*, 42; *Dunciad Variorum*, 41; *An Essay on Criticism*, 41; *First Epistle of the Second Book of Horace Imitated*, 95–96n35
Popery and Schism Equally Dangerous to the Church of England, 113–14
Pratt, Charles, 255
predestination, 182, 191, 194, 195–200, 213, 231–32n65
Presbyterian Covenant, 320–21n5
Presbyterians, 39, 60, 77, 97n45, 166, 249, 255, 281n29; and Church of England, 192; and Donatists, 145; and Horsley, 131; L'Estrange on, 29; and Methodism, 182, 187; and Protestant Association, 241; and regicide, 119, 193–94; Scottish, 249, 291; and Smollett, 208, 209, 218
Presbyterians Not Guilty of the Murther of King Charles I, 125
Priestley, Joseph, 195, 267

Progress of Methodism, The, 186
Progress of Methodism in Bristol, 187
Protestant, A, *Defence of the Act of Parliament*, 267
Protestant Appeal, 244
Protestant Association, 240, 241, 247, 248, 249–50, 254, 290; and anti-Catholic laws, 253; and Burke, 251; and class, 252; criticism of, 266, 267; and George III, 256; and Gordon, 258, 272, 291–92, 301, 318; and Gordon Riots, 259; and Gordon trial, 272–73, 275; and military, 264; and Watson, 316, 317, 319
Protestant Association, The, 265–66, 286n63
Protestantism, 10, 64, 149, 213, 248, 253, 254, 273–74
Protestant Magazine, The, 237, 244, 245, 248, 249, 253, 272, 276n1; and Catholicism, 259–60; and George III, 256; and Quebec Act, 255
Protestant Packet, The, 245, 249, 250, 256, 259, 277n9
Protestant Reformation, 55, 191, 195, 198
Prynne, William, 292
Public Advertiser, 297, 301
Puritans, 25, 32, 63, 182, 250–51, 264; and Gordon, 241, 292; and Methodism, 184, 188, 202

Quakers, 42, 48n3, 64–65, 166, 167, 170, 179n38, 249; and Defoe, 86; and genocide, 58–59; and Gordon, 317; and Leslie, 59, 90n4, 92n12; and L'Estrange, 30; as mad, 56; and Penn, 30; and religious violence, 60; and Swift, 24; Trapp on, 43
Quebec Act, 242, 254–55, 257, 318
Quesnel, Le Père Pasquier, 168

Radcliffe, Stephen, 163–64
Ramsay, Allan, 263–64
Ray, John, 4, 6
Reflections Upon a Late Scandalous and Malicious Pamphlet, 80, 81
regicide, 1, 14, 110, 111, 116, 121, 266, 267; and Bradshaw, 130; and Burnet, 117; death of, 119; and J. Hoadly, 125; and Kennett, 124; and Methodism, 202; and Milbourne, 27; and Popery, 244; and Presbyterians, 193–94; and *Presbyterians Not Guilty*, 125; and thirtieth of January sermons, 113, 114, 115, 116; and Waddington, 116

Remarks . . . by the Rev. Dr. Berryman, 135n10
Rennell, Thomas, 29
Reply to an Appeal from the Protestant Association, A, 205
Rhind, Thomas, 77
Richmond, Charles Lennox, Duke of, 265
Riot Act, 263–64, 338
Rochester, Laurence Hyde, Earl of, 11, 32, 33–34, 35–36, 47, 82
Roe, John, 298, 323n22
Roman Catholics, 15, 37, 63, 64, 166, 246, 259–60, 281n29, 353; and American war, 255–56; and Bank of England, 353; and Charles II, 26; and Church of England, 30, 245; civil rights of, 268; and Clarke, 160; and Defoe, 74, 78, 85; feelings nurtured against, 244–49; and George III, 256, 354; and Gordon Riots, 258–59; and Gordon trial, 272; and James II, 25; language used against, 243–49; as loyal, 266; and Milton, 244–45; Parliament as deaf to fears of, 251; penalties and restrictions on, 242; perpetual deprivation of rights of, 266; petitions against repeal of penalties on, 241, 249, 252–53, 259; and Protestant Association, 319; and Quebec Act, 254, 255, 257; and rage against Gordon, 266; Scottish and Irish, 256; and Swift, 245; and Synge, 162–63; and thirtieth of January sermons, 114; and Whigs, 10, 11. *See also* Catholic Relief Act (1778)
Ross, John, 125

Sacheverell, Henry, 11–12, 45–47, 48n1, 93–94n20, 115–16, 132, 240, 326n39; and anarchy, 56; and Augustine, 146; and Bisset, 91n11; and Bradbury, 202; and Burnet, 70, 71; and Carteret, 163; and Chapman, 93n19; and Defoe, 71, 73, 75, 78, 85, 86, 87, 88, 97n45, 158; and Dissenters, 307; and fence image, 248; and Free, 184; and Gordon, 307; and Kennett, 43, 82; and King, 113; and Lloyd, 203; and madness, 57; and moderation, 29–30; *The Perils*, 62–63, 71, 86, 158; *The Political Union*, 30, 67–69, 71, 246–47; and Quakers, 42; on religion, 23; and religious liberty, 39; and religious violence, 64, 65; trial of, 64, 158; and Wake, 69; in Whig/Low Church cartoon, 24
Safest-Way with the Dissenters, The, 80, 82
Sage, John, 145

Saint Bartholomew's Day Massacre, 148–50, 158, 241, 259–60, 266
Sancroft, Archbishop William, 25, 38
Satire. Also Imitation of the First Satire of Boileau, A, 305
Savage, John, 31
Savile, Sir George, 238, 243, 246, 274, 275, 345
Scarisbrike, Edward, 110, 136n17
Schism Bill, 88
Scotland, 239–40, 242, 247, 276n4, 292, 297, 316, 320–21n5; and Gordon, 291, 296; and Gordon trial, 269–70, 275
Scotland's Opposition to the Popish Bill, 293
Scott, John, 129, 194, 197, 199
Seagrave, Robert, 189, 191, 192–93, 201, 215, 222nn13, 14, 228n49
Seasonable Warning to Protestants, A, 173n10
Sense of the People, The, 253
Shaftesbury, Anthony Ashley Cooper, first Earl of, 9
Shaftesbury, Anthony Ashley Cooper, third Earl of, 40
Shakespeare, William, 26, 258
Shelburne, William Petty-FitzMaurice, Earl of, 249
Sheppard, William, 160
Sheridan, Richard Brinsley, 262, 270, 285n57
Sheridan, William, 110, 111
Sherlock, Thomas, 164
Sherlock, William, 155
Sherwill, Thomas, 37
Shipman, Joseph, 186
Shorey, William, 118
Short, John, 256
"Short Account of the Violent Proceedings," 150
Short History of the Donatists, A, 183
Short View of the Statutes at Present in Force . . . Against Popery, 239
Silvius, J., 38
Skerret, Ralph, 107, 122, 129, 130
Skinner, Quentin, 10
Smalridge, Bishop George, 29, 111
Smollett, Tobias, 203; and class, 212–14, 215, 217; *Continuation of the History of England*, 208; and family, 209, 211, 214, 217; *Humphry Clinker*, 11, 14, 190, 207–18, 248, 345
Solemn League and Covenant, 320–21n5
Somers, John Somers, Baron, 52n29
Somerville, William, 330

South, Robert, 26, 45, 54n44, 97–98n49, 110, 111, 112
Spain, 57–58, 64, 166, 241, 344
Spectator, 5, 26, 78–79, 134n3, 348–53
Spinoza, Benedict, 55
Sprat, Bishop Thomas, 110, 111
Stebbing, Henry, 184, 185, 189
Steele, Sir Richard, 64, 120–21
Stephen, Sir James Fitzjames, 296, 322–23n18
Stephens, William, 106, 113, 114, 137–38n25
Step to Oxford, A, 29
Sterne, Laurence, 198, 245
Stevenson, John Jay, 254–55
Stillingfleet, Bishop Edward, 27
St. John, Pawlet, 110, 112
Stoughton, William, 128, 142n58
Strictures on a Pamphlet, 244, 252, 256, 258, 259
Stuarts, 58, 128, 130, 131, 193, 204, 205–6, 237, 353
Stubs, Philip, 27, 55
Sunderland, Robert Spencer, Earl of, 40
Swift, Jonathan, 38, 42, 44, 55, 142n58, 153, 203; *The Battle of the Books*, 188; and church and state, 32; and Fielding, 13; *Gulliver's Travels*, 41, 245; and J. Hoadly, 124, 141n50; and human depravity, 13–14, 27; and Johnson, 4; and Methodism, 182, 191; and *Moderation Unmasked*, 256; *The Publick Spirit of the Whigs*, 64; and Quakers, 24; *Sentiments of a Church-of-England Man*, 99n55; and Smollett, 208, 215; and Stoughton, 128; and Synge, 178n31; *A Tale of a Tub*, 36, 42, 207–8; and Toland, 100n57; and Ward, 23; and West Indies, 78; and William III, 41
Sydney, Thomas Townshend, Viscount, 295
Syllabus of Lucubrations, A, 242, 278n11
Synge, Edward, 162–63, 164, 170
Synod of Dort, 192

Tale and No Tale, A, 38
Taylor, John, 226–27n37
Taylor, Sir Robert, 351
Taylor, Stephen, 134n5
Tertulian (Quintus Septimius Tertullianus), 161
Test Act, 164, 354
Third Book of the Chronicles of London, For 1780, The, 249, 281n28
thirtieth of January sermons, 24, 105–43, 158, 166, 237, 245; and Act of Toleration and 1688, 127; and Anne, 110, 112; Burnet on abolition of, 117–18; and Charles I, 57, 89, 105, 107, 108, 109, 111, 114, 118; and Charles II, 105, 111, 118; and Church of England, 110, 112; and Defoe, 120; and Dissenters, 14, 107, 108, 113, 114, 120, 121, 127, 132; and divine right of government vs. kings, 344; and divine right of kings, 344; and High Church, 107, 108, 109–16, 119, 120, 121, 122, 132; and House of Commons, 106, 108, 111; and House of Lords, 106, 107, 108, 110, 115; and James II, 105; and latitudinarians, 113; and Leslie, 114; and Low Church, 107, 109, 114, 121; and Methodism, 170; and Milbourne, 106, 107, 109, 111–12, 113, 116; and monarchy, 109, 110, 112; and Parliament, 105, 107, 112, 114, 115; and the people, 109, 112, 132; and regicide, 113, 114, 115, 116; reluctance to accept or reward fury of, 115; and Roman Catholics, 114; and royalist law, 105–9; and Smalridge, 29; and Tories, 109, 113; and Whigs, 57, 108, 109, 112, 113, 114, 116, 121, 132; and William III, 113
Thrale, Hester. *See* Piozzi, Hester Lynch Thrale
Tillotson, Archbishop John, 26, 39, 190, 244
Tilly, William, 60, 112
Tindal, Matthew, 64, 167–68
Toland, John, 58, 64, 83, 84, 100n57
toleration, 35, 41, 113, 160, 163–64, 165, 268; and Bayle, 151–52; and Defoe, 80, 81; and Gordon Riots, 354; and Grosley, 132, 330–31; Hanoverian, 199, 200, 201, 223n16, 345; and Occasional Conformity Bill, 88; and religious violence, 59; and William III, 331; and Wotton, 89
Toleration and Liberty of Conscience considered and . . . Impossible, 29
Toplady, Augustus, 204
Tories, 4, 23, 25, 29, 32, 35, 57, 317; and Anne, 82; and Clarendon, 34; and Defoe, 31, 72, 74, 80, 86, 87, 88; and *Protestant Packet*, 250; and religious violence, 65; and Sacheverell, 68, 158; and thirtieth of January sermons, 109, 113
trade and credit, 348–53
Trapp, Joseph, 28, 43, 56, 106–7, 183, 189, 191, 192, 221n10; and class, 185; *The Nature, Usefulness, and Regulation of Religious Zeal*, 185, 214, 222n14; *True, Genuine Modern Whigg-Address*, 24; *The True Spirit of the Methodists*, 200
Treatise on Christian Perfection, 219n3
Trick upon Trick, 187

Trimnell, Bishop Charles, 108
Trist, Jeremiah, 250
Truth brought to Light, 79
Tufton, Sackville, 40
Turner, Bishop Francis, 106, 113, 155
Tutchin, John, 71, 72, 77

United States, 317
University Loyalty, 46–47, 63–64

Veneer, John, 197
Veritas, Philo, 297–98
Vernon, John, 83
Villa-Real Gooch, Elizabeth Sarah, 321–22n11
Vindication of the Earl of Nottingham, 88–89
Virgil (Publius Vergilius Maro), 3, 5
Voltaire (François-Marie Arouet), 164, 175n21, 226n35
Vox populi, vox dei, 52n29

Waddington, Edward, 116
Wake, Archbishop William, 68
Wallace, James, 274
Walpole, Horace, Earl of Orford. *See* Orford, Horace Walpole, Earl of
Walpole, Sir Robert, 108, 124, 158, 344
Ward, Ned, 14, 15, 23, 24–25, 26, 37, 38, 330
Warne, Jonathan, 191–92, 225n30
War of the Spanish Succession, 25, 35
Watson, Robert, 315–20
Watts, Isaac, 168–69
Waugh, John, 122
Weaver, R. M., 163, 178n32
Webster, Samuel, 194–95, 226–27n37
Welchman, Edward, 197
Wellington, Arthur Wellesley, Duke of, 337, 354
Welstead, Henry, 42
Wesley, Charles, 181, 185, 186
Wesley, John, 168, 169, 183, 186, 203, 207, 232–33n72, 237; *A Calm Address*, 204–5, 206, 229n53, 230n55; and Calvinism, 221n10; on Catholics, 246; and Church of England, 200, 206; on dissent, 201; *Free Grace*, 182; and Gordon, 243, 287n72; and Gordon trial, 270, 271; *History of Methodism*, 181; and holiness, 182; and Johnson, 230n55; and Lancaster, 187–88; *A Letter to the Printer of the Public Advertiser*, 276n1; love for England, 201; and original sin, 198; and Oxford, 185; and perfection, 182, 219n3; reservations regarding, 189; *Scriptural Christianity*, 185; and Smollett, 208, 213, 231–32n65; and Whitefield, 182, 219n3
Wesley, Samuel, 76
West, Richard, 107, 114, 125, 134–35n9
Westmoreland, Susan Fane, Countess of, 297
Whigs, 37, 38, 42, 64, 67, 132, 165, 237; and Addison, 349; and Anne, 82; and Astell, 39, 88; and Burnet, 70, 118; and Butterfield, 354; and church and state, 157; and Clarendon, 33, 35, 36; and Defoe, 31, 72, 74, 80, 86; and Dissenters, 45, 56; and divine right of government, 130, 131; and Dryden, 9; and Hanoverians, 331; and High Church, 41, 46, 246; and history, 40; and Johnson, 11; and Leslie, 44, 88; and original sin, 193; and Protestant Association, 319; and religious violence, 59, 61, 65; and Rochester, 32, 35; and Sacheverell, 69, 158; and thirtieth of January sermons, 57, 108, 109, 112, 113, 114, 116, 121, 132; Trapp on, 43; and Watson, 317; and William III, 25; and Young, 198
Whigs No Christians, 24
Whigs Truly Christian, 24
Whiston, William, 347–48
Whitby, Daniel, 165
Whitefield, George, 176n25, 181, 183, 184, 185, 189, 207; finances of, 186; and Gibson, 190, 220n8; and Hewlett, 199; and loyalty, 201; preaching by, 189–90; *The Rev. Mr. Whitefield's Answer*, 220n8; and Smollett, 208, 213, 231–32n65; and Warne, 192; and Wesley, 182, 219n3; and Young, 198
Wilder, John, 184, 199, 221n12
Wilkes, John, 301
Wilkins, Thomas, 305, 312
William III, King of England, 81–82, 121, 126, 137n24, 243, 255, 318, 344; accession of, 25; and Act of Toleration, 25, 40, 115; anti-Catholic laws of, 238, 253, 254, 256, 257, 266, 272, 274; and Bank of England, 349; and Bell, 247; and Bennet, 248; bishops appointed by, 10; and Bradshaw, 130; and Brady, 165; and Burnet, 69, 118–19, 160; and Clavering, 123; and Cotton, 38; and Defoe, 41, 128; deification of, 127, 128; and Dissenters, 39; as Dutch Calvinist, 26; and flood imagery, 39; and George III's ministry, 256; and Gordon trial,

272; and J. Hoadly, 124; and Horsley, 132; and latitudinarian bishops, 331; and Louis XIV, 25; and the people, 40; and A. Pope, 41; and Protestant Association, 241, 319; and Protestant Dutch, 83; and Protestantism, 253, 254; and Protestant protective legislation, 253; and Rochester, 35, 36; and Sacheverell, 47, 158; and Stoughton, 128; Swift on, 41; and thirtieth of January sermons, 113; and toleration, 331; Tufton on, 40; and war, 343; and Whigs, 25
Williams, David, 262, 336
Williams, John, 110, 116
Willis, Bishop Richard, 122, 129
Wilson, Thomas, 295
Wishart, William, 177n27
Withers, John, 33, 38, 57, 125
World As It Goes, The, 257–58
Wotton, William, 88–89, 101n66
Wren, Sir Christopher, 352
Wright, Samuel, 125
Wyeth, James, 65
Wyeth, Joseph, 59, 91n11
Wyng, John, 120, 121–22, 125

York, Prince Frederick Augustus, Duke of, 243
Yorke, Henry Redhead, 315
Young, Arthur, 313
Young, Edward, 130, 198